ROAD FOOD

ALSO BY

JANE STERN
AND
MICHAEL STERN

The Lexicon of Real American Food

Confessions of a Tarot Reader
    (by Jane Stern)

500 Things to Eat Before It's Too Late

Roadfood Sandwiches

Two for the Road

Elegant Comfort Food from the Dorset Inn

The Loveless Cafe Cookbook

Southern California Cooking from the Cottage

Cooking in the Lowcountry

The Famous Dutch Kitchen Cookbook

Ambulance Girl (by Jane Stern)

Carbone's Cookbook

Harry Caray's Restaurant Cookbook

Louie's Back Yard Cookbook

The Durgin-Park Cookbook

The El Charro Cookbook

The Blue Willow Inn Cookbook

Blue Plate Specials and Blue Ribbon Chefs

Chili Nation

Two Puppies

Eat Your Way Across the USA

Dog Eat Dog

Happy Trails (with Roy Rogers
    and Dale Evans)

Way Out West

Jane & Michael Stern's Encyclopedia
    of Pop Culture

American Gourmet

The Encyclopedia of Bad Taste

Sixties People

A Taste of America

Elvis World

Real American Food

Roadfood & Goodfood

Where to Eat in Connecticut

Square Meals

Goodfood

Horror Holiday

Friendly Relations

Douglas Sirk (by Michael Stern)

Auto Ads

Amazing America

Trucker: A Portrait of the Last
    American Cowboy (by Jane Stern)

CLARKSON POTTER/PUBLISHERS
NEW YORK

AN EATER'S GUIDE

TO MORE THAN
1,000 OF THE BEST

LOCAL
HOT SPOTS

& HIDDEN
GEMS

ACROSS AMERICA

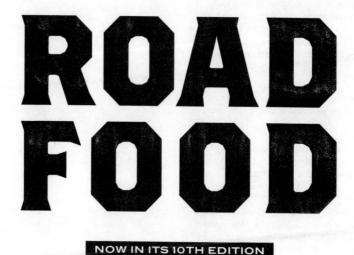

ROAD FOOD

NOW IN ITS 10TH EDITION

JANE & MICHAEL STERN

Published in the United States by Clarkson Potter/Publishers,
an imprint of the Crown Publishing Group, a division of
Penguin Random House LLC, New York.
crownpublishing.com
clarksonpotter.com

CLARKSON POTTER is a trademark and POTTER
with colophon is a registered trademark of
Penguin Random House LLC.

This work was originally published in the United States by
Penguin Random House LLC, New York, in 1978. Subsequent
revised editions were published in the United States by Penguin
Random House LLC, New York, in 1980; Alfred A. Knopf, a
division of Penguin Random House LLC, New York, in 1986;
Harper Perennial, a division of HarperCollins Publishers,
New York, in 1992; Broadway Books, an imprint of the Crown
Publishing Group, a division of Penguin Random House LLC,
New York, in 2002, 2005, and 2008; and by Clarkson Potter/
Publishers, an imprint of the Crown Publishing Group, a division
of Penguin Random House LLC, New York, in 2011 and 2014.

Library of Congress Cataloging-in-Publication Data
Names: Stern, Jane, author. | Stern, Michael, 1946- author.
    Title: Roadfood : an eater's guide to more than 1,000 of the
best local hot spots and hidden gems across America / Jane and
Michael Stern.
    Other titles: Road food
    Description: New York : Clarkson Potter/Publishers, 2017.
    Identifiers: LCCN 2016044704 (print) | LCCN 2016044800
(ebook) | ISBN 9780451496195 (hardcover) | ISBN
9780770434526 (paperback) | ISBN 9780770434533 (electronic) |
ISBN 9780451496201 (Ebook)
    Subjects: LCSH: Restaurants--United States--Guidebooks. |
Roadside restaurants--United States--Guidebooks. | Automobile
travel--United States--Guidebooks. | United States--Guidebooks.
| BISAC: TRAVEL / Restaurants. | TRAVEL / Road Travel. |
COOKING / Regional & Ethnic / American / General.
    Classification: LCC TX907.2 .S84 2017 (print) | LCC TX907.2
(ebook) | DDC 647.9573--dc23
    LC record available at https://lccn.loc.gov/2016044704

ISBN 978-0-7704-3452-6
eISBN 978-0-7704-3453-3

Printed in the United States of America

Book and cover design by Sonia Persad
Maps designed by Jeffrey L. Ward
Cover icons by Meighan Cavanaugh
Cover illustrations: (map) dovla982/Shutterstock,
(texture) ghostlypixels.com
Map texture by ghostlypixels.com

10 9 8 7 6

Tenth Edition

DEDICATED TO

JAMES BEARD and M.F.K. FISHER:

GUIDING LIGHTS

CONTENTS

INTRODUCTION

Welcome to the tenth edition of *Roadfood*. It has been forty years since we first wrote a guide to regional restaurants—a project that was hard to get off the ground because, back then, publishers doubted that there were enough decent American restaurants to fill a book. Wow, have things changed!

When we started our lifelong road trip, there were no food blogs and only a handful of food shows on television. There were no James Beard Foundation Awards, and there was scant appreciation for the nation's everyday eats. Fellow diners thought we were crazy for taking pictures of our food. Restaurateurs couldn't understand our curiosity. Few outsiders had even heard of Buffalo wings, green chile cheeseburgers, Nashville hot chicken, or Wisconsin butter burgers. Now, those dishes and countless other once-obscure local specialties are on the bucket list of traveling foodies everywhere.

In the beginning, we felt like crusaders, bound and determined to persuade people that regional food was something wonderful and that traveling to find it was a way to literally taste the nation. Mission accomplished! American cuisine, which once got no respect, now is celebrated in books, on television, and throughout the blogosphere. Whether you're talking about regional pies, local produce, or the 1,001 different kinds of barbecue from coast to coast, this country's consciousness about so many dishes and so many styles of dining has blossomed into ebullient appreciation.

Americans have come to delight in a melting-pot cuisine where tradition, creativity, and devil-may-care resourcefulness swirl together to create meals that, like the population, are boundlessly diverse.

What we especially love about finding Roadfood is that it is of the people, by the people, and for the people. Roadfood restaurants are not created by celebrity chefs, nor do they reflect of-the-moment trends. They express the combined passion and talents of cooks and staff, the hard work of farmers and fishermen and bakers and pitmasters, the enthusiasm of patrons, and the grassroots traditions from which they arose.

The purpose of this book is to help you appreciate the glory that is American food. Read it, bring it along when you travel, have cooks around the country sign their write-up, drip gravy on it, turn the pages with glistening fingers between bites of fried chicken.

On the road or at home, please join us at the website Roadfood.com, where passionate eaters come together to share the joys of appetite-adventuring. Users are welcome to post reviews, to participate in discussion forums that include trip reports, to plan meet 'n' greet get-togethers, and to voice opinions about anything food-related. Roadfood.com recently has been redesigned to be especially friendly to anyone using a mobile device, making it easy to find—and to report on—great meals wherever you go.

—Jane & Michael Stern

ROADFOOD HONOR ROLL: THE 100

We urge you to visit each and every one of the 1,000 restaurants in this book. We have included them because we think their food is great and the experience of eating in them is memorable. One hundred are starred with an asterisk to indicate that they are, to us, extra-special. We have come to love them because we believe that each is a unique expression of something wonderful about American food and foodways. A few are relatively new, but most have stood the test of time. This is the Roadfood Honor Roll.

NEW ENGLAND (11)

Frank Pepe Pizzeria Napoletana	New Haven, CT
Super Duper Weenie	Fairfield, CT
Zuppardi's Apizza	West Haven, CT
Clam Box	Ipswich, MA
Hartley's Original Pork Pies	Fall River, MA
Oxford Creamery	Mattapoisett, MA
Five Islands Lobster Co.	Georgetown, ME
Maine Diner	Wells, ME
Polly's Pancake Parlor	Sugar Hill, NH
Evelyn's Drive-in	Tiverton, RI
Parkway Diner	South Burlington, VT

MID-ATLANTIC (11)

Ben's Chili Bowl	Washington, DC
Faidley's	Baltimore, MD
Harold's New York Deli	Edison, NJ
Jimmy Buff's	West Orange, NJ
White House Sub Shop	Atlantic City, NJ
Aléthea's Chocolates	Williamsville, NY
Katz's Delicatessen	New York, NY
Nick Tahou Hots	Rochester, NY
Schwabl's	West Seneca, NY
John's Roast Pork	Philadelphia, PA
Mama's	Bala Cynwyd, PA

MID-SOUTH (11)

Peak Bros.	Waverly, KY
Keaton's	Cleveland, NC
Lexington Barbecue #1	Lexington, NC
Skylight Inn	Ayden, NC
Arnold's Country Kitchen	Nashville, TN
Cozy Corner	Memphis, TN
Prince's Hot Chicken Shack	Nashville, TN
Ridgewood Barbecue	Bluff City, TN
Metompkin Seafood	Mappsville, VA
Red Truck Rural Bakery	Marshall, VA
Coleman's Fish Market	Wheeling, WV

DEEP SOUTH (20)

Martin's	Montgomery, AL
AQ Chicken House	Springdale, AR
McClard's	Hot Springs, AR
Stubby's Bar-B-Que	Hot Springs, AR
Lynn's Quality Oysters	Eastpoint, FL
O'Steen's	St. Augustine, FL
Mary Mac's Tea Room	Atlanta, GA
Perry's Pig	Augusta, GA
Brenda's Diner	New Iberia, LA
Café des Amis	Breaux Bridge, LA
Domilise's Po-Boys	New Orleans, LA
Johnson's Boucanière	Lafayette, LA
Morning Call Coffee Stand	Metairie, LA
Doe's Eat Place	Greenville, MS
Bertha's Kitchen	North Charleston, SC
Bowens Island	Charleston, SC
Hite's Bar-B-Que	West Columbia, SC
Hominy Grill	Charleston, SC
Jackie Hite's Bar-B-Que	Leesville, SC
Juniper	Ridge Spring, SC

MIDWEST (23)

Johnnie's	Elmwood Park, IL
Poochie's	Skokie, IL
Rip's	Ladd, IL
Superdawg	Chicago, IL
Gray Brothers Cafeteria	Mooreseville, IN
Nick's Kitchen	Huntington, IN
Bob's Drive-Inn	Le Mars, IA
Coffee Cup Cafe	Sully, IA
The Cherry Hut	Beulah, MI
Jean Kay's	Marquette, MI
Krazy Jim's Blimpy Burger	Ann Arbor, MI
Hell's Kitchen	Minneapolis, MN
Lange's Cafe	Pipestone, MN
Snead's	Belton, MO
Stroud's	Kansas City, MO
Ted Drewes	St. Louis, MO
Al's Corner Restaurant	Barberton, OH
Camp Washington Chili Parlor	Cincinnati, OH
Henry's	West Jefferson, OH
Leon's	Milwaukee, WI
McBob's	Milwaukee, WI
Solly's Grille	Milwaukee, WI
Stockholm Pie Company	Stockholm, WI

SOUTHWEST (13)

El Guero Canelo	Tucson, AZ
Little Cafe Poca Cosa	Tucson, AZ
Pico de Gallo	South Tucson, AZ
Woodyard Bar-B-Que	Kansas City, KS
Frontier	Albuquerque, NM
La Posta de Mesilla	Old Mesilla, NM
Santa Fe Bite	Santa Fe, NM
Van's Pig Stand	Shawnee, OK
Bryce's Cafeteria	Texarkana, TX
Little Diner	Canutillo, TX
Louie Mueller Barbeque	Taylor, TX
Monument Cafe	Georgetown, TX
Taco Taco	San Antonio, TX

GREAT PLAINS (2)

Hudson's Hamburger's	Coeur d'Alene, ID
Eddie's Supper Club	Great Falls, MT

WEST COAST (9)

Apple Pan	Los Angeles, CA
The Cottage	La Jolla, CA
Du-par's	Los Angeles, CA
Hodad's	Ocean Beach, CA
Swan Oyster Depot	San Francisco, CA
Bowpicker	Astoria, OR
South Beach Fish Market	South Beach, OR
Freshy's Seafood Market	Mercer Island, WA
Spud Fish and Chips	Kirkland, WA

NOTES ABOUT USING THIS BOOK

If you are planning to visit a restaurant in this book, we urge you to call ahead to make certain it is open and is serving what you want to eat. Hours of operation change over the course of the year, and proprietors sometimes go fishing. Our notation of BLD—meaning breakfast, lunch, dinner—can mean different times in different places. For instance, many heartland restaurants do serve dinner, but dinner hour can end as early as seven o'clock. Also, some specialties are seasonal.

- The vast majority of Roadfood restaurants require no reservations and are come-as-you-are. We've made note of which ones get insanely crowded, and what you can do about it. But again, if in doubt, call ahead.

- We give an approximate cost guide using dollar signs, but this can vary dramatically. Many Roadfood restaurants that offer modestly priced sandwiches for lunch also can serve $50-plus dinners. Our one-to-three dollar-sign rating describes the meal we talk about most in the review (breakfast, lunch, dinner) and does not include wine, beer, cocktails, or multiple desserts.

$ = one full meal is under $15

$$ = one full meal is between $15 and $30

$$$ = one full meal is over $30

- Just because a restaurant from a previous edition of *Roadfood* does not appear here does not mean it is out of business or that we don't like it anymore. Either circumstance might be true, but it also is possible that we excised it simply to make room for new places we believe demand attention. Similarly, we have added a few new discoveries to the Roadfood Honor Roll of one hundred favorites, meaning we were forced to cut some old favorites from the list. We still love them all!

- When one-of-a-kind restaurants have prospered and become multi-location empires, the results have been mixed. Some are still so good and essential that we felt compelled to keep them in this edition. Some others we wish well, but figure there is no need for Roadfood to tell the world about them anymore.

NEW ENGLAND

MAINE

VERMONT

NEW
HAMPSHIRE

MASSACHUSETTS

CONNECTICUT

RHODE
ISLAND

VERMONT

NEW HAMPSHIRE

NORTH HERO
Papa Pete's

BURLINGTON
The Chubby Muffin
Myer's Bagels

SOUTH BURLINGTON
Al's French Frys
★ Parkway Diner

MORETOWN
Maynard's Snack Bar

MONTPELIER
Wayside Restaurant

WELLS RIVER
P&H Truck Stop

LYNDONVILLE
Miss Lyndonville Diner

LITTLETON
Bishop's

SUGAR HILL
★ Polly's Pancake Parlor

LINCOLN
Sunny Day Diner

MEREDITH
Hart's Turkey Farm

TILTON
Tilt'n Diner

CONCORD

MANCHESTER
Puritan Backroom

PORTSMOUTH
Gilley's PM Lunch

RYE
The Ice House
Rye Harbor Lobster Pound

SEABROOK
Brown's Lobster Pound

ESSEX
Essex Seafood
The Village Restaurant
Woodman's of Essex

ROCKPORT
Red Skiff

GLOUCESTER
Turtle Alley

NORTH BEVERLY
Nick's Famous Roast Beef

WEST LEBANON
Four Aces Diner

MANCHESTER
Depot Café
Mrs. Murphy's Donuts
Up For Breakfast

CHESTER
Baba-à-Louis
Country Girl Diner

PUTNEY
Curtis' All American Bar B Q
Putney Diner

WALPOLE
L.A. Burdick

BENNINGTON
Blue Benn Diner

WEST BRATTLEBORO
Chelsea Royal Diner

IPSWICH
★ Clam Box

SUNDERLAND
Smiarowski Farmstand
& Creamy

SOMERVILLE
R.F. O'Sullivan & Son

REVERE
Kelly's Roast Beef

CAMBRIDGE
Christina's Homemade Ice Cream
Toscanini's

BOSTON
Durgin-Park

EAST BOSTON
Santarpio's

WEST SPRINGFIELD
The White Hut

EAST LONGMEADOW
Donut Dip

FALL RIVER
Graham's Hot Dogs
★ Hartley's Original Pork Pies
J.J.'s Coney Island
The Liberal Club
Marzilli's Bakery
Mee Sum Restaurant and Lounge
Nick's

WESTPORT
Marguerite's

HYANNIS
Baxter's Fish & Chips

FAIRHAVEN
Elisabeth's

MATTAPOISETT
★ Oxford Creamery

MASSACHUSETTS

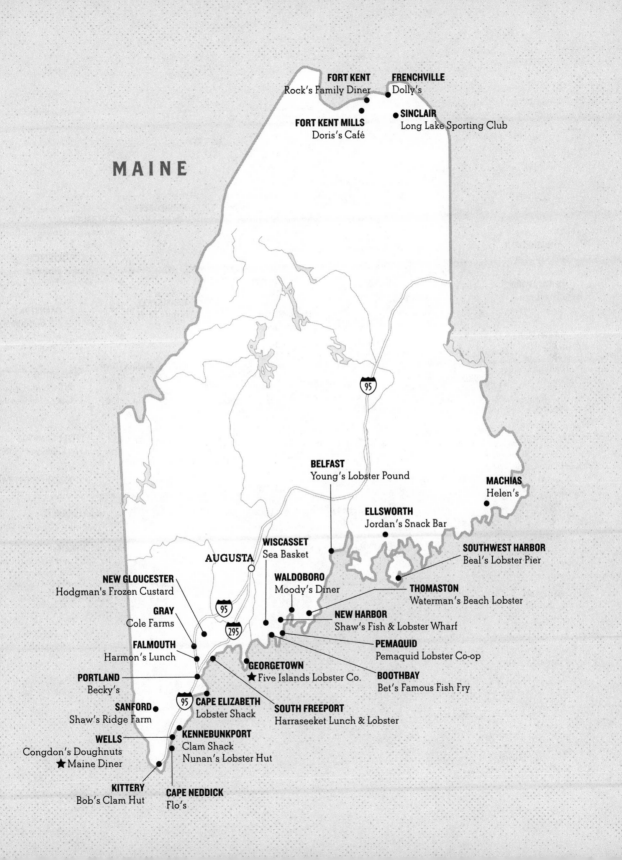

MAINE

FORT KENT
Rock's Family Diner

FRENCHVILLE
Dolly's

FORT KENT MILLS
Doris's Café

SINCLAIR
Long Lake Sporting Club

BELFAST
Young's Lobster Pound

MACHIAS
Helen's

ELLSWORTH
Jordan's Snack Bar

SOUTHWEST HARBOR
Beal's Lobster Pier

WISCASSET
Sea Basket

WALDOBORO
Moody's Diner

THOMASTON
Waterman's Beach Lobster

NEW GLOUCESTER
Hodgman's Frozen Custard

NEW HARBOR
Shaw's Fish & Lobster Wharf

GRAY
Cole Farms

PEMAQUID
Pemaquid Lobster Co-op

FALMOUTH
Harmon's Lunch

AUGUSTA

GEORGETOWN
★ Five Islands Lobster Co.

BOOTHBAY
Bet's Famous Fish Fry

PORTLAND
Becky's

SANFORD
Shaw's Ridge Farm

CAPE ELIZABETH
Lobster Shack

SOUTH FREEPORT
Harraseeket Lunch & Lobster

WELLS
Congdon's Doughnuts
★ Maine Diner

KENNEBUNKPORT
Clam Shack
Nunan's Lobster Hut

KITTERY
Bob's Clam Hut

CAPE NEDDICK
Flo's

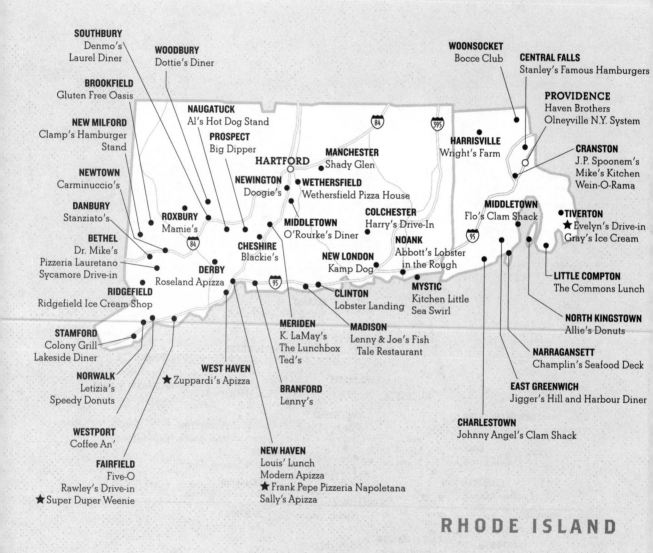

CONNECTICUT

RHODE ISLAND

SOUTHBURY
Denmo's
Laurel Diner

WOODBURY
Dottie's Diner

BROOKFIELD
Gluten Free Oasis

NEW MILFORD
Clamp's Hamburger
Stand

NAUGATUCK
Al's Hot Dog Stand

PROSPECT
Big Dipper

NEWTOWN
Carminuccio's

DANBURY
Stanziato's

BETHEL
Dr. Mike's
Pizzeria Lauretano
Sycamore Drive-in

ROXBURY
Mamie's

RIDGEFIELD
Ridgefield Ice Cream Shop

STAMFORD
Colony Grill
Lakeside Diner

NORWALK
Letizia's
Speedy Donuts

WESTPORT
Coffee An'

FAIRFIELD
Five-O
Rawley's Drive-in
★ Super Duper Weenie

HARTFORD

NEWINGTON
Doogie's

CHESHIRE
Blackie's

DERBY
Roseland Apizza

MERIDEN
K. LaMay's
The Lunchbox
Ted's

WEST HAVEN
★ Zuppardi's Apizza

BRANFORD
Lenny's

NEW HAVEN
Louis' Lunch
Modern Apizza
★ Frank Pepe Pizzeria Napoletana
Sally's Apizza

MANCHESTER
Shady Glen

WETHERSFIELD
Wethersfield Pizza House

MIDDLETOWN
O'Rourke's Diner

COLCHESTER
Harry's Drive-In

NEW LONDON
Kamp Dog

NOANK
Abbott's Lobster
in the Rough

CLINTON
Lobster Landing

MADISON
Lenny & Joe's Fish
Tale Restaurant

MYSTIC
Kitchen Little
Sea Swirl

WOONSOCKET
Bocce Club

HARRISVILLE
Wright's Farm

MIDDLETOWN
Flo's Clam Shack

CHARLESTOWN
Johnny Angel's Clam Shack

CENTRAL FALLS
Stanley's Famous Hamburgers

PROVIDENCE
Haven Brothers
Olneyville N.Y. System

CRANSTON
J.P. Spoonem's
Mike's Kitchen
Wein-O-Rama

TIVERTON
★ Evelyn's Drive-in
Gray's Ice Cream

LITTLE COMPTON
The Commons Lunch

NORTH KINGSTOWN
Allie's Donuts

NARRAGANSETT
Champlin's Seafood Deck

EAST GREENWICH
Jigger's Hill and Harbour Diner

CONNECTICUT

ABBOTT'S LOBSTER IN THE ROUGH

abbottslobster.com

117 Pearl St.
Noank, CT

860-536-7719

L D (May to Labor Day, then weekends through mid-Oct) | $$

── ★ ── ──
WATER-FRONT
DINING
── ── ★ ──

"In the rough" was never so agreeable. On an alfresco dining area perfumed by sea breezes and protected from marauding seagulls, one dines on lobster steamed to such perfect plumpness that meat erupts when the shell is broken. If cracking the carapace of a whole one seems too labor-intensive, the alternative is a hot lobster roll, which is hunks of lobster bathed in butter and sandwiched inside a warm bun. Cold lobster salad rolls are also available, as are hot and cold crab rolls.

While you can get excellent lobsters all up and down Yankee shores, one item you'll find only in this southernmost area is clear-broth clam chowder, of which Abbott's makes the best. Not nearly as creamy-dreamy as New England chowder, and lacking the cacophony of vegetables in Manhattan chowder, as well as the pink tomato blush of Rhode Island shore dinner-hall chowder, the clear-broth stuff is focused and intense. It is the essence of the ocean, and although it is dotted with bits of clam and little nuggets of potato, it is the liquid itself that commands attention. Unadulterated as it is, this is a dish strictly for seafood lovers. If you need something creamy, Abbott's lobster bisque is dramatically so.

AL'S HOT DOG STAND

248 S. Main St.
Naugatuck, CT

203-729-6229

B L D | $

Relish steals the show at many of Connecticut's big-name hot dog joints, and you will find some of the best at Al's. There are two kinds: hot relish, which will make lips glow, and Hawaiian relish, which balances the formidable heat with a shot of sweet pineapple. The dogs themselves are pork-and-beef foot-longs served in a split-top bun that gets nicely grilled on both sides. They are long enough that if you are a first-timer, you can put regular hot relish at one end and Hawaiian relish on the other and you will have multiple mouthfuls of both to compare and contrast.

Hot dogs are not the only worthies at Al's. Fried seafood, softshell crab in season, and bacon cheeseburgers all are good drive-in fare. French fries are crinkle-cuts and worth ordering. Milk shakes are the real thing.

But in truth, what we like best about Al's is not the food. It is Al's itself, a personality-plus eat shack staffed for more than three decades by family who take what they do quite seriously but offer it up with humor and charm. Dining here is light-years away from dining at a common junk-food franchise. Accommodations include outdoor picnic tables and weird indoor desks with avocado-green office chairs.

BIG DIPPER

bigdipper.com

91 Waterbury Rd.   203-758-3200
Prospect, CT   (limited winter hours) | **$**

Inspired by the traditional Good Humor bar but infinitely more delicious, Big Dipper's toasted-almond ice cream delivers the luxury of marzipan and the euphoria of Independence Day. It is but one of a multitude of flavors that include plain vanilla, silky chocolate, silly cotton candy, and a shockingly sophisticated cinnamon-coffee Café Vienna. Because it is not cloyingly rich, Big Dipper ice cream begs to be eaten in large quantities, or in such indulgences as a triple-dip fudge sundae. The line stretches far out the door on a pleasant night, and the staff is famously fun to deal with.

One thing we especially like about this place is that you are not limited to scoops as a measurement of your serving. You can buy as much or as little as you want. Each customer is charged by weight (of the ice cream).

BLACKIE'S

blackieshotdogs.com

2200 Waterbury Rd.   203-699-1819
Cheshire, CT   **L D** (closed Fri) | **$**

Hot dogs are so entirely the specialty of the house at Blackie's that regular customers walk in the door and simply call out a number, indicating how many they want. The dogs are boiled in oil to the point that their outside surface bursts apart from heat. One variation to consider is to add the suffix "well" to the integer you name. This means well-done, which adds extra crunch to the hot dogs' skin.

They are served plain in spongy buns, and it is up to each eater to spoon out mustard and relish from condiment trays that are set out along the counter. The mustard is excellent, and we recommend a modest bed of it applied to the top of each wiener, all the better for the relish to cling to. The relish is thick, luxurious, dark-green, and pepper-hot enough that the nerve endings on your lips will want to hum. Blackie's—and its devoted clientele—are happy enough with this formula for frankfurter perfection

that the kitchen doesn't bother to offer sauerkraut or chili. Service is nearly instantaneous, so if your preference is *hot* hot dogs, it is entirely practical to order them one by one until you can't eat any more.

Blackie's (since 1928) has oodles of old-fashioned charm, although you ought not come if you feel like kicking up your heels. A sign on the wall warns, "No Dancing."

CARMINUCCIO'S

carminucciospizza.com

76 S. Main St. (Rte. 25)   203-364-1133
Newtown, CT   **L D** | **$**

At the small array of bare-topped indoor tables or on the patio to the side of this inconspicuous yellow house by the side of the road, customers eat pizzas on a level with New Haven's best.

Patted out extra-thin, Carminuccio's crust has such a sturdy crunch that you can hold a hot slice by the circumference and the center will not wilt. Even with meat and vegetables on top it stays sturdy from the outer edge almost to the point, and no matter what ingredients you get, topping slippage is rare.

New Haven–made sausage, strewn edge to edge in countless little pinches, is cooked and well drained of fat before a sausage pie is assembled and baked, thus ensuring the cheese stays cheesy and the crust dry. Vegetables are pre-cooked in a convection oven, a process that not only saps crust-threatening moisture but dramatically intensifies the flavor of such toppings as spinach, onions, and tomatoes. Garlic especially benefits from the process, each whole clove caramelized to its soft, sweet essence. Before learning how it is done, we would have sworn the brilliant flavor of the kitchen's supple red pepper strips came from marinade and/or seasoning. But they are unadulterated, nothing but red peppers roasted to a sunny concentrate as vibrant as pumate. Combine the peppers with roasted garlic and sausage and you have a magisterial combo, one of the Earth's essential pizza-eating experiences.

CLAMP'S HAMBURGER STAND

Route 202   No phone
New Milford, CT   **L D** (Apr–Sept) | $

Despite its lack of a sign, street address, and telephone number, Clamp's is easy to find. Head north on Route 202 out of New Milford and when you see a crowd of cars on the right, you have arrived. Open from late April to early September from 11 a.m. to 2 p.m. and from 5 p.m. to 8 p.m., this little food stand has been a Litchfield County summertime ritual since 1939. (Those hours are exact. We arrived one day at 2:05 and got nothing to eat!)

Tables are arrayed on grassy groves on either side of the shack where you order, pay for, and pick up food. Hamburgers and cheeseburgers are the basis of Clamp's reputation. Made fresh daily and cooked the way you request, they are medium-size patties that leak enough juice to give the bun its own beefy appeal. Their edge slightly crisp, the fibers of the meat infused with a smoky taste that sings of summer afternoons, they are picnic food. All condiments are available; we highly recommend fried onions, which are cooked until caramel-sweet.

COFFEE AN'

343 Main St.   203-227-3808
Westport, CT   **B L** | $

A good donut is like a flower in bloom or a splendid sunset; the magic has something to do with the knowledge that its allure is fleeting. By tomorrow, even some of the best donuts might barely be edible. That's especially true of Coffee An's devilish devil's food sinker, which, when fresh, is as rich as expensive chocolate cake—crisp-skinned and with a roundhouse chocolate punch. Definitely one of the best chocolate donuts anywhere. The next day, when the infusion of hot oil has turned to cool fat and you sink your sorry teeth into it, you recoil as if from a hideous stranger that you find in your bed upon awakening. What possibly could have been this donut's allure?

Do return for a fresh one, and, once again, all is well with the world.

We also can recommend the plain cake and cinnamon-coated donuts, each of which has a memorably crunchy surface . . . but an equally ephemeral appeal.

COLONY GRILL

colonygrill.com
172 Myrtle Ave.   203-359-2184
Stamford, CT   **L D** | $$

Pizza is the only food on the menu of this old neighborhood tavern, and it is available in one size, about a foot and a half in diameter, with crust as thin as a saltine. Aside from the wild crunch of its crust, Colony pizza is known for locally made sweet sausage and for the optional topping called "hot oil": peppery olive oil that imbues the pie with luscious zest unlike any other. Each slice is crisp and yet so sumptuously oily that your fingers are guaranteed to glisten, even if you forgo the wonderful hot oil. Postprandial wreckage on the table is a giddy bedlam of severely battered trays piled with countless balled-up and knotted paper napkins.

Note: Three new locations have recently opened, at 1520 Post Road in Fairfield (203-259-1989), at 36–38 Broad Street in Milford, and at 515 West Avenue in Norwalk.

DENMO'S

340 S. Main St.   203-264-4626
Southbury, CT   **L D** | $$

Denmo's snuck up on us. We've been going to this picnic-table-only drive-in for years, always leaving happy and well fed. The foot-long, natural-casing hot dogs are presented in Yankee-style split-top buns, and they are beauties: slightly gnarled from getting fried, crisp-skinned, and full of garlic. The dogs are good, but it's the relish that we love. Peppery, pickly, a little bit sweet, and very hot, this relish, along with a good line of zesty mustard, will clear your sinuses and make you sing hallelujah.

Hot dogs actually are a sideshow for what Denmo's is most proud of: fried seafood. Crunchy clams with just-right bellies, sweet shrimp, and silky scallops all are fine shoreline treats (although Denmo's is a good thirty miles inland). They even have hot lobster rolls at (relatively) bargain prices, and when they are good, they are wonderful: fresh and perfectly buttered hunks of claw and tail. On occasion, however, the meat isn't as bright and sweet as one wants, and can taste like it was picked a while ago.

Among non-fried foods, the sleeper on the menu is soup. Every day there are a couple of varieties. The chowder is swell, as one might expect, but so are chicken soup and lentil soup and beef barley soup.

It is a fun place, with a big public bulletin board that is a fascinating portrait of a community's skills, needs, wants, and preferences. The only reason we can think of for not having included it in earlier *Roadfood* editions is that, as so many locals do with restaurants they frequent, we took Denmo's for granted.

DOOGIE'S

doogieshotdogs.com

2525 Berlin Tpke.   860-666-6200

Newington, CT   **L D | $**

Doogie's boasts of being "Home of the 2-foot hot dog." It is an astounding piece of food, but don't let the circus size divert attention from the fact that it is delicious. Firm-fleshed and with a chewy skin that gets charred on the grill, it has a vigorously spicy flavor that holds up under any and all toppings, especially Doogie's superb homemade hot relish. For those of meek appetite, the same good frank is available in mere sixteen-inch and foot-long configurations too.

Doogie's hamburgers, cooked on the same charcoal grill where the hot dogs are made, have a delicious smoky flavor. The top-of-the-line hamburger is listed on the menu as the MOAB (Mother of All Burgers), and while not as awesome as the elongated hot dog, it is an impressive package: a big patty buried under lettuce, tomato, chipotle mayonnaise, thousand island dressing, pickle chips, sliced red onions, provolone and pepper jack cheeses, bacon, caramelized onions, and roasted peppers—all on a garlic toasted roll.

DOTTIE'S DINER

dottiesdiner.com

787 Main St.   203-263-2516

Woodbury, CT   **B L D | $$**

LOCALS LOVE IT Dottie's is one of the few diners we know where you can still get an old-fashioned Connecticut chicken pie: savory crust loaded with nothing but warm, moist chicken meat served under a mantle of gravy. Dottie's also makes a more familiar chicken potpie that includes gravy, peas, and carrots. On the side, mashed potatoes are the genuine article.

As for donuts, which we have considered America's best since Dottie's was known as Phillips Diner and run by the Phillips family, they are, if possible, better than ever. Cinnamon donuts are creamy inside with a wickedly crunchy exterior (unless the humidity is really high that day); chocolate donuts come loaded with vast amounts of the glossy dark glaze that so perfectly complements the cake within.

Since her tenure began some four years ago, Dottie has spiffed things up with retro aqua upholstery in the booths and a new counter, and she's even gotten a liquor license and has begun serving dinners. The friendly community feeling so essential to the soul of a diner is thriving.

DR. MIKE'S

158 Greenwood Ave.   203-792-4388

Bethel, CT   (weekends only in winter) | $

Forget psychotherapy and medication! The best antidepressant we know is a visit to the good Dr. Mike of Bethel. The cones and cardboard cups dished out by this little shop are a miracle cure. As hopeless ice cream addicts, we must tell you that there is nothing quite like Dr. Mike's, and there are occasions when its ultra-richness is actually overwhelming. The longtime standard bearer, "rich chocolate," is only sweet enough to coax forth maximum cocoa flavor, its chalky chocolate and smooth butterfat body hypnotically fused. "Chocolate lace and cream" is another Dr. Mike's invention, made with wisps of refined chocolate-covered hard candy. The shards of candy are suspended in a pure white emulsion of sweetened cream: another dreamy experience, but in this case our warning is to get it in a cup. The crunch of the candy conflicts with the crunch of a cone.

We've named our two favorite flavors. Don't hesitate, though, if you find your personal favorite among the approximately eight varieties available any particular day. Each one is made the old-fashioned way, using cream from dairy buckets, in five-gallon batches, and we have fond memories of Dr. Mike's coffee, coconut, cinnamon, Heath Bar crunch, even prune, dazzling vanilla, and some real tongue-stunners made with fresh fruits in the summer.

Nota bene: Fudge sauce for sundaes is magnificent. Whipped cream is thick and fresh.

FIVE-O

1539 Black Rock Tpke.   203-330-8452
Fairfield, CT   **B L | $**

Some thirty years ago in Fairfield, Connecticut, where Tunxis Hill Road meets Black Rock Turnpike, there was a hot dog joint named Kuhn's Corner. Kuhn's is gone, replaced by a shopping center, but the four-alarm chili that made its hot dogs a local legend endures. A handful of food carts around Fairfield County offer Kuhn's chili as an optional wiener topping, and right across the street from where Kuhn's Corner used to be, a convenience store named Five-O sells quarts of the original-brew chili and serves beautiful hot dogs dressed with it.

Kuhn's chili is nothing like Texas chili con carne. Indeed, purists might argue that it isn't really chili at all. It is chili sin carne—meatless—and it also is beanless. It is not made to eat from a bowl but is a ferocious relish for a garlicky hot dog in a buttered and grilled split-top bun. The only logical improvement to the combination is a sprinkle of crisp raw onions, although Five-O also offers bacon, cheese, and all the usual frankfurter condiments.

Beyond hot dogs, Five-O's repertoire includes cold-cut sandwiches and a good Philly cheesesteak (well complemented by some of that chili). Nearly all business is takeout. In fact, the sit-down dining accommodations include exactly one little table,

nestled between the self-service coffee bar, racks of potato chips, and a shelf that holds the day's newspapers.

(Thanks to Adele O'Kane for letting us know about this place.)

★ FRANK PEPE PIZZERIA NAPOLETANA

pepespizzeria.com
157 Wooster St.   203-865-5762
New Haven, CT   **L D | $$**

Dating back to 1925, Frank Pepe Pizzeria Napoletana is a brash neighborhood joint on New Haven's pizza-parlor row that makes what we have long considered to be the best pizza on Earth. Any toppings are fine (pepperoni especially so), and the crust is sensational—brittle at its edges, ruggedly chewy where it puffs up, scattered on its crisp underside with burned grains of semolina from the oven's brick floor. The emblematic pizza is white clam, which Frank Pepe created midcentury after discussing the idea with a vendor selling littlenecks in a Wooster Street alley near the pizza parlor. It is an uncomplicated pie strewn with freshly opened littleneck clams and their nectar, a scattering of grated sharp Romano, a salvo of coarsely minced garlic, and a drizzle of oil.

In 2006, Pepe's opened a second store in Fairfield, Connecticut, and has since opened others in Manchester and Mohegan Sun, as well as in Danbury and in Yonkers, New York, with more on the way. Despite our skepticism of such proliferation, the pizzas we've had at the new places have been every bit as good as the original. Usually the wait for a table—which can be daunting in New Haven—is somewhat shorter.

GLUTEN FREE OASIS

glutenfreeoasis.net/
594 Federal Rd.   203-885-0314
Brookfield, CT   **L** (closed Sun)| **$**

──★── We're big fans of gluten and yeast and all
GREAT
GLUTEN-FREE the wonderful stuff they make when
──★── they're combined, so when locals tried
to steer us to a Brazilian bakery formerly called Mama's Cheese Bread Factory, where everything is

gluten-free and yeast-free, we dallied. When we finally walked in to order a sandwich, the man behind the counter gave us a *pão de queijo* (little cheese bun) to munch while we waited. That bun made us believers. It is lightweight yet joyously chewy—a real bread lover's delight, the sharp flavor of cheese a radically fine substitute for the tang of yeast.

While our sandwich was constructed, the boss described the process by which breads are made using tapioca flour and fermented leavener derived from yucca root. It is an ancient formula that originated in South America before Europeans and wheat arrived.

The Oasis uses this technique to make breads of various sizes, either finished or frozen and ready to bake, as well as pizza shells. For immediate satisfaction on the spot—dining in one's car or at the short window counter on one of half a dozen stools—there is a nice menu of breakfast sandwiches on cheese buns as well as some out-of-this-world lunch sandwiches. The Punta Cana is a mountain of moist, shredded roast chicken and carrots dotted with a few sweet raisins, laced with crunchy potato sticks, and garnished with lettuce leaves and mayonnaise. Hugely satisfying! Other available sandwiches include stuffed pork loin, ham-salami-mozzarella subs, sausage, grilled cheese with ham, and several vegetarian combos.

HARRY'S DRIVE-IN
harrysplace.biz

104 Broadway   860-537-2410
Colchester, CT   **L D** (summer only) | **$**

A completely alfresco eat place with wood-slat picnic tables arrayed under groves of flowering trees, Harry's has been a favorite stop for people on their way to and from the beach for more than eighty years. One of the best things about coming here is waiting for a meal to be assembled. There is no curb service. Exit your vehicle and stand in line; place an order and pay, then slide sideways to the pickup window. The view is breathtaking: two dozen hamburgers lined up on a glistening hot grill, sizzling and sputtering and oozing juice. They are formed from spheres of meat

that get slapped onto the grill and lightly squished so they flatten a bit; but the gnarled patties remain enormously juicy inside their rugged crust. With a mantle of melted cheese and a few strips of bacon, garnished with slices of summer tomato, lettuce, pickle, and mustard, sandwiched inside a fine bakery bun and held together with a long toothpick, this might be the best drive-in hamburger anywhere.

KAMP DOG
kampdog.com

15 Broad St.   860-443-3000
New London, CT   **B L** | **$**

Ironically sharing a building with a health-food store, Kamp Dog is a place to indulge in all manner of reprobate gastronomy, starting, of course, with wieners. As wieners go, in fact, these are good-quality Hummels. Grilled on the flat-top until crisp, they are bedded in buttered and grilled split-top Yankee buns. That's the basic platform; from there, chef Ken Hochstetler offers impressive variations, including a signature Kamp Dog, which features his spectacular hot-sweet-meaty "dynamite sauce," plus melted cheese and chopped raw onions. Other optional toppings are sauerkraut, chili, onions and peppers, and jalapeños. If you don't like Hummels, there are all-beef dogs, Georgia red hots, kielbasa, and knockwurst.

Hamburger variations are equally profuse, including a Reuben burger with kraut, Swiss, and thousand island dressing; a slawburger topped with house-made slaw; a bacon-egg-cheeseburger; a chili cheeseburger; and a dynamite sauce, cheese, and onion burger that is, in fact, a Kamp Dog without the dog. The menu promises that if you create a custom burger and eat ten of them, you get to name it, "unless it's a really stupid name."

Side dishes include the curiously named "chili Fritos," which Chef Ken explains is actually a Frito pie, but so named because no one in Connecticut has heard of the Southwestern classic. The chili is hot stuff. "Of course it is," he told us. "If it wasn't, it would be Bolognese sauce." And by the way, his French fries are hand-cut, cooked crisp and crunchy.

A fun, funky place. When you place an order at the counter, it is written on the back of a heavy-duty paper plate. The plate is passed along to Ken in the short-order kitchen. He makes the food, flips the plate, and uses it as your dinner dish.

K. LAMAY'S

klamayssteamedcheeseburgers.com

690 E. Main St.   203-237-8326
Meriden, CT   **L D | $**

As national interest in regional American food has blossomed in the last several years, the steamed cheeseburger has been discovered. While it is no longer an obsession known only to denizens of central Connecticut, it remains an acquired taste, the acquisition usually quite difficult for those who did not grow up eating it. Unlike renowned hamburgers elsewhere, this patty has no crunch whatsoever to its surface. At its worst, it resembles a wet sponge. But at its best, it is all juiciness and flavor.

It most definitely is at its best at K. LaMay's. Kevin LaMay began work in the burger field at Ted's, which today is the grand old institution of steamers. When he opened his own place, he decided to improve upon the formula. His burgers are bigger—one-third pound, rather than one-quarter pound; they are generously draped with steamed-soft cheese, and they are insanely juicy. One burger with the works, which would be tomato, lettuce, mustard, ketchup, and/or a dollop of the Sweet Baby Ray BBQ sauce on each table, is a big, sloppy, delicious mess. On the side there are French fries and onion rings, interesting potato chips, and locally bottled Foxon Park sodas.

KITCHEN LITTLE

kitchenlittle.org

36 Quarry Rd.   860-536-2122
Mystic, CT   **B L D | $**

Kitchen Little got big. In the spring of 2012 it moved from its minuscule location on the road to Mystic Seaport and reopened in a spacious setting that overlooks docked boats at the Mystic River Marina. You now can order beer and wine to accompany your cheeseburger, BLT, or lobster roll (available hot and cold).

Breakfast still stars, and "AM Eggstasy" remains the house motto. Omelets are impeccable, as are a variety of benedicts (California = asparagus and crab; Portuguese = *chourico* sausage and a Portuguese muffin). We love the sizzled-crisp corned beef hash, especially when customized with jalapeño cheese, onions, and sour cream. Kitchen Little's chowder is exemplary Southern New England–style: steel-gray and briny, with induplicable fresh clam flavor.

We've yet to try dinner, served in summer Thursday through Sunday.

LAKESIDE DINER

1050 Long Ridge Rd.   203-322-2252
Stamford, CT   **B L | $**

A humble eat shop literally at the foot of the southbound Exit 34 ramp off the Merritt Parkway, the Lakeside Diner is set up just like countless other diners, with a counter and stools and a scattering of tables. But there is a big difference: One whole wall is a picture window that overlooks Holts Ice Pond, where waterfowl skim past while customers fork into dandy short-order meals.

Pancakes are very good—thin and buttery, and available loaded with blueberries. Donuts are Lakeside's main claim to fame. There is no variety; these are simple cake donuts stuck with massive amounts of coarse sugar, great for dunking or eating by the bagful once you are back on the highway.

The menu is huge: all kinds of omelets and pastries, and a full repertoire of lunches that range from wraps and sandwiches to such blue-plate specials as meat loaf with mashed potatoes and gravy—all made from scratch.

LAUREL DINER

544 S. Main St.   203-264-8218
Southbury, CT   **B L | $**

Hash house connoisseurs should ignore Laurel Diner's few tables and get a stool at the counter facing the pint-sized grill. Here you have a spellbinding vision of time-space management as two short-order chefs fry, scramble, and flip eggs, fold omelets, butter toast, pour pancakes, and squish down patties of the diner's legendary corned beef hash.

The hash is a coarse-cut mélange of spicy beef shreds and nuggets of potato cooked on the griddle until a web of crust begins to envelop the tender insides. If you ask, the grill man will cook the hash until it is brittle-crisp nearly all the way through, which is a great idea if textural excitement supersedes succulence in your hierarchy of culinary pleasure; but we personally enjoy it the regular way: forkfuls of corned beef that are brick-red and moist, their pickly zest balanced perfectly by the soft pieces of potato.

You have two choices of potato: chunky home fries, which are excellent, and hash browns, which are better. While the chefs regularly scrape debris into the grill's front gutter, their touch is light enough that the flavors of bacon, ham, sausage, and hash linger, ready to be sucked into heaps of shredded potatoes piled on the hot surface. A broad cake of three or four servings is flattened and remains untouched long enough for the underside to turn gold, then the still-soft top is crowned with a scoop of butter. As the butter melts, the potatoes are flipped and worried so that by the time they are plated, they have become mostly crunchy, but with enough tender white tips to sop up at least two sunny-side yolks.

LENNY & JOE'S FISH TALE RESTAURANT
ljfishtale.com

1301 Boston Post Rd.	203-245-7289
(Rt. 1)	**L D** | $$
Madison, CT	

Lenny & Joe's opened as a roadside fried-clam stand in 1979. It has since become two large restaurants with menus that range from hot dogs to whole lobster dinners (summertime) to superior fried seafood. Whole-belly fried clams are big and succulent with golden crusts. We love the fried shrimp and scallops, even simple fried fish. All fried items are available in an ample regular size configuration as well as a "super" plate with double the amount of fish. This is one restaurant where the undecided customer who craves the crunch of fresh-fried seafood will be happy

ordering a variety platter with some of everything. It is a gargantuan meal, including crinkle-cut French fries and a little cup of sweet coleslaw. The only other necessary item would be an order of fried onions; Lenny and Joe's are wicked good!

There are two other locations, with table service: at 86 Boston Post Road (Route 1), Westbrook, CT (860-669-0767), and 501 Long Wharf Drive, New Haven, CT (203-691-6619).

LENNY'S
lennysnow.com

205 S. Montowese St.	203-488-1500
Branford, CT	**L D** | $$

A longtime fixture of the Indian Neck section of Branford's coast, this excellent restaurant is a neighborhood place with a menu that ranges from hamburgers and hot dogs to full shore dinners. The latter includes chowder (either creamy New England–style or clear-broth shoreline-style), cherrystone clams on the shell, a lobster, a heap of steamers, sweet corn, and a thick slice of watermelon for dessert.

Good as both kinds of chowder are, one should never begin a meal at Lenny's without "zuppa d'clams": steamed-open cherrystones in a bowl of spicy, lemon-laced broth, a half loaf of bread on the side for dunking. Delicious! Many of Lenny's best meals are fried: whole-belly clams, oysters, scallops, fish and chips, and huge butterflied shrimp. Crunch-crusted and clean-flavored, these are consummate fried seafoods, and proof that a crisp, clean crust can be the very best halo for seafood's natural sweetness.

Lenny's is a year-round destination. In the fall, every Sunday is turkey dinner day, featuring excellent mashed potatoes and gravy and stuffing. In the summer, diners top off meals with true Yankee strawberry shortcake, made from a sideways-split, unsweet biscuit layered with sliced berries in a thin sugar syrup, crowned with whipped cream.

LETIZIA'S

letiziaspizza.com

666 Main Ave.   203-847-6022
Norwalk, CT   **L D | $**

While the strip-mall setting isn't much, Letizia's name is part of northeast pizza history, one of the first in the region to serve it—as a weekend-only item—when Joe Letizia opened his Italian restaurant down on Norwalk's Wall Street in 1937. Well after his death in 1962, Uncle Joe's was still known as a source of fine red-sauce meals at rock-bottom prices. The family sold the old place in 1985 (it is now in others' hands), but today's Letizia's, opened by grandson Dan in 1992, still offers baked ziti and manicotti, spaghetti with marinara, and hot-parm grinders on made-here rolls. But it's pizza that matters.

The crust is terrific. Baked on a screen, then further toughened on the oven's brick floor, it is medium-thin Neapolitan-style, chewy more than brittle, with a full, earthy taste. Traditional mozzarella and sauce—the same food-service brands the family has used since the beginning—meld into a creamy Italian-American slurry with veins of tomato tang. Add discs of pepperoni, weeping oil into the mix, and you've got a mighty bite that is outrageously juicy. It is best consumed the New York City way, by pulling one triangular slice from the circle and folding it in half along the radius—the crust is pliable enough to bend, not break—creating a trough that holds everything like an open-top calzone.

LOBSTER LANDING

152 Commerce St.   860-669-2005
Clinton, CT   **L | $$**

——★--— Although lobster is considered the king
WATER-FRONT of North Atlantic seafood and tends to
DINING be priced accordingly, it usually tastes
--—★--— best when eaten in the least formal surroundings: at a picnic on the beach or overlooking a harbor, or in a place for which the term "restaurant" seems too grandiose: a shack. In this context, we present for your lobster appreciation an eatery called Lobster Landing.

Technically speaking, the dining area isn't even a shack. There is a tumbledown, hundred-year-old, wood-frame shanty by the water where you buy lobsters, oysters, and steamer clams to take home and cook. But to eat here, you sit at a plastic table in a sort of picnic area on a broken-clamshell deck that offers a makeshift tent for inclement weather. As for the choice of meals, there are hot dogs, sausage-pepper-onion subs, and lobster rolls.

The lobster roll is all that matters. It is very large—a heap of meat piled into a hollowed-out submarine loaf. The meat is bathed in butter but not swimming in it—all the better to savor the lobster itself. That's all there is to it: resilient, juicy, ocean-sweet lobster, drawn butter with a soupçon of lemon, and a toasted roll. What could be better?

LOUIS' LUNCH

louislunch.com

261 Crown St.   203-562-5507
New Haven, CT   **L | $**

You don't have to be a hamburger historian to appreciate Louis' Lunch, which claims to have invented the hamburger. The burgers are unique. They are hand-formed and cooked in ancient metal broilers that let much of the grease drip away, yet they remain juicy enough to sop the toast that encloses them. Yes, toast. There are no buns at Louis' Lunch for the obvious reason that when Louis Lassen invented the hamburger about six score years ago, there were no hamburger buns. Nor is ketchup available. You can get a slice of tomato on your burger, but ketchup always has been taboo. Other options for the burger are onions, grilled into the burger as it cooks, and Cheez Whiz.

Louis' Lunch exudes history. The small brick building is outfitted with snug school-desk seats and an ancient wooden counter with years' worth of initials carved into it. Alas, its fame has made it maddeningly popular, so waiting for a place to sit has become part of the experience.

THE LUNCHBOX

thelunchboxct.com

620 E. Main St.   203-238-0313
Meriden, CT   **B L** | **$**

A few years ago, Lunchbox proprietor Anita Dufresne won the "Most Creative" award in a Meriden newspaper's Battle of the Burgers competition for her Military Burger topped with guacamole, blue cheese, Cheddar, bacon, onion, lettuce, tomato, and mushroom. It's monumental, but even her regular steamed cheeseburger, maybe adorned with a couple of strips of bacon, packs enough convincing savor to put it in the topmost echelon of central Connecticut steamers.

While burgers are the regional specialty that makes the Lunchbox a siren song to culinary explorers, the menu beyond them is pretty great. We particularly remember a bowl of chicken soup that was as homey as Grandma's, as well as a plate of well-made Texas-style *migas*. During a recent Roadfood .com eating tour of Connecticut, several world-class eaters were stopped in their tracks by the unbelievably cheesy steamed cheeseburger omelet.

It should also be mentioned that Anita and her crew infuse the Lunchbox experience with the joie de vivre of a dream diner. They love to chat about food and everything else in the world. Even an antisocial introvert will walk out of this place not just well fed but with spring in his step.

MAMIE'S

mamiesrestaurant.com

162 Baker Rd.   860-210-0618
Roxbury, CT   **B L** (closed Tues);
                         D (Fri & Sat) | **$$**

Mamie's is glorious on a sunny day. Not that there's anything wrong with the handful of tables inside the bakeshop café, where customers come to chat, read the paper, drink coffee, and eat a handsome meal. The indoor seating is snug, sociable, and relaxed. But the more wonderful seats are outside, on a patio and at picnic tables on a sweeping lawn, where diners look out upon achingly scenic Litchfield County.

As one wants in so bucolic a setting, it is a casual place—the menu lists sandwiches, salads, and a roster of breakfast dishes ranging from familiar (bacon and eggs) to swank (crème brûlée French toast). Silverware comes wrapped in thick linen napkins, and the service, while friendly and familiar, is extraordinarily polite. If you'd like wine with dinner, BYOB.

It's weekend breakfast (aka brunch) we like best. Perfectly poached eggs come either in a cup or perched atop Mamie's autumn-root-vegetable hash or summer-vegetable hash. Toast is made from rough-textured seven-grain bread. Other breakfast highlights include banana pancakes and a chorizo omelet and—occasionally available—Mamie's freshly made beignets. Even the granola is a cut above—served warm and accompanied by fresh fruits.

Among sandwiches, we are suckers for the BLT, made with plenty of thick, smoky bacon, good tomatoes, and fresh lettuce, all best on that seven-grain toast. Locally raised Greyledge Farm beef is used for the hamburgers, thick enough to pack obscene amounts of juiciness that destroys the elegant buns.

Mamie's began as a bakery, meaning the pastries command attention. Cases display kingly coconut layer cake, banana cake, and big, chewy brownies. From the cooler come Key lime and peanut butter pies.

MODERN APIZZA

modernapizza.com

874 State St.   203-776-5306
New Haven, CT   **L D** | **$$**

While it is less famous than Pepe's and Sally's, Modern Apizza, a 1930s-era pizzeria on State Street in New Haven, is one of the Earth's best pizza parlors. Some savvy pizzaphiles consider it *the* best. "Our brick ovens reach 700 degrees fahrenheit," Modern's menu warns. "Some pizzas may blacken around the edges, and even lose their perfect shape due to contact with the brick surface of the oven." OK with us! While a few patches around the edge may be charred, the whole pizza has a swoonfully appetizing smoky taste, and you see why when you devour slices off the paper on which the pizza rests atop its round pan. The paper appears strewn with charred little bits of semolina from the oven floor, most of which cling to the underside of the crust, creating a slightly burnt hot-bread flavor that no wussy metal-floored pizza oven could produce.

Modern's specialty toppings include broccoli, sliced tomato, artichoke, and clams casino. It is known for the Italian Bomb, which is a joy to eat despite the fact that it totally overwhelms its crust: sausage, pepperoni, bacon, peppers, onions, mushrooms, and garlic. There is also a Vegetarian Bomb, topped with spinach, broccoli, olives, peppers, mushrooms, onions, and garlic. As for the New Haven favorite, white clam pizza (hold the mozzarella, please), Modern uses canned clams, not fresh, meaning there is less soulful marine juice to infuse the pizza; nevertheless, it is delicious—ocean-sweet and powerfully garlicky, and built on a crust that puffs up dry and chewy around the edges but stays wafer-thin all across the middle.

O'ROURKE'S DINER

orourkesmiddletown.com

728 Main St.   860-346-6101
Middletown, CT   **B L | $$**

★ **LOCALS LOVE IT** ★ O'Rourke's Diner almost perished in 2006 when it was ravaged by a fire. There was no insurance, but regular customers loved it so much that a fund was created to bring it back to life, as good as ever. The lustrous diner made by Mountain View Diners Company has been a Main Street fixture in Middletown, Connecticut, since 1946, and supplements familiar diner fare with the local oddity known as steamed cheeseburger, as well as unpredictable meals from relentlessly creative chef Brian O'Rourke. For example, Brian's Breakfast: "No two breakfasts are ever the same, and you do not know what you are going to get. Neither do your servers, so do not even try asking!" A few possibilities on the *petit déjeuner degustation*: duck hash, a waffle topped with barbecued pork, poached eggs with smoked salmon, a Dubliner omelet (corned beef hash and Irish Cheddar), or banana-bread French toast with clotted cream.

PIZZERIA LAURETANO

pizzerialauretano.com

291 Greenwood Ave.   203-792-1500
Bethel, CT   **L D | $$**

There are many excellent things on the menu of this gracious pizza parlor in the town that gave birth to P. T. Barnum: a just-right walnut-cranberry-gorgonzola salad dressed with lemony dressing, panini sandwiches at lunch, and pine-nut-dotted meatballs; but as the name suggests, pizzas are its glory. And glorious pizzas these are, in their own way every bit as soulful as those from Connecticut's funkier famous places. Imported flour and a wood-fired oven that proprietor Michael Lauretano brought from Naples create a crust with exquisite chewy-brittle balance. It puffs up along the edge so there may be a few spots that taste (quite deliciously) of carbon; the whole thing is insinuated with fire because just before the pizza is ready to be pulled off the oven's floor, the pizzaiolo slides his peel underneath and holds it at the very top of the oven directly over the smoldering wood pile for a few moments, making sure the top is fully cooked and at the same time giving it a smoky fragrance. We love the plain garlic pizza—really just a gilded flatbread; manna for crust lovers—as well as the mighty garlic and broccoli rabe white pizza; there are tradition-minded margheritas and puttanescas as well as occasional specials that include a ramp pizza in the spring and a fall harvest locavore's delight of multiple vegetables known as the garden pizza.

If you're lucky, when you dine here the kitchen will be passing out little lagniappes to each table to accompany salad or to munch while you wait for the pie to cook: thin strips of oven-hot crust, oh-so-ready to be dipped in seasoned olive oil.

RAWLEY'S DRIVE-IN

1886 Post Rd.   203-259-9023
Fairfield, CT   **L D | $**

Rawley's opened in 1947 and defined a way of cooking hot dogs that has become gospel for many of the important frank emporia in southwestern Connecticut. Into the deep fryer goes a substantial natural-casing dog. When plump and darkened, it is pulled from the hot vegetable oil and rolled around on the griddle with a spatula—a finishing touch that strains off excess oil and gives the exterior a delectable crackle. The dog is then bedded in a high-quality roll that has been spread open, brushed with butter, and toasted on the griddle until its interior surfaces are crisp, in contrast to the outside, which remains as soft and pliant as an oven mitt. The kitchen does the dressing, the most popular configuration being mustard and relish topped with sauerkraut and garnished with a fistful of chewy bacon shreds. To our taste, it is a perfect combination, although "heavy bacon"—twice as much—is a popular option.

The restaurant is pint-sized: four booths, plus a six-stool counter on what used to be a front porch, where an open picture window provides a scenic view into the lively short-order kitchen. As plebeian as can be, it is known for attracting celebrities who live or summer in the area. We had our first Rawley's hot dog on the recommendation of Martha Stewart.

RIDGEFIELD ICE CREAM SHOP

680 Danbury Rd.   203-438-3094
Ridgefield, CT $

A former Carvel stand, the Ridgefield Ice Cream Shop makes soft-serve ice cream by using machines from Carvel's early days, when the formula was not pumped full of air. The resulting lick is not sinfully rich or weird-flavored or in any way surprising. But in our book, it is perfect: smooth, pure, and dense, and so perfectly balanced that it tastes right no matter what the weather or time of day. While it is available with all sorts of jimmies, sprinkles, coatings, and nuts, we like ours just the way it comes from the gleaming stainless-steel machine: a swirly mound piled up on an elegant wafer cone. For those who live nearby, there are extraordinary ice cream cakes made from the same frozen manna and layered with icing and crumbled cookies.

Although it has a sunny, summertime feel, Ridgefield Ice Cream is open year-round, rain or shine. In good weather, customers have their cones while leaning on their cars in the lot, or at one of the picnic tables out front.

ROSELAND APIZZA

350 Hawthorne Ave.   203-735-0494
Derby, CT   D (Tues–Sun) | $$$

Roseland Apizza (pronounce that second word the Neapolitan way, "AH-beets") started as a bakery in 1934. Today, it is a popular neighborhood restaurant that is a shining example of Connecticut's great Italian-American cuisine: ravioli, lasagna, and nightly specials featuring shellfish and pasta, as well as brick-oven pies of the highest order. The crust is New Haven–style: thin but not quite brittle, with enough brawn to support all but the weightiest combinations of ingredients and to allay the pizza-eater's primal fears: slice collapse and topping slippage.

The luxe of some pies is surreal. High rollers can get a lavish shrimp-casino pie topped with bacon, mozzarella, fresh garlic, and too many jumbo shrimp to count. We recently enjoyed one heaped with a mountain of cool arugula salad—a yin-yang adventure of hot and cool, bread and veg, sweet cheese and bitter greens. We love the Connecticut classic white-clam pizza made without tomato sauce or mozzarella, just a crowd of clams strewn across a crust glazed with olive oil and scattered with bits of basil, parsley, and oregano, thin-sliced garlic, a twist of cracked black pepper, and a scattering of grated Parmigiano-Reggiano.

Note: Prices at Roseland are high, and some items, such as a dreamy shrimp oreganate pizza we recently had, seem outrageous. That one was more than $40. However, take into account the fact that everything served here is huge; virtually nobody leaves without boxes and bags of leftovers. That pizza satisfied two healthy appetites at dinner and provided lunch for two the next day.

SALLY'S APIZZA

sallysapizza.com
237 Wooster St.   203-624-5271
New Haven, CT   D (closed Mon & Tues) | $$

Sally's has soul. The place glows with old-neighborhood feel: wood-paneled walls, booths with well-worn Formica-topped tables, ubiquitous images of Frank Sinatra (a fan of Sal's cooking) all over the walls. And the pizza packs a wallop. It is generously topped, well oiled, and built upon a thin crust that is smudged and gritty underneath. Of special note are summertime's fresh tomato pie and broccoli rabe pie, heaped with bitter greens when they are available at the produce market. Although it is not formally listed on the menu, Sally's multi-meat "Italian bomb" (sausage, pepperoni, bacon, plus lots of onions) is also significant.

Old friends of Sally's are treated like royalty. Newcomers and unknowns might feel like they have to wait forever, first for a table, then for their pizza, and they will likely endure a staff who are at best nonchalant; but no one comes to Wooster Street for polished service or swank ambience. It's great, thin-crust pizza that counts, and on that score, Sally's delivers the goods.

SEA SWIRL

seaswirlofmystic.com

| 30 Williams Ave. | |
| Mystic, CT | **L D** (closed in winter) | $$ |

860-536-3452

Decades ago, when we played hooky from school in New Haven, we would drive along the Connecticut shoreline—a festival of good eating that always seemed to culminate in Mystic at Sea Swirl. This utterly informal former Carvel stand served some of the best whole-belly fried clams anywhere. It still does. Sheathed by ineffably tender crust, each clam is a mouthful of sweet ocean flavor that inundates the tongue with pleasure. A full order is a mountain and includes decent French fries and coleslaw. Smaller versions are available, as are clam rolls (fried clams piled into a bun). Even the clam strips are something special, delivering modest bivalve flavor in tiny bites that are amazingly tender.

We seldom venture beyond clams because they are so good, but Sea Swirl offers other excellent fried seafood, especially the scallops, as well as a capacious lobster salad roll, burgers, ten-inch hot dogs, and two kinds of chowder (New England milk and Rhode Island broth). Befitting the location's original purpose, ice cream of all sorts is available, including hard-pack or soft-serve and made-to-order milk shakes.

SHADY GLEN

| 840 E. Middle Tpke. | 860-649-4245 |
| Manchester, CT | **B L D** | $ |

Shady Glen makes baroque cheeseburgers. On a high-temperature electric grill, each circular patty of beef is cooked on one side, flipped, then blanketed with several square slices of cheese. The cheese is arranged so that only one-quarter to one-third of each slice rests atop the hamburger. The remainder extends beyond the circumference of the meat and melts down onto the surface of the grill. At the exact moment the grilling cheese begins to transform from molten to crisp, the cook uses a spatula to disengage it from the grill and curl it above the meat like some wondrous burgerflower—still slightly pliable, but rising up in some kind of symmetry. The petals of cheese, which may be topped with condiments and are crowned by a bun, are crunchy at their tips but chewy where they blend into the soft parts that adhere to the hamburger. The same cooking technique is used on hot dogs, known as cheesefurters.

The restaurant originally was opened in 1948 by John and Bernice Reig in order to put something on the menu of their dairy bar other than homemade ice cream. The ice cream is fantastic, including such seasonal flavors as minced pie, cranberry, and pumpkin in the fall and the outstanding February specialty, Bing cherry and chocolate chip. Our personal flavor faves include Grape-Nuts and Almond Joy.

SPEEDY DONUTS

| 116 Connecticut Ave. | 203-866-0044 |
| Norwalk, CT | **B L** | $ |

You need to know about one thing at Speedy Donut: the cruller. Tall and puffy, extravagantly eggy, moist within and croissant-crisp at its swirly edge, it is at once rich and featherweight, tremendously satisfying but easy to eat by twos and fours and sixes. We recommend glazed; the chocolate- and vanilla-frosted crullers are wonderful if you like chocolate and vanilla, but for us, even minimal frosting steals attention from the glory of Speedy Donut's fragile fried dough.

All kinds of other donuts are arrayed on the shelf in this humble Route 1 diner that has been earning its reputation since 1969, and they are good, albeit not divine like the crullers. Plain cake donuts are dense and creamy, ideal for dunking. Twists are heavy and substantial, the opposite of the ethereal crullers. Fritters also are hefty boys, known here curiously not as fritters but as spiders. The apple-filled glazed spider is breakfast unto itself.

It is possible to come to Speedy Donut for a full, hot meal such as bacon and eggs, breakfast sandwiches, and corned beef hash. Even lunch is served (burgers, hot dishes), but it's the magnificent crullers that call us back.

STANZIATO'S
stanziatos.com

35 Lake Ave.	203-885-1057
Danbury, CT	**L D** | $$

Pizzas are traditional Neapolitans, individually sized and baked ultrafast. It is hypnotic to stand at the counter and watch a pizza go from raw to done in less than two minutes. The crust puffs up around the edge and turns golden brown while the cheese melts in the middle and begins to spread.

The toppings roster includes familiar ingredients such as sausage, pepperoni, and mushrooms—all excellent—but this is one place where it pays to venture into the unusual options. Roasted cauliflower pie, for instance, is a devastatingly rich invention gilded with Burrata cheese and truffle oil; a soppressata pie boasts spicy salami from Arthur Avenue and very hot chile peppers; El Diablo features lime-marinated shrimp.

Pizzas star, but salads are by no means second-class menu items. We are smitten with the "winter salad": chopped romaine, sliced apples, grapes, peppery-sweet roasted pecans, and gorgonzola cheese dressed with maple balsamic vinaigrette. Other worthy dishes (after you have eaten your way through the pizza menu) include chicken wings baked in the wood-fired oven and a marvelous "mac 'n' cheese" that actually is a mix of couscous and roasted cauliflower.

★ SUPER DUPER WEENIE
superduperweenie.com

306 Black Rock Tpke.	203-334-DOGS
Fairfield, CT	**L D** | $

We've been on the Super Duper Weenie bandwagon since it was a food truck. It is now a restaurant, albeit an extremely casual one, and it has been featured on every TV show and in every publication that pays attention to hot dogs. In fact, several years ago when *Reader's Digest* asked us to name our single favorite drive-in eatery anywhere in America, this is the place to which we gave the nod. If you love hot dogs, it's a Holy Grail. (And if you don't love hot dogs, its hamburgers are terrific; from-scratch soups and sandwiches are first-rate too.)

The dogs are firm-fleshed franks made especially for SDW, which splits and grills them until their outsides turn a little crusty. They are sandwiched in fresh rolls and adorned with made-here condiments that include sweet onion sauce and hot relish. Chef Gary Zemola makes choosing easy with suggested basic configurations that include the New Englander (with sauerkraut, bacon, mustard, sweet relish, and raw onion), the New Yorker (sauerkraut, onion sauce, mustard, and hot relish), and the Chicagoan (lettuce, tomato, mustard, celery salt, relish, and a pickle spear). Whatever you get, you must get French fries: beautiful golden twigs served fresh from the fry basket and made extra-delicious by a perfect sprinkle of salt *and* pepper.

SYCAMORE DRIVE-IN
sycamoredrivein.com

282 Greenwood Ave.	203-748-2716
Bethel, CT	**B L D** | $

Hamburgers at the Sycamore Drive-In are golf-ball-sized spheres of meat that get slapped onto the grill, then spatula-flattened so intensely that edges are nearly paper thin and develop a lacy crunch. You can have one plain, doubled, sizzled with onions, topped with bacon and/or tomatoes, and if you still have questions, the menu offers "The Final Answer to the Hamburger." That's a Dagwood burger: two patties with cheese and every garnish known to mankind.

The Sycamore is rightly famous for root beer, made on premises and served in frosty glass mugs. It varies from sweet to dry, depending on where in the barrel the serving is drawn, but whatever its nature on any day, it always makes an ideal basis for a root-beer float.

The Sycamore is a genuine drive-in with carhop service (blink your lights) and window trays for in-car dining. Indoors, there are booths and a long counter. In the summer, on Saturday evenings, "Cruise Nights" attract vintage car collectors in their finest restored and custom vehicles. It's a true blast from the past!

TED'S

tedsrestaurant.com

1046 Broad St.   203-237-6660
Meriden, CT   **L** | **$**

Central Connecticut is home to about a half-dozen restaurants that all make steamed cheeseburgers, a regional specialty so geographically focused that it does not exist in eastern or western Connecticut. A steamer, as served at Ted's (since 1959), is cooked not on a grill or grate, but in a steam cabinet, the meat held inside a square tin as it browns. Adjacent to the beef in the cabinet are tins into which are placed blocks of Vermont Cheddar. The cheese turns molten and is ladled atop the burger in a hard roll (preferably with lettuce, tomato, pickle, and mustard).

If you love crusty hamburgers that crunch before your teeth sink into the pillowy meat, beware: This one is soft, inside and out, and the cheese atop it is the consistency of custard. For many otherwise broad-minded burger fans, it's just too weird. But those who become addicted to steamed cheeseburgers know nothing else that delivers its squishy satisfaction. Curiously, the dish was created in the 1920s when eating steamed food was a health fad.

WETHERSFIELD PIZZA HOUSE

955 Silas Deane Hwy.   860-529-2112
Wethersfield, CT   **L D** (closed Sun) | **$**

Despite its name, Wethersfield Pizza House makes the Roadfood roster for sandwiches. In particular, we're talking about grinders, a local term for stuffed torpedoes of bread known elsewhere as subs, heroes, po' boys, or zeps. In this family-run, thirty-plus-year-old storefront, the grinders are magnificent. Chicken cutlets head the list, offered in the traditional Italian way—topped with sauce and provolone—or American-style with lettuce, tomato, and mayonnaise. Both are grand, thanks to the cutlets themselves, which are made from chicken cooked and carved on premises every morning, breaded with homemade crumbs that feature rich, spicy seasoning and fried to a crisp in clean oil. We give the nod to the Italian-style version mostly because of the sauce, which, like just about everything else in this humble eatery, is made from scratch using old family recipes. Did we mention that each sandwich is piled four cutlets high, making it nearly impossible to fit into even the biggest mouth? A whole one, which is sixteen inches long, is a challenge for the most capacious appetite. Even an eight-inch "half" is a sizable meal.

Other hot grinders include meatball (made in house, of course), eggplant Parmesan, fried mozzarella with marinara sauce, and pepper and eggs. Among the cold grinders is an awesome Italian special—a mile-high pileup of ham, cotto salami, Genoa salami, provolone, lettuce, tomato, peppers, oil, and vinegar.

As for the pizza, it's really more like flatbread with a somewhat chewy, medium-thin crust, shockingly ungreasy. There are more interesting pizzas in the state of Connecticut. But there are no better grinders.

(Thanks to Roadfood.com contributor "ketteract" for alerting us to this gem.)

★ ZUPPARDI'S APIZZA

zuppardisapizza.com

179 Union Ave. 203-934-1949

West Haven, CT **L D | $$**

Zuppardi's is a family-run neighborhood restaurant that has earned generations of loyal clientele since 1934. You might have to wait for a table on weekend nights, but given its location far from Wooster Street's famous pizzerias, it never gets insanely crowded. The pizza it serves is every bit as good as New Haven's finest. Or is it the best anywhere?

Crust: Neapolitan-style. Thin and crisp with a puffy circumference that tilts more toward crunch than chew, it lacks a raunchy underside (the oven floors are regularly vacuumed), but it resonates with yeasty savor. Available toppings include sausage that is made on premises in two-hundred-pound batches and strewn across the pizza in rugged clumps, fresh tomato, broccoli rabe, escarole and beans, hot peppers, and roasted peppers. Clam pizza is listed twice on the menu, as whole baby clams and fresh clams, the latter twice as expensive as the former. That is because the fresh ones really are fresh, opened when you order your pizza (you will wait) and spread about the pie in superabundance. One of the Zuppardi family told us that for years vendors have tried to get them to switch over to flash-frozen, cryonautic, or otherwise pickled clams, guaranteeing the embalmed ones are indistinguishable from fresh. "Frankly, I think even the canned ones are better," she scoffed.

But freshly shucked ones are best, and the star ingredient in a magnificent pizza. They are tender littlenecks, glistening with briny-sweet oceanic liquor, complemented by a surfeit of chopped garlic and herbs. "Some customers ask for mutz [mozzarella cheese]," the pizzaiolo shared with a disapproving frown, "but that just weighs it down." Mutzless, Zuppardi's fresh white-clam pie, however perspicuous, is overwhelmingly satisfying.

MAINE

BEAL'S LOBSTER PIER

bealslobster.com

182 Clark Point Rd.   207-244-3202
Southwest Harbor, ME   **L D | $$**

Picnic tables overlook the harbor; from them, you can see the mountains of Acadia National Park in the distance and listen to the water rippling against the hulls of berthed fishing boats. At sunset, Beal's is magic.

Inside, select a lobster from the tank. While waiting for it to boil, eat your way through a bucket of steamer clams or dip into a cup of chowder. Lobsters come pre-cracked for easy meat extraction, but it's still some work. If a handsome whole one is too challenging a proposition, have a lobster roll—tightly packed, with plenty of fresh, cool meat atop a cushion of shredded lettuce. Burgers and a few other non-lobster meals also are available.

BECKY'S

beckysdiner.com

390 Commercial St.   207-773-7070
Portland, ME   **B L D | $**

Becky's has dramatically expanded since we first wrote about the little waterside diner many years ago, but it remains friendly, inexpensive, and delicious. Becky loves her varied clientele. "Side by side at my counter sit fishermen and captains of industry, college professors and paranoid schizophrenics," she boasts. "They talk to each other and they talk to those who work here. We are all family."

The breakfast menu includes homemade muffins, French toast made from locally baked Italian bread, and "loaded" hash-brown potatoes, which are mixed with peppers and onions and blanketed with melted cheese. There is a full array of usual breakfast sandwiches, and one sandwich that isn't usual at all: peanut butter and bacon. "I guess it's a breakfast sandwich," Becky chuckles. We love the "Titanic omelet," loaded with all three breakfast meats, cheese, onions, and peppers, and accompanied, preferably, with Portland's favorite morning breadstuff, Italian toast. If you are in the mood for fruit, we highly recommend Becky's fruit salad, for which everything is fresh, and is fresh-cut to order.

Lunch and dinner are equally impressive. Becky's haddock chowder is a local legend. Dinners such as pot roast with boiled potatoes and roast turkey with sausage stuffing define comfort food. Desserts include Grape-Nuts pudding, Becky's blueberry cake with cream-cheese frosting, and a marvelous Whoopie Pie cake that is like the small snack, but layered and large.

BET'S FAMOUS FISH FRY

Route 27	No phone
Boothbay, ME	**L** (Tues–Sat); **D** (Tues–Fri)
	(seasonal) | **$**

A tip of the hat to Holly Moore of hollyeats.com for directing us to this happy food truck just off Boothbay's town square. As its name says, fried fish is the dish to have—the only dish on the menu—either paired with chips (French fries) or in a gigantic sandwich or very large half sandwich. The fish is haddock, some of which is caught by Bet herself, the rest of which is secured from nearby boats. It is creamy-fresh, cased in fragile red-gold crust, and attains extra savor when dolloped with dill sauce. Get your beverage from the soda machine or bring your own.

Bet's a character, always gabbing with customers, her truck painted with a sign advertising FREE BEER TOMORROW.

BOB'S CLAM HUT

bobsclamhut.com

315 US Route 1	207-439-4233
Kittery, ME	**L D** | **$$**

Bob's motto is "Eat Clams." Fried clams, clam cakes, clam chowder, and clam burgers are all wonderful, but they are just the headliners on a long menu of excellent Downeast seafood.

Seafood rolls take center stage, and not just those piled with fried whole-belly clams or clam strips. You can have them loaded with scallops, shrimp, and oysters (all fried) or with crab, shrimp salad, or lobster. The high-ticket lobster roll is a beaut, served in a nice warm bun that is buttered and grilled until toasty golden brown on both sides; the lobster meat inside is faintly chilled, but not so much that any of the taste has been iced. On the side of most seafood dishes comes Bob's excellent tartar sauce, a perfect balance of richness and zest.

There is no table service. Either outdoors or at the indoor counter, read the posted menu, then place your order and pay in advance. You get a number, then dawdle around the pickup window (different from the order window) until the number is called. Dine either in your car, indoors at tables and counter, or at one of Bob's blue-checked picnic tables.

CLAM SHACK

theclamshack.net

2 Western Ave.	207-967-3321
Kennebunkport, ME	**L D** (summer only) | **$$**

The Clam Shack anchors one end of the bridge that connects Kennebunk to Kennebunkport. Fried clams, sold by the pint, are some of the best anywhere—crisp-crusted and heavy with juice. Lobster rolls are stratospheric. Big hunks of fresh-picked meat are arrayed across the bottom of a round bakery roll. It is your choice to have them bathed in warm butter or dolloped with cool mayonnaise before the roll's top is planted. It is not a huge sandwich, dimensionally speaking, but its flavor is immeasurable: a Maine summer pleasure to make any lobster lover weak-kneed.

Whole lobsters are boiled and sold from an adjoining store that is also a seafood market and bait-and-tackle shop. Upon receiving a cooked lobster, and maybe a half pound of steamer clams, it is the customer's job to find a place to eat. There are benches on a deck in back and seats facing the sidewalk in front, where fish crates serve as makeshift tables. (Town zoning forbids proper seating here.) Potatoes? Rolls? Corn? Dessert? You are on your own. The store does sell bottles of beer and wine.

COLE FARMS

colefarms.com

Route 100	207-657-4714
Gray, ME	**B L D** | **$**

Opened as a farmland diner in 1952, Cole Farms still can be relied on to serve such parochial arcana as boiled dinner and mince pie in the autumn, corn chowder every Wednesday, and a choice of sweet beverages that includes both milk shakes (no ice cream, just milk and flavoring) and frappes (what the rest of the world knows as a milk shake, made with ice cream). It is not, however, preserved in amber. Remodeled and expanded at least a dozen times, the building is now huge and features a gift shop as well as a banquet room. Lunch choices include wraps and modern salads with fat-free raspberry vinaigrette dressing alongside such longtime kitchen specialties as clam cakes and chicken potpie. Even morning muffins aren't quite as dour as they used to be. "We've tweaked them over the years," says proprietor Brad Pollard. "People want their muffins sweeter. You have to keep up." Such changes notwithstanding, a Cole Farms muffin is demure, nothing like a cloying cake-batter pastry.

A good measure of Cole Farms' personality is American chop suey, a *déjuner maudit* listed on the menu right below baked beans (available with or without a hot dog). Like the shockingly red hot dogs, American chop suey is an archaic New England meal once popular in institutions and on the supper tables of frugal housewives: ground beef mixed with elbow macaroni and vaguely Italian tomato sauce. It is bland as can be—closet comfort for those of us who sometimes wax nostalgic for school lunch.

The enduring regional value we like best at Cole Farms is the importance of pudding. Indian pudding, the rugged cornmeal samp sweetened with molasses, is served hot under a scoop of vanilla ice cream. Grapenut pudding comes as a cool block of custard topped by a ribbon of sweetened cereal that has an amber crust reminiscent of a swanky crème brûlée. Swanky, it is not; Yankee, it is.

CONGDON'S DOUGHNUTS

congdons.com

| 1090 Post Rd. | 207-646-4219 |
| Wells, ME | B L \| $ |

Muffins are the reigning morning pastry throughout most of Maine, but since 1955, Congdon's has built its reputation on donuts. There is a full breakfast menu, and from what we've seen, it looks pretty good. (Who doesn't like a place that includes a pot of baked beans with the meal?) But when we come to this place, we aren't going to be using up any appetite on bacon and eggs or corned-beef hash. We'll be having maple cream donuts, sugar twists, cruellers (yes, that's how they spell "cruller" here), and apple fritters. Of the many varieties, the plain honey donut is probably the best: fluffy, fresh and rich, although not so heavy that three or four aren't a reasonable breakfast. If you buy six, you get the seventh free.

Seating is diner-style, counter and booths.

DOLLY'S

| 17 US Route 1 | 207-728-7050 |
| Frenchville, ME | B L D \| $ |

Next to Dolly's cash register is a griddle about four feet square, sided by a pitcher filled with *ploye* batter. A *ploye* is an Acadian buckwheat pancake that gets cooked very briefly and never flipped. It comes off the hot iron with an underside that is slightly crisp and a top that is tender enough to beg for melting butter and maybe a dollop of molasses or maple syrup.

Unless you say otherwise at Dolly's, supper will come with *ployes* rather than rolls, and these *ployes* are memorable. They are butter-yellow with a faint green tinge created by the buckwheat (which is botanically an herb rather than a grain) and they arrive three-by-three straight off the griddle. They are a glorious companion for Dolly's Acadian chicken stew. More a curative soup than a casserole, the kindly bowl of schmaltz-rich, golden broth is crowded with large pieces of meat, nuggets of potato, and little free-form dumplings, plus a measured scattering of herbs.

Old-time Acadians ask for *creton* with their *ployes*. Creton is a crazy-fatty-good pork spread not unlike French rillettes. Dolly's version is bright and flowery, a refreshing burst of unexpected spices, including cinnamon, that harmonizes just right with a warm buckwheat crepe.

DORIS'S CAFÉ

| 345 Market St. | 207-834-6262 |
| Fort Kent Mills, ME | B L \| $ |

The Roadfood connoisseur will grin with joy upon entering Doris's Café, which shares a building with the Fort Kent Mills Post Office. On one wall hang patrons' coffee cups, which they grab upon entering (starting at 5 a.m.), then pour their own coffee while Linda Daigle (the late Doris's sister) makes sure the frying potatoes look good and the eggs are ready to crack.

With a couple of exceptions, the menu is unsurprising town-café fare, including stout toast made from baked-here bread and desserts such as pecan pie, chocolate cream pie, Boston cream cake, and "JJ apple pie," which is an obscure name for a sensational creation made from big, spicy apple chunks with a savory crust festooned with a ribbon of caramel. Hot meals come with homemade rolls, and just about anything should be sided by French fries. This is potato country, and Linda makes the most of it, producing irregularly cut, soft-centered fries from the deep fryer next to the griddle.

Fries are the foundation for the Québécois (and northernmost Maine) specialty known as *poutine*. Atop a heap of just-cooked potatoes goes a blanket of dark gravy and a big fistful of mozzarella cheese that melts from the heat of the spuds. Known in most local restaurants as "mix" or "fry mix," *poutine* delivers a roundhouse punch that makes it a nice dish to split among two (or four). The other unique treat is *ployes*, which are crepelike buckwheat pancakes cooked only on one side, resulting in a top that has a million holes and can absorb massive amounts of butter and syrup or gravy from the hot turkey plate or boiled dinner, which here is made with ham.

★ FIVE ISLANDS LOBSTER CO.

fiveislandslobster.com

1447 Five Islands Rd.	207-371-2990
Georgetown, ME	**L D** (summer only)	$$

You don't come to Five Islands, sit at a table, and get waited on. Securing dinner is part of the experience. First, go to the building with the sign above the door that says "Lobsters." Look in the tank and pick the one you want. Tell the people in here if you want clams, corn, or potatoes thrown into the net and boiled alongside the lobster. You can buy a soft drink (or bring your own wine or beer), although we had to convince one old salt to sell us a bottle of Moxie, which she promised was too bitter for travelers unaccustomed to the Yankee beverage that was originally marketed as nerve tonic. While the meal cooks, find a picnic table. If you are very hungry or for some reason don't want a lobster, go to the other building and pick up an order of fried clams, a lobster roll, fried fish, or even a hamburger or hot dog.

Good as all that other stuff is, you're crazy not to get a lobster. Proprietor Keith Langbottom says the water around here is the deepest and coldest on the coast, explaining why these lobsters yield meat that is so firm and radiant with clean marine flavor.

Tranquility reigns when you look out at the islands in the distance, even when all the picnic tables are crowded with happy eaters chattering with the joy of their sleeves-up meal. As we devoured our shore dinners, savoring the beautiful scene every bit as much as the food, a fishing boat glided into the harbor and tied up at the wharf a few yards from our table. We ate Maine blueberry cake while watching two lobstermen offload crates full of lobsters just trapped in the deep.

FLO'S

floshotdogs.com

Route 1	800-255-8401
Cape Neddick, ME	**L** (closed Weds)	$

Flo's blubbery little pink weenies are not gourmet sausages, and the place itself feels like a crowded garage. Nonetheless, there are many tube steak connoisseurs who put this wacky little place on the short list of America's must-eat hot dogs.

Hot dogs are the one and only thing on the menu, so all you need to do to place an order is to call out a number to indicate how many you want and let the staff know how you want them dressed. As far as we are concerned, there are two basic ways to go: mustard and hot sauce or mayo and hot sauce. The sauce, which is technically optional but culinarily essential, is nothing like chili on a chili dog. It is a devilishly dark sweet/hot relish of stewed onions, glistening with spice and customarily finished with a sprinkle of celery salt. With mayonnaise, it makes for a rich little weenie. With mustard, you get a dog that barks. Nestled in steamed-soft buns, the franks are small enough that two are a mere snack; four to six make a meal.

It is our duty to inform you that visitations from TV food shows have made Flo's so popular that the wait to place an order can approach an hour.

HARMON'S LUNCH

144 Gray Rd.   207-797-9857
Falmouth, ME   L | $

Doneness is not an issue at Harmon's. All hamburgers are grilled medium so they are moist but not oozing juice or pink inside. They get sandwiched inside soft Portland-bakery buns that are buttered and heated just enough that they become tender mitts for burger-holding. Among the options you do have when you order a hamburger is a slice of cheese melted on top and, better yet, grilled onions. The onions are fried until melting soft, and they add sweet vegetable savor to the little package. Also available are mustard and vivid red relish. Don't bother to ask for lettuce and tomato. They are unavailable, and if you don't like that fact, please reread the sign behind the counter that warns, "This is not Burger King. You don't get it your way. You take it my way, or you don't get the damn thing."

The only side dish is French fries, and they're super: thick-cut and delivered too hot to handle. However, when this little shop gets crowded, as it so often does, ordering French fries can delay delivery of the meal. The problem is that exactly fifteen hamburgers fit on the grill at one time, but the fry kettle has room only for four orders of potatoes. Therefore people who come only for burgers have their order put to the head of the line while potato-eaters wait.

The little wood-frame diner north of Portland was opened in 1960 by Marvin Harmon, and current boss Peter Wormell maintains the unforgiving attitude for which the place has become known over the years. He only reluctantly agreed to allow us to take pictures of the wonderful décor—row after row of old-fashioned glass milk bottles from long-gone Maine dairy farms—and he did not seem at all pleased when we started asking him about the source of his good-tasting beef. Nonetheless, after we paid at the press-button, non-digital cash register and walked out the front door heading for our car in the dirt parking lot, Mr. Wormell came running out behind us—leaving a griddle full of hamburgers sputtering—just so he could give us a small magnetic calendar, the kind you slap onto a refrigerator door, that featured the restaurant's name, address, and phone number, as well as the pacific motto, "Let's Get Harmonized!"

HARRASEEKET LUNCH & LOBSTER

harraseeketlunchandlobster.com
36 Main St.   207-865-4888
South Freeport, ME   L D (May–Oct) | $$

They tell us that it does rain in Freeport, but every visit we have made seeking lunch at Harraseeket Lobster, the sun was shining and gulls were swooping overhead through the blue, blue sky. Picnic tables overlook the Freeport town harbor; meals are perfumed by the salt smell of the ocean and serenaded by the sound of an American flag flapping overhead.

The specialty is boiled-to-order lobsters (also available live, to go), but don't ignore the seafood baskets. Whole-belly clams are giants, hefty gnarled spheres of golden crust enveloping mouthfuls of ocean nectar. On the side, you want onion rings: puffy circles of brittle sweet batter around a hoop of onion that still has crunch. Clam cakes are good too, their puffy dough holding dozens of nuggets of marine goodness. Chowder is swell, as is the cool lobster roll, served splayed open in a broad cardboard dish and packed with briny-sweet chunks of meat. Have it with onion rings and conclude with a fudgy, hand-fashioned whoopie pie.

HELEN'S

helensrestaurantmachias.com
28 East Main St.   207-255-8423
Machias, ME   B L D | $

Helen's is deservedly famous for blueberry pie. A dense slurry of cooked and fresh tiny wild Maine blueberries—one-fifth the size of the big ones you buy by the pint at the supermarket—is piled onto a flaky crust and heaped with whipped cream. If all you know are the store-bought ones, the flavor of these berries is astonishing: intensely fruity, sweet but not sugary, bright as the sun. You can get Helen's blueberry pie year-round, but the best time to have it is late summer, when fresh-picked lowbush blues are abundant.

The same fine blueberries find their way into morning muffins, and pies made from raspberries, strawberries, and boysenberries should not be ignored, nor should brownies, cakes, and turnovers. But Helen's is not merely a pastry shop. It is a dandy small-town restaurant that serves a lunch of fried clams or fried haddock, broiled halibut, hot turkey and mashed potatoes, or a simple bowl of fresh-picked lobster meat sopped with butter.

HODGMAN'S FROZEN CUSTARD

1108 Lewiston Rd.   207-926-3553
New Gloucester, ME   (Mother's Day to Labor Day)
                      (closed Mon & Tues) | $

Hodgman's custard is dense, smooth, and creamy-rich, made in vanilla and chocolate flavors, plus one special flavor each week. We loved the peanut butter flavor we tried one day, but chocolate and vanilla are so purely perfect that exotic flavors are like gilt for the lily. You can have your custard in a cone or cup, as the foundation for a sundae, banana boat, frappe, float, or what is known here as a thunderstorm, for which the custard is swirled together with toppings. If you are heading straight to a picnic or a place with a refrigerator, be aware that Hodgman's also makes custard pie with a graham-cracker crust.

There is no indoor dining area, but facilities include picnic tables and a gazebo to the side of the stand, where you can sit and lick in the shade.

JORDAN'S SNACK BAR

jordanssnackbar.com
200 Downeast Hwy.   207-667-2174
Ellsworth, ME   **L D** (Mar-Nov) | $

For three decades now, Jordan's has been a favorite stop for locals and visitors in search of good burgers, hot dogs, fried seafood, and a selection of ice cream treats, from cones and cups to banana boats and fruited milk shakes. Much business is takeout for people on their way to Bar Harbor, but you can eat here at an outdoor picnic table, in an air-conditioned dining room, or under a covered gazebo. There is a playground, and every Wednesday, Jordan's hosts a vintage car cruise night with live country music.

Among the stars of the menu are toasty, lightly battered fried clams, shrimp, and scallops, each available as a roll (sandwich), as a lunch with fries, or as a dinner with fries and coleslaw. The dinners are huge—big enough to split. Crab rolls are made with sweet, fresh meat, as are lobster rolls, although the latter seemed a bit stingy and stringy—not among Maine's finest.

LOBSTER SHACK

lobstershacktwolights.com
225 Two Lights Rd.   207-799-1677
Cape Elizabeth, ME   **L D** (closed winter) | $$

— ★ – – –
WATER-FRONT
DINING
– – ★ ——-
Some foodies like to say that ambience doesn't matter all that much; what you put in your mouth is all that counts. If you are of that persuasion, you probably want to skip the Lobster Shack and move on up the coast. Not that the seafood here is bad. In fact, it's good; but there are better fried clams and lobster rolls elsewhere.

On the other hand, nowhere else will you find a setting like that of the Lobster Shack, located in Two Lights State Park. Outside, by a rockbound cliff overlooking Casco Bay, you can sit at a picnic table and eat a lobster that really is seasoned by salty sea air blowing in. Instead of piped-in music, you will be serenaded by gulls screeching overhead.

Aside from whole lobsters, we recommend the creamy lobster stew, perhaps accompanied by a clam cake or two, and whole-belly clams, which are good and crunchy. The lobster roll is a cool one, with plenty of meat and mayonnaise applied in a single dollop on top, allowing the eater to spread it or move it aside as desired. Desserts to know about are Grape-Nuts pudding and Maine's favorite snack cake, Whoopie Pie—or as it is spelled here, curiously, Whoopy pie.

LONG LAKE SPORTING CLUB
longlakesportingclub.com

48 Sinclair Rd.	207-543-7584
Sinclair, ME	D | $$

You wouldn't call the Long Lake Sporting Club blue-chip (swank restaurants do not exist in northern Aroostook County), but neither is it blue-collar. Set in a peaceful waterside location on Long Lake and accessible by auto, boat, or seaplane (or snowmobile in season), it is a north woods supper club to which locals and visiting outdoorsmen repair for cocktails and big-deal meals of prime rib, lobster, or fried chicken.

The chicken is especially good, pressure-fried so it develops a hard, toasty crust that shores in amazing amounts of juice. Alongside the chicken comes a ramekin of translucent red barbecue sauce with spices that give the chicken a welcome jolt. Whatever main course you choose comes as part of a ritual meal that includes a finely chopped cabbage and carrot salad bathed in a spicy tomato dressing not unlike that used on barbecue slaw in the Mid-South. Well-salted French fries are thick with a tough coat enclosing creamy insides. All meals include a plate of *ployes,* the thin buckwheat pancakes that are popular in this part of Maine in lieu of dinner rolls. The *ployes* arrive wrapped in a thick white napkin accompanied by bubble packs of butter and margarine and a pitcher of corn syrup. Two plates are provided so you can pour a pool of syrup into the second plate, peel a *ploye* from the stack on the other plate, butter it, roll it into a tight tube, then dab it in the syrup for between-meat bites.

★ MAINE DINER
mainediner.com

2265 Post Rd.	207-646-4441
Wells, ME	B L D | $

For us, no trip up Route 1 is complete without a visit to the Maine Diner, whether it's for a plate of home-made baked beans, the world's most delicious seafood chowder, or grandma's-recipe lobster pie. Truly special daily specials include New England boiled dinner every Thursday and red flannel hash . . . while supplies last. We are especially fond of the fried clams, which are vigorously oceanic, just a wee bit oily, so fragile the crust seems to melt away as your teeth sink into them. Serious clam devotees can get a "clam-o-rama" lunch, which includes clam chowder, fried whole-belly clams, fried clam strips, and a clam cake!

Seafood rolls are outstanding—split buns piled with clams, haddock, scallops, or shrimp. And the lobster rolls are not to be missed. Yes, we said rolls, plural; the Maine Diner offers two kinds—a lobster salad roll, of cool meat and mayo, or a hot lobster roll with plenty of melted butter to drizzle on it. Either one is terrific; for us, the hot lobster roll is heaven on Earth.

The menu is vast, including such all-American items as buffalo wings and a barbecued pork sandwich, plus a superb chicken potpie. In our book, the single mustn't-miss dish is lobster pie—a casserole containing plump sections of lobster claw and chewy tail meat, drenched in butter and topped with a mixture of cracker crumbs and tomalley. It is a strange, punk-colored dish, monstrous green and brown and pink, shockingly rich.

To sate that after-meal sweet tooth, there are homemade pies of the day, three kinds of pudding (Grape-Nuts, Indian, bread), blueberry-chip ice cream made especially for the diner, and straw-berry shortcake.

MOODY'S DINER
moodysdiner.com

Route 1	207-832-7785
Waldoboro, ME	B L D | $

Moody's no longer is open around the clock, but it remains one of the top spots along the coast route for pre-dawn breakfast. When the doors open at 4:30 (5 a.m. in winter), morning muffins have been out of the oven long enough that you can pull one apart without searing fingertips; through the cloud of steam that erupts, a constellation of blueberries glistens in each fluffy half.

Thrift is a pillar of traditional New England cooking and a big part of Moody's echt-Maine character. This is not the place you come to splurge on a full-bore shore dinner or a $15 lobster roll; in fact the restaurant's 208-page cookbook, *What's Cooking at Moody's Diner*, doesn't contain a single recipe for lobster. But it does offer "mock lobster bake" made with haddock fillets. Haddock, which costs less than just about any other edible fish, has been served with egg sauce every Friday for as long as any of the Moody family can remember. (At last count, more than two dozen Moodys have worked in the restaurant and at the motel and cabins just up the hill.)

The menu is a primer of Northeast diner fare: meat loaf and mashed potatoes, hot turkey sandwiches, a panoply of chowders, stews and soups, red flannel hash, baked beans with brown bread, and a fabulous selection of pies, including a legendary walnut pie that is actually a gloss on southern-style pecan pie but, as Alvah Moody proudly notes, "not sickening sweet."

NUNAN'S LOBSTER HUT

nunanslobsterhut.com

9 Mills Rd.   207-967-4362
Kennebunkport, ME   **D** (summer only) | $$

LOCALS LOVE IT No frills at Nunan's will distract you from the goodness of the lobster (except maybe the view, when the panels on the sides of the dining room are raised to reveal a pleasant vista of Cape Porpoise marshlands). Each lobster is steamed in a couple inches of salty water for twenty minutes, emerging with silky tender claw meat, its knuckles and tail succulent and chewy. It comes to the table on a pizza pan with cups of drawn butter.

The Nunan family have been lobstering for three generations and running this restaurant since 1953, so by now they have the process of enjoying their catch down to its essence. In addition to whole lobsters, they serve lobster stew, lobster rolls, and lobster salad (plus a small assortment of hot dogs, hamburgers, and so on for those with lobster allergies). After supper, there are homemade brownies or a slice of pie, the recipes for which have been perfected over the last thirty years. Blueberry and apple are memorable, their subtly sweetened fruits encased in sugar-dusted crusts.

Should you desire to wash your hands before, during, or after eating, sinks are available in the open dining room, ready for immediate action. They are proletarian sinks like you'd want to have next to your workbench in the basement. For drying hands, Nunan's supplies rolls of paper towels.

PEMAQUID LOBSTER CO-OP

pemaquidlobstercoop.com

32 Co-Op Rd.   207-677-2801
Pemaquid, ME   **L D** (May-Oct) | $$

Lobster is deluxe food that many people like to eat in a primitive setting. If you're such a person, find your way to Pemaquid, Maine, and its Lobster Co-Op. And we do mean find your way: Pemaquid is not on the way to anywhere other than the famously scenic Pemaquid Lighthouse. But once you get here, you can eat some of the nicest lobster anywhere off picnic tables overlooking the harbor where co-op members berth their fishing boats.

A first-timer probably ought to have the basic shore dinner, which is a pound-plus lobster with meat that completely fills out its shell, steamer clams with broth and butter, corn on the cob, coleslaw, and a roll. Lobster options include a lobster salad roll in a split-top Yankee bun; the already-extracted lazy-lobster plate; and rich, hearty lobster stew. Fried seafood is also a specialty, and supposedly it all is local, including Maine shrimp, but we choose to devote our full appetite to lobster. BYOB.

ROCK'S FAMILY DINER

378 W. Main St.   207-834-2888
Fort Kent, ME   **B L D** | $

Rock's is ambiguously located smack between two scenic markers, one declaring itself the beginning of Route 1—2,209 miles from Key West; the other saying it is the end of Route 1—2,390 miles from Key West. We've never measured, nor do we have an opinion about whether Route 1 starts or ends in Fort Kent; but we have eaten several meals at this diner in the northeasternmost corner of the United States and recommend it with no ambiguity at all.

Walk in, study the wall menu, place your order, and pay. Then find a seat at a table or booth or one of the communal counters. In a short while, out comes a member of the staff with your cheeseburger, chili dog, sandwich, or hot-lunch plate. The burgers are thin patties, squished hard on the grill but fatty enough to be plenty juicy. On the side, fried potatoes are the order of the day, available seven ways: jo-jo's, curly fries, plain fries, fries topped with gravy, hamburger or Italian sauce, or as a mix (the local version of *poutine*): potatoes heaped with mozzarella cheese and dark-brown gravy.

In August, when Fort Kent holds its annual Muskie Derby and Ploye Festival, Rock's hosts a contest to see who can eat the most *ployes* (buckwheat crepes). They serve a traditional Acadian meal that includes some of the best pot roast anywhere, plus stacks of *ployes* to mop its gravy.

SEA BASKET

seabasket.com

303 Bath Rd.   207-882-6581
Wiscasset, ME   **L D** (closed Tues & all of Jan & Feb) | **$**

Sea Basket is a roadside café with eat-in-the-rough service: place an order and wait for your number to be called. We are huge fans of its lobster stew, which is loaded with hunks of knuckle and claw meat and is creamy but not heavy, gilded with a glistening butter slick on top. Fish chowder and clam chowder are similarly excellent, and the baskets of fried shrimp, clams, and haddock—made using a process the management calls "convection deep frying"—are all fresh and crisp. To our taste, Sea Basket scallops are especially delicious—sweet, tender, and veiled in a crust that virtually melts when bitten. We also sampled a lobster roll, which was filled with good pieces of meat bound in just enough mayonnaise, but packed into a sturdy bun similar to what you'd use for a hero sandwich—too much bun, we think.

The proper dessert for almost any Maine Roadfood meal is a whoopie pie, of which the Sea Basket has a whole selection: classic soft chocolate cakes surrounding white sugar filling, as well as raspberry crème whoopie pies made with white cookies, peanut butter cream whoopie pies, and thin-mint whoopie pies ("Tastes Just Like One!" a sign boasts).

SHAW'S FISH & LOBSTER WHARF

129 Route 32   207-677-2200
New Harbor, ME   **L D** (mid-May–mid-Oct) | **$$**

——★——
WATER-FRONT
DINING
——★——

Perched on the second floor of a building that overlooks Muscongus Bay and a small commercial harbor, Shaw's has a million-dollar view and priceless fresh seafood. Unless you happen to be driving down toward Pemaquid Point (a worthy destination, scenery-wise), you'll never accidentally pass Shaw's, a good half hour due south of Route 1. If you are hankering for impeccably fresh lobsters (brought ashore within sight of the restaurant), buttery chowder, and handsome whole-belly clams, the detour makes perfect sense.

In addition to whole lobsters, Shaw's offers cool lobster rolls and lobster pie, which is a soupy bisque decorated with crumbled Ritz crackers. There is "lazy man's lobster" too: a bowl full of picked meat swimming in butter. If there happens to be any seafood frowners in your party, they can avail themselves of a hamburger, hot dog, or chicken-finger basket. Downstairs is a small bar where locals congregate and visitors are tolerated.

SHAW'S RIDGE FARM

shawsridgefarm.com

59 Shaw's Ridge Rd.   207-324-2510
(Rt. 224)   **L D** (closed in winter) | **$**
Sanford, ME

Several years ago, when Roadfood.com's Stephen Rushmore, Amy Breisch, and Chris Ayers set out on a "Quest for the Best Ice Cream of New England," they gave Shaw's Ridge Farm five out of a possible five cones, declaring that this combination barbecue barn, miniature golf course, and creamery had "clearly perfected the art of ice cream making." Some of the flavors they liked best were coffee ("for coffee drinkers"), Indian pudding ("strong molasses flavor"), and native strawberry ("the standard by which all strawberry ice creams should be measured"). They also praised the hot fudge sauce as "thin, smooth, and slightly bitter . . . one of the greatest hot fudge sauces in the country!"

The native strawberry ice cream is not idly named: It really is made with fresh, handpicked strawberries. Likewise, blueberry, orange, lemon, and raspberry sing of the fruits at their core. Shaw's Ridge even brews its own coffee extract for the truly caffeinated coffee ice cream, which is made from a recipe developed long ago by Grammy Shaw. Among the more exotic flavors available are coconut pineapple, cashew caramel, mocha-macadamia, and that New England fave, Grape-Nut. Rococo cones, shrouded in chocolate, nuts, or jimmies, are available to hold the ice cream, but this is one place where we don't want anything distracting from the ice cream itself . . . except for a spill of that devilish hot fudge sauce.

We've heard very good things about the BBQ part of this operation but have yet to give it a try. Nor have we played the golf course.

WATERMAN'S BEACH LOBSTER

watermansbeachlobster.com

343 Waterman's	207-596-7819
Beach Rd.	L D (Jun–Sept)	$$
Thomaston, ME	

Waterman's Beach Lobster earned national fame in 2001 when it was presented a James Beard Foundation Award as one of America's Regional Classics. This came as no surprise to shore visitors who have been patronizing the traditional in-the-rough lobster shack since it opened in 1986, selling lobsters fresh off nearby fishing boats.

The menu is basic. No surprises. Choose what size lobster you want, usually between one and two pounds, and it is steamed to plump-meat perfection, then served on disposable trays and plates with corn on the cob, a bag of potato chips, coleslaw, and bread. Lobster salad rolls are made on circular buns rather than split-tops, as are crab sandwiches and tuna melts. For dessert, you want pie à la mode made with Maine's own Round Top ice cream. BYOB.

YOUNG'S LOBSTER POUND

| 4 Mitchell St. | 207-338-1160 |
| Belfast, ME | L D | $$ |

Many people come to Young's Lobster Pound as if it were a picnic, bringing just about everything except the lobster. Some even bring tablecloths, utensils, and plates (Young's serves everything on cardboard and in Styrofoam). Steamed with Penobscot Bay salt water to the point of perfect plumpness, served with a heap of steamer clams, and eaten off of picnic tables with a view of Belfast Harbor, this is one of Maine's top lobsters.

The staff will pre-crack the shell for those feeling weak. It is also possible to avoid all effort by ordering a lobster roll on a round bun, lobster stew, crab, haddock, grilled scallops, or fried clams.

Young's is a huge barn of a place with seating for five hundred and tanks that hold literally tens of thousands of live lobsters, mostly for the wholesale trade. Docking is available for those who arrive by boat.

MASSACHUSETTS

BAXTER'S FISH & CHIPS
baxterscapecod.com

177 Pleasant St.   508-775-4490
Hyannis, MA   **L D** (Apr–Columbus Day)
     | $$

Baxter's is crowded, and the prices are higher than shoreline shacks, but you cannot beat the setting, overlooking Hyannis Harbor where ferry boats set sail for Nantucket and Martha's Vineyard. While it is possible to have a big-deal meal and table service along with a famous house-made Bloody Mary, it's quicker and, in our opinion, much more fun, to go to the fish and chips part of the operation, where the modus operandi is "eat in the rough": study the posted menu, place an order, then carry your own tray to a varnished table indoors or a picnic table overlooking the water.

However you experience Baxter's, the thing to eat is summertime Yankee shore fare: crisp fried clams served with decent fries or indecently tasty clam fritters, which are deep-fried doughballs dotted with morsels of clam and served with honey for dipping. The lobster rolls are good, as are the Yankee-style (creamy) chowder and buttery, seafood-laden bisque. Or you can eat fine scallops, shrimps, or oysters. Steaks are available for fish frowners.

CHRISTINA'S HOMEMADE ICE CREAM
1255 Cambridge St.   617-492-7021
Cambridge, MA $

--★-- Christina's has two strikes against it. First,
HOT TICKET seating is severely limited and because the
--★-- place is so popular, it is not uncommon even in inclement weather for crowds to hover on the sidewalk licking cones and spooning into cups. Second, it is virtually impossible to park anywhere nearby. Roadfood.com's Bruce Bilmes offered his solution to the latter problem, which was either to take mass transit or "move to within walking distance." If you love ice cream, housing near enough to walk for a cup of Christina's would be Millionaire's Row.

Take, for example, the flavor called burnt sugar, an alchemical combination of high-butterfat ice cream and sweet sugar that teeters on the edge of bitter-burnt. It is a flavor that stimulates appetite at the same time it sates it, inevitably causing return trips in twenty-minute increments and, finally, futile alcoholic-like promises to eat moderately the next time. Burnt sugar is only one of dozens of interesting flavors at the pinnacle of greater Boston's pantheon of great ice cream shops. Seasonal specialties include eggnog, fresh rose, and pumpkin. Among the occasional must-licks are honey lavender, cinnamon rice pudding, and banana-cinnamon.

Five or more nondairy sorbets also are available each day.

★ CLAM BOX

clamboxipswich.com

246 High St.   978-356-9707
Ipswich, MA   **L D** (summer only) | $$

It's hard to believe that we ever wondered where the best fried clams are made. One taste of those served at the Clam Box is irrefutable evidence that there are none better. The whole-belly clams are not overly gooey and not too large, offering a subtle ocean sweetness that is brilliantly amplified but not the least bit overwhelmed by the crusty sheath outside. A whole clam plate is a magnificent meal, including not only the native beauties sheathed in their fragile red-gold envelope, but also elegant onion rings, French fries, and bright, palate-refreshing coleslaw. The lobster roll is loaded with meat; Jane declares the clam chowder to be among New England's best; and our friends Bruce Bilmes and Sue Boyle wrote, "Clam Box's fried clam strips are perhaps the only strips we've ever eaten that don't seem like a compromise. They are as good as the bellies, in their own way."

The place itself is a gas, shaped like a clam box, the trapezoidal container in which fried-clams-to-go are customarily served. It is a genuine roadside attraction that dates back to the 1930s and would be of interest for its looks alone. There is indoor seating, but across the parking lot are choice seats whenever the weather is nice: sunny picnic tables for open-air dining. Throughout most of the summer, expect a wait in line at mealtimes. The Clam Box is famous, deservedly so.

DONUT DIP

donutdip.com

648 N. Main St.   413-736-2224
East Longmeadow, MA   **B L** | $

"What foods these morsels be!" is the motto on the box in which your dozen is presented at the counter of a modest store that happens to be one of New England's premier donut shops. The box also boasts of forty-nine different varieties, including French crullers and long crullers, devil's-food-dark chocolate, butternuts, toasted coconut, and jelly-filled, plus fritters and fruit bars. The flagship donut is apple cider, which Roadfood.com's Chris Ayers and Amy Breisch described as "the finest we've ever eaten, the crunchy, cracked exterior bursting with cinnamon-y apple flavor."

A second shop is located at 1305 Riverside Street, West Springfield, MA.

DURGIN-PARK

arkrestaurants.com/durgin_park.html

340 Faneuil Hall   617-227-2038
Marketplace   **L D** | $$
Boston, MA

Durgin-Park attracts hordes of tourists. It is noisy and can seem impolite. It is a pillar of Yankee gastronomy that twice a day clatters out expertly made plates of regional food, many of which are getting hard to find elsewhere. Seated at the long, red-checked communal table, you holler your order to a waitress, who soon slaps down some corn bread. You then move on to such old favorites as lobster stew, Boston scrod, fishcakes and spaghetti, roast turkey with sage dressing, pot roast, or pork loin. The house specialty is prime rib, a gargantuan cut that overhangs its plate. Side that with a mountain of mashed potatoes and a scoop of fresh apple sauce, and please, please, an order of superb Boston baked beans—firm, silky, not too sweet—and you've got a meal to nourish a nation.

The dessert list is tradition itself, featuring hot mince pie in the autumn, apple pandowdy, deep-dish apple pie, strawberry shortcake on a biscuit, and the world's best Indian pudding, which is a steaming gruel of cornmeal and molasses that traditionalists love. The downright weird alternative dessert is coffee Jell-O.

ELISABETH'S
1 Middle St.   508-993-1712
Fairhaven, MA   L D | $$

For first-class seafood at the waterfront of the Acushnet River opposite New Bedford, we love Elisabeth's. Although the fare suggests fine dining, the ambience is town café: chrome-banded tables and a short counter with stools, walls decorated with mounted fish and nautical bibelots. The vibe is casual but polite, the service friendly, and prices reasonable (especially at lunch).

The menu has something for everyone, from pizza to crab-cake BLTs, but the reason to visit is local seafood: haddock, swordfish, cod, and especially scallops. The proprietors are scallopers, and the ones they serve are day-boat beauties, each at least a couple of good forkfuls, available four different ways: baked; sliced in a casserole with lobster in sherry cream sauce; dusted with porcini mushrooms in thyme beurre blanc; and grilled with a maple-bacon glaze. Any meal should start with chowder. It is more buttery than creamy, loaded with good-size nuggets of tender clam and potato.

We were skeptical about the baroque cakes featured for dessert, but Oreo cream cake and espresso chip cake with coffee icing disabused us of doubt. Far from being kitschy novelties, they are truly masterful: common flavors made aristocratic. On the side of each slice comes a mound of whipped cream. That is cream that has been whipped, not something from a spray can.

ESSEX SEAFOOD
www.essexseafood.com
143 Eastern Ave.   978-768-7233
Essex, MA   L D | $$

The sweetest, tenderest soft-shelled clams—perfect for frying—are harvested from the mudflats on Essex Bay, and here at Essex Seafood, they are expertly cooked and informally presented. This place boasts a lobster pound, where people come to buy them live to take home and boil, or boiled and ready to eat. Adjacent to the market and the holding tanks is a quiet dining room with a window to the kitchen. Here

diners select from a menu of various-sized lobster dinners as well as boats, plates, sandwiches, and side orders of fried clams, scallops, and shrimp, plus excellent clam chowder and corn on the cob. The lobsters are swell, and the fried-seafood plates are beautiful to behold: a layer of French fried potatoes, topped with a layer of onion rings, topped with a heap of your seafood of choice.

Eat inside, at booths in the wood-paneled dining room that is decorated with nautical bric-a-brac, or choose a green-painted picnic table outdoors in back—a breezy retreat from Route 133 near the Essex-Gloucester town line. Unlike many of the seafood eateries in this area, Essex is open year-round.

GRAHAM'S HOT DOGS
931 Bedford St.   508-678-9574
Fall River, MA   L | $

Franks 'n' beans are a time-honored combo almost everywhere, but there are few places where they come together as nicely as in Fall River, Massachusetts. Hot dog shops (of which the city has multitudes) offer them in a bun, the beans serving as a condiment either below or on top of the wiener. Graham's beans are especially good: brown-sugar-sweet, soft and goopy, laced with limp leaves of onion. The same good beans are available bunned with *chourico* sausage, with kielbasa, and with a hamburger. Or for all of $1.15, you can buy only beans in a bun.

Should you be interested in outfitting your hot dog with things other than beans, Graham's has a panoply: ground *chourico,* bacon, potato chips, Coney Island–style chili sauce, sauerkraut, onions sopped with hamburger juices (that one is known as a whimpy), and the moist grated Cheddar that is a local favorite.

Dating back to 1962, Graham's lacks the patina of culinary history that makes so many of the region's more ancient hot dog joints charming. Its school-desk seats along the wall are fairly modern and the façade is boring brickface. But the bean dogs and hot cheese sandwiches are exemplary.

★ HARTLEY'S ORIGINAL PORK PIES

1729 S. Main St.   508-676-8605
Fall River, MA   **B L | $**

Aside from its great food, we especially like Hartley's Original Pork Pies because its continued existence is incontrovertible evidence that regional specialties are thriving and ready to eat for anyone willing to look for them. This hundred-plus-year-old bakery continues to make and sell the meat pies introduced by British Isles immigrants as well as French Canadians who came to this region to work in the mills. The savory pies are made as family-sized nine-inchers and as individual units the size of a large cupcake. In addition to traditional ground pork with gravy, variations include chicken pie, chorizo pie, and even Buffalo chicken pie with hot sauce and blue cheese. Salmon pies are available on Friday and Saturday. The fillings are hearty and unmistakably artisan; the crust is sensational—melting-rich and flaky the way only a crust made with lard can be. In addition to meat pies, Hartley's makes stuffed quahogs and chorizo pizza. Local enough for you?

There are no dining facilities. Although infused with gravy, the pies are fairly tidy and manageable as dashboard eats with several napkins.

J.J.'S CONEY ISLAND

565 S. Main St.   508-679-7944
Fall River, MA   **B L D | $**

One of the least known and underappreciated specialties of Fall River, Massachusetts, is the hot cheese sandwich. Hot cheese, a specialty? Yes, indeed. The item so listed on J.J.'s menu is anything but ordinary. The cheese itself is different: sharp Cheddar grated into a rugged hash similar to riced potatoes. J.J.'s keeps it warm in a steam-table tureen, where, miraculously, it does not clump or melt, and from which it is retrieved by the scoopful and put into a burger bun. In the world of interesting cheeses, it alone might not achieve stardom, but it assumes beguiling buttery luxe when topped with a measure of the chili-meat sauce used on Coney Island hot dogs plus a scattering of crisp raw onions and a squirt of yellow mustard.

Aside from hot cheese and Coney Island hot dogs, J.J.'s is a terrific source of such regional favorites as *chourico* pie and stuffed quahog clams, as well as an oddity locals know as a Wimpy Burger. That's a beef patty that is cooked, then steeped in gravy and bunned with a big, soft onion petal (and, preferably, some of that good hot cheese).

J.J.'s is an extraordinarily polite place for a joint where weenies star. Proprietor Albano Medeiros once told a reporter, "We want families to come here.... We wanted to offer a classier place." The large street-corner restaurant is accoutered with comfortable booths and tables and even an espresso machine for leisurely sipping. There are no counter seats. And the management explicitly forbids swearing.

KELLY'S ROAST BEEF

kellysroastbeef.com
410 Revere Beach Blvd.   781-284-9129
Revere, MA   **L D | $**

There are a couple of other Kelly's branches, but they do not compare to the charm of the Kelly's at Revere Beach, especially on a warm spring weekend when gulls screech overhead and occasionally panhandle from the sky over diners who don't closely guard their meals. The salty air of the ocean wafts in to add ineffable savor to the roast beef sandwiches, and the sun shines down making the roast beef's special sauce glisten. While there is no indoor dining at Kelly's, the pavilions at the broad beach across the street are one of the nicest dining areas a Roadfood devotee could hope for.

The beef sandwich is a North Shore paradigm. There are many toppings available, but the primary trio—and a fine combo—are cheese, sauce, and mayo. If the beef tends to be a little bit dry—and in our experience, sometimes it is—the sauce and mayo are superb compensation, and the cheese, of course, adds extra fatty luxury to beef that is fundamentally lean. We're also fans of the tender sesame seed bun.

Beyond the signature beef, Kelly's menu is mostly beach cuisine: fried clams, lobster rolls, scallops, shrimp, French fries, and onion rings.

THE LIBERAL CLUB

theliberalclub.com

20 Star St.   508-675-7115
Fall River, MA   **L D | $$**

The Liberal Club is more than a restaurant. It is a social club, function hall, and barroom to which regulars come for shots and beers every morning. While the banquet rooms are capacious, the restaurant's dining room is modest, outfitted with Red Sox décor above unupholstered wooden booths.

The menu is South Coast Massachusetts Portuguese-American, ranging from prime rib and whole lobsters for Saturday-night feasts to marinated conch salad (what Rhode Islanders call snail salad) and shrimp Mozambique in a judiciously spiced garlic sauce. The Portuguese sausage known as *chourico* (similar to the Spanish chorizo) is huge in Fall River, available here either as *chourico,* the familiar nuggets of cased sausage presented in a bun, or *chourico* meat, something else altogether: broad, thin slices of marinated pork loin, moist and flamboyantly spiced, to be eaten with knife and fork.

When appetizers arrive—fried smelts and calamari, onion rings and stuffed quahogs—the waitress asks if we want oil and vinegar to go with them. "You do!" she says when we look puzzled by the mundane offering. Out comes a gravy boat full of marinade so crowded with herbs, minced garlic, and chopped green onion that each spoonful is a savory bouquet, delicious enough to spread like tapenade across pieces of dinner roll from the bread basket. All the seafood dishes we've tried are terrific, including fried shrimp and fried lobster tails (!), and magnificent day-boat scallops. Gilded with a translucent veil of bread crumbs and perched in a sizzling pool of garlic-charged melted butter that blends with fallen crumbs to create veins of wicked crunch on the bottom of the serving dish, the scallops are dense and cream-rich.

The Liberal Club began as a soccer club in 1915, when soccer was huge in Fall River among immigrants from the British Isles, and it continues to run the bar for the restaurant that occupies its kitchen and dining room. That means you place orders with two waitresses—one from the restaurant, one from the bar—and you pay two separate checks (cash only, please).

MARGUERITE'S

778 Main Rd.   508-636-3040
Westport, MA   **B L D** (Mon-Sat);
                               B L (Sun) **| $**

Walking into Marguerite's at noon on a rainswept winter day, the aroma in the dining room was the nicest kind of welcome: sweet clam chowder, buttery bisque ballasted with hunks of lobster, and hot crust on chicken potpie. A town lunchroom with no more than a dozen tables and a short counter, this is where folks come for honest shoreline food and the good company of waitresses who seldom stroll the dining room without a coffee pot in hand for instant refills. We love the fried bay scallops, veiled in the thinnest possible crust, and sweet-mussel billi-bi redolent of rosemary; but the dish that makes us loyal for life is stuffed quahogs: big clam shells piled with stuffing made from chopped clams, onions, and linguica sausage. Known as stuffies, these savories are found on many menus in southern New England; we've found none as good as Marguerite's. Dessert can be that New England specialty, Grape-Nuts custard.

MARZILLI'S BAKERY

marzillisbakery.com

944 Bedford St.   508-675-5551
Fall River, MA   **B L | $**

The sign outside Marzilli's Bakery is subtitled "Grinder—Pizza," and its menu is similar to what you find in sleeves-up Mediterranean places throughout southern New England. But Marzilli's offers a distinct southeastern Massachusetts flavor. In this part of the world, calzones are known as *chourico* rolls, and they come filled with the crumbled Portuguese sausage locals like so much. You can eat stuffies (stuffed quahog clams) and Portuguese custard tarts. Along with familiar soups and chowders is kale soup, a Fall River standard.

Pizza at Marzilli's is offered bakery-style, known as a tray, made medium-thin like focaccia and generally bought by the individual piece, known as a square, and served at room temperature. Toppings other than *chourico* are a rarity. The meal for which loyal customers have enshrined this humble place for decades is its grinder (the regional New England term for a hero or hoagie). All sorts of fillings are available, from seafood salad to steak and onions, but the favorite is the classic Italian combo of cold cuts, cheese, and (optional) hot and/or sweet peppers on wonderful house-baked loaves. Grinders come in three sizes, the large one a handsome meal for two . . . and at about $10, a good deal indeed.

MEE SUM RESTAURANT AND LOUNGE

1819 S. Main St.   508-678-9869
Fall River, MA   L D | $

"Have you had our Fall River chow mein before?" asks Sue the waitress. It's a question she feels she needs to ask, because the chow mein in and around the old South Coast city is different from any other. That is why Mee Sum is such a significant Roadfood restaurant, despite the fact that most of its menu and décor are standard-issue, mid-twentieth-century faux Chinese.

What makes Fall River chow mein unique is the way it is served—as a sandwich—and the goodness of its noodles, which have been made since 1926 by the Oriental Chow Mein Company over on Eighth Street. Oriental Chow Mein, now run by the son and daughter-in-law of the founder, rolls out extremely thin sheets of noodle dough, cuts them into strips scarcely thicker than a shoestring, then fries the noodles to a vivid crisp. They are nutty-rich and more addictive than potato chips, the ideal balance for soft brown gravy laced with celery and onion. Ladle the gravy atop the bottom half of a burger bun, strew it with crisp noodles, then cap the whole thing with the bun's top and you have a chow mein sandwich—a fascinating swirl of soft and crunch, moist and brittle— unique to this small part of New England (and, at one time, Nathan's of Coney Island).

Novitiates and even most regular customers eat the sandwich with a knife and fork. But there are seasoned chow mein sandwich–eaters who know to ask for theirs wrapped, and who eat the whole thing without benefit of utensils, maybe with only a couple of napkins. Sue explained to us that when the sandwich is enclosed in wax paper for even a few minutes, the gravy begins to bind it together and the tight wrapper causes the noodles to steam soft, returning to a state that is something like lo mein.

Other curious Fall River sandwiches on the otherwise classic Cantonese-American menu include egg foo yung (vaguely similar to the St. Paul of St. Louis) and a chop suey sandwich, which Sue rightly warned us was ridiculously wet, not benefiting from crisp noodles.

One of the fun things about dining at Mee Sum, aside from the unique sandwiches and ingenuously kitschy moo-goo-gai-pan repertoire, is that the menu offers exotic Polynesian potations served in tumblers shaped like the heads of Aku Aku and Fu Manchu. One drink dubbed Dr. Ming of Tahiti turned out to be a very rummy piña colada variant. After a few sips, we believed the promise on the menu, that Dr. Ming would "spin you to the island of Tahiti."

NICK'S

nickisconey.com
534 S. Main St.   508-677-3890
Fall River, MA   L D | $

Long known as Dirty Nick's, this little storefront may be the oldest weenie joint in Fall River, dating back to 1920, when Nicholas Pappas came to town with a hot-dog-sauce formula he learned in Philadelphia. Similar to the New York System weenies of adjacent Rhode Island, a hot dog at Nick's is small and pink with gentle flavor that begs to be doctored up. The standard "works" configuration is a squiggle of mustard, a thin line of the spicy, dark meat sauce, and a scattering of chopped raw onions, all loaded into a fleecy bun. No single ingredient is glorious (although an argument could be made for the sauce); nor is the whole package one of those swoonfully delicious things that induces love at first bite. No, the pleasure of these little things is more progressive, leading from taste-bud bafflement to intrigue to pleasure and, ultimately, to addiction. One is only the beginning. Two is a nice snack. Four would be a meal, except for the fact that if you buy five at Nick's ($1.26 each), you get the sixth one free. Nick's weenies are the foundation also for a Fall River delight known as the bean dog, a tube steak topped with a scattering of sweet baked beans.

Smoky *chourico* is huge in this region thanks to the Portuguese roots of so many citizens, and another local creation is the *chourico* and fry plate, which is sliced discs of sausage along with a few French fries in a bun surrounded by lots more French fries. Nick's makes its fries as needed: When you order them, someone grabs a potato, puts it in the French-fry cutter, then takes the little white spud logs and throws them into a vintage Autofry machine that automatically dispenses the cooked potatoes after their allotted cooking time.

One more local specialty not to miss: the melted cheese sandwich. "Melted cheese?" you ask. "How boring is that?" Not. While Fall River's melted cheese sandwiches are by no means epicurean tours de force, they are irresistible. Other examples around town use Cheddar so finely shredded that it seems to have been through a ricer; Nick's makes its version using tiles of sharp Cheddar that melt but don't quite drip. With some of that magic hot sauce on top, sandwiched in a supersoft bun, it's a wonderful little sandwich.

What better place to eat these nostalgic treats than in one of the hundred-year-old school desks lined up along Nick's wall?

NICK'S FAMOUS ROAST BEEF
nicksfamousroastbeef.com

139 Dodge St.	978-922-9075
North Beverly, MA	L D | $

Last we heard, Roadfood.com's Chris Ayers was engaged in a project to taste and evaluate all the roast beef sandwiches north of Boston. Although a common item everywhere in the United States, this particular sandwich is a passion hereabouts, and dozens of restaurants make it a specialty. Until Chris completes his monumental roastbeefathon, we'll be happy to maintain loyalty to Nick's of North Beverly.

Like most local roast beef houses, it is a simple, self-service sandwich shop. You can get a junior or large sandwich or a super beef sandwich on an onion roll. That last one is what we recommend. It is a hefty pile of thin-sliced, full-flavored pink beef inside a giant rectangular roll that is egg-yellow and studded with squiggles of onion. Among such add-ons as cheese, mayo, and mustard, the ones to which you should pay attention are barbecue sauce, which has a spicy sweetness, and horseradish sauce with a wicked sting. The two together are a magic halo for roast beef.

All sorts of other sandwiches and subs are listed on the menu, and there are platters that include your meat of choice (including roast beef) along with a salad, French fries, and onion rings. The onion rings are particularly good—golden brown and crunchy.

It has become a tradition for Nick's devotees who travel to take a bumper sticker with them and have their picture taken holding it. Nick's décor consists of hundreds of snapshots taken of roast beef fans all over the world.

★ OXFORD CREAMERY
oxfordcreamery.com

98 County Rd.	508-758-3847
Mattapoisett, MA	L D (Apr–Oct) | $

Mattapoisett old-timers say that hardly anything has changed since this charming little roadside eatery opened as Gulf Hill Ice Cream in 1931. In the hands of Ken and Liz Ackerman since 2003, staffed by a team of happy high school and college kids, offering seats at picnic tables in a nearby shaded grove, Oxford Creamery is a sublime summer eat-shack experience.

While you can easily pay twice as much as Oxford Creamery charges for a lobster roll, you will seldom come across one half as good. Large, resilient segments of claw, tail, and knuckle seem to be everything good in a pound-plus lobster. The pearly parts are just barely cool—not cold or icy—and veiled in a thin film of mayonnaise that provides a gauzy halo for a riptide of oceanic sweetness. The meat comes mounted on fresh leaves of lettuce in a split-top bun, sided by French fries and coleslaw.

Whole-belly clams are cased in a crisp, brightly seasoned crust and truly ooze flavor. The bill of sea fare also includes scallops, fish and chips, shrimp, and a crab roll. Fish frowners can have a hot dog, a hamburger, a linguica (sausage) roll, or any number of familiar lunch-counter sandwiches.

As for ice cream, a couple dozen flavors are available, and the options of what to do with those flavors are a primer in regional soda-fountain nomenclature. For example, in this part of the world, a milk shake is simply milk and flavoring. Add ice cream and it becomes a frappe. A milk float is a frappe that is not blended. A freeze is like a frappe, but made with soda rather than milk, and a soda float is an unblended freeze.

RED SKIFF

15 Mt. Pleasant St. 978-546-7647
Rockport, MA **B L | $**

Remodeled several years ago by new owners, the Red Skiff remains a cozy café that attracts enough tourists and locals that you can expect to wait for a table or counter seat anytime after eight a.m., especially on weekends.

The most interesting item on the menu is anadama bread, which was supposedly invented in Rockport, when a fisherman grew so angry at his lazy wife, Anna, that he baked his own loaf of bread from wheat flour, cornmeal, and molasses . . . all the while muttering, "Anna, damn her." Whatever its origins, the Red Skiff makes a dark, sweet, and high-flavored anadama loaf that tastes just great when toasted and buttered. The unique bread is used to make interesting French toast, available plain or topped with strawberries, but in truth, we like simple toasted anadama bread better. The egg dip, frying, and strawberry topping tend to detract from the solid Yankee character of the bread itself. Other good breakfasts include plate-wide pancakes (buttermilk, blueberry, or chocolate chip) and a warm pecan roll that is served adrip with caramel frosting.

R.F. O'SULLIVAN & SON

rf-osullivan.com
282 Beacon St. 617-492-7773
Somerville, MA **L D | $$**

This popular, boisterous watering hole makes quintessential pub burgers, meaning extra-large mounds of beef with a crusty surface and juice-oozing insides. A plain one is pretty sloppy, and they get sloppier when you choose one of several dozen ways the kitchen has of tricking them out. Naturally, there are cheeseburgers and bacon cheeseburgers, but opportunities to go wild abound. How about a black-and-blue burger rolled in black pepper and draped with blue cheese? Or an Empire State burger covered with Italian sausage and mozzarella cheese and festooned with peppers and onions? Thick steak fries and sweet onion rings are superb on the side.

SANTARPIO'S

santarpiospizza.com
111 Chelsea St. 617-567-9871
East Boston, MA **L D | $$**

Like so many of the great pizzerias of the Northeast, Santarpio's started as a bakery at the beginning of the twentieth century. It went to pizza in the 1930s. Arriving on battered metal trays carried by a staff of indomitable waitresses, Santarpio's Neapolitan pies are among the region's best. Their circumference is a masterful balance of crunch and chew, even if the inside has a tendency to melt like a Salvador Dalí image when ballasted with toppings. Strangely, the toppings that normally give pizza a flavor wallop, such as garlic and anchovies, even sausage, seem somewhat mild. That is a good thing because the personality of these pizzas is not overwhelming. They are pies of mild and creamy disposition, all about the interplay of tomato and cheese (and, of course, crust).

Other than pizza, you need to know about Santarpio's barbecue. Nothing like pit-cooked 'cue, this version is homemade Italian sausage, steak tips, or skewered hunks of lamb cooked over an open fire. The sausage is a taut tube with the flavor of charcoal insinuating its high-spiced insides. The lamb is quite ewey, with big flavor for lamb lovers only. Regular customers get barbecue as a pre-pizza hors d'oeuvre with hot cherry peppers and crusty Italian bread.

The second location of Santarpio's is at 71 Newbury Street in Peabody, MA (978-535-1811). Note that business is cash only.

SMIAROWSKI FARMSTAND & CREAMY

286 River Rd.   413-665-3830
Sunderland, MA   **L** (Apr–Dec) | **$**

As its name says, Smiarowski is a farm stand with an inventory of locally grown fruits and vegetables throughout the summer and gourds and pumpkins in the fall. Its name also includes the word "creamy," which refers to the fact that it is also an ice cream stand. But the reason we include it here is its Polish food, served through an order window and eaten al fresco at a picnic table.

Headlining the menu is the Polish Power Plate, a stupendously tasty double-barrel meal of *golumbki* (stuffed cabbage) and kielbasa with such side dishes as barbecue beans and "lazy pierogi," which is made of all the traditional pierogi ingredients, but not pocketed as a dumpling. It all comes on a heavy paper plate, the kielbasa bursting-plump, spicy, and smoky, the *golumbki* something you'd hope grandma would make: sweet and meaty, topped with bacon and thick tomato sauce. Lazy pierogi is pure comfort food, a mélange of noodles, onions, butter, and cheese. And the beans are extraordinary: cinnabar red, more bacon sweet than sugar sweet—a Yankee dish with a Polish twist. The short menu also includes a variety of "regional hot dogs" including the New Yorker (mustard and stewed onion pushcart sauce), the Kansas City Dog (sauerkraut, melted Swiss cheese, thousand island dressing), and the Atlanta Dog (topped with coleslaw).

Ice cream is sold in cones and cups, along with sundaes and milk shakes. We especially like maple walnut, which is packed with nuts and very creamy—just the right flavor to crown a warm square of Smiarowski's apple crisp.

TOSCANINI'S
tosci.com
899 Main St.   617-491-5877
Cambridge, MA   **$**

First, let us say that the vanilla ice cream made by Gus Rancatore at Toscanini's is some of the best there is; pure, uncomplicated, satisfying. And the regional favorite, Grape-Nuts, is as good as it gets, the familiar breakfast cereal blended into sweet cream so it becomes flavorful streaks of grain. We love such flavors as cocoa pudding and cake batter as well as such extreme exotica as black pepper bourbon. But the true call to glory is burnt caramel. If you are one who enjoys the preciousness of the crust on a flawlessly blowtorched crème brûlée, you too will understand how a controlled sugar burn creates an ice cream that transcends sweetness and makes taste buds buzz.

TURTLE ALLEY
turtlealley.com
42 Rogers St.   978-281-4000
Gloucester, MA   **L** | **$**

Mayans knew long ago what modern cooks only recently discovered, that flavoring chocolate with pepper has mouthwatering sex appeal. Our favorite way to appreciate the culinary collusion is candy made by chocolatier Hallie Baker at Turtle Alley. She creates turtles in white, dark, and milk chocolate; the stunner is an almond chipotle turtle in which the pepper's smoky bite surges through the caramel filling and around the nuts like edible adrenaline, all its excitement robed in a silky sweet chocolate coat that assures on-fire taste buds that all is well.

Not all of Hallie's vast school of terrapins are so exotic. There are plenty of normal turtles, all of which are abnormally delicious, each handmade piece as unique as a snowflake. You can get them with pecans, almonds, peanuts, and macadamias, as well as cashews, which she believes are the ideal nut, at least cosmetically, because cashews resemble turtle flippers.

Beyond turtles, the shelves are crowded with brittles, clusters and butter crunches, chocolate-robed candied fruits, nonpareils, and simple hunks of uncomplicated chocolate. Samplers are available by mail order.

There is a second Turtle Alley at 1 East India Square Mall, Salem, MA (978-740-0660).

THE VILLAGE RESTAURANT

village-essex.com

55 Main St.   978-768-6400

Essex, MA   **L D | $$**

The Village has been a Cape Ann favorite since the 1950s. It is fun to read the early menus posted in the vestibule, not only for their deflated prices ($1 for a nice dinner) but because they show that the kitchen has maintained its character. For travelers in search of traditional North Shore meals, this place is a treasure trove. Here are excellent fried clams, of course, as well as chowders and seafood stews, lobster rolls and lobster pie, and first-rate examples of such regional desserts as baked Grape-Nuts custard, strawberry shortcake on a biscuit, and Indian pudding served piping hot under a scoop of fast-melting ice cream. A fancier dessert, but true to local character, is blueberry bread pudding, made of cornmeal and molasses bread and set afloat in a pool of sweet rum sauce.

Don't get the impression that the Village is hidebound. It has changed with the times too, and stylish twists on tradition include lobster mac 'n' cheese, shrimp scampi bruschetta, and seafood Provence. While you can't go wrong ordering seafood, know that this really is the town café, where the menu is broad enough to please everyone in the family. Fish frowners can enjoy steaks, Tuscan chicken, and a beautiful Village burger—eight ounces of beef complemented by bacon–blue cheese butter and melted mozzarella.

THE WHITE HUT

whitehut.com

280 Memorial Ave.   413-736-9390

West Springfield, MA   **B L D | $**

You want a fast meal? Really, really fast? Stop in the White Hut around lunchtime, and you can be in and out—and very well fed—in less than five minutes. There are no more than a few counter seats, plus a couple of tables for eating while standing up, so it's not creature comforts that have drawn crowds to this little fortress near the Big E Fairgrounds since 1939. It is cheeseburgers. White Hut offers a modest-sized patty topped with standard American cheese. What puts it into the pantheon is the tangle of grilled onions that every regular customer knows to order as a garnish. In fact, if you forget to order onions, the waitress will ask if you want them anyway. And if you say *hamburger,* she'll shoot back, "You mean cheeseburger?" Meat, cheese, onions: It's the only way.

Sizzled on the grill alongside the hamburgers, hot dogs blossom under a mantle of mustard, relish, and raw onions (applied by the waitress, as you specify), and they are served in a bun that is soft on the inside, but buttered and toasted to a luxurious golden brown on the outside.

A second White Hut location is at 1A Boltwood Walk, Amherst, MA (413-835-0455).

WOODMAN'S OF ESSEX

woodmans.com

121 Main St.	978-768-6057
Essex, MA	**L D** | $$

Overlooking a scenic marsh in the heart of the clam belt, where towns have bivalvular names like Ipswich and Little Neck, Woodman's epitomizes a whole style of informal Yankee gastronomy known as "eat in the rough." That means you stand at a counter, yell your order through the commotion, then wait for your number. The food is served on cardboard plates with plastic forks. Carry it yourself to a table (if you can find one that isn't occupied).

A chart we made several years ago comparing and contrasting the top clam shacks along the North Shore evaluated Woodman's clams as follows: Crust crunch = crusty. Chew = resilient. Belly goo = over-flowing. Flavor = clamorama! Quantity = substantial. Whole platter presentation = merry jumble. In our experience, Woodman's clams tend to be somewhat larger and gooier than those served in other local places, sometimes a bit too large. Of course, all that depends on what the market has to offer at any given time. But whatever their size, there is no faulting the frying, which results in big mouthfuls that are shattering crisp. Also on the must-eat, fried-food roster are onion rings and French fries, and big, spherical clam fritters. Nor is clam chowder to be ignored.

Woodman's is open year-round.

NEW HAMPSHIRE

BISHOP'S

bishopshomemadeicecream.com

183 Cottage St.   603-444-6039
Littleton, NH   (April–Columbus Day) | $

Bishop's ice cream flavors range from the baroque—Bishop's Bash is chocolate chips, nuts, and brownie chunks in dark chocolate—to basic. Vanilla is pure and creamy-white; chocolate is like iced chocolate milk more than some ungodly-rich chocolate mousse cake; the coffee is reminiscent of HoJo's—smooth and creamy more than ultracaffeinated. Here too you can savor the old Yankee favorite, Grape-Nuts ice cream, in which the little specks of cereal soften into grainy streaks of flavor in pudding-smooth ice cream.

There is something unusually civilized about coming to Bishop's for ice cream. You'd think that such a happy-time product would stimulate yelps of exuberance and that the interior of the shop would ring with rapture. On the contrary, there is a reverential hush about it, even when Bishop's is jammed and every little table is occupied with ice cream eaters and a hundred are waiting to get inside. Perhaps it's due to the stately old house in which the business is located or the polite way of doing business—wooden cone holders are provided for parking the cone while you pay; or maybe the civilized demeanor is owed to the charm of the ice cream servers, who want to know, if you order a sundae with buttercrunch and coffee ice cream, which flavor you prefer on top.

BROWN'S LOBSTER POUND

brownslobsterpound.com

407 Route 286   603-474-3331
Seabrook, NH   L D (weekends only from
                      mid-Nov–Mar) | $$

For sixty-plus years now, Brown's has been a magnet for people on their way to or from the beach, hungry for all manner of Yankee seafood. It started as a lobster pound, and lobster remains its glory. Pick your own from among the tanks; it will be caught and cooked to order, preferably served with a pile of good Maine steamers. A terrific alternative to the work of a whole lobster is Brown's baked lobster pie: big chunks of meat in a savory crust. Another good lobster option: deep-fried, totally indulgent. The lobster roll is a lobster salad roll, the meat cool, bound in mayo.

Choose from among three types of chowder—corn, fish, and clam—or have a large lobster bisque. Fried seafood is double-dipped and crackermeal-coated, so it is extra-crunchy—wonderful with big, whole-belly clams, but less wonderful around scallops, which the crust tends to smother.

Brown's is a sprawling place with a dining room reminiscent of an old-time shore dinner hall. Getting the food can be a bit confusing, as you order lobster and steamers at one window, fried food at another. BYOB.

FOUR ACES DINER

4acesdiner.com

23 Bridge St.   603-298-5515
West Lebanon, NH   B L | $

There are many inviting breakfast choices at the Four Aces, a beautiful vintage diner that has been virtually swallowed up by construction around it. How about a popover with maple butter on the side? An immense maple-glazed sour-cream donut that gets cut in half, grilled, and topped with whipped cream? Other bright and shining choices include sweet corn fritters, smoked peppered salmon and cream cheese on a bagel, and—to go with just about anything—maple baked beans. We were not so impressed by Four Aces red flannel hash, although we sure appreciate it being on the menu. This version is simply corned beef hash with beets added, contributing only minimal root-vegetable flavor to the dish.

West Lebanon is north enough that road signs give distances in kilometers as well as miles, so the menu includes that Québécois passion, *poutine*. Its gravy isn't up to snuff, but we do love the French fries that are crisp and elegant and cheese that is more flavorful than most.

GILLEY'S PM LUNCH

gilleyspmlunch.com

175 Fleet St.   603-431-6343
Portsmouth, NH   L D | $

Gilley's is an old-fashioned night-owl lunch wagon now anchored on Fleet Street in Portsmouth. It was named for Ralph "Gilley" Gilbert, an employee who slung hash here for over fifty years. If it is the wee hours of the morning and all the normal restaurants are closed and even the bars are shut, you can count on this joint to be serving up hamburgers with chocolate milk on the side to a rogues' gallery of city folk who range from derelicts to debutantes. Seven days a week, Gilley's closes at 2:30 a.m.

Many dine standing on the sidewalk, but there is limited indoor seating at a thin counter opposite the order area and galley kitchen. Gathered here under some of the most unflattering lighting on Earth are insomniacs, die-hard partiers, and late-shift workers with no other place to eat, feasting on such quick-kitchen fare as chili dogs, French fries gobbed with cheese, and fried egg sandwiches with ultrastrong coffee on the side. The best dish in the house, or at least the one that seems most appropriate in this reprobate restaurant, is the hamburger; actually the cheeseburger . . . no, make that a double cheeseburger. House lingo is as follows. Works = mustard, relish, onion. Loaded = works + ketchup. Pickles and mayonnaise are available, but must be specified by name.

HART'S TURKEY FARM

hartsturkeyfarm.com

233 Daniel Webster   603-279-6212
Hwy. (Route 3)   L D | $$
Meredith, NH

At Hart's Turkey Farm, it is Thanksgiving every day of the year except Christmas, when the place is closed. Hart's is not a cozy café, that's for sure—the restaurant is gigantic with a theme-park feel—but there is no faulting the moist, full-flavored meat on the turkey dinners (white, dark, or mixed) in sizes that range from a small plate (3.5 ounces of turkey) to the jumbo plate, which is more than a pound of meat. With the turkey you get stuffing, potatoes, gravy, and cranberry sauce, and a diner with a mighty appetite can pay $6.99 extra to augment the basic meal with beverage, soup, salad, and dessert.

If sliced turkey is not your style, alternatives include turkey tempura, turkey Parmesan, turkey nuggets, turkey livers, turkey croquettes, turkey pie, turkey marsala, and turkey Divan. Not to mention big slabs of prime rib and a full repertoire of pastas and seafood. For those entertaining at home, Hart's offers roasted and ready-to-carve birds up to thirty-six pounds.

THE ICE HOUSE

theicehouserestaurant.com

112 Wentworth Rd.   603-431-3086

Rye, NH   **L D** (mid-Apr–Oct)

                        (closed Mon) | $$

Many people like the Ice House for its ice cream: Richardson's-brand, ranging in flavors from vanilla to death-by-chocolate and rum-flavored frozen pudding. It is very good ice cream, especially when used as the base for signature sundaes such as the S'Mores (vanilla ice cream, crumbled graham crackers, hot fudge, and marshmallow) and the Kitchen Sink (with strawberry, fudge, marshmallow, and pineapple toppings, plus bananas and nuts).

In addition to dessert, there is a whole menu of burgers, hot dogs, baked and broiled fish, and a superb fried fish sandwich (haddock) served with big, hand-cut, battered onion rings. Chowder lovers can avail themselves of a weeklong rotation of different choices, including corn, scallop, and clam, as well as beef or chicken chili. Coleslaw, pickled beets, and three-bean salad are all made on the premises.

Dining facilities include booths in a pine-paneled dining room decorated with an assortment of license plates, as well as picnic tables out back.

L.A. BURDICK

burdickchocolate.com/
chocolateshop-cafe-walpole.aspx

47 Main St.   603-756-2882

Walpole, NH   **B L** | $$

For chocolate bonbons, pastries, or a cup of hot chocolate, there is no place we know that delivers such impeccable satisfaction as L.A. Burdick of Walpole, New Hampshire.

Foremost is the hot chocolate, which comes either milk, dark, or white. Milk hot chocolate is daydreamy liquid velvet, while dark hot chocolate is a cocoa steamroller, the most potent chocolate food or drink imaginable. It is only sweet enough to round out the cocoa bean's inexorable intensity. Even sipped in tiny increments, it is overwhelming . . . in the best possible way.

To go along with hot chocolate (or coffee or tea, which both seem downright boring in contrast), there are fantastic pastries: Gugelhopf, the Austrian/Swiss bundt cake perfumed with lemon and vanilla, is as buttery as cake can be. The almonds and hazelnuts that go into Burdick's classic Linzer torte are balanced by a haze of cloves. A cherry Danish is more delicate than most croissants, and the croissants seem like they might actually float off the plate.

All these wonders can, of course, be taken away, along with a plethora of beautiful handmade chocolate truffles, chocolate bunnies, chocolate-covered fruits and nuts, marzipan, and other confections. Or they can be enjoyed here in a pleasant little tearoom with white-clothed tables that are topped by heavy brown paper.

There are Burdicks in Boston, Cambridge, and New York. The one in Walpole, New Hampshire, is what the management calls "home base."

★ POLLY'S PANCAKE PARLOR

pollyspancakeparlor.com

Route 117   603-823-5575

Sugar Hill, NH   **B L** | $$

A few years ago when a documentary film crew from Germany wanted us to take them to a restaurant that was echt New England, we knew exactly where to go: Polly's Pancake Parlor. They were worldly folks and knew about maple syrup, but its celebration at Polly's was, for them, a wondrous experience. If you like pancakes and maple syrup and lovely log-cabin restaurants in the heart of the White Mountain sugarbush, you too may find a visit to Polly's wondrous. We sure do.

The pancakes are made from stone-ground flours or cornmeal, either plain or upgraded with shreds of coconut, walnuts, or blueberries. One order consists of half a dozen three-inchers, and it is possible to get a sampler of several different kinds. They come with the clearest and most elegant fancy-grade maple syrup, as well as maple sugar and mouthwatering maple spread (that last one the consistency of soft cream cheese, but pure maple). You can also get maple muffins, sandwiches made with maple white bread, ice cream with maple hurricane sauce (syrup and apples stewed together), and all sorts of maple candies to take home.

Polly's is surrounded by maple trees that get hung with taps and buckets in the spring, but the most wonderful time to visit is autumn, as the trees turn color. The dining room has a glass-walled porch that overlooks fields where horses graze, and its inside walls are decorated with antiques and tools that have been in the family since the late eighteenth century.

PURITAN BACKROOM

puritanbackroom.com

245 Hooksett Rd.   603-666-9893
Manchester, NH   **L D | $$**

Puritan Backroom is not a textbook Roadfood restaurant. It is a large, well-upholstered place with a menu that has something to please everyone, a happy bar with televisions overhead, and a regular clientele of Manchester's solid citizens who come for meals that generally have little in the way of regional character.

Why include it here? Because Puritan Backroom claims to be the place chicken tenders were first served. This is a fact that will not merely please culinary history buffs; it is a fact that will feed you well if you like great big chunks of white-meat fried chicken without any of the complications that bone-in dark meat presents. (Note: Tenders are not reconstituted nuggets. They are, in fact, an actual part of the bird: the pectoralis minor from under the breast, known to butchers as the tenderloin.) They come encased in batter that is slightly sweet, or you can choose coconut-flavored or spicy ones that are shot through with pepper. A single order is absolutely immense, enough for three moderately hungry people. They come with a ramekin of clear liquid that tastes like hummingbird feed. "Duck sauce," the waitress informed us, for dipping the chicken. "Sweet and sour." Yes, it is sweet, but sour we did not taste.

Preceding our boatload of tenders, we enjoyed an expertly assembled Greek salad that comes with a block of good, tangy feta cheese and is dressed with a complicated, multi-herb vinaigrette. We also recommend the onion rings, which our waitress informed us are not the big, gross ones. Nor are they the fragile, wispy, type. They are thin hoops with crisp crust and sweet onion flavor. Like tenders, they are served in abundance.

Here you'll want ice cream for dessert. It is made on premises in small batches and tastes like good, old-fashioned ice cream: pure, not too butterfatty, and easy to eat in multiple scoops with hot fudge on top.

RYE HARBOR LOBSTER POUND

1870 Ocean Blvd.   603-964-7845
Rye, NH   **L D** (closed in winter) | **$$**

The management at Rye Harbor Lobster Pound bills its lobster roll as "infamous." For these parts, it certainly is anomalous: nine out of ten local lobster rolls are lobster *salad* rolls made with cool meat and mayo. This one is hot, and unlike the classic Connecticut-born hot lobster roll, the warm meat isn't just bathed in butter. It is sautéed in butter and sherry, giving it a perfumy twist. Per tradition, it comes in a toasted split-top bun.

Lobster also might play a part in your Rye Harbor chowder. You can have very good creamy clam chowder or ask for it "fluffy"—augmented with hunks of sherry-sopped lobster meat. Whole cooked lobsters and steamers also are available, as are lobster macaroni shells 'n' cheese and lobster gazpacho.

SUNNY DAY DINER

Route 3   603-745-4833
Lincoln, NH   **B L** (closed Tues) | **$**

--★--
LOCALS
LOVE IT
--★--
It's a sunny day indeed that starts with breakfast at the counter or in a booth at the Sunny Day Diner. A gleaming mid-twentieth-century streamliner that used to be known as Stoney's when it was parked in Dover, it was moved to Lincoln in the late 1980s, and it became the place it is today about ten years after that.

If we describe it as a diner with an elevated culinary consciousness, please do not expect a menu of striving dishes or service that's in any way pretentious. This is a heart-and-soul hash house, its goodness amplified by the fact that nearly everything is made from scratch. Corned beef hash is rich and luxurious, as are biscuits and gravy. You can have French toast made with banana bread and served, of course, with real maple syrup. On the side of eggs and omelets, the toast choice includes white, raisin, oatmeal, rye, and wheat—all made here. Bakery items are a specialty, and it would be wrong not to have at least one muffin or sticky bun. We've yet to have lunch at the Sunny Day, but its Reuben sandwich is legendary.

TILT'N DINER
thecman.com/restaurants-and-menus /tilt-n-diner.aspx

61 Laconia Rd.   603-286-2204
Tilton, NH   **B L D** | **$**

Originally built in 1952 in the American diner's heyday, the Tilt'n has a large new room and kitchen added on the back. It was bought and moved to its current location by a local restaurant group, and it is self-consciously doo-wop, with oldies on the sound system and pop culture memorabilia everywhere. Despite the nostalgic flummery, it retains authentic diner spirit in looks, attitude, and much of the no-nonsense menu.

As is true of so many vintage hash houses, breakfast is the high point of the day. Roast beef hash, made two or three times a week, is subtly seasoned, moist, and easy to fork up by the bite, with just enough spuds woven in among the beef to temper its protein potency. It's pancake-shaped and gently fried so there is a crisp web on both sides of the cake, but this hash is all about softness and comfort. Corned beef hash, on the other hand, comes from a can and tastes it.

Available sides include the usual eggs, pancakes, and so on, and baked beans, rich with porky sweetness. The rest of the breakfast menu is predictable, and lunch includes burgers, sandwiches, and locally liked hot dishes, such as American chop suey, fried cod, and shepherd's pie with creamed corn.

RHODE ISLAND

ALLIE'S DONUTS

3661 Quaker Ln.   401-295-8036
(Route 2)   **B** | $
North Kingstown, RI

Allie's is so popular that it has two doors, funneling people to separate counters to place their orders. The waiting area is fairly small, but the open kitchen behind it is an immense workspace where powerful mixers whir and deep-fryers bubble. There is no indoor seating. A couple of picnic tables are available outdoors, but most people get their dozens to go or to eat in the front seat of their car. It is common to see people buy a boxful (to take to the office), plus a bag of two or three to eat in the parking lot on the way to the car, or behind the wheel on the way to the office, before the box is opened.

The variety of donuts made each morning is vast, including honey-dipped, glazed crullers, raised jelly sticks, plain cake donuts, coconut-glazed solid chocolates, and a rainbow of jimmie-topped extravaganzas. None are fancy-pants pastries; these are big, sweet, pretty things to eat, the cake variety boasting a crisp skin and creamy insides. In addition to donuts, there are fruit squares, turnovers, and giant donut cakes suitable for slicing into a dozen or more servings.

BOCCE CLUB

226 St. Louis Ave.   401-767-2000
Woonsocket, RI   **D** | $$

It was at the Bocce Club in the 1920s where the Rhode Island tradition of big, family-style chicken dinners began when the Pavoni family decided to serve meals to friends who came to their house to play bocce. Over the decades, the ad-hoc eatery grew and became a legend, known for rosemary-roasted chicken bathed in butter and olive oil. The main course is preceded by kale soup and/or an effulgent antipasto salad, accompanied by crusty bread, penne noodles in red sauce, and a motley heap of French-fried *and* oven-roasted potatoes.

Bocce Club is famous for chicken, but it has an extensive menu that includes Italian and Portuguese dishes as well as steaks. Our waitress looked crestfallen when we chose chicken for two. "Chicken is where we started," she explained, "but our chef is so good, there is so much more to try." That may be, but to come to the Bocce Club and not eat roast chicken would be like visiting Memphis and ignoring the pork.

CHAMPLIN'S SEAFOOD DECK

champlins.com

256 Great Island Rd.   401-783-3152
Narragansett, RI   **L D** (closed in winter) | **$$**

★
**WATER-FRONT
DINING**
★

Champlin's is a seafood market and casual eatery at the entrance to Galilee Harbor. Cooked food comes on disposable plates and customers carry their own meals from the kitchen window to bare-topped tables, many of which are perched on a deck overlooking the harbor's boats.

Burgers, hot dogs, and chicken fingers are about the only non-seafood items on a menu that ranges from whole lobsters and raw cherrystones to baked stuffed shrimp and charbroiled swordfish. It is possible to buy your lobster from the retail store, then ask the kitchen to cook it. The cost is $3, including a supply of melted butter. If you come without your nutcracker, you can get one by leaving a $2 deposit with the staff. To accompany lobsters, there are buckets of steamers with broth and butter, and three kinds of chowder: creamy white, Rhode Island red, or South Coast clear broth.

You can get almost any fried seafood, including clams and really good flounder—a broad fillet of sweet, moist meat encased in unobtrusive crust. The flounder is available by the piece or as half of a fish and chips plate. While French fries are fine, we recommend substituting onion rings, which come enveloped in a hopsy batter, or boiled red potatoes, which are cream-textured with an earthy spud flavor.

The one thing we cannot figure out about Champlin's is the kitchen's apparent aversion to garlic. There seems to be none in the snail salad, a Rhode Island specialty that is customarily radiant with a garlic halo, nor in the linguine with white clam sauce.

THE COMMONS LUNCH

48 Commons   401-635-4388
Little Compton, RI   **B L D** | **$**

The Commons Lunch was ten years old when we came upon it in the mid-1970s. We were overjoyed to find so consummate an example of Ocean State roadfood, and for years it remained a favorite destination for square meals that reflected the foodways of southern New England. The place burned down in 2004 but reopened as it always was: a small-town café with authentic Rhode Island food and a clientele of authentic Rhode Islanders.

The state's signature cornmeal pancake, the jonnycake (listed on the menu as Johnny Cake), is always available. These jonnycakes are the elegant, thin variety with lacy edges and a faintly crisp surface sandwiching a fine ribbon of steamy fine yellow meal. Although they resemble pancakes and many people do eat them for breakfast with maple syrup on top, they are suitable as a side dish to lunch and supper as well. Jonnycakes are a good companion to a bowl of ocean-perfumed quahog chowder or a lobster-meat plate lunch of plump, pink claw and knuckle hunks bound in mayonnaise. The Commons Lunch menu is broad, ranging from simple sandwiches and mac 'n' cheese to plates of expertly fried shrimp, clams, scallops, and clam fritters, as well as meat pies that reflect the French heritage of some local citizens. Desserts include the Yankee stalwarts Grape-Nuts pudding and Indian pudding, plus some nice-looking pies.

★ EVELYN'S DRIVE-IN

evelynsdrivein.com

2335 Main Rd.   401-624-3100
Tiverton, RI   **B L D** (summer only) | **$$**

Most of Evelyn's regulars take a seat inside at tables or the counter, but for us travelers in search of local color as well as local food, picnic tables outside are the place to be. They provide a dreamy view of Sakonnet Bay, Newport shores, and pleasure boats skimming through the water. It is sleeves-up outdoorsy, but we have seen one couple spread a tablecloth across the weathered wood table and open their own wine to accompany lobster dinners.

Many of the locals order non-seafood meals from a broad menu of diner standards such as meat loaf, burgers, chicken pie, and the local oddity known as a chow mein sandwich. Using crisp, full-flavored noodles made by the Oriental Chow Mein Company in Fall River, Massachusetts, it is a plate of soy-sauced gravy and vegetables (and beef or chicken, if desired), made into a nominal sandwich by the addition of a hamburger bun.

Evelyn's is at its best being a seafood shack, so the chow mein is also available as lobster chow mein. But among more normal shoreline fare, you can count on good whole-belly fried clams, fish and chips, clam cakes and chowder (that's South Coast chowder, which is thin and briny), and two-pound seafood platters with some of everything.

Cocktails, beer, and wine are available, as are Grape-Nuts pudding, blueberry pie, and Buddha's chocolate—milk chocolate almond toffee.

FLO'S CLAM SHACK

4 Wave Ave.   401-847-8141
Middletown, RI   **L D** (March 1–Thanksgiving)
                    | $$

Even if you don't come away with a souvenir T-shirt emblazoned with the cry, SMACK MY CLAM AND CALL ME FLO!, you will fondly remember a visit to this good old eatery for its excellent chowders, stuffies, clam cakes, and all manner of fried seafood.

Yes we did say "chowders," plural, because three types are available: creamy New England, South Coast clear, and Rhode Island pink. With an order of clam cakes, a bowl of any of these would make a nice meal. But it would be a shame to visit Flo's without also forking into a stuffie, which is a quahog clamshell loaded with chorizo-charged stuffing, or a serving of nice whole-belly clams or batter-coated fish and chips.

Service is clam-shack casual with tote-your-own trays and disposable dishware. The drink menu includes beer, wine, and mixed drinks. One of the listed specials is a pair of hot dogs and a bottle of Champagne, for $50.

Beware of long lines. You will especially wait for a table on the weekend.

GRAY'S ICE CREAM

graysicecream.com

16 East Rd. at   401-624-4500
Four Corners $
Tiverton, RI

On a summer day in Tiverton, Gray's parking lot is packed with people who come from miles around to indulge in the time-honored ritual of standing in line at the order window and getting ice cream that ranges from normal flavors to that Yankee oddity, Grape-Nuts. Gray's also is proof that Rhode Island is one of the most coffee-conscious places in the nation. Coffee ice cream here is robust and just-right sweet. The other great Gray's flavor is ginger, made with bits of fresh root that give the creamy scoops a sparkling spicy bite. In the fall, pumpkin and then eggnog join the flavor rotation.

HAVEN BROTHERS

havenbrothersmobile.com

Fulton and Dorrance St.   401-603-8124
at Kennedy Plz.   **D** (late night) | $
Providence, RI

——★—— For anyone who thinks food-truck in-
OPEN LATE fatuation is a twenty-first-century phe-
——★—— nomenon, we recommend a visit to Haven Brothers, an enterprise that has been dishing out street food from a truck since 1888. The short-order menu includes lobster rolls and steak and cheese on toast, but most orders are for hot dogs or hamburgers. The dogs are plump and pink, served in soft steamed buns, available with chili and all the usual condiments. The hamburgers are modest-sized patties, available from plain to deluxe (lettuce, tomato, mayo, and so on). Devotees of junk food will enjoy the triple Murder Burger, which is three patties topped with every condiment in the house, plus bacon, cheese, and chili. Side a Murder Burger with cheese-glopped French fries, and you have a sidewalk meal to reckon with.

The most popular beverage at Haven Brothers is coffee milk—like chocolate milk, but flavored with coffee instead. Or you can have a frappe made with ice cream, milk, and flavoring (what the rest of the world knows as a milk shake).

Honestly, the scene is more alluring than the food. From the time it pulls up to Kennedy Plaza alongside City Hall at 4:30 p.m. to its 5 a.m. closing, the Haven Brothers truck hosts a party of Providence characters who carry on a continuous conversation with the staff, with other customers, or—if no one will listen—with the voices inside their own heads. Dining facilities include two stools at a counter inside, and the steps of City Hall. Most customers eat standing on the sidewalk.

JIGGER'S HILL AND HARBOUR DINER
jiggersdiner.com

145 Main St.	401-884-5388
East Greenwich, RI	B L | $

Jigger's, a 1950 Worcester Dining Car with gleaming silver and enamel blue exterior and polished wooden booths, has had more than its share of ups and downs since we first wrote about it in *Gourmet* in the mid-1990s. At that time, it had been closed for a decade, finally reopened with brio in 1992 by Carol Shriner. But after Carol moved away eight years later, it went through a few owners and finally was padlocked once again in 2011. Diner lovers wept. Then, in early 2012, it was brought back to life.

Rhode Island cornmeal jonnycakes continue their role as the heart and soul of the breakfast menu. They are South County–style, meaning they are silver-dollar wide and quite thick (as opposed to the superthin, lace-edged ones typical of restaurants east of the Bay). With real maple syrup ($1.99 extra), they're a great meal unto themselves or a companion to any egg dish, preferably one accompanied by pit-smoked ham or brisket hash.

The lunch menu is salads, sandwiches, wraps, grilled paninis, and hand-pressed burgers—nothing uniquely Rhode Island except for a coffee cabinet, "cabinet" being the Queen State term for milk shake, and coffee being the locally loved flavoring for dairy drinks.

J.P. SPOONEM'S

1678 Broad St.	401-941-3550
Cranston, RI	B L | $

Never mind the restaurant's cute name; pay attention to the jonnycakes (or, as they are spelled here, johnny cakes). They are iconoclastic: made with yellow cornmeal instead of white, faintly flavored with maple syrup. These are west-of-Narragansett Bay–style, meaning fairly thick, dense, and griddle-cooked until the edges are crisp. Real pressure from a fork's edge is required to sever a bite, and they are flavorful enough in their own right that only minimal butter and/or syrup is required.

We recommend getting the johnny cakes alone, or as a side dish, but it also is possible to have a johnny cake platter, which includes two of them with Swiss cheese and very good ham, accompanied by home fries and fruit.

Open only for breakfast and lunch, Spoonem's offers an extensive menu of Benedicts, omelets, frittatas, corned beef hash, salmon hash, and a veggie hash of black beans and roasted corn. House specials include French-bread French toast stuffed with fresh strawberry cream cheese (in strawberry season), spiced pumpkin, or coconut and pineapple. We enjoyed the wickedly sweet Portuguese raisin sweet-bread French toast. It comes topped with butter and brown sugar, raisins, bananas, walnuts, and whipped cream.

While the ambience is casual and diner-like, décor has a modern edge (like the menu). A U-shaped counter with chrome-pedestal stools is surrounded by a floor that is part tiny tiles, as in a vintage hash house, and part varnished wood like in a stylish twenty-first-century café.

JOHNNY ANGEL'S CLAM SHACK

johnnyangelsclamshack.com

523 Charlestown   401-419-6732
Beach Rd.   **L D** (summer only) | **$**
Charlestown, RI

A seasonal clam shack at Shelter Cove Marina, Johnny Angel's is a local fave that offers not only classic Yankee seafood but Wednesday-night pasta suppers. The good eats include New England–style chowder (thick and creamy), whole-belly clams fried to a crisp, and fish and chips. Clam cakes are superb: crisp-skinned, moist inside, and seductively oceanic. For dessert, there is good Windsor Dairy ice cream as well as a selection of donuts from Rhode Island's esteemed Allie's (p. 63).

No indoor seats, but there is a broad deck for picnic-style dining.

MIKE'S KITCHEN

170 Randall St.   401-946-5320
(at Tabor-Franchi   **L D** | **$$**
VFW Post 239)
Cranston, RI

Mike's Kitchen serves excellent Italian/Portuguese/Rhode Island food in a VFW hall at reasonable prices. The heart of the menu is a roster of well-made standards such as chicken marsala, veal Française, and tortellini marinara. You can begin a meal with a stuffie (a stuffed quahog clam), a whole artichoke loaded with sausage stuffing, or the unique Ocean State appetizer known as snail salad. Seafood pastas are especially wonderful, offered with a choice of red or white sauce. The top of the line is seafood Diablo—lobster, scallops, and shrimp spread out across a bed of noodles. While most main-course preparations involve a degree of kitchen wizardry, it also is possible to have a simple plate of broiled scallops, swordfish, salmon, or sole. On the side of anything, you want polenta—a cream-soft block of steamy cooked cornmeal that is especially wonderful when accompanied by fennel-spiked sausage. Servings are immense. The chicken Parmesan we ordered provided one full meal in the restaurant and another big one at home the next day.

To drink with your meal, wine and cocktails are available from a bar at one side of the dining room. You will pay for these separately, as the bar is run by the veterans who own the building.

OLNEYVILLE N.Y. SYSTEM

olneyvillenewyorksystem.com

20 Plainfield St.   401-621-9500
Providence, RI   **L D** | **$**

Rhode Island's distinctive New York System hot dog, known also as a hot wiener, is a small, pink, natural-casing, pork-beef-veal frankfurter that gets grilled, then inserted in a steamed bun, topped with yellow mustard, chopped raw onions, and a dark sauce of ground beef, plus a sprinkling of celery salt. It's the sauce that makes the dog unique—spicy but not hot, the meat as fine as sand, the flavor vaguely sweet, reminiscent of the kaleidoscopic flavors that give Greek-ancestored Cincinnati Five-Way chili its soul.

Olneyville was opened in the 1930s by the Stevens family, Greek immigrants who came to Rhode Island by way of Brooklyn. It is still a Stevens-family operation, and countermen use the old-time wiener-up-the-arm technique of preparing the hot dogs, lining up six to eight bunned ones from wrist to elbow and spreading sauce, onions, and mustard on all of them in the blink of an eye. A sign posted outside announces the everyday special: "Buy ONE wiener for the price of TWO and receive the second FREE!" As of 2013, the Hot Wiener Challenge record holder was John Munroe, who ate eighteen in forty-five minutes.

One curious item on the short menu is beef stew, which is not beef stew at all. It is an order of salted French fries spritzed with vinegar and ribboned with ketchup. The beverage of choice is the Rhode Island favorite, coffee milk—like chocolate milk, but coffee-flavored.

One other location: 1012 Reservoir Avenue, Cranston (401-437-8248).

STANLEY'S FAMOUS HAMBURGERS

stanleyshamburgers.com

535 Dexter St.   401-726-9689

Central Falls, RI   **L D** (closed Sun) | **$**

A swell blog called Small Bites ("spices and stories from local eateries in the smallest state") alerted us to the Stanleyburger, a crisp-edged patty customarily grilled with onions and served with pickle chips. While bigger than slider-sized, Stanleyburgers are small enough that we highly recommend a double or two, preferably with cheese, maybe also with bacon and tomato. French fries are crisp and flavorful, available plain, topped with cheese or chili, or Quebec-style, here meaning smothered with mozzarella shreds and dark gravy, a version of *poutine*. Stanley's offers milk shakes, including the Rhode Island preference, coffee shakes; for dessert, the local favorite is Grape-Nuts pudding.

WEIN-O-RAMA

1009 Oaklawn Ave.   401-943-4990

Cranston, RI   **B L D** | **$**

"The best hot weiners anywhere!" crows the menu at Wein-O-Rama, and in a state crazy for little pink weenies topped with chili, that's a bold assertion. Unlike most wiener restaurants (all of which spell the word *ei* rather than *ie*), this one has a full three-meal-a-day menu, but when the waitress caught us actually reading it, she interrupted our study and demanded to know, "You are not going to try our wieners?!"

Although the term "New York System" appears nowhere at Wein-O-Rama, the dogs served here are exactly what is known by those terms throughout the Providence area. A Wein-O-Rama frank is a small, snappy one buried inside a soft bun, dressed with meaty, vividly spiced sauce, mustard, raw onion, and celery salt. It's a fine harmony in which the several ingredients, none of which is particularly great on its own, combine to make something quite delicious. To drink: Rhode Island's favorite non-alcoholic libation, coffee milk. Rice pudding is dense and fresh, the grains of rice offering a nice al dente resistance.

WRIGHT'S FARM

wrightsfarm.com

84 Inman Rd.   401-769-2856

Harrisville, RI   **D** | **$$**

--★-- **HOT TICKET** --★-- In the early 1950s, after hosting chicken-dinner picnics for local clubs, the owner of Wright's Chicken Farm opened a restaurant. Today it is the biggest of the Blackstone Valley's chicken dinner halls—one of the biggest restaurants anywhere, with seats for up to 1,500 eaters at a time in multiple dining rooms. On a Friday or Saturday night, you'll park a quarter mile away and you might wait an hour for your party's name to be called on the speaker system. While biding time, you can shop for toys, fudge, and kitschy bric-a-brac in the 4,000-square-foot gift shop, try your luck at a window dedicated to selling lottery tickets, or play keno in one of the four bars. Tables are set up for groups of ten and twenty or more. Once seated, you will be waited on and served instantly. When you are done, you pay the waitress with cash. No credit cards are accepted (but there is an ATM machine in the lobby). Everything about the experience is so huge it is hallucinatory.

Once you are at a table, the meal comes quickly because everybody gets the same thing: hot rolls, cool salad, macaroni shells with red sauce, and fabulous thick-cut French fries all orbiting around bowls full of dripping-good roasted chicken enveloped in gossamer skin with booming flavor. What's so especially good about the chicken is that in addition to its fallapart-tender mouthfuls, there are significant surface areas where the skin has pulled away during roasting and the bare exterior of the meat itself turns firm, becoming chewy, moisture-beaded bark with flavor even more intense than the soft, juice-dripping parts within. Meals are all-you-can-eat. If ever a bowl is emptied, it gets replaced with a full one.

Chicken frowners do have an alternative: steak. It is ordered by fewer than 1 percent of Wright's customers.

VERMONT

AL'S FRENCH FRYS

alsfrenchfrys.com

1251 Williston Rd.　　802-862-9203
South Burlington, VT　　**L D** | $

Can you guess the specialty at Al's French Frys? Available by the cup, pint, and quart, these spuds are handsome, irregularly cut sticks that are fried before your eyes until their skin turns golden-brown and the edges get crisp. They arrive lightly salted, and the choice of condiments on each table includes vinegar to sprinkle on for zest. The fries are available with cheese sauce or gravy, but why goop up such perfectly made potatoes?

The hamburgers and hot dogs available to go with these fries are perfectly all right, the buns for both griddle-toasted until crisp. If you have a craving for beef, get a double burger; the patties are slider-sized. Milk shakes are made from scratch.

Al's has been around since the late 1940s, when it was known as Al's Snack Bar. Even then, Al's advertised its specialty with the unconventional spelling.

BABA-À-LOUIS

babalouisbakery.com

92 Route 11W　　802-875-4666
Chester, VT　　**B L** (closed Mon & Tues) | $

While scarcely a restaurant—no hot meals are served in the morning, and only quiche, sandwiches, soup, and a salad bar at lunch—Baba-À-Louis in Chester is one of Vermont's most noteworthy breakfast stops. Since they opened a small storefront bakery in Chester in 1976 (moved to the current location in '97), John McLure and Ruth Zezza have won a reputation for masterful yeast breads. Stop in any day after 7 a.m., find a seat at one of the tables opposite the bakery shelves, and enjoy a cup of coffee while you tear off pieces from a warm baguette, anadama loaf, or sourdough rye. Morning-specific pastries are breathtaking, especially Mr. McLure's sticky buns. Ribboned with a walnutty brown-sugar glaze, these buttery cylinders are so fragile and fine that they verge on croissanthood.

Lunch is served cafeteria-style. There is pizza on the weekends, and Tuesday through Saturday you can have a panini, open-face, or regular sandwich, quiche or soup or salad.

The place itself is beautiful: a sun-bathed cathedral with a full view of the open kitchen, where doughs are kneaded and breads pulled from ovens.

BLUE BENN DINER

314 North St.   802-442-5140
Bennington, VT   B L D | $

In the morning, it is hypnotic to watch coffeepot-armed waitresses maneuver around the cramped confines behind the counter and among the short line of wooden booths of this creaky but ultra-energetic monitor-roof diner that got planted here on Route 7 in 1949. What a joy it is to slide a fork down into a steamy slice of corn-bread French toast or a stack of crunchberry pancakes with crisp turkey hash on the side. The true-blue hash-house menu offers hearty soups and gravy-topped biscuits as well as more creative fare that includes grilled salmon Caesar salad, soya sausage, and Syrian roll-ups. Every available surface is festooned with handwritten signs advertising literally hundreds of specials, including many choices to please vegetarians...like a terrific no-meat enchilada.

CHELSEA ROYAL DINER

chelsearoyaldiner.com
487 Marlboro Rd.   802-254-8399
West Brattleboro, VT   B L D | $

Nestled at the foot of the Green Mountains, the Chelsea Royal (Worcester Dining Car #736) is like a culinary yacht: polished wooden booths and gracefully curving wood ceiling, tiny-check tile floor, everything old but oh-so shipshape. "What can we eat that's real Vermont?" we ask our waitress, who wears a "Good Food Fast" T-shirt.

"Blue Plate Special!" she shoots back. Lucky us, it is chicken potpie—comfort food supreme. We get macaroni and (Vermont) cheese and Yankee baked beans on the side and top it off with maple walnut pie and a bowl of that Yankee stalwart, Indian pudding—a luxurious hot cornmeal and molasses cereal that arrives under a crown of vanilla ice cream.

Open every day of the year, and serving breakfast all day long, the Chelsea Royal is a place to come for scrumptious corned beef hash or French toast with real maple syrup ($1.25 extra) in the morning and meat loaf with a side of baked beans at supper...or such unexpected exotica as a Cajun skillet

breakfast or Teriyaki chicken salad lunch. A full fountain offers milk shakes, sundaes, floats, and splits as well as homemade root beer and black cherry soda. The kitchen makes Mexican food Tuesday through Saturday and New England boiled dinner every Monday night. April through October, an ice cream stand offers soft-serve and hard-pack as well as burgers and foot-long hot dogs.

THE CHUBBY MUFFIN

chubbymuffin.com
88 Oak St.   802-540-0050
Burlington, VT   B L | $

The muffins are great in this cute-as-a-button café and coffee shop. Sweet favorites include lemon poppy seed with a sharp citrus kick, apple cinnamon, and banana chocolate chip. Our favorite savory flavor is Cheddar-bacon-maple, a loaf-shaped Vermont bonanza. Chubby also makes its own English muffins, and these are the foundation for the breakfast sandwich known as a Quickee (local egg and Cabot Cheddar), the Meat Quickee (add Vermont-cured bacon, sausage, or ham), and the Veggie Monster (tomato, caramelized onion, mushrooms, and spinach).

For lunch, house-made buns are used to sandwich hefty beef burgers and black bean burgers, as well as pulled pork in maple barbecue sauce. Panini options include a BLT and an Intervale, which is basil and sunflower-seed pesto with maple bacon, mozzarella, and tomato. On the side with any lunch, you want cheese curds. They are breaded, and fried to a crisp with molten cheese inside, served with ranch dressing and marinara sauce for dipping. Desserts include homemade hard ice cream and soft-serve creemees (Vermont's version of soft-serve ice cream).

While the Chubby Muffin is a breakfast-lunch-snack sort of place, it does open for supper on Wednesday, burger night, and Friday, when pizzas are featured. Coffee is always available, including scrupulously well-made lattes, cappuccinos, and the like, as well as hot cocoa, tea, and smoothies. Among available bottled drinks is a barely sweet sparkling maple seltzer that goes well with just about anything.

With its laid-back vibe and virtuous locavore credo, the Chubby Muffin is a good taste of free-wheeling Vermont. Come here ready to relax and take it easy. This is not fast food. Everything is made to order, meticulously and without shortcuts.

COUNTRY GIRL DINER
countrygirldiner.com/

46 VT Rte. 103 South   802-875-1003

Chester, VT   **B L | $**

Country Girl is an adorable vintage silver diner complete with a steel-banded counter, tile knee guard, monitor roof, and well-worn booths. Prices are low, and food is classic blue-plate fare, but with a modest modern twist. Hash at breakfast, for example, might be pulled pork hash, if it isn't the more traditional (and excellent) corned beef hash; real maple syrup is sometimes added to the waffle batter and always is served with French toast and even with oatmeal; when berries are in season, expect them to adorn pancakes.

Notable midday meals include Mexican cheese chili, Guinness-Cheddar soup, a meat-loaf melt on Texas toast, and Monte Cristo sandwiches drizzled with maple syrup. The hamburgers themselves are nothing special, but the grilled onions available to top them are swell, as are hand-cut French fries to go alongside. Peanut butter pie is an outstanding dessert.

Dinner is served Friday night only.

CURTIS' ALL AMERICAN BAR B Q
7 Putney Landing Rd.   802-387-5474

(Exit 4 off I-91)   **L D** (April–Oct, Weds–Sun)

Putney, VT   **| $$**

Curtis Tuff's barbecue is more a picnic than a restaurant. Orders are placed and food retrieved from a blue-painted school bus, one of several planted in a meadow outfitted with picnic tables. There is no indoor dining. Dishware is disposable. When you have finished, discard the dishes and drive away.

This rib-and-chicken joint has been around for more than three decades, starting in a time when decent barbecue was an extreme rarity in the Northeast. Now there are pretty fair smokehouse meals from New York to the International Boundary, but even with the growing competition, Curtis's ribs are outstanding. Available as slabs and half slabs, they are painted with a vinegar-tinted red sauce (mild or spicy) that does a fine job of underlining the piggy personality of the meat. Side dishes include corn on the cob, collard greens, baked potatoes loaded with garnishes, and saucy beans that taste especially good when topped with Vermont Cheddar cheese. We are less impressed with the chicken, which is perfectly all right but lacks the juiciness and flavor sparkle of good, smoky pork.

The picnic setting encourages strangers to share tables (especially on a really nice weekend day, when crowds come), making a meal at Curtis' a social as well as culinary event.

DEPOT CAFÉ
62 Depot St.   802-366-8181

Manchester, VT   **L D | $$**

The Depot Café is a restaurant inside a furniture store. You eat full meals in a dining room filled with lamps, settees, tapestries, tote bags, and piles of rugs, as well as customers shopping for those things. It is not textbook regional American Roadfood, as the cuisine has a strong Turkish accent, but we can't resist a restaurant that does double duty—especially when the food is so good.

Most of the interesting dishes are cooked in a wood-fired oven. That includes stylish, thin-crust pizzas available with toppings that range from a classic tomato sauce, cheese, and pepperoni to the Taste of Anatolia, with Vermont lamb, onions, and parsley. We love Hajro's Special pie, which is thin stalks of freshly roasted asparagus, feta cheese, and punchy Kalamata olive tapenade. Also wonderful is wild mushroom pie, topped with a variety of mushrooms, caramelized onions, and mozzarella.

Beyond praiseworthy pizzas, the Depot Café offers kebabs, brick-oven chicken and salmon, and brilliant salads, including one composed of arugula, sliced apples, asiago cheese, and walnuts. We cannot resist the garlicky hummus, served with extraordinary pita bread that is chewy, full-flavored, and dotted with peppery little seeds.

Do leave room for dessert. The baklava is honey-drenched and nutty. Add a cup of true Turkish coffee and you will be up all night reminiscing about a really good meal in a really interesting place.

MAYNARD'S SNACK BAR

150 Rte. 100B   802-496-3614
Moretown, VT   **L** (summer only) | **$**

We were directed to Maynard's for its fine creemees, especially the maple creemee, for which soft-serve ice cream is infused with syrup from a nearby sugar shack. This is berry country, too, and you can get a boat of vanilla soft-serve topped with freshly picked strawberries and/or blueberries almost any time Maynard's is open. (It's a strictly May to Labor Day operation.)

The savory menu is snack-bar deluxe: big, irregular hamburgers laden with juice, foot-long hot dogs available topped with cheese or a choice of spicy or mild Coney sauce, and crisp, hand-cut French fries you can decorate with either ketchup or cider vinegar. There are sundaes and milk shakes galore, including a maple shake that shouldn't be missed, even if it is somewhat redundant in a meal that includes maple creemees. It becomes even tougher to narrow down one's ice cream choice when you know about an item called the Dusty Miller, a vanilla creemee topped with hot fudge and malt powder.

Maynard's is a charming rural destination that can get pretty busy on weekends. (It's open only Thursday through Sunday, from 11:30 a.m. to 8:30 p.m.) All seating is at picnic tables on a grassy lawn out front, where rows of pink flowering trees separate diners from the two-lane road that runs past.

MISS LYNDONVILLE DINER

686 Broad St.   802-626-9890
Lyndonville, VT   **B L D** | **$**

When you see it from the outside, Miss Lyndonville does not look like a classic diner. But there is a real Sterling dining car here, now surrounded by a half century's worth of additions and extra seating. In food and in spirit, Miss Lyndonville is 100 percent diner. You can count on change from a ten-dollar bill at breakfast and lunch; the most expensive dinner on the menu—steak and shrimp—is all of $11.99. True to hash-house tradition, portions are large, service is lightning-fast, and waitresses dish out sassy repartee and wield coffeepots with the aplomb of baton twirlers.

The multipage menu devotes maximum space to breakfast. Breads are baked on-premises, meaning that even standard toast is better than ordinary; cinnamon bread is outstanding, as is French toast (especially cinnamon bread French toast).

Featured lunches include hot turkey and hot pot roast sandwiches and a North Country Special: a one-third-pound hamburg (they drop the *er* at the end of the word hereabouts) with Vermont Cheddar and sliced tomato on grilled house-baked bread. For dinner, you can choose among such blue-plate stalwarts as pot roast, liver and onions, maple-cured ham steak with raisin sauce, and roast turkey with the works. Fresh blueberry and strawberry pie lead the summer dessert menu; there always is a cream pie of the day as well as good-old pudding. Even Jell-O.

MRS. MURPHY'S DONUTS

374 Depot St. (Route 30)   802-362-1874
Manchester, VT   **B L** | **$**

A counter stool at Mrs. Murphy's is a box seat in donut heaven. You can get deluxe ones—Boston creams, jelly-filled, iced and jimmie-sprinkled—but we'll take plain sinkers every time. They are the polar opposite of the frivolous fat puffs sold by Krispy Kreme in other parts of the country (but *not* in Vermont). These hefty boys have a wicked crunchy skin and cakey insides that love to sop a while in coffee.

The storefront café is a locals' favorite. It occurred to us one breakfast hour that most customers didn't tell Cheryl the waitress what they wanted; she brought them the usual. One banker-looking guy in striped suit and brogues left his sedan idling outside, stepped up to the takeout counter, grabbed a bag, and flapped it open for Cheryl to load with six sour cream donuts. As she rang him up, he nodded thanks to her and she nodded thanks to him, then he left and drove away; not a word was spoken between them.

MYER'S BAGELS

myersbagels.com

377 Pine St.   802-863-5013
Burlington, VT   **B L | $**

———★——— You'll probably think you've lost your
OPEN EARLY way as you drive toward Myer's Bagels,
———★——— which is located well back from the road in a somewhat decrepit South End warehouse district. As soon as the car door opens, your nose will tell you that you have arrived. The aroma is vaguely like the smoldering-wood perfume that surrounds genuine barbecue parlors, but instead of pork or beef, that enticing smoke melds with the smell of baking bagels. These bagels are made the way they make them in Montreal (where bagelmeister Lloyd Squiers apprenticed at the esteemed St-Viateur), meaning they are relatively small, very chewy, slightly sweet (honey is added to the boiling water), and redolent of the wood fire that bakes them. They are nothing like aerated, balloon-style bagels that are so easy to slice and to chew. Slicing one of these requires a steady hold and a good knife. Chewing one demands healthy dentition. The reward is revelation: a great, serious, meaningful breadstuff.

They are available in every imaginable incarnation, from plain and poppy to rosemary with sea salt and sesame sunflower. One unique variation is Montreal spice, for which Mr. Squiers applies the herby mix of coriander, garlic, pepper, and salt that Quebec chefs use when they cure smoked meat. On the subject of meat, we must recommend Myer's brisket. Like the best of Texas, it is long smoked to a point of absolute tenderness, maximum juiciness, and intense beefy flavor. Inside one of these chewy bagels, it's magic.

This is a really fun place to visit, starting when it opens—at 4 a.m. It's great to watch bagels emerge from the oven in the semi-open kitchen and to get them while they are almost too hot to hold. There are a few tables scattered about for eating here, although a lot of business is takeout.

Beyond bagels and all sorts of cream cheese, and lox and brisket and the like, Myer's also happens to be home of Emily Conn, who runs a business out of here called the Bakery at the Farmhouse Kitchen. Emily makes some amazing apricot-filled Pop-Tart-like toaster pastries, savory hand pies, and almond buttercrunch cakes that are simply some of the most delicious sweet things we've ever tasted. Visit Emily's website, almondcakesvt.com, for further information.

P&H TRUCK STOP

pandhtruckstop.com

Exit 17 off I-91   802-429-2141
Wells River, VT   Always open (hot food
                             available only from 6 a.m. to
                             10 p.m.) | $

——★—— P&H is a 24/7 truck stop, not for the fastidi-
OPEN 24/7 ous epicure. You need to pass through the
——★—— aroma of diesel fuel outside to get to the fresh-baked bread and pot roast blanketed with gravy in the dining room. Soups and chowders are especially inviting: tomato-macaroni soup is thick with vegetables, ground beef, and soft noodles; corn chowder is loaded with potatoes and corn kernels and flavored with bacon. We love any kind of sandwich using thick-sliced P&H bread, but the mashed potatoes (*purée de pommes de terre* on the bilingual menu, written for French-Canadian truckers) taste like they were made from powder, and the meat loaf is strictly for die-hard diner fans.

Given the on-premises bakery, breakfast is especially worthwhile. There are big, heavy donuts that demand a dunk in coffee; there are thick slices of swirly cinnamon-raisin bread that make divine buttered toast and even better French toast. Toasted maple-nut bread is another winner, especially when spread with apple jelly. Like everything else you will eat here, pies are hale and hearty: fruit pies, berry pies, custard pies, meringue pies, Reese's pie (a peanut-cream), and maple-cream pie thick as toffee and topped with nuts.

PAPA PETE'S

35 Bridge Rd.   802-393-9747
North Hero, VT   L D (summer only) | $

As the crow flies, North Hero, Vermont, is practically a neighbor to Plattsburg, New York. But to get from Plattsburg to North Hero by car is nearly an hour's drive, out to Carry Bay in the middle of Lake Champlain. For anyone in search of Michigans, it is a worthwhile journey because it takes you to Papa Pete's and one mighty good Michigan.

In case you are not up on your tube-steak etymology, a Michigan is a style of chili dog unique to the area around northern Lake Champlain, especially Plattsburg (where, allegedly, it first was configured): a plump little dog in a large, soft roll that is closed off at its ends to hold maximum amounts of the meaty sauce. Mustard and raw onions are traditional condiments. Papa Pete's, a tiny snack shack with a walk-up window and picnic-table accommodations, offers not only classic Michigans but hamburgers enlivened by the same glowing Michigan sauce.

Beyond Michigans, this is a surprising little place, offering such non-snack-shack amenities as freshly baked rolls and hand-cut French fries. Less a surprise, considering its proximity to Canada, Pete's also serves *poutine*. On weekends, an on-premises smoker yields ribs and pulled pork.

★ PARKWAY DINER

1696 Williston Rd.   802-652-1155
South Burlington, VT   B L | $

Ever in search of great hot turkey sandwiches, we paid attention when Vermont food savant Alice Levitt wrote to say that the hot turkey sandwich at the Parkway Diner in South Burlington is "as good as it gets." We ate one, and we agree. This is the Platonic ideal of a restaurant hot turkey sandwich. Although

the menu refers to it as "homestyle," its goodness is different from the soft, tender charms of home-cooked turkey, even if a home cook were to present it in the diner way: on soft bread, under giblet gravy, sided by mashed potatoes and coleslaw. The turkey here is something else, intertwining soft white and juicy dark meats that are full-flavored and beguiling in a way that somehow seems more professional than could be achieved by even the best home cook.

Alice also recommends the VT Burger, a tour de force that begins with a thick, hand-pressed burger cooked as ordered (medium-rare, ridiculously juicy) and stacks on a melting layer of sharp Cabot Cheddar cheese, Vermont smokehouse bacon, thin slices of crisp Granny Smith apple, lettuce, tomato, and red onion, all in a fine brioche bun. This is a fantastic burger by any standards, far above any ordinary diner benchmark.

Everything about the Parkway is a cut above. Although it retains the bygone charms of a mid-twentieth-century Worcester Dining Car Company diner—chrome-banded counter stools, tiny-tile checked floor, curving monitor roof, leather and mahogany booths—it is anything but an old greasy spoon. It is, in fact, of the moment. Just look up at the movable-letter menu board next to the list of daily specials. It reveals the local farm, creamery, sugar shack, and coffee company from which the kitchen obtains its provender.

PUTNEY DINER

82 Main St.   802-387-5433
Putney, VT   B L D | $

The Putney Diner is a delightful little town eatery just minutes off I-91 at Exit 4. Although it doesn't look like a classic diner, it has the spirit . . . and the menu. In the morning, plates of plain or buckwheat pancakes come with Vermont maple syrup. Eggs can be ordered with kielbasa or corned beef hash, and broad-topped muffins are split and toasted on the grill. At lunch, you can count on square meals of meat loaf or shepherd's pie, foot-long hot dogs in grilled buns, herby-creamy mac 'n' Cheddar cheese, or—in cool weather—the arcane Yankee favorite, American chop suey.

No meal, including breakfast, should end without a slice of Putney Diner pie. There are fine fruit pies throughout the summer into fall and candy-sweet maple walnut pie year-around.

UP FOR BREAKFAST

4935 Main St.   802-362-4204
Manchester, VT   **B L | $$**

It can be difficult to order pancakes at Up for Breakfast because the menu also beckons with red flannel hash, griddle-cooked muffins, Benedicts, frittatas, and French toast. But oh, those pancakes! Three kinds are available, with or without blueberries in the batter. Buttermilk pancakes are sunny-hued and fluffy, easy to eat; those made from buckwheat batter are dark and serious; the sourdough cakes are breathtaking. The first thing you notice about the sourdoughs is the sound they make when you press the edge of a fork to one of them. You hear a faint crunch as the tine breaks through a lacy crust. Inside the chewy web that encloses them, they are thin but substantial, with the vigorous disposition of an old sourdough starter that has had years to develop its tang. Pair this with a generous infusion of sweet-tart blueberries and some of that woodsy syrup—served warm, praise be—and maybe an order of Up for Breakfast's wild turkey hash, and you'll understand why Vermont can claim the title of America's Breakfast Destination.

You really do go *up* for breakfast—to a cozy, second-story restaurant with window views of Main Street. There is pleasant art on the walls, and if you sit toward the back, you can enjoy watching goings-on in the semi-open kitchen. Seats can be scarce, but if you are looking for something extra-special in the morning, Up for Breakfast is a gold mine worth the wait.

WAYSIDE RESTAURANT

waysiderestaurant.com
1873 US Route 302   802-223-6611
Montpelier, VT   **B L D | $**

Even if you are not on a mission to eat regional arcana, you can be sure of good food, priced right, in this cheerful town lunchroom. Meals start with glossy-topped dinner rolls, warm from the oven. How nice it is to tear off a piece of roll and dunk it into a bowl of Wayside beef barley soup—a hearty brew so thick with meat and pearly grain that a spoon literally stands up in it. What a feast the Wednesday chicken pie is, piled into a big crockery boat with dressing and a crusty biscuit, with a great heap of gravy-dripping mashed potatoes on the side. Pot roast comes piled high on a plate under a mantle of good gravy.

In addition to such classic North Country sweets as Grape-Nuts pudding, mince pie, and homemade ginger snaps, the dessert repertoire includes apple pie made with densely packed hand-cut apples in a fork-crimped crust and maple cream pie. Low and flat, the filling of the maple pie is too delicious for words. Its radiant band of amber cream is complex, powerful, and elegant the way only pure maple can be, and it resonates on your taste buds after a Wayside meal like a Yankee cordial.

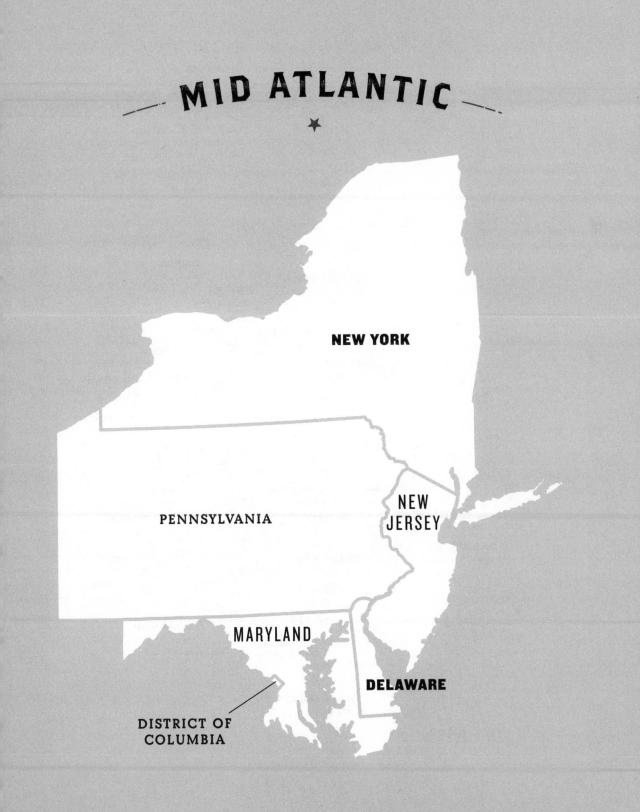

MID ATLANTIC

NEW YORK

PENNSYLVANIA

NEW JERSEY

MARYLAND

DELAWARE

DISTRICT OF COLUMBIA

PENNSYLVANIA

PHILADELPHIA
Center City Pretzel Co.
Famous 4th Street Deli
Geno's
Jim's Steaks
Joe's Steaks & Soda Shop
Johnny's Hots
★ John's Roast Pork
Lorenzo's Pizza
Pat's King of Steaks
Steve's Prince of Steaks

SCRANTON
Glider Diner

TRUCKSVILLE
Pizza Perfect

OLD FORGE
Salerno's

WHITE HAVEN
The Family Diner

GIRARDVILLE
Marrone's Cafe

PITTSBURGH
DeLuca's
The Enrico Biscotti Company
Original Hot Dog Shop
Primanti Brothers
Robert Wholey & Co.

FRACKVILLE
Dutch Kitchen

EASTON
Jimmy's Hot Dogs

NORRISTOWN
Lou's

BARTO
Longacre's Modern Dairy Bar

BALA CYNWYD
★ Mama's

HARRISBURG

FOLCRAFT
Leo's

EMMITSBURG
Chubby's Southern
Style Barbeque

PHILADELPHIA
(see above)

HOCKESSIN
Woodside Farm Creamery

HANCOCK
Park-N-Dine

WILMINGTON
Charcoal Pit

SEVERNA PARK
The Breakfast Shoppe

BEL AIR
Broom's Bloom Dairy

GLEN BURNIE
Seaside Restaurant & Crab House

BALTIMORE
★ Faidley's

ROCK HALL
Waterman's Crab House

LINTHICUM HEIGHTS
G&M Restaurant & Lounge

SILVER SPRING
Crisfield

DOVER
Countrie Eatery

SMYRNA
Helen's Sausage House

GRASONVILLE
Harris Crab House
The Narrows

LEIPSIC
Sambo's Tavern

SEABROOK
Jerry's Seafood

WASHINGTON, DC
★ Ben's Chili Bowl
DGS Delicatessen
Florida Avenue Grill

HURLOCK
Suicide Bridge Restaurant

ANNAPOLIS
Chick & Ruth's Delly

CALLAWAY
Bear Creek Open Pit BBQ

HUGHESVILLE
Randy's Ribs & Barbecue

CHARLOTTE HALL
St. Mary's Landing

DELAWARE

MARYLAND

NEW YORK

NEW JERSEY

BUFFALO
Charlie the Butcher's Kitchen
Condrell's
Mike's Candy

TONAWANDA
Ted's Jumbo Red Hots

WILLIAMSVILLE
★ Aléthea's Chocolates

SEA BREEZE
Don's Original

PLATTSBURGH
Clare and Carl's
Gus's Restaurant
McSweeney's

GLENS FALLS
New Way Lunch

CHEEKTOWAGA
Polish Villa

DEPEW
Antoinette's

WEST SENECA
★ Schwabl's

ROCHESTER
LDR Char Pit
★ Nick Tahou Hots

LIVERPOOL
Heid's of Liverpool

ALBANY

CORTLAND
Doug's Fish Fry

CHATHAM
BenGable Savories

ANCRAM
West Taghkanic Diner

ITHACA
Cornell Dairy Bar
Glenwood Pines
Shortstop Deli

WINGDALE
Big W's Roadside Bar-B-Q

HAMBURG
Nick Charlap's

BINGHAMTON
Sharkey's

BEACON
Poppy's

ENDICOTT
Phil's Chicken House

BREWSTER
Red Rooster Drive-In

LACKAWANNA
Steve's Pig &
Ox Roast

CLIFTON
The Hot Grill
Rutt's Hut

PATERSON
Libby's Lunch

NORTH SALEM
Purdy's Farmer & the Fish

WEST ORANGE
★ Jimmy Buff's

LEDGEWOOD
Cliff's Dairy Maid

PORT CHESTER
Hubba
Texas Chili

KENILWORTH
Charlie's

LINDEN
White Rose System

BRONX
Tino's

MAMARONECK
Walter's

EDISON
★ Harold's New York Deli

TRENTON

NEW YORK
Barney Greengrass
John's of Bleeker Street
★ Katz's Delicatessen
Papaya King
Patsy's
Second Avenue Deli

NEWARK
Dickie Dee's

HACKENSACK
B&W Bakery
White Manna

ROBBINSVILLE
De Lorenzo's Tomato Pies

ATLANTIC CITY
★ White House Sub Shop

DELAWARE

CHARCOAL PIT

charcoalpit.net

2600 Concord Pike   302-478-2165
(Route 202)   **L D | $**
Wilmington, DE

Charcoal Pit's hamburger is a quarter-pound patty with a smoky taste served on a big, spongy bun, either plain or in the deluxe configuration, which adds lettuce, tomato, and pickle. For those who crave extra meat, there is also a double-size eight-ounce hamburger, but in our opinion, that defeats the mid-twentieth-century charm of the meal. (The Charcoal Pit opened for business in 1956.) Fries on the side are savory, normal-size twigs with a nice tough skin and soft potato flavor. And the milk shakes are so thick that the long-handled spoon provided is much more useful than a straw. Crab cakes, while no competition for the Chesapeake Bay's best, are nice: hardball-shaped spheres with crusty outsides and a fair measure of crab. They're made here every Monday, Wednesday, and Friday.

We like this old-fashioned place with its comfy maroon booths and wall décor that includes vintage menus. Waitresses go about their job with aplomb and an attitude that make customers feel part of a cheap-eats ritual that has gone on forever.

Another Charcoal Pit is located in Prices Corner at Kirkwood Highway and Greenbank Road.

COUNTRIE EATERY

countrieeatery.com

950 North State St.   302-674-8310
Dover, DE   **B L D | $**

The Countrie Eatery is especially notable for breakfast: buttermilk pancakes filled with blueberries or chocolate chips and topped with fruits, nuts, or syrup; creamed chipped beef on toast; and three-egg omelets served in a skillet. Among noteworthy side dishes are grits, corned-beef hash, and scrapple that is fried until crunchy on the outside, but moist and porky within.

At lunch you can have a half-pound hamburger, a hot sandwich made with turkey, meat loaf, or roast beef with mashed potatoes and gravy, or a cheese-topped crab melt on an English muffin. Desserts include rice pudding, bread pudding, an apple dumpling, layer cakes, and fruit pies.

Ambience is country-craftsy Colonial with primitive art and old-time farm implements on the wall.

HELEN'S SAUSAGE HOUSE

4866 N. Dupont Hwy.   302-653-4200
Smyrna, DE   **B L | $**

If you are hungry and rushing north toward the Delaware Valley Bridge anytime between four in the morning and lunch (or on Sunday, starting at 7 a.m.), call Helen's and place a sandwich order. That's the way the truckers do it, and in this case, the truckers are on to a very good thing. Helen's Sausage House is a roadside eatery with big sandwiches at small prices.

The sausages are thick and crusty giants with plenty of Italian zest. They spurt juice when you bite them, and a normal sandwich is two in a roll (although wimpy appetites can get a single). With fried green peppers and onions, it is a majestic arrangement—a little messy to eat but nevertheless one of the great sausage sandwiches anywhere.

Helen's offers all manner of breakfast sandwich on bread or rolls, made with eggs, bacon, scrapple, and fried ham; as well as lunchtime sandwiches of steak, cheesesteak, burgers, hot beef, and hot ham. Other than the sausage, the must-eat (and must-see!) meal is Helen's pork chop sandwich. When the menu says *jumbo* pork chop, you better believe it. This slab of meat is approximately three times larger than the puny pieces of white bread that are stuck on either side of it. It isn't all that thick a chop, but it is tender, moist, and mouth-wateringly spiced.

While most of Helen's clientele stop by for sandwiches to go, it is possible to dine here. Place your order at the counter and carry it to a table opposite the instant-order counter, or proceed into a dining room decorated entirely with pictures of Elvis. Roadfood extraordinaire!

SAMBO'S TAVERN

283 Front St.   302-674-9724
Leipsic, DE   **L D** (April–Oct) | **$$$**

Bring plenty of money to eat at Sambo's, even though there is little in the way of décor and few frivolous amenities at the big waterman's tavern where cold beer goes best with just about everything. The full Mid-Atlantic seafood menu includes creamy crab soup, plush crab cakes, rockfish and chips, spiced shrimp, and fried fish of all kinds. Good as all that may be, newspapers on the table are a telltale sign that this is an establishment primarily devoted to the ritual of a crab feast. The disposable tablecloths, paper-towel napkins, hammers, and picks are at the ready to attack piles of hard-shelled crabs that radiate Old Bay spice. They're delicious, and the big ones will cost plenty; for crab fanciers, a meal like this is well worth the Benjamins.

Note: all customers must be of drinking age.

WOODSIDE FARM CREAMERY

woodsidefarmcreamery.com

1310 Little Baltimore Rd.   302-239-9847
Hockessin, DE   (closed in winter) | **$**

—★——
VEGETARIAN-
FRIENDLY
—★——

Woodside Farm is home of the Hog Trough Sundae. That's five flavors of ice cream—two scoops of each—topped with three different toppings, a fresh banana, whipped cream, and a cherry. For less gluttonous sorts, there are normal-sized cups, cones, and sundaes too, all featuring ice cream made the old-fashioned way, by taking high-butterfat milk and turning it into sweet cream. The sweet cream is mixed with fruit, flavors, and nuts and frozen in small batches to be sold at the farm's stand. Jim Mitchell, whose family settled here in 1796, likes to tell visitors, "Two weeks ago, our ice cream was grass." Mr. Mitchell credits the goodness of his ice cream to the fact that the milk's source is his herd of Jersey cows (superior to Guernseys), whom he keeps happy by grazing them on fields of sweet grass.

Flavors range from chocolate and coffee to pumpkin pecan and butter brickle toffee. It is wonderfully normal ice cream, by which we mean it is not sickeningly butterfatty or cloying with too many mix-ins. The ingenuous true-farm flavor is especially welcome in varieties made with fresh fruit: peach, strawberry, black raspberry, and black cherry.

★ BEN'S CHILI BOWL

benschilibowl.com

1213 U St. NW
Washington, DC

202-667-0909
L D | $

★
OPEN LATE
★

It is possible to get only chili at Ben's Chili Bowl, the landmark lunch counter on U Street in the nation's capital; but regular customers know that the best way to enjoy the mahogany-brown ground-meat stew is atop a half-smoke. That's the city's unique tube steak—a plump, gently smoked beef-and-pork sausage link that gets sizzled on a hot griddle until its skin turns snapping-crisp. Served in a bun with mustard and onions, it's swell without chili; but when smothered, it may well be the ultimate chili dog. Ben's half-smokes are presented in a red plastic basket and hopefully accompanied by the kitchen's fine French fries, then topped off with a slice of sweet-potato pie, sweet-potato cake, or strawberry layer cake.

Big as its reputation is, Ben's remains a relaxed and easygoing diner, part of the neighborhood since 1958, surviving urban unrest and economic ups and downs. In 2001, its founders, Ben and Virginia Ali, were inducted into the Washington, DC, Hall of Fame. Today the restaurant is run by their sons.

DGS DELICATESSEN

dgsdelicatessen.com

1317 Connecticut Ave.
NW
Washington, DC

202-293-4400
L D | $$

We were tipped off to DGS Delicatessen by Abby Durlester, who promised that the pastrami here would make us weep. It did, with joy. Sliced extra thick, it is moist and fatty, rimmed with a dark halo of assertive spice and smoke, glowing with brined-meat savor. Several bread varieties are available to sandwich it (including, if you wish, Montreal bagels), the natural choice being rye. Like the pastrami, DGS double-baked rye is old-fashioned good: glossy-crusted, dense and chewy, spangled with caraway seeds. Both items are reminiscent of the great days of urban delis, most of which are gone with the ages.

In fact, DGS (which stands for District Grocery Store) calls itself a "next generation delicatessen," which means an elevated consciousness that includes a back-to-basics attitude about food quality and preparation. "We brine, cure, smoke, slice, and pickle daily in the house using only the finest ingredients from our trusted farmers and purveyors," the menu promises. In addition to classic deli dishes—corned beef sandwiches and Reuben variations, lox and bagels and latkes—the kitchen offers intriguing modern variants such as Reuben fries: thin, crisp-edged fries topped with pastrami, sauerkraut,

Swiss cheese, Russian dressing, and Fresno chiles. A smooth paste of chopped liver comes with old-time *gribenes* (a Jewish cognate of southern cracklins, made with chicken skin rather than pork) and also new-age sweet onion marmalade.

DGS is an achingly narrow storefront with a small dining room upstairs and a happy hour bar downstairs. The space feels especially boisterous, crowded with people who aren't necessarily crying over the goodness of their pastrami, but are audibly happy to be in a place where deli standards are so high.

FLORIDA AVENUE GRILL

floridaavenuegrill.com

1100 Florida Ave.   202-265-1586
Washington, DC   B L D | $

America is overpopulated with subpar or merely adequate biscuits, which is why discovery of excellent ones is cause for joy. In the cool, pre-dawn hours at the counter or in a booth at the Florida Avenue Grill, they are served two by two, warm enough so you can only gingerly grab the top and bottom of one to pull it into halves, all the better for the fleecy interior to absorb a cascade of spicy, sausage-crowded, cream-thick gravy. A smothered pair is adequate breakfast for modest appetites or an awesome side dish with fried pork chops, grits, and stewed apples. Alternate breakfast meats include crisp-fried scrapple and bisected half-smoke sausages.

Breakfast is the best meal of the day, but lunch and supper are special too. It is possible to order such soul-food standards as pigs' feet and chitterlings, but unless you are already a feet or intestine aficionado, we suggest you begin with more familiar things to eat. Spare ribs, for example, glazed with breathless hot sauce, are rugged and satisfying. For a tender meal, how about meat loaf, served with a side of mashed potatoes and a heap of collard greens? True to southern custom, there are lots of sides to accompany the entrees: candied sweet potatoes, mac 'n' cheese, lavish potato salad, rice, beans, peas, and always sweet corn bread for mopping up a plate.

Long a favorite destination for Washington's power brokers as well as blue-collar folk, and just a quick cab ride from Capitol Hill, the Grill's walls are plastered with 8 × 10 photos of officeholders and sports stars who all are fans of the long-lasting soul-food diner. If you value honest eats, this humble restaurant with its sprung-spring booths, pink counter, and red plastic stools is choice. It is cheap, fast, and the motherly waitresses make even pale-faced strangers feel right at home.

MARYLAND

BEAR CREEK OPEN PIT BBQ

bearcreekbarbq.com

20294 Point Lookout Rd.   301-994-1030
Callaway, MD   L D | $

Over a capacious open pit, chef Curtis Shreve cooks pork and beef so tender that if you look at it hard, it falls apart. We are especially fond of the pork, either hand-pulled into shreds or sliced. It has a smoky flavor and a piggy richness that defies description. It is good enough to need no sauce whatsoever, all the better to savor the flavor of the meat. (Mr. Shreve's sauce, we should say, is excellent: sweet, gently spicy, and mildly addictive.)

Mr. Shreve originally hails from the Louisiana/Texas area, so his cooking reflects southwest roots too. Corn dogs are reminiscent of those at the Texas State Fair, and chili is the sleeper on the menu. It's a meat-and-bean stew with assertive but not incendiary spices, served under a mantle of grated cheese. Here also is that miraculous Texas twist on chili known as Fritos pie: a bed of crisp corn chips topped with chili and spangled with Cheddar cheese and chopped raw onions. Shreve remembered, "When I was a kid years ago, they used to take a scoop of chili and put it right in the bag of Fritos and you ate it just like that. Now the bags are made of plastic that does not withstand the heat. So we serve our Fritos pie in a dish."

THE BREAKFAST SHOPPE

thebreakfastshoppe.com

552 Ritchie Hwy.   410-544-8599
Severna Park, MD   B L | $

Start with fresh OJ, then move on to buckwheat pancakes with molasses syrup, omelets and egg scrambles, eggs Benedict in various configurations (including one made with Nova Scotia lox), or a megameal known as the Backpacker. That's eggs, sausage, ham, bacon, potatoes, peppers, onions, spinach, broccoli, tomatoes, and jack cheese all loaded into a hot iron skillet that is set upon a trivet on the table.

Pancakes are terrific, available as tall stacks (five), normal stacks (three), short stacks (two), and singly. In addition to buckwheat, there are banana-nut cakes and pancakes topped with strawberry marinade. Creamed chipped beef, a fairly scarce Mid-Atlantic delight, is a house specialty, served on thick-cut challah bread with fried potatoes on the side.

The staff of swift waitresses makes life here friendly. Ours was always ready to refill coffee cups and to offer her own huzzahs about the menu items she likes best. When we told her how much we were enjoying our meal, she responded, "I know; it's so good. This is where I eat on my days off!"

BROOM'S BLOOM DAIRY

bbdairy.com

1700 S. Fountain Green Rd.
Bel Air, MD

410-399-2697
L (closed in Jan) | $

"Pastoral heaven" is how Roadfood.com's Buffet-buster described Broom's Bloom Dairy out in the Harford County countryside. It's an ice cream place with a roster of over one hundred flavors, at least a dozen of which are available every day. These include intense coffee, truly fruity banana, red raspberry (with lots of berries), red velvet with real cake in the mix, and sweet corn, that last one described by Buffetbuster as delivering "a powerful new wave of fresh, sweet corn flavor."

Pre–ice cream, Broom's Bloom is a good place for lunch—the main attractions are smoky Gouda-rich mac 'n' cheese and Maryland crab soups, either tomato-spicy or rich and creamy. The two soups can be combined in what's called a Maryland Half and Half, and it's also possible to combine mac 'n' cheese with either crab soup. Sweet-sausage-based chili is a kitchen specialty, and it, too, is available in a combo plate, ladled atop the mac 'n' cheese.

Dine inside or al fresco at wooden picnic tables.

CHICK & RUTH'S DELLY

chickandruths.com

165 Main St.
Annapolis, MD

410-269-6737
B L D | $

Being near the District of Columbia, Chick & Ruth's Delly has its own twist on the kosher-style restaurant theme of giving celebrity monikers to sandwiches. Here house specialties carry the names of politicians ranging from Sen. Barbara Mikulski (open-face tuna and cheese on a bagel) to Annapolis Fire Chief David Stokes (ham, turkey, Swiss, lettuce, and tomato on whole wheat toast). Traditional deli-meat sandwiches are swell and, satisfying as the regular-sized ones are, Chick & Ruth's has a separate category of novelty sandwiches dubbed "colossal," which means up to three pounds per sandwich. (You might want to accompany that with a colossal milk shake, which is all of six pounds and costs $17.95.)

Improbable specialties of the kosher-style (but definitely not kosher) eatery include barbecued ribs, fried shrimp, and crab cakes. "I know most people don't think of crab cakes when they think about good deli food," says Teddy Levitt, whose father started the business in 1965, "but this is crab country. We get the best crab and I believe we make the best cakes." They are available on a surf 'n' turf platter with a T-bone steak or as a seafood combo with fried clams and shrimp. Levitt attributes their moistness to the fact that the meat is cooked quickly at a high temperature. "The longer you take, the greater the chance it will dry out," he explains.

As you may have ascertained by now, Chick & Ruth's is not the place to come for a quiet, private, or intimate conversation. It is fun and disheveled, full of life, and so cramped that if you sit in one of the booths opposite the counter, you will be within inches of the stranger next to you.

CHUBBY'S SOUTHERN STYLE BARBEQUE

chubbysbbq.net

16430 Old Frederick Rd.
Emmitsburg, MD

301-447-3322
L D | $$

A plain place in the beautiful countryside south of Gettysburg, Chubby's has become a destination dining spot for lovers of barbecued pork. Smokemeister Tom Caulfield marinates and dry rubs ribs, cooking them low and slow until drippingly tender, serving them with a choice of sauces that includes South Carolina mustard–style, North Carolina vinegar-pepper, and the most familiar tomato sweet/tangy. Caulfield's pulled pork is soft and smoky, and baked beans are liberally laced with shreds of it. Side dishes are fine smokehouse standards such as collard greens, French fries (superb), corn bread, and in-season corn on the cob.

The menu is broad and also includes non-barbecued daily items that range from cream of crab soup to a fried bologna sandwich to a tilapia platter. Several years ago Washington Redskins lineman Randy Thomas made pig-out history by consuming six pounds of Chubby's food in less than an hour. His menu included a pound of brisket, two and a half pounds of ribs, a pound of shrimp scampi, a pound of chili, three-quarters of a pound of crab dip, cheese-garlic toast, cheesecake, and a pumpkin parfait. His beverage of choice was a gallon of iced tea. Anyone else seeking glory is invited to take the "Avalanche Challenge": Eat a pair of Avalanche Burgers (each of which is composed of four quarter-pound cheese-burgers, four hot links, and all the fixins on a triple-decker roll) in one sitting, in one hour, with no bathroom visits, and you get it for free, plus a $100 gift certificate, a T-shirt, and your picture on the wall of fame. If you fail, the meal will cost $39.95.

CRISFIELD

8012 Georgia Ave.	301-589-1306
Silver Spring, MD	**L D** | $$$

Crisfield's is expensive, but no-frills. The room you enter is like a bar, with a long counter running along both sides and stools where people sit to eat and drink. The adjoining dining room has walls covered with white tile and cinderblocks, with all the charm of a locker room. Service is brusque and efficient, yet dinner for two can eat up most of a hundred-dollar bill.

We'll happily pay the prices because some of the food served here is top-drawer. Crisfield is a fish house with regional specialties you simply don't find many places anymore: seafood Norfolk-style (that is, swimming in butter), and huge fillets of flounder, broiled or fried or heaped with fresh lump crabmeat, as well as oysters and softshell crabs in season.

We have found the "Crisfield special" (lump crabmeat mixed with a bit of mayo and baked until golden brown) to be erratic: one time fresh and sweet, another tired; but the crab-stuffed flounder has never been a disappointment. It is a gigantic, milky-white fillet covered with a full-flavored crown of crab. We also liked the "Combination Norfolk"—hunks of crab, whole shrimp, and pieces of lobster all crowded into a skillet up to their waistlines in melted butter. It's a simple preparation, but unbeatable.

★ FAIDLEY'S
faidleyscrabcakes.com

203 N. Paca St.	410-727-4898
Baltimore, MD	**L D** | $$

You may think you know what a great crab cake tastes like, but until you have eaten one at Faidley's, you cannot be sure. Forget all the spongy, bready, fishy blobs that pass as crab cakes in most other places; here is the paradigm: a baseball-sized sphere of jumbo lump crab meat held together with minimal crushed-saltine filler and a whisper of mayo and mustard that is just enough to be a foil for the marine sweetness of the meat. While Faidley's offers "regular" crab cakes, made from shredded claw meat, and backfin crab cakes, made from slightly larger strips of body meat, the one you want is the "all lump crab cake." It is significantly more expensive than the others, but the silky weight of the big nuggets, which are the choicest meat picked from the hind-leg area of the blue crab, is what makes these cakes one of the nation's most memorable local specialties.

Operated by the same family that started it in 1886—and who still form each jumbo lump cake by hand—Faidley's is fortuitously located on one side of the boisterous, centuries-old food emporium known as the Lexington Market. Amenities are minimal. Stand up to order, then stand up to eat at chest-high tables provided. You can down raw oysters at the oyster bar, and in addition to crab cakes, the menu includes both Maryland crab soup (red) and cream of crab soup, as well as the Baltimore fish cake known as a coddie, composed of cod, mashed potato, and onion. Whereas jumbo lump crab cakes are the top of the line at well over $10 each, a coddie costs less than $3.

G&M RESTAURANT & LOUNGE

gandmcrabcakes.com

804 N. Hammonds	877-554-3723
Ferry Rd.	L D	$$$
Linthicum Heights, MD	

G&M is practically the only restaurant where we would recommend ordering stuffed shrimp. Given the usual flaccidity of the dish, we were not inclined to do so until our waitress passionately recommended them, guaranteeing that the stuffing of these shrimp was all crab. We took the plunge and got a trio (at nearly $30; G&M is not cheap). Each of three big, buff shrimp was heaped with its own virtual crab cake—a pile of pearly white lumps separated by one-dimensional lines of spicy filler that do for crab what salt does for sirloin.

G&M's crab cakes, which come two to an order, sport the biggest possible lumps. You can count the pieces of meat in each one, those from the interior glistening, resilient and all white, those forked off the outside offering a browned facet with faint crunch. The crab is so regal that it is a perfect fit for crab imperial, the butter-rich casserole infused with a shot of Greek spice.

As noted above, G&M is at the high end of the Roadfood cost scale. A nice dinner for two with a few drinks easily can hit triple-digit prices. But if you are looking for a grand Baltimore meal in a dining room with such amenities as nondisposable flatware and white tablecloths, it's hard to beat. Beyond legendary crab meat, the menu is extensive, including such local specialties as broiled rockfish and fried oysters as well as yet-to-be-sampled temptations like Chesapeake chicken (stuffed with crab meat) and Baltimore's take on German sauerbraten—sour beef and potato dumplings.

HARRIS CRAB HOUSE

harriscrabhouse.com

433 N. Kent	410-827-9500
Narrows Way	L D	$$$
Grasonville, MD	

★ WATER-FRONT DINING ★ Long tables are covered with brown wrapping paper. The big, airy dining room and outdoor deck pulse with the beat of crab shells cracking and people slurping up sweet pink meat. Buy big ones by the dozen and feast, the Chesapeake Bay way. Alternatives to the full-bore crab feast include steamed spiced shrimp and fried shrimp, cherrystone clams by the pail, snow crab by the bucket, stuffed softshells, even steak and chicken and ribs. One appetizer known as Cajun mac 'n' cheese is not particularly Cajun, but is pretty damn wonderful: shrimp and crawfish plus bacon are mixed into the noodles along with sharp, smoky cheese. None of this food is inexpensive, but it tastes as rich as it costs.

Of the several profligate desserts (fudge brownie cake, Key lime pie, turtle cheesecake), one holds tremendous appeal to those of us who share a forbidden love of gas-station ice cream—those inexcusably bad but somehow alluring King Kones, Drumsticks, and so on. This is Harris's own Nutty Buddy, made with actual quality ice cream, crisp nuts, and decent chocolate.

JERRY'S SEAFOOD

jerrys-seafood.com

9364 Lanham-Severn	302-645-6611
Rd.	L (Mon–Fri); D (Tues–Sat)
Seabrook, MD		$$$

Surefire tipster Joe Heflin described Jerry's Seafood to us as the "best overall Maryland seafood restaurant without a view." He warned that the ambience is nondescript—Jerry's is located in a strip mall—and we should expect long lines any evening, especially weekends.

No problem. We'll gladly wait for this extraordinary DC-area seafood treasure. Nor do we need to be soaking up ambience when we have one of Jerry's Crab Bombs on a plate in front of us. This is a fairly gigantic (ten-ounce) and expensive (more than $30) crab cake that is nothing more than fresh jumbo lump meat, Old Bay seasoning, and just enough mayonnaise to make it cling together, baked until a fragile crust develops all around the edges but the inside is still dripping-sweet. Even better for those with a yen for spice thrills is the firecracker crab bomb, to which mustard and pepper are added. Jerry's also makes a six-ounce Baby Bomb and ordinary-sized crab cakes about which the menu boasts, "Absolutely no filler!"

Mr. Heflin's other recommendation was crab soup, a virtuoso balance of creaminess, crabbiness, and sharp spice. You can also eat velvety crab imperial perked up with peppers, crab dip, and crab bisque made with sherry. Those who are anti-crab can revel in fried shrimp, scallops, and oysters, all with a light fragile crust, as well as good side dishes that the menu promises are from Jerry's mom's recipes: stewed tomatoes and coleslaw.

Jerry's has a second location at 15211 Major Lansdale Boulevard in Bowie, MD (301-805-2284).

THE NARROWS

thenarrowsrestaurant.com

3023 Kent Narrows	410-827-8113
Way S.	L D | $$$
Grasonville, MD	

★ —— Here is an extraordinarily handsome
WATER-FRONT Eastern Shore restaurant in a breath-
DINING taking setting overlooking the Kent
—— ★ —— Narrows at the eastern end of the Chesapeake Bay Bridge. The menu is broad, including $30+ steak dinners, sandwiches and salads, hamburgers, cioppino, and barbecued quail accompanied by Smithfield ham in a balsamic glaze.

Great stuff, what little of it we have sampled, but we likely wouldn't include this fairly pricey place in *Roadfood* if it weren't for two great local specialties, crab cakes and oysters. The crab cakes are the purest ever: jumbo lump crab piled into a mound and just barely kissed by a bit of spice in the ridiculously minimal filler. As your fork touches the cake, chances are good it will tumble into big lumps, their outside surfaces faintly brown and barely crisp, the interior nothing but moist, warm, and fragrant.

Oysters, breaded in cornmeal and fried, are known hereabouts as White Gold, and what's so magnificent about them is that although they have been cooked, the meat of the oysters retains all of its fluid sensuousness—as much as a raw one, but even more intense because of its warmth and the frail cornmeal crust with which the oyster melds. You can get a great big plate of them or have them as the ne plus ultra topping of a Caesar salad.

PARK-N-DINE

park-n-dine.com

189 E. Main St.	301-678-5242
Hancock, MD	B L D | $

If you are traveling through the narrowest part of western Maryland in Hancock and find yourself hankering for meat and potatoes or a bountiful breakfast, pull up to Park-N-Dine. Located alongside I-70 and at the end of the bike trail from Indian Springs along the C&O Canal, this venerable establishment is a blast from the past (1946) where uniformed waitresses are pros and where the kitchen still practices the craft of from-scratch cooking.

Kudos to the old-fashioned roast turkey dinner with mashed potatoes, stuffing, and gravy. Sandwiches and hamburgers are available, but the charm of Park-N-Dine for us is its seven-day-a-week roster of Sunday dinner—that is, pork chops, meat loaf, and plates of corned beef and cabbage. Portions are big and prices are moderate.

RANDY'S RIBS & BARBECUE

randysribs.com

7744 Leonardtown Rd.	301-274-3525
Hughesville, MD	L D | $

Randy's opened in 1981 as a weekend-only roadside stand, and while its catering business has become large, the eatery remains charming. The sweet perfume of slow-smoking pork fills the air seven days a week throughout the year, and if you are one who considers barbecue foremost among the food groups, you will love what you find.

Sandwiches and platters are available: minced or sliced pork, ribs and ham, whole chickens, and slabs of ribs. "Slaw on that?" the order-taker will ask if you get a sandwich. "Yes!" we say, and then unwrap the foil around a big bun loaded with chunks of moist, full-flavored pork bathed in Randy's excellent sweet hickory sauce, with which sweet slaw sings happy harmony. Ribs are large and chewy, their meat infused with smoke.

Randy also offers a mighty fine half-smoke, which is a local variant of a hot dog: a plump sausage bisected lengthwise and smoke-cooked until its skin is taut and dark red, its insides succulent. All the usual hot dog condiments are available, but we recommend topping it with only one thing: Randy's sauce. That good sauce is available by the pint and gallon: an excellent investment in one's future culinary happiness.

SEASIDE RESTAURANT & CRAB HOUSE

theseasiderestaurant.com

| 224 Crain Hwy. N. | 410-760-2200 |
| Glen Burnie, MD | L D \| $$ |

Beautiful steamed crabs (preferably jumbos, if available) come to the table stuck with a peppery, salty spice mix and too hot to handle. Grab your knife to pry away the outer shell, pick up the mallet to start pounding, and soon you will be rewarded with fat nuggets of sweet meat. Toss your shells into brown paper bags on the floor and hoist an ice-cold beer to quench the thirst that spicy crabs inevitably provoke.

Beyond blue crabs, the Seaside Restaurant has a menu of other specialties worth sampling, especially if crabmeat-extraction is too daunting a task: broiled shrimp, scallops, and flounder, and zesty crab cakes, plus fine crab soups, both Maryland-style (red, with vegetables) and creamy.

A busy place, especially on weekends. Expect to wait at mealtime.

ST. MARY'S LANDING

| 29935 Three Notch Rd. | 301-884-6124 |
| Charlotte Hall, MD | B L D \| $$ |

St. Mary's County stuffed ham is a seasonal dish, generally served between Thanksgiving and Easter, but you can get it year-round at St. Mary's Landing. It's wonderful stuff: a corned ham packed with heaps of kale, cabbage, onions, and spice, served for breakfast on a plate with delicious potato cakes or for supper as a main course.

Lucky for us, they were out of stuffed ham when we came for supper. That meant we discovered the kitchen's good crab cakes, a plate of big, snapping-firm spiced boiled shrimp, and barbecued ribs that had a delicate crunch to their edges and meat that slid right off the bone.

This is a fascinating restaurant—a drinker's tavern as well as a family-friendly eatery—with a wall-mounted TV monitor that displays keno numbers and a countdown to the next game. One morning when we arrived at 7 a.m., we were the first customers to take seats in the restaurant, but bar stools in the tap-room were already occupied by ladies and gentlemen having shots and beers to start their day.

SUICIDE BRIDGE RESTAURANT

suicide-bridge-restaurant.com

| 6304 Suicide Bridge Rd. | 410-943-4689 |
| Hurlock, MD | L D \| $$$ |

On two occasions, men shot and killed themselves on the bridge over Cabin Creek, then fell into the water. Another guy drove off the bridge. A subsequent jumper's body was fished from the creek and laid out on the wooden bridge, where his blood soaked into the boards, which stayed stained for five years. All this we learned from the takeout menu at this rather eerily named restaurant that is—bridge notwithstanding—extremely charming. Located on an Eastern Shore inlet from which paddlewheel boats glide into the Choptank River for dinner cruises, its broad windows offer views of the boats, the water, and the notorious bridge.

While the menu has a small section for "land lovers" that lists steaks, ribs, and chicken, the reason we recommend eating here is seafood—primarily broiled rockfish, fried oysters, cream of crab soup with a shot of sherry, and first-rate crab cakes. There are backfin cakes, available either fried or broiled, their fine and wispy meat humming with a devilish pepper glow, and there are the fancier (and more expensive) "Kool's Deluxe Crab Cakes" made with jumbo lump crab meat and available only broiled. Kool's Deluxe cakes also have some sharp seasoning, and their snowy hunks of meat are speckled with green herbs; nevertheless, the overwhelming goodness of those big pieces of crab puts all other seasoning into the background.

Suicide Bridge also makes a specialty of crab balls—peppery little orbs of deep-fried crabmeat, a crunchy pop-in-the-mouth bar snack or hors d'oeuvre.

WATERMAN'S CRAB HOUSE
watermanscrabhouse.com

21055 E. Sharp St.	410-639-2261
Rock Hall, MD	**L D**	$$

A big, breezy eatery with a deck overlooking Rock Hall Harbor and shuttle service for those who arrive by boat at one of the nearby marinas, Waterman's is a good-time place. Blues, rock, and 1950s oldies bands perform on weekends, and at dusk merrymakers gather at the forty-foot-long bar to savor cocktails, beer, and a spectacular sunset.

Many regulars come for steamed crabs by the dozen, but the rest of Waterman's menu is broad and inviting. Other seafood temptations include crab soup served with a shot of sherry, crusty-creamy jumbo lump crab cakes (fried or broiled), stuffed flounder, spiced steamed shrimp, softshell crabs, and a gorgeous broiled rockfish available with or without a side of crab imperial. Even fish frowners will find plenty here: baby-back ribs, ten-ounce hamburgers, and one-pound "Admiral's cut" prime rib.

Recommended desserts: lemonade cake, Smith Island cake, and hot apple dumpling à la mode drizzled with caramel sauce.

NEW JERSEY

B&W BAKERY

614 Main St.   201-342-5383
Hackensack, NJ   **B | $**

--★-- **LOCALS LOVE IT** --★-- In a wide orbit around New York City, crumb cake is not just a generic term for coffee cake with some crumbs on top. It refers to a pastry that is significantly more crumb than cake. The benchmark version, as made by B&W Bakery, has so little cake that you might think of it as merely a conveyance mechanism to hoist streusel from plate to mouth. But that would be wrong. The cake provides creamy balance for the crumbs; the two elements together make a fine friend for morning coffee.

Whole cakes are huge, as are single slices; one of them will cover most of a nine-inch plate. Beyond the crumb cake, B&W makes a full array of regular pastries. Among the highlights are éclairs loaded with creamy filling, crumb-raisin buns, black-and-white cookies, and a killer banana cream pie.

There are no dining facilities on premises.

CHARLIE'S

18 S. Michigan Ave.   908-241-2627
Kenilworth, NJ   **L D | $**

While you can order what the menu calls a "push cart dog"—an ordinary street weenie on a blah roll with mundane condiments, Charlie's raison d'être is its Italian hot dog: one or preferably a pair of deep-fried, crisp-skinned, bursting-with-flavor franks stuffed into a half circle of what's known hereabouts as pizza bread. It's a round loaf that resembles a pita pocket with muscle. The bread is chewy, soulful, and absorbent, that last quality essential for engulfing the traditional garnishes that an Italian hot dog demands. These include fried peppers and onions and crisp-fried potato discs. The same ingredients can be used to accompany a sausage sandwich, also packed into pizza bread.

Service is do-it-yourself. There are tables but a majority of business is takeout.

CLIFF'S DAIRY MAID
cliffsicecream.com

1475 Route 46   973-584-9721
Ledgewood, NJ   **L D | $**

Cliff's is a great place to know about if you and your appetite are traveling along Route 80 through New Jersey. The 1975 drive-in is most famous for its ice cream but is also a worthy source for foot-long hot dogs and chili dogs (especially good when topped with a tangle of sautéed onions), hamburgers, and buckets of French fries.

Cliff's ice cream menu lists a few dozen "original homemade flavors," which range from utterly familiar chocolate and strawberry to bubble gum, cotton candy, and banana walnut chocolate chunk, plus another few dozen "fantasy flavors": sticky bun, holy cannoli, Bavarian cream raspberry truffle, and so on. In addition to these hard-pack ice creams, Cliff's boasts several soft-serves, which are dense and rich. There is always a flavor of the month—and it can be swirled together with one of the regulars. We very much enjoyed a twist of chocolate and the March flavor, mint.

No indoor seating at this drive-in, but there are picnic tables out back.

DE LORENZO'S TOMATO PIES

delorenzostomatopies.com

| 2350 US-33 | 609-341-8480 |
| Robbinsville, NJ | **L D** \| $$ |

De Lorenzo's makes what many connoisseurs consider to be America's best pizza. It is certainly among the top ten for its impeccable pizza harmony: crisp crust, creamy mozzarella, fruity crushed tomatoes, and zesty, fennel-laced Italian sausage. DeLo's calls them tomato pies, the old Napoli term, and one reason the toppings blend so well is that the pizza men first apply some cheese to the unbaked crust, then sauce and toppings, then another sprinkle of mozzarella. In the oven, they all swirl together just right.

For decades located in an extremely humble neighborhood storefront (so primitive that it had no restrooms!), De Lorenzo's moved to a modern place a few years ago, expanding its menu to include fine salads that include fresh berries and interesting cheese.

DICKIE DEE'S

| 380 Bloomfield Ave. | 973-483-9396 |
| Newark, NJ | **L D** \| $ |

No ordinary weenie, Dickie Dee's specialty is an Italian-style (aka Newark-style) hot dog, meaning one or a pair are deep-fried and stuffed into half a loaf of Italian bread along with fried peppers, onions, and big chunks of crisp-edge, soft-center fried potatoes. All the ingredients are cooked in the same vat of oil next to the order counter, and they are plucked from the oil and inserted directly into the bread (no draining!), making for a wondrously oily double-handful of food.

Be prepared for a faceful of attitude from behind the counter of this brash lunchroom. When it's crowded—it usually is—the line moves fast, and woe to he who hesitates when placing an order. As the sandwich is made, the cook will demand to know what you want on it in the way of condiments, and this is another time you don't want to be slow responding. (We suggest that a spritz of ketchup is a nice complement for the potatoes that go atop all the other ingredients in the sandwich.)

Carry your tray to a table and ease into a molded plastic chair. Lay out plenty of napkins and dig into a hot dog that is a true North Ward original.

★ HAROLD'S NEW YORK DELI

haroldsfamousdeli.com

| 3050 Woodbridge Ave. | 732-661-9100 |
| Edison, NJ | **B L D** \| $$$ |

Just because Harold's is comical doesn't mean it isn't seriously great. It may just be the best New York deli anywhere, even if it is in Edison, New Jersey. For intensely chickeny chicken soup with matzoh balls, for spice-edged pastrami that is melting-rich, for creamy blintzes and even creamier egg creams, for the best rugelach anywhere and a pickle bar to make the famous Guss' of New York blush, Harold's is the gold standard. The menu is vast, ranging from kosher hot dogs to triple-decker sandwiches, cold fish plates to hot suppers—all of it exemplary.

What's funny about the big, boisterous eatery is the size of its portions. While most New York delis offer sandwiches stacked extra-high and soup with very large matzoh balls, Harold's ups the ante to sur-real proportions. A single matzoh ball is bigger than a softball, and yet, rest the edge of a spoon at its top and gravity is all that's needed to send the spoon sliding smoothly down into the ball's fluffy center. It is impossible not to gasp when you enter and see shelves of whole, wedding-sized cakes, each two feet tall. When a towering "large sandwich" gets carried past your table to a party of four (who will divvy it up, eat their fill, and each take home enough meat for more sandwiches the next day), no superlatives seem adequate to express the awe it inspires. Ridiculous, insane: the biggest food anywhere! While such pro-tean portions of protein might seem wasteful and/or expensive, remember that everyone walks out with leftovers. On a recent visit, a single brisket sandwich provided a very filling lunch for one. Its remains became the basis of an excellent beef hash lunch for two the next day, and leftovers of the leftover hash became a pair of hearty breakfasts on day three.

THE HOT GRILL

thehotgrill.com

669 Lexington Ave.   973-772-6000
Clifton, NJ   **B L D | $**

Texas weiners (spelled *ei*, not *ie*) are a big deal in this part of New Jersey, the word "Texas" being Northeast hash-house code for chili. One of the best places to sample this Garden State specialty is the Hot Grill of Clifton.

Step up to the order counter and order a pair. *Nobody* gets just one Texas weiner! The counterman will holler out to the back kitchen, "Two, all the way!" And within ninety seconds, a pair of handsome hot dogs will appear on the tray in front of you. Each is a deep-fried pup with rugged skin nestled in a too-short bun topped with mustard, onion, and sweet beef-chili sauce. On the side you definitely want gravy fries, or fries topped with gravy plus cheese and/or sauce.

Many customers come for hamburgers, in single or double configurations, served plain, all the way, or ultra all the way, which augments the onions-mustard-chili topping with a slice of grilled pork roll and a fried egg.

It's fun to dine in the Hot Grill's vast, modern dining room where, instead of music, you listen to the calls of the countermen back to the kitchen, and instead of sports, the overhead TV is tuned to "The Hot Grill Channel," which is a continuous program of hosannas to the hot dog.

★ JIMMY BUFF'S

jimmybuff.com

60 Washington St.   973-325-9897
West Orange, NJ   **L D | $**

James Racioppi, proprietor of Jimmy Buff's, believes it was his grandparents, James and Mary Racioppi, who created the Newark hot dog, in 1932. Mr. Racioppi says, "He played cards there every week. My grand-mother served sandwiches to him and his associates. After a while, people started coming just to eat." As for the name of the store, James explains: "My grand-father Jimmy was an excellent card player. He was known for his talent to bluff, but with their Italian accents, they used to call him Jimmy Buff."

A Newark hot dog is built in a round of fresh, chewy Italian bread that is nothing at all like a flimsy, sponge-soft hot-dog bun. It *must* be tough to hold all the ingredients that get piled into it. The bread is cut in half, forming two half-circles. Each gets squeezed open to become a pocket like a robust pita. Into the pocket go a pair of all-beef hot dogs that have been fried in hot fat until crunch-crusted, a heap of onions and peppers that have been sautéed until limp, and a handful of crisp-fried potato discs. Options include ketchup and/or mustard and/or marinara sauce, and fire-hot onion relish.

A second Jimmy Buff's in Kenilworth is at 506 Boulevard (908-276-2833).

LIBBY'S LUNCH

98 McBride Ave.   973-278-8718
Paterson, NJ   **L D | $**

Texas weiners were invented in New Jersey prior to 1920 by John Patrellis, who worked at his father's hot dog stand at the Manhattan Hotel in Paterson. According to hot dog historian Robert C. Gamer of Wyckoff, Mr. Patrellis devised the formulation of a deep-fried frankfurter in a too-short bun topped with mustard, onions, and spicy-sweet meat sauce, traditionally accompanied by French fries and a mug of root beer. In 1920 the hot dog stand was renamed the Original Hot Texas Weiner because Mr. Patrellis believed the sauce to be like Texas chili (and, presumably, because he wanted the spelling of weiner to set his invention apart from ordinary wieners). In fact, a Texas weiner is more Greek than Texan; but the Lone Star moniker has stuck, and today the region is rich with Texas weiner shops.

Libby's Lunch, since 1936, serves 'em with an impeccable pedigree, dishing out dogs all the way, meaning topped with mustard, chopped onions, and sauce. Good as the spicy chili sauce is (you can buy it by the pint), it is the hot dog itself that makes this a memorable eating experience. Its insides are tender and succulent, while the exterior is blistered and chewy because of its hot-oil bath. Extra-large dogs (and cheese dogs) are available, but we believe the original size works best. A pair of these tube steaks with a side of crisp French fries blanketed with gravy is a grand plate of food: true New Jersey, and uniquely American.

Beyond weiners, Libby's has a full short-order menu of burgers, sandwiches, and a homemade soup of the day.

RUTT'S HUT
ruttshut.com
417 River Rd.   973-779-8615
Clifton, NJ   **B L D | $**

Rutt's Hut "rippers" are a cheap-eats legend among Garden State frank fanatics. They got their nickname because their skin tears and crinkles as they cook in a vat of hot oil and their exterior turns rugged and chewy. Weenie wimps can ask for an "in and outer," which gets plucked from the boiling fat more quickly and remains thoroughly pink and plump. Extremists get "cremators" (well-done), which are so porcine they remind us of fried pig skin.

The stellar condiment for a ripper is Rutt's spicy-sweet relish, a dense yellow concoction made from onions and finely chopped carrots and cabbage. Hamburgers and hot-from-the-kettle French fries are all right too, and we are fond of Rutt's chili: a chunky Mid-Atlantic brew of clods of ground beef with an occasional bean among it, suspended in a vividly spicy tomato emulsion. With crumbled crackers on top, it's a formidable meal.

Rutt's serves hot-lunch meals as well as real drinks in an adjoining taproom with a separate entrance. Here, amid wood-panel décor, one can quaff many beers with platters of such blue-plate fare as chicken croquettes, stuffed cabbage, Jersey pork chops, and that Garden-State favorite, Taylor Ham on a bun. Prices are low, and the food we have tasted is satisfying. But if you are coming to Rutt's only once, eat hot dogs at a counter. It's a Roadfood experience to remember: Dine in a wide-open mess hall with high counters that provide a view of the parking lot. Stand and eat off paper plates, and enjoy the calls of the countermen as they sing out, "Twins, all the way," meaning a pair of rippers with mustard and relish.

★ WHITE HOUSE SUB SHOP
whitehousesubshop.net
2301 Arctic Ave.   609-345-1564
Atlantic City, NJ   **L | $**

What makes a White House sub so good is more than superb bread and quality cold cuts. Its virtue is imparted by the artistry of its builders—the profusion of cold cuts without a hint of glut, the symmetry of ingredients, the spring of the lettuce applied in all the right places, the perfect splash of oil. And there's the astounding size. One whole sub is close to a yard long, requiring a string of paper plates to hold it. Even a half sub will challenge all but the healthiest appetites. Ingredients range from fancy white tuna fish to meatballs and sauce, and the Philly cheesesteak (arguably a sub corollary) is excellent. The traditional favorite is an Italian special or its big brother, the White House Special—Genoa salami, ham, capicola, and provolone cheese all rolled and tightly packed inside the loaf, lubricated with olive oil, and decorated with lettuce and bits of sweet pepper.

The White House is a landmark for sandwich connoisseurs, and like the cheesesteak shops of Philadelphia, it boasts of a glitterati clientele. Pictures of famous customers line the walls, inscribed with praise for the excellence of the cuisine. News clippings tell of the time the astronauts came to scarf down subs, and of Frank Sinatra once having a bunch of them shipped from New Jersey across the world to a movie location. For all its stardust, the White House remains a humble Naugahyde-and-neon eatery with a row of booths along the wall and a counter up front. The lighting is harsh, the napkins are paper, and the service is lightning fast: It would be a sin to sell subs any other way. Expect a long wait at noon.

WHITE MANNA

358 River St.   201-342-0914
Hackensack, NJ   B L D | $

With good reason, New Jersey is famous for its vibrant hot dog culture; but here is one great hamburger joint that earns high marks from cheap-eats devotees. White Manna's burgers are paradigmatic sliders: little balls of freshly ground chuck that get slapped down onto a greasy griddle, preferably along with a handful of thin-sliced onions, mashed with a spatula, flipped, topped with cheese if requested, then crowned with the top of a tender potato roll. The roll is soft enough to sop up massive amounts of protein nectar that oozes from the beef as well as sweet perfume from the steamed onions, and its yeasty blandness is just what the forceful ingredients need to hit their peak. Heaps of thin-sliced pickle chips come alongside. Four or six of these make a nice meal.

The place is a minuscule diner with hardly more than a dozen seats and minimal counter space. We've never been to White Manna when it isn't very crowded, meaning that although the hamburgers are definitive fast food, you might wait a while to get some.

WHITE ROSE SYSTEM

whiterosediner.com
1301 E. Elizabeth Ave.   908-486-9651
Linden, NJ   B L | $

Roadfood pillars Bruce Bilmes and Sue Boyle referred to pork roll, egg, and cheese on a bun as the "unofficial state sandwich of New Jersey," the context for which was their review of White Rose System. Now, these two know New Jersey like nobody else in the state, so when they said this sandwich is the best, we were on our way.

We're the first to admit that we are not connoisseurs of pork roll (aka Taylor ham), but we do have high appreciation for this tremendously fatty, salty loaf of pork products that is sliced thin and usually fried. Together with egg and cheese in a hard roll or, better yet, as per Bruce and Sue's advice, in a hero roll, and maybe with some fried potatoes added to the sandwich, it makes up virtually an entire day's recommended intake of just about everything we're supposed to be afraid of eating. In diner slang, the combo is known as a triple bypass.

White Rose System provides the ideal ambience for ingesting pork roll. It is a sassy diner with counter seats that provide a view of short-order cooks at work. The menu includes such other Garden State delights as an Italian hot dog (with fried potatoes, onions, and peppers), an Italian cheesesteak (also with potatoes), a super-hot sausage sub, greasy little oniony sliders (here known as little bullets), and—of all things—fish and grits!

NEW YORK

★ ALÉTHEA'S CHOCOLATES
aletheas.com

8301 Main St.   716-633-8620
Williamsville, NY $

———★——— Aléthea's is a top-tier source for such
VEGETARIAN- Buffalo specialties as sponge candy
FRIENDLY (chocolate-coated spun sugar) and
———★——— Charlie Chaplins (marshmallow, coconut, cashews,
and chocolate). Here too you will find fudge, turtles,
barks, and chocolate-covered ginger and chocolate-
covered raspberries to die for. All these can be purchased in the impeccably clean showroom in front of
the large area in which everything is made, or via mail
order.

The Roadfooder passing through who wants to
sit down and have something more than bonbons
needs to know about Aléthea's adjoining ice cream
parlor, where truffled hot fudge, dark-amber caramel sauce, freshly made marshmallow topping, and
crunchy-crisp, well-salted nuts crown luxurious ice
cream. Have a classic "Mexicano" (chocolate sauce
and Spanish peanuts) or a Delphi Maiden of chocolate
chip and coffee ice cream topped with marshmallow, chocolate sauce, and toasted almonds. Or just
a regular sundae topped with devilishly chocolaty
hot fudge.

ANTOINETTE'S
antoinettesbuffalo.com

5981 Transit Rd.   716-684-2376
Depew, NY $

There are two Antoinette's in greater Buffalo: the
original on Transit Road and a second, around the
corner from Schwabl's Restaurant at 1203 Union
Road in West Seneca. Either one demands attention
from the devotee of ice cream and/or masterfully
made chocolates. Simply walking into the store will
make you smile: The air is cocoa-scented. Watching
a sundae being constructed is enchanting gastronomic foreplay. Starting at the top, nuts are fresh
and crunchy. Whipped cream is, in fact, cream that
is whipped. Nothing else, not even sugar, is added. It
gets piped onto the ice cream from a pastry tube in
thick, luxurious swirls. Fudge sauce? Caramel sauce?
Better yet, fudge and caramel and pecans on cream-
pure vanilla ice cream to make a turtle sundae? It
doesn't get better than this.

Spend enough time here and you will earn
an advanced degree in soda-fountain mixology.
Sundaes are available with twenty different toppings, including six different chocolate variations:
cinnamon-chocolate, chocolate-mint, hot fudge,
French chocolate pudding, bittersweet chocolate, and
regular chocolate. "Classic sundaes" include a rum-n-
butter frappe, cara-mallow, a crunchy coffee special,

and French chocolate nutty nut. There's a variety of sodas, milk shakes, floats, and fancy frappes.

The candy selection is magnificent, including Buffalo's own sponge candy and Charlie Chaplin logs as well as an assortment of barks, clusters, molasses pops, truffles, cordials, chocolate pretzels, and chocolate popcorn.

BARNEY GREENGRASS

barneygreengrass.com

541 Amsterdam Ave.   212-724-4707
New York, NY   **B L** | $$

The food that put Barney Greengrass on the map is smoked fish. In the glass case of this restaurant and takeout store between 86th and 87th streets, you will find lean and silky sturgeon, salty cured salmon (known as lox), not-so-salty cured salmon (novie), snow-white whitefish, and luscious sable. In the dining room adjacent to the takeout counter, the fish are available on platters, with bagels and/or bialys, cream cheese, onions, tomatoes, and olives. These are the makings of a grand New York breakfast, and there isn't a restaurant in town that does it with the aplomb of bare-tabled Barney Greengrass.

BENGABLE SAVORIES

bengablesavories.com

17 Central Sq.   518-392-0205
Chatham, NY   **B L** (closed Mon & Tues) | $

BenGable Savories is primarily a bakeshop: quiche and frittatas, loaf cakes and scones, potpies and tarts. Melt-in-your-mouth crème fraîche biscuits with crusty edges and fluffy insides are served warm with fresh fruit jam and premium butter from local dairies. In fact, much of what's served here is local: fruits and vegetables in season, eggs and cream from nearby farms. Baguettes used for many of the sandwiches are not local, though. They come from Tribeca Oven in New Jersey and are chewy, crusty, and full-flavored.

There could be no better bread for wrapping salami, roasted fennel, arugula pesto, and orange aioli in a tremendously satisfying sandwich. Slices of good sourdough are the right thing for BenGable's

fine turkey sandwich, in which thick slices of bird are dressed with a layer of pimento cheese and crisp bread-and-butter pickles. A whole other kind of sandwich is the croque monsieur: ham and gruyère cheese on peasant bread, dipped in egg, and baked until the outside is brittle and the ingredients have melded together and become as tender as custard. When you slice through the crust, the very aroma of this sandwich is intoxicating. Add a fried egg on top and it becomes a croque madame.

Given BenGable's focus on baked goods, it's not surprising that breakfast is stellar. Aside from a sour cherry scone and blueberry corn bread, our favorite thing to eat is a simple length of toasted baguette, available a few ways. You can have it plainly buttered with good jam on the side; you can have it buttered and salted and drizzled with honey—a devastating sweet-salty powerhouse; or you can have it buttered and lightly salted and spread with a slick emulsion of dark, barely sweet chocolate. The mix of bread, butter, and chocolate, pinged with salt, is a dizzying combination, intense but elegant.

BIG W'S ROADSIDE BAR-B-Q

bigwsbbq.com

1475 Route 22   845-832-6200
Wingdale, NY   **L D** | $$

Big W's began as a food truck and roadside smoke pit but subsequently moved to permanent quarters in a small cluster of buildings by the side of the road. While the new accommodations are more commodious and the place is able to stay open year-round, the move in no way diminished the in-your-face authenticity of this excellent barbecue.

When we say "excellent barbecue," we do not feel the need to qualify our kudos with such phrases as "for New York" or "for the Northeast." This is good meat by any standard. We are particularly impressed by the brisket, which is fatty enough to outrage a prim cadet from the nutrition police, and therefore dripping flavor. You can get it by the plate along with side dishes, by the pound, or in a sandwich, of which the menu lists three sizes: Truly Sensible (one-third pound meat), Sensible (one-half pound meat), and

Roadside (one and one-third pounds meat). Pulled pork also is available in all those configurations, and it is handsome pig meat—shreds and hunks meticulously separated from their fat. Other smokehouse choices include spare ribs, chicken, and burnt ends. On the side, you can have sweet corn pudding that is as dense as bread pudding, mac 'n' cheese, greens, hush puppies, or mashed potatoes. If you're lucky, the potatoes will be garnished with porky cracklins.

Part of the fun of dining at Big W's is the presence of pitmaster Warren Norstein, who seems always busy carving meat, pulling things from the oven, and kibitzing with customers like a loquacious deli man.

CHARLIE THE BUTCHER'S KITCHEN

charliethebutcher.com

1065 Wehrle Dr.	716-633-8330
Buffalo, NY	**L D** | $

According to Charlie Roesch, proprietor of Charlie the Butcher's Kitchen, it was beer that inspired the invention of beef on weck. He believes that back in the 1880s a now-forgotten local tavern owner decided to offer a sandwich that would induce a powerful thirst in his patrons. He had plenty of coarse salt on hand for the pretzels he served, so he painted a mixture of the salt and caraway seeds (*kummelweck*, in German) atop some hard rolls, cooked a roast and sliced it thin, and piled the meat inside the rolls. As a condiment, he served hot horseradish. Slaking the thirst these sandwiches induced, beer sales soared. And Buffalo's passion for beef on weck was born.

Charlie's father was a butcher, as was his grandfather (their slogan: "You Know It's Fresh if It Comes from Roesch"). To honor the family trade, he wears a white hard hat and a butcher's smock and necktie as he carves beef in the open kitchen at the center of his restaurant. The beef on weck sandwiches are protein ecstasy, the rolls delicate but tough enough to sop up gravy and still stay strong.

Charlie's menu extends well beyond beef on weck, and everything else we've sampled is first-rate: Buffalo-made hot dogs and sausages grilled over coals, chicken spiedie (a boneless breast that is marinated and grilled), full-flavored roast turkey, and such daily-special sandwiches as meat loaf, double-smoked ham, and prime rib. The beverage list includes the local favorite, loganberry juice, as well as Charlie's personal favorite, birch beer.

CLARE AND CARL'S

4727 State Route 9	518-561-1163
Plattsburgh, NY	**L D** (summer only) | $

A newspaper story posted on the wall at Clare and Carl's says that the region's unique weenie, the Michigan, owes its name to a Michigander named Eula Otis, who came to work for Clare Warn in the early days of the drive-in (it opened in 1943) and went around to area restaurants saying, "I'm from Michigan. Would you like to try one of our chili dogs?" The state's name clung to the hot dog topped with Warn's sauce, which she had invented because New York–style hot dogs with mustard and sauerkraut weren't selling well. The Michigan became a passion of New York's North Country between the Adirondacks and Lake Champlain, served at summertime stands, in grocery stores, and even in the cafeteria at the Champlain Valley Physicians Hospital Medical Center.

Clare and Carl's presents its Michigans in a cream-soft bun that is similar to the Northeast split-top, but is thicker at the bottom and closed at both ends, forming a trough to shore in the sloppy topping. The chili is thick with meat, intriguingly spiced, not at all sweet, and just barely hot.

There is another Clare and Carl's at the marina in town, but the original is a wonderful vision of long-gone roadside Americana, its clapboard walls so old that they appear to have settled deep into the earth. Carhops attend customers in a broad parking lot, and there is a U-shaped counter with padded stools inside. A menu posted above the open kitchen lists Michigans first; signs outside advertise the house specialty as Texas red hots.

CONDRELL'S

condrells.com

2805 Delaware Ave.   716-877-4485
Buffalo, NY   L D | $

We're not sure if the formal name of this place is Condrell's or King Condrell's; both are used on menus, on signs, and when employees speak of it. No matter, because what's important here are sundaes—some of the best on the planet. Atop locally made Perry's ice cream you can have basso profundo hot fudge, warm French chocolate sauce that is lighter-flavored than fudge and more pudding-like, or traditional chocolate sauce that is thin and innocent. Marshmallow topping is smooth as cream, caramel is extra-buttery, whipped cream is utterly fresh, and nuts are crisp and salted just enough to be a perfect foil for everything sweet. Portions are big.

Do not neglect Condrell's candies. There are exemplary sponge candies and Charlie Chaplins (Buffalo faves), as well as more universally known delights, including molasses paddles and molasses chips enrobed in dark or light chocolate, truffles of every kind, cashew or pecan turtles, chocolate-covered chunks of candied orange, pineapple, and ginger, dozens of varieties of cream centers, nut barks, chocolate-covered pretzels, and malted milk balls. To shop at Condrell's is truly to be a kid in a candy store. No metaphor exists to express the bliss of a Condrell's sundae.

CORNELL DAIRY BAR

living.sas.cornell.edu/dine/wheretoeat/ cafescoffeehouses/cornelldairybar.cfm

411 Tower Rd.   607-255-7660
Ithaca, NY   B L | $

If you believe that food is best when it comes directly from the source, have a dish of ice cream or a glass of milk at the Cornell Dairy Bar. The dairy products served in this on-campus eatery are produced by the College of Agriculture and Life Sciences, whose herd of cows is only a few miles away. A glass wall provides a view of the ice cream being made.

The Dairy Bar is a casual joint in Stocking Hall (remodeled in 2013) with tables inside and out. Sandwiches, salads, cheese curds, coffee drinks, and even sushi are available, but of course, ice cream is the star. Choose from such student-conceived flavors as Kahlúa Fudge (coffee-flavored with a fudge swirl), Mexican Sundae (with peanuts and fudge chunks), Sticky Bunz, even Green Tea. Order a cone, cup, or sundae and carry it to a seat. This is excellent ice cream: just rich enough to fully satisfy without being cloying, and without the complications and cost of boutique ice cream.

In addition to praising the good ice cream, we must also note that the whipped cream that tops sundaes is superb: thick, sweet, and dairy-fresh. And finally: chocolate milk. It's a beautiful thing, so smooth, so gently chocolaty, so perfectly juvenile. Cornell's director of sports nutrition once called it "the gold standard for a recovery beverage."

DON'S ORIGINAL

donsoriginal.com/seabreeze

4900 Culver Rd.   585-323-1177
Sea Breeze, NY   L D (summer only) | $

Say "New York hot dog" and most people will conjure up a street-corner dirty-water dog or a kosher frank from an urban deli or Nathan's of Coney Island. But culinarily, as in every other aspect of its culture, New York has two personalities: downstate and everything else. Hot dogs on the far side of the Southern Tier are a food group unto themselves, known as hots. There are two primary subcategories: white hots and red hots.

The white hot, as served by Don's Original at the Lake Ontario summer playground known as Sea Breeze, is an all-pork tube steak (which locals call a porker) that wants to spurt juice when teeth sink into it. Split and grilled to sputtering succulence, a white hot is dressed with mustard and diced onions. Don's red hot, known as a Texas hot, is firmer and looks more like a traditional weenie and is dressed with finely ground chili.

Frankfurter frowners love this happy Rochester landmark (since 1945) because of its one-third-pound hamburger, known here as a "ground steak sandwich." It is cooked to order and brought to its best self by an application of bright-red hot sauce. Big, fat onion rings are made here, as is custard, available inside or at the walk-up window.

DOUG'S FISH FRY

dougsfishfry.com

3638 West Rd.	607-753-9184
Cortland, NY	L D | $$

★
LOCALS
LOVE IT
★

Doug's is a fish-and-chips lover's dream. Your choice is either a sandwich, a fish dinner, or a fish onion dinner. The titles are misleading because the sandwich is in fact two or three large hunks of fried fish piled in and around a modest bun that is in no way large enough to hold even half its ingredients. Like a tenderloin from the southern Midwest, the presentation pushes the envelope of what defines a sandwich. A fish dinner adds chunky French fries to the pseudo-sandwich; a fish onion dinner means onion rings.

The fish is Atlantic cod, bought fresh in Boston five times a week. It is moist, sweet, and meek-flavored, encased in a sandy crust with just the right amount of crunch. It comes with pickly tartar sauce that is surprisingly unsweet. Sweetness comes in the form of Doug's superb coleslaw, which is finely chopped and fetchingly spicy. And then there is sweet dessert: excellent soft-serve custard, dense and alabaster-pure. Throughout summer the custard is a foundation for warm fruit sundaes. The available compote, made right here from the fruit of the season, begins with strawberries and blueberries early in the summer, then moves to peaches and finally to apples in the fall. Glorious!

Service is eat-in-the-rough-style: Place your order at the stand-up counter (from which you have an appetizing view of fish and fries coming out of the hot oil), pay for the meal, and wait for your name to be called. Fetch your own utensils from a table in the center of the dining room that holds plastic forks and knives, ketchup and mustard, and malt vinegar for spritzing on fries.

GLENWOOD PINES

glenwoodpines.com

1213 Taughannock Blvd.	607-273-3709
Ithaca, NY	L D | $

The primary attraction of this friendly roadhouse overlooking Cayuga Lake is a Pinesburger. That's a six-ounce beef oval topped with a couple of slices of cheese wedged into a length of Ithaca Bakery French bread with lettuce, tomato, onion, and your choice of Thousand Island dressing or mayonnaise. Connoisseurs told us that we had to have it with the Thousand Island; the sweetness of the dressing is a grand complement for the smoky meat and all its dressings. On the side, good companions include ultra-crunchy fried onion rings and creamy coleslaw. Anyone who eats four Pinesburgers in less than an hour gets their picture on Glenwood Pines' Facebook Wall of Fame.

We said the Pinesburger was the primary reason to visit. The secondary one is the fish fry. A huge, thick length of haddock is breaded and fried crisp and served with either tartar sauce or cocktail sauce. It is sweet, moist, flavorful fish, and a giant meal.

Ambience at the 1946-vintage Glenwood Pines is old-time tavern. When you walk in, you see a few pinball machines and a bowling game on the right, a pool table ahead of you, and, beyond that, the bar where folks sit and imbibe beers with (or without) their Pinesburgers.

GUS'S RESTAURANT

3 Cumberland Head Rd.	518-561-3711
Plattsburgh, NY	B L D | $

In the same phylum as the Coney Islands of the heartland and New York Systems of Rhode Island, the Michigans of New York's North Country are primarily summertime food. They are little porkers that come nestled in a soft bun and topped with a fine-grained, mildly spicy meat sauce.

Gus's serves Michigans year-round. It started as a dog stand in 1951, but it has grown to a three-meal-a-day restaurant with a full menu that boasts, "The restaurant features just about everything [even Lake Champlain perch], including their famous 'Michigan red hot,' which they invite you to try while dining." Each Michigan you order arrives in a cardboard boat. The heft of the sauce contrasts with the fluffy bun and fatty frank, and while each separate ingredient is inarguably loutish, the combo achieves a satisfying dignity—especially when topped with a judicious line of yellow mustard and a scattering of crisp, chopped raw onions.

HEID'S OF LIVERPOOL
heidsofliverpool.com

305 Oswego St. 315-451-0786
Liverpool, NY **L D | $**

Heid's has been around as long as the hot dog, and for as long as any living human can remember, hot dogs have been its claim to fame. For a while there were branches of the original, but today only one remains: a fast-food dog house with some tables inside and picnic tables outdoors under a tent.

The menu is wienercentric. German franks, Texas hots (red wieners), or Hofmann brand white hots made of beef, pork, and veal are quickly grilled, a process you can watch after placing your order. These are handsome sausages with a delicate casing and dense insides. In the old days the one and only available condiment was mustard. But since John and Randall Parker started running Heid's back in 1995, the topping choices have expanded to include chili, onions, sweet onion relish, and ketchup.

As always, the beverage list is a short one, including milk shakes, sodas, beer, and chocolate milk.

HUBBA
24 N. Main St. 914-939-7271
Port Chester, NY **B L D | $**

OPEN LATE In southeastern New York, central New Jersey, and western Connecticut, the word "Texas," when used to modify the words "hot," "hot dog," or "weiner" (yes, *ei*), means chili. A Texas hot is a chili dog. The long-standing chili dog king of Port Chester is Hubba, formerly known as Pat's Hubba Hubba and, before that, Texas Quick Lunch. While there is a full menu written in permanent marker on white paper plates tacked to the wall, nine out of ten meals served are the same: two, four, or six split and grilled weenies blanketed with no-bean, ground-beef chili and garnished with crisp chopped onions. It is a wanton combo—hot, greasy, and messy—but with a personality so intense that when the yen for one strikes, not even prime filet mignon will cut the mustard. Those who need more sustenance than a brace of chili dogs get chili cheese fries on the side. To drink: Hubba water, which is tap water tinted pink by a dash of Hawaiian Punch.

Hubba's chili dogs are famous as the kill-or-cure conclusion to a night of heavy drinking. The restaurant stays open until just before dawn on weekends. No wider than an apartment hallway, with only about a dozen counter seats, it is known also for its eye-boggling décor: every available piece of wall and ceiling is papered with dollar bills.

JOHN'S OF BLEECKER STREET
johnsbrickovenpizza.com

278 Bleecker St. 212-243-1680
New York, NY **L D | $$**

There are nearly as many John's pizza shops in New York as there are Ray's, but the one to know about is John's of Bleecker Street. It looks well lived-in and well eaten-in, its walls and the wooden backs of its rickety booths covered with a thicket of graffiti that represents the countless enthusiastic visitors who have dined here since 1929. At the back of the front dining room, photographs of famous fans are displayed. They include former Mayor Rudy Giuliani and former Chairman of the Board Frank Sinatra.

Pizzas come large (eight slices) or small (six slices). There are no surprises on the ingredient list, except taste-wise: the sausage is especially delicious, the mushrooms are fresh, and the mozzarella has a creamy goodness that makes magic with the brightly herbed red sauce. What makes John's pizza taste important is its crust. Cooked in a coal-fired oven at 850 degrees, it has a dough that turns almost brittle at its outer edges in places where it blisters and blackens from the heat, and yet just fractions of an inch inside that circumference, it has a wondrous chew. Flip over a slice—you can do this, for the toppings cling well and each slice has enough structural integrity to stay together as it's handled—and gaze upon the bottom. It is crunchy from its stay on the floor of the old oven. For serious bread-and-pizza lovers, this crust verges on a spiritual experience.

★ KATZ'S DELICATESSEN

katzsdelicatessen.com

205 E. Houston St.   212-254-2246
New York, NY   B L D | $$

Katz's has been about to be demolished for a half-dozen years, but until that happens, it's one of New York's Lower East Side relics, remaining as it was a century ago. It is a gymnasium-sized eating hall with lined-up tables, the air filled with the noise of shouted orders and clattering carving knives and the aroma of the odoriferous garlicky salamis hanging along the wall. Pictures of happy celebrity customers ranging from comics Jerry Lewis and Henny Youngman to former Police Commissioner Ray Kelly are everywhere.

Ordinary table service by waiters is available, and quite easy. But the better way to do it is to personally engage with a counterman. Here's how: Make eye contact with one of the white-aproned carvers who are busy hand-slicing meats and making sandwiches behind the glass. Once you've gotten his attention, be quick and tell him what you want: pastrami on rye or on a club roll, or corned beef or brisket. They portion out meat and assemble sandwiches with the certainty and expertise of a Dutch diamond cutter.

King of Katz's sandwiches is pastrami—not the hugest in the city, but very possibly the best: three-quarters of a pound, expertly severed into pieces so chunky that the word "slice" seems too lightweight to describe them. Each brick-red, glistening moist hunk is rimmed black, redolent of garlic, smoke, and pickling spices, as savory as food can be. You can pay a dollar extra to have it cut extra-lean, but that would be sad.

Beyond superb cured meat: Katz's hot dogs just may be the city's best all-beefers; omelets are made deli-style, meaning open-face and unfolded; there are tender-souled matzoh ball soup and chicken noodle soup as well as potato latkes and blintzes; and to drink you can have a classic New York egg cream, chocolate or vanilla.

LDR CHAR PIT

ldrcharpit.com

4753 Lake Ave.   585-865-0112
Rochester, NY   L D | $

When you first see an LDR steak sandwich, you will likely be suspicious. The single, broad cut of meat in its bun looks like a challenging chew, especially considering the bargain price of $6.25 and the fact that the LDR Char Pit is a booth-and-counter diner, as far from a prime steak house as a restaurant can be. But when you take a bite, the preconception vanishes. This slim steak, which is maybe a quarter of an inch thick and cooked to order, is tenderness incarnate, oh-so-easy to chew and a joy to savor, as buttery-beef-flavored as a KC strip: a miracle sandwich.

It arrives completely unadorned. Condiments, including a meaty hot sauce, are available at a help-yourself counter; but we highly recommend you forgo them. The beauty of this steak sandwich is its simplicity: meat and bread. Anything else is only a complication.

LDR's menu also lists red hots and white hots—traditional upstate New York frankfurters—as well as grilled chicken and ham steaks, none of which we've tried. The steak is too compelling. When you are finished, walk a half block toward Lake Ontario and you will find an Abbott's custard shop. Creamy, dense, dairy-pure, it is wonderful dessert. Our favorite flavor is chocolate almond.

MCSWEENEY'S

mcsweeneysredhots.com

535 N. Margaret St.   518-562-9309
Plattsburgh, NY   **L D | $**

A style of chili dog unique to New York State's Northland, the Michigan goes back to the early 1940s. Each place that makes Michigans in and around Plattsburgh has its own formula, but the basic idea is a piggy-pink wiener in a split-top bun, topped with dark-orange chili sauce in which the meat is sandy smithereens.

McSweeney's, which bills itself as Plattsburgh's Red Hot Car Hop Stop, is a relative newcomer to the area, opened in 1991 and now boasting three locations. We visited the one on Route 9 North (Margaret Street), which features old-time carhop service and an inside counter as well as comfortable sit-down tables indoors. Its sauce is especially beefy, flecked with pepper that kindles a nice glow on the tongue. The package is substantial enough that Michigans come with a fork. Looking around the dining room and at people eating off trays hung on car windows, it appeared to us that most customers forgo the utensil. A few people we observed had perfected a technique of hoisting the entire cardboard boat to chin level with one hand, then using the other hand to ease the Michigan from boat to mouth, bite by bite.

McSweeney's sells Michigan sauce by the pint ($11.50) and offers a Michigan without the hot dog: mustard, onions, and plenty of sauce in a hollowed-out bun. This configuration is known as a sauce-burger, and as much as we like the sauce, we much prefer it in concert with a weenie.

MIKE'S CANDY

mikescandies.com

2110 Clinton St.   716-826-6515
Buffalo, NY   **$**

-- ★ --
LOCALS
LOVE IT
-- ★ --
Of Buffalo's several claims to culinary fame (wings, beef on weck, char-cooked hot dogs), one of the lesser-known stars is sponge candy. Made of sugar that is cooked and spun and leavened to a state of desiccated near-weightlessness, then cut into diaphanous, double-bite-sized hunks and sheathed in dark chocolate (or milk chocolate, if you prefer), it is similar to candy known in some parts of the Midwest as seafoam or fairy food.

We well remember our first bite at Mike's, a Buffalo chocolate shop where everything is made from scratch in a small backroom kitchen, and where sponge candy is an obsession. We stood at the counter and sampled a piece, remarking that the molasses interior seemed actually lighter than air, as if it would float upward without the ballast of its thick chocolate coat. As soon as it was bitten and slightly moist, it evaporated into pure flavor with no corporeal residue at all. Susan Walter, daughter of founders Mike and Anastasia Melithoniotes, listened to us, but not to our words. "It sounds a little crisp today," she said, noticing the faint crunch it made when our teeth first met the sponge underneath its chocolate sheath. "It's breaking hard." The subtlety of her evaluation was lost on us, for it seemed absolutely perfect. Susan also clued us in to the uniquely Buffalonian favorite the Charlie Chaplin, which is a log of freshly made marshmallow laced with coconut and rolled with cashews and chocolate. Neither she nor any other confectioner in town had a convincing explanation for how the Buffalo obsession got its name.

Sponge candy is almost always available in-store at Mike's, as well as for mail order throughout the year except in the hottest months of summer, when heat and humidity preclude shipping.

NEW WAY LUNCH

newwaylunch.com

21 South St.   518-792-9803
Glens Falls, NY   **B L | $**

New Way Lunch, which longtime residents know as Dirty John's, has a sign outside boasting that it has been world famous since 1919, and although it now occupies a new, modern building, its way with hot dogs (or, as locals call them, dirt dogs) is timeless. They are slim, non-kosher franks that are griddle cooked and slipped into soft, warm buns. The fundamental dressing formula is a trio of mustard, diced onions, and a finely textured beef sauce that has a peppery tang. It is a small package, costing just over a dollar. Takeout customers come in for dozens.

There's a brief menu of other items too: char-cooked burgers, a Philly cheesesteak, fried fish and chicken, and a Greek salad. For a quick lunch not far from the New York Thruway, New Way is an easy detour.

NICK CHARLAP'S

7264 Boston State Rd.   716-312-0592
Hamburg, NY   **L D | $**

"Vat pasteurization is the key," Mr. Charlap told us, explaining that most ice cream makers pasteurize their product as quickly as possible for efficiency's sake. But he holds his at 180 degrees for a full twenty minutes. The result is flavor that tastes deep rather than superficial, cooked-in rather than added-on. You can savor it easily in plain vanilla, but the depth is there too in chocolate and coffee, as well as in more complicated flavors such as cashew caramel crunch, raspberry chocolate chip, deep-dish apple pie, burgundy cherry, cinnamon, and caramel brownie overload. Charlap's hard ice cream is scooped and served at a temperature that makes it nearly as soft as custard, meaning the flavor glows.

Dine outside at a picnic table, or inside, where the ambience is 1950s retro with neon signs, glass-brick counter, and checkered tile floor. Adjoining is a grill serving hot dogs, hamburgers, sandwiches, and fries.

★ NICK TAHOU HOTS

garbageplate.com

320 W. Main St.   585-436-0184
Rochester, NY   **L D | $**

Don't confuse a Rochester Garbage Plate with junk food that is tossed willy-nilly into a paper bag or bucket. At Nick Tahou Hots, where it was invented, a Garbage Plate is a carefully assembled meal. It demands a table and utensils, not to mention a big appetite and courage.

Construction of a Garbage Plate begins with your choice of two items from among home fries, French fries, macaroni salad, and baked beans. The duo is marshaled half-and-half onto a carton-weight cardboard plate. Atop the foundation of starches are positioned a brace of hot dogs, hamburgers or cheeseburgers, Italian sausage or steak, or fried eggs. Piled onto the protein layer are meaty hot sauce and onions, and bread comes alongside to push, mop, and scoop.

The Garbage Plate was created by Nick Tahou during the Great Depression, when it was known as hots and potots—"hots" being the upstate New York term for hot dogs. The maximum-food/minimum-cost meal was renamed by happy customers and has been embraced by Rochesterians as a hometown specialty as dear as wings in Buffalo.

To its loyal clientele, Nick Tahou's is more than a restaurant. It is home, it is family, it is a spirit of ragtag generosity with which Nick's son Alex Tahou feeds needy kids at Christmas and takes care of neighbors and friends as well as newcomers all year round.

PAPAYA KING

papayaking.com

179 E. 86th St.   212-369-0648
New York, NY   **L D | $**

Incredibly, Papaya King began as a health-oriented juice store. That was 1932, when original proprietor Gus Poulos hired waitresses to do the hula on the sidewalk and lure people inside to taste "nature's own revitalizer." You still can have papaya juice, which is frothy and sweet if not necessarily salubrious, but it's for the hot dogs this popular street-corner eatery has earned its stripes. A sign boasts that they are "tastier than filet mignon." They do pack a booming garlic taste inside natural casing that pops when you bite it. Available toppings include chili, sauerkraut, even coleslaw; the essentials are New York–style stewed onions and good ol' mustard.

Dine at an eating shelf that affords a nice view of the passing scene along Third Avenue and 86th Street.

PATSY'S

thepatsypizza.com

2287 1st Ave.	212-534-9783
New York, NY	**L D | $**

New Yorkers think nothing of picking up a slice of pizza for eating on the go. Patsy's is the Italian landmark in the midst of Spanish Harlem where street slices first were served back in the 1930s. To this day, customers stand around on the sidewalk or lean on an open-air counter facing First Avenue wolfing down slices of pizza, which is the only thing on the menu. These are some of the most elegant slices you'll find in the city: wafer-thin charcoaled crust, minimal tomato, and just enough cheese to make it rich.

Whole pies are served at tables and booths inside. While all sorts of toppings are available, we like the most basic tomato-cheese combo: easy to hoist slice by slice, built on that marvelous fragile crust. Two versions of plain cheese pizza are available: fresh mozzarella, with thin pools of creamy sliced cheese spread out within the microthin layer of tomato sauce, and regular mozzarella on which saltier, slightly oilier shredded cheese is spread evenly all across the surface.

PHIL'S CHICKEN HOUSE

philschickenhouse.com

1208 Union Center	607-748-6855
Maine Hwy.	**B** (weekends) **L D | $**
Endicott, NY	

Phil's Chicken House was opened a half century ago by Phil Card, who learned his skills at Endicott's Chicken Inn. His folksy wood-paneled restaurant is decorated to the hilt with country-crafty knickknacks (souvenir plates, angel statuettes, lighthouse miniatures) and it attracts customers that range from local families to well-armed state police SWAT teams (who practice marksmanship nearby).

As you might suspect by the name of this restaurant, its featured attraction is chicken—slow cooked, and relentlessly basted on a rotisserie until the skin is glazed gold and the meat drips juice. The breast meat is velvet soft; thighs and drumsticks pack a roundhouse flavor punch; wings, which carry maximum marinade, reverberate with exclamatory gusto. The marinade is the classic Cornell chicken formula, devised by a professor by the name of Dr. Robert Baker in 1946—a tomato-free vinaigrette, enriched with eggs and shot through with poultry spice, now used as a marinade and/or basting sauce by cooks throughout the region.

While nine out of ten customers come to Phil's for a half or a quarter barbecued chicken, square meals of all kinds are available, including pot roast, meat loaf, grilled ham, and steak. There's a lunch buffet every day and a breakfast buffet on weekends.

POLISH VILLA

2954 Union Rd.	716-683-9460
Cheektowaga, NY	**B L D | $**

One of the chief culinary assets of America's heartland is its bounty of Eastern European restaurants. Polish Villa is one of the best. Look, for example, at the pierogies, stuffed with sauerkraut, their soft and tangy filling robed in dough that gets quick-sautéed to a crisp just before being served: magnificent! Sweet-and-sour cabbage—available as a side dish for any meal—is soft but not mushy, balanced perfectly between sugar and tang. Other menu highlights include *czarnina* soup, kielbasa, *golabki,* and fruit crepes for dessert. One course after another, everything you eat is Mom's-home-cooking good: slightly sticky potato pancakes served with either sour cream or applesauce (but you must pay extra if you want both); firm-fleshed, smoky sausages; crisp wiener schnitzel sided by creamy mashed potatoes, *kluski* noodles topped with chicken and mushrooms.

Such a welcoming restaurant! It's informal, but so polite. At the door, you are greeted by a hostess who seems genuinely grateful you have arrived. Waitresses are able to explain anything that needs explaining. And the room's tone is that of a huge family reunion, where nearly everybody present seems very happy to be plowing into such exquisite Old World meals.

PURDY'S FARMER & THE FISH
farmerandthefish.com

100 Titicus Rd.   914-617-8380
North Salem, NY   **L D | $$$**

--★--
HOT
TICKET
--★--

The name of this restaurant is no affectation. The salad you eat is grown in a five-acre terraced field out back. The fish comes from a co-owner's seafood business, most of it from nearby waters. Describing itself as a "community-oriented restaurant where people can meet and enjoy reasonably priced, locally grown food and high quality seafood," Purdy's Farmer & the Fish is a casual destination for anyone who appreciates the freshest possible food made with skill and style and served in helter-skelter dining rooms that ring with cheer. Located in an old farmhouse and surrounded by effulgent blossoming plants, it has earned tremendous kudos (and sometimes long waits for a table) since opening in 2012.

On the Roadfood scale, the meals are a splurge. Entrees go for $25 to $30, but you can get a softshell crab sandwich or Big Eye Tuna Burger for under $20. A block of Scottish salmon, perched atop a base of black barley with a subtle sweet twist, along with baby beets, turnips, and carrots, seems worth every penny of its $24 price. The impeccably fresh salmon, cooked medium-rare as ordered, is velvet-soft except

at its well-seasoned, crusty edges—a true melt-in-your-mouth dish. A lobster roll, available either cool with lemon aioli and cucumbers or warm with only butter, contains massive chunks of juicy meat from the tail, claw, and knuckle. The bun is a bore, but who cares? The meat is ocean-sweet. On the side come hefty steak fries that are crisp-skinned and creamy inside.

Among hors d'oeuvres, we love the calamari veiled in an elegant thin crust, each little circle shockingly tender, delivering that subtle seafood taste that even a fish frowner will love. An order of Buffalo shrimp yields three breaded colossals on a field of piquant hot sauce scattered with blue cheese, presented with a ramekin of cool ranch dressing. One of the most amazing starters is cucumber salad, an off-the-menu special in which the bright, sunny flavor of just-picked cukes tangles with other garden greens in a pool of cucumber squeezins. On the subject of appetizers, we should mention that there is a full raw bar menu that includes East Coast and West Coast oysters, clams, shrimp or lobster cocktails, crab legs, and cornucopian "seafood towers" for two or more people.

There is a nice card of desserts with some wild chocolate creations, but if it's summer, who can resist freshly picked berries with just-whipped cream—a fitting end to a truly farm-fresh meal.

POPPY'S
poppyburger.com

184 Main St.   845-765-2121
Beacon, NY   **L D | $**

Poppy's hamburger is not extreme. An honest quarter-pounder (unless you get a Classic Big, which is two quarter-pound patties on one bun), the burger itself is hand-formed and grilled to crusty succulence. It comes on a bun that is soft and tender but somehow substantial enough to hold up to the onslaught of juices that ooze. And they do ooze. Unless you get yours well done, aka dried out, a first bite releases torrents of delicious beefy juices.

The luscious beef is accompanied by a scattering of chopped red onions and a mantle of locally produced Cheddar cheese that melts beautifully into every fissure and crevice in the burger. The cheese is only moderately sharp, just sharp enough to sing harmony with the radiant protein luxury of the meat. On the side, a little ramekin of crisp dill-pickle chips adds a twangy twist. Other topping options include Hudson Valley tomatoes and lettuce, bacon, sautéed onions, barbecue sauce, a fried egg, and aioli. Vegetarians can get a veggie patty made of beans, which we are told by devout meat frowners is very good. Beyond burgers, Poppy's offers a short list of rice bowls and salads.

Potatoes are a must, either sweet-potato chips, which are see-through thin, or French fries, which are thin, crisp, and flavorful, each order laced with crunchy little brown twigs.

Poppy's is a bare-table, paper-napkin sort of place where burgers come wrapped in foil. Indoor seats are at handsome wood-back booths, and there is now a patio out back for al fresco eating when weather permits.

RED ROOSTER DRIVE-IN

1566 Route 22   845-279-8046
Brewster, NY   L D | $

Although a roadside archeologist would categorize the Rooster as a drive-in, there is no car service and there are no carhops. Still, plenty of people eat in their cars, and the service, cuisine, and ambience are *Happy Days* incarnate.

The hamburgers are not too big, not odd in any way, just pleasant handfuls fashioned by proprietor Jack Sypek or Andy the grill chef and sizzled on a charcoal grill. We are particularly fond of cheeseburgers gilded by onions that have been grilled until limp and slippery. They are served on tender buns—deluxe, please, with lettuce and tomato—and accompanied by French fries, milk shakes, ice cream floats, or egg creams.

In nice weather, customers can choose to eat at one of several picnic tables spread across the lawn in back. Adjacent to this open-air dining room is a miniature golf course where kids and carefree adults while away pleasant evenings in the Red Rooster's afterglow.

★ SCHWABL'S
schwabls.com
789 Center Rd.   716-675-2333
West Seneca, NY   L D | $$

Now operated by former waitress Cheryl Staychok and her husband, Gene, Buffalo's best-known beef house didn't miss a beat when the Schwabl family left the business. Here is the benchmark version of that glorious Buffalo specialty, beef on weck. The beef itself is superb: thin slices (preferably rare) severed from a center-cut round roast just before the sandwich is assembled. The pillow of protein is piled high inside a *kummelweck* roll heavily crusted with coarse salt and caraway seeds, the roll's top momentarily dipped in natural gravy before it sandwiches the meat. The only thing this package could possibly want is a dab of horseradish, which is supplied on each table.

Of the several side dishes, mashed potatoes are very good (and topped with excellent gravy), but tangy-sweet German potato salad is our pick. That is all you need to know about Schwabl's, except for the nice hot ham sandwich on white bread in a pool of tomato-clove gravy. The ham is an interesting alternative to the beef, although it has none of the clout.

Schwabl's is a casual, well-aged eatery, attended by businesspeople at noon and families at suppertime. While liquor is served, the best beverage to pair with beef on weck is birch beer, which is available here on draft: a local brew with the faint twang of spearmint.

SECOND AVENUE DELI
2ndavedeli.com
162 E. 33rd St.   212-689-9000
New York, NY   B L D | $$

The Second Avenue Deli has moved closer to Third Avenue, on Thirty-Third Street, but it remains one of the ever-scarcer true Jewish delicatessens. You can smell its culinary character the moment you walk in and inhale the swirling perfume of sour pickles, aged salami, hot chicken broth, steamy corned beef, and pastrami. Where else can you begin a meal with *gribenes*, which are the leftovers from rendering chicken fat? The Second Avenue Deli makes them in big batches, so they aren't as refined or as delicate as you might find on the kitchen counter at Grandma's house, but they are nonetheless irresistible: squiggles and nibbles of skin along with limp caramelized shreds of onion that have been fried in the full-flavored oil. Dangerous to munch before a meal because they are so addictive and so corpulent, *gribenes* are the world's best complement to chopped liver, which here is smooth-flavored but ragged enough for textural excitement, rich the way only organ meat can be, and yet fresh and sparkling the way liver so seldom is.

Smoked fish platters are silky luxury, soups—especially the legendary mushroom barley—are some of the city's best, and deli sandwiches are delightful. While the sandwiches are not gargantuan, they are piled high enough that they are barely pickupable. Pastrami is especially excellent, more smoky than spicy, and unless you pay $2 extra for lean meat, it comes just-right fatty. Our only complaint is the rye bread, which, as in so many otherwise first-rate delis nowadays, is second-class, pale and flabby.

Meals are topped off with a complimentary shot-glass chocolate phosphate ("Bosco and seltzer," explains the waitress). Second Avenue's kitchen actually is kosher, meaning you can't get cheese on a sandwich.

SHARKEY'S

56 Glenwood Ave.   716-729-9201
Binghamton, NY   L D | $$

Larry Sharak's father started making spiedies at a cookfire in the window at the family's tavern over sixty years ago. Skewered, marinated hunks of lamb were cooked on a charcoal grill and served with broad slices of bread. The custom was to grab the bread in one hand and use it as an edible mitt to slide a few hunks off the metal rod, thus creating an instant sandwich. Spiedies are still served and eaten this way at the bar and tables of Sharkey's. Lamb has grown

too expensive, however, so today's spiedies are made from either pork or chicken. When you bite into a piece, it blossoms with the flavorful juice of a two-day marinade that tastes of garlic and vinegar, peppers and oregano and, according to Larry Sharak, for whom the recipe is a family heirloom, "a lot of pinches of many spices."

Sharkey's is a local institution to which families have come for generations. Old-timers know to enter through the back door rather than the front. Here, you walk into a dark dining room outfitted with ancient wooden booths and long family-style tables formed from pushed-together dinettes. Between courses, the young folks get up to play a few lines on the old Tic Tac Strike game, a pre-electronic diversion that seems at home in this historic tavern.

SHORTSTOP DELI

shortstopdeli.com
200 W. Seneca St.   607-273-1030
Ithaca, NY   Always open | $

— ★ —
OPEN
24/7
— ★ —
Any hearty eater who attended Cornell University in Ithaca in the last half century knows about Hot Truck, the mobile food wagon that invented French bread pizzas in the early 1960s. As served every night starting at 11 p.m. during the school year, these fusions of pizza and submarine sandwich are piled with ingredients then baked open-face until the bread is shatteringly crisp, the cheese bubbles, and the meats sizzle.

The Hot Truck's hours are extremely limited, which is why we love the Shortstop Deli, which features Hot Truck cuisine and never closes. More a big convenience store than a sit-down eatery, the Shortstop features shelves of snack foods, countless varieties of coffee, and a counter where you write down your order. There are no tables and chairs, just some concrete benches outside the front window to bring your wrapped sandwich and your cup of soda (10¢ with a meal!) and dine alfresco with a view of the parking lot.

The pizza subs are made on loaves of Ithaca Bakery French bread, and they range from the basic PMP (Poor Man's Pizza), which is nothing but bread, sauce, and cheese, to the extravaganza known as a Suicide (garlic, sauce, mushrooms, sausage, pepperoni, and mozzarella). These sandwiches have inspired a language all their own. For example, a "Triple Sui, Hot and Heavy, G and G" is a full Suicide with three extra homemade meatballs, a sprinkle of red pepper, extra garlic, mayonnaise, and lettuce. (G and G = grease and garden—that is, mayo and lettuce.) A Flaming Turkey Bone (which contains no turkey and no bones and is not served on fire) includes chicken breast, tomato sauce, cheese, onions, extra hot and heavy, plus "spontaneous combustion" (double-X hot sauce).

STEVE'S PIG & OX ROAST

951 Ridge Rd.   716-824-8601
Lackawanna, NY   L D | $

Here is one of the Buffalo area's more interesting beef on weck sandwiches. The beef is not sliced thin into rose-red slices like at most local beef houses. It is thicker and cooked through, tender like pot roast. It comes with a cup of natural gravy for dipping or pouring into the sandwich and a mountain of French fries. The spuds are long and thin with lots of crunchy squiggles throughout. Bruce Bilmes and Sue Boyle, who tipped us off to this neighborhood roaster-café, warned that unless we specifically asked for a *kummelweck* roll, sandwiches are served on regular buns. Weck is the way to go.

At $5 each—for pork, lamb, or turkey, as well as for beef—these mountainous sandwiches are a great bargain, available with Buffalo's beloved loganberry juice to drink. Meats are cooked on an impressive rotisserie adjacent to the dining room. If you arrive early, chances are you will see the meat still in motion.

TED'S JUMBO RED HOTS

tedshotdogs.com
2312 Sheridan Dr.   716-836-8986
Tonawanda (Buffalo),   L D | $
NY

Ted's began as a horse-drawn hot dog cart in Buffalo in the 1920s. It became a permanently anchored hot dog stand under the Peace Bridge in 1927 and opened as a bigger store on Sheridan Drive in 1948. There are now eight Ted's in western New York, and one in Tempe, Arizona; but the one to which we always want to return is Ted's of Tonawanda. It has modernized since 1948 and is as clean and sanitary as any fast-food franchise, but the hot dogs are like no others. Natural-casing Sahlen's-brand franks, available regular-length or foot-long, are cooked on a grate over charcoal that infuses each one with pungent smoke flavor and makes the skin get crackling-crisp. As they cook, the chef pokes them with a fork, slaps them, squeezes them, and otherwise abuses them, thus puncturing the skin and allowing them to suck in maximum smoky taste.

In consultation with a person behind the counter known as "the dresser," you decide how you want to garnish your tube steak. The standout condiment is Ted's hot sauce, a peppery concoction laced with bits of relish. You also want onion rings, sold as tangled webs of crisp fried batter and limp onion. The beverage of choice in these parts is loganberry juice, which is a kind of grand cru Kool-Aid.

TEXAS CHILI

texaschilirestaurant.com
36 Broad St.   914-937-0840
Port Chester, NY   B L D | $

 Although Texas Chili is neat, clean, and well-lit, it delivers all the funky soul you expect in a chili-dog joint. Opened in 2009 by two partners who had worked down the street at the legendary greasy spoon Hubba (p. 101), it has a three-meal-a-day menu on which nearly everything, from omelets at dawn to wieners at 4 a.m. on Saturday night, features chili. It is a beanless, ground-beef brew glistening with oil, so peppery that it is not listed on the menu as a stand-alone—although serious chiliheads do get it solo. It is best as an eyebrow-raising complement for little tube steaks that are split and grilled until their edges get crusty. Atop the chili on the hot dog, chopped onions are the standard garnish. Crisp, cool, and refreshing, they are a marvelous counterbalance for the chili dog, doing what onions so seldom do: carrying the banner for an actual vegetable. It is traditional for hot dogs in this area to be served in little white-bread buns; Texas Chili grills its buns in butter (or maybe buttery-flavored grease), adding a note of opulence to a package that is unctuous in so many other ways.

While a full array of soda pop is available to drink, the connoisseur's choice is what's known here as Texas water: plain water turned pink by an infusion of Hawaiian Punch.

TINO'S

tinosdeli.com

2410 Arthur Ave.   718-733-9879
Bronx, NY   **L | $**

The Bronx originally was part of Westchester County, so it makes sense that when you go to Tino's for a chicken parm hero, you'll hear some fellow eaters refer to it by its Westchester moniker, a wedge. Whatever you call it, this mighty log of lunch is authoritative. First, there's the bread. Many sandwiches of chicken parmigiana (and eggplant parmigiana) are built upon a toasted loaf. Not that there's anything wrong with that, but all too often toasting is simply a way of disguising a stale or inferior length of bread. Tino's doesn't toast, but if you want that crunch, get yours on a crisp-crusted Italian roll that is impeccably fresh and Arthur-Avenue soulful. Soft club rolls also are available. Then there's the chicken itself, a cutlet that's lightly breaded and glazed with fantastic sauce that tastes like it's really made from tomatoes, all of this crowned with creamy-fresh mozzarella. We nominate Tino's handsome hunk as king of hot Italian sandwiches.

If you are in the market for a cold-cut sandwich that is super-hot, we recommend what Tino's calls Bocca di Fuoco: hot soppressata, hot capicola, and hot peppers with mozzarella cheese. Tino's combo is a classic Italian sub of salami, ham, mortadella, and provolone with lettuce, tomato, and roasted peppers, and the only proper condiments: oil and vinegar.

WALTER'S

waltershotdogs.com

937 Palmer Ave.   No phone
Mamaroneck, NY   **L | $**

Even if you have another weenie you love more, it is hard to deny that Walter's belongs on any list of America's top dogs. Each begins as a beef-pork-veal frank made exclusively for Walter's, as they have been since 1919. The frank is bisected lengthwise and cooked on a grill coated with secret-formula sauce. It's a buttery sauce with an ineffable spice that insinuates flavor into the cut-flat surface of the weenie and gives it a faint crunch that is a joy to bite, especially inside a soft bun that has been toasted on an adjacent grill. Some customers ask for their hot dog well-done and therefore more crisp than usual (not a bad idea) and others get a double dog (in our opinion, an imbalance of dog and bun), but whichever way you like it, please have it with mustard. It is Walter's own mustard, grainy and dotted with pickle bits. To drink? Walter's makes a fine malted milk shake.

The place is a vernacular-architecture hoot, designed to evoke a pagoda, complete with lanterns and a sign that spells out WALTER's in letters that look vaguely like Chinese brushstrokes from a distance but turn out to be images of hot dogs strung together. On a pleasant day, you can dine in a grove of picnic tables suited to devouring multiple hot dogs; but in inclement weather, you are on your own. Walter's has no inside seats.

WEST TAGHKANIC DINER

Route 82 &
Taconic Pkwy.
Ancram, NY

518-851-7117
B L D | $

When we first walked into the West Taghkanic Diner, a beautiful streamliner from 1953, we passed two women dressed in business suits in the silver vestibule. They stopped, blocking our way, and one furtively whispered a single word: "jitterbug." Then they let us pass.

When the waitress came to take our order, we mumbled, "Um, er, 'jitterbug'?" We said the secret password, having no idea if it was a clue or the ranting of a crazy woman. "Fine," she said. "You want your bread toasted?" We said no, wondering what exactly we had ordered. The jitterbug, it turns out, is a mid–Hudson Valley specialty of a hamburger between two pieces of bread or toast, sided by potatoes and covered with gravy. The burger is juice-laden, the gravy thick, the mashed potatoes lumpy-good and tinged with garlic.

The rest of the menu is vast and inviting, a wide array of sandwiches, salads, and hot dishes. Among daily specials written on a board above the counter are homemade stuffed cabbage, pot roast, chicken Parmesan, and tuna noodle casserole. A bowl of chili is not huge, but it is dense and thick, loaded with chunks of meat that taste like (and may be) broken-up meat loaf. It's a Northeast classic, slightly sweet and just a bit spicy, thick with meat and beans and onions and peppers.

Despite its age, the West Taghkanic is spanking-clean and like new: boomerang-pattern Formica tabletops, baby-blue upholstered stools that match the blue tiles in the floor and arched blue ceiling, and a counter where you can watch the waitress mix an egg cream (chocolate or vanilla).

PENNSYLVANIA

CENTER CITY PRETZEL CO.
centercitypretzel.com

816 Washington Ave.   215-463-5664
Philadelphia, PA $

★ OPEN LATE ★ Bad-tasting water = good-tasting food. There is no other logical explanation for the excellence of Philadelphia soft pretzels. There is a brackish tang to the flavor of the pretzel, especially to its tan skin, that puts it a cut above pretzels from any other city. If it's morning when you get one—or, preferably, a bag of several—it likely will still be oven-warm, the absolute freshness bold-facing its dense, chewy nature. Some pretzel lovers like to have a little mustard as a condiment. As far as we're concerned, these big softies need nothing to attain street-food perfection.

Notes: Center City pretzels are all-natural (nothing but flour, yeast, water, and salt), made in a nut-free environment, and are kosher-certified.

DELUCA'S

2015 Penn Ave.   412-566-2195
Pittsburgh, PA   B L | $

If you crave maximum breakfast in Pittsburgh, visit DeLuca's. There are frittatas, pumpkin pancakes, extra-large egg sandwiches, and a showstopper called mixed grill: sausage or ham sizzled with a huge heap of peppers, onions, tomatoes, mushrooms, and zucchini, crowned with a couple of eggs (optional) and sided by home-fried potatoes and a couple of slabs of toast. Among the available varieties of toast are cinnamon-raisin, rye, wheat, and white.

For many visitors, DeLuca's is an opportunity to indulge in one of the really outrageous breakfast items, such as the chocolate chip hotcake sundae, which is a stack of pancakes chockablock with melted and melting chocolate chips, topped with ice cream and strawberries. We are fond of blueberry French toast made with that sweet-smelling raisin bread.

Expect to wait for a seat at peak mealtime hours, especially on weekends when Pittsburghers throng to the Strip on a kind of eaters' holiday. For us, the choice place in DeLuca's is at the counter, with a good view of the short-order chefs flipping eggs and hotcakes at lightning speed.

DUTCH KITCHEN
dutchkitchen.com

433 S. Lehigh Ave.   570-874-3265
Frackville, PA   B L D | $

The Dutch Kitchen is really convenient. At Exit 124B off I-81, it always seems to be just where we need it when hunger strikes south of the I-80 junction. It is a big, friendly place, a former dining car to which has been added a whole dining room decorated to the max with country crafts, speckleware, homily plaques, and souvenirs of Pennsylvania.

In some ways, the Dutch Kitchen is a traditional diner where you can come for bacon and eggs or a nice hamburger or sandwich. But beyond good versions of standard fare are such hearty Keystone State dishes as smoked pork chops, turkey croquettes, and a stupendously good potpie with homemade noodles, chicken and turkey, potatoes, and vegetables. One of our favorite daily specials is a stew of ham, cabbage, and potato sided by a block of brown-top corn bread nearly as sweet as cake. For dessert, we like shoofly pie—a ribbon of molasses filling topped with a crumbly top—or shoofly cake, a dark spice cake that is a supreme coffee companion and easy to eat while driving.

THE ENRICO BISCOTTI COMPANY

enricobiscotti.com

2022 Penn Ave.	412-281-2602
Pittsburgh, PA	B L D | $

One of the fringe benefits of coffee's ascendance in recent years is the discovery of biscotti, the firm, twice-baked Italian cookie that dunks so well. Alas, like coffee itself, there are a lot of lame versions around. We didn't even think we liked them . . . until we visited the Enrico Biscotti Company in Pittsburgh's historic Strip District. Here baker Larry Lagattuta makes them by hand using the finest ingredients, turning out such flavors as anise-almond, apricot-hazelnut, and pineapple-vanilla with white chocolate. They are firm enough that you'd never call them soft, but they do offer a tooth-pleasing resistance completely different from the desiccated, cellophane-wrapped variety.

Attached to the bakery is a European-style café where you can eat individual-sized brick-oven pizza, *torta rustica* (quiche), beans and greens, soup, or a "big fat salad." Here too is the espresso machine, as well as a handful of tables both inside and outdoors in a makeshift patio along the sidewalk. We know of no nicer place to start the day with strong coffee and biscotti, or to have a leisurely lunch of true Italian food. Bring your own wine.

THE FAMILY DINER

302 Main St.	570-443-8797
White Haven, PA	B L | $

Interstate 80 through Pennsylvania is a challenging route for people who like to eat. There are truck stops and restaurants at nearly every exit, but most are mediocre. That is why we like the Family Diner, just a few minutes' detour from the highway. There is something for everyone in this friendly place, from blue-plate liver and onions or meat loaf and mashed potatoes to a fourteen-ounce burger (preferably with cheese and bacon) that eclipses both its bun and the plate it comes on.

As in so many diners, breakfast is deeply satisfying, served here from dawn until the middle of the afternoon. Pancakes, while not what you'd call elegant, are colossal. To add ballast, have them blanketed with gooey hot apple or blueberry topping. The Pennsylvania favorite, creamed chipped beef, comes sided by home fries or bite-sized potato cakes. Eggs are available any way (including soft-boiled and poached) with bacon, ham, sausage, pork roll, or scrapple. Scrapple is a Mid-Atlantic passion—thin slices from a loaf of ground pork and cornmeal that are sizzled in a pan until crisp.

FAMOUS 4TH STREET DELI

famous4thstreetdelicatessen.com

700 S. 4th St.	215-922-3274
Philadelphia, PA	L D | $$

Since it opened in 1923, the Famous 4th Street Deli has had its ups and downs, but today it is a consummate kosher-style eatery: glass cases up front full of smoked fish, wrinkly salamis hanging from the ceiling, colossal sandwiches of cured meat, and a vast menu of such classic Jewish fare as matzoh ball soup, noodle kugel, and chicken-in-the-pot.

Sinatra and Sammy Davis Jr. croon on the sound system in the background. A plate arrives with crisp coleslaw and a half-sour pickle. Dr. Brown's soda comes in a can along with an immense tumbler full of ice. And finally—ta-da!—the sandwich arrives. You can have it regular-sized, which is quite large, or zaftig, meaning cartoon-large. We love the pastrami, which is only modestly spiced even at its blackened edges. It is rich enough to feel like wanton indulgence, but not obscenely fatty.

While not cloyingly so, décor truly is nostalgic: an ancient black-and-white tiny-tile floor, vintage mirrored cabinets at the back of the dining area, and walls crowded with press accolades and pictures of the still-famous and long-forgotten personages who have eaten here.

GENO'S

genosteaks.com

1219 S. 9th St.   215-389-0659
Philadelphia, PA   **L D | $**

--★-- **OPEN 24/7** --★-- Whichever of Philadelphia's cheesesteak shops we happen to consider our favorite at any particular time, we have always appreciated Geno's classicism. This is the cheesesteak as it originally was served (by Pat's [p. 118], virtually across the street). It seems that here the meat is cut a little thicker than at other places (although it's still thin enough to be cooked through almost instantly when it hits the griddle), the rolls are sturdy, and the cheese choice includes Provolone, American, and Whiz. Open into the wee hours of the morning, Geno's is a magnet for night owls who eat standing under carnival-colored neon lights, leaning forward at the waist so shreds of beef that fall from the sandwich hit the sidewalk rather than their shoes.

Be sure to order your steak properly: First give your choice of cheese, then say the word "with" or "without," indicating your decision on whether or not you want onions. In other words, "Whiz without" means a cheesesteak made with Cheez Whiz but no onions. Red sauce is another option, but for most aficionados, sauce is not an essential cheesesteak ingredient. On the other hand, you must have fries—or cheese fries—on the side.

GLIDER DINER

gliderdiner.com

890 Providence Rd.   570-343-8036
Scranton, PA   **B L D | $**

Named because it originally was built from the packing crates that held a glider airplane, the wood-sided Glider Diner was replaced by a shiny silver Mountain View dining car in 1952. A large annex known as the Fireside Lounge was added in the early 1960s, but for blue-plate traditionalists, the old silver streamliner is the place to be. Here breakfast is served 'round the clock. Lunch and supper specialties include Gliderburgers and milk shakes and hot sandwiches of roast beef, meat loaf, Virginia ham, and turkey.

Roadfood stalwarts Bruce Bilmes and Sue Boyle clued us in to the real specialty of the house, listed on the menu as roasted porketta and available in a toasted hard roll as the centerpiece of a hot platter, accompanied by mashed potatoes and blanketed with gravy. Porketta is well-seasoned roast pork, sliced thin and dripping moisture: delish!

JIMMY'S HOT DOGS

2555 Nazareth Rd.   610-258-7545
Easton, PA   **L D | $**

We're not cheapskates, but we must confess that there is something irresistibly alluring about a decent meal that costs considerably less than coffee at Starbucks. Maybe *decent* isn't the exact right term to describe what's served at Jimmy's Hot Dogs, for these skinless dogs are sinful little steamers—piggy and juicy and priced under one dollar each. This means you can have two hot dogs, dressed, of course, the Jimmy's way—with mustard, onions, and pickle spears—along with a bag of potato chips and a Coke or chocolate milk for about three dollars. If you've got a big appetite, you might want three or four hot dogs; but even if you and a friend indulged in four apiece, you could still walk out with change from a ten-dollar bill.

Want something other than a hot dog and chips? Too bad, because that is the extent of Jimmy's menu. There is no extra charge to kibitz with members of the Apostopolous family, who have run the joint for decades . . . and who have perfected the art of freezing and overnight-shipping their beloved weenies to ex-Eastonites desperate for a taste of home.

Note: There are no seats. Business is takeout only.

JIM'S STEAKS

jimssouthstreet.com

| 400 South St. | 215-928-1911 |
| Philadelphia, PA | **L D** \| $ |

Opened in 1939, Jim's is Philadelphia's second-oldest cheesesteak shop (after Pat's [p. 118]), and it is definitely the sharpest-looking with its deco black-and-white tile décor. It's a very popular place, which is a good thing, because your wait in line will provide ample time for deciding how you like your steak garnished—"wit" or "witout" (onions), and whether you want the standard Cheez Whiz or optional American or provolone. The wait takes you past the back of the store, where an automatic slicer produces heaps of rosy-colored beef ready to be fried.

The steaks are made by hacking up the meat on the grill so it becomes hash. If you get sliced cheese, it is layered in the roll before the meat and melts underneath it. Whiz is ladled atop the meat. The bread is excellent, the fried onions are appropriately slippery, and the optional hot peppers are breathtaking.

JOE'S STEAKS & SODA SHOP

joessteaks.com

| 6030 Torresdale Ave. | 215-535-9405 |
| Philadelphia, PA | **L D** \| $ |

Joe's Steaks & Soda Shop (formerly Chink's) is an old-fashioned cheesesteak shop staffed by young women who delight in what they do, which includes building banana splits supreme and blending chocolate milk shakes thick enough that trying to suck one up a straw will cause serious hollows in your cheeks.

The open kitchen—little more than a griddle—is up front at a picture window that allows pedestrians to watch the cooks fry meat, scoot sizzling onions around, layer on slices of cheese, then hoist the jumble into a long, chewy, toasty-edged roll. The result: a well-balanced, buttery confluence of meat and dairy

and weeping sweet onion that welcomes a spill of sharp yellow peppers and pickle chips, arriving on a square of butcher paper.

Joe's interior is vintage Americana: old wooden booths and a short, five-stool counter. A sign up front reads "Please do not lean on the counter. This is our work space. Thank you."

JOHNNY'S HOTS

| 1234 N. Delaware Ave. | 215-423-2280 |
| Philadelphia, PA | **B L** \| $ |

The name of this restaurant refers to a tube steak that is similar to a half-smoke or Georgia hot: finely ground pork and plenty of spice packed into a taut casing. While it is not brutally hot, your tongue will glow, and if you like that glow, get your hot with hots, long hot peppers with exclamatory punch.

Johnny's is known for top-ranked cheesesteaks and breakfast sandwiches that include eggs along with the hot sausage, but the one item that most deserves attention if you are a devotee of recherché local taste is what wiseacres know as Philly surf 'n' turf: a hot dog and fish cake sandwich. Yup, snugged into a single sturdy roll is a split hot dog (or hot sausage, if you prefer) with a fish cake smooshed right on top of it. We got ours with that ever-rarer local condiment, pepper hash. The hash is wonderful. The fish cake and wiener combo demands more culinary mercy than we can muster.

Located on the Fishtown waterfront, Johnny's has no indoor dining room or tables and chairs. Place your order and pay for it at one window, pick it up at a window a couple of yards to the right, then marshal the meal onto one of the metal counters provided at chest level against the shop's stone block wall and on the pillars in front. When finished—ten, fifteen minutes at most—gather crumbs in the papers in which the food was wrapped, dispose of your refuse in a garbage can, and drive away.

★ JOHN'S ROAST PORK

johnsroastpork.com

14 E. Snyder Ave.   215-463-1951
Philadelphia, PA   B L | $

John's roast pork sandwich is one of Philadelphia's culinary treasures, made from "Pop Pop's original recipe," cooked and boned on premises. The slices of pale, sweet meat are forked from a drippy trough and piled into a superb Carangi Bakery seeded roll, then preferably supplemented by clumps of spinach sautéed in olive oil with plenty of garlic. While the tonic shot of spinach is a welcome addition, we recommend forgoing optional cheese toppings. They detract from the essential piggy pleasure of the pork itself.

John's cheesesteak, ordered from a separate station at the walk-up counter, also is one of the city's best. John Bucci Jr., whose family started the place, explains why he thinks the steaks are so good. "When you order one, there is nothing on the grill. We start clean," he says. "Onions are not precooked; every steak is made for the person who orders it. I am a cheese fanatic. We put five slices on every sandwich, eight if you order extra." There is so much meat in a John's sandwich that the server tears out some of the roll's insides to make room. The onions are sweet, the beef juicy, the cheese abundant, the roll fresh: Is there a better formula for cheesesteak perfection?

John's original customers were shipyard personnel who went home for dinner, so it closes midafternoon. Heavy industry no longer dominates the neighborhood, which has become a Monopoly board of big-box stores, strip malls, and discount warehouses that dwarf the modest sandwich shop and its patio picnic tables. There is no indoor dining; but heat lamps and shutters are set up for cool weather.

LEO'S

leossteaks.com

1403 Chester Pike   610-586-1199
Folcroft, PA   L D | $

A full-sized Leo's cheesesteak is enough for two normal appetites. A half yard of excellent Amoroso Bakery bread is split open and loaded with an incalculable amount of sliced-thin beef that has been sizzled and trowel-cut on the griddle, interlaced with caramelized onions, and saturated with melted cheese. Steaks are available without cheese, as hoagies (meaning lettuce and tomato added), as well as in the configuration known as a pizza steak: with sauce. But there is no improving on the classic configuration, plus a scattering of peppers and pickles to add a bit of sparkle.

Leo's offers no indoor seating. It is a counter where you place your order and can watch the grill man cook it. Picnic tables are provided outside.

LONGACRE'S MODERN DAIRY BAR

longacresicecream.com

1445 PA Route 100   610-845-7551
Barto, PA   B L | $

The rolling land of eastern Pennsylvania, dotted as it is with black-and-white bossies roaming farm fields, is a perfect appetizer for one of Longacre's excellent milk shakes or malts, or an old-fashioned ice cream soda in a tall tulip glass. If you need an ice cream dish that is more substantial, choose a sundae made from your choice of more than a dozen flavors of ice cream and nearly two dozen toppings, including the usual fudge and marshmallow and butterscotch as well as such old-time fountain oddities as wet maple walnuts and crushed cherries. The supreme concoction is known as the Longacre Special Garbage Sundae and features ten scoops of ice cream, ten toppings, whipped cream, and a cherry.

It is also possible to come to Longacre's for a hamburger, a double hamburger, or a California burger (all dressed-up); a hot dog; or a tuna salad sandwich. Side dishes include red beet eggs and mac 'n' cheese.

Longacre's little eating area—a short counter and a handful of booths and tables (plus picnic tables outside)—opens at 7:30 a.m., when customers come for eggs with bacon, ham, or pork roll. But the waitress assured us that it is not uncommon for the doors to open at dawn for customers to order up a cookie-dough sundae or a CMP (chocolate marshmallow peanut sundae) for breakfast. Humankind's fundamental need for excellent ice cream is a craving that cannot be controlled by the hands of a clock.

LORENZO'S PIZZA

lorenzospizza.net

900 Christian St.   215-922-2540
Philadelphia, PA   **L D | $**

Located on a corner near the Italian Market, Lorenzo's is a real neighborhood place with little tourist traffic. Its cheesesteaks are superb, made from frozen sheets of lean meat, which is not really a bad thing—after all, we are not talking about prime beef here. Anyway, the frozen sheets get thrown onto the grill along with a pile of raw onions. As the meat and onions sizzle together, the chef hacks away at them with a spatula, winding up with a hodgepodge of meat and soft-cooked onions. The aromatic combo is shaped into an oval about the length of the Italian bread for which it's destined and infused with molten Cheez Whiz.

The pizza is street food–style, not artisan in any way, available by the whole pie or slice, thin crust or Sicilian. White pies and cheeseless tomato pies frequently are available, as are Stromboli, hoagies, and burgers.

LOU'S

414 E. Main St.   610-279-5415
Norristown, PA   **B L | $**

Lou's is a vintage booth-and-counter sandwich shop that starts serving immense and excellent short-order breakfasts at 5:30 in the morning and offers cheesesteaks and sandwiches of all sorts, with such fine companions as fried hot peppers, cheese fries, and thick milk shakes. It is the place to go if you want to savor a sandwich unique to Norristown: the zep.

The zep is in the hoagie family, but differs from the more familiar Delaware Valley super sandwich in at least a couple of significant ways. For one thing, a zep never includes lettuce. For another, it always is stacked with an abundance of onions. Lou's makes its traditional zep with a couple of slices of mild cheese (provolone is preferred) and cotto salami, a semisoft cold cut that is like lightly seasoned bologna. It also includes slices of tomato, and a sprinkling of oregano, olive oil, salt, and pepper. (A spritz of vinegar or a dollop of peppery relish is an acceptable addition.) In addition to its definitive zep, Lou's offers zeps made with tuna salad, ham, turkey, and even burgers. They all are available in three sizes: on a round roll, on an eight-inch loaf, or on a sixteen-inch loaf. As is true of all proper zeps, the rolls are fresh and chewy and come from Conshohocken Bakery in nearby Conshohocken.

★ MAMA'S

426 Belmont Ave.   610-664-4757
Bala Cynwyd, PA   **L D | $**

Although the cheesesteak was invented in the hubbub of Philadelphia's Italian Market, the best one we've ever eaten is far from the urban core, in the suburb of Bala Cynwyd. In fact, the cheesesteak made at Mama's might be too good. Although the place is a modest pizza parlor and sandwich shop, one local we know contends that Mama's cooking is too masterly and that its refined cheesesteak defies the proletarian nature of a street-food sandwich most commonly made from stringy beef and Cheez Whiz. OK, then, let's call this the übercheesesteak.

Chef Paul Castellucci's beef is thin-sliced, lean, and scarlet, hitting the hot griddle in clumps that get hacked up with a trowel as they brown. He then applies a great mound of what looks like shredded mozzarella but is in fact a proprietary mix that, incredibly, does not stick to the hot iron surface. The beef and cheese are worked over so thoroughly that cheese nearly disappears into the finished product, but its luxury saturates every bite. The onions are not cooked on the grill among the shreds of beef, which is the customary way steak chefs do it. Instead,

Castellucci sautés them separately until they tip from sharp to sweet and crisp to limp. They are added after the loose log of meat and cheese is hoisted from the griddle into the jaws of a length of muscular Italian bread. Long hot peppers, roasted in Mama's pizza oven, add brilliant red and jade green hues as well as hot sparkle to the earthy combo.

Mama's standard cheesesteak weighs a pound and a half. The mini is three-quarters of a pound.

MARRONE'S CAFE

31 W. Main St.   570-276-6407
Girardville, PA   L D | $

Marrone's of Schuylkill County serves its own unique variation of Old Forge pizza. Presented on a thin sheet of paper in a metal pan, it is rectangular with a lightweight crust that is about a half-inch thick and crisp around the edges but chewy-bready toward the middle. Most regular pizza toppings are available in addition to the standard gobs of cheese, and on the side comes a plastic cup full of bright-red, crushed-pepper hot sauce. A plastic spoon is provided to spread the sauce atop the pizza, and it is a brilliant addition. The pizza is mild-mannered; the sauce packs a punch. Beyond pizza, the Italian-American menu includes lasagna that Roadfood.com's Buffetbuster deemed "the best I have had, with a dark, sweet, and chunky sauce."

Marrone's is a seventy-plus-year-old, brick-front tavern where many people come only to drink in the bar next to the dining room. The ideal beverage to accompany its distinctive pizza is locally brewed Yuengling beer, known here in coal country as Pottsville Punch.

ORIGINAL HOT DOG SHOP

theoriginalhotdogshop.com

3901 Forbes Ave.   412-621-7388
Pittsburgh, PA   L D (late night) | $

The Original Hot Dog Shop, aka the O or the Dirty O, has quite a large menu, including pizza, hoagies, fish sandwiches, and hamburgers; but if the name of the place doesn't clue you in to what's good, the view behind the counter will. There on a broad grill are row upon row of hot dogs—pale pink ones barely warm, and darker ones cooked through and ready to be bunned. Regular or all-beef, these are fine franks with a loud meaty flavor, available plain or gooped with cheese or in a "Super" configuration with cheese and bacon, and with a full array of condiments that include ketchup, mustard, relish, onion, pickle, chili, mayo, and kraut.

On the side of whatever hot dog suits your taste, you must get French fries. O fries are legendary, twice-fried to a crisp with clean flavor and a wicked crunch that makes them such a good companion for just about any sandwich. Even a small order is a substantial dish.

Aside from great fast food and post-midnight hours, one reason Pittsburghers are so fond of the Original Hot Dog Shop is that it can trace its heritage back to the Original Famous Sandwich Shop, where the foot-long hot dog was introduced in 1928. Syd Simon, who opened the Original Hot Dog Shop in 1960 (just as the Pirates won the World Series in Forbes Field across the street), worked fifteen years at the old Famous.

PAT'S KING OF STEAKS

patskingofsteaks.com

1237 E. Passyunk   215-468-1546
Philadelphia, PA   Always open
                             (except Thanksgiving and
                             Christmas) | $

—★—
OPEN
24/7 Street-food historians believe that Pat
—★— Olivieri invented the cheesesteak in Philadelphia in 1933. His family continues to operate the restaurant he began, and while aficionados of the cheesesteak enjoy debating the merits of the city's many cheesesteak restaurants there is no denying the absolute authenticity of Pat's sandwich, which is oily, salty, and meaty—in other words, everything nutrition prigs dislike. Thin flaps of less-than-prime beef are sizzled on a grill alongside onions and hefted into a roll (with or without onions), then a trowel of melted Cheez Whiz is dripped on top. Peppers, mushrooms, pizza sauce, and double cheese are all extra-cost

options, and if you wish to dude it up further, there are big glass jars with hot sauce and peppers near the takeout windows.

The combination of plebeian ingredients adds up to something that is certainly not aristocratic but carries a distinction all its own. Side your sandwich with a cup full of cheese fries (more of that melted Whiz), and eat standing on the sidewalk under harsh lights. Observe the splattered hot sauce and dropped French fries crushed underfoot. Listen to the rumble of trucks going past on their way to or from the Italian Market. Smell the mingling of cheap aftershave lotion and fancy fragrances on customers in line—both aromas overwhelmed, as the line approaches the take-out window, by the powerhouse aroma of steak and onions sizzling on a hot grill.

PIZZA PERFECT
pizza-perfect.com

16 Carverton Rd. 570-696-2100
Trucksville, PA **L D | $**

Trucksville is just southwest of Old Forge, Pennsylvania, a fact apparent to any culinary anthropologist who looks at the signature dish of Pizza Perfect. A pizza here is not referred to as a pie; it is a "tray." And it is not divided into slices, but into "cuts." A cut is not a triangle, but a rectangle, and it usually comes heaped with enough ingredients that it looks more like an exuberantly American open-face sandwich than a traditional Neapolitan pizza. The toppings are traditional—pepperoni, sausage, olives, peppers, and the like—and onions always are part of the picture unless you specifically request that they are removed from your order. The pizza is baked in a well-oiled tray that turns the crust crunchy, and while it offers none of the vigorous chew of the southern Italian pizza, it has a unique character all its own.

When Bruce Bilmes and Sue Boyle reviewed Pizza Perfect for Roadfood.com back in 2012, they wrote that it "falls into that beloved sub-genre of Pennsylvania/New York cuisine, the family tavern. It's a bar, all right, but one where the food is upfront. We spied most of the other customers eating their

cuts as part of a multicourse feast that included the likes of wings, fried mushrooms, and sandwiches."

PRIMANTI BROTHERS
primantibros.com

46 W. 18th St. 412-263-2142
Pittsburgh, PA Always open | $

OPEN 24/7 When we first wrote about Primanti Brothers, it was one of a kind. Now with twenty-one locations, including three in Florida, and more on the way, we're hard-pressed to justify its inclusion in a book devoted to unique eateries. Nevertheless, a Primanti's *sandwich* is unique, and while we've never had one anywhere else, we do highly recommend having one in the original eatery in the Strip District of Pittsburgh.

The astonishing sandwiches were designed in the 1930s for truckers who hauled produce to the nearby wholesale market. While their trucks were being unloaded, they dashed over to Primanti Brothers with a big appetite but little time to eat a Dagwood, slaw, and potatoes separately. The solution was to load hot French fries directly into the sandwich atop the customer's meat of choice, then top the fries with Pittsburgh-style (no mayo) coleslaw and a few slices of tomato: an all-in-one meal. The sandwiches are assembled at the grill behind the bar at the speed of light, so when delivered, the fries and grilled meats are still steaming hot, the slaw and tomato cool. The barely hoistable meal is presented wrapped in butcher paper.

ROBERT WHOLEY & CO.
wholey.com

1711 Penn Ave. 412-391-3737
Pittsburgh, PA **L D | $**

Located in Pittsburgh's appetite-inducing Strip District, Robert Wholey & Co. seems more like a culinary amusement park than a mere store. It has a toy train running around and singing mechanical pigs to amuse children and an extensive kitchenware department to amuse recipe-obsessed adults.

Once strictly a wholesale fish market, Wholey now carries a vast inventory of foodstuffs that range from baked ham by the haunch to sides of tuna that are cut into steaks to order. For those of us who demand immediate gratification, there are a few makeshift tables for sit-down meals at the end of a cooked-food line, and more tables upstairs in the Pittsburgh Room. While you can order crab cakes, shrimp, and even chicken, the meal most people come to eat is a fish sandwich on a tender, butter-rich bun. Whiting and cod are both available, the king of sandwiches being the Wholey Whaler: a pound of whiting sizzled crisp in the bubbling fry kettles toward the front. If that's not enough to sate you, simply ask the staff to fry (or broil) as much fish as you want to eat and they will charge you by the pound.

SALERNO'S

139 Moosic Rd.   570-457-2117
Old Forge, PA   **L D** | $$

Salerno's is a tavern where many people come only to drink. We recommend a visit for Old Forge pizza, a style of pie unique to the area around Scranton. An Old Forge pie is squared off rather than round, airy-crusted, and topped with sweet marinara sauce and a mild blend of Italian and American cheese. It's an easy-to-eat pizza, simple and friendly.

At lunch Salerno's serves only red pizza, which is a twelve-slice pie big enough for two healthy appetites. At dinner, the better-known creation is a white pizza—a double-cruster made with a blend of several cheeses between the crusts. BTW, a slice of this pizza is called a cut, and a whole pie is a tray.

There is a broad menu beyond pizza in this neighborhood tavern: spaghetti and meatballs, sausage and peppers, chicken Parmesan sub sandwiches, *pasta e fagiole*. Many customers take their food at the bar, where they can knock back draft beers and watch the wall-mounted TV.

STEVE'S PRINCE OF STEAKS

stevesprinceofsteaks.com
7200 Bustleton Ave.   215-338-0985
Philadelphia, PA   **L D** | $

"The perfect balance of flavors and textures" is how Roadfood.com's Bruce Bilmes and Sue Boyle described the cheesesteak at Steve's Prince of Steaks in northeast Philadelphia. Unlike steak places that chop their meat into hash on the grill, Steve's slices it into flaps and sizzles the pieces in the traditional Italian Market way. The meat is not prime cut, that's for sure, but its flavor is a welcome, oily blast of beefy protein. Combine that with a load of Cheez Whiz and a heap of fried-soft, sweet onions all piled into a chewy tube of fresh bread and you've got a picture of cheesesteak perfection.

Here are the choices you'll need to make when you dine at Steve's: plain steak, cheesesteak, pizza steak (with sauce), or steak hoagie (with lettuce and tomato); normal weight or double-meat. If you choose cheese: American, Whiz, provolone, or mozzarella. Extras? They include pizza sauce, mushrooms, and house-roasted hot red and green peppers. Dill pickles, relish, cherry peppers, yellow peppers, and hot sauce are available as garnishes. The French fry selection features cheese fries and pizza fries. Soft drinks include birch beer; or you can have a chocolate soda, which is nothing but chocolate syrup mixed with seltzer water.

The dining experience is unequivocal street food. Read the menus posted on the wall, place your order at two different windows (one for sandwiches, the other for fries and drinks, each paid for separately), then dine at the easy-wipe silver counter that runs along the wall.

Steve's two other locations are at 2711 Comly Road in Philadelphia (215-677-8020), and 1617 East Lincoln Highway in Langhorne (215-943-4640).

MID-SOUTH

KENTUCKY

WEST VIRGINIA

VIRGINIA

TENNESSEE

NORTH CAROLINA

KENTUCKY

LOUISVILLE
Homemade Ice Cream and Pie Kitchen
Mike Linnig's Place
Nord's

HENDERSON
Mr. D's
Thomason's Barbecue

WAVERLY
★ Peak Bros.

SEBREE
Bell's Drug Store

MARION
Marion Pit

KEVIL
Leigh's Barbecue

PRINCETON
Heaton's

OWENSBORO
Moonlite Bar-B-Q Inn

FRANKFORT

WINCHESTER
Hall's on the River

BLUFF CITY
★ Ridgewood Barbecue

ANTIOCH
Hot Stuff Spicy Chicken and Fish

NASHVILLE
400 Degrees
★ Arnold's Country Kitchen
Bolton's Spicy Chicken & Fish
Ed's Fish & Pizza House
Elliston Place Soda Shop
Loveless Cafe
Pancake Pantry
Pepperfire Spiced Chicken
★ Prince's Hot Chicken Shack
Rotier's
Swett's
TJ's BBQ & Fish

FRANKLIN
Merridee's Breadbasket

BON AQUA
Beacon Light Tea Room

KNOXVILLE
Litton's

MASON
Bozo's Hot Pit BBQ

MEMPHIS
A&R Bar-B-Que
Alcenia's
Bryant's Breakfast
Coletta's
★ Cozy Corner
The Cupboard
Dyer's Burgers
Gus's Fried Chicken
Interstate Barbecue
Leonard's
Little Tea Shop
Payne's
The Rendezvous

GERMANTOWN
Germantown Commissary

CHATTANOOGA
Bluegrass Grill
Nikki's Drive-In
Zarzour's

TENNESSEE

WEST VIRGINIA

VIRGINIA

ORLEAN
Orlean Market

WINCHESTER
Snow White Grill

LINDEN
The Apple House

WARRENTON
★ Red Truck Rural Bakery

WHEELING
★ Coleman's Fish Market

FAIRFAX
Chutzpah

MORGANTOWN
Ruby & Ketchy's

NEW MARTINSVILLE
Quinet's Court

FLINT HILL
24 Crows

ARLINGTON
Weenie Beenie

CHARLOTTESVILLE
Ace Biscuit and Barbecue
Brown's
Preston Avenue Shell
Wayside Take Out & Catering

CLARKSBURG
Julio's Cafe
Oliverio's Cash and Carry
Ritzy Lunch

SPERRYVILLE
Rudy's

NEW MARKET
Southern Kitchen

NITRO
Diehl's Family Restaurant

FULKS RUN
Fulks Run Grocery

WOODBRIDGE
Dixie Bones BBQ

MAPPSVILLE
★ Metompkin Seafood

HUNTINGTON
Stewart's Original Hot Dogs

CHARLESTON

STAUNTON
Mrs. Rowe's
Wright's Dairy-Rite

GORDONSVILLE
Barbeque Exchange

CROZET
Brownsville Shell

FREDERICKSBURG
Goolrick's Pharmacy

NORTH GARDEN
Dr. Ho's Humble Pie

LOVINGSTON
The Chicken Coop

RICHMOND
Sally Bell's Kitchen
Stuart's Fresh Catch

WAKEFIELD
Virginia Diner

EXMORE
Exmore Diner

ROANOKE
Roanoker

ROCKY MOUNT
Franklin Restaurant

CAPE CHARLES
Sting-Ray's

GALAX
Galax Smokehouse

REIDSVILLE
Short Sugar's

NORFOLK
Charlie's Café
Doumar's

MOUNT AIRY
Snappy Lunch

DURHAM
Dame's Chicken & Waffles

WINDSOR
Bunn's Bar-B-Q

STATESVILLE
Jay Bee's

GREENSBORO
Stamey's

RALEIGH

JAMESVILLE
Cypress Grill

CLEVELAND
★ Keaton's

SILER CITY
Brownie-Lu

LEXINGTON
★ Lexington Barbecue #1

GOLDSBORO
Wilber's Barbecue

WILSON
Flo's Kitchen
Parker's

SHELBY
Bridges Barbecue Lodge

CHARLOTTE
Bar B Q King
Bill Spoon's
Lupie's
Nana's Soul Food
Price's Chicken Coop
South 21 Drive-in
Zada Jane's Corner Cafe

AYDEN
Bum's
★ Skylight Inn

GASTONIA
R. O.'s Barbecue

DALLAS
Long Creek Fish Fry

CHAPEL HILL
Allen & Son
Mama Dip's Country Kitchen
Sunrise Biscuit Kitchen

NORTH CAROLINA

KENTUCKY

BELL'S DRUG STORE

bellsdrugstore.wordpress.com

7107 Kentucky Route 56   270-835-7544

Sebree, KY   **L | $**

As we drove into the small town of Sebree on a backroads eating tour in the company of Kentucky-food authority Louis Hatchett, Louis suddenly called out, "Orangeade!" We pulled up at the sturdy old brick-facade building that is Bell's Drug Store. It is a working pharmacy with shelves of patent medicines for sale and a short soda fountain counter up front.

We placed our orangeade orders and then a moment later, the soda jerk turned to us with a tragic look on his face. "We have run out of oranges," he lamented. But there was still a good supply of lemons, so we ordered lemonade made with an extra lemon (50¢ surcharge): what a mighty sweet/tart wallop that delivered! Then there is lemon ice, a Bell Drug specialty: nothing but fresh lemon juice poured over crushed ice and seasoned with a dash of salt. When the mixologist handed it to us, he pointed to a large sugar dispenser that had been filled with salt (and conspicuously so labeled!). "There's more salt if you'd like," he said. To our taste, it was just right as presented, the sprinkle of salinity enriching the pure citrus power.

HALL'S ON THE RIVER

hallsontheriver.com

1225 Athens   859-527-6620

Boonesboro Rd.   **L D | $$**

Winchester, KY

Hall's really is on the river—the Kentucky River—perched high above it, to be precise: a scenic setting for a fine Kentucky meal. The hot brown is a mighty version of the Louisville-ancestored open-face sandwich that includes both turkey and country ham, great gobs of melted cheese, bacon, and a slurry of cream sauce. A seafood version also is available, the toast topped with shrimp and scallops, then sliced tomatoes, cream sauce, and cheese. Strange platefellows, indeed, as the cheese and seafood do not quite harmonize. We'll take the classic version every time.

Another good regional specialty is fried green tomatoes, notable for its truly elegant crust. The crunch and tartness inherent in the tomatoes are well-balanced by a duet of smooth sauces, one of which has a sweet-pepper edge.

From shrimp and grits to frog legs and wedge salad to rib-eye steak, Hall's menu offers something for everyone. The place is perhaps most famous for its beer cheese, a zesty, yeasty spread well suited as an hors d'oeuvre or as the topping for a cheeseburger.

HEATON'S

495 Marion Rd. 270-365-3102
Princeton, KY B L | $

We admit to getting perverse pleasure from dining at a table opposite shelves of motor oil and other automotive necessities. Located in a Marathon service station, Heaton's resembles a thousand other quick-stop, quick-eat mini-marts around rural America. But the barbecue it serves is superb. It is real Kentucky 'cue—in this case pulled pork, served in a sandwich, large or small, as a plate with two side dishes, by the pound, and whole shoulder. It is hickory smoked, rugged-textured, and comes with a fascinating sauce that is slightly sweet with a bright citrus flavor. Ribs also are available, as are breakfast sandwiches and hamburgers.

HOMEMADE ICE CREAM AND PIE KITCHEN

piekitchen.com

2525 Bardstown Rd. 502-459-8184
Louisville, KY $

Because we visit Louisville only for short periods of time, coming to this place is inevitably frustrating. There is no way two people or even five people can sample a significant fraction of the tempting desserts available on any one day. The good news is that nearly every pie and cake is available by the slice, maximizing opportunity to taste the greatest number of things. All the usual suspects are available, from red velvet cake to Key lime pie, and several desserts are little known outside the South: chess pie that is purity itself; hummingbird cake sweet enough to please a nectar-crazed avian, sweet-potato pie, Italian cream cake (a Kentucky favorite), and praline ice cream. In addition to regular chess, which is little more than cream, sugar, and eggs, there are lemon chess and chocolate chess.

Many of the handsome layer cakes come swirled with sweet buttercream icing, but our favorite variety is yellow cake with caramel icing. Or perhaps Georgia cake, which features mandarin oranges and pineapple whipped topping. Among pies, the one not to miss is Dutch apple blanketed with molten caramel.

Note: There are a handful of other locations around Louisville.

LEIGH'S BARBECUE

9405 US Route 60 270-488-3434
Kevil, KY L (closed Weds) | $

Not for barbecue milquetoasts, Leigh's pork packs punch—even before the application of vinegar-pepper sauce. Sandwiches come light, medium, or heavy, referring to the amount of sauce desired. The 'cue itself is of the ridiculously tender sort—cooked in the hickory haze of an open pit for a full twenty-four hours, emerging smoky-sweet the way only long-cooked pork can be. Regulars know to ask for inside or outside pieces, or a mix of both; the pork is chopped when a sandwich is ordered. On the side, you definitely want Leigh's potato salad and maybe baked beans too. Coleslaw is good, in or out of the sandwich.

Opened in 1950 and now in a third generation of the Leigh family, Leigh's is a stark cinder-block bunker by the side of the road just west of Paducah. Seating is at a curved counter, or at the picnic table outside. Note that Leigh's is open only for lunch, and closes when the day's meat supply runs out (sometimes before 2 p.m.).

MARION PIT

728 S. Main St. 270-965-3318
Marion, KY L D | $

Marion Pit, known also as Jack's By the Tracks, has been around nearly four decades, long enough to become a Crittenden County institution. Proprietor Jack Easley said that he usually cooks an especially large number of pork shoulders on Saturday because so many local churches purchase meat by the pound for Sunday suppers. His place is the oldest smokehouse around, and certainly the most unpretentious—a hut on the outskirts of town with a few picnic tables for dining outdoors or inside a screened patio.

Place your order at a window in the small building, to which hickory-cooked shoulders are brought from an adjoining cookhouse and readied for eating. Mr. Easley told us that he cooks his meat for seventeen hours, using no seasonings and no sauce. The long smoke at low temperature results in pork that is unspeakably tender, so soft that it cannot be sliced, because it would fall apart. You can buy it by the pound to go, by the sandwich, or by the plate (billed here as a "big pile of bar-b-q"). It is some of the best Q anywhere, served with a delicious sauce, the recipe for which is known only to Mr. Easley, his wife, and his son.

MIKE LINNIG'S PLACE

mikelinnigsrestaurant.com

9308 Cane Run Rd.   502-937-9888
Louisville, KY   L D (closed Mon) | $$

Mike Linnig's opened some ninety years ago as a fruit and vegetable stand on the Linnig family farm. It is now a big restaurant with beer-garden accommodations outside and cavernous dining rooms indoors. The menu includes just about every kind of seafood that can be fried, including sea scallops, crawfish, and salmon, but its highlights are such heartland fish-camp specialties as catfish, whitefish, and frog legs—all served in immense portions. We are especially fond of the spicy fish nuggets and the freshly breaded shrimp. The frog legs, the scallops, and the oysters have a nice crunch to their crust but are not otherwise memorable.

Onion rings are a specialty. They are big chunky things, extremely brittle, and mostly crust with just a hint of onion flavor emanating from the slick ribbon within. By the way, the tartar sauce and cocktail sauce, while served in the sort of individual cups typical of institutional meals, are Mike Linnig's own recipe, and both are outstanding.

Among the beverage choices are iced tea (sweet or not), lemonade (which tastes a lot like the tea), and genuine Kool-Aid, listed as fruit punch.

MOONLITE BAR-B-Q INN

moonlite.com

2840 W. Parrish Ave.   270-684-8143
Owensboro, KY   L D | $$

There is a printed menu of dinners and sandwiches at the Moonlite Bar-B-Q, but nearly everyone who isn't crippled avails themselves of a spectacular buffet that occupies one large room with salads and desserts on one side, vegetables and meats on the other. There are barbecued chicken, ribs, pulled pork,

spectacularly succulent beef brisket, and even a pan of non-barbecued sliced country ham that is firm and salty, as well as a tray of ready-made ham biscuits. And there is western Kentucky's favorite barbecue meat, mutton. Cooked until pot-roast tender, it is set out on the buffet two ways: chopped or pulled. Chopped mutton is pulverized to nothing but flavor: tangy lamb and woodsmoke in a bold duet. The pulled version is a textural amusement park—rugged and chunky with a lot of hard outside crust among soft, juicy chunks of interior meat. Apply your own sauce at the table from the pitchers the waitress brings. One is a dark orange emulsion with gentle vinegar-tomato zest; the other is known as "mutton dip," an unctuous gravy that is used to baste the mutton as it cooks. For those who need heat, Moonlite also supplies bottles of "Very Hot Sauce," which is brilliantly peppered and will set your lips and tongue aglow.

An impressive deployment of vegetables: cheesy broccoli casserole, creamed corn niblets, and butter-drizzled mashed potatoes, plus the western Kentucky soup/stew of mutton and vegetables known as burgoo (pronounced BUR-goo). Other notable sides: crusty corn muffins, mac 'n' cheese, baked apples, and ham and beans. We also sampled a silly but intriguing banana salad made with Miracle Whip and chopped nuts, plus a couple of tables of terrific Kentucky pies. On Thursday and Friday nights, shrimp and catfish are added to the buffet.

MR. D'S

1435 S. Green St.   270-826-2505
Henderson, KY   L D | $

A fiberglass chicken as tall as a grizzly bear stands outside of Mr. D's, beckoning customers to drive in. While Mr. D's is a full-menu drive-in with a repertoire of hamburgers, hot dogs, and sandwiches, the chicken rules. It is made from a recipe popularized decades ago by a legendary chicken man named Colonel Jim, and has a wickedly crunchy crust spicy enough to make your eyes water.

Because Mr. D's is a quick-service drive-in with car-service only, the chicken you order will be delivered to your window in five minutes or less, meaning that the kitchen cooks it ahead of time rather than to order. This is good if you are really, really hungry, but not so good if you are a crisp-skin connoisseur, because the crust loses its crunch. Make no mistake: This is four-star fried chicken, and puts just about any non-Kentucky fried chicken to shame. But the next time we order some, we are going to do as Henderson tipster Louis Hatchett IV advises: request that it be cooked to order. If that twenty-minute wait means crust that cracks when bitten, we'll happily endure it.

NORD'S

nordsbakery.biz

2118 S. Preston St.   502-634-0931
Louisville, KY   **B | $**

Nord's is a full-service bakery with a vast menu of pastries that will send sweets fanciers into orbit. Among the highlights are iced sugar cookies in the shape of Kentucky, long johns frosted with maple spread and topped with crisp bacon, donuts shaped like pretzels, glazed bear claws, knobby apple fritters, plump Boston creams filled with luxurious custard, and ooey-gooey cinnamon-veined pecan rolls. Even if you are not a buttercream fan, we suggest you try at least one cream puff filled and topped with buttercream. The word "buttercream" attains full meaning here, as that's what the stuff tastes like: butter and cream (and just enough sugar).

While most business is takeout, there are a handful of tables up a flight of stairs in back. A sign posted above the little dining area proclaims, "It's all good!" Amen to that.

★ PEAK BROS.

6353 US Hwy. 60   270-389-0267
Waverly, KY   **L D | $**

Peak Bros., which had become a legend among western Kentucky barbecue parlors since it opened in 1948, burned down in 2006. It has been rebuilt and is as good as ever. Originally guided here by Kentucky tipster Louis Hatchett, who referred to Waverly as "the western edge of barbecued muttonland," we began our Peak Bros. love affair with chipped mutton sandwiches. Chipping, a local term for intensive chopping, turns the meat into a hash sopped with the potent natural gravy known as dip.

Debbie Britt, whose father and uncle started the restaurant, assured us that chipped is good, but sliced is even better. At her urging, we got some slices and they were really good, although our preference is chipped. Peak Bros.' ham, edged with pepper, was a sweet harmony of pork and smoke, luxuriously tender; the sliced mutton was moist and mellow with none of the rank bite typical of mature lamb elsewhere.

Come November, Peak Bros. becomes a favorite source among locals and fans from around the country for Thanksgiving and Christmas hams. They are sweet and smoky with a hugely savory blackened crust all around their vast lode of pink meat. Lady Bird Johnson once declared Peak Bros.' ham to be the best "this side of Texas."

THOMASON'S BARBECUE

701 Atkinson St.   270-826-0654
Henderson, KY   **L D | $**

Thomason's barbecued beans are magnificent—rich and smoky, laced with shreds of meat and so vividly spiced that they taste like Kentucky Christmas. The barbecue itself is worth a trip too.

Thomason's barbecues everything: pork, mutton, beef, spare ribs, baby-back ribs, chicken, ham, and turkey. You can get your choice of meat on a plate, which includes pickle, onion, bread, and beans; on a tray, which includes only pickle, onion, and bread; or in a sandwich. Like all other sandwiches in this area, Thomason's can scarcely be picked up by hand because juice from the meat saturates the lower piece of bread, causing it to disintegrate. The pork is velvet-soft, moist, and seductively smoky; the mutton is sopped with gravy and gentle-flavored.

A simple, freestanding eatery with an order counter and a scattering of tables, Thomason's does a big carry-out business, selling its specialties by the pound and gallon. On a shelf below the order counter are for-sale bottles of dip, which is a sauce with natural "au jus" character.

NORTH CAROLINA

ALLEN & SON

6203 Millhouse Rd.   919-942-7576

Chapel Hill, NC   **L D | $**

Cinder-block walls, plastic tablecloths, and pork slow-smoked over hickory coals: Here is a consummate North Carolina barbecue parlor. Sandwiches are available, but we recommend getting Allen's meat on a plate, which includes a pile of sparkling coleslaw and about a half-dozen spherical, crisp-skinned hush puppies. Meat is served just barely moistened with sauce, but you can boldface it with further applications of Allen & Son's butter-rich, vinegar-based hot sauce loaded with spice and cracked pepper.

If you get the combination plate known to some locals as "stew and que" (highly recommended), the pile of good smoked meat is supplemented by a bowl of Brunswick stew, another traditional companion to smoked pork in these parts. Unlike the meatier Brunswick stews of southern Virginia, this luscious stuff is mostly vegetables with a few shreds of meat, all cosseted in a tomato-rich sauce. It is a hearty, rib-sticking food that makes a wonderful contrast to the exquisite pork. On the side: sweet, sweet tea.

BAR B Q KING

barbqking.com

2900 Wilkinson Blvd.   704-399-8344

Charlotte, NC   **L D | $**

Bar B Q King is an American drive-in par excellence, complete with a vintage "Servus-Fone" ordering system whereby you study the menu, then press a button to speak with the kitchen, and place your order. Meals are brought to the car on blue plastic trays.

Our first visit, we made the mistake of asking for a "pork sandwich." What we got was a perch sandwich. We ate it anyway, and it was marvelous—moist, sweet white meat so satisfying it reminded us of the best pork, but encased in a golden crust. In fact, the perch was so good, we subsequently ordered trout, shrimp, and oysters—all fried in that only-in-the-South soulful way that's guaranteed to convert even a diehard fish frowner.

What we learned from our experience—other than to recommend BBQK as a fried-fish restaurant—is that if you want smoked pork hereabouts, you don't say "pork"; you say "barbecue." Of course it is pork, available sliced or minced, and it too is a winner—tender, succulent, veiled in a vinegar sauce that does not overwhelm the meat's fundamental fineness and always paired with a layer of coleslaw in the bun. Fried chicken also is barbecued: first fried, then quickly dipped in hot sauce long enough to get hot, but not so long that it doesn't stay crisp.

BILL SPOON'S

spoonsbarbecue.com

5524 South Blvd.   704-525-8865
Charlotte, NC   L (closed Sun) | $

A sign on the front of Bill Spoon's announces, "We've cooked the whole pig since 1963." That's no lie. As swell as slow-smoke-cooked shoulders and butts may be, they cannot match the rousing diversity of hacked-up whole hog, from creamy to crunchy, which you can have here with a couple of side dishes or packed into a bun and crowned with bright mustard slaw.

Spoon's Brunswick stew is so dense with meat and vegetables that you can clean the bowl using only a fork, and tubular hush puppies with vivid onion punch provide a cornmeal counterpoint to the spice of barbecue or barbecue-laced beans. If there is a pork frowner at your table, Spoon's chicken, cooked ultra-tender and encased in succulent skin, is a fine alternative.

To drink: sweet tea, refilled approximately every ninety seconds by roving waitstaff. For dessert: banana pudding. It all adds up to an archetypal barbecue meal, just what you'd hope for in a place that's built a grand reputation pit-cooking pig since 1963. Founder Bill Spoon learned the barbecue trade from John Skinner, who learned his craft at North Carolina's first sit-down barbecue restaurant, opened by Bob Melton in Rocky Mount in 1924.

BRIDGES BARBECUE LODGE

bridgesbbq.com

2000 E. Dixon Blvd.   704-482-8567
Shelby, NC   L D (closed Mon & Tues) | $

--★--
LOCALS
LOVE IT
--★--
Bridges has no written menu, just the slip of paper used by the waitress to take orders: sandwich, tray, or plate. A tray is barbecue and barbecue slaw; a plate also holds French fries, lettuce, tomato, and pickle. Both are accompanied by hush puppies, and whether you select sandwich, tray, or plate, you must decide if you want your meat (pork shoulder) minced, chopped, or sliced. It is a major decision, for they are almost like three different foods. Bridges is one of the few places that offers minced barbecue, an old-time configuration from traditional pig-pickin's. It is pulverized into moist hash with some little shreds of darkened, chewy crust among the distressed pork. The mound is held together by a good portion of uniquely North Carolinian sauce with a strong vinegar punch. Chopped is the more typical way modern North Carolinians like it—chunky and easily chewable, and with only a smidgen of sauce. Sliced barbecue comes as big, soft flaps. With the pork comes a Styrofoam cup of warm sauce for dipping.

Tubular hush puppies, some of the best in the South, sport a sandy-textured crust and creamy insides. Bridges' slaw is *barbecue* slaw, meaning finely chopped cabbage bound together with—what else?—barbecue sauce! It's got a brilliant flavor and a pearly-red color that handsomely complements your pork of choice. The small tray, by the way, is only about three by five inches and an inch and a half deep, but it is astounding how much meat and slaw get packed into it.

Bridges' dining room is plain and soothing, with the kind of meditative atmosphere unique to the finest pork parlors of the Mid-South. Square wooden chandeliers cast soft light over green-upholstered booths and a short counter up front where single diners chat quietly among themselves as they sip buttermilk or iced tea and fork into barbecue. During our first meal here, five police officers with gleaming nickel-plated pistols occupied a table toward the back. Even they spoke in hushed tones, as if it would be sacrilegious to be raucous in this decent eat place.

BROWNIE-LU

919 N. 2nd Ave.   919-663-3913
Siler City, NC   B L D | $

Brownie-Lu, which opened in 1960, earned the Golden Chicken Award from the Broaster Company, which makes equipment that simultaneously fries and pressure cooks the bird. The result is meat so tender that it barely clings to the bone, encased in crunchy-brittle skin. It has a full but mellow flavor, like something an ideal grandma might make. At Brownie-Lu, a counter-and-booth diner loved by locals, it is served with such laudable side dishes as black-eyed peas, genuine mashed potatoes, and butter beans cooked with ham. There are enough good vegetables on the menu that a health-food type could come here and have a totally meatless, delicious meal. A full breakfast is served—country ham is a must— and lunch and supper demand a slice from one of the kitchen's homemade cream pies.

BUM'S

bumsrestaurant.com

566 3rd St.   252-746-6880
Ayden, NC   **B L | $**

Many people think of Bum's as a barbecue restaurant, and that in itself is a high compliment, considering its "competition" in Ayden is the Skylight Inn (p. 136), which any sane person must agree is one of the best barbecue restaurants on Planet Earth. Some others think of it as a chicken restaurant. You'll wait a good twenty minutes for the bird to fry, but the reward for your patience is crisp-crusted chicken on a par with North Carolina's finest. We love Bum's most for its vegetables and side dishes.

It's a small torture to go through the cafeteria line and have to choose among corn sticks, corn bread, porky boiled cabbage, pieces of crisp pork skin, butter beans, and collard greens. The last, those greens, are actually grown by proprietor Latham "Bum" Dennis in his home garden (Ayden is the collard capital of the world), and they are cooked to a point of supreme tenderness. There are a few desserts from which to choose; warm banana pudding is the one not to be missed.

Breakfast features excellent biscuits (with or without gravy) and a choice of pig meats that includes homemade sausage, pork tenderloin, and fried ham.

BUNN'S BAR-B-Q

127 N. King St.   252-794-2274
Windsor, NC   **L | $**

Bunn's building started life in the mid-1800s as a doctor's office. It became a filling station in 1900, and in 1938 barbecue was added to the menu. There's still an old Texaco pump outside, and the place is decorated with vintage signs, ads, and ephemera. The atmosphere is vaguely similar to what the Cracker Barrel chain aims to create; but in this case, it is real.

You eat pork, with or without Brunswick stew, accompanied by crisp, fresh coleslaw. The pork is chopped ultra-fine, a mix of soft white meat from the inside of the shoulder laced with chewy brown bark from its surface. It comes ever-so-lightly sauced with what the locals like: vinegar and spice; but if you want it moister or hotter, other sauces are provided. Each plate is topped with a square of thin, unctuous corn bread that has a serious chew and is the ideal medium for pushing around Brunswick stew on the plate. Two slices of this corn bread stand in for normal bread on Bunn's barbecue sandwich, which also contains a measure of slaw.

CYPRESS GRILL

1520 Stewart St.   252-792-4175
Jamesville, NC   **D** (Jan-Apr) | **$$**

For those of us who grew up thinking of herring as a pickled hors d'oeuvre, North Carolina river herring is a shock. For one thing, it looks like a fish. Second, it tastes like fish, not the least bit like chicken or anything else. There is no better place to get to know it than at the Cypress Grill on the banks of the Roanoke River. Here is the last of the old-time herring shacks, quite literally a cypress wood shack, open only for the herring run, mid-January through April. (In recent years, even in those months, herring depopulation has sometimes meant a no-herring menu early in the year.)

There is no meal on the Cypress Grill menu other than fish. Other than herring, you can have rock (striped bass), perch, flounder, shrimp, oysters, devil crab, clam strips, trout fillet, or catfish fillet. Side dishes include a choice of vegetables, which are fine but not particularly interesting: boiled potatoes, fried okra, or slaw.

The herring are served with their heads lopped off, each one's flesh scored with notches and veiled in the thinnest possible sheath of cornmeal, so that when it was tossed into the boiling oil, it cooked quickly deep down to the bone. The big issue among river herring lovers is degree of doneness. Some ask for it sunny-side up, meaning minimal immersion in the fry kettle, resulting in a fish from which you can peel away the skin and lift moist pieces of meat off the bones. The opposite way to go is to ask for your herring cremated: fried until hard and crunchy and so well cooked that all the little bones have become indistinguishable from the flesh around them. The meat itself is transformed, its weight lightened so the natural oiliness is gone, but the flavor has become even more intense. The crust and the interior are melded, and they break off in unbelievably savory bite-sized pieces, finally leaving nothing but a herring backbone on the plate.

While herring-crazed patrons fill up on four, five, six, or more of the plush fish, we advise first-time visitors to the Cypress Grill to leave appetite for dessert. That's the one non-fish item on the menu worth singing about. Every morning, proprietors Leslie and Sally Gardner make pies. When we stopped to visit one day around 10 a.m., Mr. Gardner led us right over to the pie case—a wooden cupboard built by a neighbor to be so sturdy, he says, "you could dance on it." He insisted we feel the bottom of a pie pan, still nearly too hot to touch. We sat down then and there and forked up a piece of chocolate pie that was modest-sized but intensely fudgy.

DAME'S CHICKEN & WAFFLES
dameschickenwaffles.com

317 W. Main St.	919-682-9235
Durham, NC	**L D** | **$**

Thanks to Roadfood.com correspondent Jim Pfefferle for tipping us off to this excellent eatery in Durham (with another location in Greensboro). Jim declared that Dame's was his favorite chicken and waffle restaurant, for all sorts of reasons. First, the chicken is perfectly spiced, crisp-crusted, and juicy. Waffles are Belgian size but fluffy and refined, head and shoulders above the typical doughy ones; they come plain or gingerbread flavored, with blueberries or sweet potatoes mixed into the batter. The coup de grace is a schmear of flavored butter that accompanies every configuration—peach-apricot, vanilla-almond, orange-honeycomb, maple-pecan, or chocolate-hazelnut.

Dame's virtues extend beyond chicken and waffles to include pan-seared salmon, shrimp and grits, and a few salads, plus outstanding side dishes that include vigorously spiced greens and ultrarich triple mac 'n' cheese.

Crowded and celebratory, Dame's enthusiastically carries on its mission of upholding culinary and cultural tradition. Expect classic jazz on the sound system and on-the-ball waitstaff. Also expect to wait quite some time for a table. Dame's enjoys well-deserved popularity.

FLO'S KITCHEN

1015 Goldsboro St. S.	252-237-9146
Wilson, NC	**B** (closes at noon; closed Sun & Mon) | **$**

If you are hungry on the north–south interstate or meandering around the Coastal Plain in North Carolina, head to Flo's for southern-biscuit breakfasts at bargain prices in a decades-old café. Prepare to play virtual bumper cars with other vehicles in the lot, some of which are aiming for the drive-through window, others for a parking spot. Once inside, you might feel claustrophobic, for Flo's is small and always crowded. But oh, the biscuits! They're mighty catheads—big and gnarled, good and buttery, and substantial with nothing added, but even more rewarding when split to sandwich egg and cheese, pork tenderloin or country ham, or a big slab of wicked-good fatback. Biscuits are pretty much the menu, with side dishes limited to hash browns, grits, or a cup of molasses.

JAY BEE'S

320 Mocksville Hwy.   704-872-8033
Statesville, NC   **L D** (closed Sun) | **$**

The brash personality of this drive-through (or dine-in) eat place is hard to resist. "This Ain't No Fast Food Joint!" a sign outside brags. "We Proudly Make All Our Menu Items to Order and It Takes a Little More Time." That would be about a three-minute wait until you are presented with a bacon-Cheddar dog, a Northerner's Fancy with sauerkraut and mustard, or a Prairie Dog topped with barbecue sauce, chopped onions, and melted cheese. They come all-beef or not, in regular and foot-long sizes. You can also get a double—two in one bun. Hamburgers are less impressive, although their institutional blandness is overcome by adding sautéed onions to the package.

The beverage menu ranges from sweet tea and milk shakes to Dr Pepper and Mountain Dew, and if you dine inside, a refill of any soda is free. Don't tell former Mayor Bloomberg of New York, but thirty-two-ounce drinks are available at the drive-through window.

★ KEATON'S

keatonsoriginalbbq.com
17365 Cool Springs Rd.   704-278-1619
Cleveland, NC   **L** (Tues & Weds);
                           L D (Thurs–Sat) | **$**

A cinder-block bunker in North Carolina cattle land between the High Country's natural beauty and High Point's unnaturally low-priced furniture outlets, Keaton's serves some of the best fried chicken you ever will eat.

Step up to the counter and order an upper or a lower (the polite country terms for breast and wing or thigh and drumstick). Pick side dishes from a soulful repertoire of mac 'n' cheese, baked beans, hot-sauce slaw, or white-mayo slaw; choose iced tea (sweet, of course) or beer; then go to your assigned table or booth, to which a waitress brings the food.

In Keaton's kitchen, the chicken is peppered and salted, floured and fried, at which point it is simply excellent country-style, pan-cooked chicken. Then comes the distinctive extra step: just-fried pieces are immersed in a bubbling vat of secret-formula red sauce, a high-spiced, opaque potion similar to what graces High Country barbecued pork. This process takes only seconds, but the throbbing sauce permeates to the bone. You eat this chicken with your hands, pulling off crisp strips of sauce-glazed skin, worrying every joint to suck out all the flavor you can get.

★ LEXINGTON BARBECUE #1

lexbbq.com
100 Smokehouse Lane   336-249-9814
Lexington, NC   **L D** | **$**

"Monk's Place," as locals know it (in deference to founder Wayne "Honey" Monk), looks like a barn with six smelters attached to the back. From their tall chimneys issues the scent of burning hickory and oak wood and slow-cooking pork, one of the most appetite-arousing perfumes in the world. Honey Monk's is a straightforward eatery with booths and tables and carhop service in the parking lot. Much business is takeout.

There are no complicated techniques or deep secrets about Lexington Barbecue. After about ten hours basking in smoke, pork shoulders get chopped into a hash of pieces that vary from melting soft (from the inside) to chewy (from the "bark," or exterior). Nothing like pyrotechnic barbecue of the Midwest or balls-out beef from the pits of Texas, this is subtle stuff, a graceful duet of pork and smoke, full appreciation of which demands a well-honed palate. The meat is served on a bun with finely chopped coleslaw or as part of a platter, on which it occupies half a small yellow cardboard boat, with slaw in the other half. Like the meat, the slaw is flavored with a vinegar/sweet red barbecue sauce. As part of the platter you get terrific, crunch-crusted hush puppies. For dessert, there's peach cobbler and, on rare occasions, berry cobbler too. Cheerwine is available on draught.

LONG CREEK FISH FRY

1301 Lower Dallas Hwy.   704-922-3998
Dallas, NC   **L D** (closed Mon & Tues) | **$**

If you are only a little bit hungry, go somewhere else. Long Creek Fish Fry is all about eating large, even if you order the "small" plates that are available for most entrees. But it's not just quantity that marks this out-of-the-way fish camp as a worthy destination. It is simple and delicious food. Since the mid-twentieth century, Long Creek has drawn crowds of locals—very large crowds on weekends—for its crisp-crusted fried catfish (whole or filleted), green shrimp (small and crunchy), oysters, and salt-and-pepper flounder, accompanied by French fries or onion rings, tubular hush puppies, slaw, and sweet iced tea. Tartar sauce that comes alongside is bright and pickly.

Dining is fish-camp casual. Find a place to park, maybe along the road. Dine off disposable dishware at unclothed tables.

LUPIE'S

2718 Monroe Rd.   704-374-1232
Charlotte, NC   **L D** | **$**

LOCALS LOVE IT Lupie's is the sort of place locals love but outsiders seldom discover. It's been part of the Elizabeth neighborhood since 1987, and it has unvarnished charm that is increasingly rare in a world of corporate restaurants. Prices are in the single-digit range. Sweet tea is served in mason jars. Décor includes odes to Elvis as well as portraits of the waitstaff from years past. Lupie's isn't just a restaurant; it is a part of its community.

Much of the food is true South. The four-vegetable plate is a meat-and-three benchmark. We had one with painfully tender discs of yellow squash and sweet onions, green beans (non-canned, well cooked) saturated by waves of pork flavor, large hunks of carrot sweetened with brown sugar, and super-cheesy mac 'n' cheese. On the side came a square of corn bread. The menu lists three kinds of chili: Texas, vegetarian, and Cincinnati-style. We've enjoyed them all. Burgers too are beautiful: thick and craggy, all the better to hold massive quantities of melted Cheddar cheese. You get your choice of Kaiser or onion roll, potato chips or coleslaw.

For dessert, we've yet to go beyond banana pudding, which is thick with crumbled vanilla wafers. One portion will feed two or three.

MAMA DIP'S COUNTRY KITCHEN

mamadips.com
408 W. Rosemary St.   919-942-5837
Chapel Hill, NC   **B L D** | **$$**

"Mama Dip" is Mildred Council, founder/owner/chef at Chapel Hill's beloved soul-food restaurant. Ms. Council, nicknamed "Dip" by her siblings because she was tall with long arms that enabled her to dip water from the very bottom of the rain barrel, wrote *Mama Dip's Kitchen* in 1999, a valuable cookbook that includes many of the restaurant's recipes.

Three meals a day are served in Dip's nouveau rustic quarters. Lunch and dinner offer great southern classics—fried chicken, chitlins, Brunswick stew; at breakfast, you can't go wrong with eggs, pork chops and gravy, and regular or sweet-potato biscuits. The morning menu also includes trout fillets, whole catfish, and fried salmon cakes.

Later in the day, what we like best about Dip's meals, aside from the lumpy, crunchy, brightly salty crust of the fried chicken, are the vegetables. The daily list includes long-cooked greens, black-eyed peas, crunchy nuggets of fried okra, mashed potatoes and gravy, porky string beans, okra stew with tomatoes, corn-dotted coleslaw, always a sumptuous vegetable casserole, and cool sweet-potato salad. For mopping and dipping, there are buttermilk biscuits, corn bread, and yeast rolls.

NANA'S SOUL FOOD

nanassoulfoodkitchen.com

2908 Oak Lake Blvd.   704-357-3700
Charlotte, NC   **L D** | **$**

Nana's was named for the proprietor's grandmother, but it looks nothing like grandma's house. Packed into a strip mall among such soulless franchised eateries as Jersey Mike's and Hibachi Express, it evidences no charm from the outside, and the interior is squeaky-clean to the point of sterility. The food you eat here, however, tells another story. It is extremely grandmotherly—that is, if grandmother happened to be an excellent African American cook who specialized in classic soul food.

Dark-meat fried chicken is luscious; even the big white breasts, which do tend to be on the dry side, are saved by a thick coat of chewy-crisp, bacon-rich skin that is itself worth the price of admission. If you are anti-fried, there is moist baked chicken and smothered chicken, curried chicken, chicken Alfredo (Thursdays only), and barbecued chicken. Don't like chicken? Have meat loaf, pork chops, fried catfish, or tilapia.

Do pay attention to vegetables. Or even skip the main course and have nothing but vegetables and side dishes, for these are dandy. Collard greens are spicy-sweet, painfully tender, bracing; lima beans are soft and silky and sopped with piggy liquor from the pot; curried rice is dirty rice of the best sort, laced with meat and packed with flavor; mac 'n' cheese is as rich as butter with just enough tang to make every forkful slightly exciting.

Food is obtained by standing in a cafeteria line and telling the servers what you want. This can be a problem, since much of what's available is kept in serving trays with covers, preventing you from seeing it all. The staff is more than willing to lift the covers to show you anything, and to describe it as well, but the visual experience of going through the line—so much fun at cafeterias where everything is out in the open—does little to prepare you for the deliciousness of what finally winds up on your Styrofoam plate.

PARKER'S

2514 Hwy. 301 S.   252-237-0972
Wilson, NC   **L D** | **$**

Parker's goes back to the 1940s when Wilson was the place tobacco farmers sold their crop. A big barbecue meal was how they celebrated the harvest; buyers ate here and spread the word up and down Highway 301, which was the main north-south road prior to I-95. Still, the interstate is only seven miles away, making Parker's an extremely convenient stop.

It is a spacious eating facility with multiple dining rooms. Customers crowd the lined-up tables for family-style combo platters of chopped pork, fried chicken, Brunswick stew, boiled potatoes, corn sticks, and sweet coleslaw with a mustard tinge. Cooked in hardwood smoke and chopped into hash, the pork is moist and scarcely sauced. If you do want to doll it up, tables are set with plain vinegar and a hot sauce that has a vinegar base. As for the Parker's chicken, we like it even better than the pork. Its brittle crust encloses juice-dripping meat, the dark pieces especially luscious. Family-style dinners, including all-you-can-eat barbecue, two pieces of fried chicken per customer, and all the fixins are available for under $10 per person.

From the moment it opens each day, Parker's always seems to bustle. As you enter, it's an adventure maneuvering your way to a table as waiters zoom past toting platters piled high with food.

PRICE'S CHICKEN COOP

priceschickencoop.com

1614 Camden Rd.   704-333-9866
Charlotte, NC   **L D** (takeout only) | **$**

Once inside the door of this little South End storefront, two-thirds of which is dedicated to cooking and one-third to ordering (no dining facilities), you pick your place in one of six or seven lines leading to a counter with three cash registers, each of which is flanked by white-uniformed servers. The cinderblock room thunders with kitchen clatter undershot by the syncopation of bubbling oil, and everything happens double-fast.

Order a quarter or half, white or dark, wings, gizzards, or livers, and it will all be assembled by the time you draw your wallet. Box of chicken in hand, you exit and find a place to eat: back at work, in your car, or on the pleasant grassy berm of the light rail line across the street.

Amenities are minimal, but the fried chicken is maximal. There is nothing dramatically unusual about it. It is cooked in peanut oil, and while brothers Steve and Andrew Price keep their seasonings a secret, it is not spice that makes it unforgettable. What's so great is the surfeit of crunchy skin imbued with the silky goodness of chicken fat. The skin is substantially chewy and you can hear its juices when you apply your teeth to it—just before it dissolves into a flood of chicken flavor on your tongue. Expectedly, the meat of the dark parts oozes savory juice. Not so predictably, even the breasts are moist and big-flavored in a way that white meat seldom is.

We love the express guarantee on Price's menu: ALL FOOD GUARANTEED SATISFACTORY.

R.O.'S BARBECUE
rosbbq.com

1318 Gaston Ave.	704-866-8143
Gastonia, NC	L D (closed Sun) | $

Barbecue slaw, which amends the familiar chopped-cabbage salad with sauce, is a big deal in this part of North Carolina, but nowhere is it more important than at R.O.'s. Billed on the menu as a "sauce, slaw & dip," the soupy emulsion is so significant a presence in the kitchen's repertoire that some customers come for a slaw sandwich—a broad, well-toasted bun filled with a thick layer of the stuff and no meat whatsoever. R.O.'s sauce is a shade darker than coral pink, reminiscent of thousand island dressing (but only vaguely), pickly sweet with enough cayenne pepper to rouse taste buds to full attention. Is there a hint of pimento cheese in it?

R.O.'s slaw is bought by customers not only to accompany barbecue or to eat solo but also as an ingredient in meat loaf, a sauce for cocktail shrimp, as a hamburger condiment, and a dip for chips or crudités. The recipe dates back to 1946 when Robert Ozy Black opened his barbecue restaurant and made his wife Pearl's specialty condiment part of the menu.

It is at its best in concert with R.O.'s barbecued pork, which is some of the best anywhere. Cooked the old-fashioned way with hickory smoke, the pale meat is creamy and rich and so moist that even the extraordinary sauce seems unnecessary. The pork is available sliced or chopped; the latter is more fun, although the slices are tenderness incarnate.

Ice tea and soda are sold in sixteen-, twenty-four-, and thirty-two-ounce tumblers, but if you really want to go local, have the R.O.'s specialty, Cherry-Lemon Sun Drop. It's something like a cross between Mountain Dew and Hawaiian Punch.

Aside from good food and drink, R.O.'s is memorable because it is such a nicely weathered place. It is casual to the extreme—what Yankees would call "eat in the rough": order at the counter and fetch your own tray when your number is called. But the dining room to which you take the tray (after stocking up on napkins at a service bar) is quite civilized. Décor includes potted plants, wallpaper of which a Victorian grandmother would approve, and a hushed, reverent room tone that is the mark of so many great barbecue parlors.

SHORT SUGAR'S
shortsugars.com

1328 S. Scales St.	336-342-7487
Reidsville, NC	B L D | $

At the tap of a horn, carhop service is still available at Short Sugar's, which opened as a hamburger joint in 1949. It now serves three meals a day, and the menu is vast, including breakfast, sandwiches, and a burger roster with a "teenage burger" (a double cheeseburger). Chili dogs are raunchy little things topped with chili so fine that it is more paste than hash. Barbecue is the featured attraction, a point that is obvious if you walk in the door that leads to the takeout counter, for here you have a view of quarter hogs on the grate, soon to be chopped and served on a plate (with fries, slaw, and hush puppies), on a tray (with just slaw and hush puppies), or as a sandwich. The meat is sweeter than most, due to Short Sugar's fascinating sauce, which is mixed in and also available on the table if you want more. The slaw is brilliant, fresh as can be, and the hush puppies provide a welcome crunchy counterpoint for the tender pork. Our only disappointment was a bland ham biscuit.

A big restaurant with a long counter, booths, and tables, Short Sugar's has the patina of a place that has been around many decades. Most of the clientele are regulars, but the staff treats strangers as welcome guests.

★ SKYLIGHT INN
skylightinnbbq.com

4618 S. Lee St.   252-746-4113
Ayden, NC   **L D** (closed Sun) | **$**

Hickory-smoked, whole-hog barbecue, unaffected by time or trends, has made the Skylight Inn a legend. Unlike pyrotechnical kick-ass Q's, Skylight's marriage of smoke and pork is a subtle nuptial, elegantly abetted by the addition of a little vinegar and Texas Pete hot sauce, salt and pepper—nothing more—as it is chopped with cleavers on a hard-rock maple cutting board. Beyond exquisite flavor, what is most striking about whole-hog barbecue is the texture. Along with soft shreds from the interior are chewy strips from the outside as well as shockingly crunchy nuggets of skin. The cooked skin conveys terabytes of lusciousness, its firmness adding drama that is lacking in barbecue made only from upscale hams or shoulders. Any sauce beyond the vinegar and Texas Pete is anathema. There are two and only two ways to have meat at the Skylight Inn: in a cardboard tray or on a bun. Other than a tile of unleavened corn bread and some coleslaw, there is nothing else on the menu.

Sandwiches are a twentieth-century addition to the Jones family repertoire, but their pairing of barbecue and corn bread goes back to 1830 when ancestor Skilton M. Dennis, who cooked whole hogs in pits dug in the ground, brought some of the meat to sell at a nearby Baptist convention. "As far as we know, that was the first time barbecue was served to the public in North Carolina," says Samuel Jones, Dennis's seventh-generation descendant, who operates the Skylight Inn along with his father, Bruce. Sam is the grandson of Pete Jones, the longtime pitmaster who started in the business with his uncle, Emmett Dennis, when he was six years old. Pete built the current Skylight Inn in 1947, and in 1988 he put a jumbo replica of the Capitol Dome atop the building after a journalist declared his place the Barbecue Capital of America.

SNAPPY LUNCH
thesnappylunch.com

125 N. Main St.   336-786-4931
Mount Airy, NC   **B L** (closed Sun) | **$**

As Yankees, we'd never heard of a pork-chop sandwich until we traveled south. Even in Dixie, it is not all that common. One of the very best is the boneless beauty at Snappy Lunch. It is a broad slab of meat that is breaded and fried similar to the tenderloins of the Midwest, but with more pork, and battered rather than breaded. It is soft and juicy, as tender as a mother's love.

Few customers of Snappy Lunch get a plain pork-chop sandwich. The ritual here in Mount Airy (Andy Griffith's hometown, and the inspiration for TV's Mayberry) is to have it *all the way,* which means dressed with tomato, chopped onion, mustard, meaty/sweet chili, and fine-cut cabbage slaw speckled with green peppers and onions. The total package is unwieldy in the extreme. Served in booths or at the counter in a wax-paper wrapper, this is a sandwich that requires two hands and a meaningful grip. There are no side dishes available other than a bag of potato chips, and the beverage of choice is tea—iced and presweetened, of course.

There are, however, other items on the menu, including a weird Depression-era legacy known as the breaded hamburger, for which ground beef is extended by mixing it with an equal portion of moistened bread. The result is a strange, plump hamburger that resembles a crab cake. There's an all-beef burger too; but the pork-chop sandwich is what you want.

SOUTH 21 DRIVE-IN

south21drivein.net

3101 E. Independence   704-377-4509
Blvd.   L D | $
Charlotte, NC

If you like classic American drive-ins and don't already know about Charlotte's South 21, allow us to introduce you to your new best friend.

When South 21 Drive-In boasts that its Super Boy burger is a meal in itself, that's only partially true. It's a lot of food, for sure: two good-sized patties with the works in a sesame bun crowned with a quartered pickle spear and sided by a heap of French fries. While that may indeed be a meal, all aficionados of this vintage 1955 drive-in know that no meal is complete without an order of onion rings. They are individual hoops that arrive so greaseless that they first appear to have been baked, not fried. But after a few bites, the lavishness of the fry kettle becomes apparent. With some salt added, these are four-star O-rings. The other thing necessary to complete the meal is either cherry-flavored lemon Sundrop (a tradition hereabouts) or one of South 21's excellent milk shakes, blended to order.

While we love this old-fashioned drive-in with its articulated windowside trays and Servus-Fone ordering equipment at every car slip, we do believe the hamburgers need doctoring up; they tend to be dry enough to beg for extra condiments. That's why many regulars prefer the heftier and juicier hamburger steak platter or fried chicken.

STAMEY'S

stameys.com

2206 W. Gate City   336-299-9888
Blvd. (formerly High   L D (closed Sun) | $
Point Rd.)
Greensboro, NC

Stamey's dates back to 1938 and pretty much defined what is now known as Lexington-style North Carolina barbecue: pork shoulder pit-cooked over smoldering hickory coals until eminently tender, then chopped or sliced. Chopped means nearly pulverized. Slices are more like shreds of varying sizes, some soft, others crusty. The sauce is peppery with a vinegar twist, and thin enough to permeate the soft pork rather than blanket it. If you get a platter (as opposed to a sandwich), it will be accompanied by a powerfully zesty red coleslaw and odd-shaped, deep-fried corn squiggles that are Stamey's version of hush puppies. This is a Piedmont meal that connoisseurs put in the top tier of a state that is fanatical about barbecue. Be sure to leave room for dessert: the peach cobbler is nearly as famous as the barbecue.

There is a second Stamey's at 2812 Battleground Avenue (US 220 North) in Greensboro (336-288-9275).

SUNRISE BISCUIT KITCHEN

1305 E. Franklin St.   919-933-1324
Chapel Hill, NC   B L | $

If you have a cramped and uncomfortable car, you might find Sunrise Biscuit Kitchen problematic. It is drive-through only, offering no place to eat. But if you are a biscuit lover, you will want to come here even if you're the filling of a Smart Car. Sunrise biscuits are big and buttermilky with an outside surface that is golden-crisp. The kitchen pulls them into halves and loads in resounding slices of grilled country ham, pork tenderloin, or pillows of expertly fried white-meat chicken. Coffee is available, but so is sweet tea, which is a good biscuit's soul mate.

There is another Sunrise Biscuit Kitchen at 208 S. Bickett Boulevard in Louisburg (919-496-2609). It has indoor seating.

WILBER'S BARBECUE

wilbersbarbecue.com

4172 US Hwy. 70 E.   919-778-5218
Goldsboro, NC   B L D | $

Pilots who take off from Seymour Johnson Air Force Base have flown the fame of Wilber's far and wide, and legends abound regarding the pounds of barbecue carried aboard strategic flights. Even if it weren't at the end of the runway, Wilber's reputation for serving first-class Lexington-style North Carolina barbecue could never have remained merely local.

This place is world-class! Since 1962, when Wilber Shirley stoked the oak coals in old-fashioned pits, he has been known for whole-hog barbecue, chopped and shrewdly seasoned with a peppery vinegar sauce. After eight hours over coals, the meat is soft as a sigh, its natural sweetness haloed by hardwood smoke. It is served with potato salad, coleslaw, Brunswick stew (a pork hash with Veg-All type vegetables), and squiggly hush puppies.

Beyond terrific barbecue, the original Wilber's has the added attraction of serving breakfast, in the form of a buffet with smoked sausages, thick-cut bacon, cracklins, biscuits and gravy, grits, and sweet muffins. By late morning, chopped barbecue reigns, and it is served until about nine at night . . . or until the day's supply runs out. When that happens, the management locks the door and hangs up a sign that advises, OUT OF BARBECUE!

ZADA JANE'S CORNER CAFE

zadajanes.com

1601 Central Ave.   704-332-3663
Charlotte, NC   B L D | $$

--★--
LOCALS
LOVE IT
--★--
When the old Coffee Cup bit the dust, we despaired about the dearth of great breakfast in Charlotte, but a visit to Zada Jane's restored our faith. Not that the two places are similar. Zada Jane's is fashionable and modern, with a menu that includes gluten-free pancakes as well as soysage and tofu for non-carnivores. Situated in the same once-shabby, now upwardly mobile neighborhood as the old Penguin, the stylin' eatery is a favorite of local foodies. It is small and cozy, making it a sociable dining experience whether or not you want to socialize. Expect to wait for a seat, at table or counter, especially on weekends.

Buttermilk biscuits come with apple jam and multiberry jam obtained from a small farm outside of Asheville. Hash, made from sweet potatoes, is like the tenderest home fries but with a spicy-sugary edge. It shines in the Booker T's East Side Hasher breakfast, where it is topped with a couple of eggs cooked frittata-style and topped with cheese and sausage, plus green onions. (That last ingredient is inspiration for the dish's name.) Among the sausage choices is beautifully seasoned, locally made Grateful Grower's pork. Thick slices of challah-bread French toast are dipped in batter flavored with amaretto and are served with orange butter. Coffee is served in an assortment of kitschy souvenir mugs.

TENNESSEE

400 DEGREES

www.400degreeshotchicken.com

319 Peabody St.   615-244-4467
Nashville, TN   **L D** | $

At 319 Peabody in Nashville, Tennessee, is a Quizno's food court with a difference. The difference is that in addition to the mass-market sub shop, it contains 400 Degrees, which is one of the premier sources for Nashville hot chicken. Here you will find mercilessly spiced leg-quarter sandwiches, quartets of wings, and pork chops sided by sweet baked beans.

The menu item titled "400 Degrees" is the hottest chicken you can order. It is taken from the fry basket and painted with a thick pepper impasto that is as dark as antique bronze. "200 Degrees" chicken is brighter red and still sinus-clearing. "100 Degrees" is just a bit spicy, and there is "Zero," which is fried but not at all peppered. What's truly grand about the hot chicken is how the pepper paste fuses with its fried skin, forming a coat that you can lift away in bite-sized masses of pure, hot savor.

Proprietor Aqui Simpson originally opened for business in a two-table dive out on Clarksville Highway, but success eventually led her to this incongruously bland location, where there is plenty of seating at laminate tables under bright, mall-like lights. Aqui reminded us that regular customers call ahead so their chicken is ready when they arrive. Hot chicken is always made to order, meaning a twenty-minute wait is mandatory.

A&R BAR-B-QUE

aandrbbq.com

1802 Elvis Presley Blvd.   901-774-7444
Memphis, TN   **L D** | $

At the counter where you stand and place your order at A&R you can hear a blissful smokehouse lullaby coming from the kitchen: chop-chop-chop on the cutting board, as hickory-cooked pork gets hacked into mottled shreds and pieces for plates and sandwiches. The sandwich is Memphis-style: pork mixed with tangy red sauce piled in a bun and crowned with coleslaw. The slaw in a Memphis barbecue sandwich is as important for its texture as for its taste. The cabbage adds nice little bits of crunch to velvety pork.

Beyond pig sandwiches, the A&R menu is full. You can have pork or beef ribs, catfish dinner, hot tamales, smoked sausage, a turkey-leg plate, and that only-in-Memphis treat, barbecue spaghetti. That's a mound of soft noodles dressed not with ordinary tomato sauce, but with—what else?—barbecue sauce, laced with shreds of pork. For dessert, you want fried pie, warm, with ice cream.

The ambience of A&R is unadulterated BBQ parlor: quiet enough so you can hear the chopping in the kitchen. It is a big place with a lot of elbow room. Raw brick walls and fluorescent lights set a no-nonsense mood, and however hot it is outside, you can count on the air-conditioning system to be running so high that it's practically like going into hibernation. Or is the trance we experience a result of hypnotically good food?

There are three other A&Rs in Memphis.

ALCENIA'S

alcenias.com

317 N. Main St.   901-523-0200
Memphis, TN   **L** | **$**

Everyone who eats at Alcenia's gets a hug from proprietor B. J. Lester-Tamayo, either on the way in or out, or both. "I feel so guilty if I haven't hugged you, I'll chase you down the street when you leave," she says with a laugh. Her restaurant, named for her mother and granddaughter, is a modest lunchroom decorated in a style that is an intriguing mix of 1960s psychedelic beaded curtains, primitive folk art, odes to African American culture, and white wedding-veil lace strung up across the ceiling over the large table.

B.J. learned to cook from her mother, who lives in Meridian, Mississippi, but comes to visit and makes tea cakes and egg custard pie and coaches B.J. on the phone when she is making chowchow or pear preserves. B.J.'s turnip greens are extraordinary, flavored not with pork but with what she calls turkey "tails." Even more wondrous is cabbage, which we first assumed was steamed with greens because dark leaves were laced among the white ones. B.J. explained that those are the cabbage's outer leaves. "The best part!" she declared. "Most people throw them away because they are tough. They need an hour extra steaming; that makes them soft and brown." Flavored with a hail of spice that includes jerk chicken seasoning and lots of pepper, this is cabbage with tongue-searing punch. On the side comes a basket of hot-water corn bread: cushiony-moist, griddle-cooked cakes that are the perfect foil for ecstatically seasoned vegetables.

Aside from Alcenia's vegetables, dining delights here include a fried pork chop that is crisp and dripping with juice, crunchy fried chicken, and bread pudding that the Memphis *Commercial Appeal* declared to be one of the ten best desserts in the city.

★ ARNOLD'S COUNTRY KITCHEN

arnoldscountrykitchen.com

605 8th Ave. S.   615-256-4455
Nashville, Tennessee   **L** (Mon–Fri) | **$**

If you have time to experience just one meat-and-three restaurant in Nashville (perish the thought), please consider Arnold's Country Kitchen. Service is cafeteria-style, tables are shared by strangers when the place is crowded (it always is), and the food is beautiful. Not beautiful in a glossy-magazine sense, but beautiful the way plate lunch ought to be: messy, colorful, breadcrumb-crusted, cheese-dripping, hog-jowl-flavored soulful. The meats include moist and mighty meat loaf, exemplary fried chicken, pulled pork, and catfish; among the side dishes that command attention are greens, squash casserole, and most especially that distinguished "vegetable," mac 'n' cheese. Two kinds of corn bread are available, both essential: muffins and skillet-cooked cakes, the latter especially useful for mopping gravy, sopping the liquor under porky green beans, and dipping into the creamy emulsion in which black-eyed peas are suspended.

If only for its banana pudding, we would put this place on any hit list of great Music City destinations. But if by choosing pudding you neglect the pies, you will be sorry, because Arnold's pies are some of the best anywhere. Especially the chess pie: smooth, simple, butter-rich, and sugar-sweet.

BEACON LIGHT TEA ROOM

beaconlighttearoom.com

6276 Hwy. 100   931-670-3880
Bon Aqua, TN   **D** (Tues–Thurs);
                            B L D (Fri–Sun) | **$**

Opened in 1936 by Lon Loveless, who went on to open the renowned Loveless Cafe (p. 147) in Nashville, the Beacon Light Tea Room is a lesser-known gem of Tennessee country cooking. Longtime Loveless fans will have déjà vu upon opening the menu, for it is the same as the Loveless's used to be. Fried chicken and country ham with red-eye gravy are the entrees to know about, and among essential sides is the sumptuously rich midcentury Home-Ec triumph, hash brown casserole. Potato shreds are mixed with cheese, sour cream, and—you guessed it—a can of chicken soup, then baked until bubbly with a crust on top.

Meals are sided by biscuits with homemade peach and blackberry preserves. They are set out on the table in spoon-it-yourself crocks. There are soft hunks of peach in the amber one, and the blackberries have a sultry flavor that is a brilliant counterpoint to supersalty country ham.

Although it was originally named for the revolving spotlight that directed planes flying mail between Memphis and Nashville, the term "Beacon Light" now has another meaning. For the proprietors, the beacon is Jesus, and his image is everywhere in art on the old wood-paneled walls. Each table, which is clad with a leatherette cloth, is outfitted with a "Scripture Bread Box," a small plastic loaf hollowed out to contain cards about the size of fortune-cookie fortunes, but with scriptural advice on each side.

BLUEGRASS GRILL

bluegrassgrillchattanooga.com

55 E. Main St.   423-752-4020
Chattanooga, TN   **B L** (closed Sun & Mon) | **$**

We get lots of suggestions about where to eat. Some pan out, others don't. Ever since John Reed tipped us off to Zarzour's (p. 151), we have learned to put full faith in any of his suggestions. That is how we came upon the Bluegrass Grill, to which Mr. Reed directed us for "heavenly muffins, granola, cinnamon rolls, biscuits and breads all made from scratch starting at 3:30 a.m. by Father Jonas." Fr. Jonas Worsham, along with his family, including wife Joan Marie, have created a beckoning breakfast destination that also is open for lunch.

Big, squared-off biscuits, given extra character by the inclusion of whole wheat flour, arrive hot enough to melt butter pats. Add gravy on top and get a bottomless cup of coffee, and you will have a mighty morning meal for under $6. French toast is made from a choice of house-baked breads, including multigrain; superb home fries—red potatoes sautéed with

onion and garlic—are offered as a side dish to omelets or as a bed for toppings that range from gyro meat to chorizo to beans and cheese. Muffins, cinnamon rolls, whipped-cream-topped brownies: all first-class!

The lunch menu is soup, chili, sandwiches, and salads. If you have a party of fifteen or more and want dinner, the Worsham family also offers a "Greek feast" for which you consult about the menu. For that, of course, advance notice is required.

BOLTON'S SPICY CHICKEN & FISH

624 Main St.   615-254-8015
Nashville, TN   **L D** | **$**

Bolton's manager Dolly Graham once said, "Our chicken is hot, but it won't cause you to lose your composure." That depends. If you are leery of high-capsicum fare, Bolton's chicken might be reason for a meltdown, especially if you ask for it hot. Those who do like inflammatory food love it because the heat is deep in the meat, right down to the bone itself. It is much more spicy than it is salty, making for a meal's worth of taste-bud kicks.

It is beautiful chicken with a thin, red-gold crust that flakes off in delicate strips. You can get breast, leg, or wings, and side dishes include turnip greens, sweet coleslaw, strangely soupy mac 'n' cheese, and that Nashville soul-food favorite, spaghetti. In addition to chicken, Bolton's sells a whiting sandwich that is available garnished in the locally favored way, with mustard, onion, pickles, and enough hot sauce to make your tongue glow.

A tiny East Nashville shop with a carry-out window to its side and a dining room with a handful of tables (oilcloth-covered), Bolton's is a vital stop for anyone in search of a true taste of Music City.

BOZO'S HOT PIT BBQ

342 Hwy. 70   901-294-3400
Mason, TN   L D (Tues–Sat) | $$

Since it opened in 1923, Bozo's has earned a sterling reputation for barbecue. Slow-smoked shoulder is served white or dark, the former unspeakably tender shreds, the latter more chewy and crusty outside meat. (Many savvy eaters get a combination of the two.) You can have it the classic Memphis way, in a sandwich with slaw (although here the slaw has a more pronounced vinegar tang), or on a plate with beans and/or onion rings. Sandwiches are immense, loaded with more meat than any bun could possibly contain. Tables are armed with three sauces: mild, sweet, and hot. Hot is very hot.

Although barbecue is the must-eat meal, Bozo's menu also includes steaks, shrimp, and pies made by Ms. Perry, known for years among Bozo's aficionados as the Pie Lady. Named for founder Thomas Jefferson "Bozo" Williams, the restaurant was engaged in a trademark battle with Bozo the Clown back in the 1980s. *Bozo v. Bozo* went all the way to the US Supreme Court, which refused to hear it. So Bozo's is still Bozo's, its well-worn Formica tables showing only sixty-four years of use. (The original Bozo's was destroyed by fire in 1950.)

BRYANT'S BREAKFAST

bryantsmemphis.com
3965 Summer Ave.   901-324-7494
Memphis, TN   B L (Wed–Sun) | $

Bryant's Breakfast is a likeable destination for southern-style morning meals shared with locals. Order your food from the stand-up line, which likely will be well populated before 8 a.m. The bustle of the crowd, the high spirits of conversations that bounce around the room, and the warm aroma of bacon, ham, and hot biscuits make this a fine place to start the day.

Many house specialties, like the glazed and glistening cinnamon roll and ham biscuit, are presented in line, as you pay your bill. Those that take time to cook, such as bacon pancakes or omelets, are brought to your table by members of the staff. Biscuits are outstanding: Mid-South beauties, large, substantial, and unctuous enough to leave fingers glistening when you pick one up. They may be ordered plain or stuffed with country ham or city ham, with smoked sausage, bologna, bacon, chicken, steak, or pork tenderloin. To go whole hog, the meat inside can be supplemented with eggs or cheese. It also is possible to get a breakfast sandwich on toast, but with biscuits this good, why bother? Those of robust appetite should consider the grits bowl. The grits are good and creamy, laced with your choice of bacon or sausage and topped with an egg and grated cheese.

Bacon pancakes are a good idea, but disappointing: a stack of ordinary flapjacks with fistfuls of crumbled bacon that, although abundant, is not abundantly flavored. Likewise, sausage gravy, while thick and hearty, is timid in taste.

Breakfast is the house specialty, but Bryant's also is a destination for a plate lunch built upon such square-meal cornerstones as fried chicken, grilled pork tenderloin, meat loaf, and, on Friday, catfish. With any of these items, you get biscuits and corn bread and can choose from a long list of Dixie sides, including mac 'n' cheese, fried okra, squash casserole, braised cabbage, turnip greens, field peas, and white beans. Meatless four- and three-veggie plates also are available.

COLETTA'S

colettas.net
1063 South Pkwy. E.   901-948-7652
Memphis, TN   L D | $

At Coletta's Restaurant, a medium-thick-crust pizza pie with a glaze of melted mozzarella is topped not with Italian sauce and sausage or pepperoni, but with a bouquet of barbecued pulled pork in a zesty cinnabar pit sauce. No, it is not one of the world's great pizzas; nor is it in the highest echelon of Mid-South barbecue; but it is a specialty worth noting—and eating—for all who want to savor America's rules-be-damned cuisine.

Coletta's also serves barbecue salad, which is like any ordinary salad (iceberg lettuce, carrot shreds, tomatoes) but adorned with barbecue—the same moist mix of fine shreds and a few chewy nuggets as on the pizza. The meat on the salad is unsauced. Dressing is the customer's choice, and it makes all the difference. Italian vinaigrette nudges it in the direction of minimally sauced eastern North Carolina 'cue; thousand island or Russian is more like mountain smokehouse meals; ranch dressing brings it close to that strange Alabama variety of sauce that is based on mayonnaise.

Barbecue pizza and salad are just two items on a full-range menu of familiar Italian-American fare, including more universally known pizzas, housemade sausage, ravioli, and spaghetti and meatballs.

Around the corner from Graceland, Coletta's has a sad look from the outside, but red-checked tablecloths in the dining room, which sport paper place mats that explain Italy's many charms, set a hospitable tone. The cognitive dissonance of barbecue pizza defines the ambience as well: a vintage Italian-American dining room where the wood-paneled walls hold massive amounts of Elvisiana and where waitresses speak in syrupy southern drawls.

★ COZY CORNER
cozycornerbbq.com

726 North Pkwy.   901-527-9158
Memphis, TN   **L D** (Tues-Sat) | **$**

In America's premier barbecue city, the number one barbecue restaurant is the Cozy Corner. The house specialty in this family run storefront is Cornish hen, a plump little bird that emerges from its long smoke bath with fragile, burnished skin wrapping meat that throbs with spicy flavor. Cozy Corner's sauce-glazed spare ribs pack huge sweet-pork punch; baby-backs boast meat that slips from the bone in glistening ribbons; thick discs of barbecue bologna are a revelation; and whatever meat you get, you can side it with that delightfully monomaniacal Memphis side dish, barbecued spaghetti. There are two wonderful desserts: sweet-potato pie and banana pudding.

Despite its reputation among barbecue connoisseurs, the Cozy Corner remains humble, its front room clouded with haze from the Chicago-style aquarium smoker behind the self-service counter. It

was established back in 1977 by Raymond Robinson, who, until his death early in 2001, oversaw his empire from a seat behind the order counter, haloed by the glow of his smoke pit. Today his widow, Desiree, keeps up the high culinary standards and the friendly air that has always made this such a happy place to visit.

THE CUPBOARD
thecupboardrestaurant.com

1400 Union Ave.   901-276-8015
Memphis, TN   **B L D** | **$**

★ VEGETARIAN-FRIENDLY ★ The Cupboard is a hugely popular restaurant in what used to be a Shoney's, where a sign outside boasts, "Freshest Veggies in Town." Proprietor Charles Cavallo is a fresh-food fanatic, a joy he credits to his uncle, who sold watermelons. He drove a produce delivery truck for ten years, and in 1993 bought the Cupboard (then, a much smaller place) with the goal of making it a showcase for vegetables. Tomatoes direct from the field in Ripley, local squash, crowder peas, onions, cabbage, and sweet potatoes appear not only on the menu (which features a four-vegetable, no-meat meal), but also on the floor of the restaurant, in the vestibule, and around the cash register, from which they are sold by the peck and bushel when they are in season.

One of the best-cooked vegetables here is the simplest: a whole baked sweet potato, starchy-sweet and soft as pudding. Corn pudding is stellar; ditto the baked apple. The Cupboard's full-flavored turnip greens are made without pork or poultry, just boiled and seasoned. "My greens taste like greens," Charles says, stating the obvious. "Sometimes I have people who come in and say, 'You've changed the recipe. These are different.' Yes, they are different, I say: maybe younger, maybe winter greens, which have a softer taste, maybe they are from Georgia instead of Tennessee. Every bunch has a flavor of its own."

Non-vegetable notables include corn bread gem muffins and yeast rolls, warm fruit cobbler, and brilliant lemon icebox pie.

DYER'S BURGERS

dyersonbeale.com

205 Beale St.   901-527-3937
Memphis, TN   **L D | $**

A round of raw ground beef is held on the cutting board under a spatula, and the spatula is whacked a few times with a heavy hammer, flattening the meat into a semi-compressed patty at least four inches wide. The patty is submerged into a deep, black skillet full of hot grease that the management boasts has not been changed since Dyer's opened in 1912. The hot oil bath gives a Dyer's burger a severe crust outside, while the inside stays juicy. For those who flout all conventional wisdom about healthful eating, there's a variation called the dip: The whole assembled hamburger, bun and all, is dunked in the bubbling grease just before it gets plated.

Our waitress explained that the grease is strained every night; besides, the old grease is always burning off, so the supply that supposedly never changes is, in fact, always changing. Anyway, the fact is that this is one heck of an interesting hamburger, if for no other reason than its ability to drive nutrition wardens wild. Burgers are assembled in many ways: as doubles or triples, or as double or triple "combos" (with layers of cheese). Good hand-cut French fries are available on the side.

If hamburgers are not your passion, allow us to suggest another Dyer's specialty: the Big Rag Baloney sandwich. That's a half-inch-thick slab of baloney (or two slabs, if desired), fried to a crisp in the same skillet, and in the same vintage oil, as the burgers.

ED'S FISH & PIZZA HOUSE

1801 Dr. D. B. Todd Jr.   615-255-4362
Blvd.   **L D | $**
Nashville, TN

Fried fish has been a staple at soul-food restaurants for as long as there have been soul-food restaurants, but Nashville has a very specific way of serving it: the hot fish sandwich. A couple of crisp-fried whiting fillets—often totaling a pound, spritzed with hot sauce—are arranged between two to four slices of white bread with sliced raw onion, pickle chips, and mustard. Various accompaniments are available, including coleslaw and fried potatoes, but the classic companion is a serving of sweet-sauced spaghetti noodles.

The goodness of a hot fish sandwich depends to a large degree on its being eaten within moments of the fish being pulled from the fry kettle. We are happy to report that at Ed's we waited a good fifteen or twenty minutes for our sandwich to be presented, the fish still sizzling hot.

What a magnificent sandwich: plump, moist fillets in a golden crust, splotched with only enough hot sauce to tease forth their flavor. The spaghetti we ordered on the side left its al dente character long behind, and its chunky red sauce was nearly chutney-sweet. The bright innocence of these noodles is just the right partner for hot and funky fish.

ELLISTON PLACE SODA SHOP

2111 Elliston Pl.   615-327-1090
Nashville, TN   **B L | $**

It bills itself as a soda shop, and a fine one it is; but we like Elliston Place more for meat-and-three lunch. Choose sugar-cured ham, salt-cured country ham, southern-fried chicken (white or dark meat), a pork chop, or liver and onions, then select three vegetables from a daily roster. On Mondays and Thursdays the house special is turkey and dressing, a casserole of shredded roasted white and dark meat with steamy corn-bread dressing: delicious! If you want to skip meat altogether (Elliston Place vegetables are so good, such a strategy makes sense), there is a four-vegetable plate, accompanied by hot bread, for about $5. The vegetable repertoire includes whipped potatoes, turnip greens, baked squash, fried rounds of okra, black-eyed peas, and congealed fruit salad (the Dixie name for Jell-O). Banana pudding, streaked with fluffy veins of meringue, is exquisite.

Breakfast biscuits are crunchy brown on the outside with a soft interior that begs to wrap itself around a slice of salty country ham. On the side comes a bowl of firm, steamy white grits—a mild-mannered companion for full-flavored breakfast meat.

A city fixture since 1939, this is a restaurant with personality! Its tiny-tile floor is well weathered and its tables wobble. Above the counter, vintage soda fountain signs advertise banana splits, fruit sundaes, sodas, and fresh fruit ades. Each green-upholstered booth has its own jukebox with selections that are, suitably enough, country classics.

GERMANTOWN COMMISSARY
commissarybbq.com

2290 S. Germantown	901-754-5540
Germantown, TN	L D	$$

The most exalted barbecue often is served in the lowliest dives, but here is fine smokehouse fare in decorator-rustic surroundings. Give your car to the valet and enter dining quarters, where barnboard walls sport collectible old tin signs, wind-up telephones, and vintage advertisements . . . and the air is filled with the unmistakably seductive aroma of real barbecue.

It is best known for ribs, which truly are first-rate: crusted with sauce, scented by hickory, meaty as hell with enough chew to provide maximum flavor. You can order them by number of bones, from five to twelve (a full rack), or as part of a combo plate with one to three other meats. We suggest the sampler, because it would be a crime to come to the Commissary and *not* have pulled pork. It is shoulder meat, pulled into slightly-more-than-bite-sized strips and hunks, some edges crusty, some parts velvet-soft. You can also get the meat chopped, which is OK but deprives your tongue of the pleasure of worrying those long strips of meat you get when it's pulled.

For dessert, we like banana pudding with softened vanilla wafers in the custard, tongue-soothing lemon icebox pie, and caramel cake.

GUS'S FRIED CHICKEN
gusfriedchicken.com

310 S. Front St.	901-527-4877
Memphis, TN	L D	$

Each piece of Gus's chicken, dark and white, is encased in a zesty envelope that vigorously crunches then offers plenty of rewarding chew, all the while radiating the ecstatic flavor combo of chicken fat and pepper.

Other than catfish a couple of nights a week, chicken is Gus's only entree; any pieces are available in any combination; side dishes include baked beans, coleslaw, fried rice (!), fried okra, and spiced French fries. Even those who aren't fans of fried green tomatoes and fried dill pickles should consider ordering some of Gus's to start the meal. No novelty in this kitchen, the pickles maintain nice al dente firmness inside their crunchy coat, which, like the batter on the chicken, is an elegant balance of spice and lusciousness.

To call the restaurant casual underestimates its humility. On a crappy street the wrong side of Beale, it regularly posts a security guard on the sidewalk so that visitors will feel safe between car and front door. The interior, where mismatched chairs are arranged around a couple dozen tables topped with easy-wipe tablecloths, seems like a chaotic madhouse as customers mill around near the door waiting for their turn to sit. Once seated, you will deal with a staff who are nothing but courteous and efficient.

Note: Gus's has gone national. This original is unique.

HOT STUFF SPICY CHICKEN & FISH
hotstufftn.com

1309 Bell Rd., Ste. 218	615-712-6100
Antioch, TN	L D	$

Fast food this is not. The kitchen starts cooking only after an order is placed, and since there is no jiffy way of frying chicken right, time passes while appetite builds. The twenty minutes spent waiting is the best argument you'll ever know in favor of the slow food movement. What you get, served in a Styrofoam clamshell with white bread, French fries, and pickle chips, is Nashville hot chicken at its finest.

Compared to some of the other chicken shacks around town, the heat levels at Hot Stuff seem relatively sane. Hot is very hot but not killer. Even X-hot is more pleasure than pain. As for XX and XXX . . . we'll leave them to the asbestos-tongue crowd. Hot Stuff also offers Li'l Spice, Mild, Lemon Pepper, Cajun, and Sweet Heat versions that will not set taste buds on fire.

The chicken is ravishing red-gold. Press it gently with fork or finger and juices start oozing. Dark meat is especially luscious, but Hot Stuff's breasts drip savor too. The crust is crisp and thin, radiant with that magic combination of palliative chicken fat and incendiary spice.

When we placed our order, co-owner Kiki Montgomery suggested house-made sweet tea to deal with the chicken's heat, and in one way, she was right. It is so sweet that it manages to divert attention from tongue fires. But it does little to actually tamp them down. A thick piece of mocha layer cake, made by local baker Spencer D. Middlebrooks and available by the slice at Hot Stuff's counter, was more effective (and really delicious) relief.

INTERSTATE BARBECUE

interstatebarbecue.com

2265 S. 3rd St.   901-775-2304
Memphis, TN   **L D** | $$

Interstate's Jim Neely is a master barbecue man, and in the city of Memphis, to be a respected pitmaster is to be a god. His restaurant is a modest pork house serving ribs, shoulder meat, sausages, and bologna with all the proper fixins, including barbecue spaghetti (soft noodles in breathtaking sauce).

Each rib exudes the perfume of woodsmoke; chewing it generates massive infusions of flavor that literally exhaust taste buds after a while. Chopped pork shoulder is a medley of shreds, chunks, wisps, and ribbons of smoky meat, all crowned with Neely's spicy-sweet red sauce. A chopped pork sandwich is the most Memphian dish on the menu, made with a layer of cool coleslaw atop the well-sauced meat.

A second location is at 150 West Stateline Road, Southhaven, Mississippi (662-393-5699).

LEONARD'S

leonardsbarbecue.com

5465 Fox Plaza Dr.   901-360-1963
Memphis, TN   **L** (Sun–Thurs);
                                   L D (Fri–Sat) | $

In 1922 Leonard Heuberger configured the barbecued pork sandwich that has become a regional icon: shreds of smoked shoulder meat topped with tomato-sweet, vinegar-tangy sauce, festooned with creamy coleslaw. It is a mesmerizing confluence of sugar and spice, meat and bread and sauce.

Choices at Leonard's include slabs of ribs, platters and plates, barbecued bologna, and even a roster of Italo-Dixie combo plates that include spaghetti with ribs and barbecue with ravioli. Big eaters avail themselves of the lunch buffet Sunday through Friday and the evening buffet Friday and Saturday.

Leonard's is worth visiting not only for its pork but for its sign, which is one of the great images in porklore: a neon pig, all decked out in top hat and tails, captioned "Mr. Brown Goes to Town." Years ago, a waitress explained its significance: "Mr. Brown was the term used for brown-meat barbecue. It is the outside of the shoulder that gets succulent and chewy from the sauce and the smoke in the pit. The inside part of the roast, which is moist but has very little barbecue flavor, is known as Miss White. People in Memphis used to ask for plates and sandwiches of 'Mr. Brown and Miss White.'"

LITTLE TEA SHOP

69 Monroe Ave.   901-525-6000
Memphis, TN   **L** | $

— ★ —
LOCALS
LOVE IT
— ★ —

Memphis is our favorite place to eat pork, but there's none served at the Little Tea Shop down by old Cotton Row. Proprietor Suhair Lauck is Muslim, and yet despite her religion's prohibition against pigs, she serves some of the most soulful eats in the city. We were aghast when Sue told us that her greens were in fact completely meat-free. It had always seemed to us that the opulent "likker" in which they wallow in their serving bowl—a spruce-green broth retrieved from the pot in which they have boiled—gets its intoxicating character at least as much from the hambone as from the collard, turnip, or mustard leaves that the boiling process turns soft and mellow.

But tasting is believing, and let us tell you that a serving of pork-free turnip greens with pot likker at the Little Tea Shop is positively tonic. If a flavor can be verdant, here it is: the heady soul of a plant with leaves that marinate in sunlight. Turnip greens are the centerpiece of Sue's most popular lunch, on the printed-daily menu every day of the week. It is a bowl filled with sultry dark greens sodden in their likker, the once-tough leaves cooked so limp that you can easily separate them with a soup spoon and gather it up with plenty of the liquid. Atop the greens are slices of raw onion, leaching pungent bite into the leaves, and atop the onions are bright red slices of tomato, which are shockingly sweet compared to everything below. On the side are crisp-edged, cream-centered corn sticks well suited for crumbling into the bowl.

The process for ordering food is do-it-yourself. Every customer gets a one-page printed menu of the day with a little box next to each item. Like voting with an old-fashioned ballot, you put a check mark in the box next to each dish you want to elect for your lunch. Other than pot likker, some of the outstanding choices are the Lacy Special (named for a cotton trader), in which corn sticks sandwich a chicken breast topped with gravy, and such vegetables as sliced candied yams, fried corn, baked squash, black-eyed peas, and scalloped tomatoes. The longtime favorite dessert is a frozen pecan ice cream ball topped with hot fudge.

LITTON'S
littonsburgers.com

2803 Essary Rd.   865-688-0429
Knoxville, TN   **L D** (closed Sun) | **$**

With a catalogue of hamburgers that range from minimalist beef patties to a "Thunder Road" burger (named for the movie about moonshining in the Appalachians) topped with pimiento cheese, onions, and hot peppers, Litton's is a burger lover's paradise. Freshly ground meat is formed into a patty that is nearly half a pound and it is cooked to order, then

sandwiched in a made-here bun, preferably with at least lettuce, tomato, and onion and, at most, bacon, pickles, or chili.

At least as famous as the hamburgers are Litton's desserts: coconut cream pie, chocolate chess pie (Tuesday only), old-fashioned red velvet cake, banana pudding, and cream-cheese-frosted Italian cream cake, a buttery concoction that goes perfectly with a cup of after-meal coffee.

LOVELESS CAFE
lovelesscafe.com

8400 Hwy. 100   615-646-9700
Nashville, TN   **B L D** | **$**

Eating at the Loveless Cafe isn't only a matter of fried chicken and biscuits. It is all about the South, Tennessee in particular, and Nashville, heart and soul. Three or four decades ago, when it was known only to cognoscenti and accidental tourists, the Loveless could get crowded; if you knew you were coming during peak mealtime, you could call and make a reservation. When you did, you said whether you were planning on having fried chicken or ham. That was pretty much the extent of the menu . . . along with the immemorial companions: biscuits, cream gravy, red-eye gravy, peach preserves, blackberry preserves, honey, and sorghum syrup. Now the kitchen's repertoire has grown—although country ham and fried chicken remain the anchor meals—and the Loveless Cafe has itself become a national celebrity. Among luminaries who have visited in recent years are Britain's Princess Anne (in the neighborhood for a horse show) and Sir Paul McCartney (who spontaneously sang "Happy Birthday" to a sixteen-year-old customer who had come to celebrate with friends).

Despite its renown, the Loveless remains faithful to its roots, and like a true-hearted singing star who hits the big-time, it has never strayed from the fundamental good things that led to its original success. First among them is fried chicken . . . the original meal served by Lon and Annie Loveless back in the early 1950s when they began offering picnic suppers to passersby along Highway 100. The major alternative to chicken is country ham, and the newly expanded menu includes the likes of pulled pork, green tomato BLTs, and what is perhaps the most elegant banana pudding anywhere.

MERRIDEE'S BREADBASKET
merridees.com

110 4th Ave. S.   615-790-3755
Franklin, TN   **B L; D** (Thurs–Sat) | **$**

--★-- **LOCALS LOVE IT** --★-- Merridee's is a casual bakery-café where people come early in the day to buy breads and pastries to take home or to sit down for breakfast or lunch. Place an order at the counter and they'll call your name when it is ready, by which time, hopefully, you will have found a seat. The repertoire includes hot breakfasts and a vast array of oven-fresh rolls (almond swirl, cinnamon twist, sticky bun, muffins, biscuits, scones, and so on) as well as lunch of sandwiches, salads, and crescents ("No, not croissants!" says the menu), which are homemade bread doughs wrapped around turkey and honey mustard, spinach and feta cheese, or roast beef and Swiss.

Pimiento cheese, a Mid-South passion, is the essential sandwich. It is not dramatically different from ordinary cheese spread, but subtle difference is just the point. Pimiento cheese is all about nuance: the slight zip of chopped pimientos and sweet relish and their red and green sparkle in the gentle-flavored cheese. While hearty and satisfying, it has a refined character that sings of ladies' lunchrooms, afternoon tea, and Dixie finesse.

For dessert: cake, pie, fudge brownies, and sugar tea cakes, available with espresso coffee drinks.

NIKKI'S DRIVE-IN
899 Cherokee Blvd.   423-265-9015
Chattanooga, TN   **B L D** | **$**

Although carhop service no longer is available, Nikki's remains a timeless mid-twentieth-century drive-in, complete with long counter, jukebox at every booth, and Coke served in glass bottles. Signs atop the brick building do not boast of hamburgers (although the burgers are very nice lunch-counter patties); they advertise the house specialties: Gulf Coast shrimp and southern fried chicken. The fried shrimp are relatively pricey (over $20 for a dozen), but meaty enough that six of them, with salad, fries, and hush puppies, make a fine meal. We thank tipster John Reed for telling us we had to have bacon-wrapped, deep-fried chicken livers (oh, Mama, are these ever rich!) as well as Nikki's justifiably famous big-hoop battered onion rings. We topped things off with very good pecan pie.

PANCAKE PANTRY
thepancakepantry.com

1796 21st Ave. S.   615-383-9333
Nashville, TN   **B L** | **$**

We suffer from anxiety at the Pancake Pantry. First we worry about getting in. There is almost always a line of hungry Nashvillians waiting for a precious seat in this singular restaurant that transcends generic pancake-house dining. Second, simply choosing from the menu induces paroxysms of indecision. If we order sweet-potato pancakes that are so good drizzled with cinnamon cream, then it doesn't make sense also to eat onion-laced potato pancakes. And if we get stacks of pancakes, how much appetite can possibly remain to enjoy what are surely the best hash browns in the South? We don't know if they're cooked on the same griddle as the pancakes, or if it's just pancake scent in the air, but Pancake Pantry potatoes are as buttercream fluffy as the best flapjack. Fried to a golden crisp, they are counterpoise for the salty punch of a brick-red slab of griddled country ham.

A few other favorites from the broad and inviting menu: Smoky Mountain buckwheat cakes, which appear dark and somber, but are featherlight, arriving as a stack of five with plenty of butter and a pitcher of warm syrup to pour on top; Caribbean buttermilk pancakes; and thin and eggy Swedish pancakes wrapped around lingonberry preserves.

The Pancake Pantry is a big restaurant with plenty of space among the tables and a high-spirited ambience throughout the dining room. It is impossible to imagine being in a bad mood when eating here.

PAYNE'S

1762 Lamar Ave.   901-272-1523
Memphis, TN   **L** | $

As in most barbecue parlors of the Mid-South, the counter man at Payne's will not ask if you want cole-slaw when you order a pulled pork sandwich. It is auto-matic: tender pork shoulder is hacked with a cleaver on a wooden block and piled into a bun with hot or mild sauce, and to balance the meat's smoky profundity, pickly sweet, mustard-tinged slaw goes on top. This configuration, formally known as a pig sandwich, is a brilliant, wide-spectrum presentation that combines warm meat with cool slaw, spicy sauce with creamy dressing, piggy pork with crunchy cabbage.

Expect no frills in this fundamental place, where accommodations are just a few scattered tables to which you carry your own food, presented ready-wrapped. The menu is posted on a moveable-letter board above the order counter, where the short list includes beef barbecue, sausages, rib tips, and bolo-gna, with sides of beans, slaw, and French fries. In our experience none of these is stellar; but the pig sand-wich is.

PEPPERFIRE SPICED CHICKEN

pepperfirechicken.com
1000 Gallatin Pike   615-582-4824
Nashville, TN   **L D** (closed Sun) | $

Isaac Beard opened Pepperfire in the fall of 2010. Although a native of Nashville, Beard wasn't all that impressed with hot chicken until a revelatory moment several years ago when he visited Prince's and suddenly was struck with its glory, becoming a two-times-a-day extra-hot eater. Despite its built-in inefficiencies, he is convinced hot chicken has poten-tial to become popular all over the country, just as its profile in Nashville has gone from being a strictly black-neighborhood specialty to a source of citywide pride and inspiration for an annual hot-chicken festi-val every Independence Day. "I believe I was born to do something with hot chicken," he says. "I am a hot-chicken evangelist."

He makes what is perhaps the most beautiful hot chicken in the city: cinnabar-red, glistening with fat and heat, oozing juice at the slightest poke. In addition to breast quarters and leg quarters, as well as half and whole chickens, Pepperfire offers jumbo hot wings and tenders as well as a tender royale—a deep-fried cheese sandwich topped with chicken. Side dishes are mere palate-salve: crinkle-cut fries, potato salad, coleslaw, baked beans, and green beans.

★ PRINCE'S HOT CHICKEN SHACK

princeshotchicken.com
123 Ewing Dr.   615-226-9442
Nashville, TN   **L D** (Tues–Sat) | $

Pay attention to the name: Prince's *Hot* Chicken Shack. Available mild, medium, hot, and extra-hot, be forewarned that even mild packs a punch. We tried hot and it had us tearing up . . . with joy! What's great about this crisp-fried wonder is that it isn't merely hot. It is radiant with flavor; its chewy skin has soul-ful character; the meat is moist and luxurious. To say it is addictive is not hyperbole: We have met devotees who told us they come to Prince's five times a week (it's closed Sunday and Monday), and any day they didn't get their extra-hot was a sad one.

Chicken is all you need to know, except for French fries, which are terrific too. The chicken comes in halves and quarters. It is delivered in a paper bag near the window where you placed your order and paid. There are a handful of tables in the restaurant and many people simply step outside to dine on the walkway of the small strip mall where Prince's is located. Beverages are sold from vending machines inside.

THE RENDEZVOUS

hogsfly.com
52 S. 2nd St.   901-523-2746
Memphis, TN   **D** | $$

Famous as they are as a symbol of Memphis barbecue, the Rendezvous's ribs technically are not barbecued; they are charcoal broiled. Instead of being bathed in sauce, which is the more typical Memphis way, they are dry. Dry, but not drab. Indeed, these are some of the most flavorful ribs you will eat anywhere. Instead of sauce, the meaty bones arrive at the table encased in a crust of powerful spice. The spice accentuates the sweetness of the pork and also contains and concentrates its succulence. Rendezvous ribs are the juiciest.

With its semi-subterranean dining room where the décor is antique bric-a-brac and thousands of business cards left by decades of happy customers, the Rendezvous is more reminiscent of a beer hall in *The Student Prince* than a Mid-South barbecue. To accompany the beer you must drink before (as well as during) any meal, there are plates of sausage and cheese that are a merry hors d'oeuvre. Sound like a lot of food? Eating large is part of the Rendezvous experience; of all the restaurants in town, we nominate this one as the worst to visit on a diet.

★ RIDGEWOOD BARBECUE

900 Elizabethton Hwy.   423-212-4813
(Old 19E)   **L D** | $$
Bluff City, TN

When we first came upon the Ridgewood Barbecue in Roadfood's earliest days, we knew we had found a benchmark. The food was sensational, and Mrs. Proffit, who ran the place, along with her good ol' girl staff, were a vision of no-bull country hospitality. The queenly Mrs. Proffit and her gals are gone, but the place is pretty much the same, as are its priceless recipes.

Hams are hickory-cooked in a pit adjacent to the restaurant, sliced into fairly thin pieces, then reheated on a grill when ordered. The meat is souped with a tangy, dark-red, slightly smoky sauce (available by the pint and quart near the cash register) and served as a platter with terrific dark-gold French fries, or in a sandwich that spills out all sides of the bun. We like the platter because it allows one to fork up a French fry and a few flaps of sauced meat all at the same time, making for one of the world's perfect mouthfuls. Prior to the arrival of the platter, you will be served a bowl of coleslaw—cool, crisp, sweet—surrounded by saltine crackers. We also recommend ordering a crock of beans. They are laced with meat and have a fetching smoky flavor.

A word of warning: If you arrive at a normal mealtime, expect to wait. Despite its fairly remote location, Ridgewood's excellence has earned it fame. It attracts barbecue pilgrims from far and near.

ROTIER'S

rotiersrestaurant.com
2413 Elliston Pl.   615-327-9892
Nashville, TN   **L D** (closed Sun) | $

LOCALS LOVE IT — ★ — A longtime favorite of Vanderbilt students, Rotier's is a blast from the past, its burger one-of-a-kind. A thick, irregularly shaped patty of ground beef is grilled to glistening perfection and stacked with lettuce, tomato, pickle, and hopefully a layer of bright-orange cheese and a good squirt of mustard between two handsome tiles of toasty French bread. The package is tall enough that it arrives stuck together with a toothpick.

Although everyone in town knows Rotier's as the hamburger place, it also happens to be one of Nashville's premier hot-lunch restaurants, where you can choose from a menu of such entrees as pork barbecue, country-fried steak, fried chicken, and meat loaf. On the side, pick two vegetables from a list of southern classics: black-eyed peas, turnip greens, fried okra, baked squash casserole, crowder peas, white beans, and more. Or, it is possible to get a plate of nothing but vegetables—an excellent strategy if for some reason you are going meatless. With the vegetables come good rolls or warm corn bread, and if you don't want to drink beer, the menu lists milk shakes, chocolate milk, sweet milk, and buttermilk. And, of course, sweet tea.

SWETT'S

www.swettsrestaurant.com

2725 Clifton Ave. 615-329-4418
Nashville, TN **L D | $**

Swett's is a visible success story: opened in 1954 as a small soul-food meat-and-three café, it became a large, modern cafeteria, burned down, and was built again. Portraits of the founding Swetts adorn the walls, and their legacy is reflected by a kitchen serving hearty southern meals at reasonable prices.

Like so many cafeteria lines, this one starts with dessert: pie ranging from low-profile chess to lofty meringues, plus a couple of hot fruit cobblers. Beyond the sweets are the meats: masterful fried chicken, spice-encrusted baked chicken, sausages, country steak, and beef tips. Now comes the real fun: vegetables. Swett's repertoire is a symphony of steamed or fried okra, fried corn, squash casserole, candied yams, mashed potatoes, mac 'n' cheese, stewed cabbage, candied apples, baked beans, turnip greens, rice and gravy, et cetera. Most customers get one meat and two or three vegetables. Some fill their tray with nothing but four or five vegetable dishes . . . accompanied, of course, by corn bread, either baked as a loaf and sliced or in the more typical local formation, as a cake fried on a griddle.

Draw your own tea (sweet or unsweet) at the end of the cafeteria line.

TJ'S BBQ & FISH

1104 Ed Temple Blvd. 615-329-1200
Nashville, TN **L D | $**

A few years back, Jim Myers of *The Tennessean* declared the hot fish sandwich at TJ's BBQ & Fish to be one of the best in Nashville. The same story noted that TJ's pitmaster happened to be the son-in-law of the pitmaster at Joe's Bar-B-Que & Fish, and that the two places' fish sandwiches were remarkably similar. We came to the same conclusion during an eating expedition of Nashville. Now that Joe's is gone, TJ's stands alone.

The menu lists whiting and catfish, and we do love the whiting. But it's TJ's pork for which we'll make return visits. It is lasciviously tender and plays crazy chords of flavor all over one's tongue. Sauce is available hot or not; the former is a little sweet and a lot hot. Griddle-cooked corn bread makes a wonderful companion. Other available sides include turnip greens, fried okra, mac 'n' cheese, and spaghetti.

As it was at Joe's, service is strictly drive-through (no indoor seating). Once you place an order, you pull around to an adjacent parking lot and when it is ready, someone from the kitchen runs it out to the car.

ZARZOUR'S

1627 Rossville Rd. 423-266-0424
Chattanooga, TN **L** (Mon-Fri) | $

When you walk into Zarzour's, you will be greeted by chef Shannon Fuller, who wants to know, "Are you having a cheeseburger, or dining off the menu today?" The burgers are not to be slighted: hand-pattied, thick and juicy and satisfying. But the menu, a 5×7 piece of paper with three entrees handwritten every day above a printed list of vegetables, is irresistible. If turnip greens are on it, they're a must: murky, pork-sweet, as tender as long-steamed cabbage, and heavy with tonic pot likker. We adore the antediluvian baked spaghetti, which is toothless pasta laced with crumbled beef, chewy shreds of cheese scraped from the edge of the casserole, and a web of hardened noodles from the top. No hot meal is more popular than the every-Wednesday salmon croquettes (known to some fans as "redneck crab cakes"). "I make twenty-five or thirty plates of them," Shannon says, showing how she forms each one from a mix of salmon, egg, onion, flour, and milk, then pan-fries it so the pink mash inside is encircled by a good crunch.

Shannon's mother-in-law, Shirley (granddaughter of the man who first opened Zarzour's in 1918), developed the recipes for dessert. Her glories include lemon icebox pie, peach ice cream in season, banana pudding, and the amazing millionaire pie. That's pineapple chunks, walnut pieces, green grapes, and mandarin orange slices suspended in a mix of frozen Cool Whip and sweetened condensed milk.

VIRGINIA

ACE BISCUIT AND BARBECUE

acebiscuitandbarbecue.com/index.html

711 Henry Ave.   434-202-1403
Charlottesville, VA   **B L D** (closed Mon & Tues)
| $

An Ace biscuit is a substantial square, not angelically light but a big-flavored presence to reckon with, speckled throughout with sharp grains of black pepper. Its heft makes it ideal for sandwiching a gnarled, boneless buttermilk fried chicken thigh, country ham, or sausage. The blackboard menu has a long list of ingredients from which you can create your own biscuit sandwich—meats, eggs, cheeses—or you can opt for such house specialties as a brisket biscuit (beef, caramelized onion, Cheddar cheese, egg) or a devil-may-care dirty biscuit (fried chicken, peppery sausage gravy, house-made dill pickle chips, and a schmear of pimento cheese). Or get an unadorned biscuit and apply intense-flavored local honey or blackberry-peach jam that is the darkest possible purple, thick with big, limp hunks of fruit.

Barbecue gets equal billing in the restaurant name, and deserves it. Pulled pork is extraordinarily smoky, a mélange of shreds and chunks. Brisket, sliced thin and redolent of oak and hickory smoke, is heavy with juice—especially good when enlivened by horseradish mayonnaise. Nine different sauces are available, including North Carolina vinegar, Virginia red, bold and spicy, and cider mustard. On the side,

check out the tremendously creamy macaroni and cheese, collard greens that are pungent and sharp, and stewed apples that provide sweet harmony for just about any meat.

Such a friendly place! Give the order taker your name to call out when the meal is ready to fetch. Later, when we are halfway through, we hear, "How's everything, Michael?" At first, we assume she is talking to a friend, but no, she is addressing Michael Stern, and she really is interested in knowing if we are enjoying our dirty biscuit. Yes, indeed!

THE APPLE HOUSE

theapplehouse.net

4675 John Marshall   540-636-6329
Hwy.   **B L D** | $
Linden, VA

For many regular travelers along I-66 or the Skyline Drive, the Apple House isn't a restaurant at all, but rather a place to stock up on crunchy apple-butter donuts plastered with sugar. They're four-star donuts, radiant with fruit flavor and all the luxury of fried dough.

Meals are served too, and they are good. Breakfast includes a roster of eggs and flapjacks; the hickory-smoked pork barbecue available at lunch is satisfying. There are soups and salads and specialty sandwiches that range from BLTs to one-pound hamburgers. If you do have a meal, save room for dessert.

The next-best items on the menu, after the apple-butter donut, are the apple fritter—sugar-glazed and chock-full of fruit—and the baked apple dumpling with a caramel glaze.

BARBEQUE EXCHANGE
bbqex.com

| 102 Martinsburg Ave. | 540-832-0227 |
| Gordonsville, VA | **L D** \| **$** |

Pay attention to the name of the Barbeque Exchange. The kitchen offers no hamburgers, hot dogs, fried chicken, or anything else that is not barbecue or barbecue related. A first quick look at the menu might suggest that hot wings are available, but careful reading reveals that the item is in fact "hog wings," which are crisp-fried pork shanks with hot sauce.

There is a slew of side dishes such as baked beans, mac 'n' cheese, pepper cabbage, collard greens, Brunswick stew, hush puppies, and coleslaw, and there is a huge variety of house-made pickles, including sweet, garlic, dill, spicy, and horseradish. But it is meat that counts: hickory-smoked pork shoulders and spare ribs, brisket, ribs, pork belly, sausage, and charcoal-cooked chicken. There's even barbecued tofu!

BROWN'S

| 1218 Avon St. | 434-295-4911 |
| Charlottesville, VA | **L** \| **$** |

Brown's, formerly known as Stoney's Grocery, is now helmed by Mike Brown, who became known to local chicken devotees for the superior quality of what he served at his mini-mart in Esmont, south of Charlottesville. From the outside, you'd never know it's worth a stop, except as a bargain—a sign in the window advertises ten pieces of chicken for $10.99. But once you walk in the door, a first drawn breath will sound the good-eats alert, for the air is redolent of good cooking—not just fried chicken, but also collard greens, spuds, and fruit cobblers to accompany it. Yes, this nondescript place serves four-star bird: drippy and juicy, fine and fatty, tingling with pepper and a shot of some subtle, sneaky spice that veritably glows on your tongue, commanding you to want more and more. At first crunch through the luscious crust, it seems merely well salted, but as you devour it, spices keep rolling across your tongue, making this an incessantly intriguing eating experience.

There are no dining facilities indoors. Everything is takeout.

BROWNSVILLE SHELL

| 5995 Rockfish Gap Tpke. | 434-823-5251 |
| Crozet, VA | **B L D** \| **$** |

★ OPEN EARLY ★ A first glance inside the Brownsville Shell station does nothing to raise one's hopes of finding anything other than beef sticks, fried pork rinds, energy drinks, and horrid plastic-wrapped honey buns. As for dining facilities, there is one small glass-top table with two wire-backed chairs opposite an enormous wall cooler filled with a thousand brands of beer. The store may look ho-hum, but focus on the back corner of the big room, beyond the cash register, and you see a small food-prep area that yields four-star fried chicken.

Nobody at Brownsville Shell was willing to reveal anything about the recipe, but we can tell you that the red-gold crust, fairly glowing with spice, is egg-wash thin, not batter-thick; as our teeth made it crack and break, we knew instantly that we were in the presence of greatness. Curiously, even the dark meat does not ooze rivers of juice when you bite it. All its lusciousness is held within the meat itself, making each bite outlandishly succulent. There are other items on the Brownsville menu, and we do have a soft spot for the chicken broccoli casserole, made with tender noodles and gooped with cheese—a well-balanced home-ec classic from the mid-twentieth century—but it's fried chicken that makes this place a must.

CHARLIE'S CAFÉ

1800 Granby St.   757-625-0824
Norfolk, VA   **B** L | $

When we asked locals for Roadfood suggestions in Hampton Roads, many recommended Charlie's Café, describing it as a great greasy spoon. The wood-frame house does have a well-worn feel and cheap-eats accommodations: bare tables, counter with stools, unbreakable heavy-duty china. And the menu is hash-house cuisine par excellence. But if Charlie's is a greasy spoon in ambience, it is a cut above in food and service. Even the walls are interesting: a gallery for strange and intriguing paintings that are a far cry from standard-issue diner décor.

There is a full lunch menu with burgers of all kinds, sandwiches, salad, and homemade soup, as well as daily specials that always include a full turkey dinner every Thursday; but it's breakfast that is the big draw (very big on weekends; prepare to wait for a table). Omelets are notable. Ingredients are not unique—choices range from fajita chicken or chili filling to vegetarian specials—but the eggs from which they're made are grand. I sat at the counter and watched my potato omelet made (at the suggestion of regional food savant Patrick Evans-Hylton, a potato omelet topped with "habinaro salsa") and didn't see the cook do anything special; yet the fluffy cloud of eggs that arrived on my plate was sheer elegance. In concert with a filling of crisp-fried potatoes and melted jack cheese, it was one splendid breakfast. Potential accompaniments include biscuits, corn bread, Texas toast, and butter-gobbed grits. Coffee is bottomless and tea is sweet.

THE CHICKEN COOP

40 Front St.   434-263-7818
Lovingston, VA   **L D** | $

Perhaps the richest genre of unusually situated excellent food is what's served in gas stations—functioning gas stations like the P&H Truck Stop in Vermont for freshly baked bread (p. 73) and former gas stations like Taco Garage (p. 382) in San Antonio and Freshy's Seafood Market (p. 442) out in Mercer Island, Washington. In and around Charlottesville, Virginia, you will find some of the Mid-South's finest fried chicken served in the most boring, cookie-cutter service stations that look just like a thousand other Citgos, Valeros, and BPs.

The best of the best is at an Exxon Mobil station south of the city along Route 29 in Lovingston. A food-service area known as the Chicken Coop is off to one side, accessible via a walk-up window out on the tarmac where the gas pumps are, or from inside the convenience store, which is known as the Nelson Food Mart. After you place your order, you are given a little tab of paper with the price marked on it. Take the paper to the cash register, where you wait in line with people buying lotto tickets and cigarettes and paying for their gas. Back at the Coop, food is presented on heavy cardboard plates. This chicken features a thin, abundant crust with so many facets and angles you want to call it rococo. It sports a toasty herbal twist—more about comfort than culinary pyrotechnics.

We oohed and ahhed so loudly as we savored Chicken Coop chicken that a lone eater in workman's coveralls at a nearby table asked if this was our first visit. We said it was and expressed our wonder at just how amazingly good the fried chicken is in so many of the area's gas stations. He nodded in knowing agreement, then gestured out to cars passing on the highway, proclaiming, "People out there, they drive right by without a clue. They have no idea what they're missing."

CHUTZPAH
chutzpahdeli.com

12214 Fairfax Towne	703-385-8883
Center	**B L D** | $$
Fairfax, VA	

Located at the far end of a nondescript Fairfax shopping center, Chutzpah is a modest-sized storefront with an immodest personality. Billing itself as a *real* New York deli, it features gigantic sandwiches, smoked fish platters, bagel plates, hot or cold borscht, and a full repertoire of Dr. Brown's sodas. While it is in no way regionally unique, it's a good spot to know about if you want authentic deli food on Interstate 66 west of DC.

Meals begin with bowls of sour and half-sour pickles and creamy coleslaw. We spooned into matzoh ball chicken noodle soup, which was as homey as can be, then feasted on wiener schnitzel—a big, thick slab of juicy meat in an envelope of crunchy, dark-brown crust. It is served with lemon wedges and a large side dish of serious meaty gravy. We thought the gravy superfluous; but the latke (potato pancake) on the side was excellent. Of course, we also had to have a sandwich, but which to choose? Pastrami (annotated on the menu with the advice "Please don't embarrass yourself and ask for mayonnaise"), hot brisket, or chopped liver? We went for a Reuben, which is an extremely unwieldy tower of steamy corned beef, sauerkraut, melted Swiss cheese, and Russian dressing between two crisp-grilled slabs of rye bread. It comes with thick-cut steak fries and it is delicious!

For dessert, we walked out with a nice black-and-white cookie, forgoing the seven-layer cake, carrot cake, and genuine New York cheesecake.

DIXIE BONES BBQ
dixiebones.com

13440 Occoquan Rd.	703-492-2205
Woodbridge, VA	**L D** | $$

Cooked at least a dozen hours over smoking hickory logs, Dixie Bones pork is velvet-soft and gentle-flavored, served in sandwiches heaped on a platter with such side dishes as Laura's favorite creamy-lush macaroni salad, French fries, baked beans, limp greens, and a terrific item known as muddy spuds. That last item is chopped-up baked potato dressed with barbecue sauce.

There are three heat levels of Carolina-style sauce (tomato-sweet/vinegar-tangy), the hottest of which is not incendiary. In addition to boneless pork, there are ribs sold by the rack and half-rack, pork sausage, beef brisket, pulled chicken breast, and fried catfish fillets.

Pies are made here, and we found the individual fried apple pie endearingly soulful—well-sweetened and cooked long enough that the pieces of apple inside were as tender as the barbecued pork. Thursday is lemon pie day. Saturday's pie is sweet potato. Bread pudding with caramel sauce is always available.

DOUMAR'S
doumars.com

1919 Monticello Ave.	757-627-4163
Norfolk, VA	**B L D** (closed Sun) | $

Doumar's has been at the corner of 20th Street and Monticello Avenue in Norfolk since 1934, but it was thirty years before that and in the city of St. Louis that the Doumar name first gained fame. At the World's Fair of 1904, Mr. Doumar introduced a novel way of serving and eating ice cream: the cone. The cone made it possible for fairgoers to walk and eat ice cream at the same time—surely one of the great ideas in culinary history.

Today's Doumar's of Norfolk is marked by a sign with two big ice cream cones on either side, but it's known also for pork barbecue, double-meat hot dogs, burger-and-French-fry plates, and flat grilled cheese sandwiches. As for ice cream, if you choose not to get a traditional waffle cone (still made the old-fashioned way), you can order what is here known as a Reggie (a chocolate milk shake with crushed cone chips), a June Bride (chocolate ice cream topped with strawberry sauce), or a Kingston Flat (strawberry shortcake with bananas). Milk shakes are served in glasses made of . . . glass!

There's plenty of indoor seating, but Doumar's also delivers its classic fare on trays that hang on the window of your car.

DR. HO'S HUMBLE PIE
drhoshumblepie.com

4916 Plank Rd.   434-245-0000
North Garden, VA   L D | $$

This hip, high-spirited place is designed to look like a converted old garage. It is a big space with exposed heat ducts above, vintage signs on the wall, unupholstered chairs and booth benches, bare tables, a poured floor, a high ceiling, and a semi-open kitchen.

Boasting that it serves Charlottesville's best pizza, Dr. Ho's makes pies with a thin, chewy crust topped with ingredients that range from meatballs to crawfish tails, including hen eggs, ground beef, and andouille sausage that all are local. Our favorite is the Bellissima, a gloss on the traditional margherita pizza that also includes arugula, lemon vinaigrette, and thin shavings of country ham from Turner's Ham House at Fulks Run Grocery (p. 157). It is a bewitching combo, the ham a Virginia analog of fine prosciutto di Parma.

Pizza is just one portion of a menu from which we have relished a dish called Crispy Grits-n-Greens, which is spinach, salsa, and red quinoa accompanied by flavorful triangles of crisp-edged grits cakes. We also unequivocally recommend the pickled okra and country ham salad, spicy fried calamari with sesame ginger vinaigrette, and a roasted sweet-potato salad.

Among standout desserts is a baroque chocolate-cookie caramel ice cream sandwich drizzled with chocolate sauce, for which a fork is necessary, and an utterly simple hot milk cake. The latter is a home-cooking paradigm, such a simple and straightforward dessert that it rarely appears on restaurant menus and is often referred to, even in vintage cookbooks,

as "old-fashioned" hot milk cake. Made right, as it is here, and crowned with uncomplicated buttercream frosting, it is not even a little extravagant. It is moist, eggy, and ingenuous—a mother's-hug Dixie classic.

EXMORE DINER
exmorediner.com

4264 Main St.   757-442-2313
Exmore, VA   B L D | $

The Exmore Diner is a wood, tile, and stainless-steel streamliner just off the main highway on Business Route 13 heading into town. It's the sort of place Roadfooders prize not just because it has good things to eat but because it is an ad-hoc community center—the gastronomic version of what now takes place mostly in cyberspace: human interaction. Counter and booths arrayed beneath the curving monitor roof are close enough that unless you speak very quietly, your conversation is open to the public. We first had breakfast here shortly after a fluke blizzard and the place was buzzing with tales of shoveling, busted pipes, frozen gas lines, and treacherous backroads snowdrifts.

Breakfast is an especially good time to come to the Exmore Diner, not just for local color but for such Mid-Atlantic signatures as creamed chipped beef, sausage gravy biscuits, and scrapple with grits. Fried chicken, along with such soulful sides as collard greens, mac 'n' cheese, and braised cabbage, are everyday winners, and the kitchen is known for its seafood, including pancake-flat, griddle-cooked blue crab cakes ("shell is possible," the menu warns); beautiful fried butterflied shrimp; and a platter of all the seafoods in the kitchen, which is, the house boasts, the "largest plate anywhere." Extremely local dishes frequently offered as specials include swelling toads (little panfish that taste great sautéed in butter) and fried ribs from the black drumfish.

You can top things off with rice pudding or bread pudding, but we'll always go for sweet-potato pie. Sweet potato crops are especially bounteous on Virginia's Eastern Shore.

FRANKLIN RESTAURANT

20221 Virgil H. Goode   540-483-5601
Hwy.   **B L D | $**
Rocky Mount, VA

Traveling from Roanoke toward Winston-Salem along the Virgil H. Goode Highway (Route 220) early one morning, we spotted a bunch of vehicles with local license plates pulled into the parking lot at the Franklin Restaurant in Rocky Mount. Upon opening the car door, we were suddenly intoxicated by the smell of sizzling country ham. This is the real stuff, salt cured to a concentrated essence-of-pig flavor that no other meat can match. You can get a big serving as part of a meal with eggs and such or have it more simply sandwiched in one of Franklin's tender, crumbly, homemade biscuits, which have enough body to sop up a full charge of ham essence.

A return trip confirmed that breakfast may be the most important meal of the day, but it's not the only good one in this friendly diner. Supper of turkey with all the trimmings was glorious. It is nothing out of the ordinary: a meal where the much-abused saw "home cooking" would seem to fully apply, except for the fact that salad is retrieved from a (very nice) salad bar. We only wish the wonderful warm peach cobbler that came for dessert had been served alongside the full-flavored ham steak that was our other main course. There aren't too many taste sensations more thrilling than the sweet-salty punch of these two.

FULKS RUN GROCERY

turnerhams.com
11441 Brocks Gap Rd.   540-896-7487
Fulks Run, VA   **$$**

As its name suggests, Fulks Run Grocery is a grocery, not a restaurant. Other than Friday-only ham sandwiches on a makeshift table in back, you can't eat here. But you can buy out-of-this-world Turner Ham. Available with or without the bone and even by the slice or as trimmings for flavoring soups and vegetables, it is cured with brown sugar as well as flake salt, which makes for a ham that is nut-rich, mellow, and memorable. Other highlights of shopping here: pimiento cheese, Virginia peanuts, Red Rooster barbecue sauce, and raspberry-Dijon ham glaze.

Many people who know Turner Hams never even go to Fulks Run; it has been a thriving mail-order business for years. But there is a special pleasure in visiting the wood-floor market and inhaling its smoky perfume. Whole hams, wrapped in nets, are displayed in shopping carts. Merely finding the place is a pleasure. Located along the North Fork of the Shenandoah River just south of the West Virginia border, it is surrounded by nothing but countryside.

GALAX SMOKEHOUSE

thegalaxsmokehouse.com
101 N. Main St.   276-236-1000
Galax, VA   **L D | $$**

A sign on the front of this friendly corner storefront announces "Genuine Pit Barbecue," and that is a promise you can believe. Ravishing ribs, available in slabs from four to twelve bones, come with hush puppies, corn on the cob, sauce-absorbent bread, and such other sides as barbecue beans, fried potatoes, corn nuggets, and smoked mashed potatoes. Brunswick stew, generally served as a side dish but also available by the bowl, is a fork-thick gallimaufry of hunky vegetables. No less than seven different barbecue sauces are available, from Tennessee Sweet to South Carolina Mustard.

If ribs are not your dish, the Smokehouse also offers pulled pork, brisket, and chicken (white or dark), as well as handsome half-pound hamburgers and all-beef hot dogs. Big smoked potatoes are available with just butter and sour cream or loaded with your choice of barbecued meat. Smokehouse banana pudding is some of the best anywhere: big-flavored and soulful.

GOOLRICK'S PHARMACY

901 Caroline St.   540-373-9878
Fredericksburg, VA   L | $

Goolrick's is a vintage pharmacy lunch counter where shakes are still assembled from ice cream, syrup, and milk, whirled by wand, and served in the tall aluminum beaker in which they were mixed. Not only are the shakes great, so is the lemonade, which is freshly squeezed. And while nothing on the lunch menu will win huzzahs on the Food Network, we love a roster of nice, modest sandwiches such as BLT, chicken salad, grilled cheese, cream cheese and olive, and even peanut butter and jelly. If a shake or lemonade doesn't suit your fancy, how about a cherry Coke, vanilla Coke, or chocolate Coke—each made by squirting fountain syrup into the bottom of the glass before the Coke is drawn.

Accommodations are limited to counter stools and a handful of tables along the wall. In back, a compounding pharmacist can actually fill prescriptions the old-fashioned way, by customizing medicines.

★ METOMPKIN SEAFOOD

14209 Lankford Hwy.   757-824-0503
Mappsville, VA   (Tues–Sat 9–6)
                              (closed winter) | $

Cruising along Highway 13 between Temperanceville and Modest Town on Virginia's Eastern Shore, there is no ignoring Metompkin Seafood. Brightly painted yellow sign boards set up by the roadside like a flurry of vintage Burma-Shave ads are emblazoned with red script calling out "soft crabs," "steamed shrimp," "fried fish," "oysters," and "homemade crab cakes." The place is a shack with a wooden crab mascot hung on its clapboards overlooking picnic tables and handwritten menus posted on the wall. Inside is a seafood market and takeout counter, along with a single round table and a couple of rocking chairs where customers who have placed their orders can sit and wait for them to cook.

Fast food this is not. When owner Ellen Hudgins takes your order at the counter, she writes it on a slip of paper and carries it to the back room where the fish is fried, oysters opened, and shrimp steamed. While you wait, you can peruse raw seafood in the case, shop for seasonings and hush-puppy mix on the wall shelves, and watch TV at the single table that is outfitted with paper towels, hot sauce, a local real estate guide, and a Bible. After about fifteen minutes, Ellen announces, "I've got some orders here." Hungry hopefuls listen to see if their time has come. Platters come in Styrofoam clamshells, sandwiches are wrapped in foil; serve yourself canned beverages from the cooler, then dine at a picnic table or in your car.

MRS. ROWE'S

mrsrowes.net
74 Rowe Rd. (Exit 222   540-886-1833
off I-81)   B L D | $
Staunton, VA

Mrs. Rowe's is not what it used to be, but that doesn't mean you won't enjoy its freshly baked biscuits and sticky buns, crunchy fried chicken with mashed potatoes and/or mac 'n' cheese on the side, the pork chop and stewed apple plate, and creamy, meringue-crowned banana pudding. Opened by the late Mildred Rowe decades ago as a mom-and-pop café, the once-homey eatery has become a big roadside enterprise. Its long-lasting fame and its location at the end of a highway exit ramp attract crowds on busy travel weekends (a million people per year!) and sometimes it can seem like an assembly-line eatery. But we've never found the staff less than courteous, and once the food starts coming we easily drop prejudice engendered by Mrs. Rowe's conspicuous success and eat hearty.

ORLEAN MARKET

orleanmarket.com
6855 Leeds Manor Rd.   540-364-2774
Orlean, VA   B L D | $

-- ★ --
LOCALS
LOVE IT
-- ★ --
The Orlean Market really is a market, with an inventory that ranges from mousetraps and 30-weight motor oil to Cheerios and Jell-O. Above the counter up front, a blackboard menu offers ham biscuits, barbecue, and sandwiches, plus such daily specials as Cuban paninis and chili. Place your order, grab a drink from the cooler and maybe a bag of

Mama Zuma's Revenge potato chips, and find a seat at one of the sundry tables scattered around the store or in an adjoining dining room.

We very much enjoyed the crisp-grilled Cuban sandwich and made-to-order house salad with its balsamic reduction decoration, and the hamburgers are first-rate, but the one thing for which we will forever love Orlean Market is coconut layer cake. Made by a local baker, it is fresh and sunny, the frosting extra-thick and sweet but not cloyingly so. The lady who makes it regularly bakes cakes for the Market, about one every other day, her specialties also including caramel cake and hummingbird cake.

PRESTON AVENUE SHELL

601 Preston Ave.   434-296-2004
Charlottesville, VA   **B L D | $**

Preston Avenue Shell is one of several otherwise humdrum gas stations in the Charlottesville area that make and serve superb fried chicken. For the last dozen years, this unlikely eatery with no dining facilities other than a short row of tables up front has earned its reputation for chicken that is crisp on the outside and oozy-juicy within. The most succulent part of all, the thigh, is enveloped in a salty coat that peels away in thick, chewy strips, revealing dark meat that is unconscionably moist.

No one on premises wants to reveal the precise recipe, but we do know that the frying medium is peanut oil, the breading is generously packed with seasoned salt, and the egg wash is just that—eggs without buttermilk.

Among side dishes, collard greens are soft and clumpy, laced with plentiful slivers of pork. We also really like the stewed apples, which are tender and sweet and dusted with cinnamon—a good balance for salty chicken and pungent greens.

★ RED TRUCK RURAL BAKERY

redtruckbakery.com
8368 W. Main St.   540-364-BAKE (2253)
Marshall, VA   **B L | $**

There now are two Red Truck Bakeries: the original, cute little café in Warrenton and a larger main location in nearby Marshall. The new place has more seating and more to eat; both sell the magnificent baked goods that have made this rural bakery a runaway success. These include such palate-boggling creations as moonshine double-chocolate cake, real suet-rich mince pie, bourbon cake, and fruit pies based on what happens to be ripe at that time of year. Plus the best granola on earth.

In addition to the baked pastries (and weekend donuts) that always have been available at the Warrenton location, the Marshall store also offers biscuit sandwiches for breakfast, ham and cheese croissants, Baker Brian Noyes' aunt's smoky pimento cheese, seasonal flatbreads, and even ice cream with Red Truck mixins (cinnamon ice cream packed with granola). Both places feature a soup of the day—a sensationally piggy black-bean soup with bacon, sausage, and ham, for instance—as well as a small selection of sandwiches: chicken salad made from local chickens, egg salad made with eggs laid by those local chickens, ham and cheese, meat loaf, and spectacularly succulent meatless beet loaf. All sandwiches, of course, are made with freshly baked bread.

The cafés are eminently hospitable, staffed by folks who obviously like being surrounded by some of the best baked goods anywhere. If you can't get to them, the Red Truck Bakery is all set up for mail-order sales.

The original location is at 22 Waterloo Street in Warrenton (540-347-2224).

ROANOKER

theroanokerrestaurant.com

2522 Colonial Ave.   540-344-7746
Roanoke, VA   **B L D** (closed Mon) | **$**

When we first came across the Roanoker while researching the first edition of this book, it was a snug little downtown café with a front window full of burlap-wrapped country hams. When it moved to its present location in 1982, it became a sanitary middle-class lunchroom and lost its vintage ambience. But breakfast of ultrathin "wafer-sliced" country ham with red-eye gravy, fried apples, and biscuits remained the menu headliner. The ham still is good, as are crunchy corn sticks, candied yams, peppery boiled cabbage, congealed salads (aka Jell-O), and always several highly seasoned greens and beans. Of course, there is fried chicken, and a dinner-thick country ham steak also is available, served with red-eye gravy.

Dessert pies include sweet potato, egg custard, peach, and apple.

RUDY'S

thorntonrivergrille.com/#/rudys-pizza

3710 Sperryville Pike   540-987-9494
Sperryville, VA   **L D** (closed Mon & Tues) | **$**

Having lived in the Northeast, where excellent pizza is commonplace, we tend to be snobbish on the subject. But every once in a while we are surprised by good pizza in an unlikely place. "Not bad pizza for the middle of nowhere," boasted one of the pizzaioli at Rudy's in Sperryville, Virginia, just east of Shenandoah National Park. We say it's better than that. Rudy's makes pretty darn good pizza by any standard, and while it isn't going to knock Pepe's, Zuppardi's, or Pizzeria Bianco off anybody's top-ten list, it is a very worthy Rappahannock County destination.

Located in a vintage grocery store and adjoining the Thornton River Grille, the pizza parlor offers a scattering of tables and stand-up viewing of the pizzas being made. They are handsome pies, Neapolitan-thin with a puffy collar. The mozzarella is creamy, the crust is chewy, and the locally made sausage is pig-perfect.

All the usual toppings are available, plus fancier items such as artichoke, sun-dried tomato, and prosciutto. Build your own or choose from a roster of house specialties that includes Skyline BBQ Chicken (feta cheese, barbecue sauce, and a balsamic vinegar glaze), Maui Wowi (pineapple, ham, onion, jalapeño, and teriyaki glaze), and Rappahannock Veggie.

One thing we like about Rudy's, other than the fact that the pizza is good, is its prices. What is here known as a "personal pizza" is sized for one very hungry person. Costing all of $5, plus 75¢ per extra topping, it is a tremendous bargain. A large pie, which will easily satisfy three normal appetites, goes for $13, plus $1.75 per extra ingredient.

SALLY BELL'S KITCHEN

sallybellskitchen.com

708 W. Grace St.   804-644-2838
Richmond, VA   **L** (Mon-Fri) | **$**

Sally Bell's Kitchen was conceived in 1924 as a bakery, and that is what it is today—a charming relic from the past, with Sally Lunn muffins, pies, tarts, and that nearly lost icon of the Old South kitchen, beaten biscuits. The biscuits are crisp, tan rounds with silky tops that are an ideal companion for bisque or Sally Bell's tomato aspic. Cupcakes are notable because they are iced all over, not just on top. We love the strawberry cupcakes, so pretty in pink.

There is no place to eat on premises, but boxed lunch is a specialty. Inside a white cardboard box, inscribed with the trademark feminine silhouette, you will find a sandwich on a made-here roll or bread, a cup of macaroni or potato salad, a cupcake . . . and this marvelous thing called a cheese wafer. Topped with a single half pecan, it is delicate and fragile—a couple of bites and it is gone—a taste of a more refined era long before supersizing. Among available sandwich ingredients are chicken salad, egg salad, Smithfield ham, cream cheese with nuts or olives, and, of course, pimiento cheese.

SNOW WHITE GRILL

snowwhitegrill.com

159 N. Loudoun St.   540-662-5955

Winchester, VA   L D | $

The star dish on the menu of this adorable 1949 diner is known as a Mini-Burger. It is a chunky little patty served with de rigueur grilled onions and pickle chips on a steamed roll. (Cheese, lettuce, and tomato also are available, but they do tend to overwhelm the package.) It is not the King of All Burgers, but in the world of satisfying sliders, it is a prince. We were less impressed by Snow White hot dogs. Even if ordered deep-fried and therefore offering admirable crunch, and despite options of chili, cheese, and thirteen different condiments, the all-beef dogs themselves are blah. A good alternative is the grilled cheese sandwich, for which the bread (rye, please) is buttered enough to turn crisp on the griddle. "We have white or orange cheese," advises the counterman before he assembles it, recommending a double-barrel version made from slices of each. The two identical-tasting cheeses do create a cheerful swirly pattern when they melt together and start oozing from the sides of the sandwich.

Dine at the counter or in a small al fresco area on the pedestrian mall on Loudon Street. Nice as the outdoor area is, we prefer inside seats, which allow more interaction with the staff. They all seem to enjoy working in the vintage diner, our grill man explaining that the top-of-the-line milk shake is Chocolate-Covered Cherry, a chocolate shake laced with maraschino cherry juice. It is served in a tall silver beaker.

Note to competitive eaters: The Snow White Grill hosts an ongoing contest to see who can eat the most burgers in ten minutes. Last we looked, the first-place holder had consumed twenty-one.

SOUTHERN KITCHEN

9576 S. Congress St.   540-740-3514

New Market, VA   B L D | $

If you want something genuine to eat, something genuinely southern, bypass the junk-food restaurants clustered near I-81 and find a seat in the dining room, at the counter, or in one of the old booths of the Southern Kitchen. Here you will find country ham at breakfast and Virginia peanut soup at lunch. The soup is the consistency of light cream, nutty-flavored but not like liquid peanut butter, and laced with fetching onion sweetness. A little goes a long way; it is an Old Dominion specialty whose svelte character is a perfect hors d'oeuvre before a supper of powerhouse country ham.

If a thick slice of that good ham is just too intense for dinner, consider fried chicken, encased in a succulent golden crust, or even fried oysters, which, considering the location hundreds of miles from seawater, are surprisingly bright. Among noteworthy sides are stewed tomatoes made the traditional southern way—extra-sweet; a welcome balance for the ham. Pies are homemade and worth saving appetite for—especially coconut meringue.

STING-RAY'S

cape-center.com

26507 Lankford Hwy.   757-331-1541

Cape Charles, VA   B L D | $$

Located on Virginia's Eastern Shore and known to locals as Chez Exxon, Sting-Ray's shares space with fuel pumps, a pottery shop, and a boat-storage facility. Instead of the familiar gas station repertoire of corn dogs and cellophane-wrapped honey buns, it is a source of superb local cuisine.

Oysters and shrimp are expertly fried (marinated shrimp are gorgeous too). A not-to-be-missed kitchen specialty is sweet-potato biscuits. Made from a recipe that is decades old, they are particularly good sandwiching thin slices of country ham, which, being Virginia ham, isn't all that brackish. Regional highlights also include ultra-luxurious crab imperial and flounder stuffed with crab imperial as well as a creamed crab dish that isn't really a stew but is too thick to pass as a soup.

Deluxe though some dishes may be, service at Sting-Ray's is down-home. Place your order at the counter and pay. Find a seat (which can be difficult on weekends) and your food will be brought out by one of a staff of professional waitresses. One named Etta turned out to be a fount of Sting-Ray's history as well as a top-notch adviser when it came to ordering, steering us toward the sweet-potato pie for dessert. Its creamy goodness was accented by a dollop of bright-flavored damson plum preserves.

STUART'S FRESH CATCH

stuartsfreshcatch.com

2400 Mechanicsville Tpke.   804-643-3474
Richmond, VA   **L D** (closed Mon) | $

Stuart's is a storefront seafood market with no place for customers to eat. Everything is sold fried (or grilled), either ready to eat by the tray, dinner, piece, and sandwich, or ready to take home and cook. We accompanied our sandwich of cream-fleshed fried lake trout, fried oysters, and fried shrimp with individual orders of exemplary collard greens, fried okra, macaroni and cheese, and, best of all, spoonbread. A rarity in any other region and ever more difficult to find even in the South, this billowy corn pudding has a kind of gaiety that tastes as much of corn as any outside sweetener. It is earthy but elegant, and even though it does require a spoon, it makes an ideal companion for hunks of golden-crusted lake trout with its dense meat and crisp golden crust that is so right to pick up and eat with fingers.

VIRGINIA DINER

vadinerrestaurant.com

408 County Dr. N.   757-899-3106
Wakefield, VA   **B L D** | $

The sign outside Wakefield's Virginia Diner declares it to be the Peanut Capital of the World. Here you can buy pounds of Virginia peanuts, which are 100 percent better than any other peanuts: big, crunchy, dark, and rich. They come salted or unsalted, spiced with Old Bay seasoning or Cajun pepper, butter-toasted, in the shell or shelled, and as the foundation for a truly aristocratic peanut brittle.

Curiously, there are not a lot of peanuts served in the restaurant, although it used to be that Virginia ham had to be made from peanut-fed pigs (no more). This diner's ham is terrific, available baked or fried. Fried chicken, having nothing to do with peanuts, is also mighty good, sheathed in a brittle crust. With these fine southern entrees, you can choose turnip greens, candied yams, spoonbread, black-eyed peas, or stewed tomatoes.

For dessert, you definitely want peanut pie. Served warm, it is a simple dish similar to pecan pie but not so plush.

WAYSIDE TAKEOUT & CATERING

waysidechicken.com

2203 Jefferson Park Ave.   434-977-5000
Charlottesville, VA   **B L D** (closed Sun) | $

Gordonsville, Virginia, was once known as the fried chicken capital of the world. In the years after the Civil War, emancipated slaves used to sell their chicken, along with biscuits and pie, to train passengers who came through what was then a major transportation hub of the Mid-South. Today, Gordonsville continues to host an annual Fried Chicken Festival, but to eat it at its best in a restaurant, head twenty miles southwest to Charlottesville to an outfit called Wayside Takeout & Catering.

All parts of the chicken are available, but for us, thighs rule. Wayside's thighs are crunch-crusted, juicy, and so subtly seasoned that you don't at first fully appreciate the mastery until you are already down to the bone and find yourself hunting for another piece or any little shred or patch of crisp skin that has fallen into the Styrofoam dishware. Drumsticks are great too: oozingly yummy when warm, but also a great room-temperature snack any time of day.

As its name says, a large portion of business is takeout (everything is presented in to-go containers), but there are picnic tables outside as well as a scattering of seats indoors. Dining companions will likely include students from the nearby University of Virginia, here to take advantage of the low prices, casual setting, and better-than-home fried chicken.

WEENIE BEENIE

2680 S. Shirlington Rd.	703-671-6661
Arlington, VA	**B L D** (closed Sun)	**$**

Weenie Beenie is the sole survivor of a small Washington-area chain of drive-ins specializing in half-smokes. No one knows for sure how the half-smoke got its name (perhaps because it's only half-smoky or because many places, like Weenie Beenie, bisect them horizontally before they are grilled), but it is unique to the area around the District of Columbia. Here you can have one at lunch dressed with chili (known as a chili smoke), mustard, onions, and relish. At breakfast your half-smoke will be matched with a fried egg and a slice of bright orange cheese.

Regular hot dogs also are available, but they look pretty boring to us. You also can order barbecue pork or just a bowl of beef chili. Picnic tables are arrayed along the side of the takeout-only restaurant for those who choose not to eat in their cars.

WRIGHT'S DAIRY-RITE

dairy-rite.com

346 Greenville Ave.	540-886-0435
Staunton, VA	**L D**	**$**

The star of the menu is a Superburger: two beef patties with cheese and lettuce, topped with special sauce and layered in a triple-decker bun. First served in 1952, it is still served as it was then, by carhops at the window of your vehicle in a car slip at the side of the restaurant. Wright's added a dining room in 1989, so it is also possible to eat inside, where décor includes a Wurlitzer jukebox and vintage Wright's menus from the 1950s and 1960s. In 1958, the Superburger cost 55¢.

Handsome as the Superburger is, we prefer a Monsterburger (a half-pound patty) or a Carolina burger (with cheese, chili, slaw, and onion); they tend not to lose their juice, which can be a fault of the smaller ones. On the side, you want Wright's homemade onion rings. Milk shakes are the real thing, available in chocolate, strawberry, or vanilla, as well as with bananas or strawberries, with or without malt powder for additional richness. It is, after all, Wright's *Dairy*-Rite, so don't hesitate to have a banana split, a float, or a flurry (candy and/or cookies blended into soft-serve ice cream).

Wright's menu goes well beyond burgers. There are regular and foot-long hot dogs, corn dogs, pork barbecue on a bun, sandwich baskets, submarines, chili with beans, even a veggie wrap with fat-free dressing. In addition to milk shakes and soda pop, the beverage list includes freshly brewed iced tea (sweet or not) served in twenty-ounce cups.

★ COLEMAN'S FISH MARKET

2226 Market St.   304-232-8510
Wheeling, WV   L D | $

Coleman's fish sandwich is simplicity itself: two pieces of soft white bread holding a cluster of steaming-hot fried-fish fillets. It is delivered across a counter, wrapped in wax paper. Find a table on the broad floor of the renovated century-old Wheeling Centre Market House, unwrap, and feast!

The crust on the North Atlantic pollock fillets is made of cracker meal, thin as parchment. When you break through it, your sense of smell is tickled by a clean ocean perfume, and as the pearl-white meat seeps warm sweetness, you taste a brand-new food, like no other fish sandwich ever created.

After you've eaten several dozen over time, you might want to branch out and try some of the many other excellent foods Coleman's makes: a Canadian white sandwich (a bit blander and "whiter"-tasting than the regular fish), shrimp boats and baskets, fried clams, oysters, deviled crabs, and Cajun-spiced catfish. Coleman's really is a fish market, and if you wait in the "Special Line" (as opposed to the "Regular Sandwich Line"), you can ask the staff to cook up just about any raw fish in the case, and pay for it by weight. On the side of whatever fish you get, there are good French fries and Jo-Jo potatoes, and onion rings every day but Friday (when the deep fryers are totally devoted to making only fish sandwiches).

DIEHL'S FAMILY RESTAURANT

152 Main Ave.   304-755-9353
Nitro, WV   L D | $

Now run by a third generation of the Diehl family, this gem of a restaurant seems never to have heard of convenience cooking. Everything is made from scratch. "Do you know?" asks the paper placemat, and several bulleted points give you the facts, including, "We make our own Thousand Island dressing," "Cornbread and hot rolls made daily," and "Special hot bologna sauce since 1960." Whether you come for a $5 pulled-pork sandwich or a $7 twelve-ounce cheeseburger, we guarantee that you will be whistling a happy tune when you are finished. Big-deal dinners, selling for about $10, include bone-in country ham, roast beef and mashed potatoes with gravy, and huge plates of spaghetti with meat sauce or marinara. On the side come such country veggies as creamed tomatoes, buttered corn, fried apples, and sage dressing.

Whatever you eat, save room for dessert. Creamy-sweet graham-cracker pie is the highlight, but when Roadfood.com's Dale Fine visited in 2011, he reported that the chocolate peanut butter pie was not to be missed, describing it as "moist, rich, and truly decadent."

Interior décor consists of enthusiastic odes to NASCAR and local sports teams, including model cars, pennants, and a fender that came off Dale Earnhardt's car when he hit the wall at Bristol Motor Speedway.

JULIO'S CAFE

501 Baltimore Ave.   304-622-2592
Clarksburg, WV   **L D** (closed Sun) | **$$**

Across from the train station in the old Glen Elk section of Clarksburg, Julio's is a first-rate Italian restaurant with a tin ceiling, carved wooden bar, and plush leather booths. While the food is prepared by a chef with culinary expertise and prices are fairly high, service is neighborhood-friendly.

The bill of fare includes four different versions of *pasta e fagiole*—with cream sauce, with marinara, with potatoes and kale, and *en brodo* that twinkles with fennel. There are Italian-American standards such as lasagna, spaghetti with meatballs, and pasta primavera made with uncooked vegetables in red sauce. Waitresses recite what is available for any given meal.

For an hors d'oeuvre, we love the "paisano salad," a cold antipasto plate topped with the kitchen's jade-green garlic-basil dressing, and roasted pepper–gorgonzola bruschetta. Other favorite dishes include red peppers stuffed with hot ground sausage atop a bed of al dente spaghetti noodles and a stylish plate of tuna pomodoro. Meals commence with a basket of garlic toast and conclude with an outrageously rich house-made éclair loaded with French cream and blanketed with chocolate.

OLIVERIO'S CASH AND CARRY

427 Clark St.   304-622-8612
Clarksburg, WV   **$**

"This was once *the* spot in Clarksburg," Angela Oliverio told us several years ago as she slid a long length of pig gut onto the spout of her hand-cranked sausage-making machine. "We had everything here in Elk Point [the Clarksburg neighborhood where her grocery is located]: prostitution, gambling, big business, street-corner business, thriving industry."

While not by any means a bustling metropolis, Elk Point is coming back and, most important, Oliverio's is as wonderful as ever: a vintage, family-run grocery store where Angela sits in back and with the help of her brother John cranks out lengths of Italian pork sausage seasoned with paprika, fennel seed, and hot pepper. She also prepares bowls full of peppered green and black olives that she will sell you by the pint.

Note that Oliverio's is not a restaurant. It is a little grocery store, and unless Angela takes a liking to you and you happen to arrive just when she's cooked up a batch of her sausage for tasting, you cannot eat here.

QUINET'S COURT

quinetscatering.com
215 Main St.   304-455-2110
New Martinsville, WV   **B L D** | **$**

★ LOCALS LOVE IT ★ "We use the area's finest hobby chefs' recipes often," boasts the printed menu of Quinet's Court, where the choice of items on multiple buffet tables is cornucopic. Although presented in big institutional pans on room-length steam tables, most of the dishes seem like home cooking at its finest—from cake-smooth corn bread to stuffed peppers to cream pies, cobblers, cookies, and pudding.

To accompany baby-back ribs, kielbasa, chicken casserole, or ham loaf with pineapple glaze, customers avail themselves of a side-dish smorgasbord to make even a devoted vegetarian smile. Silk-tender butter beans, sweet hunks of carrot, scalloped potatoes, homemade noodles, five-cheese mac 'n' cheese, and baked beans can fill a plate.

The buffet rule is that you pay one price and help yourself to as much as you want. A sign at the beginning of the first table does warn, however, that a $2 surcharge will be added to the bill of anyone who wastes food. Our waitress was especially generous. As we walked in the door, early during lunch hour, we noted a couple of beautiful sticky buns in a pan left-over from breakfast. When we asked her if we could have one, she brought it, no charge, and told us simply to consider it part of our lunch buffet.

Accommodations are appropriately vast: big tables in several spacious dining rooms. Décor includes an awesome picture of prizefighter Jack Dempsey (who ate here in the 1940s) and thousands of pictures of town history and local citizens. It is possible to dine non-buffet-style: breakfast, lunch sandwiches, and a selection of hot meals listed on the menu under the heading "Great Specials for Our Not-So-Hungry Friends."

RITZY LUNCH

456 W. Pike St.   304-622-3600
Clarksburg, WV   **B L** (closed Sun) | **$**

Hot Dog John Selario's parents opened Ritzy Lunch in 1933. "Ritzy Lunch has always been known for hot dogs," he tells us. "Clarksburg itself is an important hot dog town, not so much because of the weenies but because of the way we make our chili. There are so many immigrants and sons and daughters of immigrants—Greeks and Italians, mostly—that when we spice up our chili, we know how to do it right!" He will get no argument from us. His dogs are lovely little puppies, buried deep inside a steamed-soft bun and topped with a zesty ground-beef sauce that is lightly peppered and earthy-flavored. If you want to add a sweet note, get a layer of coleslaw atop the chili—a popular configuration throughout West Virginia.

Note also the Giovanni, a burger topped with melted cheese and roasted peppers served between two slices of butter-and-garlic-infused toast. Excellent!

Ritzy Lunch is an immensely happy place, a sort of non-alcoholic tavern where old friends and town characters hang out on the ancient counter stools to kibitz back and forth among themselves and the waitresses and where, on any pleasant day, two or three wiseacres are likely to be found out on the sidewalk making friends with newcomers.

RUBY & KETCHY'S

2232 Cheat Rd.   304-594-2004
Morgantown, WV   **B L D** | **$**

LOCALS LOVE IT Ruby and Ketchy's is an out-of-the-way diner in the Cheat Lake area east of Morgantown. It's open for three meals a day, and its knotty-pine booths and counter are usually occupied by locals who come for good eats and conversation. Opened by Ruby Nicholson in 1958, who was soon joined by husband Ketchy, it's still run by their descendants, and many of the recipes, including the vegetable soup, chili, and every-Tuesday meat loaf, are Ruby's.

Hot meals range from crab cakes to sirloin steak, and such lunch specials as bean soup and corn bread (every Thursday) and salmon patties with mac 'n' cheese on Friday. We enjoyed our ham dinner, of which the menu boasts "served over 30 years." The ham was pan-sizzled and had a rewarding chew. Hot roast beef was also good: pot-roast tender and accompanied by a sphere of mashed potatoes covered with gravy. If you come for dinner on Friday, you can order stuffed cabbage, which Roadfood.com's Buffetbuster has declared his favorite Ruby & Ketchy's dish.

Blackberry pie is the go-to dessert. It is dark purple and winey, with a rugged berry texture. The crust could have been flakier, but the filling was first-rate.

STEWART'S ORIGINAL HOT DOGS

stewartshotdogs.com
2445 5th Ave.   304-529-3647
Huntington, WV   **L D** (closed Mon) | **$**

With countless stands and storefronts that specialize in spicy little weenies topped with chili and coleslaw, West Virginia considers itself the hot dog capital of the universe. The best place to test that claim is Stewart's, a curb-service drive-in since 1932. The formula includes local Logan hot dogs and Heiner's buns and, most important, all the trimmings: onions, mustard, and—drum roll, please—Stewart's secret-recipe chili sauce. The sauce is thick and pasty, not too hot. West Virginia hot dog connoisseurs believe the picture is not complete unless it also includes coleslaw as part of the trimmings constellation; Stewart's is creamy with a bit of pickle bite.

To drink, nearly everybody swills renowned Stewart's root beer, available in quantities that range from a four-ounce mug for kids to a thirty-two-ounce drink to a gallon jug. Or you can enjoy it as the basis of an ice cream float.

Note: There is another Stewart's location in the Huntington area: 1025 Oak Street in Kenova (304-453-3647).

DEEP SOUTH

ARKANSAS

SOUTH CAROLINA

ALABAMA

GEORGIA

MISSISSIPPI

LOUISIANA

FLORIDA

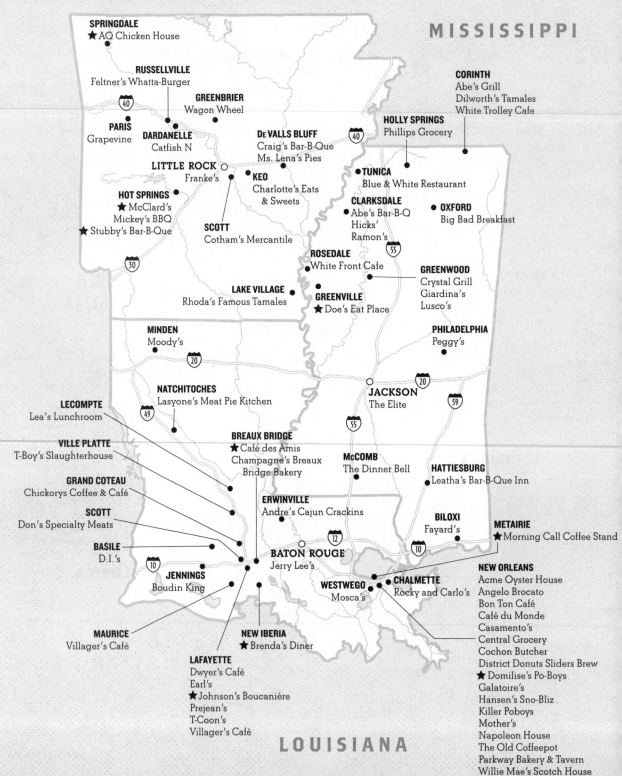

ARKANSAS

MISSISSIPPI

SPRINGDALE
★ AQ Chicken House

RUSSELLVILLE
Feltner's Whatta-Burger

GREENBRIER
Wagon Wheel

CORINTH
Abe's Grill
Dilworth's Tamales
White Trolley Cafe

PARIS
Grapevine

DARDANELLE
Catfish N

De VALLS BLUFF
Craig's Bar-B-Que
Ms. Lena's Pies

HOLLY SPRINGS
Phillips Grocery

LITTLE ROCK
Franke's

KEO
Charlotte's Eats
& Sweets

TUNICA
Blue & White Restaurant

HOT SPRINGS
★ McClard's
Mickey's BBQ
★ Stubby's Bar-B-Que

CLARKSDALE
Abe's Bar-B-Q
Hicks'
Ramon's

OXFORD
Big Bad Breakfast

SCOTT
Cotham's Mercantile

ROSEDALE
White Front Cafe

GREENWOOD
Crystal Grill
Giardina's
Lusco's

LAKE VILLAGE
Rhoda's Famous Tamales

GREENVILLE
★ Doe's Eat Place

MINDEN
Moody's

PHILADELPHIA
Peggy's

NATCHITOCHES
Lasyone's Meat Pie Kitchen

JACKSON
The Elite

LECOMPTE
Lea's Lunchroom

BREAUX BRIDGE
★ Café des Amis
Champagne's Breaux
Bridge Bakery

McCOMB
The Dinner Bell

VILLE PLATTE
T-Boy's Slaughterhouse

HATTIESBURG
Leatha's Bar-B-Que Inn

GRAND COTEAU
Chickorys Coffee & Café

ERWINVILLE
Andre's Cajun Crackins

SCOTT
Don's Specialty Meats

BILOXI
Fayard's

METAIRIE
★ Morning Call Coffee Stand

BASILE
D.I.'s

JENNINGS
Boudin King

BATON ROUGE
Jerry Lee's

NEW ORLEANS
Acme Oyster House
Angelo Brocato
Bon Ton Café
Café du Monde
Casamento's
Central Grocery
Cochon Butcher
District Donuts Sliders Brew
★ Domilise's Po-Boys
Galatoire's
Hansen's Sno-Bliz
Killer Poboys
Mother's
Napoleon House
The Old Coffeepot
Parkway Bakery & Tavern
Willie Mae's Scotch House

WESTWEGO
Mosca's

CHALMETTE
Rocky and Carlo's

MAURICE
Villager's Café

NEW IBERIA
★ Brenda's Diner

LAFAYETTE
Dwyer's Café
Earl's
★ Johnson's Boucanière
Prejean's
T-Coon's
Villager's Café

LOUISIANA

ALABAMA

MADISON
Greenbrier Restaurant

BESSEMER
Bob Sykes Bar B-Q

BIRMINGHAM
Bogue's
★ Niki's West

TUSCALOOSA
The Waysider

PHENIX CITY
13th Street Bar-B-Q

MONTGOMERY
★ Martin's

MOBILE
The Brick Pit
Cream & Sugar Café
Dew Drop Inn
Wintzell's Oyster House

PANAMA CITY
J.R.'s Rib Shack

PENSACOLA
Captain Joey Patti's
Seafood Restaurant
Jerry's Drive-in
Marina Oyster Barn

PORT ST. JOE
Indian Pass Raw Bar
Smiley's Chicken

APALACHICOLA
Apalachicola Seafood Grill
Boss Oyster

CARRABELLE
The Fisherman's Wife

EASTPOINT
★ Lynn's Quality Oysters

TALLAHASSEE
Olean's Cafe

WAKULLA SPRINGS
Wakulla Springs Lodge

CRAWFORDVILLE
Mineral Springs Seafood
by the Bay
Spring Creek Restaurant

PANACEA
Posey's Steam Room
and Oyster Bar

FLEMING ISLAND
Whitey's Fish Camp

JACKSONVILLE
Beach Road Chicken Dinners
Jenkins Quality Barbecue

FERNANDINA BEACH
T-Ray's Burger Station

MAYPORT
Singleton's Seafood Shack

ST. AUGUSTINE
Barnacle Bill's
★ O'Steen's
Saltwater Cowboys
Schooner Seafood House

DE LEON SPRINGS
Old Spanish Sugar Mill Grill

NEW SMRYNA BEACH
JB's Fish Camp

MAITLAND
Gordon's Be Back Fish House

WINTER PARK
Toasted
Winter Park Fish Co.

ORLANDO
Chef Eddie's
Cuban Sandwiches
P & D Soul Food Kitchen

TAMPA
La Teresita Cafeteria

WEST PALM BEACH
Havana

FLORIDA

KEY WEST
Blue Heaven
El Siboney
Louie's Backyard
Pepe's Café & Steakhouse

MARATHON
Keys Fisheries

SOUTH CAROLINA

GEORGIA

JOHNSTON
Triangle Restaurant

BELTON
Grits & Groceries

GREENVILLE
Northgate Soda Shop

WASHINGTON
Big Chick

LANDRUM
Southside Smokehouse

SOUTH LYMAN
Hot Dog Cafe

CLARKS HILL
La Cantina

GRANITEVILLE
Bush's

TUCKER
Matthews Cafeteria

GROVETOWN
Perry Foster's BBQ

RIDGE SPRING
★ Juniper

WATKINSVILLE
Hot Thomas' Barbeque

SPARTANBURG
Beacon Drive-in

DECATUR
Community BBQ

DILLARD
Dillard House

FORT MILL
521 BBQ & Grill

CHATSWORTH
Edna's

DAHLONEGA
Smith House

LEESVILLE
★ Jackie Hite's Bar-B-Que
Shealy's Bar-B-Que

WEST COLUMBIA
★ Hite's Bar-B-Que
True BBQ

KENNESAW
Stilesboro Biscuits

SOCIAL CIRCLE
Blue Willow Inn

MONETTA
Peaches 'n' Such

COLUMBIA
(see below)

HEMINGWAY
Scott's Bar-B-Que

MARIETTA
Mountain Biscuits

SMYRNA
Old South Bar-B-Q

CAYCE
The Kingsman

SALLEY
Hilltop Café

COLLEGE PARK
Barbecue Kitchen
Big Daddy's Dish

ATLANTA
(see below)

THOMSON
Sweet T's

AIKEN
(see below)

SUMMERTON
Summerton Diner

HEPHZIBAH
Dennis' BBQ

NEW ELLENTON
Carolina Bar-B-Que

AWENDAW
SeeWee Restaurant

JACKSON
Buckner's Family Restaurant

AUGUSTA
(see below)

BEECH ISLAND
Freeman's BBQ

NORTH CHARLESTON
★ Bertha's Kitchen
Evo

JOHNS ISLAND
Fishnet Seafood

WARM SPRINGS
Bulloch House

WAYNESBORO
Taylor's Bar-B-Que

NORTH AUGUSTA
DeShawn's Seafood
and Chicken

CHARLESTON
82 Queen
★ Bowens Island
Dave's Carry-Out
★ Hominy Grill
Hyman's Seafood
Martha Lou's Kitchen
Middleton Place Restaurant
WildFlour Pastry

MOUNT PLEASANT
The Wreck

FORT VALLEY
Peachtree Café

COLUMBUS
Dinglewood Pharmacy

SAVANNAH
Mrs. Wilkes' Dining Room

DARIEN
Skipper's Fish Camp

BEAUFORT
Sgt. White's

TYBEE ISLAND
The Crab Shack

ATLANTA
The Colonnade
★ Mary Mac's Tea Room
Silver Skillet
Varsity Drive-In

BLUFFTON
Cahill's Chicken Kitchen

AIKEN
Betsy's on the Corner
Charlie's Fish Market
City Billiards
Dukes
Track Kitchen

AUGUSTA
Hildebrandt's
Honey From the Rock Café
★ Perry's Pig
Ruth's Family Restaurant
Sconyer's Bar-B-Que
Sports Center

COLUMBIA
Big Boy's Original Smokehouse
Ray's Diner
Rockaway Athletic Club

ALABAMA

13TH STREET BAR-B-Q

13thstbbqofladonia.com

3869 US Hwy. 80 W   334-291-1855
Phenix City, AL   **L D** (closed Sun & Mon) | **$**

We've eaten a few memorable pork chop sandwiches around the country, from Helen's Sausage House in Delaware to Pork Chop John's in Montana and, of course, the hallowed Snappy Lunch in Mount Airy, North Carolina. Here's a real beauty, in an inconspicuous smokehouse that bills itself as "Home of the Original Pork Chop Sandwich." You get a pair of thick, boneless slabs dressed with a measure of slaw and your choice of mild or (very) hot mustard sauce. The sandwich arrives in a tender, poppy-seeded roll that serves not only as a good mitt for lifting the chop but as a quiet bready counterpoint for the succulent meat and spicy sauce.

The full barbecue menu also includes ribs crusted with vivid glaze as well as barbecue sandwiches and plates: chipped, chopped, or sliced. 13th Street also makes its own version of the scrambled dog, which here is two hot dogs topped with chili, cheese, onions, and coleslaw. Yet to be sampled: a five-pound "Hawg Dog," selling for $24.95.

BOB SYKES BAR B-Q

bobsykes.com

1724 9th Ave. N.   205-426-1400
Bessemer, AL   **L D** (closed Sun) | **$$**

Bob Sykes opened in 1957, and at one time there were fourteen Bob Sykes barbecues in northern Alabama, but in 1977 the Sykes family decided to concentrate on one location in Bessemer, southwest of Birmingham. Since then, this smokehouse, now run by a third generation of Sykeses who still uses the original recipes, has been a smoke signal of good eats.

Cooked over smoldering hickory wood, the pork is finely chopped and succulent; ribs are beautiful burnished mahogany with great hefty ribbons of meat around each bone; chopped beef is particularly flavorful. "Big Bob" specials include your barbecued meat of choice with baked beans, coleslaw, and French fries or potato salad, plus rolls. For those with a lot of hungry mouths to feed, Sykes's menu lists extra-large orders for five or ten (the latter is based on two and a half pounds of barbecue and comes with a gallon of tea). Carry-out meals and big feeds for twenty-five people and more are sold at a drive-through window. Pies are excellent, sold by the slice, whole pie, or junior pie. You can get chocolate, pecan, and coconut. The one that must be sampled is the meringue-topped lemon pie: sweet, creamy, and southern to its soul.

BOGUE'S

3028 Clairmont Ave.   205-254-9780
Birmingham, AL   **B L D** | $

--★--
LOCALS
LOVE IT
--★--
Despite the motto "It's Vogue to Eat at Bogue's," you won't have to worry about those bothersome paparazzi when you dine here. If you seek an epicurean breakfast, obsequious service, or the trendy restaurant where fashionistas dine, Bogue's is all wrong. If, on the other hand, you want a cheap, rib-sticking breakfast featuring grilled country ham, buttered grits, and biscuits so richly endowed with cooking grease that your fingers glisten after you split one in half, this is where you want to be. If for some reason you don't want biscuits, we highly recommend the caramel sweet rolls.

All the usual subjects are available as breakfast meat, plus flavorful boneless pork chops that look especially right sandwiched between biscuits.

THE BRICK PIT
brickpit.com

5456 Old Shell Rd.   251-343-0001
Mobile, AL   **L D** (closed Sun & Mon) | $$

Pitmaster Bill Armbrecht operates a room-sized pit into which he piles hickory and pecan logs and cooks meats at the lowest possible temperature for the longest possible time. Pork shoulder basks in smoke for some thirty hours; ribs for twelve; chicken for six. During the process, the meats' natural fat becomes their basting juices; by the time they are done, each piece of pork and chicken is virtually fatless, yet moister than moist.

We're especially smitten with the pulled pork. It is presented as a pile of motley chunks and shreds—some as soft as warm butter, others with a crunchy crust. Ribs are blackened on the outside but extravagantly tender, with many areas so gentled by their tenure in the smoke pit that the lightest finger pressure causes pieces of meat to slide off the bone.

The low-slung dining room at the Brick Pit is painted white and completely covered in signatures, tributes, and other happy graffiti. Orders are taken at a back window; once you've said what you want, you find a seat, and in no time a waitress brings the meal

in a partitioned plate that holds the meat of choice separate from the beans and coleslaw that come with it.

CREAM & SUGAR CAFÉ
creamandsugarmobile.com

351 George St.   251-463-8359
Mobile, AL   **B L** | $

Cream & Sugar is a laid-back old house in Mobile's Oakleigh Garden District—a dandy place for coffee, breakfast, or lunch, indoors or al fresco.

On the breakfast sandwich, a grilled, split link of Conecuh sausage (an Alabama brand), vibrantly spiced and resounding with hickory smoke flavor, is tucked into a plush biscuit. The biscuit absorbs good drippings from the sausage, becoming even more luxurious. Sausage gravy on the side is porky with slow-rolling pepper heat.

House-made granola is extraordinary. It is tremendously nutty with a minimal fruit allotment. Unlike so many candy-bar granolas, it tastes nearly sugarless, its sweetness coming from a handful of dried cranberries and the fresh pecans and almonds that are its essence. Those with an especially hearty breakfast appetite need to know about Ya Ya Grits, which are topped with Conecuh sausage gravy, sautéed shrimp, and shredded Cheddar cheese.

There are all kinds of lattes and coffee drinks, our favorite being the special cold-brew coffee, infused with milk and almond flavor. Even if you prefer your coffee straight, as we do, try it. We found this smooth creation, so dairy fresh and nutty, impossible to resist.

DEW DROP INN

1808 Old Shell Rd.   251-473-7872
Mobile, AL   **L D** (closed Sun) | $

South Alabamians put ketchup on their hot dogs—an anomaly in most places, a criminal act in most of the Midwest. But talk to any wiener lover who grew up in Mobile, and you will see eyes mist with nostalgia for the unique joy of their hometown hot dog as dished out by street vendors during Mardi Gras and as served at the Dew Drop Inn year-round. They are bright-red steamed franks of medium size, their presentation a work of art. The wiener, nestled in a toasted bun, is topped with cool sauerkraut and a layer of warm, beefy chili with spicy-sweet zest. Standard condiments include mustard and pickles as well as ketchup. Aesthetes order them upside down (the dog sits atop the condiments) and others like them "shaved" (without kraut).

A comfy, wood-paneled roadhouse that opened in 1924 and introduced hot dogs to southern Alabama, the Dew Drop Inn also offers a full menu of po' boys, gumbo, Gulf shrimp, and hot dinners accompanied by such vegetables as turnip greens and rice and gravy. Coca-Cola is served the true-South way, in its shapely bottle alongside a glass full of ice. Banana pudding is the choice dessert. Service is speedy; checks are delivered with meals.

GREENBRIER RESTAURANT

oldgreenbrier.com

27028 Old Hwy. 20	256-351-1800
Madison, AL	L D | $

Mike Stroud, the Roadfooder who pointed the way to this fine old country café, warns, "Beware of confusing this place with 'Greenbrier Bar-B-Que.' . . . It has a similar menu but nowhere near the charm and spaciousness." The spaciousness to which Mr. Stroud refers is at least as much outside as in. Surrounding Greenbrier are endless acres of cotton fields.

Inside, there is elbowroom aplenty; walls are corrugated metal and hand-hewn wooden tables are covered with easy-wipe cloths. The two big main edible attractions are pork shoulder and catfish fillets—available separately or on a combo platter with pickle-topped, tart coleslaw and spuds (baked or fried)—preceded, always, by a basket of squiggly hush puppies. Within moments of one's sitting down, the pups arrive hot from the fryer. Some visitors consider them to be bland as-is, and so bring them to life by applying one of the barbecue sauces on the table: traditional vinegar-pepper hot sauce or the Alabama-only curiosity, white sauce, based on mayonnaise and containing a rousing shot of pepper.

The menu also includes barbecued chicken, on which that white sauce sings, and ribs, which benefit from a third, tomato-based sweet sauce. Pork and catfish frowners can order fried or boiled shrimp.

★ MARTIN'S

1796 Carter Hill Rd.	334-265-1767
Montgomery, AL	L D | $

Oh, such biscuits begin supper at Martin's! Warm with gossamer insides, they would be insulted by the use of butter. The only thing better than biscuits is corn bread, in the form of soft-textured muffins, also warm.

The dinner menu offers such main-course choices as whole fried catfish, stuffed deviled crabs, and fried chicken livers. At lunch, there are daily specials: catfish fillets, smoked sausage, country-fried steak, chicken and dumplings. You always can count on a roster of side dishes that honor the southern way with vegetables: velvet-soft cooked cabbage, pot-likker-sopped collard greens, pole beans, buttery mashed potatoes, plus, of course, Jell-O salad in rainbow hues. The standout meal is fried chicken. Its crisp crust has a nice jolt of spice, it is easy to handle (that is, grease-free), and it is dripping moist inside. One serving includes a meaty white breast and a dark-meat thigh. With biscuits, mashed potatoes, and greens, it makes a memorable meal, especially when followed by Martin's coconut meringue pie.

A wood-paneled, colonial-themed restaurant in a strip mall, Martin's is busier at lunch than at supper. At noon, you will likely have to wait as early arriving customers devour their plates of fried chicken with hedonistic gusto.

★ NIKI'S WEST

nikiswest.com

233 Finley Ave. West	205-252-5751
Birmingham, AL	B L D (closed Mon) | $

In the Deep South, vegetables are grown nearly year-round; and many of those vegetables are trucked to the produce center in Birmingham, where they are then shipped to destinations all over the East. Niki's West, surrounded by warehouses and loading docks, is where the produce-haulers come to eat. We counted more than three dozen vegetables along the steam-table line—far too many to even contemplate sampling some of each; so prepare yourself to make some hard choices among the likes of yellow squash casserole, fried green tomatoes, black-eyed peas, and three different kinds of seasoned greens (turnip, collard, and spinach). Some items from the market are austere enough to please even the strictest dieter: unadorned sliced tomatoes, raw vegetable vinaigrette, and baby lima beans. But the more tempting segment of Niki's produce repertoire is prepared according to voluptuous southern-café tradition. Broccoli is mixed with cheese and rice in a crazy-rich mélange; tomatoes are stewed with sugar and shreds of torn white bread until they become as sweet as cobbler; bright-orange yams are infused with sugar; crunchy-fresh okra is sheathed in a deep-fried crust.

The decorative theme at Niki's is the Aegean Sea (fishnets, scenic art of fishing boats), and when it comes to choosing an entree, we recommend baked fish Creole, broiled mackerel, and grilled amberjack. For fish frowners, there is always a selection of beef and pork as well as a terrific baked Greek chicken.

We used to not like dessert here, but recent visits have made us happily eat our words. Lemon meringue pie is lofty and light, lemon icebox pie is vibrant, and banana pudding, as rich as caramel, is one of the South's best.

THE WAYSIDER

1512 Greensboro Ave.　　205-345-8239
Tuscaloosa, AL　　**B L** (closed Mon) | **$**

--★--
LOCALS
LOVE IT
--★--
For decades now, the Waysider has been the breakfast spot of choice in Tuscaloosa, especially well known for its airweight biscuits, served with honey and, preferably, a slab of country ham with red-eye gravy and a side of hearty cheese grits. On weekends, the place is breakfast-only, but during the week you can count on lunch of such Dixie café fare as fried chicken with fried okra, field peas,

collard greens, squash soufflé, candied yams, or fried corn. Warm fruit cobbler and cream pies top things off with a super-sweet exclamation mark.

WINTZELL'S OYSTER HOUSE

wintzellsoysterhouse.com
605 Dauphin St.　　334-432-4605
Mobile, AL　　**L D** | **$$**

Wintzell's used to be one-of-a-kind. There now are six of them in Alabama and one in Hattiesburg, Mississippi. We've heard mixed reviews about the others, but have only good things to say about the original in downtown Mobile. Aside from impeccable, opened-as-you-watch raw oysters, grilled oysters, oysters Bienville, and oysters Rockefeller, you can sample such definitive Gulf Coast specialties as seafood gumbo and crisp-fried crab claws, po' boys, and crusty-fried catfish. This is a good place to eat the unique Mobile specialty, West Indies salad. It's nothing more than crab meat marinated in oil and vinegar with grated onions. If the crab is good—and you can count on that here—it is a dish that is rich and ocean-sweet, so good that many customers forgo it as an appetizer (its usual role) and get a couple of large orders for their main course, accompanied by saltine crackers.

The restaurant itself is heaps of fun. Opened by Oliver Wintzell as a six-stool oyster bar in 1938, it has survived hurricanes and floods, and has been rebuilt and expanded into a big place. There still is an oyster bar where you can sit and knock 'em back by the dozen, and the ongoing contest continues to see who can eat the most raw oysters in one hour. The walls are plastered with thousands of little signs offering bons mots and rules of life put there by the late Mr. Wintzell, starting in the 1950s. For example: "If you want to save face . . . keep the lower half shut." *Bits of Wit and Wisdom* (*The Signs at Wintzell's Oyster House*) and *Oysters and Politics*, Mr. Wintzell's self-published books, are available for sale at the cash register.

ARKANSAS

★ AQ CHICKEN HOUSE

aqchickenhouse.net

1207 N. Thompson St.	479-751-4633
Springdale, AR	**L D** | **$**

Fried chicken? There is none better. Charcoal-cooked chicken? AQ's is the best. Barbecued chicken? These crusty pieces, sticky with dark-red, spicy-sweet sauce, will never get kicked off our plate. The point is: If you like chicken, you need to come to Springdale (or AQ's second location on Highway 71B in Fayetteville) and test this fine bird for yourself. Fried is juice-spurting tender, encased in a chewy-crisp envelope of well-seasoned crust. Charcoal-cooked is nearly as indulgent, its spicy skin imbued with the flavor of smoke and a vigorous lemon-pepper smack. If you can't make up your mind, the menu does offer a sampler platter of three pieces, each cooked a different way. An all-you-can-eat plan is available for $11.99 per person.

Meals at this big, family-friendly restaurant begin with glossy-topped cloverleaf rolls hot from the oven, and among essential side dishes are sweet-potato casserole, batter-dipped French fries, seasoned green beans, baked beans, and mashed potatoes. Unless you have a note from your doctor, you must order fried peaches for dessert: slices of al dente peach are battered and fried and served hot under a pile of ice cream.

CATFISH N

catfishn.com

210 Dardanelle Dam Rd.	479-229-3321
Dardanelle, AR	**D** (closed Sun & Mon) | **$$**

Catfish N is an eating barn above the Arkansas River where you can pile your plate with whole mud-cats or fillets (and, if you wish, fried chicken and boiled shrimp), along with hush puppies (regular or jalapeño-spiked), fried biscuits, assorted vegetables, and salad fixins. Help yourself to as much as you want; everything is set out in an open-access buffet. Beneath its thick, golden crust, the whole catfish is moist and sweet, the fillets somewhat less so. For dessert, there are usually a couple of cobblers from which to choose. They are sweet and gooey, equal amounts crust and cooked-soft fruit.

CHARLOTTE'S EATS & SWEETS

290 Main St.	501-842-2123
Keo, AR	**L** | **$**

One of the most prolific contributors to Roadfood.com is a gent who goes by the screen name Buffetbuster. There is no food or food group Buffetbuster doesn't like, but of all the good eats a traveler can discover along the American road, pie is his special field of expertise. So when Buffetbuster declares the pies at Charlotte's Eats & Sweets to be "world-class," pastry lovers among us pay serious attention. In his words,

"They are such masters of the meringue. . . . The filling of the chocolate pie is deep, dark, and fudgy, while the silky smooth, rich custard of the caramel pie is unmistakably homemade. The delicate meringues are a brilliant white and reach an impressive five to six inches high."

The quality of Charlotte's pies is no secret to the people who live around Keo (population 235). They know to come at 11 a.m., when the restaurant opens, or even earlier to avoid a line. If you come too late in the lunch hour, chances are your favorite kind of pie will be all eaten up.

Pre-pie soups and salads include very nice garlic cheese biscuits, but most people who don't go directly to dessert avail themselves of a grill-toasted Keo Klassic, which is smoked turkey, Monterey Jack cheese, tomato, onion, and avocado on sourdough.

COTHAM'S MERCANTILE
cothams.com

5301 Hwy. 161 S.   501-961-9284
Scott, AR   L (Mon-Sat); D (Fri-Sat) | $

★
LOCALS LOVE IT In the Grand Prairie southeast of Little Rock, Cotham's Mercantile is perched on stilts
★ above a slow-flowing river. Built in 1917, it has been a general store, a jail, and a military commissary. Since 1984, Arkansans have come to know it as a plate-lunch destination.

The old wood building is fronted by a broad porch. Enter a swinging door into a dining room packed literally to the ceiling with vintage house and farm bric-a-brac, from garden tools to primordial television sets. Remote the restaurant may be, but it is rare to see an empty chair. Bare wood tables are surrounded by customers who come for meals built around catfish, chicken-fried steak, or chicken-fried chicken, and such daily lunch specials as fried pork chops (Monday), chicken and dumplings (Tuesday), meat loaf (Wednesday), and southern-fried chicken (Thursday). Side dishes include corn fritters, hush puppies, collard greens, and fried green tomatoes.

Cotham's calls its burger a Hubcap Hamburger. It is an immense circle of cooked ground beef—close to a foot in diameter and half an inch thick—that comes in a bun that nearly fits, dressed with a salad's worth of mustard, lettuce, tomato slices, pickles, and hoops of onion. The outlandish specialty has earned such renown that the store's pushpin map of the United States has no room left to show where Hubcap-loving customers have come from; business cards from visitors around the globe are tacked up all around it.

Desserts include Arkansas fried pies and peach or blackberry cobbler.

CRAIG'S BAR-B-QUE

Hwy. 70 W.   870-998-2616
De Valls Bluff, AR   L D | $

Craig's pork is deeply smoked and brushed with thick, orange sauce that is big on spice and nearly sugarless, with a twist that tastes vaguely like citrus. To balance the devilish sauce, which is available ultra-hot if specially requested, sandwiches are constructed with a layer of sweet coleslaw inside the bun. That bright slaw sings a fine tune when it dresses one of Craig's Polish sausages, also lined with mustard and topped with hot sauce. Dinner plates include beans and slaw; the only other available side dish is a bag of chips. The proper thing to drink is iced tea—very sweet tea, of course.

Ambience is hunting-lodge rustic. Pinned to the walls are business cards and hand-penned ads who-knows-how-old: lost dogs, pre-owned shotguns, beauty salons, deer processing, and taxidermy. Diners' attire ranges from still-wet camouflage waders to pressed pinstripe suits and well-worn overalls. Although the dining room is bisected (a legacy of segregation days), quarters are close enough that conversations are wide open among seated eaters as well as takeout customers hovering around waiting for their food.

FELTNER'S WHATTA-BURGER
whatta-burger.com

1410 N. Arkansas   479-968-1410
Russellville, AR   **L D** | **$**

There are Whatta-Burger shops throughout the Southwest, but none like this one, where the "custom made hamburgers," served with crisp French fries and thick milk shakes are a cut above.

In addition to big and good meals, Feltner's offers the kick of an only-in-America experience that is fast food at its finest. The instant you enter the low-slung brick building, an order taker virtually accosts you at the door to find out what you want. At the head of the line, you convey the precise details of your order, from a simple Whatta-Burger (a quarter-pound patty on a five-inch bun) to a Whatta-Burger with double meat and double cheese. At the end of the line, you pay and receive your meal on a tray in a white bag. Find a booth in the big dining room, where the walls are lined with humorous and inspirational homilies: "We guarantee fast service no matter how long it takes"; "The hurrier I go, the behinder I get"; "Cherish yesterday, dream tomorrow, live today."

Feltner's is *the* town burger joint, a favorite for families, teens on dates, and Arkansas Tech students. We well recall our first visit, when we shared the dining room with a happy stampede of approximately three dozen fresh-faced six-footers attending basketball camp at the college, each of whom carried a tray with a brace of double-doubles and a heap of French fries.

FRANKE'S
frankescafeteria.com

11121 N. Rodney Parham   501-225-4487
Little Rock, AR   **L D** | **$**

Where to begin? As is the custom in bountiful cafeterias, let us begin with dessert. Custard pie in particular is a study in culinary clarity: egg-rich and cream-smooth, it fairly floats in its fine, flaky crust. There are cobblers, hot custard and banana pudding, cheesecake, and brownies—not a clinker among them—but pie is king at Franke's. If not custard, then coconut cream, Karo nut (pecan), chocolate, or apple.

As you might extrapolate from the pie selection, Franke's is a Dixie classic. In fact, it's the oldest restaurant in Arkansas (since 1919). The only bad thing to say is that there are too many wonderful items to eat on any one day, forcing those of us passing through to leave town longing for all the good stuff we did not taste. For example, if you come on a Thursday, the day's special entrees will include chicken and dumplings, fried chicken livers, and fried chicken in addition to such everyday items as baked pit ham and roast beef. Choosing vegetables is an even more daunting task; Thursday's are fried okra, rice pilaf, okra and tomatoes, Brussels sprouts, and pinto beans. Every day there are mac 'n' cheese, greens, candied yams, from-scratch mashed potatoes, and an absolutely sensational eggplant casserole that includes tomatoes, onions, bread crumbs, and a layer of melty cheese on top. Breadstuffs? Choose from white rolls, whole wheat rolls, biscuits, garlic toast, and hush puppies.

We were clued in to this grand place by tipster Michelle Little, a New Orleans resident who grew up in Little Rock. Michelle wrote, "Franke's is the best. This is a part of my childhood that makes me happy—good food, lots of tasty vegetables, fluffy rolls, sweet tea, and most of all, those cream pies at the end of the line.... Even though I live in a food heaven here in New Orleans, I still miss those meat-and-threes (plus cream pies) from home."

There is another location of Franke's at 400 Broadway in Little Rock (501-372-1919).

GRAPEVINE
thegrapevinerestaurant.com

105 E. Walnut   479-963-2413
Paris, AR   **B L D** (closed Sun) | **$**

The Grapevine defies categorization. It is a worldly restaurant in a country town. Its repertoire ranges from catfish to coconut shrimp, veggie plates to surf 'n' turf, sweet tea to chocolate milk to wines from France and Arkansas. The staff is folksy and down-home but able to walk you through the menu with the savvy of a learned gastronome. It's the finest food for miles around, and you will be hard-pressed to spend more than $10 for a meal.

You know you are in for something special when the bread basket arrives. Crisp-crusted tawny loaves with a slightly sweet edge are cut into irregularly sized slices and served with a ramekin of honey butter. Hamburgers are one-third-pound beauties; the salad selection includes Greek, Cobb, and a "Santa Fe" concoction topped with unbelievably tender grilled chicken and served with creamy avocado dressing. Full dinners, including barbecued beef, chicken-fried steak, and house-smoked brisket, come with such sides as fried okra and mac 'n' cheese.

Bread pudding is huge: physically and flavorfully, a dense block of bread that has become custard, served floating in a pool of sweet praline sauce.

★ MCCLARD'S

mcclards.com

505 Albert Pike   501-623-9665
Hot Springs, AR   **L D** (Tues–Sat) | **$$**

Pork is king in this legendary smokehouse, the pulled pork ineffably tender, its smoky sweetness especially radiant when spread with hot sauce. The standout dish is a rib and fry plate. The ribs are a meat-heavy slab with a sticky glaze of peppery red sauce. They are presented under a tangle of gorgeous honey-brown French fried potatoes and sided by coleslaw to create what may be the most perfectly balanced barbecue meal anywhere.

A whole section of McClard's menu is devoted to tamale plates, ranging from plain tamales with beans to a full "spread"—a pair of tamales topped with sauce-sopped chopped smoked meat, beans, crisp Fritos chips, raw onions, and shredded orange cheese. Spreads remind us of the locally favored Fritos pie, but with the added zest of genuine pit barbecue.

The neon-lit 1942 stucco building that houses McClard's once offered toot-your-horn carhop service but now hordes of happy eaters line up to fill the booths inside. The recipe for its sauce supposedly dates back to 1928, when a customer at the McClard family trailer court couldn't pay his bill and so offered his barbecue sauce recipe instead.

MICKEY'S BBQ

mickeysbbq.net

1622 Park Ave.   501-624-1247
Hot Springs, AR   **B L D** (Tues–Sat) | **$**

Hot Springs is a barbecue hot spot, its highlights including not only ribs and pulled pork but also great beans and pit-cooked potatoes. You'll find all of the above at Mickey's, a snug hut where the "Hickory Nut" dining room features napkin holders carved from tree limbs, as well as wood paneling branded with scenes of deer, ducks, and pheasants. The beef and pork are terrific, ham is exemplary, and Mickey's hot, complicated sauce infuses each of them with a delicious glow.

And what fine side dishes. The potato, slow cooked over hickory smoke just like the meats, has a leathery skin and cream-soft center. You can have it gobbed with butter or, even better, stuffed with the barbecue meat of your choice (beef, pork, or ham) then heaped with just-right spicy-sweet barbecue sauce, coleslaw, and beans. That treatment is more of a meal than a side. Beans, by the way, are also top-drawer, larded with shreds and chunks and chewy debris off the good ham roast.

MS. LENA'S PIES

2885 Hwy. 33 S.   870-998-1385
De Valls Bluff, AR   **L** (Thurs–Sat) | **$**

De Valls Bluff, Arkansas, is a culinary Shangri-la. This White River town of 619 citizens, just off I-40 between Memphis and Little Rock, is home of the thriving Craig's Bar-B-Que (p. 176), the erstwhile Family Pie Shop, and a recent inamorata Ms. Lena's Pies. Operating out of a house trailer, Ms. Lena's makes all kinds of pies, but it's the fried pies we love most. Flaky-crusted turnovers with a savory crust that is nearly parchment-thin, they come with fillings that include sunny-tart apricot, buttery-soft apples, smooth chocolate, and a curious autumn specialty called Hunter's Pie that is chocolate and cherries blended with marshmallows that melt and give the chocolate a dreamy, creamy nature. Coconut, pecan, and pumpkin-pecan are some of the others we found when we stopped in the third week of October.

These are truly elegant pastries, even if there is no place on premises to eat, so you dine standing in the parking lot.

Fried pies tend to be a weekend thing. The rest of the week, count on four-star regular pies, both cream and fruit-filled. They are sold whole or by the slice.

RHODA'S FAMOUS TAMALES

714 Saint Mary St.   870-265-3108
Lake Village, AR   **B L | $**

Rhoda Adams's tamales deserve the fame they have earned throughout the Mississippi Delta. Made with a mixture of beef and chicken, they emanate an irresistibly appetizing aroma and are a joy to eat any time of day.

Beyond tamales, the menu at James and Rhoda Adams's little eat place by the side of the road is a roster of soulful regional specialties. For fried chicken or pigs' feet, pork barbecue or catfish dinner, you won't do better for miles around. Early one morning Rhoda made us a breakfast of bacon and eggs with biscuits on the side. Rhoda is one of those gifted cooks who makes everything she touches something special.

We've always considered Arkansas one of America's Big 7 pie states (along with Iowa, Wisconsin, Minnesota, Virginia, Texas, and Maine). Rhoda's pies are proof. She makes small individual ones as well as full-size pies. Sweet-potato pie, lemon pie, and pecan pie are world-class.

★ STUBBY'S BAR-B-QUE

stubbysbbq.com
3024 Central Ave.   501-624-1552
Hot Springs, AR   **L D | $$**

Chris Dunkel, whose family bought Stubby's from founder Richard "Stubby" Stubblefield Sr. in 1977, is known now to regulars as "Stubb" because he carries on the traditions that have made this place a hallowed barbecue destination since 1952. "There are three things that mark a good barbecue," Chris told us. "A wood pile, mismatched chairs, and high-quality meat."

Stubby's has all of those, and is delicious. Ribs, pork, and ham each in its own way presents the magical duo of swine and smoke; even the brisket is Texas-tender and dripping juice. Chicken, which in our book of barbecue tends to be a secondary consideration, is not to be dissed in this place; its skin is nearly blackened by smoke exposure in the pit, its meat is moist and ludicrously tender. No matter what your meat preference, two side dishes are essential. The smoked pit potato is a pound-plus spud that emerges from a long, slow heat bath with insides that are fluffy and delicious even before butter and sour cream are applied. Stubby's pot-o-beans is laden with smoky ham and a blanket of sauce. That sauce, made in the back room daily, is so beguilingly spiced that we find ourselves dipping plain old white bread in it after the beans are gone and the meat on our plate is a glowing memory.

WAGON WHEEL

166 S. Broadview St.   501-679-5009
Greenbrier, AR   **B L D | $**

Chocolate gravy is not the invention of some chef pandering to chocoholism but is, in fact, a time-honored Appalachian cook's recipe, albeit rare nowadays. So when we saw it on the menu of the Wagon Wheel, a friendly café on the road from Little Rock up to Branson, MO, we had to give it a try. Fascinating stuff, at first shocking, smooth and only moderately sweet, blasting normal standards for gravy into foggy puzzlement. We're not sure we'd order it again, but that's OK, because Wagon Wheel's more familiar sausage gravy is excellent: thick, meaty, and powerfully peppery. The biscuits these gravies blanket are top-drawer: big, knobby critters, served hot and fresh. They're also wonderful when paired with eggs and Petit Jean bacon.

Even if you come to the Wagon Wheel only for breakfast (there is a full-plate lunch menu and supper menu too), you must have pie. In the pie-rich state of Arkansas, Wagon Wheel is a standout. In particular, we like the classic coconut meringue; for those who want to go for broke there is banana split pie, containing banana, pineapple, and chopped pecans.

FLORIDA

APALACHICOLA SEAFOOD GRILL

100 Market St.   850-653-9510
Apalachicola, FL   **L D | $$**

During a weeklong trip along Florida's so-called Forgotten Coast, we ate many excellent shrimp. The very best were grilled in this modest town lunch-room. They come spangled with oregano and parsley, with a tingle of pepper spice and a wisp of smoke in their seasoning. They are remarkably tender but not the least bit flabby, modest-sized but huge-flavored.

Another out-of-this-world dish is Apalachicola gumbo—spicy, robust, earthy, loaded with beauti-ful oysters and shrimp and forkfuls of flatfish. It is aggressively seasoned but without the complica-tion of Creole gumbo. Instead, it glows with cordial Dixie charm. Apalachicola is known for its deep-cupped oysters, in their glory raw, steamed, or fried. The fried ones are astonishingly temperate: sweet, nutty, gentle-flavored. Crab cakes, scallops, grouper, salmon, and the "world's largest fried fish sandwich" round out the menu, but if you are a seafood frowner, you'll do pretty well here too. Hamburgers are no afterthought. They are half-pound hunks of beef, nicely accoutered and served with good potato salad or equally good French fries.

A few steps along the raised sidewalk from the Seafood Grill is a collectibles-and-knickknack shop called Retsyo (spell it backwards), where proprietor John Lee sells the Tupelo honey that is unique to the Apalachicola River basin. Billed as the champagne of honey, it is light amber with a crisp floral flavor. Mr. Lee reminded us that it was the subject of the 1997 Peter Fonda movie *Ulee's Gold* and also assured us it would lower our cholesterol and blood pressure and strengthen our heart. "Even diabetics can eat all they want!" he promised. We cannot guarantee the health claims, but it sure is an ideal sweetener for hot or iced tea and a winning drizzle for hush puppies.

BARNACLE BILL'S

barnaclebillsonline.com
14 W. Castillo Dr.   904-824-3663
St. Augustine, FL   **L D | $$**

Barnacle Bill's is not an undiscovered Roadfood hole in the wall. It is big and popular and in fact there are two of it, the second location (dinner only) at 451 A1A Beach Boulevard in St. Augustine, phone: 904-471-2434. (But these two are no relation to the other Barnacle Bills found along the Atlantic coast.)

Shrimp brought in on boats to nearby Mayport are the main attraction: They are firm, juicy butter-flies available simply fried in an envelope of melting-crisp crust, in a coconut crust or, most exciting of all, in a crust enhanced by the heat of locally grown datil peppers. The pungent datil, which seems to be a sport variety of the habanero, has become St. Augustine's signature flavor agent.

For first-timers and those who have a hard time making up their mind what kind of shrimp they want, there are plates of a dozen, four of each variety. You can get stuffed shrimp, blackened shrimp, teriyaki shrimp, shrimp scampi, and steamed peel-your-own shrimp. The menu offers all sorts of other seafood and even a selection of "landlubber fare," but we agree with tipster Meg Butler, who first clued us in to this restaurant: "I can't say much other than fried shrimp, fried shrimp, fried shrimp."

BEACH ROAD CHICKEN DINNERS

4132 Atlantic Blvd.   904-398-7980
Jacksonville, FL   **L D** (closed Mon) | **$**

Jacksonville is America's shrimp central, but don't let that make you disregard Beach Road Chicken Dinners. Fried shrimp indeed are on the menu, and we suspect they are good, a suspicion based on the fact that the fried chicken is first-rate. Served family-style with biscuits and gravy and honey, corn nuggets, fried okra, French fries, coleslaw, and creamed peas, white and/or dark parts come encased in a crisp, red-gold crust and drip with flavorful juices. Adventurous chicken eaters can get livers, gizzards, or hearts, and should there be someone with an allergy to fried food, baked chicken is available (if you are willing to wait forty-five minutes).

A low-slung building that has expanded in all directions since opening day in 1939, Beach Road offers little in the way of polite amenities (when the staff isn't feeling gruff, they'll call you hon), and chances are you will wait in line for a table.

BLUE HEAVEN

blueheavenkw.com
729 Thomas St.   305-296-8666
Key West, FL   **B L D** | **$$**

Off the beaten path in the Bahama Village area of the sunny neverland known as the Conch Republic, Blue Heaven is a breakfast lover's dream. Dining is *en plein air* on a broad outdoor patio under a canopy of opulent banyan trees, where your companions include the café's flock of hens and roosters who hop and peck around tables and chairs. Their cock-a-doodle-doing is a natural companion for hefty omelets, but our favorite dishes are the tropical-tasting banana pancakes and seafood benedict built upon ocean-fresh fish and topped with lime hollandaise. To drink? Who can resist a mimosa made with fresh-squeezed OJ? Lunch items include wonderful barbecued shrimp, fresh local fish, and jerk chicken.

An incredibly colorful place to eat, Blue Heaven has been the home of a boxing ring (Ernest Hemingway sparred here), a bordello (the tiny rooms upstairs are now part of an art gallery), a bookmaking parlor, and a cockfighting pit (heroic roosters are buried in a little graveyard behind the dining area), as well as inspiration for Jimmy Buffett's song "Blue Heaven Rendezvous."

BOSS OYSTER

bossoyster.com
123 Water St.   850-653-9364
Apalachicola, FL   **L D** | **$$**

★
WATER-FRONT
DINING
★

Route 98 east of Panama City and south of Tallahassee borders what is known as Florida's Big Bend because it is shaped like the one in Texas. But unlike the desert land west of the Pecos, Florida's Big Bend is lush: cool blue waters of Apalachee Bay to the south and Spanish moss–draped forest on the other side of the road. Beyond the natural beauty of a blessedly underdeveloped stretch of Florida's panhandle, a trip along this road provides access to culinary treasure in the form of oysters harvested from the fresh/saltwater mix where the Apalachicola River flows into the Gulf of Mexico.

At river's edge in Apalachicola (which has dubbed itself Florida's Oyster Capital), Boss Oyster runs its own boat from which oystermen harvest, chill (on board), and bring oysters directly to the restaurant's dock, where they are washed and refrigerated. Is it any surprise that the raw ones served here are spectacularly bright, fresh, and just-right briny with that magic liquid richness that is luxury incarnate? We order a half dozen but are given eight because three are on the small side.

When the big ones get fried, each is a great mouthful of bursting flavor enveloped in a thick, spicy coat of gold. They're also available steamed or baked, or gilded with Thai chile, wasabi and ginger, or flying fish roe. If you are allergic to oysters, we recommend Grand Grits—cheese grits topped with cream sauce, tasso ham, and shrimp so juicy that they are a revelation for those of us accustomed to wooden, pale-flavored ones.

Because the restaurant is on the water, its deck is outfitted with signs warning "Please do not feed the birds," and despite wooden scarecrow owls perched along the rail, if you sit at an al fresco picnic table you can expect to dine with an audience of greedy-looking gulls perched on nearby pilings.

CAPTAIN JOEY PATTI'S SEAFOOD RESTAURANT

captainjoeysdeli.com

610 S. C St.   850-434-3193
Pensacola, FL   **L** (closed Sun & Mon) | **$**

Located behind the circus-sized Joe Patti's Seafood Market, Captain Joey Patti's restaurant offers a full repertoire of Gulf Coast favorites. Here are vividly peppered crab cakes, Apalachicola oysters, and steamed U-peel-'em or fried butterflied shrimp. On the side come steak fries or hearty cheese grits. Everything is served in abundance. The Panhandle-favorite fried mullet is a best dish, its cracker-meal-crunchy skin enveloping fillets that are oily and luxurious. Fried shrimp are large and tasty, if a bit overzealously breaded; ditto oysters.

The ambience is casual in this family-friendly diner: paper place mats, quick and affable service, reasonable prices, and a menu that even includes chicken fingers and hamburgers for members of your party who don't like fish.

CHEF EDDIE'S

chefeddies.com

595 W. Church St.   407-826-1731
Orlando, FL   **B L D** | **$**

Chef Eddie's used to be Queen Bee's, which gained renown for smothered pork chops, a tradition Chef Eddie James upholds. The chops are not too thick, but they are intensely porky, smothered with onions and peppers in a long-simmered brown sauce. Beef short ribs are another top-notch entree, cooked a full five hours in a wine and vegetable marinade.

While we are pondering chicken and waffles, unable to choose between a regular waffle and a red velvet waffle, waitress Debbie says, "I'll take care of you," and comes out with a half-and-half waffle she had Chef Eddie make. Kitsch it may be, but the red velvet half is really very good—not too sweet, and with a buttermilky smack that welcomes the warm syrup that comes alongside and proves to be fine company for juicy, dark-meat fried chicken. Ribs also are outstanding, cooked in a big smoker out front, arriving at the table so tender that you literally cannot pick one up without the bone sliding out from the great cylinder of meat that surrounds it.

Worthy side dishes include peppery steamed cabbage that is as rich and oily as a vegetable can be, and sweet-potato casserole topped with a melting marshmallow and a crunchy crust of brown sugar. We also recommend the huge-flavored collard greens. Parmesan cheese grits are thick and satisfying, with a flavor we cheerfully identify as bacon, but which waitress Debbie later advises is in fact smoked Gouda cheese, adding an extra note of dairy richness.

Sunday is a big deal at Chef Eddie's, a banquet-hall-size place where a man comes in after church to play the white baby grand piano and sing gospel tunes to a packed house. With none of the festive after-church ambience of Sunday, weekdays offer a quiet setting for community members who come to sit alone and read, text, or watch an overhead television while they eat.

CUBAN SANDWICHES

1605 Lee Rd.	407-578-8888
Orlando, FL	**L** (closed Sun)	$

"We are not a FAST food franchise, so please hurry up and *WAIT!*" orders a sign in the window of this happy drive-in. "Our Cuban sandwiches are made fresh to order then grilled (*slowly*) to perfection." Ingredients are immemorial: thinly sliced pork, salty pink ham, cheese, pickle chips, and mustard. The sandwich spends enough time in the *plancha*, which presses it like a hot vise, for the outside of the bread to become sensuously brittle. It is cut on a rakish diagonal from end to end, making the sandwich into two long-legged triangles. Despite its having been compressed during the toasting process, you need to hold it gingerly, lest the mustard lube the ingredients enough that they begin to slide out when pressure is applied.

Available variations on the traditional Cubano are a *media noche*, which is a Cuban on sweet bread; a roast pork sandwich (basically a Cuban without the ham), and an intriguing item described as a Cuban tradition, the *pan con timba*: guava and cream cheese on sweet bread. On the side, you can get black bean soup with rice and onions, fried plantains, tamales, or chips. The drink roster includes Cuban coffee, Latin sodas, and tropical shakes made with mango, papaya, or mamey.

Accommodations are limited to six al fresco picnic tables. Many customers dine in their cars or buy sandwiches to take elsewhere.

EL SIBONEY

elsiboneyrestaurant.com

900 Catherine St.	305-296-4184
Key West, FL	**L D**	$$

When you consider El Siboney is just ninety miles from Cuba itself—closer to Havana than to Miami—you understand why its Cuban food tastes so right. This is the best place we know on Key West to taste grilled garlic chicken, a half bird with a crisp skin and meat so tender that going at it with utensils feels like overkill. Plantains on the side are slightly crusty and caramelized around their edges. And yuca, served with roast pork, beans, and rice, is a revelation. Soft and glistening white hunks, reminiscent of a well-baked potato but more luscious and substantial, are served in a bath of heavily garlicked oil and garlanded with onion slices.

The Cuban mix sandwich is a beaut, made on a length of fragile-texture toasted bread cut in half at a rakish angle and loaded with ham, roast pork, salami, and cheese with pickles, lettuce, and tomato. Conch chowder is thick with conch meat, and provides a great opportunity for dunking shreds of the buttered Cuban bread that comes with every meal. The grandest dish in the house is paella Valenciana for two (call ahead; it takes an hour to prepare), a vast fisherman's stew served with rice, black beans, and plenty of Cuban bread for mopping juices. Dessert choices include Key lime pie, flan, and rice pudding, accompanied of course by espresso or café con leche.

El Siboney is a clean, pleasant place with red-striped tables topped with easy-wipe plastic and silverware presented in tidy little paper bags. If you don't speak Spanish, the waitresses do their best to help you. The name of the place is a variation of the word Ciboney, who were occupants of Florida and the Caribbean region since the Stone Age. The restaurant was established in 1984.

THE FISHERMAN'S WIFE

201 8th St.	850-697-4533
Carrabelle, FL	**L D**	$

Pam Lycett, who really is a fisherman's wife (hubby was out on his shrimp boat when we stopped in), runs a gracious little café with pastel-colored walls, slow-spinning overhead fans, and a sound-dampening rug on the floor. There is no throbbing music or raucous conversation in this peaceful place, which is so right for contemplating an oyster po' boy that comes splayed open on the plate, too large and overflowing to pick up and eat like a sandwich. So you pluck at it, oyster by oyster, savoring the warm luxury of sweet meat and zesty crust, occasionally punctuating the melty-crunchy ecstasy by forking up the sandwich's lettuce, tomato, onion, and mayo, along with pinches of good bread.

The same excellent oysters come as the featured presence in a basket, which includes French fries, slaw, cheese grits, and hush puppies; and there are baskets also of shrimp, the catch of the day, and—on Thursday, Friday, and Saturday—crab cakes. The same seafood also is available in even larger portions as part of a dinner. Or, if you are a couple, there is a seafood platter for two that includes fried grouper, shrimp, and oysters, plus all the fixins. One extra side dish we highly recommend is fried green tomatoes, which are resplendent in their veil of see-through crust.

Miss Pam's Key lime pie is a triumvirate of creamy luxe, sweetness, and citrus twang—a modest wedge, pale yellow with a thin graham-cracker crust and no adornment whatsoever. This classic cannot be improved.

GORDON'S BE BACK FISH HOUSE

558 E. Kennedy Blvd.   407-644-6640
Maitland, FL   **L D** (closed Sun & Mon) | **$**

In the orbit of Orlando, where the towns of Maitland and Eatonville meet, there is Roadfood paydirt in the form of Gordon's Be Back Fish House. What curious eater could resist visiting a place with a handwritten sign outside boasting "YES WE HAVE MULLET" and a somewhat more formal sign, planted in the lawn, advertising "Hot Fish and Grits"? This corner café, the name of which was devised to suggest that if you eat here once, you will be back for more, is presided over by Abraham Gordon Jr., who has been in the food-service business well over half a century, having started as a short-order cook in a diner at the age of twelve. Mr. Gordon, who spent some time as mayor of Eatonville, sits at the cash register taking orders, holding forth for all in the restaurant to hear (it's that small), and giving advice about whether he thinks you are a mullet person or a catfish person.

Crisp-fried catfish is boneless and meaty, clean and mild. It's good, but we prefer the mullet, which is ineluctably unctuous, its succulent flesh fairly wallowing in a golden envelope of seasoned crust. We also love the flounder, which is moist and cream-soft, breaded only enough to envelop the pure white meat. "Butter and cheese?" Mr. Gordon asks, regarding grits

that are fish's de rigueur partner in this place. They are stout grits, sopped with butter and capped with a puddle of molten yellow cheese. Fried okra sports a thick, crunchy coat but is intensely green-tasting once bitten—a serious vegetable presence. Naturally, hush puppies are included in every Styrofoam dinner tray (all dishware is disposable). They are crunchy and sweet, oily enough to make fingertips glisten.

HAVANA

havanacubanfood.com
6801 S. Dixie Hwy.   561-547-9799
West Palm Beach, FL   **L D** | **$**

There is something especially right about a *media noche* from the walk-up window of Havana restaurant because the window is open 'round the clock. *Media noche* means midnight, which traditionally is when this unique variant of the Cuban sandwich is the snack of choice. It is suitable for late-night eating because it is somewhat lighter than a dinner-sized Cuban . . . but only somewhat. The ingredients are the same—roast pork, ham, and Swiss cheese—but instead of a hearty Cuban loaf, it is made on sweet, eggy bread. When grilled, the sweet bread develops a light crunch that is completely different from the chewier nature of the traditional baguette.

In addition to the twenty-four-hour walk-up window, Havana is a full-service, sit-down restaurant with a king-sized Cuban menu ranging from white bean soup on Sunday to guanabana milk shakes and café con leche. The *media noche* and classic Cuban are supplemented by an "Especial de West Palm Beach"—a similar Dagwood but with a full deck of ham, turkey, Swiss cheese, bacon, lettuce, and tomato. Note: Pickles are a standard Cuban sandwich ingredient, but here they must be requested.

INDIAN PASS RAW BAR

indianpassrawbar.com

8391 County Rd. 30A   850-227-1670

Port St. Joe, FL   **L D** (closed Mon) | **$**

"Oysters & Music, Beer & Wine, Family & Friends" are the watchwords of the Indian Pass Raw Bar. A vintage eat-shack along Florida's Forgotten Coast, this jolly outfit started over a century ago as the commissary for a turpentine factory. It became a wholesale oyster business, then in 1986 opened as a restaurant.

Oysters on the half shell are magnificent—reason enough to drive along this colorful coast. They are deep-cupped Apalachicolas, each glistening with oceanic liquor, painfully tender, ocean-sweet, overwhelmingly satisfying. Those who like their oysters gilded will find nirvana in the kitchen's baked oysters: cooked only long enough for the marine meat to warm but not toughen or dry, and for all the butter, Parmesan cheese, and garlic on top to melt into a luxurious golden veil.

Smoked fish dip, a Panhandle passion, is creamy with the harmonious duet of smoke and fresh fish. Also notable are seasoned, steamed peel-and-eat shrimp, simple seafood gumbo, and classic Key lime pie. For seafood frowners, there is a short menu of burgers, hot dogs, and barbecue.

Seating is at commissary-style tables, and service is the charming antiquated method by which customers check off what they want on a paper menu and hand that menu to a waitress. The décor is a wildly eclectic pastiche that includes dollar bills plastered everywhere on the wall and a map of the United States with pushpins showing where customers have come from.

JB'S FISH CAMP

jbsfishcamp.com

859 Pompano Ave.   386-427-5747

New Smyrna Beach, FL   **L D** | **$$**

————★———

WATER-FRONT
DINING

———★———

The cracker fish camp is a vanishing species, its unapologetic rural nature out of step with twenty-first-century life in general and with the ever-denser population of waterside Florida in particular. Nowhere is the culture clash more apparent than on the road to JB's Fish Camp at the southernmost end of Turtle Mound Road (Route A1A) outside New Smyrna Beach. Other than by boat along the Intracoastal Waterway, the only way to get to JB's is to drive past miles of new high-rise housing and recently built shopping malls. The bourgeois landscape shifts dramatically the moment you pull onto Pompano Avenue and find the white-sand parking lot that surrounds the helter-skelter restaurant and its annex trailer selling T-shirts that depict the mosquito as the Florida state bird. A bumper sticker plastered to the dining room door announces, "Slow Down. You're Not on the Mainland," and shows a slovenly catfish who appears to be drunk or hungover.

The menu offers every kind of Florida seafood, including rock shrimp and pompano. Capt. John A. Bollman III, who runs the place, is a passionate crabber. The restaurant nabs its own, a fact evident in the snowy crab cakes and a "Crabulous Sandwich," which is nothing more than cool, fresh crab meat, mayo, and a sprinkle of spice. Blue crabs are sold by the dozen, infused with whatever degree of JB's spice mix you specify, and there are softshells, stone crab claws, and snow crab clusters. There's also a full array of fresh oysters, scallops, pink shrimp and rock shrimp, and clams.

JB's really is a fish camp, offering kayak rentals, bait to catch redfish, and slips for arriving boaters. Located along the Canaveral National Seashore between the Mosquito Lagoon and the Atlantic Ocean, it does have indoor dining, but the choice seats are outside on a broad deck by the water, where lucky ones glimpse manatees and porpoises cavorting nearby. Private and commercial fishing boats come and go and ever-present sunshine muffles even the high-spirited chatter of JB's raucous clientele. Among those eating at the breezy picnic tables are local anglers, tourists, and road-tripping bikers, as well as a large number of people for whom Florida is a second home and who come here to enjoy what the state was like before they arrived.

JENKINS QUALITY BARBECUE

jenkinsqualitybarbecue.com

830 N. Pearl St.   904-353-6388
Jacksonville, FL   **L D** | $

Jenkins smokes beef, pork, and chickens in a pit fired by oak logs, then serves them with sauce made from a recipe that is a long-held family secret. The sauce is unusual stuff, peppery but not ferocious, mustard-orange and as thick as Thanksgiving gravy—a righteous companion especially for Jenkins's superb roast chicken, but also swell on ribs or beef and delicious soaked up straight with the white bread that is used for sandwiches.

The sandwiches are sandwiches in name only. The spare rib sandwich is four slices of white bread surrounding four or five big spare ribs, the whole thing drenched with enough sauce that picking it up whole is impossible. Instead, one folds back the thick butcher paper in which it is presented and alternately gnaws a rib and peels off pieces of sauce-drenched bread. Very good! On the side, you want an order of corn nuggets, which are creamy-centered corn fritters. For dessert, there is fine red velvet cake.

The store on Pearl Street, in a fairly desolate part of downtown Jacksonville, is the main location. There are a few other Jenkins around the city. Dining facilities include a handful of booths and a couple of picnic tables outside.

JERRY'S DRIVE-IN

jerrysdrivein.com

2815 E. Cervantes   850-433-9910
Pensacola, FL   **B L D** (closed Sun) | $

Jerry's opened for business in 1939 and, frankly, it doesn't look like it's changed much since then. It is a Formica-counter café with a few tables and booths and help-yourself rolls of paper towels for customers to use as needed. The walls are decorated with college pennants, silly homilies, and beer ads going back decades. Jerry's has character to spare . . . but it also has important hamburgers—good-sized, juicy patties of beef beautifully dressed with lettuce, tomato, chopped onions, mustard, and mayo, served with sweet coleslaw and crisp French fries. Not gourmet burgers, not unusual burgers: just good, satisfying hamburgers . . . in a classic lunch-counter setting.

Although many visitors to the "Redneck Riviera" know Jerry's as the hamburger place, regulars come for three square meals a day. The breakfast menu features all the usual configurations of eggs and luncheon meat (with grits and/or hash browns), plus an extraordinarily luxurious chicken liver omelet. At lunch, you can have such regional delights as smoked mullet, deviled crab, and broiled grouper, as well as big deep-fried oysters with hush puppies and cold beer on the side.

J.R.'S RIB SHACK

jrsribshack.com

281 N. Star Ave.   850-871-5601
Panama City, FL   **L D** (closed Sun) | $

As one might infer from the name, J.R.'s ribs are something to boast about. They are tender, but not baby-back soft, their heavy-flavored meat offering chew that sets forth waves of smoky, piggy flavor. Barbecued chicken is another four-star feast, so tender that juice-saturated dark meat quite literally falls from the bones of a drumstick when it is lifted from the plate. Chopped barbecue pork can be listless, but that situation is easily bettered with one of the restaurant's excellent sauces: mild, sweet, or hot. There is white sauce too, available on request, but in our opinion, this Alabama-style emulsion works only on chicken, which doesn't really need it.

Side dishes are swell: thick, firm mac 'n' cheese, meat-laden barbecue beans, crisp and refreshing coleslaw. While Brunswick stew can elsewhere seem like leftovers, J.R.'s is nothing short of magnificent—packed with big shreds of pork, sweet tomato-fruity, and tongue-tickling spicy. Iced tea is served in thirty-two-ounce cups.

J.R.'s is a somewhat ramshackle building with interior décor that includes a bevy of pig figurines, game animal trophies, and signs with slogans such as "A bad day of fishing beats a good day at work" and "If my pickup truck ain't here, I'm in the woods chasin' deer . . ." Bathrooms are labeled for Bucks and Does.

KEYS FISHERIES

keysfisheries.com/restaurant

3502 Gulfview Ave.   866-743-4353
Marathon, FL   **L D** | $$

The most famous place to eat stone crabs is Joe's Stone Crab of Miami, and there is something right about eating the regal food in so fancy a setting. On the other hand, it's also good to get stone crabs at a bargain price (relatively speaking), fresh off the boat, and eat them at a picnic table.

If you like the sound of the latter and are traveling the Overseas Highway, pull over in Marathon and have a meal at Keys Fisheries. In contrast to ordering from one of Joe's formally attired waitstaff, the process of getting crabs at Keys Fisheries is purposely goofy. The custom is to place your order at a counter and give the order taker a celebrity name, not yours, to call out when it's ready. Plates and utensils are disposable, dining is virtually outdoors (with plastic sheeting to keep out wind and rain, if necessary), and the view is fishing boats coming or going and a nightly ooh-and-ahh sunset. The menu is replete with local seafood dishes from conch chowder to Key West pink shrimp, and many habitués swear by the lobster Reuben, a locally loved grilled sandwich of lobster meat, Swiss cheese, sauerkraut, and thousand island dressing on rye. But it's stone crabs that steal the show. Nowhere will you find them cheaper or more perfectly fresh.

LA TERESITA CAFETERIA

lateresitarestaurant.com

3248 W. Columbus Dr.   813-879-9704
Tampa, FL   **B L D** (open all night Fri
                                  & Sat) | $

A Cuban sandwich is a beautiful thing: ham, roast pork, and cheese, along with mustard, mayonnaise, and pickles encased in elegant bread that is toasted to a crisp. There is no better place to eat one than Tampa, especially at the neighborhood café called La Teresita.

While La Teresita is a full-scale restaurant and banquet hall, the Roadfooder's choice will likely be in the lunch-counter part of the operation, where choice seats (and swift service) are at a sweeping serpentine counter at which whole families line up on the rows of stools, dawn to dark. Regulars come for breakfast of buttered Cuban bread and café con leche; lunch favorites include carne asada, *ropa vieja, vaca frita,* and the best black beans and rice in town. Throughout the day, you'll see groups of happy gents gathering in the street after dining at La Teresita. Here they fire up big made-in-Tampa cigars and look like kings who have just enjoyed a royal feast.

LOUIE'S BACKYARD

louiesbackyard.com

700 Waddell Ave.   305-294-1061
Key West, FL   **L D** | $$$

★
WATER-FRONT
DINING
★

Louie's is not cheap or in any way typical. It is one of a kind. But when we visit Key West and think about dinner, our thoughts immediately take us to a table at Louie's Backyard, where the best seats are located on a multileveled terrace overlooking the Atlantic. Here you dine while pleasure boats sail past and pelicans graze the waves.

The gracious pink classic-revival house could serve TV dinner and it would be irresistible on a moonlit night, but it happens to be one of the innovators of Key West cuisine, known for such tropical delights as Bahamian conch chowder with bird-pepper hot sauce, grilled local shrimp with salsa verde, and cracked conch with pepper jelly and ginger daikon slaw. The Louie's supper forever etched in our book of great culinary memories was our first: a pair of lovely grilled strip steaks glazed with hot chipotle chile sauce, sided by garlic mashed potatoes and red onion corn relish. To top things off, we had fancy coffee and feathery Key lime tarts. Soft island breezes made hurricane lamps flicker. Bulbs strung among branches in overhead trees formed a radiant canopy above the patio. The ocean glowed cobalt blue when distant lightning storms ignited over the horizon.

★ LYNN'S QUALITY OYSTERS

lynnsqualityoysters.com

402 Hwy. 98   850-670-8796
Eastpoint, FL   **L D | $**

It's hard to find a bad oyster along Florida's Forgotten Coast, but if you are looking for the best, put Lynn's high on the hit list. Supplier to restaurants throughout the Panhandle, it serves Apalachicolas at their finest: raw on the half shell, cool and utterly fresh, perfectly salty-sweet, and sized to be a yummy mouthful.

Baked oysters also are outstanding. They're cooked just enough to be warm and so the cheese on top melts and the copious bits of garlic soften, but the oyster meat itself retains the moist, sensual mouthfeel that makes oyster eating downright erotic. We like them simply baked with cheese, but other available varieties include Rockefeller (with spinach), Margherita (mozzarella and tomatoes), Capt. Jack's (jalapeño, bacon, cheese, hot sauce), as poppers (jalapeño and cream cheese), or just plain steamed with drawn butter. Beyond oysters, Lynn's menu includes spicy steamed shrimp and mahimahi dip with a smokehouse punch. Meringue-topped Key lime pie is available for dessert.

Lynn's is small and cozy, humming with happy customers at the raw bar and at tables as staff carries boxes of freshly harvested oysters to the shuckers who open them with ease. There are outdoor seats too, with a scenic view of the Gulf, but the good vibes inside make indoor dining a delight.

MARINA OYSTER BARN

marinaoysterbarn.com

505 Bayou Blvd.   850-433-0511
Pensacola, FL   **L D** (closed Sun & Mon) | **$$**

------★------
WATER-FRONT
DINING
------★------

You can count on good oysters at the Marina Oyster Barn, even if sometimes, especially early in the season, they're from Louisiana rather than the East Bay. They are available raw, steamed, or steamed supreme (the latter being topped with cheese), Rockefeller, Texas-Crabster style (with crabmeat stuffing and cheese), or Texas-Shrimpster style. The back of the menu advises that a dozen raw ones are a mere 114 calories and that "there is some evidence that certain types of seafood protect against heart disease."

Good as oysters can be, the Oyster Barn offers a tempting selection of other seafood dinners—including catfish, grouper, crab, flounder, and mullet—that can be fried, broiled, or grilled. The standout dish for us is jumbo grilled shrimp. A dozen of them come on a wooden skewer. They are nicely charred and modestly seasoned—firm, juicy, and fresh. The cocktail sauce is a nice condiment; even better is tartar sauce, which is just-right sweet, balanced by a good pickle tang. They come with crisp-skinned, creamy-centered hush puppies and sides like "Mom's baked beans," new potatoes, French fries, or cheese grits. Speaking of grits, the dish called Grits A-Ha-Ha is a dandy, laced with Gouda cheese, shrimp, and bacon.

For dessert, there is good banana pudding and store-bought Key lime pie that is a perfectly all right, no-frills classic.

This place is perched right at Rooks Marina overlooking Bayou Texar, making it easy for customers to arrive by boat and for diners to watch their comings and goings, as well as the comings and goings of local pelicans. Most tables are windowside.

MINERAL SPRINGS SEAFOOD BY THE BAY

1612 Coastal Hwy.   850-984-2248
Crawfordville, FL   **L | $**

Mineral Springs Seafood by the Bay is a smokehouse, seafood store, and bait shop, not a restaurant. Here you can buy raw oysters and clams that are local and impeccably fresh, but you need to be willing and able to open them yourself. Here, too, you will find grand Florida shrimp and snapper to take and cook elsewhere.

For those in search of easy and immediate appetite satisfaction, this place has plenty to offer in the way of Florida Gulf Coast specialties at their informal best. Out front a smoker billows, so you enter the shop through a thick haze that smells of sweet, smoldering hardwood. When we walk in, proprietor Kim Williams tells us that he's just about to put mullet in the smoker, so it won't be ready for several hours, but salmon is freshly done. It is firm and agreeably oily. A taste of that and of delicately flavored grouper, and we think we're done, but Kim insists we try his spreads.

Each spread, made with mullet, salmon, or grouper, is smooth, smoky, and masterfully seasoned to highlight whichever fish it features. Then there is Leftover Spread, which is hardly an afterthought. Leftovers never tasted so good in what may be the best smoked-fish spread ever. It contains good-size hunks of all three very different-tasting fish, and it is thick and creamy with a pickle twist—one of those foods so flavorful that you keep eating even after your appetite has become a memory. Lacking crackers or suitable crudités, we consumed a pint with a plastic spoon as we peeled off the Coastal Highway and headed north toward Tallahassee.

OLD SPANISH SUGAR MILL GRILL

oldspanishsugarmill.com

601 Ponce de Leon Blvd.   368-985-5644
De Leon Springs, FL   **B L | $**

Cook your own pancakes at the Old Spanish Sugar Mill Grill in De Leon Springs State Park. Tables have griddles built into their center. The staff brings two pitchers from the kitchen—a milled-here, stone-ground, buckwheat-style batter as well as more traditional buttermilk batter—plus whatever mix-ins you need (bananas, blueberries, pecans, apple chunks, peanut butter, chocolate chips, and apple sauce are all available for a slight extra cost). You pour and flip the flapjacks as you like them. Sausage, bacon, and ham are also available . . . but cooked in the kitchen.

It's fun to punctuate the process of eating pancakes by cooking them at your speed and in your size; you can keep pouring batter until you bust. At $4.95 per person (plus the park entrance fee and obligatory 18 percent tip), this is one of the bargain breakfasts of the South. The pancakes are served from morning until midafternoon, but if you're not in the mood to cook, the kitchen also will make a fine sandwich on house-made whole-grain bread (the BLT is extremely well endowed with bacon) or a salad.

The restaurant is located in an old mill building in the beautiful area where explorers once sought the Fountain of Youth. The park around it is an idyllic recreation area with boat rides and picnic tables and opportunities to hike and bird-watch. It is a popular destination and the restaurant is a small one, so almost any time of day you will likely wait for a table.

OLEAN'S CAFE

1605 S. Adams St.   850-521-0259
Tallahassee, FL   **B L | $**

The hungrier you are when you come to Olean's Cafe, the better. It is practically impossible to get a meager meal in this one-room eatery where you step up to the counter and make your choices either by reading the moveable-letter menu on the wall or by looking at the food arrayed on the steam table. Whatever you select is put into a Styrofoam clamshell container by servers who do employ some utensils—a brush to drip butter onto grits (or cheese grits) or a big spoon to separate a serving of the Olean omelet. But mostly, they use their (gloved) hands to select clusters of bacon to push into a little segment of the tray, throw sheaves of sausage patties in with scrambled eggs, and place fried chicken parts atop hot waffles.

The star of the breakfast menu is the Olean omelet, which is more casserole than omelet, each serving a block of food about the size of a brick. It reminds us of a high-rise frittata: eggs baked with sausage, ground beef, potatoes, onions, peppers, and tomatoes, all under a mantle of melted cheese. Every forkful is a different medley of taste and texture. Fried chicken, which is available with or without a waffle as its trivet, comes encased in gnarled, crust-hugged skin that fairly drips fatty juice with every crunch. It is the most flavorful chicken imaginable.

Jesus Christ has a significant presence at Olean's. Testaments to him are everywhere on the walls, in the form of bumper stickers ("Try Jesus: If You Don't Like Him, the Devil Will Always Take You Back") as well as posters for church events and gospel sings, plaques with religious homilies, and bas-relief praying hands. If you don't drink iced tea with your meal, an equally sweet alternative is Hawaiian Punch–colored "Jesus Passion Juice."

At lunch, Olean's offers a full repertoire of classic southern side dishes such as collard greens, mac 'n' cheese, fried okra, braised cabbage, black-eyed peas, and candied yams. Everyday entrees include catfish, smothered pork chops, baked or fried chicken, and chitlins. Ribs are featured Thursday, mullet Friday and Saturday. Of course, Olean's is closed on the Sabbath.

★ O'STEEN'S

osteensrestaurant.com

205 Anastasia Blvd.   904-829-6974
St. Augustine, FL   L D | $$

With about a dozen tables and a six-stool counter, O'Steen's is a minimalist kind of place: no credit cards, no tablecloths, no cocktails, no wine or beer. A sign on the wall reads "If you have reservations, you are in the wrong place." It is so popular that there always is a wait, even at 11:30 a.m. and 5 p.m. There's good reason for the crowds. The north Florida coast is the center of America's shrimping industry, a fact immediately apparent when you bite through the crunchy veil that encloses the dense pink flesh of O'Steen's fried shrimp, which are as rich as nutmeat and ocean-sweet. O'Steen's sells them by nine, twelve, eighteen, or twenty-four; they are medium-sized and each butterflied to resemble the lines inside a peace symbol.

"Have you been here before?" the waitress asks as she sets down a plate of them. When we say no, she points to a plastic ramekin that holds the kitchen's special pink sauce for dipping. She then hoists a Grolsch beer bottle. "And this is the datil pepper sauce we make. Don't start with it alone. Mix it with the pink." O'Steen's hot sauce, turbocharged with datil peppers, is bright and fragrant and even when prudently blended with the milder pink stuff engenders a back-of-the-throat roar that rumbles forward with inexorable titillation.

P&D SOUL FOOD KITCHEN

soulfoodkitchenorlando.com

927 S. Goldwyn Ave.,   407-730-3486
Ste. 120   L D | $
Orlando, FL

Orlando is best known as the epicenter of fabricated family fun. It also happens to be a gold mine of soul food restaurants that are anything but corporate in character. Take P&D Soul Food Kitchen, for example. Meals served here are like home cooking if you happened to grow up in a home with an African American mom who was a culinary wizard. "We use no cans," explains Dennis Cox, who runs the place with his wife, Paula. "We snap our own string beans; we're getting our collard greens now from Valdosta, Georgia, but the main thing is that we cut them right." He and Paula use their parents' recipes, but with a healthful twist: smoked turkey necks replace ham hocks to add meaty savor to greens and cabbage.

Open Tuesday through Sunday, P&D offers a roster of everyday entrees such as fried chicken, pork chops, and chicken wings that are fried crisp and a joy to worry down to bare bone. Sunday's baked half chicken is divine—butter-rich, drenched with natural juices, and so tender that applying knife and fork seems sadistic. We love it on a platform of herby, slightly sweet corn-bread dressing, which imbibes all the seeping juices. Essential side dishes beyond the collard greens include extraordinarily dark glazed beets and peppery rutabaga served in big, velvety hunks. Stewed cabbage is insanely tender, vegetable-sweet, and more luxurious than cabbage has a right to be. And no matter what else a person eats, it is de rigueur to get an order of baked macaroni and cheese on the side. Dennis makes his using four different cheeses and—although he is mum on the specifics of the recipe—we suspect a measure of sour cream.

If you are planning to visit, we need to warn you that P&D Soul Food Kitchen looks boring. No personal photos or memorabilia cover the walls, as in the other worthy soul-food places around town. Located in a newish but somewhat forlorn commercial building known as the Village Square, it is a miniscule carry-out storefront with scarcely room for half a dozen people to stand and place orders. There is no table service. All meals are packed (abundantly) into Styrofoam containers and bagged with plastic utensils. While most people take their food elsewhere, P&D does offer three tiny tables in the hallway just outside the door for those who crave immediate satisfaction. On Sunday, Dennis adds a couple of party-sized round tops in the larger hall around the corner so big families have a place to dine together after church and strangers can join others for a meal.

PEPE'S CAFÉ & STEAKHOUSE

pepescafe.net

806 Caroline St.   305-294-7192
Key West, FL   **B L D** | $$

Breakfast at Pepe's, from 6:30 every morning, is heaps of fun, always featuring a bread of the day in addition to omelets, pancakes, homemade granola, and creamed chipped beef on toast. Later in the day, Apalachicola Bay oysters make Pepe's a destination for oyster lovers who consume them raw, baked, or roasted Mexican-style. Weekly traditions include a Sunday-night barbecue that features steak, pork ribs, tenderloin, chicken, salmon, and mahimahi. The lunch menu offers both a blue-collar burger and a white-collar burger. (The former is six ounces, the latter four.)

Pepe's boasts that it is "the eldest eating house in the Florida Keys," and it sure does have the feel of a place that's seen it all. The well-burnished dining room is covered with knickknacks as miscellaneous as Grandma's attic, including pictures of famous people and nobodies, a nude painting, nautical bibelots, and scenes of old Key West. Each varnished wooden booth is outfitted with a shelf that holds about a dozen different hot sauces for oyster eating. Out back is a bar where locals congregate. (The bar opens at 7 a.m.) And to the side on an open patio strewn with mismatched tables, illumination is provided by an array of fixtures that includes a crystal chandelier, green-shaded billiard lamps, and year-round Christmas lights.

POSEY'S STEAM ROOM AND OYSTER BAR

1506 Coastal Hwy.   850-984-5243
Panacea, FL   **L D** (closed Mon) | $

Just north of Ochlockonee Bay in Panacea, Posey's Steam Room and Oyster Bar is a happy dive with picnic-style seating in folding chairs at long tables outfitted with rolls of paper towels. Bring your own fish and they'll cook it for you, or choose expertly steamed and seasoned (Cajun or Old Bay) shrimp or blue crabs, or oysters any which way; on the half shell, steamed, fried, or baked with bacon and cheese. Thursday is all-you-can-eat shrimp night; the cornmeal-crusted fried mullet is rich and meaty, a strictly local delicacy; and flounder is always a house specialty—moist, pure white, falling into glistening flakes when prodded with a fork. We were impressed by the kitchen's fine version of the elegant Mobile Bay specialty, West Indies salad, which is creamy white crabmeat marinated with onions and served with crackers.

Prime rib, baby back ribs, steaks, and fried chicken are available for seafood frowners.

SALTWATER COWBOYS

saltwatercowboys.com

299 Dondanville Rd.   904-471-2332
St. Augustine, FL   **D** | $$

Named for founder Howard Dondanville, who was affectionately called Cowboy, and designed to look like a salt-marsh fish camp from long ago, this way-too-popular restaurant serves excellent Minorcan clam chowder (a St. Augustine specialty) and a slew of southern seafood: freshly opened oysters and fancy-cooked ones, boiled crawfish with Cajun vibes, snapper, deviled crabs, softshells, and shrimp. A whole portion of the menu is headlined "Florida Cracker Corner" and is devoted to frog legs, cooter (soft-shelled turtle), catfish, alligator tail, and even fried chicken with a vividly flavored bread-crumb crust. We suggest starting a meal with oysters Dondanville, served on the half shell glistening with a mantle of garlic, butter, wine, and finely chopped onions, then moving on to Cowboy's jambalaya, which is a profusion of shrimp, oysters, chicken, ham, and sausage on a pile of seasoned rice.

Fish-camp-fare frowners can have open-pit barbecue, including ribs, chicken, and shrimp. What we saw on other people's plates looked good, but the opportunity to indulge in so much inviting seafood precluded a sample.

When we wrote "too popular," we meant that chances are good you will wait for a table at any normal suppertime. It's a big place with four dining rooms, but reservations are not accepted. Waiting facilities are an open-air deck where cool frozen drinks (and sweet tea in mason jars) are served. The place exudes ramshackle beauty, occupying a restored old home with its bentwood chairs and walls decorated with antique fishing gear, snakeskins, and cracker memorabilia. Windows look out over marshland and dusk on the Intracoastal Waterway.

SCHOONER'S SEAFOOD HOUSE
schooners-seafood.com

3560 Ponce De Leon	904-826-0233
St. Augustine, FL	L D (closed Sun) | $$

Pilau, which has twins and cognates known variously as *perloo, perlau, pilaw,* and *purlieu* from America's Low Country to the Middle East, is always based on rice. The common history of all of them is that of cooks making something bountiful out of what they happened to have on hand. Pilau can be a side dish or a meal, pyrotechnical or bland. Familiar as it is to so many cooks, it tends to be fairly rare on restaurant menus.

In St. Augustine, while looking for Minorcan clam chowder, we came across a lovely chicken perloo while sitting at the counter of Schooner's Seafood House. It was not a regular menu item but the daily special. "This here pilau is good but needs a kick in the you-know-what," suggested a cologne-scented customer in beltless high-pocket slacks and a torso-hugging, no-iron short-sleeved shirt. He threw his tie back over one shoulder and poured dark red datil pepper sauce atop the old-time coastal casserole of chicken and rice, then forked into it with a madman's glee.

"Excuse me," the waitress piped in. "It is *perloo,* not pilau!"

"Says who?" said he.

The waitress pointed both thumbs at her chest. "Cracker, here; born and bred. Do not question authority."

Schooner's perloo, served with candied yams and stewed okra, proved to be a welcoming tableau for the locally favored datil pepper sauce, which transformed it from palliative comfort food into a meal so exhilarating that a cool piece of Key lime pie became a necessary conclusion.

Everyday menu items include very good local shrimp, fried oysters, scallops, crab cakes, and clam strips, as well as catfish, gator, and frog legs.

SINGLETON'S SEAFOOD SHACK

4728 Ocean St.	904-246-4442
Mayport, FL	L D | $$

Singleton's is a delightfully déclassé nautical wreck with a low ceiling, listing wooden floors, bare wood tables, and hard benches. Everything is served in Styrofoam. Utensils are plastic. Waitresses reward customers with such appellations as hon, babe, and dear. And the cuisine is North Coast seafood in all its glory. Yes, there are burgers and barbecue and slaw dogs on the menu, but they are immaterial. What matters is fried shrimp that fairly burst with flavor, briny oysters sheathed in fragile crust, and devil crab that is moist and seasoned with eye-opening panache.

Dinners come with a pair of hush puppies, clad in a red-gold crust that surrounds insides that are as moist as cake. Collard greens are vaguely sweet, limp leaves, as earthy-tasting as tobacco and yet deliriously healthful. You also can have a good bowl of Minorcan clam chowder, a St. Augustine specialty that is like Manhattan clam chowder but kick-ass hot.

The entrance to the restaurant features a large case full of raw seafood, and seats afford a view of fishing boats rocking in their berths. Nautical bric-a-brac is everywhere, and there is a large annex that is a makeshift museum of wooden model ships.

SMILEY'S CHICKEN

405 Baltzell Ave.   850-227-9353
Port St. Joe, FL   **L | $**

Smiley's is a dual-purpose establishment that details cars and serves fried chicken. We did not stick around long enough to evaluate the former, but we can tell you that the chicken is mighty fine. Made from a recipe that Smiley, the proprietor, learned from his mother, it is sensibly seasoned fried chicken with an abundance of crust poised perfectly between crunch and chew, the meat within good and moist. On the side come nuggets of fried okra with al dente oomph and see-through crust, as well as fairly mild mac 'n' cheese plus a biscuit or dinner roll.

There is no place to eat here. Smiley's is a shack with an order window, and all food is served in Styrofoam containers, ready to go. Everything is cooked to order. Expect a fifteen-plus-minute wait once your order is placed. Regular customers know to call ahead.

SPRING CREEK RESTAURANT

33 Ben Willis Rd.   850-926-3751
Crawfordville, FL   **L D** (closed Mon) **| $$$**

With dinner entree prices topping out around $30, Spring Creek Restaurant is hardly eat-in-the-rough cracker dining. But neither is it the least bit swanky. Although it only dates back to 1977, it feels more like a taste of laid-back Florida from a century ago—a tree-shaded fish-camp lodge that catches its own mullet and crabs and even farms its own extraordinary oysters. Flavored by the springs that surround the restaurant and feed straight into the salty waters of the Gulf, Spring Creek oysters deliver exceptionally briny flavor in cup or bowl, perfectly abetted by nothing more than a spritz of fresh lemon.

It is also possible to start a meal with a small portion of Spring Creek's tomato-cheese pie topped with broiled shrimp. If that sounds really good (it is!), note that the tomato pie also is available as a main course. Other entrees we've enjoyed are softshell crab (fried or broiled), shrimp stuffed with deviled crab and wrapped in bacon, and crisp-fried fillets of mullet. If you bring your own cleaned fish, the kitchen will cook it for you and serve it with salad, rolls, spuds or grits, and hush puppies, all for $12.

TOASTED

igettoasted.com
1945 Aloma Ave.   407-960-3922
Winter Park, FL   **L D | $**

Toasted is the brainchild of Jeff Yarmuth, who made Sonny's BBQ into a national success. Clearly, this Winter Park restaurant is a bellwether for future expansion. (As of 2016, another had opened in Orlando.) Despite a ready-to-franchise fast-food mien that includes an amusing periodic table of cheeses decorating one wall, it is a warm and friendly place with staff who really seems proud of what they are doing.

The theme is grilled cheese sandwiches. Options range from The 101, simply Cheddar and tomato, to the likes of Truffle Melt (Havarti, truffle oil, and arugula) and Braised Brisket (fontina, brisket, barbecue sauce, and caramelized onions). For $1 extra, you can add bacon or a fried egg to any sandwich. Side dishes include apple compote, which goes so well with anything cheesy, and French fries flavored with a heady perfume of rosemary and truffle oil. Mac 'n' cheese, a house specialty, is made with a blend of Jarlsberg, Cheddar, and gruyère,

Sandwiches are handsome packages, made using tiles of significant bread and enough griddle grease to create a rich crunch. Most sandwiches ooze just enough cheese to provide great eye appeal but remain wieldy.

There is a whole array of cheeseburgers, bacon cheeseburgers, and turkey burgers, plus a vegan menu of pretend-cheese sandwiches, pretend-meat burgers, and salads.

T-RAY'S BURGER STATION

traysburgerstation.com

202 S. 8th St.   904-261-6310

Fernandina Beach, FL   **B L** (closed Sun) | **$**

As the name suggests, burgers are what's to eat. They come in two sizes and dressed in many ways. We like the Big T Bacon Burger—extremely juicy and full-flavored. For beef frowners there is a portobello mushroom burger. Beyond burgers, T-Ray's offers salads and fried chicken and delicious cheese grits too. Locals know it as the place to get superb chicken and dumplings every Thursday as well as banana pudding for dessert every day. They flock here in the morning for masterful hot-from-the-oven biscuits.

It's easy to drive right past. It looks like every other Exxon station, except for the cars circled every day around it at breakfast and lunchtime. Dine at the counter or one of the mismatched tables. Ray's the guy who does the cooking. His father, Terrell, runs the gas station.

WAKULLA SPRINGS LODGE

wakullaspringslodge.com

550 Wakulla Park Dr.   850-421-2000

Wakulla Springs, FL   **B L D** | **$$**

In the heart of Edward Ball Wakulla Springs State Park, a 6,000-acre wildlife sanctuary populated by manatees, alligators, and waterfowl, the Wakulla Springs Lodge is an amazing place to stay and to eat. "Welcome to the REAL Florida" reads a sign as you enter the park and wend through a canopy of hardwood forest toward the two-story Moorish-deco edifice built in the 1930s and little changed since then. There are no TVs in guest rooms (but there is Wi-Fi); the lobby ceiling is a glorious painted tableau that melds Teutonic folk art with Arabic and Native American symbols and crests of Europe's noble families; and the lobby walls are adorned with backlit transparency photos that show life at the lodge in the mid-twentieth century: bathing beauties frolicking, glass-bottom boats gliding over the spring basin. A placard at the front desk advises that the air-conditioning system is unique, cooling the inn using pumped-in fresh spring water. Does that explain the sweet, moss-green scent that gives this place such a dreamy feel? Next to the original walnut-walled elevator (close the iron gate yourself, please) is a poster from the 1954 movie *Creature from the Black Lagoon*, which was filmed hereabouts to take advantage of the primeval ambience.

The setting is echt Florida, and the menu is an upscale reflection thereof. Dinner is a big-deal meal—and priced accordingly—featuring such local delights as oysters, deviled crab, shrimp, and ham-laced navy bean soup that has earned legendary status over the years. But our favorite meal is breakfast. Bright and early, birds outside the great arched windows of the dining room are busy on their morning errands, providing a colorful backdrop to a table crowded with sizzled ham steak, cheese grits, biscuits and sausage gravy, and, best of all, fried chicken. The chicken is cooked to order (expect a twenty-five-minute wait) and arrives at the table too hot to handle. Its crunchy-chewy crust outdoes bacon as a luxury breakfast meat. This is fried chicken at its finest—a reminder that northernmost Florida is America's deepest South.

WHITEY'S FISH CAMP

www.whiteysfishcamp.com

2032 CR 220   904-269-4198

Fleming Island, FL   **L D** | **$$**

We came upon Whitey's Fish Camp researching the first edition of this book more than thirty years ago. We ate wild-caught catfish, which was so delicious it made us instant fans. Subsequent encounters with farm-raised catfish revealed that the flavor of genuine, bottom-feeding river cats is something special. Pond-raised are fine—mild and polite, receptive to all kinds of character-building treatments such as blackening and Cajun-spicing. But farmed fish are no comparison to the wild ones at Whitey's, where the menu and the place have expanded dramatically but where catfish still reigns.

Served AYCE (local fish-house shorthand for All You Can Eat), the cats vary from three inches to over a half-foot long. Unless you specify what size you want, each plate delivered to the table will hold one or two big ones and two or three little ones. The tiniest are so fragile that experienced diners eat even the tender rib bones, leaving nothing but vertebrae. Big ones, with a skeleton that demands respect, provide easy access to meat. Simply poke the tines of a fork through the sandy cornmeal girdle just below the backbone, then pull downward. A nice mouthful slips cleanly off the ribs. Atop the patch of brittle crust on your fork is dense meat as luxurious as prime beefsteak but with a freshwater sparkle that evokes vacation campfires and balmy summer nights. We have never eaten anything so indisputably outdoorsy in a normal cloth-napkin restaurant. (In lieu of napkins, Whitey's supplies each table with a roll of paper towels.)

It wasn't only the robust character of the fish that impressed us when we first found Whitey's. It was the place itself, which today remains a community center as much as it is a restaurant: boat launches, bait-and-tackle shop, oyster bar and beer bar, and a campground and RV park complete with hair-styling salon. With its out-of-fashion video games for kids and two-dollar claw machine that grabs a live lobster rather than a stuffed toy, Whitey's is not quaint like some bucolic farm-town café or vintage diner. It is a taste of what locals like to call cracker culture, meaning it evokes the old, pre-air-conditioned Florida that had its own special brand of sporting lifestyle long before the great influx of retirees. A blatant patch of cracker living such as Whitey's is a good reminder of the old saw that the farther north you go in this state, the deeper south you are.

WINTER PARK FISH CO.

thewinterparkfishcompany.com

761 N. Orange Ave.   407-622-6112
Winter Park, FL   **L D** (closed Sun) | $$$

It would take countless visits to sample a significant portion of the menu in this cheerful place. Decorated like an oceanside shanty, with fishing rods and buoys hanging overhead, the Fish Company sports bare tables made from local wood. It is a tiny place with a total of six tables indoors (frequently shared by

strangers) and an outdoor bar where you can dine and drink. Expect to wait for a place at prime mealtimes.

It is the customer's job to step up to the order counter and devise a meal. First, choose a fish. When we visited in January, the roster included Tasmanian trout, stone bass, halibut, king fish, striped bass, swordfish, ahi tuna, mahimahi, grouper, scallops, salmon, and snapper. Next, decide how it should be cooked. The choices are dizzying: grilled, broiled, blackened, seared, Cajun, jerked, TNT crusted (very peppery), chili crusted, macadamia buttered, tempura battered, lightly fried, or buttermilk fried. Third, pick a topping from among mango ginger glaze, tartar sauce, olive tapenade, garlic, chile, and soy, green-tomato chowchow, Cajun remoulade, white cocktail, lemon caper butter, habanero BBQ, sun-dried tomato truffle basil butter, or orange beurre blanc.

Finally, select two side dishes from a list that includes sweet puppies (hush puppies dusted with powdered sugar), French fries, mango coleslaw, coconut rice, black beans, fried okra, squash cassoulet, black-eyed pea ragù, zucchini stir-fry, roasted Parmesan-topped tomato slices, sweet potato fries, grits, mashed sweet potatoes, green beans, bok choy, spinach pie, Parmesan couscous, mac 'n' cheese, and potato salad.

If all these decisions are too much of a challenge, one can forgo the step-by-step order system and instead go for one of the Fish Company Classics, which are complete meals such as fish and chips, bacon-wrapped trout, Florida grouper cheeks in parchment, and buttermilk fried shrimp. We love the shrimp and grits, which is an abundance of seared pink shrimp with real snap to their flesh cosseted in a very peppery lobster gravy enriched with melted Cheddar cheese, all piled atop a mound of luxurious creamy grits. On the side comes a chewy Cheddar-jalapeño biscuit.

GEORGIA

BARBECUE KITCHEN

1437 Virginia Ave.   404-766-9906
College Park, GA   **B L D** | $

Atlanta's Hartsfield Airport is surrounded by ho-hum strip-mall cafés and fast-food franchises, but those who crave an authentic Dixie meal have another choice: the Barbecue Kitchen. It's an old-time restaurant practically around the corner from the airport, right next to a Waffle House. And while barbecue is its name and, rightfully, its fame, a sign outside boasts of fresh vegetables. These are superb, nutritious southern kitchen classics: collard greens, rutabagas, speckled butter beans, pole beans, simple sliced tomatoes, and stewed squash. On a slightly less salubrious note, choices include fried okra, baked potato casserole, creamed corn, and baked apples.

Each item arrives in its own little bowl atop a partitioned unbreakable plate, the largest section of which can be filled not only with hickory-smoked barbecue (the real deal) but with such items as fried chicken, grilled ham, or corned beef hash. On the side come corn muffins and/or biscuits, the former not the least bit sweet (a perfect companion for those greens), the latter a good moppin' sop for barbecue. Of course, the libation of choice with such a model meat-and-three meal is sweet tea. For dessert: coconut layer cake.

BIG CHICK

204 E. Robert   706-678-2214
Toombs Ave.   **L D** (closed Sun) | $
Washington, GA

Big Chick has earned a sterling reputation for its fried-to-order chicken. White and dark parts, gizzards, livers, strips (regular or spicy), and wings all come crusted with a brightly salted skin that shatters at first bite, then melts in your mouth.

"Fried" is the word that describes almost all the side dishes, each of which is a vegetable with only enough flavor to make its presence known within the main ingredient, which is batter. Onion rings are modestly oniony; fried okra strikes a nice balance of green pod and golden crust; hush puppies are super crunchy; corn balls are spheres of creamed corn with a crisp coat.

There is no seating on premises. All food is presented in paper bags for taking elsewhere.

BIG DADDY'S DISH

bigdaddysdish.com

5549 Old National Hwy.   678-859-5191
College Park, GA   L D | $

The extraordinary hospitality of the staff makes visiting Big Daddy's Dish a heartening experience. Delicious meals put it on the itinerary of all hungry travelers who appreciate soul food prepared with flair and expertise. Service is cafeteria-style, with staff all along the way to dish it out and to explain what goes best with what. Among entrees, ribs and fried chicken are essential. Big spare ribs are cooked to a point of such tenderness that when the server tries to grab a few with his tongs, he frequently winds up lifting the bone straight out of the meat, then having to return to pick up hefty ribbons of nothing but rib meat. Fried chicken seems to have twice as much crisp, crusty skin as most fried chicken. It is flamboyantly seasoned, a sheer joy to savor. Other options include pork chops, catfish and whiting, jerk turkey, meat loaf, and smothered chicken livers.

Side dishes are a register of southern standards: earthy rutabagas with an enticing bitter twist, creamy mac 'n' cheese, collard greens cooked with or without smoked turkey, carrot soufflé, yam soufflé, corn-bread dressing, broccoli-rice casserole thick with molten cheese, and more. Even plain steamed cabbage is anything but plain. Somehow the slow cooking brings out vivacious cruciferous flavor. As for dessert, peach cobbler is smoky-good, but apple cobbler is even better; banana pudding, available with or without whipped topping, is a classic; and there is an entire case of rainbow-hued layer cakes.

BLUE WILLOW INN

bluewillowinn.com

294 N. Cherokee Rd.   770-464-2131
Social Circle, GA   L D | $$

"We have two rules," says the waitress when you are seated at a table and receive your sweet iced tea (known here as the Champagne of the South). "Rule one is that no one goes home hungry. Rule two is that everybody has to have at least two desserts." Each guest is given a plate and invited to go to the serving tables as often as possible to help himself. Every day here is Sunday supper, southern-style. The beautiful, bounteous buffet is located in a room that includes far more dishes than any one appetite can sample in a single meal. A few of the must-eats are fried chicken, fried green tomatoes, collard greens that are long-cooked to porky tenderness, chicken and dumplings, and, of course, biscuits. Using a recipe from Sema Wilkes's legendary boardinghouse in Savannah (p. 203), the Blue Willow kitchen creates tan-crusted domes with fluffy insides and a compelling fresh-from-the-oven aroma. Their tops are faintly knobby because the dough is patted out rather than rolled.

For dessert, there are pies, cakes, cookies, and pudding, but the one we recommend (assuming you have an inkling of appetite by the end of the meal) is warm fruit cobbler. The Inn provides rocking chairs on its broad front porch for postprandial snoozing. It is a magnificent place, a grand mansion that is said to have inspired Margaret Mitchell to conceive of Tara in *Gone With the Wind*. Although meal service is help-yourself, the serving staff couldn't be more gracious.

BUCKNER'S FAMILY RESTAURANT

bucknersfamilyrestaurant.com

1168 Bucksnort Rd.   770-775-6150
Jackson, GA   L D (Thurs–Sun) | $$

The full name of this restaurant is real in many ways. First, it really has been family-run, by the Buckners, since it opened in 1980. More important, the food is cooked from family recipes and served family-style. Seating is at banquet-sized round tables with lazy Susans in the middle, on which are placed platters of fried chicken, barbecue, and at least a dozen side dishes. These likely will include Brunswick stew, corn-bread dressing, whipped sweet potatoes and hunks of yam, black-eyed peas, and speckled butter beans. Plus, of course, corn bread and yeast rolls. Spin the lazy Susan, and keep helping yourself until you've had enough. Then dig into fruit cobbler. It's a consummate southern-comfort feast, shared with family, friends, and perfect strangers with whom you likely will share a table.

Note: On Friday and Saturday nights, after-dinner entertainment (included in the prix fixe) includes live bluegrass and/or gospel music from 7 p.m. to about 9 p.m.

BULLOCH HOUSE
bullochhouse.com

70 Broad St.   706-655-9068
Warm Springs, GA   **L** (closed Mon);
                     D (Fri & Sat) | **$**

Benjamin Bulloch's home, built in 1893, became a restaurant in 1990. The menu reflects both vintage and modern taste. Twenty-first-century types can come for fruit in a shell (that's a tortilla shell), a turkey burger (or beef burger), a veggie wrap, or a grilled chicken panini. Classicists come for the buffet, available at lunch every day and at dinner Friday and Saturday. While the specifics of the buffet change, depending on which vegetables look good at the market, you can always count on fried chicken, biscuits, and corn bread, as well as fried green tomatoes and fried apples, plus soufflé-light mac 'n' cheese. Desserts, ordered from the waitress, include to-die-for caramel cake, a six-layer chocolate cake, pecan pie, and banana pudding.

THE COLONNADE
colonnadeatlanta.com

1879 Cheshire   404-874-5642
Bridge Rd. NE   **L D** | **$$**
Atlanta, GA

It is unlikely one of television's food showboats will soon be reporting on the Colonnade. There is nothing about this vintage eatery that's outrageous, outlandish, outsized, or in any way vulgar enough to succeed on the boob tube.

On the other hand, people with a honed Roadfood sensibility will find a meal at the Colonnade to be pulse-quickening nurture for the spirit as well as for the appetite. In this polite place, a bastion of square meals since 1927, waitresses speed trays of southern comfort food to families who have been customers for generations. The specialties, which never change, include fried chicken, pork loin, pot roast, and roast turkey breast, served with your choice from a roster of over two dozen soulful southern vegetables, including sweet-potato soufflé, turnip greens, rutabagas, and fried okra. The whole wonderfully predictable experience begins with a lovely bread basket piled with corn muffins, yeast rolls, and whole wheat rolls, and perhaps a Waldorf salad or tomato aspic. Our next meal will be the one Roadfood.com's Dale Fine, who goes by the screen moniker Wanderingjew, reported on back in 2012. He called it "spruced up" liver and onions: calves' liver smothered with not only bacon and onions but with sautéed-soft Granny Smith apples, all in a rich demiglace.

Among the flawless desserts are strawberry shortcake, hot fudge cake (with ice cream, of course), and an only-in-the-South coconut icebox pie.

COMMUNITY Q BBQ
communityqbbq.com

1361 Clairmont Rd.   404-633-2080
Decatur, GA   **L D** | **$**

"We cook fresh every day . . . that means we have to guess how much we will need . . . Please understand that we will run out of meat occasionally." Fair warning from the Community Q menu. Do plan to arrive early, because this is one barbecue you do not want to miss. It is among Atlanta's best; maybe it is the best, since Harold's hit the skids and finally closed.

Pulled pork is a mélange of velvety strips and chewy bits of bark, brought to full flower by the application of vinegar-pepper sauce (or a sweeter, more tomato-based sauce). Dry-rub ribs ooze juice as soon as tooth pressure is applied. Strangely enough—this being the Deep South—Community Q brisket delivers beefy satisfaction reminiscent of the benchmark Q's of Texas. Brunswick stew is hearty enough that it easily could be a meal. Sandwiches come on buttery Texas toast. Among side dishes, mac 'n' cheese, made with penne noodles, is a standout: chewy, gooey, cheesy, and greasy.

Our only disappointment was a rather monotone banana pudding at dessert. Next time, we'll try the cobbler or bread pudding.

THE CRAB SHACK

thecrabshack.com

40 Estill Hammock Rd.   912-786-9857
Tybee Island, GA   L D | $$

——★—— It may not be the most romantic come-
WATER-FRONT on in the restaurant world, but what
DINING
——★—— Roadfooder could resist the Crab Shack's catchphrase, "Where the Elite Eat in Their Bare Feet"? Need we say that this is not a formal dining room? Park among heaps of oyster shells and eat off paper plates at picnic tables to the sound of Jimmy Buffett tunes. The deckside view of the broad tidal creek is lovely—a true waterside picnic—but even lovelier are the great heaps of sloppy, hands-on seafood that Savannahians come to gobble up with beer and/or frozen margaritas.

The fundamentals include boiled shrimp (served the Lowcountry way with corn, potatoes, and sausage), steamers by the bucket, oysters on the half shell, crawfish in season, and your choice from a list of several crabs: Alaskan, blue, Dungeness, snow, and, when available, stone crab (claws only, of course). In addition to these simple seafoods, the Crab Shack offers deviled crabs, crab stew, and shrimp and crab au gratin. Couples and groups of three or four can opt for a seasonal shellfish feast, accompanied by corn, potatoes, and sausage.

DENNIS' BBQ

dennisbbq.com

3639 San Sebastian Dr.   706-790-5477
Hephzibah, GA   L D (closed Sun-Tues) | $

Dennis's ribs are outstanding, each bone impossibly heavy with meat that has been brought to utmost tenderness and delirious smokiness. The chopped pork isn't quite so intensely flavorful, but it has all the subtle sweetness that slow smoking evokes. Great as those barbecue classics are, the #1 entree on the menu is chicken, its skin crisp as bacon, its meat infused with enough spice to make taste buds cry for mercy. Top any of these meats with house-made sauce, which has the locally loved mustard twang and a sweet undernote to balance it, and you have the anchor of a memorable smokehouse meal. (The sauce is available in degrees of hotness, the hottest being incendiary.)

On the side, you want hash, the porky gallimaufry that is sweet and sour and luridly spiced—so intense that the downy bed of rice upon which it sits provides essential stability. Other fine sides include creamy mac 'n' cheese, gentle-flavored collard greens, supersweet yams, and fried okra. Little squares of red velvet sheet cake are available for dessert.

An out-of-the-way restaurant that is primarily in the takeout business, Dennis's does provide five tables with molded plastic bench seats for on-premises dining. Its motto is inarguable: "If you want good food, then come to where the good food is."

DILLARD HOUSE

dillardhouse.com

768 Franklin St.   706-746-5348
Dillard, GA   B L D | $

——★—— Dillard House isn't really a boarding-
MOUNTAIN house, but it serves its meals
VIEWS
——★—— boardinghouse-style. Everything is set out on the table on platters and in bowls. Friends, family, and strangers reach, pass, and grab for what they want. There is no fixed menu; the meal consists of everything the kitchen is offering at the time you sit down, the blackboard list changing hour by hour as new dishes are cooked and others are eaten up. It is essential to come to Dillard House with a big

appetite; it would be wrong to practice moderation. And be prepared to grab what you like. At a boardinghouse feed like this, nobody wants to waste time being polite.

Fried chicken always is on the table, and it's crunch-crusted gold. Country ham, prime rib, and barbecue chicken are the other entrees. But it's the vegetables we like. They are lavish, ultra-flavored, stars-and-bars Dixie vegetables such as acorn squash soufflé loaded with coconut and raisins, creamy vanilla-scented yams streaked with minimarshmallows, and limp-leaf collard greens pungent with the smack of a salty hambone. Plus dinner rolls and biscuits and, of course, iced tea in mason jars. The dessert to eat is peach cobbler.

The Dillard House dining room is huge and boisterous, just one part of a vast good-time complex in the scenic mountains that includes a hotel and cottages, hiking trails, and opportunities to whitewater raft, fish, and golf.

DINGLEWOOD PHARMACY

1939 Wynnton Rd.　　　706-322-0616
Columbus, GA　　　　　**L** (closed Sun) | **$**

The Northeast, where we live, has plenty of excellent hot dogs of all kinds, but nothing like a scrambled dog. When you sit at Dinglewood's counter (or at one of a few tables and booths) and receive your dog, you will not recognize it as a member of the wiener family. A shallow rectangular dish comes with the handle of a spoon sticking out from below a pile of oyster crackers, meat-and-bean chili, pickle slices, and chopped raw onions. Use the spoon to poke around a bit and you soon will discover the hot dog, a neon-red weenie already cut into bite-sized pieces, buried underneath everything else. The spoon, of course, is essential. This take on the scrambled dog cannot be picked up. It doesn't even pretend to have a bun. The movable-letter menu above the counter lists a few other sandwiches, a chili dog and a bun with nothing but chili in it, as well as milk shakes, sundaes, and fresh lemonade.

EDNA'S

1300 Hwy. 411 S.　　　　706-695-4960
Chatsworth, GA　　　　　**L D** | **$**

Every day Edna's puts out a short list of entrees and a long list of vegetables from which you choose one main course and three side dishes. In many meat-and-three restaurants, it is the vegetables that matter, and some customers forget the meat altogether, getting a four-vegetable plate for lunch. At Edna's the all-vegetable strategy would be a big mistake. We don't know about the meat loaf or the country-fried steak, but we can tell you that the fried chicken is delicious, a fact that becomes apparent if you look around the restaurant and note that probably half the clientele chooses it. Edna's logo is a chicken wearing a chef's toque with the proclamation, "Our chicken dinners are worth crowing about."

The side dishes include not only vegetables such as mashed potatoes, fried potatoes, green beans, pole beans, and so on, but also mac 'n' cheese and Jell-O salads. Whatever you get comes with a cornbread muffin that crumbles very nicely over cooked greens. For dessert, there is no better choice than one of Edna's pies—peanut butter and coconut cream preferred.

HILDEBRANDT'S
dasdeli.us

226 6th St.　　　　　　706-722-7756
Augusta, GA　　　　　　**L** | **$**

When Hildebrandt's opened for business, Rutherford B. Hayes was president. It was a grocery store then, but sometime in the last seven-score years, a kitchen was added in back and tables were set up for people to have a sit-down lunch on premises. There still is a bit of produce for sale, plus a large inventory of hard-to-find candy and soft drinks, as well as endless shelves of curios, but the main reason people come to this colorful institution in downtown Augusta is lunch.

Sandwiches reign; big, stuffed beauties are listed on the white-board menu under three categories: Italian (your choice from among salami, pepperoni, capicola, prosciutto, provolone, etc.), German (braunschweiger, yachtwurst, or zungenwurst on pumpernickel or rye), and hot (pastrami, corned beef, Buffalo chicken). Or, devise your own. For a side dish, warm German potato salad is marvelous, a wee bit pickly and very bacony. Starting in the fall when the weather cools, Hildebrandt's offers chili, a robust, mild-mannered bowlful heavy with drifts of ground beef and a few beans, available with grated cheese and sour cream on top.

Service is personal and delightfully antiquated. When you place your order at the front counter, it is written on a little menu pad that is brought back to the kitchen. Meanwhile, help yourself to lemonade or tea at the beverage station and find a seat at either a front-room table, with a view of the vast inventory of curios and antiques for sale, or at one of the backroom marble tables, where you can eavesdrop on kitchen chatter. The written order, which has become your check, is delivered with lunch. Pay at the register on your way out.

The food is very good, but it is the experience of simply being in this 1879 store, run with genuine hospitality by the family that founded it, that makes visiting Hildebrandt's a high-water mark of Roadfood delight.

(Thanks to Roadfood.com's Keith McLendon for leading the way.)

HONEY FROM THE ROCK CAFÉ
honeyfromtherockcafe.com

2621 Washington Rd.   706-434-1098
Augusta, GA   **L** (Mon–Fri) | $

If you are hungry in Augusta, Georgia, it's OK if you don't subscribe to the aim of Whole Life Ministries: "To Grow Up the Body of Christ and Teach Them Victory." Whoever's your savior, your appetite will have no trouble believing in Honey from the Rock Café, where Whole Life serves munificent cafeteria-style lunch every weekday. The tradition-minded bill of fare includes baked or fried chicken, baked ham with pineapple sauce, chicken and dumplings, and meat loaf sided by the likes of sweet-potato casserole, fried green tomatoes, broccoli casserole, and macaroni and cheese. Have a couple of crisp discs of corn fritter and top off the meal with banana pudding, coconut pie, or house-churned peach ice cream, and you will be in Dixie-dining bliss. This is first-rate fare, and you pay accordingly. A nice meal for two can easily cost $30.

Given the spiritual mission of the enterprise, it is no surprise that the food is served with unabashed goodwill. Expect your glass of sweet tea to be topped off about every third sip. And talk about helpful: If you are too busy, too lazy, or too weak to pray, write a prayer request on a piece of paper and drop it in a slot. A member of the staff will fetch it and pray on your behalf. The décor showcases Bible verses everywhere, and the background music is gospel too rousing to fade into the background. The name of the place comes from Psalms 81:16: "With honey out of the rock would I satisfy thee."

HOT THOMAS' BARBEQUE
hotthomasbbq.com

3753 Greensboro Hwy.   706-769-6550
Watkinsville, GA   **L D** (Tues–Sat) | $

Hot Thomas' used to be a peach orchard. It grew into a country store in the middle of fruit-growing country, then a barbecue restaurant. The peach trees are no more, but the barbecue is well worth a trip.

Step up to the counter inside the sunbleached white building, order a plate of 'cue, and nab yourself a Coke or Mr. Pibb from the cooler. Find a seat and fork into moist hickory-cooked pork, hacked to smithereens with a good measure of "Mr. Brown" (crusty dark meat from the outside) laced among the supple, sweet pieces from the center of the shoulder. Side dishes to accompany this lovely entree include Brunswick stew, sweet coleslaw, and soft, white bread suitable for dunking in the stew and mopping up hot sauce. There are ribs too, as well as hamburgers, chili dogs, and chicken mull (a creamy stew), but chopped pork is what you want.

★ MARY MAC'S TEA ROOM

marymacs.com

224 Ponce de Leon Ave.   404-876-1800
Atlanta, GA   **L D** | $$

Originally opened in 1945, Mary Mac's is an old-fashioned urban lunchroom in the heart of Atlanta that offers a broad menu of Dixie cooking. You can start a meal with pot likker—that's soft turnip greens wallowing in a bowl with their flavorful cooking liquid—sided by a corn-bread muffin. Entrees include baked chicken with corn-bread dressing, pork barbecue with Brunswick stew, and country-fried steak with gravy. Fried chicken is crust-crunching, moisture-spurting delicious.

Many customers come only for vegetables. Stand-outs include sweet-potato soufflé that is spiced Christmas-sweet, mac 'n' cheese in which the noodles are suspended in an eggy cheese soufflé, tomato pie that is fruity and cheese-enriched, hoppin' John, and crisp-fried okra.

An airy place with soothing pastel yellow walls and tables covered with white oilcloth, Mary Mac's offers old-style tearoom service, which is great fun. When you sit down, you are given an order pad and menus. Once you've made your decisions, you write your own order and hand it to your waiter or waitress who, in the meanwhile, has brought you an immense tankard of what the menu lists as the table wine of the South—sweet iced tea.

MATTHEWS CAFETERIA

matthewscafeteria.com

2299 Main St.   770-939-2357
Tucker, GA   **B L D** (closed Sat) | $

Matthews Cafeteria is 100 percent Roadfood. To fully understand its appeal, you need a deep appreciation of *cuisine maudite* cues such as ancient walls painted institutional beige, a raucous cafeteria line where food is marshaled upon the steam table with little regard for beauty, vegetables that are purposely overcooked, creamed corn that is crazy-creamy to the point where the kernels are a minor element, mac 'n' cheese with macaroni so soft that it is inseparable from the cheese, and strawberry shortcake sweeter than a Twinkie. Yes, we actually do like all these things ... and, more important, we love Matthews's fried chicken, for which no apology need be made. It bears a fine, fragile crust, just salty enough to enhance the meat, which ranges from dripping-moist to chewy bark.

You can argue that there are better vegetables and fried chicken around Atlanta, but you will not find another place with the unvarnished charm of Matthews Cafeteria. We hesitate even to call it charming, because most common markers for charmingness are lacking, but if you check it out and fall in love with it as we did, you will have earned your Roadfood colors.

MOUNTAIN BISCUITS

1718 Old 41 Hwy. NW   770-419-3311
Marietta, GA   **B L** | $

Mountain Biscuits is one of a few excellent little eateries northwest of Atlanta where biscuits rule. Here they are broad and cushiony, soft with a faintly crisp exterior. While good all by themselves or with a bit of butter and/or molasses, they come into their own when sandwiching generous portions of smoky bacon, country ham, crisp-fried chicken, or chicken-fried steak.

The specialty of the house is a fried biscuit. It gets dunked in boiling oil and served under a blanket of powdered sugar. Neither puffy like a beignet nor fluffy like an oven-hot biscuit, it is dense and chewy—a substantial breakfast breadstuff. Cinnamon rolls are also available fried and covered with a glistening glaze, a wanton indulgence.

Warning: Mountain Biscuits is a small place (a former gas station) and can get very crowded, especially on Saturday mornings.

MRS. WILKES' DINING ROOM

mrswilkes.com

107 W. Jones St.
Savannah, GA

912-232-5997
L (Mon–Fri; closed in Jan)| **$**

West Jones Street is a boulevard of antique brick houses with curving steps and graceful cast-iron banisters. At eleven o'clock each morning a line begins to form at #107. At 11:30, the doors open and the lunch crowd finds seats at tables shared by strangers. And so begins Mrs. Wilkes' daily feast, boardinghouse-style.

The tabletops are crowded with platters of fried chicken and corn-bread dressing, corn muffins, and biscuits. As at any southern banquet worth its cracklin' corn bread, there are constellations of vegetable casseroles: great, gooey, buttery bowls full of mac 'n' cheese, candied yams, butter beans, squash casserole, okra and tomatoes, rice and gravy, and Savannah red rice. The food comes fast, and everybody eats fast in a joyful camaraderie.

When the late Mrs. Wilkes first started serving meals in this dining room in 1943, there were many similar places throughout the region, where boarders as well as frugal local citizens gathered to enjoy the special pleasure of a meal shared with neighbors and strangers. Now, the take-some-and-pass-the-bowl style of the old boardinghouse is a rarity. Mrs. Wilkes' is a prized opportunity to indulge in the delicious dining style of a culinary tradition that values sociability as much as a good macaroni salad.

OLD SOUTH BAR-B-Q

oldsouthbbq.com

Windy Hill Rd.
Smyrna, GA

770-435-4215
L D (closed Mon) | **$$**

We first ran into barbecue salad in Memphis, but have since seen a claim for its invention in Alabama and found the exemplary one in Georgia, at Old South Bar-B-Q, a family-run eatery that's been slow-smoking meats since 1968. No paradigm exists telling exactly what such a salad should be; there are more ways to make it than there are to spell the word "barbecue." Some are regular green salads topped with barbecue sauce and/or salad dressing; Jim Neely's in Memphis adds bacon bits but no other meat; others pile dressed salad greens on top of sauced barbecue.

Old South calls its version a "chef's bar-b-q salad." It is a big plate of cold, crisp lettuce and grated orange cheese topped with pork (pulled, chopped, or sliced), beef brisket (chopped or sliced), or chicken, the whole meal-on-a-plate accompanied by your choice from a selection of eight salad dressings and four sauces (original, sweet, hot, or sweet-hot). Pour or dip: It's up to you. Our first-timer recommendation is pulled pork with hot or hot-sweet sauce and honey mustard dressing. Purely speaking, it's neither salad nor barbecue. But what it is is weirdly satisfying.

If you are a traditionalist, be assured that the regular barbecue plates and sandwiches are first-rate, the latter available on either bun or garlic toast.

PEACHTREE CAFÉ

lanesouthernorchards.com

Lane Packing Company
50 Lane Rd.
Fort Valley, GA

800-277-3224
L | **$**

The Peachtree Café at the Lane Packing Company, which farms over 2,500 acres of peach trees, has a nice lunch menu of barbecue, sandwiches, and salads; but it's dessert that is compelling. That is especially true during summer peach season, when over two dozen different varieties ripen, week by week, on company trees. Peach muffins and peach ice cream are swell, as are warm peach cobbler and butter pecan ice cream made from Lane Company nuts. Best of all is pecan pie, crowded with Lane Company nuts that are sweet and just-cracked crunchy. Top this with fresh peach ice cream, and your taste buds will be humming "Georgia on My Mind."

PERRY FOSTER'S BBQ

4314 Wrightsboro Rd.   706-869-7759
Grovetown, GA   **L D** | $$

For three decades before coming to Georgia in 2013, Perry Foster built his reputation as a barbecue man in Warrensburg, Missouri, about an hour southeast of Kansas City. When he returned to Georgia, he brought back some of the best of the Midwest's smokehouse traditions. Mutton, for example (here called lamb), used to be a sleeper go-to dish at the legendary Arthur Bryant's. Mr. Foster's mutton won't win a beauty contest: It appears dry and juiceless. But a good chew liberates great waves of concentrated flavor—a smoke-saturated mineral smack unique to ewe meat. With a full ration of spicy red barbecue sauce, it is divine.

As for ribs, those of pork are definitely juicier, but beef ribs here pack three times as much flavor. Hugely satisfying beef! Likewise brisket, which is in the Texas league of succulence. Sliced pork is quite all right, especially when painted with Perry Foster's good sauce, but there's better pork around Augusta. We've yet to find better barbecue beef.

Terrific side dishes include super-creamy mac 'n' cheese; greens that are oily and fetchingly bitter; gorgeous French fries that are each a significant cut from a potato, the outside logs still bearing skin; and baked beans that are thick and hammy, as satisfying as a main-course stew.

Don't forget your pig skins. When ours arrived at the table, they were so fresh from the fry kettle that they were still hissing, popping, and crackling. They are an amazing snack, hitting your mouth all crunchy, then dissolving into pure pig flavor.

★ PERRY'S PIG

1957 Old Savannah Rd.   706-724-2387
Augusta, GA   **L D** (closed Sun & Mon) | $

A ragtag shack on a rough city road, offering only chest-high counters outside for on-premise dining (nearly all business is takeout), Perry's Pig is a Roadfood prize sure to thrill aficionados of southern barbecue. It offers meaty ribs and tender chicken, a potent version of the Central Savannah River Area's favorite hash on rice, even turkey legs and red velvet cake (or, sometimes, Key lime cake, which is as bright green as the velvet is red).

The must-eat specialty is Perry's barbecue sandwich. It is a motley pile of succulent, hacked-up pork dressed with sweet-hot sauce and, if you request it (you must!), a great spill of crumbled cracklins. The cracklins are wickedly crunchy compared to the soft meat they adorn, and their indulgent flavor, which Roadfood.com contributor Chickenplucker described as something like pork candy, adds a whole other dimension of luxury to what is already a very plush assembly of food. We were told that topping pork with cracklins is an old-time tradition; they are billed on the sign outside as "washpot skins," dating back to the days when pork skin, fat, and scraps got boiled in an old pot.

Perry's has been crafting sublime 'cue for over forty years now, and the family has it down to a fine art. Meeting the staff adds extra pleasure to the experience—such nice people! If you visit, please say hello to Maria, Desmond, and Leroy from the Sterns.

RUTH'S FAMILY RESTAURANT

3843 Washington Rd.   706-863-5616
Augusta, GA   **B L** | $

Breakfast is served all day at Ruth's (until its 2:30 p.m. closing), and it is good. There is genuine country ham—chewy, salty, flavorful—accompanied by biscuits that are hefty, but still nice to eat despite their density, and a fine sop for sausage gravy. Sorry to say that grits are nothing more than a perfunctory grain. Catfish makes a wonderful breakfast. It is an extraordinarily moist fillet, arriving in a falling-apart jacket of brightly seasoned batter.

Catfish also can be the anchor of a meat-and-two lunch. Other everyday lunches are diner standards such as liver and onions, country-fried steak, fried chicken, and hamburgers, along with a selection of at least a dozen vegetables. Among the veggies, we like sweet and spicy candied yams, rutabagas, and fried okra. Mac 'n' cheese is bland. Comfort-food fanciers will want chicken and dumplings, frequently a daily special. It is as homey a dish as can be—tender pieces of chicken and fluffy ribbons of dough in aromatic white sauce. It is bland, but generous sprinkles of salt and pepper bring forth blissful chicken savor.

Even if you come for breakfast, do consider dessert. Cakes, puddings, and cobblers all are made by Ruth's waitresses or the waitresses' mothers, and they are church-bake-sale-good. Diana's blackberry cobbler is our favorite, served warm, with ice cream on top, of course.

SCONYER'S BAR-B-QUE

sconyersbar-b-que.com

2250 Sconyers Way   706-790-5411

Augusta, GA   **L D** (Thurs-Sat only) | $$

Sconyer's is an immense barbecue complex with seating for hundreds in multiple dining rooms, plus drive-through service. Hams are cooked a full twenty-four hours over oak and hickory, resulting in meat that is ridiculously tender and sopping in its own smoke-perfumed juices. Curiously, it is a lot like Lexington-style barbecue, but with a sauce that has more of a pepper punch. It comes on a plate along with hash and rice, pickles and coleslaw, and plenty of nice soft white bread for mopping, or in a sandwich or à la carte by the pound.

For people afraid of their food, Sconyer's offers 97 percent fat-free turkey as well as something called T-loin, which is billed as 96 percent fat-free, low sodium and low cholesterol "choice pork." Ribs, chopped beef, turkey, and chicken are also available off the pit. Wine is served in addition to sweet tea and Coke.

SILVER SKILLET

thesilverskillet.com

200 14th St.   404-874-1388

Atlanta, GA   **B L** | $

The Silver Skillet diner is a charismatic blast from the past, its glass windows tilting outward like mid-century tailfins. Booths are upholstered in green and orange Naugahyde, tables topped with boomerang-pattern Formica, and the clientele ranges from blue-collar boys in overalls to visiting celebrities with an entourage in tow.

Breakfast is fine: skillet-cooked ham afloat in a pool of dark, red-eye gravy with biscuits on the side; plate-wide pancakes; fried pork chops with grits. At lunch, there is meat loaf or fried chicken and always a list of southern-style vegetables from which you can make a bounteous four-vegetable plate.

And for dessert? Ah, dessert. The banana pudding is dandy, as is peach or blackberry cobbler, and the lemon icebox pie is stellar. Cool, creamy, and neatly poised between sugar-sweet and lemon-zesty, it is a superlative exclamation point after any meal, but especially after a slab of country ham.

SKIPPER'S FISH CAMP

skippersfishcamp.com

85 Screven St.   912-437-FISH

Darien, GA   **L D** | $$

Unlike most fish-camp restaurants, Skipper's is refined, its walls decorated with handsome nautical décor and a whole stuffed alligator. Service is solicitous; meals come on non-disposable plates. There is a boat launch next door that dates back to the time this place really was more like a fish camp; but now Skipper's is adjoined by a prestigious waterside condominium development where no worms are sold.

The handsomest meal here is crisp-fried flounder, a fish so big that it hangs over both ends of a good-sized plate. The plateau of meat below its craggy orange-gold crust is moist and sweet, easy to lift in bite-sized nuggets right off the skeleton. Fried shrimp, caught locally, are firm and fresh, accompanied by red-crusted hush puppies in which the cornmeal is infused with a beguiling swirl of sweetness and garlic. By comparison to the muscular shrimp, fried oysters are shockingly fragile, so tender that they virtually melt in the mouth. Excellent sides include brown-sugary sweet-potato casserole and bitter greens. Brunswick stew is available as a formidable hors d'oeuvre or entree companion.

The essential dessert is Georgia peach cobbler, a one-two punch of fruity sweetness and buttery crust. It is served hot, making a globe of vanilla ice cream perched on top melt fast.

SMITH HOUSE

smithhouse.com

84 S. Chestatee St.   706-867-7000
Dahlonega, GA   L D (Tues–Sun) | $$

Did you know that Dahlonega, Georgia, had a gold rush in 1828? Proprietors of the Smith House like to say their building sits atop an untapped vein, but today's treasure is in the form of puffy yeast rolls, cracklin' corn-bread muffins, fried chicken, ham with dumplings, and vegetables that range from candied yams to chestnut soufflé.

Since 1922, when Henry and Bessie Smith turned the old house into an inn, service has been family-style: Pay one price and eat your fill. There is no menu to look at; there are no choices to make. Everything the kitchen has prepared that day is brought to the communal tables in large serving dishes. Local folks and visitors all behave as though they were at a family party, passing platters back and forth, chattering happily about the good ol' southern food they are eating.

SPORTS CENTER

594 Broad St.   706-724-9307
Augusta, GA   L D | $

Sports Center is not for those of delicate disposition. It's a pool hall and bar in downtown Augusta with beer-sign décor and waitstaff who takes no guff. When a freight train rumbles past on 6th Street, the loudest conversation is drowned out. The air inside is thick with two perfumes: onions frying on the flat-top and cigarette smoke. Even the cook periodically takes occasional short breaks to set down her spatula and suck on her unfiltered butt.

The raffish setting may not be your idea of fun, but you still should know about this place for hamburgers and onion rings. The burgers are hand-patted half-pounders so well-fatted that even hard pressing with a spatula on the grill does not deprive them of extreme juiciness. Piled into a bun with lettuce, tomato, mayo, mustard, grilled onions, and optional cheese, they are an oozy delight. And one needn't be a fan of déclassé dining to appreciate Sports Center's scrumptious onion rings, which get breaded just

before lunch and emerge from the deep fryer with a thin, fragile coat that barely hugs the onion.

STILESBORO BISCUITS

3545 Stilesboro Rd. NW   770-429-5552
Kennesaw, GA   B L (Wed–Sat) | $

———★——— A tiny, focused restaurant open only
MOUNTAIN until 11:30 in the morning and popular
VIEWS enough that you will wait in line, espe-
———★——— cially on a weekend morning, Stilesboro Biscuits is a Roadfood treasure. The biscuits are creamy catheads, rich enough to make fingers glisten. Sandwich ingredients are superb, light-years beyond the fast-food versions: well-seasoned fried chicken, thick-cut bacon, red-hot sausage, and the like.

If you are looking for a powerhouse meal, consider a sausage biscuit with gravy. It comes split open and smothered with rich, peppery gravy and massive amounts of fragrant pork sausage. Also of note is the house-made cinnamon roll, served hot and wallowing in a sugar glaze that has a captivating orange twist.

On the last Saturday of the month, customers are treated to live bluegrass music.

SWEET T'S

352 Gordon St.   706-595-7753
Thomson, GA   L (Mon–Fri) | $

Weekday lunch is the only meal served here—a cafeteria line of country cooking that is a vision of beauty. We don't mean studio-photographer beauty, but the kind of beauty one hopes to see at potluck supper. Crisp-edged pork cutlets are hoisted from a pan with savory gravy and sided by fragrant dressing that has its own chicken gravy, dotted with chopped egg whites. Chicken is frequently among the entree choices, both baked (ridiculously tender, vividly spiced) and fried (inside a potently seasoned golden coat). There are rice and gravy, mashed potatoes and gravy, and macaroni and cheese, as well as beautiful pods of fresh okra (boiled), cabbage cooked with enough pork to become as meaty as a vegetable can be, cheese-enriched squash casserole, and sweet-potato casserole. Accouterments to go alongside might include biscuits and cracklin' corn bread, hush puppies, crisp sticks of fried fatback, and pretty little deviled eggs.

Unless one gets more than three or four side dishes, there will be enough room left on the tray for dessert. Banana pudding is a perfect swirl of custard, bananas, large pieces of vanilla wafers at an ideal point of tenderness, and meringue that is lighter than air. Other possible sweets include peach cobbler, pecan pie, pound cake, individual fried apple pies, and chocolate layer cake.

Sweet T's is an extraordinarily cordial place, a shining example of no-frills southern hospitality. Décor is a curious mix of slogans—some devotional, some cute ("God created man . . . then he had a better idea")—and photos and posters of Elvis in his prime. In fact, diners are serenaded by Elvis tunes playing quietly in the background. Elvis would have liked this food.

TAYLOR'S BAR-B-QUE

112 E. 13th St.   706-554-9752
Waynesboro, GA   B L D | $

_____ ★ _ _ _ _   Barbecue is second fiddle at Taylor's.
OPEN EARLY Yes, the pulled pork is satisfying, as are
_ _ _ ★ _ _ _ _   meaty, easy-to-eat spare ribs, but what's outstanding is everything else, especially a grand formation of vegetables to round out a meat-and-three plate. These include extremely creamy creamed corn, pungent turnip greens, buttery mac 'n' cheese with just as much crunchy edge as you request from the server, hunks of sweet potato that are uncharacteristically not-too-sweet but full of earthy satisfaction, butter beans, black-eyed peas, and two kinds of corn bread—baked and served in squares as well as fried and served as a pancake. All these side dishes can be anchored by fried or baked chicken, smothered pork chops, catfish, pot roast, meat loaf, or lengths of rugged beef and pork sausage.

Hamburgers also are available, as are the usual array of breakfast sandwiches (on biscuits of course) starting at 4:30 a.m., but plate lunch is the draw—that, plus Taylor's vibrant personality. At the height of mealtime, a crowd of servers all along the cafeteria line take care of business, among them four generations of the Taylor family. Open since 1966, this is a town-favorite eatery, crowded with happy customers carrying overloaded trays to tables and wooden booths in a dining area that used to be a private home.

VARSITY DRIVE-IN
thevarsity.com

61 North Ave.   404-881-1706
Atlanta, GA   B L D | $

Like a nation unto itself, the Varsity is a teeming, overpopulated place that has its own language. If you order "a heavyweight, a ring, and a string," you will receive a hot dog with mustard and extra chili, onion rings, and French fries. Although curb service is an option, full and true communion with the V requires that you get out of your car and stand in line at the inside counter. Here, as you go eye-to-eye with an order taker, he will bark out "What'll ya have?" with all the urgency of a Marine drill sergeant. The food will appear before you have a chance to reach for your wallet.

To drink, there's a full menu of reliable southern favorites: ice-cold buttermilk, gigantic cups full of Coke, PCs, and FOs. PC is Varsity lingo for chocolate milk ("plain chocolate") as opposed to a chocolate milk *shake* (with ice cream). FO means frosted orange, reminiscent of a Creamsicle. With or without chili dogs, frosted oranges are one heck of a way to keep cool.

Lest you have any doubts, this is health food. Varsity founder Frank Gordy, who lived well into his seventies, once proclaimed, "A couple of chili dogs a day keep you young."

LOUISIANA

ACME OYSTER HOUSE

acmeoyster.com

724 Iberville St.   504-522-5973
New Orleans, LA   **L D** | $$

As Roadfood.com contributor Anne Ritchings put it, when you get to Acme Oyster House, "you have found paradise." The only problem is that you are not the only one who wants admittance. In the heart of the French Quarter, this place overflows with customers. Expect an extended wait to be seated.

The rewards for patience include impeccable raw oysters, char-grilled oysters cooked with butter and grated cheese, overflowing oyster po' boys, even an oysters Rockefeller soup. Beyond bivalves, Acme offers gumbo, jambalaya, red beans and rice, and fine-crusted softshell crab.

Note: Seats at the oyster bar itself are especially precious, providing a view of master shuckers at work.

ANDRE'S CAJUN CRACKLINS

12608 Hwy. 190 West   225-627-4600
Erwinville, LA   **L** | $

Located next to a convenience store, Andre's is a roadside stand that offers a full measure of Cajun takeout food to eat in the car or bring home and put on a plate. (No seating is available here.) We relish the fried turkey wings, big handfuls with a crunchy crust and dripping-moist meat that slides away from the bone with ease. Boudin is great too. A sharp knife comes in handy, as the natural casing doesn't tear easily. Inside is a savory soft mélange of pork and rice with a gentle spice kick. A link such as this probably ought to be fork food, eaten off a plate. But we managed to rip ours open and devour its filling with only minor grease drippage on hands and lap. Crunch-coated, fried boudin balls also are available.

As the name suggests, cracklins are the star of the show: long, crisp, meaty, melt-in-your-mouth delights that are seasoned to bring out maximum piggy flavor. The menu also includes crawfish pie and meat pie, gumbo, and hot tamales, as well as pickled pig lips, pig tails, and pig feet. And, for home cooking, buckets of lard.

ANGELO BROCATO

angelobrocatoicecream.com

214 N. Carrollton Ave.   504-486-0078
New Orleans, LA   (Tues-Sun) | $

Honestly, we rarely eat cannoli. Not because we don't like them, but because so many are so bad: cold and tasteless, hard-shelled rather than crisp, filled with white paste that is a ghost of ricotta. Angelo Brocato restores one's faith in cannoli. Here, each one is made to order, the crunchy, full-flavored pastry tube loaded with just-right sweet cheese that is barely cooler than room temperature, thus blooming with flavor. Once filled, its ends are dipped in ground pistachio nuts and each elegant tube is topped with a dusting of powdered sugar and cinnamon.

At this neighborhood sweet shop that opened in 1905 on Ursulines Street in the French Quarter, gelato also is a specialty. It is dense, custard-rich, and bright with flavors that range from amaretto to zuppa inglese. Other menu highlights include strudel and baba au rhum, éclairs and cream puffs, napoleons and *sfogliatelle*, and baked Alaska that is a textbook combo of ice cream, cake, and meringue.

Seating is on wire-back ice cream parlor chairs under spinning overhead fans. A friendly and conscientious staff makes the experience truly personable— a blissful taste of old New Orleans.

BON TON CAFÉ

thebontoncafe.com

401 Magazine St.   504-524-3386
New Orleans, LA   **L D** (Mon-Fri) | **$$$**

Magazine Street was laid out in 1788; the building holding the Bon Ton Café is slightly newer, going back to the 1840s. The restaurant opened in 1953. Its menu is old-time Louisiana cuisine that is *not* kicked up a notch, not overspiced or overhyped or blackened or infused, but simply delicious. This is the place to know the joy of crawfish étouffée, an unspeakably luscious meal especially in the spring, when crawdads are plumpest. You can have étouffée as a main course or as one part of a monomaniacal meal of bisque, étouffée, Newburg, jambalaya, and an omelet, each of which is made with crawfish. Or you can start dinner with fried crawfish tails. They look like little fried shrimp but taste like shrimp's affluent relatives.

Dinner begins with the delivery of a loaf of hot French bread, tightly wrapped in a white napkin. When the napkin is unfurled, the bread's aroma swirls around the table. Then comes soup—either peppery okra gumbo made with shrimp and crab or turtle soup into which the waitress pours a shot of sherry. Other than crawfish in any form, the great entree is redfish Bon Ton, which is a thick fillet sautéed in butter until just faintly crisp, served under a heap of fresh crabmeat and some gigantic fried onion rings. For dessert, you want bread pudding, which is a dense, warm square of sweetness studded with raisins and drenched with whiskey sauce.

A big, square, brick-walled room with red-checked tablecloths, Bon Ton is soothingly old-fashioned. There is no music, just the sounds of knife, fork, and spoon and happy conversation. Service, by a staff of uniformed professionals, is gracious and Dixie-sweet. As we prepared to take a picture of our redfish, a waitress rushed over and insisted on taking the picture herself, so she could include the two of us along with the lovely meal.

BOUDIN KING

906 W. Division St.   337-824-6593
Jennings, LA   **B L D** | **$**

Yes, the boudin at Boudin King is wonderful—densely packed, spicy, and deeply satisfying. Buy it mild or hot, by the link; it is a Cajun classic. Here also is fine gumbo, smoky-flavored and thick with sausage and big pieces of chicken. And speaking of chicken, we would rate the fried chicken served by Boudin King as some of the most delicious in southern Louisiana, a part of the world where frying chicken is a fine art. Other specialties include crawfish and fried pies.

The late Ellis Cormier, who founded this place back in the 1970s, once told us, "Nowhere else in America, except perhaps where the Mexicans live, is food properly spiced." Monsieur Cormier was one of the leading lights in America's rediscovery of its regional food, of Cajun food in particular. It was primarily thanks to his good cooking that in 1979 the Louisiana state legislature proclaimed Jennings "the Boudin Capital of the Universe."

★ BRENDA'S DINER

411 W. Pershing St.   337-367-0868
New Iberia, LA   **B L** (Mon-Fri) | **$**

Brenda's brought tears of joy to our eyes. "It doesn't get better than this," we agreed out loud halfway through a lunch of fried chicken, fried pork chops, red beans with sausage, rice and gravy, candied yams, and smothered cabbage. Each dish Brenda Placide had cooked was the best imaginable version of itself. The pork chop was audibly juicy with a tender taste that had us gnawing to the bone. The chicken's fragile crust shored in juice-dripping meat. The red beans were New-Iberia *hot*, crowded with thick discs of sausage; smothered cabbage, speckled with nuggets of garlicky sausage, brought high honor to the vegetable kingdom.

We had to ask Brenda how she cooks such magnificent food, but we weren't surprised when she had no satisfactory answer. "It's from my mama's kitchen," she said. "I cannot tell you how to do it because she never taught me to measure anything. You add seasoning and spice until it's right." It occurred to us that even if we studied Brenda as she cooked, taking scrupulous notes about every grain of every ingredient she used, we couldn't in a lifetime make food like this. It would be like watching Isaac Stern play the violin, then copying his every move.

★ CAFÉ DES AMIS
cafedesamis.com

140 E. Bridge St. 337-332-5273
Breaux Bridge, LA **B** (Fri–Sun);
L D (Tues–Sat) | $$

A sign in the window of Café des Amis boasts that it is "The essence of French Louisiana." It's the real deal, all right, a French-accented mix of South and soul, with a dash of Caribbean spice and Italian brio.

At breakfast, it is beignets, crisp-edged twists of fried dough under an avalanche of powdered sugar; it is "Oreille de Couchon," a strip of fried dough that resembles a pig's ear, available plain or filled with boudin. It is biscuits topped with crawfish étouffée, omelets filled with tasso ham, and cheese grits with andouille sausage.

The menu for lunch and supper is a veritable encyclopedia of local favorites, including turtle soup, andouille gumbo, barbecue shrimp, corn bread filled with crawfish tails, softshell crab, and crawfish pie. Desserts include bread pudding with rum sauce, which is more of a New Orleans thing than a Cajun one, and gateau sirop, which is extremely local. Made from sugar cane—grown and processed all around here—it is a block of moist spice cake with the distinctive smoky sweetness of cane sugar.

A friendly old brick-wall storefront that has been renovated to serve as an art gallery and live-music venue (check out the Saturday-morning Zydeco breakfast) as well as a restaurant, Café des Amis is a gathering place for locals and an easy destination for passersby. If you are looking for a full, joyous taste of Acadian Louisiana, make Breaux Bridge your destination.

CAFÉ DU MONDE
cafedumonde.com

800 Decatur St. 504-525-4544
New Orleans, LA Always open | $

★ OPEN 24/7 ★ Café Du Monde is a New Orleans institution, serving café au lait and beignets to locals and tourists for more than a century and a half. It is always open, and the characters you'll meet here—any time of day, but especially at odd hours in the middle of the night—are among the Crescent City's most colorful.

There is not much to the menu: chicory coffee, either black or au lait (with a lot of milk), white or chocolate milk, orange juice, and beignets. Beignets are dense, hole-less donuts, served hot from the fry kettle and so heaped with powdered sugar that it is not possible to eat one without getting white powder all over your hands, face, and clothes.

After leisurely coffee-sipping and beignet-eating, you can buy New Orleans souvenirs inside the restaurant, then stroll across Decatur Street to the place where fortune-tellers, tarot-card readers, and palmists set up shop every evening and, for the right price, reveal your future.

CASAMENTO'S
casamentosrestaurant.com

4330 Magazine St. 504-895-9761
New Orleans, LA **L D** (Thurs–Sun)
(closed in summer) | $$

Oyster loaves are served throughout New Orleans and Cajun country, and it is rare to find one that's bad. But for many loaf lovers, Casamento's is the ultimate. Oysters aren't the only dish of note in this spanking-clean neighborhood oyster bar that closes for a long summer vacation when oysters aren't in season. You can also have fried fish and shrimp and springtime softshell crabs, and there's even a plate of that arcane Creole Italian meal, daube, which is pot roast in gravy on spaghetti noodles. (Need we mention that shucked-to-order raw oysters by the dozen are a specialty too?)

Casamento's oyster loaf is nothing short of magnificent: a dozen crackle-crusted hotties piled between two big slabs of what New Orleans cooks know as pan bread, aka Texas toast. Each single oyster is a joy, its brittle skin shattering with light pressure, giving way to a wave of melting-warm, briny oyster meat across the tongue. When we asked proprietor Joe Gerdes what made his oysters so especially good, he modestly replied that his method is "too simple to call a recipe." Of course, he uses freshly shucked local oysters, and he does recommend frying in lard, but the real secret is ineffable. "Everything is fried by feel and sound," he said. "It requires a lot of personal attention and experience."

CENTRAL GROCERY

centralgrocerynola.com

923 Decatur St.   504-523-1620
New Orleans, LA   **L D** | **$**

The name "muffuletta" once referred to a round loaf of chewy bread turned out by Italian bakeries in New Orleans. Grocery stores that sold muffulettas got the fine idea to slice them horizontally and load them with salami, ham, and provolone, then top that with a wickedly spicy mélange of chopped green and black olives fragrant with anchovies and garlic. The place that claims to have done it first is the Central Grocery on Decatur Street.

While it has become a tourist attraction and muffulettas are now the only sandwich on the menu, the Central Grocery still feels like a neighborhood store, its yellowed walls decorated with travel posters, the air inside smelling of garlic and sausage and provolone cheese, its shelves stocked with such imported canned exotica as sardines, kippered snacks, hearts of palm, and octopus. There is no table service. Step up to the counter and order a whole or half. Whole

sandwiches are cut into quarters (enough for four modest appetites) and wrapped, at which point you can take it to a counter toward the back of the store to unwrap and eat it.

CHAMPAGNE'S BREAUX BRIDGE BAKERY

champagnesbakery.com

105 S. Poydras St.   337-332-1117
Breaux Bridge, LA   **L** (closed Sun & Mon) | **$**

This charming nineteenth-century one-room bakery in the crawfish capital of the world caused us to stomp the brakes as we drove past early in the morning. The smell of just-baked bread was irresistible. Inside the door, a small card table was arrayed with loaves. They are the familiar-looking south-Louisiana torpedoes, like French baguettes but about half the weight. Some are wrapped in paper, the others in plastic bags. "You want soft, you get the plastic," advised the gent behind the counter. "For crisp, paper." Our paper-wrapped loaf had a refined crunch to its crust and feathery insides. It's delicious just to eat, but oh, how well this would scoop out to become a seafood boat filled with fried oysters or shrimp!

Cooked meat pies were displayed along the bakery counter, and good as they looked, we hesitated about getting one because who wants a cold meat pie? "We have a microwave," said the woman behind the counter, and although a regular oven is kinder to the crust, the pies she warmed for us were nothing short of spectacular: rich, moist, and vividly spiced.

CHICKORYS COFFEE & CAFÉ

219 E. Martin Luther   337-886-5770
King Dr.   **B L** (closed Mon) | **$**
Grand Coteau, LA

A large, airy space with plenty of elbow room between the tables, Chickorys is a coffee house on the main drag of the charming old St. Landry Parrish town of Grand Coteau. At first glance, it's the sort of place you'd expect good coffee but not good food. But this is Cajun country, where some of the most excellent food is found in some of the most unlikely eateries.

Take the chicken and sausage gumbo, for example. Nearly as thick as syrup and as brown as chocolate, it is a smoky, spicy-hot brew based on a long-stirred roux—made the old-fashioned way, low and slow. It may not be as complex and kaleidoscopic as the very best Creole gumbos, but it has an authentic country charm that we find even more beguiling.

Pork is the meat of choice hereabouts, but Chickorys' brisket sandwich is a royal exception. It is made of magnificent beef, as tender as the finest pot roast, super-moist and resonantly beefy. Great long shreds and clumps of it, piled into a loaf of fine Gambino's Bakery bread and fully dressed with mayo, lettuce, and tomato, make for a memorable local meal.

A few other winners from the short menu include deeply sweet, crusty-edged white chocolate bread pudding, served warm, of course; breakfast biscuits made with eggs, cheese, and, if desired, boudin instead of regular sausage. The boudin is dense and moist with a gradual pepper punch that will make your mouth glow midway through the sandwich. Made-to-order smoothies include the Berrylicious Bluejay, made with blueberries, blackberries, raspberries, and strawberries blended with yogurt, and the Who Dat, which is peanut butter, banana, chocolate syrup, and milk.

COCHON BUTCHER

cochonbutcher.com/new-orleans

930 Tchoupitoulas St.   504-588-7675
New Orleans, LA   L D | $

Cochon Butcher calls itself a "swine bar," and, sure enough, the pork is splendorous. Boudin sausage is moist and meaty, edged with the sultry savor of poblano peppers. Barbecue pork is very smoky, a heterogeneous heap of chunks, shreds, and nuggets of tender meat. It is billed as Carolina-style, meaning it has a touch of vinegar tang. The Cajun pork dog is a dramatically plump, bursting-at-the-seams sausage served on a toasted pretzel bun and dressed "all the way" with chili and sauerkraut. (The bill of fare does include non-pork items such as smoked turkey, brisket sliders, duck pastrami, and pretty little pimento cheese sandwiches on crustless white bread.)

Good as the meats and side dishes are, it is wise to save appetite for dessert, Key lime pie in particular.

It is a double-tall masterpiece on an extra-thick ribbon of graham-cracker crust.

D.I.'S

discajunrestaurant.com

6561 Evangeline Hwy.   337-432-5141
Basile, LA   L D (closed Sun & Mon) | $$

★
LOCALS
LOVE IT
★
Set back from the two-lane in the middle of nothing but rice fields and crawfish ponds, D.I.'s is a brimful measure of Acadian pleasure. If it hadn't been for Sulphur policeman and good friend Maj. Many McNeil, we never, ever would have come across it. When we told Many we were on the lookout for a true Cajun eating experience, he said D.I.'s was it.

Daniel Isaac ("D.I.") Fruge has been known to neighbors for his well-seasoned crawdads since the 1970s. He was a rice and soybean farmer who began harvesting the mudbugs, boiling and serving them on weekends to friends and neighbors. They were served in his barn the traditional way, strewn in heaps across bare tables with beer to drink on the side.

D.I. and his wife, Sherry, now run a restaurant with a full menu that includes steaks, crabs, oysters, frog legs, flounder, and shrimp, but vividly-spiced crawfish are the draw. The classic way to enjoy them is boiled and piled onto the beer tray—a messy meal that rewards vigorous tail pulling and head sucking with an unending procession of the vibrant sweetwater richness that only crawdads deliver. You can have them crisp-fried into bite-sized morsels, and there are crawfish pie, étouffée, and bisque.

No longer a makeshift annex to Monsieur Fruge's barn, D.I.'s is a spacious destination with multiple dining rooms and a dance floor. The Cajun music starts at seven.

DISTRICT DONUTS SLIDERS BREW

donutsandsliders.com

2209 Magazine St.   504-570-6945
New Orleans, LA   B L D | $

Beignets are the #1 fried dough to eat in New Orleans, but this cheerful place makes the case for donuts. Here are donuts of every imaginable (and unimaginable) variety, from relatively simple cinnamon-sugared or salted-caramel-glazed puffies to such outlandish inventions as a sriracha donut, a Vietnamese iced-coffee donut, and a variety of croquenuts (griddled donut sandwiches). Everything is impeccably fresh. Walk to the back of the long storefront and you can watch the donuts slid into boiling oil and, beyond that, observe cream puffs filled and chocolate donuts iced.

The breakfast menu also includes baked *kolaches* made with sweet dough, pork belly tacos, bacon biscuits, and cinnamon rolls. While donuts always are available, after 11 a.m. sliders come into play. These include the juiciest possible cheeseburgers and fried chicken with peppery gravy. As for the brew part of the restaurant's name, that refers not to beer, but to coffee: all the usual espresso variations, cold-brew coffees, and a puzzling but not totally disagreeable concoction called a Sproca-Cola. That's cola, espresso, and chocolate milk.

★ DOMILISE'S PO-BOYS
domilisespoboys.com

| 5240 Annunciation St. | 504-899-9126 |
| New Orleans, LA | **L** (closed Sun) \| $ |

You won't likely come upon Domilise's bar/sandwich shop by accident, for it is located in an unscenic blue-collar neighborhood, and if you did accidentally drive by, you might not guess that it is the source of great New Orleans sandwiches. It looks like a small, no-frills neighborhood tavern, and in some ways, that is what it is. We guess it would be possible to walk in, sit at the bar, and have nothing but a liquid diet of long-necks or boilermakers. To do so, you'd have to have no sense of smell, for the air of this tavern is wildly perfumed with shrimp, oysters, and catfish hoisted from the fry basket.

You may have to take a number before you can place your order. At the height of lunch hour, Domilise's is packed, for its superior po' boys attract eaters from all over the city; table space is precious (strangers often share); and the house phone rings unanswered.

For the newcomer, delay provides an opportunity to read the menu on the wall and to observe the sandwich makers constructing different combos before you decide which is the right one for you. Hot smoked sausage with gravy is the one we recommend above all others. Get it "dressed," meaning topped with tomato, lettuce, and grainy Creole mustard. A large one is assembled on a length of bread so long that it must be cut in thirds. While the sandwich is being made, buy your drink at the bar and hope that by the time you are ready, space at a table is available.

DON'S SPECIALTY MEATS
donsspecialtymeats.com

730 I-10	337-234-2528
(S. Frontage Rd.)	**L** (butcher shop is open daily
Scott, LA	from 6 a.m. to 7 p.m.) | $

A big modern building located just off the interstate, Don's is a destination for boudin and cracklins, hot lunch, po' boys, fried pork chops, fried chicken, hot meat pies, and just about any kind of Cajun-butcher fixins you need for cooking at home. There is a large indoor dining room as well as picnic tables outside. Service is do-it-yourself.

Weekends are an especially good time to eat at Don's. Saturday, the smoked pork chop draws fans from Lafayette Parish and beyond. Slices of white bread hold a giant, bone-in chop that oozes juice at first bite and is even messier if you have it dressed with barbecue sauce. Sunday, the place is thronged with locals who come for pork steak, stuffed brisket, and ribs.

DWYER'S CAFÉ

| 323 Jefferson St. | 337-235-9364 |
| Lafayette, LA | **B L** \| $ |

No one makes lunch sound as good as Mike Dwyer does. You will hear his pitch as you approach the cafeteria area of Dwyer's Café, where he enumerates the day's choices, one by one, with pride and exuberance to make appetites growl. In fact, this food needs no hard sell. The proof is in the tasting.

Dwyer's is a meat-and-three affair, the daily meats including such expertly cooked stalwarts as smothered pork chops, lengths of pork sausage, roast beef with dark gravy, and chicken-fried steak with white gravy. When we visited, Mike was pitching crawfish fettuccine, a fabulous cross-cultural Franco-Italian-Cajun noodle casserole loaded with high-flavored crawdads. Among the notable sides are dirty rice, eggplant casserole, red beans, and sausage jambalaya. On cold days, you can get gumbo or chili.

Dwyer's is also a notable breakfast opportunity. We love the tender sweet-potato hot cakes with their faintly crisp edge (which Mike says he added to the menu for low-carb dieters!). When you order pancakes, the waitress will ask what kind of syrup you want: cane or maple. Sugar cane is a major crop around here, and the pancake syrup made from it is thick, dark, and resonantly sweet . . . very different from white-sugar sweet.

EARL'S

earlscajunmarket.net

510 Verot School Rd.   337-237-5501
Lafayette, LA   **L | $**

West of New Orleans from Baton Rouge to St. Charles and from the swamps of Avery Island to the prairies of Evangeline Parish, hundreds of places sell boudin sausage. Among the best of them is Earl's, which sells it by the link from a hot box near the cash register. Customers buy it to take home or to eat in the car. There are no dining tables on premises.

Earl's boudin is ideal for off-the-dashboard dining, the links so dense that once their casing is breached with a sharp knife, you can fork out pieces in tidy clumps. Each bite is a country-style symphony of pork and rice, pepper and onion, needing only beer (or Barq's root beer) on the side.

Earl's also offers plate lunch, including fried chicken, po' boys, red beans and rice, and catfish on Friday—again, all on a takeout basis.

GALATOIRE'S

galatoires.com

209 Bourbon St.   504-525-2021
New Orleans, LA   **L D** (closed Mon) | **$$$**

HOT TICKET ─★─ Galatoire's is more formal than any other Roadfood restaurant—no jeans allowed, jackets are required for men. And at $50+ per person, it is beyond this book's normal price range. But if Roadfood is all about finding unique regional meals, meals that reflect the culture that gave birth to them, Galatoire's goes to the top of the list. It is the definitive Creole dining experience. With its mirrored walls, bright lights and dark woodwork, white linen tablecloths and black-tie waiters, it is a crystalline image of a bourgeois dining room from the turn of the nineteenth century: solid, dependable, with a bounteous larder of the highest quality. The staff is polite but not obsequious. They are able to clearly and appealingly describe every item on the multipage menu without making the description a grocery list or trying too hard to sell it. Nor will these pros offer the ridiculous "Good choice!" if you happen to select something of which they approve.

A surfeit of options makes deciding sweet agony. Do you like crab meat? You can have it au gratin, ravigote, Sardou, Saint-Pierre, maison, or Yvonne. There's shrimp Clemenceau, Creole, Marguery, au vin, étouffée, deep-fried, and the remoulade (which bears little resemblance to remoulades anywhere else). There are seven kinds of potato, nine omelets and egg dishes, and a choice of soups that includes oyster-artichoke, Creole gumbo, and turtle.

We've sampled only a fraction of what Galatoire's offers. Not once have we been disappointed; more often, we rave that the plate before us holds the paradigm of whatever it's supposed to be. Highest on our honor roll are the shrimp remoulade, trout amandine, crab Sardou (with spinach, artichoke hearts, and hollandaise sauce), softshell crabs (the tenderest, ever!), and the inconspicuous but conspicuously potent garlic green salad.

Meals begin with warm loaves of the fragile-skinned, fluffy bread found nowhere outside of southern Louisiana and, if you're a tippler, the classic New

Orleans aperitif, a Sazerac. And they can end with a fiery climax: *café brûlot* for two, flamed tableside.

(Guys: House jackets are available if you come without yours.)

HANSEN'S SNO-BLIZ
snobliz.com

4801 Tchoupitoulas St.   504-891-9788
New Orleans, LA   (closed Mon) | $

The shave ice served by Hansen's Sno-Bliz resembles a snow cone but is a world apart. Yes, it is ice and flavoring, but rather than being chopped and clumpy, shave ice is as fluffy as freshly fallen snow. Whereas the ice and syrup in a normal snow cone never quite blend, shave ice literally sops up its flavor and delivers such compelling refreshment that brain freeze is a near-certain side effect.

With historical antecedents in Asia and in Hawaii, shave ice had always been a time-consuming product to make, requiring that the ice actually be shaved from a block with knives. That changed in 1934 when Ernest Hansen of New Orleans invented a machine that shaves ice. Five years later he opened Hansen's Sno-Bliz, where homemade tropical syrups were applied to the ice in layers. Now run by Hansen's granddaughter, the little shop continues to set the gold standard, offering shave ice with such special flavors as cream of peach and cream of coffee, tart satsuma and limeade, as well as luxury toppings that include condensed milk, marshmallow, crushed pineapple, and whipped cream.

Expect to wait in line. Service is meticulous and therefore slow. Other than a few benches outside, there are no dining facilities.

JERRY LEE'S
jerryleescajunfoods.com

12181 Greenwell   225-272-0739
Springs Rd.   L (closed Sun) | $
Baton Rouge, LA

Like most of the boudin makers in southern Louisiana, Jerry Lee's is a store rather than a restaurant. It is common to see customers sitting in their trucks or cars and dining off the dashboard or, on a nice day, eating off the tailgate. A neon sign in Jerry Lee's window shows a boiling pot (presumably where the pork is cooked) with this legend underneath: "If it's not Jerry Lee's, it's not Boudin." While a lot of Cajun boudin is fire-hot, Jerry Lee's is only haloed by pepper . . . all the better to savor the flavor of the rice that is its dominant ingredient, along with the luxe of ground pork that is its soul.

In a heated case near the cash register, you will find the boudin already extracted from its casing and piled into rolls along with cheese. In our opinion, the cheese is all wrong, completely overwhelming the refined flavor play of the sausage. The better choice is to forgo the fixins and get a couple of links, which cost about $1.75 each. Their casing is really tough, virtually impossible to cut with teeth alone, but once it is opened up with the plastic knife provided by the management, out wafts a balmy aroma that is unique to southernmost Louisiana. Grab a bag of Zapp's potato chips and a Barq's root beer and you have the makings of a five-dollar feast.

★ JOHNSON'S BOUCANIÈRE
johnsonsboucaniere.com

1111 St. John St.   337-269-8878
Lafayette, LA   L (closed Sun) | $

Boucanière means smokehouse in Cajun, and smoking pork and beef is what the Johnson family has done since they opened up a grocery store in Eunice in 1937. Today they live above their smokehouse in Lafayette, making it easy for them to come downstairs about 3:30 in the morning to get meat on the grate, where it cooks low and slow. The results compose a lunch menu featuring pillowy pulled pork, beef brisket, tasso ham, and sausage made from pork or turkey. There's even a barbecue salad of your choice of pork, brisket, or chicken combined with lettuce, onions, tomatoes, and shredded cheese, dressed with Johnson's barbecue sauce.

Finally, but by no means the least of Johnson's accomplishments, is boudin sausage, the savory Cajun treat that may be eaten with a fork or hand-squeezed directly from its natural casing. The authoritative website boudinlink.com gave Johnson's Boucanière an A+ rating, declaring it to be the ideal blend of rice and meat with an overall flavor that is complex but clean. Boudin balls are crumbled and sandwiched with cheese in a grilled bun for a signature Parrain's Special, about which Stephen Rushmore wrote, "If the Cajuns were to create a cheesesteak, this would be it."

Much business is takeout. A covered porch provides casual accommodations for those who come to eat plate lunch.

KILLER POBOYS

killerpoboys.com

219 Dauphine St.   504-462-2731
New Orleans, LA   **L D** (closed Tues) | **$**

— ★ ---
VEGAN
FRIENDLY
— ★ ---
A Killer Poboy sandwich looks more like an ovoid *bánh mi* than a traditional stretched-out submarine. In fact, the rolls are not the New Orleans standard Ledenheimers; they come from Dong Phuong Vietnamese bakery. Ingredients are unusual, too, even those that sound familiar. A debris po' boy, for instance, does contain the expected heap of gravy-sopped shredded braised beef, but with it come pickled jalapeño chips, red peppers, onions, and long green beans. A shrimp po' boy is made of seared, not fried, shrimp—big, firm-bodied crescents—and their companions in the loaf are coriander lime spice, sriracha aioli, pickled daikon radish, carrot, and cucumber. When we ask if it is possible to get a shrimp po' boy without all the folderol, the girl behind the counter kindly informs us that it is not possible because that would "ruin the integrity of the sandwich." The house mission statement describes its fare as "internationally inspired, chef-crafted New Orleans–style sandwiches."

A sign announces that vegans will be happy here, but you don't have to be an animal-product frowner to enjoy the brilliant sweet-potato po' boy that contains tender discs of verge-of-caramel yam along with great amounts of succulent, barely-bitter smothered greens and a lavish tapenade of black-eyed peas and pecans. Vegan options also include an intriguing

roasted cauliflower sandwich with avocado, radishes, and peppery Spanish romesco sauce.

Killer is an eat-in-the-rough outfit: Place your order at the counter and pay there, after which you find a seat at one of the copper-topped tables. Breakfast options include a Cheddar omelet po' boy and a smoked salmon po' boy with remoulade, onions, capers, and hard-boiled egg.

Note: The original location of Killer Poboys, inside the Erin Rose Bar at 811 Conti Street, is open from noon to midnight and is adults only (504-252-6745).

LASYONE'S MEAT PIE KITCHEN

lasyones.com

622 2nd St.   318-352-3353
Natchitoches, LA   **B L** (closed Sun) | **$**

When we surveyed visitors at the first annual Louisiana Roadfood Festival of 2009 to find out what food they liked best from among the several dozen specialties sold by street vendors, the winner by a landslide was the meat pie dished out by Lasyone's. Second place was Lasyone's crawfish pie. Lasyone's has returned to the festival every year and it always wins a unanimous thumbs-up.

Half-circle pastry pockets about the size of tacos with a rugged crimp around their edges, these deep-fried pies have golden crust that is brittle and crunchy near the crimp, pliant near the mounded center. Inside each flaky sheaf is a good-sized portion of deftly seasoned ground beef, moist enough to make gravy irrelevant. Spicy but not fire-hot, complex and succulent, it is an honest piece of food that satisfies in an old-fashioned way. Lasyone's serves them for breakfast, accompanied by eggs and hash browns, but most customers come midday to get a pair of them for lunch, with soulful dirty rice on the side, darkened with plenty of gizzards and topped with zesty gravy.

LEA'S LUNCHROOM

leaslunchroom.com

1810 US 71   318-776-5178
Lecompte, LA   **B L** (closed Mon) | **$**

Many of Lea's biggest fans and most devoted customers never eat on premises. They come for ham and pies to take home. Luckily for us travelers, there is seating inside and a limited menu that includes chicken and corn-bread dressing, red beans and rice, and, on Sunday, southern fried chicken and turkey. Dough-baked ham is the main attraction—the dough wrap ensuring that the pink meat stays super-juicy. A balance of sweet, spicy, and salty, the ham is available on platters, but the signature specialty is a ham sandwich. Served in a lightly toasted bun, it contains a surfeit of ham, along with mayonnaise, lettuce, tomato, and pickles.

Lea's is equally famous (since 1928) for its daily baked pies: soaring meringues, double-crusted fruit pies, insanely sweet pecan pie, and—in season—blueberry, blackberry, sweet potato, and pumpkin.

MOODY'S

601 Martin Luther   318-377-5873
King Dr.   **L** | **$**
Minden, LA

If you are traveling through Webster Parish along Interstate 20 east of Shreveport, we highly recommend taking Exit 47 and driving five minutes to the north. Here in Minden (where Hank Williams married his Billie Jean in 1952) you will find Moody's, where heavy-duty partitioned plates carry some of the highest-quality, lowest-priced meals in the South. Expertly made fried chicken, pork chops, or meat loaf is accompanied by such soulful vegetables as turnip greens, cheese-enriched broccoli, and candied yams. Filling out the plate are cylinders of hot-water corn bread—baked, then fried to a crisp. Peach and blackberry cobblers compete for your dessert vote with coconut pie and strawberry cream pie.

★ MORNING CALL COFFEE STAND

morningcallcoffeestand.com

3325 Severn Ave.   504-885-4068
Metairie, LA   Always open, except
                          Christmas | **$**

--★--
OPEN
24/7
--★--
Crisp-edged and nearly as light as air, Morning Call beignets arrive three to an order, hot from the fry kettle. It is the diner's job to apply powdered sugar. This can be an arduous task if you prefer a thick blanket of the white stuff, because Morning Call offers it in shakers that have to be vigorously shaken to extract maximum sugar. Long ago, the restaurant supplied broad bowls full of powdered sugar so customers could simply sweep their hot beignet right through it. Worrying about the hazards of double dipping, health department authorities forbade that practice.

Café au lait is the time-honored beignet companion, and here is the best anywhere. What joy it is to look to the back of the dining room and watch it being concocted. The waitress holds a big pitcher full of ink-dark chicory coffee in one hand, pouring it into a cup in a long, flowing stream. When the cup is about half full, she takes a smaller pitcher in her other hand, hoists it high, and adds warm milk so that both streams swirl together, filling the cup to its top and creating a frothy head.

Morning Call has a second location at City Park Casino. It is always open, except on Christmas Day.

MOSCA'S

moscasrestaurant.com

4137 US 90 W.   504-436-8950
Westwego, LA   **D** (Tues–Sat) | **$$$**

Despite catastrophic hurricanes and cataclysmic changes in the American diet, Mosca's never seems to change. All the great things about this legendary destination still deserve legendary status, especially Oysters Mosca—a festival of garlic, olive oil, Parmesan cheese, and bread crumbs all cosseting little nuggets of sweet oyster meat.

The parking lot remains a gravel wreck; the outside is dark and nefarious. In fact, on a recent trip to New Orleans, we were told that Mosca's for many years was the hangout of the region's chief mafioso. If it's your first time, we guarantee you will think you are lost when you make the drive. And even when you find it, you will wonder: Can this two-room joint with the blaring jukebox and semi-secret kitchen dining area really be the most famous Italian roadhouse in America? Inside, conviviality reigns, and we saw only friendly sorts of folks eating; no one looked like a cast member of *The Godfather* or *The Sopranos*.

Aside from the setting and location, the primary thing you'll notice upon arriving at Mosca's is the sweet, provocative smell of roasting garlic. There are whole cloves of it in Chicken à la Grande—painfully tender pieces that arrive in a pool of rosemary-perfumed gravy. Thank God for spaghetti bordelaise, which is little more than a heap of thin noodles bathed in oil, butter, and garlic. It is an ideal medium for rolling up on a fork and pushing around in extra chicken gravy or the last of the Oysters Mosca bread crumbs.

Go with friends: The bigger the group, the more different dishes you can sample, and you do need also to taste Mosca's sausage, chicken cacciatore, and Louisiana shrimp. Everything is served family-style.

MOTHER'S
mothersrestaurant.net

401 Poydras	504-523-9656
New Orleans, LA	**B L D** | $

Mother's began in 1938 as a family-run diner specializing in po' boy sandwiches for a clientele that included working men from the waterfront as well as lawyers and newspaper reporters who had business in the nearby courthouse. Today it attracts hordes of tourists as well as locals who come for heroic sandwiches available in full-sized and two-thirds-sized portions, with fillings like smoked or hot sausage, shrimp, oysters, softshell crabs, and catfish. Most famous is called a Ferdi Special, after the local merchant who asked to have ham added to his roast beef po' boy, along with a spill of debris (meat scraps) and gravy. What a wonderful mess!

During World War II, Mother's became such a favorite haunt of US Marines that they named it "Tun Tavern—New Orleans" after the old Tun Tavern of Philadelphia, where the Marine Corps recruited its first members in 1775. The original mother, Mary Landry, who opened the restaurant with her husband, Simon, passed it on to her sons, who in 1986 sold it to Jerry and John Amato. The Amatos kept Mother's menu of effulgent po' boys, adding a repertoire of New Orleans classics such as filé gumbo, jambalaya, red beans and rice, black ham, and, of course, bread pudding for dessert. Today, there is probably no other restaurant in the city that so completely defines blue-collar Creole cuisine.

NAPOLEON HOUSE
napoleonhouse.com

500 Chartres St.	504-524-9752
New Orleans, LA	**L D** | $$

Images of Napoleon are everywhere at Napoleon House, a big, three-story home that legend says was built late in the eighteenth century as a refuge for Napoleon Bonaparte. (He never did show up.) It was then the residence of Nicholas Girod, New Orleans' mayor, and one of the most elegant homes in town. Like so much of old New Orleans, it has aged tremendously but endured heroically; today it is a bar and restaurant popular among tourists as well as locals and most famous for its Pimm's Cup (the Wimbledon drink of Pimm's, lemonade, lemon-lime soda, and a cucumber garnish).

The menu is classic Creole: gumbo, jambalaya, red beans and rice. They're fine, but the reason we come here, aside from the charmingly outré bodice-ripper ambience of peeling paint, dingy walls, and ancient Deep South history, is the muffuletta sandwich. It differs from most because the kitchen heats it up, warming it enough for the salami to turn limp and the cheese to melt and meld with the olive salad. The olives are fairly tame—easy on the garlic and spice—making this sandwich a paragon of what might be called Italian Creole comfort food.

THE OLD COFFEEPOT

theoldcoffeepot.com

714 St. Peter St.   504-524-3500
New Orleans, LA   **B L D** | $$

Calas, an old New Orleans specialty now nearly forgotten, are deep-fried rice balls traditionally eaten for breakfast. The Old Coffeepot serves them in orders of four, with or without pecans. A heavy white dusting of powdered sugar makes them vaguely resemble beignets, but calas are denser with creamy centers, more like Italian *arancini* with a delectably leathery exterior. The quartet comes with a pitcher of syrup, which the waiter advised we apply "temperately but not timidly." On the plate along with the four calas is a large spill of thick, creamy grits—a welcome, dairy-rich addition when you realize just how sweet calas are with all that sugar and syrup.

The Old Coffeepot opens at 8 a.m., and the first time we stopped in, calas were slated to be just one of many meals on a daylong restaurant crawl all around New Orleans. The plan was to reserve our appetite by sampling just one cala before we moved on to breakfast #2. But as we laid waste to the plateful, we loved them more and more. The process of separating a small bite-sized piece from the ball with equal amounts of rugged, chewy skin and creamy inside, then gathering just the right amount of powdered sugar and pushing this through the syrup, and finally separating a small clump of grits, added up to such satisfying forkfuls that by the end of breakfast we were hunting every last grain of rice and spot of sugar on the ravaged plate.

More familiar breakfasts include such Creole eye-openers as *pain perdu* (French-bread French toast) and eggs Sardou (poached, atop spinach and artichokes, topped with hollandaise sauce). For lunch, choose from chicken and andouille sausage gumbo, seafood gumbo made with crab and shrimp, jambalaya with blackened redfish, and a whole roster of po' boy sandwiches. Bread pudding, made from a recipe created by Mrs. Pearl, a fifty-plus-year employee in the Old Coffeepot kitchen, is luxuriously eggy, more like custard than bread, and is topped with an intoxicating flourish of whiskey sauce.

PARKWAY BAKERY & TAVERN

parkwaypoorboys.com

538 Hagan Ave.   504-482-3047
New Orleans, LA   **L D** (closed Tues) | $

After much arduous research, it is our opinion that the best roast beef po' boy in New Orleans (a city that takes its roast beef po' boys very seriously) is made by the Parkway Bakery & Tavern, overlooking Bayou St. John. The sandwich is presented tightly wrapped in a tube of butcher paper that already is mottled through with gravy splotches when you pick it up at the kitchen window. Unwrap it and behold a length of fresh, brawny bread loaded with beef so falling-apart tender that it seems not to have been sliced but rather hand-pulled, like barbecued pork, into myriad slivers, nuggets, and clumps. It is difficult to discern where the meat ends and gravy begins because there is so much gravy saturating the meat and so many carving-board scraps, known as debris (say DAY-bree), in the gravy.

That meaty gravy makes the city's ultimate dining bargain. At $4.85 for a full-length sandwich, and $3.65 for an eight-incher, Parkway's gravy po' boy is a minimalist sandwich of the good, chewy bread filled only with gravy. The bread is substantial enough to absorb massive amounts of the liquid and a booming beef scent, becoming the most appetizing savory loaf imaginable, its surface crowded with the concentrated essence of roast beef.

Parkway has a full repertoire of po' boy fillings, including oysters, crunchy fried shrimp (a fabulous partner with roast beef in the surf 'n' turf po' boy), and a brunch version that includes sausage, bacon, eggs, and cheese and is served with a side of syrup!

Note about the restaurant name: The original Parkway on this site indeed was a bakery, so beloved that lines of customers would stretch out the door at times when it was known fresh bread would be coming out of the brick oven. The bakery closed in the early 1980s and today's Parkway does not make its own, but the name lives on.

PREJEAN'S

prejeans.com

3480 I-49 N.   337-896-3247
Lafayette, LA   **B L D** | $$

Prejean's is big and noisy (the live music starts every night at 7, and be sure to wear your dancing shoes), and the food is classic Cajun. In some other part of the country, a restaurant this brash might seem too "commercial" to qualify for Roadfood—walls hung with Acadiana, a stuffed alligator in the center of the dining room, a gift shop with tacky souvenirs—but for all its razzle-dazzle, Prejean's is the real thing, a fact about which you can have no doubt when you dip a spoon into the chicken and sausage gumbo or the dark andouille gumbo laced with smoked duck.

The menu is big and exotic, featuring dozens of dishes you'll not find on menus outside Louisiana, from crisp-fried crawfish boudin balls and catfish Catahoula (stuffed with crawfish, shrimp, and crab) to eggplant *pirogues* ("canoes" of bread) hollowed out, fried, and filled with crawfish and red snapper fillet, drizzled with buttery lobster sauce. It is possible to get a monomaniacal all-crawfish meal of crawfish bisque, fried crawfish, crawfish étouffée, crawfish pie, crawfish boulettes, and a salad dotted with crawfish. There are two significant desserts: red velvet cake and bread pudding with Jack Daniel's sour mash sauce.

ROCKY AND CARLO'S

613 W. St. Bernard Hwy.   504-279-8323
Chalmette, LA   **L D** (closed Mon & Fri) | $

Way out in St. Bernard Parish, Rocky and Carlo's opened in 1965 and has since survived hurricanes, floods, and a devastating fire in 2012. In this spacious eating hall you will find meals that reflect that essential trinity of south Louisiana cuisine—Italian-Cajun-Dixie. Walk along the cafeteria line and select from a hot-lunch menu that includes pork chops with greens, braciola, veal parm, stuffed peppers, muffulettas, fried shrimp or oysters, and gorgeous baked chicken. Rocky and Carlo's seafood gumbo, loaded with shrimp, crab, and crawfish and thickened with okra, just may be the best in or out of New Orleans.

The blackboard menu also lists wop salad, the locals' politically incorrect term for garlicky iceberg lettuce with green olives, and many customers come for the excellent roast beef po' boys. Platters of wispy, deep-fried onions adorn almost every table.

No matter what you eat at Rocky and Carlo's, the single dish that you likely will remember best is the inconspicuous menu listing "macaroni." There is none better. Very different from typical mac 'n' cheese made with elbow noodles, this mountain of baked pasta is built from substantial perciatelli tubes that come plastered with orange cheese—tender gobs from the heart, chewy strips from the top, and crisp webbed bark from the casserole's edge. It is fine as it is, but some people get it topped with sweet red marinara sauce or glistening mahogany brown gravy.

T-BOY'S SLAUGHTERHOUSE

tboysboudin.com

2228 Pine Point Rd.   337-468-3333
(Hwy. 104)   **L** (closed Sun) | $
Ville Platte, LA

The trip from the swamplands of the South to T-Boy's Slaughterhouse winds through Evangeline Parish prairies, where cattle and horses graze and native zydeco music sets the cultural beat. Once you arrive, you are in for a true taste of country life. As its name suggests, this place is not a restaurant. It is a from-scratch butcher and convenience store selling sausages and meats from the smokehouse, including paunce (stuffed stomach) and tasso ham. For those just passing through, it is a premier source of the moist and visceral Cajun sausage known as boudin. In the spring crawfish season, especially during Lent, crawfish boudin is a Friday special. It is moist, sweet, and swampy, with a slow-rolling pepper kick.

Boudin is sold hot by the long link, which proprietor T-Boy Berzas is happy to scissor into pieces two or three inches long, making it easy simply to squeeze the luxuriant filling from casing to mouth without the trouble of utensils. We strongly suggest accompanying boudin with some of T-Boy's fabulous hot cracklins, which are assertively seasoned, pop-in-the-mouth chunks and squiggles of deep-fried pig skin, fat, and shreds of meat that shatter when you bite into them, then dissolve into an ethereal slurry of pork and pepper—the flavor of Cajun Louisiana in bite-sized pieces.

T-Boy's has a second location in Eunice.

T-COON'S

tcoons.com

1900 West Pinhook Rd.   337-233-0422

Lafayette, LA   **B L | $**

--★--
LOCALS
LOVE IT
--★--
From its parking lot, T-Coon's looks like any ordinary short-order café, but here in south Louisiana, "ordinary" is a word that rarely applies to restaurants. T-Coon's serves what you might call Cajun food, except that its chef and owner, David Billeaud, prefers to call it Zydeco (after the local music), because that implies a mix of Creole and Cajun. However you define it, the cooking is extraordinary. Everything is from scratch, and it is all brilliantly seasoned.

Breakfast potatoes, for example, are no forgettable side dish. They are griddle-cooked with onions and Chef Billeaud's proprietary spice mix to the point that they could be a main course by themselves. Bread for toast that goes with eggs is baked in-house. It comes in thick half slices that are ideal for dipping into the yolk of a fried egg or for mopping up gravy. The kitchen offers sausage in broad, juicy, rugged patties that glow with exuberant spice. Even the simplest over-easy eggs are extra-good, glistening with the butter in which they have been basted.

Lunch specials include red beans and rice (with sausage), smothered rabbit (on Monday), crawfish étouffée, and chicken and sausage gumbo when it's cold outside.

VILLAGER'S CAFÉ

villagerscafe.net

8400 Maurice Ave.   337-898-1554

Maurice, LA   **L D** (closed Sun) **| $**

The sign out front announces that Villager's is "Louisiana's Best-Kept Secret." Unfortunately for those who want to eat in this very small, lively po' boy shop with electrical spools for tables, the secret is out and chances are good you will wait for a seat. It's worth it.

Made on toasted lengths of Langlinais French bread and available full size or half, the big sandwiches range from fried shrimp or oysters to sauce-drenched meatballs to the meatless Villager Veggie. Our favorite is a fully dressed pot-roast po' boy, dripping with beef juices that mingle with the mayo, lettuce, and tomato packed into the distinguished bread. The waitress will ask if you want cheese on it. Much as we love cheeseburgers and cheesesteaks, our experience is that cheese actually detracts from the direct deliciousness of the pot roast.

Do have a side dish or two. French fries are atypical chunks rather than twigs: lots of crisp exterior around soft insides. Corn nuggets are little deep-fried fritters with a center of sweet, creamy kernels. For dessert, funnel cake fries are squiggles of freshly fried state-fair midway food, dusted with powdered sugar.

Note: If you cannot wait for a seat to dine here, it is possible to call ahead and pick up po' boys from a drive-up window.

WILLIE MAE'S SCOTCH HOUSE

williemaesnola.com

2401 St. Ann St.   504-822-9503

New Orleans, LA   **L D** (closed Sun) **| $$**

Willie Mae's, a formerly obscure eatery in New Orleans' Lower Ninth Ward has, over the years, become a destination for fried-chicken devotees. It was raggedy before Katrina's devastation, but the reborn restaurant is bright, clean, and welcoming. And the chicken really is something special—moist and luscious inside an amber crust so fine and fragile that it tends to flake into savory shards when you bite into it. The same luxurious envelope is available on what the menu lists as a chicken-fried pork chop, the chop's meat far chewier than chicken, but in its own way a grand crust companion.

If you are allergic to boiled-in-oil food (why are you here?), you can order a simple grill-cooked pork chop. There is no crust or batter. It is just a hunk of pork plastered with an intensely flavorful coat of seasonings.

MISSISSIPPI

ABE'S BAR-B-Q
abesbbq.com

616 N. State St.   662-624-9947
Clarksdale, MS   **L D | $**

Folklore designates the crossroads of Highway 61 and 49 in Clarksdale as the spot Robert Johnson sold his soul to the devil in exchange for music mastery. In 1924, when Johnson was thirteen, Abraham Davis began selling sandwiches in Clarksdale. After World War II, he opened Abe's Bar-B-Q at the crossroads, and today his grandson Pat Davis runs the place, which is known for pecan-smoked pork and hot tamales.

Abe's barbecue is Boston butt that is cooked over pecan wood, cooled overnight, then sliced and heated again on the griddle when it is ordered. While on the grill it gets hacked up. The result? Pork hash with lots of juicy buzz in its pale inside fibers and plenty of crusty parts where it has fried on the hot iron of the grill. You can have it on a platter or in a sandwich, the latter available in two sizes—normal and Big Abe, which is twice the pork loaded into a double-decker bun. Clarksdale is close enough to Memphis that it is served city-style—that is, with the slaw inside the bun.

Abe's sauce is dark red and tangy, with the resonance of pepper and spice—a sublime companion for the meat. Pat Davis told us that it is made from the original recipe his grandfather developed, except for one ingredient, which he swears he doesn't use

anymore. We wondered aloud if that secret ingredient might be opium, considering its addictive qualities. Pat denied it with a sly smile.

Served three to an order, with or without chili on top, Abe's tamales are packed into cayenne-red husks, their yellow cornmeal moist with drippings from a mixture of beef and pork. The recipe is Abe Davis's, unchanged. "No doubt Granddaddy got it from someone in town," Pat suggests, reminding us that Abe had come to the United States from Lebanon, where tamales aren't a big part of the culinary mix. Why Abe thought they would sell well in his barbecue place is a head-scratcher. "There were no Mexican restaurants here then," Pat says. "And as far as I know, not many Mexicans."

ABE'S GRILL
abesgrill.com

803 Hwy. 72 W.   662-286-6124
Corinth, MS   **B L** (Mon–Fri) **| $**

A tip of the hat to Michael Medley, whom we met in Salt Lake City, where he slipped us a tempting list of eateries in northern Mississippi. Otherwise, we might never have traveled out Highway 72 to Abe's Grill. What to eat at Abe's? "Breakfast!" Michael said, and sure enough, if you are looking for hot biscuits made the true-South way with Martha White flour, for country ham and eggs, or even for a plate of pork brains, you must stop at this colorful roadside attraction that is plastered inside and out with vintage advertising signs, license plates, postcards, calendars, and old-time photographs.

No praise is too high for Abe's biscuits, which are lightweight but substantially savory, and especially delicious when oven-fresh. Sawmill gravy is a well-known classic to top them, but, curiously enough, chocolate gravy is a classic too. (Ari Weinzweig of Zingerman's Deli [p. 285] did the research on this.) While it takes some getting used to, the chocolate makes a seductive alternative to ordinary biscuit companions. Split and buttered or sandwiching sausage or bologna is good too. Coffee is included with most breakfasts, but if you eat enough pig meat to rouse a powerful thirst, consider Abe's iced tea, served in a one-quart frosted mason jar.

We have yet to have lunch at Abe's, but we do look forward to a hamburger, which Abe's makes from beef ground here daily, as well as to Abe's "original recipe" corn dog along with fresh-cut French fries.

BIG BAD BREAKFAST
bigbadbreakfast.com

719 N. Lamar Blvd.	662-236-2666
Oxford, MS	B L | $$

Chef John Currence's Big Bad Breakfast has been a shining star of cutting-edge diners since it opened in 2012. Currence, who is known for the exquisite Dixie/Creole dinners he serves at his very successful City Grocery restaurant in Oxford, said, "I want to give breakfast the same consideration we give lunch or dinner."

To that end, he serves outstanding cathead biscuits either with house-made jellies or as the exoskeleton of a lasciviously rich breakfast sandwich. French toast is spiked with brandy and served with fresh strawberries and whipped cream. Shrimp and grits outdo their Lowcountry inspiration. What devoted diner lover could resist a kitchen that proudly announces that it cooks omelets in a blend of butter and bacon fat? BBB is definitely the place to come if you drank too much the night before, because here you can order what the menu boasts is "a hangover's worst enemy": a chili dog with slaw, Cheddar cheese, pickles, onions, and jalapeño peppers all atop a waffle.

The lunch menu includes artisan burgers, BLTs made with Tabasco aioli, and an Elvis griddle-fried sandwich of peanut butter, bananas, and bacon on white or whole wheat. To drink, choose from among really good coffee, freshly squeezed juices, milk shakes, and a roster of alcoholic "big bad libations."

House motto: "Lard Have Mercy."

BLUE & WHITE RESTAURANT
blueandwhiterestaurant.com

1355 US Hwy. 61 N.	662-363-1371
Tunica, MS	B L D | $

Tunica has gone from cotton fields to gamblers' paradise, but out on Highway 61, the old Blue & White Restaurant is operating pretty much the same as it's been since opening here in 1937 as a Pure service station. The gas pumps are gone, but if you are looking for good southern food at reasonable prices in an atmosphere that is more down-home than high-stakes, this is the place to go.

"You have ten more minutes to order breakfast," our waitress warned. "Then the lunch buffet will open." We started with a country ham plate, the vigorous, well-aged slab of pig accompanied by eggs, biscuits, chunky sausage cream gravy, coffee-flavored red-eye gravy, and a bowl of stout, buttery grits. What a great morning meal!

When the buffet opened up, we helped ourselves to chicken and dumplings, which was superb: powerfully chickeny, loaded with meat, and laced with free-form mouthfuls of tender dough. On the side, we spooned up black-eyed peas, creamed corn, escalloped potatoes, and some of the most amazing turnip greens we've ever eaten. These greens were oily, salty, luscious, and rich, more like the pork used to flavor them than the green vegetable they appear to be. On the side came a sweet-dough yeast muffin and a crisp corn stick, both oven-hot and delicious.

We paid extra for an order of that weird specialty invented several decades ago in the Delta, fried dill pickles. Blue & White's are ultrathin slices with a veil of crust, nearly weightless, served with ranch dressing as a dip. Light as they are, the pickles have a resounding brine flavor that induces a mighty thirst. If you are a beer drinker, you will have instant cravings.

CRYSTAL GRILL
crystalgrillms.com

423 Carrollton Ave.   662-453-6530
Greenwood, MS   **L D** (closed Mon) | *$$*

LOCALS LOVE IT — ★ — Years ago, the Crystal Grill was known for a neon sign that glowed NEVER SLEEP. Open from 4 a.m. until midnight, it hosted the locals for their pre-dawn coffee klatch as well as C&G Railroad men who'd stop their train on the tracks just across the street for late-night supper. Breakfast no longer is served; at lunchtime, townsfolk flock here with the gusto of celebrants arriving at a church picnic. Multiple remodelings have created a labyrinth of small dining rooms that can seat over two hundred people.

The menu is an eccentric spectrum of local treasures (peppery Delta tamales, Biloxi flounder, Belzoni catfish) and such saccharine Dixie oddities as pink velvet frozen salad (crushed pineapple, Cool Whip, cherry pie filling, and condensed milk). Proprietor John Ballas said that spaghetti sauce is made from a recipe that his father obtained years ago by writing a letter to Heinz. Our favorite dishes on the menu are shrimp and crab Newburg, fried oysters, turnip greens, and sweet, sweet tea. And pie.

Oh, what pie! Mile-high slices are significantly taller than they are wide, the great meringue triangle on top about twice the height of the ribbon of cream it surmounts. It's an adventure to ease the edge of a fork onto the top of the fluffy white crown and allow nothing more than gravity to carry it through to the filling, where its downward progress slows but doesn't stop. Finally the fork hits lard-laced savory crust that shatters under an ounce of pressure. Not to slight coconut cream, which is fantastic, but chocolate cream is Crystal Grill's crowning glory. It is like Swiss milk chocolate, its creamy soul as prominent

as its chocolate flavor. It reminds us of fine chocolate pudding, all the more delicious for being sandwiched between a cloud of delicate meringue and a stratum of meltingly flaky crust.

DILWORTH'S TAMALES

702 Wick St.   662-223-3296
Corinth, MS   **L D** | *$*

At $3 per dozen, Dilworth's tamales are a terrific bargain. You actually can eat a dozen, maybe even two dozen if you're hungry, for they are panatela-thin. Wrapped in parchment, they are a simple mixture of beef, cornmeal, and spice steamed in a parchment wrapper long enough to become a single, pleasing chord. Dilworth's sells them hot or mild, the former bright but not incendiary, the latter sheer Miss-Mex comfort.

All business is drive-through, and while your dozen will come well wrapped inside a brown paper bag, we advise being armed with napkins when you open up the butcher paper that contains them.

These tamales have a long history in Corinth. Proprietor Lisa Edmond's father used to ride through town on a three-wheel bike with a large basket, hawking tamales. The house motto is: "Dilworth's Are the Best Yet."

THE DINNER BELL
thedinnerbell.net

229 5th Ave.   601-684-4883
McComb, MS   **L** | *$$*

The Dinner Bell is the place to go in Mississippi to experience revolving-table dining.

The tables are large and circular, and in the center of each is a lazy Susan that those seated at the circumference can set in motion. It is piled with a lavish array of food. Spin it and take what you want. When a serving tray starts getting empty, out comes a full one from the kitchen. Grab as much as you want and eat at your own speed.

This is classic Dixie food: chicken and dumplings, catfish, ham, corn sticks, sweet-potato casseroles, black-eyed peas, and fried okra. The spinach casserole enriched with cream cheese and margarine and cans of artichoke hearts is good for the soul . . . not to mention scrumptious. To drink, the right stuff is sweet tea.

★ DOE'S EAT PLACE

doeseatplace.com

502 Nelson St.   662-334-3315
Greenville, MS   D (closed Sun) | $$$

LOCALS LOVE IT — Located on the wrong side of town in the back rooms of a dilapidated grocery store, Doe's does not look like a restaurant, much less a great restaurant. Its fans love it just the way it is. Mississippians have eaten here since 1941, when segregation was a way of life. Back then, blacks entered through the front door for meals of fried fish and tamales; white patrons came in the back door and ate in the kitchen. Today, many dining tables still are located in the kitchen, spread helter-skelter among stoves and counters where the staff fries potatoes in big iron skillets and dresses salads. Plates, flatware, and tablecloths are all mismatched. Newcomers may be shocked by the ramshackle surroundings, but Doe's is easy to like once the food starts coming.

Begin with tamales and a brilliantly garlicked salad made of iceberg lettuce dressed with olive oil and fresh-squeezed lemon juice. Shrimp are usually available, broiled or fried, and they are very, very good. It is steak, however, for which Doe's has earned its reputation. "Baby Doe" Signa, son of the founder, told us that it is merely "US Choice" grade, which, frankly, we don't believe. Booming with flavor, oozing juice, tender but in no way tenderized, it is the equal or better of any expense-account chain restaurant steak. Choices range from a ten-ounce filet mignon up to a four-pound sirloin. Our personal preference is the porterhouse, the bone of which bisects a couple of pounds of meat that is very different in character on either side of the bone. The tenderloin side is zesty and exciting; the other side seems laden with protein, as deeply satisfying as beef can be. With steak come delicious French fries—dandy to eat "neat," even

better when dragged through the oily juices that flow out of steaks onto the plate.

Note: Please do not confuse this great eat place or its family-run sibling in Little Rock with franchised Doe's throughout the South.

THE ELITE

141 E. Capitol St.   601-352-5606
Jackson, MS   B L D (closed Sun) | $

Despite its name, the Elite is a restaurant for people of every social class: white-collar downtowners at breakfast, white and blue collars at lunch, whole families and even starry-eyed couples on dates for supper. A Jackson fixture now for one hundred years, it belongs to a little-acknowledged genre of the southern restaurant: the square-meals café with a Greek accent.

Most of what you'll eat is textbook southern-comfort fare: country-fried steaks and veal cutlets with gravy, Delta-style tamales, fried crab claws from the Gulf, Mobile Bay West Indies salad, crisp-fried shrimp, and a choice of vegetables from simple sliced tomatoes to elaborate casseroles. The Elite also offers a selection of Mexican food, including an enchilada plate that Roadfood.com's Bruce Bilmes and Sue Boyle described as "simply as good as it gets: gooey, laced with raw chopped onions, topped with a mantle of orange cheese." Breakfast biscuits are delicate; yeasty dinner rolls are famously good. There is excellent house-made baklava for dessert, but do not ignore the intense lemon chess pie.

FAYARD'S

fayards.biz

1757 Popps Ferry Rd.   228-388-1021
Biloxi, MS   B L D (closed Sun) | $

OPEN EARLY — Located in the back of a gas station / convenience store on a commercial strip of road, Fayard's is a delicious, quick and easy waystation for travelers along I-10. There's a full menu of sandwiches and hot lunches, but the thing to know about are the po' boys, "dressed and pressed." "Dressed" means slathered with mustard and mayo and garnished with lettuce and tomato; "pressed" refers to the fact that the assembled sandwich is cooked in a press, which compacts the top and bottom of the long, house-baked roll, toasting the bread's surface and causing its ingredients to meld into a sloppy slurry of deliciousness.

The sandwich we like best is called a Country Roast: sirloin tips roasted long and slow until falling-apart tender, reminiscent of what a New Orleans po' boy chef would call roast beef debris. Other possible ingredients range from tuna and burgers to softshell crab, shrimp, and oysters, plus Boom shrimp and Boom oysters. "Boom" refers to the addition of vivid hot sauce that makes the well-fried Gulf seafood a very exciting bite.

Although a passing glance makes it look like just another service station, Fayard's is in fact a very personal and personable place. As we dined at one of the indoor tables, we very much enjoyed a conversation with Mr. Fayard, the seemingly omnipresent host, who told us of his love for thoroughbred horses and pointed out the country-craftsy décor that was created by his late wife.

GIARDINA'S
giardinas.com

314 Howard St.   662-455-4227
Greenwood, MS   **D** | $$$

Opened in 1936, Giardina's started as a fish market but soon became a restaurant popular among cotton growers, who dined in private, curtained booths where bootleg booze could be drunk in secrecy. As King Cotton lost its economic hegemony late in the twentieth century, Giardina's fortunes waned, along with those of Greenwood, the South's cotton capital. But then the Viking Range Corporation came to town in 1989 and turned everything around. The Mississippi Heritage Trust Awards that Viking has won for rehabilitation of local properties include the transformation of the historic Irving Hotel from a ratty embarrassment to a stylish boutique hotel called the Alluvian. What we like about the Alluvian, beyond its feather beds, is the fact that it is the new home of Giardina's (pronounced with a hard G).

Giardina's is stylish, modern, and expensive. Service is polished. Tables are outfitted with thick white cloths and snazzy Viking cutlery. The wine collection—stored in state-of-the-art Viking wine cellars—is impressive. And yet for all that, dinner is down-home Delta. You still sit in a private dining compartment. The menu is upscale cotton-country fare, including hefty steaks and elegant pompano, hot tamales, and a bevy of dishes that reflect the powerful influence of Italian immigrants on Greenwood's cuisine. These include garlicky salads and a marvelous appetizer called Camille's bread, which our waiter described as "like a muffuletta but without the meat"—a hot loaf stuffed with olives, sardines, and cheese.

HICKS'

305 S. State St.   662-624-9887
Clarksdale, MS   **L D** (closed Sun) | $

"I am sixty-one years old, and I made my first tamales at age sixteen," Eugene Hicks told us years ago when we asked him why the ones he makes are so especially good. Laced with a hard kick of pepper spices, each one is hand-shucked, and they are available by threes, sixes, and twelves. A plate is served with chili and cheese, baked beans, and Italian-seasoned coleslaw.

Tamales are what put Hicks' on the map, but there is a whole menu of ribs, rib tips, and chopped pork shoulder cooked over hickory and topped with house-made sauce. In addition, there are Hicks-made pork sausages, fried catfish, and a "Big Daddy" sandwich that is made with a combination of sliced barbecued pork and smoked turkey.

LEATHA'S BAR-B-QUE INN
leathasbbq.com

6374 US Hwy. 98   601-271-6003
Hattiesburg, MS   **L D** (Tues–Sat) | $

There's a sign for Leatha's on Highway 98, but it can be a challenge to see it behind the RV sales lot. In this case, your nose is more useful than your eyes, because if you roll down the windows you will smell it before you see it. The air is threaded by wisps of smoke puffing from the pit located next to a rickety building that is the restaurant.

Beautiful baby-back ribs come heavily painted with warm red sauce. Pulled pork is more lightly glazed, available on a plate or in a sandwich. Side dishes are de rigueur alongside any meat: There are sweet, soupy beans, mustard-powered coleslaw, and potato salad, and if you arrive before it's all sold out, memorable pecan pie. Tea is sweeter than sugar itself.

Everyone we know who has gone to Leatha's comes back raving not only about the food but about the kindness of the staff. Disheveled it may look from the outside, but you will feel extremely well taken care of.

LUSCO'S

luscos.net

722 Carrollton Ave.   662-453-5365
Greenwood, MS   **D** (Wed-Sat) | $$$

To occupy one of Lusco's backroom private dining booths and to hear the plaint of blues musicians that floats from the sound system above the partitions that segregate each party of diners is a weird and compelling taste of cotton-country history. Planters around Greenwood came to know Charles "Papa" Lusco as a grocer in the 1920s. His wife, Marie "Mama" Lusco, sold plates of her spaghetti at the store, and Papa built secret dining rooms in back where customers could enjoy his homemade wine with their meals.

Mama and Papa were Italian by way of Louisiana, so the flavors of the kitchen they established are as much Creole as they are southern. Gumbo, crab, and shrimp are always on the menu, and oysters are a specialty in season—on the half shell or baked with bacon. The menu is best known for its high-end items. Lusco's T-bone steaks are some of the finest anywhere: sumptuous cuts that are brought raw to the table for your approval, then broiled to pillowy succulence. Pompano has for many years been a house trademark (when available, usually in the spring), broiled and served whole, bathed in a magical sauce made of butter, lemon, and secret spices.

Lusco's is also known for its New Orleans–style salad of iceberg lettuce dolled up with anchovies, capers, and olives and liberally sopped in a fragrant vinaigrette; but third-generation Lusco Karen

Pinkston is a serious salad buff who has made it her business to concoct more modern alternatives. One evening's choices included Mediterranean salad, made with feta cheese; traditional Caesar salad; and a salad billed as Gourmet Delight, made with arugula, radicchio, endive, red lettuce, and spinach. "Andy [Karen's husband] likes to tease me about that one," Karen said about the latter. "He tells me it's just weeds I've picked by the side of the highway. But the fact is that the Delta is different now than it used to be, and the new people have more educated palates. Even this place has to change with the times."

PEGGY'S

512 Bay St. E.   601-656-3478
Philadelphia, MS   **L** (closed Sat & Sun) | $

Peggy's started in the 1950s as a private home serving lunch to friends and passersby. You helped yourself and put some money in the cigar box. It is now officially a restaurant, but the folksy informality and down-home food scarcely have changed. The place is still an old house, the day's dishes set out on a card table in the hallway near the kitchen, where you grab a plate and dip your own. Chances are good you will share a table with strangers.

There are always a couple of entrees, such as pork chops, baked ham, and chicken and dumplings, but if you come on Tuesday, Wednesday, or Friday, you will have a chance to sample what is Peggy's culinary pennant: fried chicken. It's soulful chicken, with plenty of crunch and juice and chicken fat dripping down your chin when teeth sink into a thigh. Sides are classic Dixie fare: greens, butter beans, vegetable casseroles, corn sticks, and yeast rolls. Desserts include sheet cakes and lemon icebox pie.

Payment for lunch is on the honor system: Put your money in the bowl near the door as you leave.

PHILLIPS GROCERY

541 E. Van Dorn Ave.   662-252-4671
Holly Springs, MS   **L | $**

Located in a two-story wood-frame house that was a saloon in the nineteenth century, Phillips became a grocery store in 1919 and has built its reputation on hamburgers since the 1940s.

The menu is written on a blackboard that lists side dishes, including fresh-from-the-freezer tater tots and morsels of deep-fried, bright-green okra enveloped in a golden crust. Corn nuggets are something special—bite-sized fritters with lots of kernels packed inside a sweet hush-puppy-like jacket. You can get spicy or regular French fries. And if a MoonPie off the grocery shelf isn't your dish for dessert, Phillips also offers fried pies for a dollar apiece: a folded-over half-circle of dough fried until reddish brown and chewy, enclosing a heavy dollop of sugary peach or apple filling.

Hamburgers are presented wrapped in yellow wax paper. When you peel back the wrapping, particularly on a one-third-pound Phil-Up Burger, you behold a vision of beauty-in-a-bun: a thick patty with a wickedly good crunch to its nearly blackened skin, adorned with two kinds of cheese, bacon and ham, lettuce, tomato, and mayonnaise. The meat itself is smooth-textured and moist enough to ooze juice when you gently squeeze the soft bun wrapped around it. The flavor is fresh, beefy, and sumptuous: an American classic.

RAMON'S

535 Oakhurst Ave.   662-624-9230
Clarksdale, MS   **D** (closed Sun & Mon) | **$$**

We thank Roger and Jennifer Stolle, infallible tipsters for all things relating to food and culture in the Mississippi Delta, for taking us to Ramon's. "I wouldn't tell everyone to eat here," Roger said, pointing at the water-damaged acoustical ceiling tiles and explaining that local lore blames a lax landlord for the decomposition that makes the place a bona fide dump. Still, Thomas and Barbara Ely, the couple who run Ramon's, valiantly create a pleasing milieu in the form of empty fifths of Jack Daniel's and three-liter jugs of Taylor Chablis that have been made into decorative lamps, and they serve magnificent butterflied fried shrimp nearly as big as MoonPies. "We were taking bets in the kitchen if y'all would be able to finish," the waitress admitted when we left two of his dozen shrimp uneaten on the plate.

Roger said his favorite thing to eat was a plate of chicken livers and spaghetti. The livers are sensational: unspeakably rich and luxuriously crunchy. They are so filling that we barely forked into the heap of noodles that came alongside them.

WHITE FRONT CAFE

902 Main St.   662-759-3842
Rosedale, MS   **L** (closed Sun & Mon) | **$**

Joe Pope is gone, but the little wood-frame house still attracts pilgrims from miles around for tamales—the one and only meal on the menu. Many people buy them to take home, but customers are welcome to sit at one of four kitchenette tables in the front room. Order three or four and they are served tightly wrapped in their corn husk. You can eat them one of two ways: pick up a tamale and squeeze out a mouthful of the succulent insides or peel away the husk and use a saltine cracker to scoop some up.

Mr. Pope once told us that he got his recipe from the daughter of John Hooks, who learned how to cook tamales from a Mexican from Texas who traveled through the Delta back in the 1930s. We believe they are some of the very best: all-beef (no pork), a well-nigh perfect blend of meat, cornmeal, and just enough peppery spice to excite but not overwhelm your tongue.

WHITE TROLLEY CAFE

1215 Hwy. 72 E.   662-287-4593
Corinth, MS   B L | $

The "slugburger" originally was configured in Corinth, Mississippi, during the first World War. The pint-sized patty, sometimes called a doughburger, was formed by mixing ground beef with potato flakes and flour. At first it was called a Weeksburger because the man who invented it was a diner owner named John Weeks. Over the years, grits have become the meat-extender of choice for the oddball blimpy, which gets deep-fried to a crisp and garnished with mustard, pickle chips, and onions. The name slugburger came about during the Great Depression, when you could buy one for a nickel and the five-cent piece was known as a "slug." The belief that the recipe calls for ground-up garden snails is a culinary canard.

With its dozen counter stools, mostly male clientele, and in-your-face hash-house ambience, the White Trolley Cafe is an ideal place to confront a slug. White Trolley's is thicker than most, with a crust that's tough or—if you ask for yours well done—brutally crunchy. The interior, however it's cooked, is soft but not too juicy. (Many years ago, the custom was to briefly dip the bun in cooking grease, thus adding succulence.) Native Corinthians adore them; for those accustomed to a red-meat hamburger that oozes juice, the slug is a demanding dish. The White Trolley also offers all-beef burgers, but if you don't say beef when you order, you get a slug.

Much business at the White Trolley is takeout, hence it makes sense that the popular dessert is a Mrs. Sullivan's pre-wrapped individual pie—pecan, coconut, or chocolate. Mrs. Sullivan's pies are another old-time inamorata, invented during the Depression in Jackson, Tennessee.

82 QUEEN

82queen.com

82 Queen St.   843-723-7591

Charleston, SC   **L D** | $$$

─★── 82 Queen is not typical Roadfood. At a good
HOT $50+ per person, maybe it isn't Roadfood at
TICKET
─★── all. But if you want to eat some of the most
inspired versions of coastal Carolina's regional specialties, it is a destination to treasure. For instance,
there are good versions of shrimp and creamy grits
throughout the Lowcountry, but 82 Queen chef Brad
Jones enhances the formula by making his with barbecued shrimp—muscular sweeties whose coat of
fire is dramatic balance for the earthy grits below.
Enriched with cheese, sprinkled with a bounty of
crisp bacon pieces and chopped green onions, this is
an unforgettably good meal. The same good grits
serve as a pedestal for grilled mahimahi, adorned
with pumate butter and crisp fried green tomatoes. If
you need to wait at the bar for your table, the not-to-
be missed plate is fried oysters, little lodes of marine
meat encased in crisp, Tabasco-charged crust, served
with crushed red pepper marmalade.

A whole section of the menu is devoted to
"Lowcountry Specialties": crab cakes with hoppin'
John, Frogmore stew (a hearty gallimaufry of shrimp,
sausage, corn, okra, and potatoes), and good ol' buttermilk fried chicken served with skillet corn bread
and a luxurious portion of mac 'n' cheese. Sunday
brunch features a spiced shrimp boil, crab Benedict,
French toast casserole, and a BLT that promises a
quarter pound of apple-smoked bacon. Desserts
include bourbon pecan pie, peach praline cobbler,
raspberry glazed Key lime pie, and outrageously
indulgent Toll House pie.

521 BBQ & GRILL

521bbq.com

6257 Carolina Commons   803-548-7675

Dr.   **L D** | $

Fort Mill, SC

521 BBQ & Grill is a conspicuously worthy barbecue
destination. Not that there's anything wrong with
the menu's extra-thick fried bologna sandwich, but it
would be a crime to come here and not eat chopped
pork and/or ribs. The former—Boston butt that is
slow-smoked for fourteen hours—becomes rough-
hewn hash that is served sauceless. Please, savor
some unadorned forkfuls for full appreciation of the
refined synergy of swine and smoke. But then, bring
on the sauce. Two kinds are arrayed in squeeze bottles on every table (next to the roll of paper towels):
a thin, pepper-powered vinegar dressing that adds an
exclamation mark to the flavor, and a thicker, sweeter,
and extremely tangy tomato sauce. Both are winners.

The ribs are just about the meatiest baby backs
we've ever run across. Huge amounts of juice-sopped
meat slide off the bone at the slightest provocation.

Like the pork butts, the ribs are slow-smoked so the woodsy flavor of the pit completely insinuates itself into every fiber of the meat. Then they are painted with some of that tangy sauce and grilled until the sauce begins to caramelize and hug the pork.

We haven't yet mentioned what some people consider to be the very best thing on the menu, included on every plate: hush puppies. Irregularly shaped with dark, red-gold skin that offers both crunch and chew, their interiors are moist and sweet-corn sweet, laced with perfumy onion. Neither are the baked beans to be ignored. They fairly vibrate with barbecue zest.

And finally we need to mention the staff: a corps of waitresses who are as much fun as they are efficient, eagerly replacing a couple of hush puppies that accidentally tumbled into the baked beans and taking great joy when a customer is caught licking every bit of sauce off his fingers. In short: If you like barbecue, put 521 on any short list of must-visits in the Carolinas.

There's a second 521 in Tega Cay at 1135 Stonecrest Boulevard, 803-548-0123.

BEACON DRIVE-IN

beacondrivein.com

255 John B. White Sr.   864-585-9387
Blvd.   L D | $
Spartanburg, SC

Drive-in service at the Beacon is swell, but any newcomer must avail himself of the serving line inside. Here, you enter a fourth dimension of restaurant-going, unlike anywhere else. As you approach the counter, an employee will demand, *"Call it out!"* Give your order quickly, or else stand back and allow other, swifter folks to say their piece. On a good weekend day, the Beacon serves five thousand people.

Once you give an order, it is shouted back to the huge open kitchen, then you are asked in no uncertain terms to *"Move on down the line!"* Grab a tray, and by the time you have moved twenty paces forward, there your order will be—miraculously, exactly as you ordered it, with or without extra barbecue sauce, double bacon on the burger. A bit farther down the line, you get your tea, lemonade, or milk shake and pay the cashier, then find a seat. Total time from entering to digging in—maybe two minutes.

The menu is big, ranging from gizzard plates to banana sandwiches. We recommend Pork A-Plenty, which is chopped and sauced hickory-cooked hot barbecue on a bun that also contains cool coleslaw. The "A-Plenty" designation, applied to burgers and even pimiento cheese sandwiches, indicates the addition of intertwined deep-fried onion rings and French fries. The only correct libation is sweet tea, served in a tall tumbler over crushed ice so cold that gulpers run the risk of a brain-freeze headache. The Beacon sells more tea than any other single restaurant in the USA.

★ BERTHA'S KITCHEN

2332 Meeting St. Rd.   843-554-6519
North Charleston, SC   L | $

Bertha's Kitchen, an out-of-the-way, soul-food eatery now in its fourth decade, is small enough that the cafeteria line isn't so much a line as it is a counter where you stand and tell one of the several kitchen staff if you want your pork-rib niblets on rice, which parts of the fried chicken you prefer, and if you're having just lima beans or lima bean dinner. The beans alone are a soupy, khaki-colored side dish. Dinner pairs them with hunks of neck from which weighty nuggets of meat are easily detached by probing with a fork. With the neck, or in place of it to accompany the beans, you also can choose pig tails, which are little more than cylinders of glistening, warm pork fat that melts as it hits your tongue. Who knew a menu item called lima beans could be so mighty a meal?

Beyond those great beans, the menu is a primer in Lowcountry soul food: red rice with sausage, fried chicken encased in fissured red-gold crust, pork chops with meat as wanton as gravy itself, turkey *prileau* (a doppelgänger of pilau), hoppin' John, and mac 'n' cheese with shards of crunchy-chewy crust. Every meal is prepared exactly as you order it. Do you want more pig tails or less in the limas? Will you have red rice, white rice, or hoppin' John—on the side or underneath? How much gravy will you have with your stewed gizzards? For all the precision ordering, meals come on disposable plates and it is difficult for one person to spend more than $10 for a tray-filling feast.

BETSY'S ON THE CORNER

betsysonthecorner.com

159 Laurens St.   803-226-0078

Aiken, SC   **B** (Sat); **L D** (closed Sun) | **$**

Betsy's is a soda fountain, a diner, and a lively town café—a fine place for an honest meal with a southern accent or for an all-American ice cream splurge. Its big menu offers salads, soups, sandwiches, and rugged burgers with all sorts of toppings (turkey or veggie patties also available), including a Corner Burger that is a South Carolina paradigm topped with fried green tomatoes and pimento cheese. All-beef hot dogs come nestled in New England–style split-top buns that are griddle-toasted to a crisp. Onion rings available on the side are fragile-crusted and fresh, needing only a sprinkle of salt to attain perfection.

Betsy's serves a blue-plate special every day, a meat-and-two affair that includes a couple of side dishes (try the rich, motley-textured mac 'n' cheese), a corn muffin, and a drink, all for $9. Friday's fried haddock is sweet, fresh, and hearty. On a recent Saturday when we stopped in, the day's special was chicken and waffles. On Sunday only, Betsy's also serves breakfast.

Ice cream service is a kick, ranging from cones and cups to sundaes to a top-of-the-line Heavens to Betsy that is eight scoops of ice cream, hot fudge, butterscotch, caramel and marshmallow toppings, pineapple, strawberries, bananas, Heath Bar crunch, Oreo crumbles, peanuts, whipped cream, and cherries. There is nothing extraordinary about the ice cream or the toppings, but everything is well-constructed and will likely satisfy all but the fussiest ice cream epicure.

BIG BOYS ORIGINAL SMOKEHOUSE

8604 Farrow Rd., Ste. A   803-788-6822

Columbia, SC   **L D** (Weds–Sun, closes at 6 p.m.) | **$**

Among the South Carolina Midlands' many fine barbecue parlors, Big Boy's is a standout. Here you eat pulled pork that is a tangle of tender, smoke-infused filaments, fibers, nuggets, chunks, soft inside meat, and chewy bark. It's lavishly juicy and would be delicious with no adornment whatsoever, but the two available sauces are both hard to resist. Mustard sauce—a local tradition—is not too sharp, quite sweet, and a little tangy; red sauce adds a peppery exclamation point.

This is pork country, but Big Boy's beef brisket, infused with smoke and literally dripping juices, is fabulous—a fatty orgy for carnivores, all the more sensuous when humming with a mustard sauce tingle.

To go with its magnificent meats, Big Boy's offers regular sides and "premium sides," the latter being pig feet and rice, hash and rice, or gumbo and rice. Any one of these could be a whole meal. Regular sides include custard-rich macaroni and cheese and a heap of collard greens that maintain tremendous vegetable potency.

With meals this good, it's a challenge to save room for dessert, but worth the effort. Banana pudding is based on a remarkable custard, which is so rich and substantial that it reminds us of cheesecake. Sweet-potato pie is lighter, brighter, cheerfully spiced, and not too sweet.

There is no table service at Big Boy's. Place an order at the counter and pay, then wait for your name to be called. Everything is served in disposable containers, for eating at a handful of tables or for taking away.

★ BOWENS ISLAND
bowensisland.biz

1870 Bowens Island Rd. 843-795-2757
Charleston, SC   **D** (Tues–Sat) | **$$**

Bowens Island oysters are hideous to see, all gnarled and splotched with pluff, which is the oysterman's term for the fine silt that is stuck on them when they are harvested and clings to them when they are roasted so that merely touching a cooked cluster will smudge your fingers. Experienced customers, who come for the all-you-can-eat deal ($20+), bring their own oyster-eating gloves. Amateurs, who might eat only a cafeteria tray's worth, are given a clean-looking washcloth, along with a dull knife for prying the shells open (an easy task on roasted oysters) and cutting the meat loose. However you do it, eating pluff is an inevitable part of the meal, and while it has what proprietor Robert Barber calls "a unique stinky smell," it is a good stink, an oceany aroma that adds mineral salubrity to the flavor. On the door of the hut where you go to place your order, a bumper sticker reads "Pluff Mud: The Goo That Holds the Earth Together."

"Most people who aren't from around here think of oysters as cold on the half shell, all wet and slimy," Barber told us. "They've never had them steamed, hot and juicy." The cooking process infuses the meat of the oyster with its own juices, concentrating the flavor, and while it takes nothing away from the sensual mouthfeel of a raw one, the lick of fire adds balmy bliss.

Oysters are the reason to come to Bowens Island, but they are not the whole story. You can eat expertly fried shrimp or fish or hearty Frogmore stew (a Lowcountry slumgullion of sausage, shrimp, corn, and potatoes). The hush puppies served alongside are among the best anywhere, their dark-red, spherical surface hard and crunchy, their insides creamy rich.

Ambience is fish-camp rough-and-tumble, tables outfitted with holes in the center where you conveniently can throw shells after you have extricated the meat from the inner tidal bivalves that are shoveled onto the table hot from the roaster. (The verb "shovel" is not a metaphor; a garden shovel actually is used to serve the oysters.) The heavy kerplunk of emptied shells is the backbeat of dining at Bowens Island; the melody is the slurp of sucking slippery nuggets of marine meat straight off the oyster knife, then drinking down warm, salty liquor from the shell.

BUSH'S

409 Main St.   803-663-1073
Graniteville, SC   **L D** | **$**

South Carolina cooks are masters of fried seafood; Bush's is evidence that the talent is not just a coastal trait. Inland, just across the river from Augusta, Georgia, Bush's flies the frying banner with pride. It is a humble fish and chips shack that offers firm, sweet shrimp (jumbos or Calabash minis), creamy slabs of flounder, lasciviously large oysters, tender scallops, soulful catfish, and a wide variety of other flatfish such as whiting, croaker, mullet, and bream, all encased in a thin, crisp, vividly seasoned coat that is positively addicting.

If you are allergic to fried food, there is an all-you-can-eat crab legs deal in the $20 range—about twice the price of most other meals. And if you are a fish frowner, try the pork chops. They are boneless and haloed by that fine, fragile crust that gives the seafood its flavor glow. Visitors in a more adventurous mood can opt for less mainstream menu items, such as catfish stew or chitlins (by the pint). The menu even offers Buffalo wings and a half-pound hamburger billed as "incredible." We recently asked a waitress how incredible the burger actually is and she replied, "Not."

Good side dishes enhance the meal. They range from uniquely South Carolinian hash and rice to all-American mac 'n' cheese. We especially like the collard greens, which have all the tonic punch one expects, but with a completely unexpected sweetness that makes them into a very happy vegetable. Yams are very sweet and spiced to be a nice complement for either pork chops or fried fish. For dessert, there is mom's-home-cooking cake. While whole cakes are available to order—red velvet, caramel, carrot, pineapple, lemon, strawberry, and carrot—you can't beat the simple perfect pound cake. It is rich and creamy but not overly dense.

The dining room is fairly small, and tables are set up in rows reminiscent of a commissary. This makes for an agreeably social tone; while we were strangers, the staff and other customers soon had us feeling like regulars.

CAHILL'S CHICKEN KITCHEN

cahillsmarket.com

1055 May River Rd.   843-757-2921
Bluffton, SC   **B L D** | **$**

Fried, broiled, blackened, or on top of waffles, chicken is Cahill's leading light. But the sprawling menu also includes half-pound hamburgers accoutered every which way, red snapper tacos, locally harvested May River oysters, and more than a dozen vegetables, some of which come directly from the farmer's market to which the restaurant is attached.

Vegetables are special enough that many customers choose the Field & Fork option, which is a plate of four of them without meat. Highlights include peppery homegrown rutabaga, oily and intense collard greens, spice-whirled sweet-potato soufflé, stout stone-ground grits, meaty little butter beans, and preposterously cheesy broccoli casserole.

The fried chicken is good (we wish the crust was crunchier), but the main dishes we'll be back for are fried oysters veiled in a well-seasoned crust, and shrimp, which are firm and sweet either fried or broiled.

Eating at Cahill's feels like going to a happy potluck supper at a farmer's barn. The setting is casual and rustic, and the air resounds with energetic chatter among diners who all seem to be having a wonderful time.

Note: Breakfast and dinner are served Monday through Saturday; lunch is served only Monday through Wednesday; brunch is served Sunday from 9 a.m. to 3 p.m.

CAROLINA BAR-B-QUE

109 S. Main St.   803-652-2919
New Ellenton, SC   **L D** (Thurs–Tues)
                         (closed Sun) | **$**

The name Carolina BBQ is the truth, but not the whole truth. This restaurant is *South* Carolina barbecue, faithful to the likings of the south-central area of the Palmetto State. For one thing, it is open only Thursday through Saturday (plus Wednesday lunch); for another, service is buffet-style, all-you-can-eat. While neither trait is unique to South Carolina, both are true of nearly every great South Carolina barbecue. Most important, of course, is the food. This is all-about-the-hog barbecue, featuring a rugged mélange of meat that is smoky and sweetly piggy, ranging from velvet-soft hunks to shreds to crunchy shards. Alongside are trays of white rice and pork hash, the latter a South Carolina favorite comfort food that packs pure pork satisfaction.

And, oh, what side dishes! Most are familiar southern staples: crisp-fried okra; sweet and oniony hush puppies; mac 'n' cheese that is wildly funky-textured, from leathery top to soft elbow noodles stuck with cheese; greens and beans and candied yams. One jaw-dropper is fried squash—a simple dish, just discs of yellow squash that are fried up in a thin, well-seasoned batter, becoming the essence of vegetable with a crisp, warm halo. The big surprise among sides is sweet-potato tater tots, which look something like fried okra but are rolled in sugar, the yam inside the breading melting-soft and sweet. We returned for seconds, then thirds.

At the table, dress the pork with either red barbecue sauce or a true South Carolina mustard sauce that delivers a slow-rolling heat that is just what this subtle-flavored pork wants. Pitchers of iced tea are included with the price of the buffet, which is $9 for anyone ages eleven to sixty, $8.50 for those older, $6.25 for children ages six to ten, and $2.50 for ages three to five. Customers under three years old eat free.

CHARLIE'S FISH MARKET

813 Richland Ave. E. 803-649-2131
Aiken, SC L (closed Sun) | $

There are a few tables at Charlie's Fish Market, but hardly anybody eats here. Some come to buy raw fish—brim, whiting, mullet—for cooking at home; others have their fish fried and wrapped, ready to eat. You can even bring in your own fish (cleaned) and they will fry it for you. It's a bare, no-frills sort of place, but it is hospitable and friendly to newcomers. Family-run since 1909 (originally in the main business district), Charlie's is Aiken's oldest restaurant.

Mullet, sheathed in a crisp, lightly seasoned crust, is oily and unctuous, rich but only mildly fishy. Brim presents many bones, but its flesh is sweet enough to make working around them worthwhile. Whiting is easy to eat and to like—virtually boneless. Dinner-sized portions come with French fries and hush puppies that are cooked in a regular fryolator, as opposed to the huge cast-iron skillet in which the fish is fried. The preferred way to dress all these fried fish is with a double whammy of mustard and hot sauce.

CITY BILLIARDS

citybilliardsaikensc.com

208 Richland Ave. 803-649-7362
Aiken, SC L D (closed Sun) | $

City Billiards' sign boasts of "the best cheeseburger you'll ever eat." If not quite that, it is a mighty good one: velvety ground beef, thickly pattied and griddle-fried, plush enough to ooze rivers of savory juice into a steamed-soft bun, its condiments including mayonnaise, mustard, shredded lettuce, sliced tomato, and onions. Eighteen different burgers are listed on the menu, including ones topped with blue cheese or jalapeño cheese, with bacon or mushrooms or barbecue sauce or Jamaican jerk seasoning. We haven't tried the oddities but can vouch for the basic cheeseburger.

You also can get chili on your burger, which we find redundant, since it is a thick, beefy chili. But this same chili is the star ingredient in what may not be the best chili dog you'll ever eat, but one that will give the best of them a run for the money. The sauce, which the menu touts as "made from a 50-year-old recipe," is dense, sweet, and spicy, pairing beautifully with cheese, chopped raw onions, and yellow mustard. (Coleslaw is another good optional topping.) The dog itself is a blubbery pale pink one. At first sight of it, you might wish for a better class of wiener, but a fancy frank would be as wrong here as Luciano Pavarotti covering the Dead Kennedys. Its pallid cheapness is an ideal palette for the pyrotechnics that go atop it. The bun, too, is soft and squishy; an artisan roll would be sacrilege.

DAVE'S CARRY-OUT

42 Morris St. 843-577-7943
Charleston, SC L D (closed Sun & Mon) | $

Not to disregard Tuesday's jumbo turkey wings and red rice or Thursday's melting-tender Cornish hen with hoppin' John, but it is Dave's everyday shrimp that must be eaten. These taut pink crescents are veiled in a film of elegant crunch reminiscent of the legendary frying done by the long-gone Edisto Motel. It is hypnotic to watch the cook bread them one by one, then toss them into a fry basket that gets dropped into hot oil above the pieces of fish and pork chop that sizzle down below. Yes, everything goes into the same soup and comes out with its own flavor—pork, fish, chicken—complicated by a multi-flavored zest that is the hallmark of Lowcountry cooking.

Dave's is a tiny corner storefront with only two tables for eating on premises and a reputation for staying open long into the morning when everything else in town has closed. A few years ago it moved from its original oil-saturated disreputable location to the current corner storefront, which is freshly painted and shipshape. While purists bemoan the cultural elevation, the current Dave's is a restaurant where anyone will feel welcome, any time of night. As the name suggests, it is designed mostly for the takeout trade. Still, when it's crowded, as it inevitably is late at night, you can wait up to an hour for your food to be cooked and plated (in Styrofoam). Everything is cooked to order, order by order.

DESHAWN'S SEAFOOD AND CHICKEN

10316 Atomic Rd.   803-442-4444
North Augusta, SC   L D (Wed–Sun) | $$

"Let's get crackin" say the T-shirts worn by waitresses at DeShawn's, which is famed for its under-$30 all-you-can-eat crab legs special. The legs are grand, and if you are someone who never can get enough of them, this could be the deal of the century. But it's all the other great seafood—and consummate fried chicken—that will keep us coming back. Fried shrimp are medium-sized beauties, firm and sweet and encased in vividly spiced breading; flounder is skin-on flavorful, also sheathed in a full-flavored crust; catfish, whole or filleted, sings of the great outdoors. Fry frowners can get their seafood broiled, and there even is a classic Lowcountry boil of shrimp, potatoes, sweet corn, and sausage.

Chicken is no second-class citizen in this kitchen. It is breaded and fried to crispy-crunchy succulence, each piece sporting an embarrassment of peppery gnarled crust. Side it with soulful mac 'n' cheese or a stupendously indulgent hot baked potato salad (larded with bacon, cheese, and mayo), plus turnip greens with large pieces of zesty turnip, and you have a grand Deep South meal.

DeShawn's, named by combining the first names of owners Shawn Thomas and Deanna Brown Thomas (yes, Soul Man James Brown's daughter) is as much an eating hall as it is a restaurant. The cinder-block walls are painted blue. Tables, available normal height or higher for easier sitting down and getting up, are made of polished wood-grain material. Décor is a typical array of nautical knickknacks. Just inside the front door behind the hostess's station is a bell with a long chain on its clapper. A sign suggests, "If you are a first time customer and you enjoyed your meal . . . RING THE BELL." We sure did, with enthusiasm.

Do note that, although DeShawn's is off the beaten path, it has enough of a reputation that it can get dauntingly crowded, especially on weekend nights. We prefer to go for lunch, when seating is ample.

DUKES

dukesbarbque.com
4248 Whiskey Rd.   803-649-7675
Aiken, SC   L D (Wed–Sun) | $

There are Dukes barbecues throughout South Carolina's Midlands, named for the Dukes family that opened the first of them in the 1950s. None are part of any sort of chain, but they all specialize in the barbecue meal that has become a culinary signature of the Palmetto State: the grand, hog-centered, all-you-can-eat buffet.

Pulled pork is a dazzling jumble of light and dark, soft and chewy meat that is slightly smoky and intensely piggy. It is wonderful with no adornment whatsoever, but South Carolina mustard sauce, bright and tangy-sweet, is oh-so-right. The buffet line includes a pan that is full of fried chicken parts, freshly fried extra-thick potato chips, and lots of little squiggles and ribbons of fried chicken skin that really do melt in your mouth.

Among the more than two dozen available side dishes are rice and hash (a savory pork-products stew), squash casserole, macaroni with yummy cheese impasto, hush puppies, fried okra, and deep-fried corn nuggets. Beyond the buffet is a separate table that holds white bread and a bin full of cracklins—large and small, chewy and melty, indescribably piggy. For dessert, choose from among warm peach cobbler that is as dense as bread pudding, cool banana pudding streaked with cookie crumbs, and that seldom-seen legacy of the 1970s, Watergate salad, which is a Frankenstein-green pistachio pudding that includes mini marshmallows and pineapple.

Dukes' phone number, by the way, can be dialed as 803-649-PORK.

EVO

evopizza.com
1075 E. Montague Ave.   843-225-1796
North Charleston, SC   L D | $$

While the Palmetto State is not famous as a source of great pizza, Lowcountry cooks are famously talented. And Evo—an acronym for "extra-virgin oven"—is evidence that those creative juices combined with local products and a wood-fired oven can equal outstanding pizza.

But before we get to the pizza, may we dally at hors d'oeuvres? . . . There's a peak-of-summer panzanella salad, starring big chunks of boomingly delicious heirloom tomatoes and significant house-made croutons along with pickled red onion, crumbles of creamy local blue cheese, and basil, all dressed with bright balsamic vinaigrette. For a simpler starter, you can get something called an olive plate. It is more than a plate. It is a big, fragrant bowlful of black and green ones—many dozens—along with a bunch of whole garlic cloves that have been roasted until they are soft and sweet, the gorgeous cornucopia marinated in oil rich with basil.

Now, about the pizza. Cooked briefly in a roaring wood-fired oven, it comes out with a crust that is thin and lightweight, easy to chew. Toppings range from basic margherita to such inventions as pistachio pesto topped with mozzarella (made here daily) and just enough crème fraîche to elevate the eating experience into wanton excess. We have enjoyed a special of locally made feta along with fresh okra and a purée of roasted garlic and corn as well as the oh-so-southern "pork trifecta" of house-made sausage, pepperoni, and smoked bacon.

For dessert, it is hard not to indulge in a sampler of Sweet Teeth brand chocolates (made by a former employee) that includes a salted caramel heart and a peach cobbler bonbon; but you should also consider reserving a significant amount of appetite for the outsized blueberry calzone—a pocket of pizza dough filled with dark chocolate melting around local blueberries and drizzled with South Carolina honey.

FISHNET SEAFOOD

3832 Savannah Hwy.   843-571-2423
Johns Island, SC   **L D** (closed Sun) | **$**

A fundamental rule for finding good things to eat while traveling is to look for restaurants located in former gas stations. We don't know why, but they're some of the best Roadfood stops. To wit: Fishnet Seafood. It isn't really a restaurant at all; it is a fish market with no tables, not even provisions for stand-up eating. But if you point to just about any fish in the house, the staff will bread it and fry it to order, and in this part of coastal South Carolina, cooks know how to fry things. Flounder is particularly wonderful, sheathed in a brittle gold crust, its sweet white meat dripping moisture. If you order it as a sandwich, you get one huge, falling-apart-tender fillet with two token slices of white bread: finger food, for sure!

Another fine dish is Jesus crab, which is the management's name for what other places refer to as devil crab. A woman behind the counter explained that the dish was simply too good to be named for the prince of darkness. Indeed, Fishnet is a very religious place, its décor featuring signs reminding guests of Jesus's ultimate importance. We've seen a lot of barbecues where religion is a fundamental aspect of the dining experience, but not so many seafood places. This is one where the original fisher of men is the star of the menu.

FREEMAN'S BAR-B-Q

1060 Sand Bar Ferry Rd.   803-827-1623
Beech Island, SC   **L D** (Thurs–Sat only) | **$$**

WEEKEND ONLY We have a friend who regularly drives along Sand Bar Ferry Road, and even when she does not have time to stop and eat at Freeman's Bar-B-Q, she slows the car and rolls down the windows just so she can inhale as she passes. She calls the beguiling aroma of hickory smoke and pork an "amuse-nez." In fact, smell is a key element in what makes James Freeman's barbecue outstanding. He says that he uses no thermometer, nor does he poke the meat to check resiliency. He inhales, and because he has been barbecuing long enough, his nose tells him exactly when it is done just right.

Whatever the alchemy, the results are incontestable. Chopped meat is a motley festival of creamy-sweet shreds and nuggets and long strips of smoke-haloed pork that need only the slightest application of house-made sauce to attain simple perfection. That's the way it is served—lightly sauced—and there is more of the pungent potion available in bottles. Heat-seeking diners can ask for extra-hot sauce, which is so ferocious that it is kept in back unless specifically requested.

The pork is available in a sandwich or on a platter. We like the latter, mostly because it is such a joy to fork through the beautiful meat, but also because platters come with side dishes, which are excellent. Hash on rice is notable for the fresh, luxurious nature of the hash, made with both beef and pork. Mac 'n' cheese is a comfort-food classic. Collard greens are fresh and forceful.

Dessert is the one menu item that Mr. Freeman does not make himself. Lemon pound cake comes from a local woman named Tricia. It is good cake, especially welcome as a tender final note after a meal of such kaleidoscopic flavors. Sweet-potato pie looks ordinary, but it is not. A citrus twist makes the earthy tubers glow.

GRITS & GROCERIES

gritsandgroceries.com

2440 Due West Hwy.   864-296-3316
Belton, SC   **L** (closed Sun & Mon) | **$**

Grits & Groceries is a sophisticated restaurant with ingenuous country charm. Because the proprietors earned their kitchen chops in New Orleans, many featured dishes have a Louisiana accent, such as pork steak with Creole gravy, a shrimp po' boy, and praline-crusted bacon. Among deep Dixie delights on the menu are a juicy pimento cheeseburger draped with bacon, okra fritters with corn relish (a Wednesday special), and an appetizer of crisp-fried spheres of country ham, pimento cheese, and cream cheese rolled in cornflakes and presented on a puddle of sweet-hot pepper jelly. If we have a problem with this place, it's that there are too many outstanding things on the menu to taste them all, even in multiple visits.

Dessert is as good as it gets. Banana pudding is loaded with cookies and topped with real whipped cream. Crisp-crusted fried apple pie is served warm, inducing ecstasy when sided by a scoop of house-made cinnamon ice cream. Chocolate Coca-Cola cake is moist and powerfully chocolaty. Other inviting sweets include coconut bread pudding, chocolate coconut cheesecake, peanut-butter crunch bread pudding, Acadian fig cake, and whiskey egg nog ice cream.

Befitting the country-crossroads setting, Grits & Groceries service is casual and friendly. Dine indoors or out on a covered patio. There's also a long picnic table out by the side of the road.

In addition to daily lunch, breakfast is served Friday and Saturday until 10:30 a.m. Dinner is served Thursday nights only.

HILLTOP CAFÉ

1130 S. Dixie Rd.   No phone
Salley, SC   **L** | **$**

The only decision to make when lunching at the Hilltop Café is whether you want pie or pudding for dessert. Everything that comes before that is preordained. Hattie Williams, owner and chef for more than twenty years, cooks a different meal every day, and that is the meal you will get. It might be pork roast or neck bones or meat loaf, and there's almost always fried chicken too, along with rice and gravy, collard greens, black-eyed peas, and, of course, a square of corn bread.

It's messy-looking food, all the more appetizing for the way savory gravy from the rice swirls into potlikker-soaked collard greens and the square of corn bread sops up juices from the thick, fork-tender slices of pork roast. The fried chicken is outstanding, its brightly seasoned crust balancing delectably between crunch and chew, the meat inside luxuriously moist.

The Hilltop Café is as ramshackle as a building can be, located at country crossroads with only a tiny placard outside reading "Hilltop." Business is cash only and, at $7 per meal, a tremendous bargain.

★ HITE'S BAR-B-QUE

hitesbbq.com

240 Dreher Rd.	803-794-4120
West Columbia, SC	L D (open only Fri & Sat)	$

WEEKEND ONLY John Hite began offering barbecue to the public in 1957. True to local custom, it was a weekend-only deal. Grandson David Hite continues that tradition: Whole hogs cooked the old-fashioned way—slowly, over hickory coals—are sold only on Friday and Saturday.

Here you find central South Carolina barbecue without frills or distractions. There aren't even tables other than a few picnic-style ones at the far edge of the parking lot. Everything is packed in Styrofoam to take and eat elsewhere. The menu is elementary: ribs, chopped meat, ham, chicken; side dishes: coleslaw and hash on rice. The best item in the house, when it is available (early in the day) is what's known as the rib cut. This is a massive cross-section of the smoke-cooked hog that includes luxuriously crisp skin, velvet-soft meat, and hefty spare ribs. In all Hite's meats, the duet of pork flavor and smoke is hard to improve, but there is sauce, and it too is classically South Carolinian: a tangy mustard-based emulsion that does a good job of haloing the sweet meat on which it's brushed.

Located a quarter mile from a crass commercial strip of Route 1, Hite's is another world: peaceful and out of the past. Generations of the Hite family live and work here, fish in the pond next to the picnic tables, and do an admirable job welcoming visitors and introducing them to the time-honored rituals of barbecue.

★ HOMINY GRILL

hominygrill.com

207 Rutledge Ave.	843-937-0930
Charleston, SC	B L D	$$

Our first meal at the Hominy Grill was breakfast, and it was spectacular. The sausage patties that came alongside our sunnyside-up eggs were rugged and crusty and brilliantly spiced—a joy when pushed through some yolk or sandwiched inside a tall biscuit. Bacon was excellent too—double-thick, crisp, and full-flavored, just begging to be cosseted in that biscuit or eaten in alternating mouthfuls of smooth-textured grits. A great breakfast option, even if a bit biscuit-redundant, is house-made bread, either pumpkin-ginger or banana-nut, both of which are moist, full-flavored, and elegant.

We were equally impressed when we returned for lunch and plowed into thick shrimp gumbo and Brunswick stew. We love the distinctly southern BLT made with crunchy discs of fried green tomato. Buttermilk pie is the perfect dessert, surpassed only by what we both agree is the best chocolate pudding anywhere. And did we mention caramel layer cake, the hugely wonderful Charleston fave?

The Hominy Grill building was at one time a barber shop, and striped poles still flank the inside of the front door. It's a spacious room with an old stamped tin ceiling, wood-slat walls, and slow-spinning fans overhead. There also is an outdoor patio. You can expect to wait for a table, especially on weekends. It is no secret that this place serves some of the best Lowcountry food anywhere, and at very reasonable prices.

HOT DOG CAFE

605 Spartanburg Hwy.	864-439-3647
South Lyman, SC	L D (closed Sun)	$

South Carolina is not one of the great hot-dog states, but wiener lovers should know about the Hot Dog Cafe. This merry stand serves Dixie dog classics. The franks themselves are nothing special: basic porky pink tube steaks presented in steamed-soft buns. But add meaty chili and sweet slaw and you have a package that is better than the sum of its parts. The ultimate variation, known as a Dump Dog, gets not only chili and slaw but also mayonnaise, mustard, ketchup, chopped onion, and shredded cheese.

Do not ignore hamburgers at the Hot Dog Cafe. They are large, hand-formed patties, thick enough to be plenty juicy even if they are cooked through. All condiments known to mankind are available, including that combo of slaw and chili.

French fries are a must. Raw, skin-on potatoes are cut one by one on a vintage potato slicer and tossed directly into boiling oil. The result is fries with a full spuddy flavor, albeit lacking the crunch of ones that have been chilled and twice-fried.

Do consider dessert. A sign on the wall above the counter advertises Hot Moon Pie—a simple idea, and a good one. The pie is removed from its wrapper and put into the same steam cabinet used to heat buns. The marshmallow inside the Moon Pie doesn't quite liquefy, but it softens, as do the cookie layers, and the dark chocolate coat develops an inviting oily sheen.

HYMAN'S SEAFOOD

hymanseafood.com

215 Meeting St.   843-723-6000
Charleston, SC   **L D** | $$

What we didn't eat one evening at Hyman's Seafood: amberjack, cod, flounder, mahi, mako, monkfish, snapper, hokie, salmon, tilapia, trout, tuna, and black drum. Those were the fish of the day on the blackboard, and below them were grouper, stuffed wahoo, and fried lobster tails, which we didn't sample either. Local oysters were coming in and available on the half shell or fried, and we didn't even have appetite enough for them. The point is that Hyman's has a big, big menu—mostly seafood, with a few token meats and pastas—and it's a little frustrating to pass up so many good things.

What we *did* have was swell: she-crab soup that is ridiculously thick, rich as cream sauce itself and loaded with meat; a broad dish with thirty steamed spiced shrimp; and a house specialty, crispy flounder. This is one large, beautiful fish that has been scored in a diamond pattern and broiled so the fork-sized sections of meat get a crusty edge and seem to virtually lift off the bone: one of the East Coast's top fish-eating experiences.

Hyman's is a tremendously popular place, frequented by tourists and locals alike. If you're looking for a romantic restaurant or an undiscovered hole in the wall, Charleston and vicinity have plenty, but for large-party ambience and impeccable local seafood, Hyman's is a good choice.

★ JACKIE HITE'S BAR-B-QUE

460 E. Railroad Ave.   803-532-3354
Leesville, SC   **L** (Weds–Sun) | $

Jackie Hite's is now in its fourth decade, using the cooking methods that Jackie learned from his father. A meal here, served in an unassuming building next to the railroad tracks, reflects South Carolina Midlands–style barbecue in all its glory.

Whole hogs are cooked slowly over hickory coals, their smoke-perfumed meat chopped and pulled into hunks of ham, loin, shoulder, and ribs and laid out on a buffet. The sauce is tangy mustard, although much of this meat, the loin especially, is so succulent that sauce is only an afterthought. Barbecued chicken, on the other hand, benefits tremendously from a mustard sauce that has a sweeter tone than the sauce customarily applied to pork. (A vinegar-pepper sauce also is available.)

In addition to smoke-pit meats, here you can eat buttery hash atop Carolina rice, weekend fried chicken that is toasty comfort food, bacon-sopped beans, black-eyed peas, potato salad, slaw as rich as cream, and also kitschy pastel puddings for dessert.

Jackie Hite's is open only for lunch. Friday is the best day to come, for that is pig-pull day, when in addition to the more familiar meats, the buffet contains patches of skin. Because the hog is mopped with a salt mix as it cooks, the semi-charred skin absorbs briny smack that combines with its inherent fatty luxury to create crunchy melt-in-the-mouth morsels: divine swine!

★ JUNIPER

640 E. Main St.   803-685-7547
Ridge Spring, SC   **L D** (dinner Thurs–Sat only)
                          (closed Wed) | $$

Juniper defies pigeonholes. You can come for lunch and enjoy a dandy sandwich of tuna salad or ham and Swiss along with sweet tea and a slice of chocolate cake. Cost? About $10. Or you can come on a weekend evening for glazed quail atop stone-ground grits under a crown of flash-fried collard greens, along with an amuse-bouche or two, and pay a good $30, plus the cost of wine.

Whether dining on bare, chrome-banded kitchenette tables or on the white cloths that are laid across them for evening meals, Juniper's customers can count on a few consistent values: the provender is local, the recipes are southern, and the meals are delicious.

Southern, yes. Southern at its finest. Grits, for instance, are far from the white cereal that all too often is a perfunctory side dish. Juniper's grits are dense and creamy, butter-rich, and absolutely wonderful with no adornment whatever. Add red-eye gravy or side them with a couple of the chef's excellent crab cakes or top them with spicy shrimp and they become the best supporting player imaginable. (These are Adluh brand grits, stone-ground over in Columbia since 1900.)

From corn chowder at the beginning of a meal to maple-bourbon pecan pie at the end, every item served in this place bears the mark of a kitchen that is at once respectful of tradition but also adamantly creative. A few other menu faves: Monday meat loaf made using Yon Farms beef from just up the road, crab-stuffed southern fried chicken, and a fine house salad loaded with smoky bacon and glistening with blue cheese vinaigrette.

Always, always reserve some appetite for dessert. The cakes are not to be missed, especially Italian cream cake and caramel layer cake.

THE KINGSMAN
thekingsmanrestaurant.com
936 Axtell Dr.   803-796-8622
Cayce, SC   **L D** (closed Sun) | **$**

The Kingsman is a locally loved meat-and-three café that serves what might be the best pimento cheeseburger anywhere. It is listed on the menu as the Palmetto: ten ounces of ruggedly ground rib eye hand-formed into a tremendously succulent mound, grilled, and put into an enormous bun along with a massive amount of rich pimento cheese, thick strips of bacon, and crisp-fried chips of jalapeño pepper. It is huge just like that, but even better when dressed to the nines with mayonnaise, mustard, lettuce, tomato, onion, and pickle chips. A "regular" pimento

cheeseburger made with six ounces of ground Angus beef also is available, and it's very good, if not in the stellar league of the rib-eye-rich Palmetto.

LA CANTINA
lacantinaclarkshill.com
1750 Garrett Rd.   864-333-5315
Clarks Hill, SC   **D** (Fri & Sat only) | **$$$**

WEEKEND ONLY Open only two nights a week, with reservations essential and the cost of a full meal in the $50 range, La Cantina is hardly a typical Roadfood restaurant. It is not a typical restaurant of any kind. When we first were told about it, we were scared off. Rusty Lindberg—proprietor, host, and chef—is known to put on puppet shows after dinner, or to sing the songs he writes. Ummm, maybe not, thanks.

Finally, we relented, and were guided there by friends Rose Lee Hayes and David Stinson. They suggested we eat early to avoid any possible after-dinner entertainment (they're grouchy like us), which we did. And lo, we were rendered rapt by four-star steaks. Seated on the outdoor patio, we watched chef Rusty cook the meat in a dramatic fashion. Slid into a 1,800-degree wood-burning *horno* (oven) on iron skillets that rest directly upon red-hot logs, sirloins are enveloped in flame for no more than a couple of minutes, emerging in a swirl of smoke that sends red-meat perfume wafting over the tables. They are beautiful steaks with crusty, blackened edges that shore in tidal waves of succulence.

Beyond the steaks (which are available topped with pico de gallo or shrimp), menu highlights include almond-crusted herbed salmon; Lamb Istanbul, seasoned with rosemary, garlic, and tamarind; a lavish Seafood Macarhena that includes shrimp, chicken, and sausage; and an immense, almond-crusted chicken breast stuffed with house-made herbed cheese and presented atop a bed of pasta with potent marinara sauce.

La Cantina is in the middle of nowhere: a surreal (and very delicious) dining adventure.

MARTHA LOU'S KITCHEN

marthalouskitchen.com

1068 Morrison Dr. 843-577-9583
Charleston, SC **L D** (closed Sun) | **$**

We have driven past Martha Lou's Kitchen a few times when it was supposed to be open, but was not, so we suggest calling ahead. Persistence will pay off, for this place is a gem in the rough. The word "casual" doesn't begin to describe how casual it is. The window air-conditioning unit is propped up by a pepper dispenser; framed encomia from the press hung helter-skelter on the walls have not recently been dusted; a television is tuned to an evangelical station to which no one pays attention. And yet Debra Gadsden, who runs the place with her mother, Martha Lou, greets customers with genuine hospitality offered by few formal maître d's.

Debra guides newcomers through a menu that includes fried chicken every day and such specials as fried fish, pork chops, ribs, and chitterlings. Sides are Lowcountry paragons: mac 'n' cheese, red rice and white rice, collard greens, lima beans, okra soup, and corn bread.

Subtlety is not Martha Lou's culinary signature. Everything she cooks is boldly flavored. Even iced tea is supersweet and superlemony. Mac 'n' cheese is less comfort food than exciting food, the creamy cheese vibrant with pepper punch. The crust on fried chicken and fish is big-flavored salty; okra soup smacks you with a one-two punch of tomatoes and okra. Bread pudding, chockablock with fruit cocktail, is as sweet as candy.

We liked our first lunch in this place so much that we returned the next day. Debra offered suggestions of what we ought to eat so that we would get a full taste of her mother's skills, and she led us to one of the other tables so that this day's meal would provide a fresh point of view.

MIDDLETON PLACE RESTAURANT

middletonplace.org

4300 Ashley River Rd. 843-556-6020
Charleston, SC **L D** | **$$$**

It costs a lot of money to have lunch at the Middleton Place Restaurant: You easily can spend $20 for the food, plus you will pay $28 just to get on the grounds where the restaurant is located. It is part of a vast interpretive environment built on the plantation that once was the home of Henry Middleton, president of the First Continental Congress. If you have a taste for Colonial history, the cost of admission is money well spent, providing access to sweeping terraces, gardens, walks, and artificial lakes that proffer beauty from a bygone age. Attractions include "Eliza's House," a freedman's dwelling that shows what life was like for African Americans who stayed on the plantation after the Civil War, and the stable yards where blacksmiths, potters, and coopers demonstrate their eighteenth-century skills. Mounted trail rides (right past sneaky-looking alligators) are available at the nearby Equestrian Center, and the mansion itself is full of priceless antique furniture.

The restaurant is very much part of the effort to honor the Lowcountry's cultural heritage. When it opened as a tearoom run by the Junior League in 1928, its specialties were okra soup and sandwiches. In more recent times, southern cook Edna Lewis came on board with recipes that provide a sampler of beguiling southern specialties. We don't know any other restaurant in town that continues to serve Charleston's own Huguenot torte, a sticky-gooey apple dessert that is something like cobbler, but more intense. Peanut soup, thickened with sweet potatoes, is smooth and smoky, the earthy duet becoming a single note rather than two. Even the more ordinary dishes tend to be extraordinarily good. Fried chicken is hugged by thin buttermilk batter that is radiant with spice, its skin succulence incarnate. Greens are totally tender, not limp but pungent with tonic punch. Pulled-pork barbecue—smoke-cooked on premises—has simple authenticity that puts it right up there with South Carolina's best.

The dining room overlooks green grass and grazing sheep.

NORTHGATE SODA SHOP

northgatesodashop.com

918 N. Main St.   864-235-6770
Greenville, SC   **B L D** (closed Sun) | $

An atmospheric relic from the heyday of soda fountain dining, this eatery is a neighborhood experience where regulars enter, wave to old friends, and easily drop into conversations among staff and customers seated at the counter or at a scattering of bare-top tables.

We originally came for the well-respected pimento cheeseburger, which is a handsome package dressed with lettuce and tomato. The hand-formed burger has a fresh, meaty savor, even if it is cooked through. Overcooking is a nonissue, thanks to the liquid luxury of smooth, melting pimento cheese piled on top.

Fried bologna fanciers will delight in what is called the Cincinnati steak—a thick, griddle-cooked round of spicy pink meat adorned with cheese, fried onions, and a spill of meaty (beanless), slightly sweet chili. Another dandy package is the slaw dog: a spicy little frankfurter, chunky beef chili, and creamy-sweet coleslaw all piled into a spongy bun.

If there's a caramel cake on the counter, you want a slice. We counted twelve thin layers of cake and frosting.

PEACHES 'N' SUCH

3771 Hwy. 23   803-685-5838
Monetta, SC   **B L D** | $

Peaches 'N' Such is a roadside stand with a huge inventory of peach products from the orchards that surround it. When strawberries are in season, beautiful baskets of them are sold here; asparagus is another local crop that is sold picked-that-morning fresh in the spring. Peaches 'N' Such also is a wonderful place to have a meal. A limited menu of sandwiches, plus daily special entrees with down-home vegetables to match can be enjoyed on premises at picnic tables indoors and, weather permitting, outside. Breakfast also is available, including such delights as peach bread French toast with warm peach syrup.

There's always a burger of the week, and Friday is fried chicken day. It's terrific fried chicken. Pieces of indulgently moist meat are hugged by a seasoned crust poised perfectly between crunch and chew, oozing its own full-flavored juices with every bite. On the side, we love the broccoli casserole, a country classic that presents well-cooked stalks and florets in a melted web of chewy orange cheese and bread crumbs. Butter beans are simple and al dente with real legume earthiness. Another fine vegetable is fried eggplant, nuggets of the vegetable turned ethereal inside a frail jacket of salty breading.

Desserts include red velvet cake, triple-layer Neapolitan cake, and hummingbird cake. That last one is a Dixie delight loaded with bananas and pineapple. Peach cobbler is huge and indulgent. And, of course, there is smooth, soft-serve peach ice cream.

RAY'S DINER

3110 Two Notch Rd.   803-661-8175
Columbia, SC   **B L; D** (Weds-Sat) | $

Breakfast at Ray's presents a dilemma: hash browns or grits? Starch redundancy aside, both must be savored. The hash browns are irregularly sized nuggets of potato laced with onions and cooked on a flat-top aged enough to impart profound hash-house soul. They come off the grill with crunchy edges and tender centers—magnificent potatoes!

The grits are billed on the menu as creamy grits, and they are. No wishy-washy side dish, they are a stout cereal, fully satisfying plain and even more so when augmented with melty cheese.

To go with grits and hash browns, Ray's offers beautiful omelets. They are large and fluffy, the sunny eggs just-right soft, the ingredients of choice piled in and atop the great yellow crescent in abundance. There's also a handsome chicken-fried steak with a choice of white or brown gravy, and decent pancakes too.

Lunch is a whole other story, and a very good one. It's meat-and-three with a soul-food edge, featuring vegetables such as squash casserole, collard greens, fried okra, candied yams, and braised cabbage to accompany smothered or fried chicken, fish fillets, or smoked sausage. We were less impressed by the somewhat pedestrian pies than by the kitchen's stout banana pudding.

Ray's is a charming place in its spare urban way, located in a strip of three stores that also includes Auto Zone and Heavenly Hands Hair Studio. Returning customers (who seem to be about 90 percent of Ray's business) are greeted by waitress Stacy, who knows exactly what they want, and newcomers are greeted by either Stacy or Vernell, the lunch chef, who makes sure they order whatever is especially good that day.

ROCKAWAY ATHLETIC CLUB

2719 Rosewood Dr.   803-256-1075
Columbia, SC   L D | $$

Don't worry, you will not work up a sweat when you visit the Rockaway Athletic Club, which regulars know as Rockaway's. It's not a club; it's a pub, and although there is a full menu of sandwiches, salads, and fried seafood, the Roadfood headliner is a pimento cheeseburger. Columbia is supposedly where this delightful southern gloss on the cheeseburger was created (sometime in the 1960s), so it is fitting that they make a big deal of it here. The burger is a big, rugged hunk of beef smothered with the grated Cheddar–mayo mix dotted with countless bits of red pepper that is, make no mistake, about zero on the Scoville scale. In other words, the pepper has flavor but virtually no heat. The standard configuration includes lettuce, tomato, raw onion (grilled onions are available), mayonnaise, and a few pickle chips on the side. Crinkle-cut French fries are swell, available plain and crisp or smothered with pimento cheese, which turns them into delicious mush.

You might have a hard time finding this place because there is no sign on Rosewood Drive to let passersby know they have arrived. There is a very tiny sign in back at the entrance to the parking lot.

SCOTT'S BAR-B-QUE

thescottsbbq.com
2734 Hemingway Hwy.   843-558-0134
Hemingway, SC   L D (Weds–Sat) | $

Whole-hog pork, cooked all night over smoldering oak and hickory coals, is pulled into shreds and served with hunks of pig skin and servings of peppery, just-barely-sweet sauce for dipping. Two kinds of skin are available—either fried to a crisp or stripped off the hog, the latter as chewy as they are crunchy. White bread comes alongside, and you can get boiled peanuts for munching. Chicken and steak, also slow-smoked, are sometimes available.

Founded in 1972 by Ella and Rosie (short for Roosevelt) Scott, and now presided over by the Scotts' son, Rodney, this much-loved local place was anointed as authentic by the national press a few years ago and thereafter declared itself world-famous. Add to the fame Scott's proximity to Myrtle Beach and the result is big crowds, especially on weekends. Tourists notwithstanding, the meal on the plate and the place itself are the real deal.

SEEWEE RESTAURANT

4808 US 17 N.   843-928-3609
Awendaw, SC   L D | $$

A former grocery north of Charleston along US 17, SeeWee is now a hugely popular restaurant that includes an outdoor patio for alfresco dining. It still looks a bit like a roadside store—shelves stocked with supplies, higgledy-piggledy décor of nautical bibelots.

Daily specials are chalked up on a board: country-fried steak, whole catfish, Jamaican jerk chicken, Buffalo shrimp or oysters (fried in a spicy Buffalo-wing style), fish stew by the cup or bowl. We are partial to the regular menu and its roster of fried seafood. You can get a platter or a sandwich with very good extra-large French fries and coleslaw on the side. Our shrimp were snapping-firm and veiled in a fine, crisp crust.

One of the great only-in-the-South meals to get here is an all-"vegetable" plate. Choose four from a list of more than a dozen available, including such local likes as red rice, butter beans, fried squash, fried okra, and rice and gravy. We went for fried green tomatoes (deliciously al dente with a tangy smack), sweet-potato casserole (super spicy), mac 'n' cheese (dense and thick with cheese), and collard greens (salty, oily, luxurious).

As you walk into the restaurant you will see a shelf of the day's layer cakes, and desserts are listed on a blackboard. When we saw chocolate cake with peanut butter icing, we knew we had to have a piece. So we ordered it as we ordered lunch. The cake came before the meal. "I cut this for you because I was worried there wouldn't be any left by the time you were ready," our waitress kindly explained as she set it down with our sweet teas. We are so grateful she was watching out for us, because this cake was superb . . . as was our caramel layer cake and goober pie.

No bill arrives after the meal. When you're done eating, the waitress will instruct you to go up to the cash register and tell the man your table number. He's got your check and will tally it up and get you squared away.

SGT. WHITE'S

1908 Boundary St.   843-522-2029
Beaufort, SC   L D | $

Upon entering this little restaurant, you are faced with the steam table from which the server puts together your plate. While it is possible to order off a menu—and the fried chicken and shrimp therefrom are excellent—we cannot resist the array of barbecue and side dishes in the trays. You get either pulled pork, which is a medley of velvet-soft shreds from inside and crunchy strips from the outside of the roast bathed in the Sergeant's brilliant tangy-sweet sauce, or ribs, which are crusty and unspeakably luscious, also caked with the good sauce. Each side dish is a super-soulful rendition of a southern classic: smothered cabbage richer than ham itself, broccoli gobbed with cheese, brilliantly seasoned red rice, a vivid mix of collard and turnip greens, *real* mashed potatoes, candied yams, and so on. A normal meal is one meat and two sides, served with a block of corn bread. Even that corn bread is extraordinary: rugged-textured and sweet as cake.

SHEALY'S BAR-B-QUE

shealysbbq.com
340 E. Columbia Ave.   803-532-8135
Leesville, SC   L D (closed Weds & Sun) | $

We found out about Shealy's thanks to tipster Paul McCravy, who wrote that "the vegetables surpass any I've had at the three family reunions I attend each year in Pickens County." Greens and beans, boiled, fried, and mashed, served plain and in elaborate casseroles—the array of vegetables is awesome. And they are merely the side dishes to outstanding fried chicken with cream gravy, including pulley bones for those who are feeling lucky.

For us, the main attraction is pork barbecue, which is presented at the buffet with all the folderol of a traditional South Carolina barbecue feast, meaning you will find just about every part of the pig from the rooter to the tooter. That includes meat, ribs, hash, skin, gravy, and a rather bizarre creamy/spicy mush apparently quite popular in these parts known as liver nips. Of special interest on the tender shreds of smoked pork is Shealy's sauce (available by the bottle), an alluring mustard-tinged sweet-and-sour condiment unique to the South Carolina Midlands.

SOUTHSIDE SMOKEHOUSE

southsidesmokehouse.com
726 S. Howard Ave.   864-457-4581
Landrum, SC   L D (closed Sun) | $$

Since they were invented at the Dairy Bar of Columbia, South Carolina, in the early 1960s, pimento cheeseburgers have become a signature dish of the Palmetto State. The Southside Smokehouse takes the concept to a higher plane not only by topping its juice-laden meat patty with pimento cheese (plus onion, lettuce, and mayo) and putting it in a brioche bun, but also by bedding it on a couple of discs of crisp-fried green tomato.

As its name suggests, the Southside Smokehouse is at heart a barbecue parlor—a good one, for sure. Pulled pork is soft and radiant with sweet pig flavor, succulent ribs are served by the rack or half-rack, pork hash over rice (a South Carolina passion) is always available, and there is even barbecue salad: cabbage, cheese, onion, peppers, and tomato adorned with your choice of smoke-cooked pulled pork or chicken.

The Southside Smokehouse may look like an extra-large double-wide mobile home, but it is, in fact, a colorful and creative restaurant. Chef Sarah McClure (daughter of proprietor Robbie McClure) is all about diversity, using whatever local vegetables are available and offering specials that range from lamb pizzette topped with caramelized onions and pomegranate to brandy-laced she-crab soup, catfish tacos, and flat-iron steak with green herb chimichurri sauce. She's happy to accommodate vegetarians, vegans, and those intolerant of gluten.

If you dine at the Southside Smokehouse in summer at the height of peach season, you'll have an opportunity to dig into the kitchen's outstanding grilled pound cake topped with crisp pecans and slices of incredibly flavorful fresh peaches, a dreamy conclusion to a hugely satisfying meal.

SUMMERTON DINER

33 S. Church St.	803-485-6835
Summerton, SC	**B L D** (closed Thurs) | $

Since Lois Hughes opened it for business in 1967, this little café on the outskirts of town has been a favorite of locals and a beacon for travelers along I-95. After Lois's daughter Lynelle Blackwell took over in 1987, she enlarged and remodeled it, but the diner has the feel of an ageless eatery: well-worn Formica counter, blond wood-paneled walls, each table set with bottles of hot vinegar peppers for brightening up orders of collard greens.

There's a full menu, and such items as fried chicken or steak and quail are always available, but at lunchtime the thing to order is the special. For well under $10, you get an entree, three vegetables, dessert, and tea, plus corn bread and biscuits. We love baked chicken supreme, which is crusty and fallapart tender; the waitress asks if you want white or dark meat. Like all entrees, it comes on a partitioned plate along with two of the vegetables. (The third vegetable comes in its own bowl.) As you might expect in a true-South café such as this, the side dishes are superb: earthy fresh rutabagas, spicy stewed apples, porky

sweet greens with an al dente oomph to their leaves, mashed potatoes blanketed in gorgeous, beef-shred gravy, hefty blocks of mac 'n' cheese with crusty edges and creamy insides, rice infused with soulful gravy. Et cetera!

TRACK KITCHEN

420 Mead Ave.	803-641-9628
Aiken, SC	**B** (closed in summer) | $

--★--
LOCALS
LOVE IT
--★--

To the side of a rutted red-dirt road, Track Kitchen is a café in an old wood-frame building. It barely looks open for business. Inside, the menu is written with marking pen on a board above the order counter and tables are unceremoniously lined up like in a mess hall. If you want coffee, go back to the kitchen, grab a mug, and pour your own. Into this extremely humble dining room come trainers, riders, owners, and aficionados of some of the finest horseflesh on Earth. Aiken has long been a vacation destination for the horsey set—until 1954 train service direct from New York served wintering horses, horse owners, and their staff—and this is where a large number of them come for breakfast. If you get here much after 8 a.m., when it opens, most seats will be occupied by people who all seem to know one another and table-hop continuously.

Everybody is friends with Carol Carter, who runs the place with her husband, Pockets. (Pockets used to be a groom for King Ranch horses.) Carol commands the kitchen and does all the cooking. There is no fast food here: Service is deliberate, and you can be sure that each plate that comes from the kitchen is scrupulously prepared. Even the simplest meal of bacon and over-easy eggs gleams with that buttery, good-cook luster that makes the yolks taste extra sunny and the baked bacon break just right. Pancakes are fluffy, omelets are cooked through but never dried out, and country ham is a big, fibrous slab that requires (and rewards) serious chewing.

The restaurant is named because about twenty-five yards behind it is a training track where thoroughbreds are exercised. If you like watching these athletes work out, it's a great bonus of eating here.

TRIANGLE RESTAURANT

335 Lee St.   803-275-0034
Johnston, SC   **L D** | $$

A jaunty architectural legacy of mid-twentieth-century Populuxe design, the Triangle is, in fact, triangular. In back at the triangle's hypotenuse, there's a Monday through Friday lunchtime cafeteria with a meat-and-three menu featuring southern classics from fried chicken to vegetable casseroles to Watergate salad (a green ambrosia variant). Up front at the triangle's point is a whole separate restaurant, a dinner-only, table-service operation where steaks star. Filet mignon, sirloins, and a broad "John's rib eye" are grilled on a flat-top, developing savory skin with delectable crunch at its edges. On the side come French fries, sweet potato fries, or a foil-wrapped baked potato, plus a dinner roll that has been well lubricated and grilled to a crisp.

Homemade cakes are cut into big, happy slices, the repertoire including red velvet, Key lime, coconut, and the Dixie fave, hummingbird, as well as strawberry shortcake. They're not sophisticated, but they will make a sweet tooth very happy.

TRUE BBQ

true-bbq.com

1237 D Ave.   803-791-9950
West Columbia, SC   **L D** (Wed–Sat) | $

The sign outside advertises "Best hash & rice in SC." If that claim is accurate, True BBQ probably could boast of the best hash and rice on Earth, since South Carolina is the only state where hash and rice is a common and significant menu item at nearly every place that slow-smokes swine. It is a side dish that comes with just about every meal: white rice topped with a finely chopped gravy made from the lowlier parts of the hog, but in some ways the most deliciously piggy—slightly sweet, a little bit tangy, a seductive food that both appeases and teases the appetite.

Along with the likes of collard greens, mac 'n' cheese, and baked beans, hash and rice is just one companion to well-crafted meats cooked in a smoker right in front of the restaurant. Available in large and small sizes, dinner choices include baby-back ribs and spare ribs, hacked-up pork, chicken, pork chops, and turkey wings. No matter which meat you get, we suggest first tasting it as it comes. It needs no sauce. On the other hand, the three sauces True BBQ serves are intriguing: Sexy Lady, which is tomato-based; Pretty Lady, which has a mustard twang; and Vinegar Red.

WILDFLOUR PASTRY

wildflourpastrycharleston.com

73 Spring St.   843-327-2621
Charleston, SC   **B L** | $

Roadfood pathfinders Chris Ayers and Amy Breisch told us that the one thing we mustn't miss when visiting WildFlour Pastry was the sticky bun. We *did* miss it because baker Lauren Mitterer makes sticky buns only on Sunday. But after morning visits on Wednesday and Thursday, we hardly feel deprived. We ate what may be the best turnover anywhere—a fine, flaky pastry, served warm, radiant with butter flavor, and filled with a mix of Nutella and fresh raspberries. Lauren's coffee cake muffin is packed with crunchy pecan halves; her raspberry scone strikes an ideal biscuity balance of savory and sweet; and her red velvet cupcake should be a lesson for lesser bakers who try their hand at the red velvet fad but wind up with duds.

Traveling gourmands intent on tasting the most different dishes will love WildFlour because so many of the specialties are offered in single-serving sizes. Not just cupcakes and morning pastries, but lemon chess tarts, Key lime pies, milk chocolate crème brûlée, and passion-fruit pot de crème. Lauren's whole repertoire is not available every day, but count on enough selections to sate the most voracious appetite.

THE WRECK
wreckrc.com
106 Haddrell St.   843-884-0052
Mount Pleasant, SC   **D** | **$$**

The docks at Shem Creek in Mount Pleasant, just north of the city, are lined with seafood restaurants, all quite pleasant-looking and with similar shoreline menus; but if you meander farther along the water, out Live Oak Road to Haddrell Point, you will find a Roadfood jewel in the rough. And we do mean *find*, for the restaurant known as the Wreck (formally named the Wreck of the Richard and Charlene, for a boat hit by Hurricane Hugo) has no sign outside, and we also mean *in the rough*, for it is located in a former bait locker, and décor is mostly piles of cardboard beer cartons. Seats are plastic lawn chairs at tables clothed with fish-wrapping paper (but romantically lit by candles at night). If the weather is cool, you are warmed by a couple of fireplaces in the concrete-floored dining room. The view of docked shrimp trawlers couldn't be more appetizing. And the food is impeccable.

Place your order by using a marking pen to circle what you want on the paper menu. Meals begin with a bowl of soft-boiled peanuts. She-crab soup is served in the traditional manner with a shot of sherry to pour on top just before spooning in. Then come crunchy fried shrimp, scallops, oysters, or broiled fish accompanied by zesty slaw and tubular hush puppies. Depending on your appetite, you can get a meal either "Richard-sized" (copious) or "Charlene-sized" (normal portion). Everything is presented on cardboard plates with plastic utensils; beer comes in the bottle. Dessert is a choice of Key lime pie, Key lime bread pudding, or banana pudding.

If you are a fish frowner, the Wreck offers London broil. However, the menu warns, "This is a seafood house claiming no expertise in the preparation of red meat. So, when you order red meat it is yours . . . No returns!!!!!"

MIDWEST

MINNESOTA

WISCONSIN

IOWA

MOORHEAD
M&H Restaurant

PARKERS PRAIRIE
Chet's Lakeside Inn

ANOKA
Swedish Crown Bakery

GRAND MARAIS
World's Best Donuts

TWO HARBORS
Betty's Pies

DULUTH
Northern Waters Smokehaus

BAYFIELD
Maggie's

SUPERIOR
Anchor Bar

FISH CREEK
White Gull Inn

LINDSTROM
Lindstrom Bakery

ROSEVILLE
Maverick's

BLAINE
Carol's

ST. PAUL
Bread & Chocolate
Cafe Latté
Tavern On Grand

COLUMBIA HEIGHTS
Johnson's Bacon and Egg Cafe

MINNEAPOLIS
Al's Breakfast
★ Hell's Kitchen
Matt's Bar
Pumphouse Creamery

STOCKHOLM
★ Stockholm Pie Company

GREEN BAY
Chili John's

MANITOWOC
Beernsten's Confectionary

SHEBOYGAN
Charcoal Inn

EDINA
Convention Grill

WINONA
Bloedow Bakery

PLAIN
Ring's Bar

WHITEFISH BAY
Jack Pandl's Whitefish Bay Inn

PIPESTONE
★ Lange's Cafe

MASON CITY
Birdsall's Ice Cream Co.

MADISON
Plaza Tavern

RACINE
Bendtsen's Bakery

LE MARS
Archie's Waeside
★ Bob's Drive-Inn

ST. OLAF
St. Olaf Tap

DUNLAP
Dairy Sweet

SIOUX CITY
Miles Inn
Milwaukee Wiener House
Tastee Inn & Out

AUDUBON
The Chatterbox

HAMLIN
Darrell's Place

AMES
Grove Cafe

DeWITT
TC's Point After

MILWAUKEE
Benji's
Jake's
Jo's Café
Klinger's East
Kopp's Custard
★ Leon's
Mazo's
★ McBob's
Mr. Perkins' Family Restaurant
Real Chili
★ Solly's Grille
Speed Queen
Three Brothers

ELK HORN
Larsen's Pub

SULLY
★ Coffee Cup Cafe

WILTON
Wilton Candy Kitchen

DES MOINES
B&B Grocery
Bauder Pharmacy
Iowa Machine Shed
Jesse's Embers
Mr. Bibbs
Smitty's Tenderloin Shop

EXIRA
The Red Barn

OTTUMWA
Canteen Lunch in the Alley

PELLA
In't Veld's Meat Market

EAGLE HARBOR
The Jampot

LAURIUM
Toni's Country Kitchen

HOUGHTON
Suomi Home Bakery & Restaurant

MARQUETTE
Crossroads Lounge
★ Jean Kay's

ISHPEMING
Lawry's Pasty Shop
Ralph's Italian Deli

NEGAUNEE
Irontown Pasties

TRENARY
Trenary Home Bakery

BREVORT
Gustafson's

MICHIGAN

BEULAH
★ The Cherry Hut

TRAVERSE CITY
Don's Drive-In

DETROIT
Johnny's Ham King
Lafayette Coney Island

PARMA
Little Polish Diner
Perla Homemade Delights
State Meats

LUDINGTON
Bortell's Fisheries

ANN ARBOR
★ Krazy Jim's Blimpy Burger
Northside Grill
Zingerman's Deli

CLEVELAND
Balaton
Slyman's Restaurant
Sokolowski's University Inn

GRAND RAPIDS
Yesterdog

LANSING

CONNEAUT
White Turkey
Drive-In

SANDUSKY
New Sandusky
Fish Company

INDEPENDENCE
Babushka's Kitchen

SCHERERVILLE
Teibel's

MIDDLEBURY
Village Inn

CUYAHOGA FALLS
Cathedral Buffet
Flury's Cafe

FORT WAYNE
Coney Island Wiener

AKRON
New Era Restaurant
Swensons

NORTH MANCHESTER
Mr. Dave's

BARBERTON
★ Al's Corner
Restaurant
Belgrade Gardens
White House Chicken

INDIANAPOLIS
Hollyhock Hill
John's Famous Stew
King Ribs Bar-B-Q
Mug 'n' Bun
Nick's Chili Parlor
Shapiro's
Workingman's Friend

HUNTINGTON
★ Nick's Kitchen

WEST LIBERTY
Liberty Gathering Place

WALDO
G&R Tavern

ANDERSON
Lemon Drop

URBANA
Crabill's

COLUMBUS

MOORESVILLE
★ Gray Brothers Cafeteria

DAYTON
The Pine Club

WEST JEFFERSON
★ Henry's

YELLOW SPRINGS
Young's Jersey Dairy

CANTON
Kennedy's Bar-B-Que
Taggarts Ice Cream

STARLIGHT
Joe Huber's

CINCINNATI
Aglamesis Bros.
Avril-Bleh & Sons
★ Camp Washington Chili Parlor
Eckerlin Meats
Hathaway's Coffee Shop
Price Hill Chili
Putz's Creamy Whip
Tucker's

OHIO

INDIANA

CHICAGO
Al's #1 Italian Beef
Byron's Hot Dog Haus
Corned Beef Factory
Doughnut Vault
Garrett Popcorn Shop
Harry Caray's
Hoosier Mama Pie Company
Lem's
Manny's
Mr. Beef
★ Superdawg
Vienna Beef Café
The Wiener's Circle

DES PLAINES
Paradise Pup

ELMWOOD PARK
★ Johnnie's

SKOKIE
● Poochie's

CICERO
Freddy's Pizza

RIVER GROVE
Gene & Jude's

MOLINE
Lagomarcino's

LADD
★ Rip's
Torri's Ice Cream Parlor

OTTAWA
Wedron Office

CREST HILL
Merichka's

MISSOURI

PERU
The Igloo

LEONORE
Smitty's Tap

HUDSON
Green Gables

BLOOMINGTON
Shannon's Five Star

SPRINGFIELD
Charlie Parker's
Cozy Dog
D&J Café
Joe Rogers Original Recipe
Chili Parlor

BELTON
★ Snead's

COLUMBIA
Booches

FERGUSON
Natalie's Cakes & More

KANSAS CITY
Arthur Bryant's
Jess & Jim's
LC's Barbeque
Niecie's
★ Stroud's

JEFFERSON CITY

BRENTWOOD
Carl's Drive-in

ST. LOUIS
Amighetti's
C&K Barbecue
Chris's Pancake & Dining
Crown Candy Kitchen
Donut Stop
Goody Goody Diner
Hodak's
O'Connell's Pub
Riley's Pub
★ Ted Drewes

ILLINOIS

ILLINOIS

AL'S #1 ITALIAN BEEF

alsbeef.com

1079 W. Taylor St.   312-226-4017

Chicago, IL   **L D** (closed Sun) | **$**

Al's, which claims to have invented the Chicago Italian beef sandwich, started as Al's Bar-B-Q in old Little Italy with no seats for dining, just waist-high counters along the wall. Some thirty years ago *Chicago* magazine named it the city's best beef, at which point it became Al's #1 Italian Beef. In 1999, Chicago Franchise Systems got involved and there now are more than a dozen around the city, as well as branches as far as California. The original Al's is especially worth visiting because it is directly across the street from Mario's Italian Ice.

Al's sandwich is thin-sliced, gravy-sopped, garlic-charged beef piled into a chewy length of Italian bread. You can ask for big beef (about twice as much) or have your sandwich double-dipped, which means totally immersed in a pan of natural gravy so the bread is soaked through. "Beef with hot" is a request for the relish known as *giardiniera,* an eye-opening garden mélange of finely chopped marinated vegetables, capers, and spice that is roast beef's perfect complement. "With sweet" is what you say if you prefer the popular alternative to *giardiniera*: big, tender flaps of roasted green bell pepper with a charcoal taste.

"Combo!" or "Half and half!" is a call for a sandwich that contains not only beef but also a plump, four-inch length of Italian sausage, retrieved from the appetizing haze that hovers over the hot metal grate just behind the order counter. Taut-skinned, succulent, and well spiced, the sausage is itself a major lure for many customers who sidestep beef altogether and order double-sausage sandwiches, hot or sweet.

BYRON'S HOT DOG HAUS

byronschicago.com

1017 W. Irving Park Rd.   773-281-7474

Chicago, IL   **L D** | **$**

As plump Polish sausages sizzle on the grill, the counterman dips a ladle into the fryolator to get some hot fat to pour over the grilling tube steaks. The grease helps give them a blackened, crisp skin; it also produces a look of glistening, sinfully swollen plumpness. These are some of the burliest Polish sausages in a city where Polish sausages, along with their all-beef brothers, hot dogs, are matters of serious culinary consideration. If you are a Polish sausage fanatic, it isn't likely you will be blasé about the big, charred tubes they serve up at Byron's dog haus; you will love them or hate them.

The hot dogs are more civil; we recommend them to all who appreciate a substantial, all-beef frank. They are Vienna brand, steeped to full succulence, with a faint crackle as you sink your teeth into them. Our only complaint is about the buns. They are a bore—small, plain (no poppy seeds), forked straight from their plastic-wrapped container (not warmed).

But Byron's condiments are fine: eleven different toppings that include strips of green pepper, cucumber discs, piccalilli, squeeze-on yellow mustard, onions, and sport peppers (hot!). And resting atop your hot dog and its condiments is one tomato, not quite still round, because it has been cut into slices. But because the slices don't go all the way through, it stays in one piece . . . until you try to eat the dog, at which time everything falls into a splendid mess. The tomato is customarily gilded with a sprinkle of celery salt.

Alongside this good specimen of frankfurter pulchritude, you want French fries. They are skinny and crisp—a suitable spuddy companion to the highly seasoned sausages that are this restaurant's specialty. Unless you really love French fries, one order is plenty for two.

A second Byron's is at 1701 Lawrence Avenue (773-271-0900).

CHARLIE PARKER'S
charlieparkersdiner.net

| 700 North St. | 217-241-2104 |
| Springfield, IL | B L \| $ |

Don't rely on your GPS if you come hunting for Charlie Parker's, an out-of-the-way trackside Quonset hut that has a sense of scale as out of whack as its lat-long coordinates. One single pancake is the size of a large pizza—flipped on the griddle with a pizza peel and served in a pizza pan. No one ever has been able to eat a Four Giant Stack (but if you do, they're free). Even a single one is enough for two to four people. What's most amazing is that it's very good, made from a fresh, farmy batter and griddle-cooked so that it develops a faintly crisp skin.

Charlie's is also an appropriate place to eat a horseshoe, that outrageously huge Springfield specialty that is basically a pile of everything on a plate. Breakfast 'shoes are especially awe-inspiring: big oval mountains built upon a foundation of white bread. Atop the bread are eggs, breakfast meats, hash browns, and cream gravy and/or hot cheese sauce.

CORNED BEEF FACTORY
cornedbeeffactorychicago.com

| 1009 W. Lake St. | 312-666-2535 |
| Chicago, IL | B L (closed Sun) \| $ |

The Corned Beef Factory really is a corned beef factory, having corned and packed briskets for Chicago-area restaurants and grocery stores since 1948. Only recently, it added a retail operation up front selling sandwiches of what they do so well in back. It is barely a restaurant. Seating is limited to one large communal picnic table on the sidewalk. Everything is presented in a cardboard box tied with string.

The corned beef sandwich is magnificent, the meat sliced thin, the Chicago way. Moist and tender, minimally briny, remarkably lean, and yet dramatically flavorful, it comes piled high on rye with either yellow or spicy mustard and a pickle spear. On the side are gorgeous house-made potato chips: see-through thin, lightweight, and crisp. Pastrami, like the corned beef, is alarmingly lean but somehow luxurious. A combination sandwich of both meats is known as a Tom and Jerry Combo.

The Corned Beef Factory also serves a grand Chicago-style red hot, the Vienna all-beef hot dog nestled in a steamed-soft poppy-seed bun and fully dressed with mustard, bright green relish, sport peppers, and a pickle spear. Nor is Italian beef an afterthought; it is top-notch, available dry or wet, with sweet peppers or hot *giardiniera*, in a nice length of crusty bread with mozzarella cheese, if desired.

COZY DOG
cozydogdrivein.com

| 2935 S. 6th St. | 217-525-1992 |
| Springfield, IL | B L D (closed Sun) \| $ |

Invented during World War II by Ed Waldemire when he was in the Air Force stationed in Texas, the corn-clad, deep-fried Cozy Dog was originally called Crusty Cur and was a big hit with flyboys at the Amarillo PX. After the war, Waldemire's wife convinced him that his wiener needed a more appealing name, and in 1946, they opened Cozy Dog (so christened because no one eats a single, lonely one). You don't have to be a street-food connoisseur to savvy the difference between a Cozy Dog and an ordinary corn dog. The cozy's batter jacket has a vivid crunch and earthy corn flavor; the dog within is plump with juice. Family baskets include four Cozy Dogs and a large order of (freshly-cut) French fries.

D&J CAFÉ

915 W. Laurel St.   217-753-1708
Springfield, IL   **B L D** | **$**

The horseshoe is one of the most regionally restricted of all local specialties, found nowhere beyond Springfield, where it was first devised at the Leland Hotel back in 1928. It is one of America's most out-landish meals, in a class with the Rochester Garbage Plate (p. 104) and super nachos. Historians say it was named because it originally resembled a horse's shoe (a slice of ham) on an anvil (a hot metal plate) with farriers' nails (French fries) scattered around. But over the years, 'shoes have been supersized to the point that they no longer bear any resemblance to equine footwear. Drizzles of cheese have become gobs; a few French fries have become mountains. The original ham-and-cheese configuration has been aug-mented by 'shoes based on burgers, sausage, Buffalo-sauced chicken, and even vegetarian combos.

And, naturally, there is now the breakfast 'shoe, which may or may not contain ham (or bacon or sau-sage patties), and which will more likely be heaped with hash browns than French fries. It will contain two to four eggs. Cheese sauce may be supplemented by or replaced by cream gravy.

At the humble D&J Café, everything on the breakfast 'shoe is completely blanketed by hash browns that have a crisp outside coat and enough thickness that below the crunch is plenty of plush spuditude—essential for mopping eggs if you like runny yolks. What's notable about this particular 'shoe is its balance—a magnificent harmony of gravy, cheese, meat, and potatoes.

DOUGHNUT VAULT

doughnutvault.com
401 N. Franklin St.   No phone
Chicago, IL   **B** | **$**

The Doughnut Vault shows just how cruel the law of supply and demand can be. About 1,000 donuts are made each morning and 10,000 Chicagoans want them. So the line forms before opening at 8:30 and the donuts can be gone before noon.

The buttermilk donuts are dense and cake-like, eminently suitable for dunking. Glazed donuts are lighter, and generally available in such flavors as chestnut, chocolate, and vanilla. While these donuts are big enough so that one will satisfy a mod-est appetite, you also can get stacks of three smaller ones. Daily specials include double-chocolate old-fashioneds, powdered sugar stacks, mocha-glazed toasted almond, and pistachio.

FREDDY'S PIZZA

freddyspizza.com
1600 S. 61st Ave.   708-863-9289
Cicero, IL   **L D** (closed Sun) | **$**

--★--
LOCALS
LOVE IT
--★--
It is almost as hard to start describing Freddy's as it is to choose something to eat at Freddy's. The problem is that there is so much, and so much is so good. For a pint-sized corner grocery store, the menu is huge. Well, no, that's not quite right, because there is no menu. Customers choose what to eat by crowding into the little space and perusing what's laid out: pizzas thick and thin and calzones large and small, three kinds of chicken, pastas and *arancini*, vegetable salads, pasta salads, seafood salads. That's not even talking about the big shelf of just-baked loaves of bread on the counter at back—round ones and long ones—and assorted sala-mis and house-cured prosciutto, nor can we describe the virtually infinite number of sandwiches available, hot and cold, and the extremely interesting groceries on the shelves. Selecting and getting a meal is all the more challenging because there seems not to be any logic as to who among the many staff behind the counter is helping whom on the other side, and who to pay, and who's presenting the food you ordered.

But the real challenge is that nearly everything is drop-dead delicious. Strangely, despite the name of the place, pizzas may be the least interesting thing available. Oh, they're good, with chewy, faintly charred crust and quality toppings, but compared to, say, the brilliantly citrusy lemon chicken or the ridiculously fluffy veal stuffed into rolled, baked sheaves of eggplant or the gnocchi that are light as a cloud, the pizzas aren't all that exciting. Any pasta with tomato sauce is fantastic—sweet and tangy—and the seafood salad is like a gust of fresh ocean air. The bread that holds such sandwiches as eggplant parm or meatballs is crusty and chewy and impeccably fresh.

After all this hyperbole, will you believe us when we say that the gelato made by Freddy's owner, Joe Quercia, is the best anywhere? It is smooth as top cream, rich but not the least bit cloying, intensely charged with whatever flavor is its essence, from hazelnut to fruits of the forest.

Thanks to Gregg Pill for showing it to us.

GARRETT POPCORN SHOP

garrettpopcorn.com

625 N. Michigan Ave.   312-943-4200
Chicago, IL $

Most candy-coated popcorn is frivolous junk food. CaramelCrisp—Garrett's name for caramel corn—is serious and soulful. It scarcely tastes candied. The popcorn is an earthy note within a deeply buttery caramel sheath and has dark flavor that teeters at the edge of tasting burnt. Like singed crust atop a crème brûlée, the corn's coat smacks of fire as much as sugar.

Another thing that makes it good is that it is served hot and fresh. Once mixed with caramel it is spilled into a trough against the front wall, where a woman worries it with two large scoops, ensuring the caramel corn doesn't clump into pieces larger than three or four popped kernels. As it achieves perfect consistency, it is shoveled into the other end of the trough, where it is scooped into bags that are weighed out for customers. Almost equally excellent is Garrett's cheese corn, which is impossible to eat without your fingers turning bright orange from the cheese that coats and infuses the hot popped kernels. The cheese immeasurably enhances the starchy corn flavor of the puffy kernels, making a savory snack that is almost unimprovable.

But it can get better. Instead of ordering either CaramelCrisp or cheese corn, you can ask one of the women working the counter for a "mix," also known as the Chicago Mix. She fills a bag half full with caramel corn, tops it off with cheese corn, and then shakes. The combo is a giant taste sensation that seems to cover the whole spectrum of what a tongue can appreciate: salty, sweet, buttery, earthy, crisp, and chewy. Even a mini-mix, which is a mere eight ounces, exhausts our ability to eat anything else for hours.

Note: There are Garretts elsewhere; none we have tried can compare to those in Chicago, of which there are ten. The Michigan Avenue location is best of them all.

GENE & JUDE'S

geneandjudes.com

2720 N. River Rd.   708-452-7634
River Grove, IL   L D | $

Gene & Jude's has no tables or chairs. As is Chicago custom, it offers a counter to which you may bring your meal, unwrap it, and eat standing up. When finished, use the wax paper in which the food was served to gather up scraps and heave them into one of the garbage cans. The arrangement is comfortable and practical for eating extremely messy food; however, many customers choose to dine in their cars.

You get a hot dog or a double dog. The natural-casing, all-beef Vienna brand links are slim and snappy; they are inserted into soft buns and dressed with mustard, onions, piccalilli, and sport peppers. Tipster Glen Stepanovic told us that some hot dog historians consider this the "original" Chicago-style dog, before the more baroque garnishes of pickle spear, tomato slice, and celery salt. Whatever toppings are included, each dog gets heaped with a large fistful of freshly made French fries.

GREEN GABLES

greengablesgrill.com

17485 E. 2500 North Rd. 309-747-2496
Hudson, IL   **B L D | $**

--★-- **LOCALS LOVE IT** --★-- Green Gables is a restaurant like no other: Walk into a dark bar with a pool table. Beyond that is a brightly lit room with picnic-table seating, and beyond that are grocery shelves with products lined up in eye-boggling perfection. To the left is a refrigerator full of bait for people who want to fish in nearby Lake Bloomington, and up behind the tables is the stock of liquor for sale by the bottle. The menu in this polymorphous establishment tells customers they are in the "resort capital of the world" and they are about to experience "the best food known to man."

We wouldn't go quite that far, but the hamburgers are something special. They are cooked central-Illinois-style, meaning that they are pressed flat on the grill, so flat that their edges turn crisp and lacy as they cook. They're plenty fatty and stay juicy, however much they are pressed, but they are thin enough that a double makes sense, preferably a double with cheese, pickle, tomato, onion, ketchup, and mustard. Each burger is presented swaddled in paper so that the whole package has quickly steamed into a great mound of savory goodness by the time it's unwrapped.

Three meals a day are served, but hamburgers are the reason to detour deep into farmland to find this unique place. Side dishes, all fried, are OK: cheese balls, corn nuggets, mozzarella, cauliflower, onion rings, and so on. Italian beef goes on the menu when the weather gets warm, and chili is featured when it's cold.

HARRY CARAY'S

harrycarays.com

33 W. Kinzie St.   312-828-0966
Chicago, IL   **L D | $$$**

--★-- **HOT TICKET** --★-- Beyond his antics in the broadcast booth, especially as the voice of the Chicago Cubs, Harry Caray was known as a man who loved to eat. The place he opened is testimony to that passion. It is fancier and pricier than most Roadfood, but we include it here because it is the essence of edible Chicago. For example, there is not a better prime steak in town. We like the sirloin best, grilled in a coat of cracked peppercorns. Other highlights include such Italian specialties as lasagna, veal parmigiana, and a risotto of the day.

Among the "Italian" dishes is one that we've found only in Chicago, and it is magnificent: chicken Vesuvio. Chicken Vesuvio is several bone-in pieces of chicken, sautéed then baked to utmost succulence, encased in a dark, red-gold crust of lush skin that slides from the meat as the meat slides off its bone. The dark meat in particular sets new standards for chicken tenderness. Piled among the chicken are wedges of potato, long-sautéed in a bath of white wine, garlic, olive oil, and spice until they are soft as mashed inside, but with crunchy edges. Even if you don't get chicken Vesuvio, Vesuvio potatoes are available as a side dish to go with any steak or chop. The only problem about ordering them is that you likely won't also be ordering the superb garlic mashed potatoes.

The setting is vintage: an 1895 Dutch Renaissance–style limestone building now on the National Register of Historic Places, its interior a luxuriously muscular space of mahogany woodwork and broad tables covered by thick white napery. Although an opulent place to which many customers come in pinstriped business suits, there is a democratic feel about this dining room that makes any decently dressed customer feel right at home. Harry Caray was a people's hero, and that's the way he liked it.

HOOSIER MAMA PIE COMPANY

hoosiermamapie.com

1618½ W. Chicago Ave.   312-243-4846
Chicago, IL   (closed Mon) | $

Hoosier Mama is mostly a kitchen and takeout shop with a mere three tables on premises. Pies are sold whole and by the slice. They are among America's best.

Standout varieties include chocolate cream, chocolate chess, ginger custard, oatmeal, Grape-Nuts, and banana cream. We love apple cherry with oat crumble, a balancing act of sweet and tart, soft fruit and streusel top, but our favorite is Hoosier sugar cream. It is a simple mix of butter, sugar, and vanilla-flavored cream, baked to become a sort of fudgy custard that is like a Midwestern analog of dulce de leche, but richer.

Friday nights, Hoosier Mama offers "pie flights," which are three small slices of different pies, providing maximum variety.

A second, larger Hoosier Mama is located at 749 N. Chicago Avenue in Evanston (847-868-8863). Espresso is served, as are savory pie plates and sandwiches.

THE IGLOO

igloodiner.com

2819 4th St.   815-223-0848
Peru, IL   L D (closed Tues) | $

Generations of Peruvians know and love the Igloo for hamburgers, chili, and pork tenderloins. Rich Decker, who, along with his brother Chris, bought the seventy-five-year-old drive-in in 2010 from the family who started it, explained that he serves "true tenderloin, not a chop, not just some loin, but the really good part." The wavy cutlet does have a regal bearing—thin and rich, offering just the right amount of succulent meat hugged by brittle crust, garnished with onion, pickles, and ketchup. Ketchup is an unusual tenderloin condiment, but it sings a sweet song with the tangy pickles, crunchy onion, sandy crust, and dense, moist pork. French fries are medium-thin, good lunch-counter potatoes, nothing unusual, but just right. Mid-sandwich they tend to soften, but the fresh potato flavor remains.

Even better than the tenderloin is a double tenderloin—two cutlets in one sandwich, accentuating the crispness—a sandwich that is as thrilling to bite as it is to taste. Igloo regulars do not order "tenderloins." They ask for a "pork," or a "double pork," and then for a malt.

"Is the malt real?" we ask Chris.

"I've got malt, I've got ice cream, I've got syrup," he answers, enumerating a flavor choice that includes vanilla, chocolate, root beer, cherry, and papaya. The malt comes with a broad straw, but even so, its thickness demands so much cheek-hollowing suction that we forwent the straw and gulped.

JOE ROGERS ORIGINAL RECIPE CHILI PARLOR

thechiliparloronline.com

820 S. 9th St.   217-523-4989
Springfield, IL   L (closed Sun) | $

Springfield chili, as made at Joe Rogers, is wild stuff, definitely not for the fastidious epicure. Cooked ground beef, which resembles loosemeats, comes afloat in grease—known more politely as hot oil—and is almost always accompanied by beans. It is possible to ask for the oil to be skimmed off when you order a bowl, but that would negate the purpose of the little oyster crackers that come alongside. They are a nice sponge for the oil, sopping up its chili-pepper zest. The chili comes in six different degrees of hotness, from mild to Firebrand, the latter known as the J. R. Special. If you eat a bowl of Firebrand, your name will be inscribed on the honor roll posted on the wall so that your survivors can come and salute your daredevil spirit.

Note that Joe Rogers spells chili the normal way, with a single L. That is unusual in Springfield, Illinois, because in 1993, when the state legislature formally declared the downstate capital to be the "Chilli Capital of the Civilized Universe," it purposely used the rare double-L spelling of the word, ordained by force of Senate resolution.

★ JOHNNIE'S

7500 W. North Ave.   708-452-6000
Elmwood Park, IL   L D | $

LOCALS LOVE IT
--★--
-★-
We do not eat Italian beef often enough to anoint one place the best. Chicago (and Chicago alone) has so many good ones, and as a native, Michael gets too sentimental at the very sight (and smell) of shaved-thin, garlic-sopped beef loaded into a brawny length of bread and crowned with pickly-hot *giardiniera* to make any sort of reasoned judgment. But the last time we were at Johnnie's and had a combo sandwich (that's beef plus sausage), we found it hard to believe that Chicago's great signature sandwich can get any better than this. The beef is soft and fairly softly seasoned—just garlicky enough to halo its protein magnitude—and the char-cooked sausage is dense, taut, and chewy. This glorious duo, plus Johnnie's vibrant *giardiniera*, compose a taste-bud epiphany. To accompany Italian beef or to savor its afterglow, Johnnie's makes delicious Italian ice, a tantalizing balance of sweet and tart.

LAGOMARCINO'S

lagomarcinos.com

1422 5th Ave.   309-764-1814
Moline, IL   L D | $

Started as a Moline, Illinois, candy store in 1908, Lagomarcino's is still renowned for hand-dipped chocolates. You won't find better sponge candy anywhere, here known as sea foam (not available in hot summer months). Turtles, aka pecan dainties, are superb. In addition to familiar chocolate barks, Lagomarcino's offers lemon bark and peppermint bark.

What we like best is the hot fudge sundae, its fudge made from a recipe acquired in 1918 from a traveling salesman for the princely sum of twenty-five dollars. It is a bittersweet, not-too-thick elixir that just may be the best hot fudge in this solar system or any other. When you order a sundae, the great, dark stuff is served in a manner befitting its distinction: in a small pitcher alongside the tulip-glass full of ice cream and whipped cream, so you can pour or spoon it on to taste. This serving technique provides a fascinating demonstration of how soda-fountain habits reflect one's personality. Do you pour on all the fudge at one time, willy-nilly, risking that some will spill over the sides of the serving glass? Do you pour it on spoonful by spoonful, carefully ensuring that every bite will have just the proper balance of ice cream and fudge? Or do you eat all the ice cream, with maybe just a dash of fudge poured on, so you can then conclude your snack by downing all the hot fudge that remains in one dizzy chocoholic binge?

LEM'S

lemsque.com

311 E. 75th St.   773-994-2428
Chicago, IL   L D (closed Tues) | $$

Lem's is a South Side barbecue that dates back to 1954, when brothers Bruce and Myles Lemons created the aquarium smoker, named because its tempered glass walls show the meat as it slow-cooks. This type of barbecue pit has since become a signature of Chicago's South Side, along with the rib tips that Lem's introduced as a less expensive but succulent alternative to whole racks.

The rib racks are sensational: big, meaty bats with all the lascivious fatty flavor and satisfying chew that baby backs simply cannot deliver. Also not to be missed are Lem's hot links—plump, rugged-textured sausages served with barbecue sauce, French fries, and white bread for sopping up the last of Lem's kaleidoscopic sauce.

Note: There are no dining facilities at Lem's. All business is takeout.

MANNY'S

mannysdeli.com

1141 S. Jefferson St.   312-939-2855
Chicago, IL   B L D | $$

We usually return to our favorite Chicago cafeteria-style deli with the vow to *not* eat corned beef sandwiches. There are so many other good-looking things to eat: kasha and bowtie noodles, short ribs of beef, oxtail stew, and pierogies, not to mention matzoh ball soup, blintzes, and potato latkes. But all too often, the beauty of the warm corned beef, thin-sliced before one's eyes and piled between slices of glossy-crusted rye bread, wins out and that's what we eat, sided by potato latkes.

Gino Gambarota, Manny's corned beef man for more than a quarter century, will cut the meat the way you like it—lean, fatty, or regular—but he will not cut it thick. "The art of cutting corned beef is to cut it as thin as possible, and against the grain," Gino says. His slices are shaved so thin they verge on disintegration, but they stay intact and miraculously succulent.

At the edge of Chicago's Loop, not far from where the everything-goes bazaar known as Maxwell Street once thrived, Manny's remains a magnet for Chicagoans of every stripe. Dining-room tables are occupied by politicians and other crooks, captains of industry and university professors, and cured-meat lovers from distant suburbs. When a newspaper photographer joined us at a recent meal, a nearby cop couldn't resist coming over to investigate. When he saw the lensman focusing on a corned beef sandwich, he beamed with understanding and gave us the high sign.

MERICHKA'S

merichkas.com

604 Theodore St.	815-723-9371
Crest Hill, IL	**L D** | $$

Merichka's opened in 1933 and has since grown to include a dance hall, banquet facilities, and a large parking lot for weekend crowds. The menu has something for everyone, with steaks of every size and cut, fried chicken, wild salmon and lobster tails, mini-cheeseburger appetizers, and special-occasion cakes for dessert. We advise taking a cue from Chicago food authority Gregg Pill (who goes by the handle Chitowndiner) and going for a Poorboy Steak.

Marichka's poor boy is simplicity itself: a long cube steak in a tube of chewy bread. The bread is good, the steak is moderately flavorful and tender. What makes the sandwich memorable is its condiment, what Merichka's calls "butterine," which is melted margarine mixed with an outlandish amount of chopped garlic. It soaks into the meat and the

bread, infusing both with intense garlic flavor, transforming what would otherwise be an ordinary sandwich into a fragrant bombshell.

MR. BEEF

666 N. Orleans St.	312-337-8500
Chicago, IL	**L D** (closed Sun) | $

Mr. Beef is a premier source for the Second City's #1 street food, Italian beef. Great heaps of ultra-thin-sliced, garlic-infused beef are piled into a length of muscular Italian bread that gets soft as beef juices soak into it, but retains the oomph to stay in one piece even if you order your sandwich "dipped," which means double-soaked in gravy. An important choice you'll need to make is if you want your sandwich topped with roasted peppers or the peppery vegetable mélange known as *giardiniera,* which is crunchy, spicy, and a brilliant contrast to the full-flavored beef.

Sausages are excellent as well—cooked on a grate until they sweat juice. You can get a sausage sandwich in similar configurations as beef, and it is also possible to have a combo, a length of both sausage and beef.

Accommodations are minimal. There is an adjoining dining room, ironically titled the Elegant Dining Room, with actual tables at which to sit as well as a counter up front with stools, but the Italian beef connoisseur's choice is to stand at the chest-high counter that rims the perimeter of the main room. Here, the wax paper that wraps the sandwich can catch all the spillage and keep it at handy plucking distance.

PARADISE PUP

1724 S. River Rd.   847-699-8590
Des Plaines, IL   **L | $**

The name is Paradise Pup and the hot dogs are excellent—Chicagoland classics that are available topped with a wheelbarrow's worth of condiments. Italian beef sandwiches are top-tier. But the Pup's primary attraction is its cheeseburger. A hefty patty charcoal-grilled to crusty succulence, all the more delicious with a sheaf of bacon on top or perhaps raw or grilled onions, it comes on a seeded Kaiser roll. You get your choice of cheese—American, mozzarella, or the connoisseur's choice: Merkt's, a tangy Cheddar from Wisconsin that matches perfectly with the beef.

Seasoned French fries are excellent too, whether you order them plain or loaded, which means heaped with cheese, bacon, and sour cream. To drink: a cream-rich milk shake.

Dining accommodations are virtually non-existent—a handful of counter seats and outdoor tables with umbrellas—and the small eat shack is almost always crowded. Expect to wait.

★ POOCHIE'S

poochieshotdogs.com

3602 Dempster St.   847-673-0100
Skokie, IL   **L D | $**

Poochie's red hots are the best. Standard hot dogs are all-beef Vienna franks, boiled to perfect plumpness and served in tender, seeded Rosen's-brand buns. Char dogs, cooked over coals, are crusty, blackened versions thereof. Polish sausages are plumper, porkier variants slit in a spiral pattern to attain maximum crunchy surface area. If one in a bun of any of these tube steaks is insufficient for your appetite, you can get either a jumbo dog or a double. Our personal favorite meal is a jumbo char dog with Cheddar fries (superb fries!) on the side.

Poochie's is proud of its char-cooked hamburgers, and we like them very much. But if you are passing through Chicago and stop at Poochie's with time for only one street-food indulgence, make it a red hot with the works.

★ RIP'S

ripschicken.com

311 N. Main Ave.   815-894-3051
Ladd, IL   **D** (closed Mon & Tues) **| $**

LOCALS LOVE IT In matters of food, as in politics, the state of Illinois gets eclipsed by the city of Chicago. But when it comes to fried chicken, Chicago cannot hold a candle to LaSalle and Bureau Counties. If you are a fried-chicken pilgrim, this big-sky prairie belongs on the essential itinerary right along with Nashville, Kansas City, and western Kentucky.

The region boasts literally dozens of good chicken places, nearly all of them taverns, most serving only supper. Rip's is the best—so good that fans don't mind an hour's wait for a table on weekends. Waiting in line with beer or cocktail in hand and telling other devotees how far away you live and how often you come is part of the experience.

Rip's is all about chicken (plus fish on Friday), and amenities are minimal: dishware is disposable, forks are provided only when requested. Rip's quarters, light or dark, are encased in a significant crisp crust. While much surplus skin has been trimmed away, there are places on each piece, such as the underside of the breast, that carry brittle little clumps of batter infused with chicken-fat flavor—some of the most sumptuous bites anywhere. Below the crunch is impeccable meat, bursting with juice all the way to the bone, thanks in large part to a prep process that includes brining. Pieces are served on a pallet of white bread, but the bread remains surprisingly dry and intact. As lubricated as this chicken is—it *is* all about deep-frying—it does not shed surplus grease.

One big reason for loyalty to Rip's is a unique item known as crunchies. Every table gets a cardboard boat full of them while waiting for quarters to fry. Hot morsels of batter retrieved from the cooking oil with a broad, long-handled screen, they are reminiscent of southern cracklins or, more to the point, Jewish *gribenes*, glowing with the silky luxury of fried chicken fat. Pure shattering flavor, crunchies are an item virtually impossible to stop eating once you start. They are served with a cup of tart dill pickle chips. Rip's bartender, Betha, demonstrated that the custom is to fold a pickle chip around a little cluster of crunchies, creating what regulars call a finger taco. She explained that the puckery pickles are an important part of the meal because their pungency gives the tongue endurance to eat more fried food.

SHANNON'S FIVE STAR

shannonsfivestar.com

1305 S. Mercer Ave.	309-664-0808
Bloomington, IL	**B L D** | $

Located where the Five Star Truck Stop used to be on old Route 66, Shannon's is a diner serving three square meals a day Monday through Saturday and breakfast on Sunday until noon. Daily specials range from meat loaf on Monday to walleye on Friday, but the meal we've liked best is breakfast. A huge and hearty hash brown potato plate includes thin-sliced ham (or sausage or bacon) laced among spuds, along with grilled onions, melted cheese, and sausage gravy . . . plus eggs, if desired. It is not technically a Springfield horseshoe (Illinois' unique 10,000-calorie kitchen-sink platter), but it has all the sledgehammer authority of one. Insatiable appetites also will want to know about the breakfast skillet: another mammoth meal of fried potatoes, onions, and peppers topped with ham, bacon, and sausage, eggs, and sausage gravy.

Shannon's is a large, friendly place with speedy service that includes coffee refills throughout the meal. While we wouldn't drive out of our way to eat here, we will return when hankering for a big breakfast in Bloomington.

SMITTY'S TAP

308 Gary St.	815-856-2030
Leonore, IL	**L D** | $

Among the several Illinois River Valley restaurants known for good fried chicken, Smitty's Tap is listed among the top contenders, but when we came to this friendly crossroads tavern one Thursday, we ate none. Smitty's serves its chicken, which is broasted, only on Wednesday and Friday nights.

It was a good stop anyway, because Smitty's offers tenderloin every day. And oh, what a tenderloin: a foot across, piled with lettuce, tomato, and onion, and sandwiched—if that is the right word for it—in a ridiculously little-looking (but actually normal-sized) burger bun. The pounded-thin pork is sweet and moist, its crust a blond halo of crunch. For most folks, it is knife-and-fork food, but the waitress assured us that there are people who manage to fold the cutlet over on itself a few times so they can hoist it off the iron skillet in which it is served, using the bun in a normal way.

★ SUPERDAWG

superdawg.com

6363 N. Milwaukee Ave.	773-763-0660
Chicago, IL	**L D** | $

Many savvy Chicagoans believe Superdawg's all-beef tube steaks are the city's best. If not, they are surely among the top two or three. Contrary to Chicago custom, these proprietary franks are skinless, and yet they are burstingly juicy. And while they do have the garlic edge that defines red hots hereabouts, their dominant flavor is quality beef. Condiments are impeccable. Buns are fresh and soft, spangled with sesame seeds. Other super menu items include Superfries, Superonionchips, Superburgers, and Supershakes. Or you can have a Whoopskidog (the house name for a Polish sausage).

It is easy to spot Superdawg as you approach a pair of ten-foot statues of a male and female wiener (Flaurie and Maurie) wearing leopard-skin togas and standing high atop the roof, winking electrically. Opened in 1948, this Roadfood landmark still features the once-modern "Suddenserver" automated order system and serves its dogs in cardboard boxes that announce, "Your Superdawg lounges inside contentedly cushioned in Superfries, comfortably attired in mustard, relish, onion, pickle, and hot pepper."

TORRI'S ICE CREAM PARLOR

115 N. Main Ave.	815-894-9316
Ladd, IL	**B L**	$

Tom Torri, who opened his first business, the Fruit Store, in Ladd, Illinois, in 1911, became so well known for the ice cream he made that people traveled from Chicago and the Quad Cities to buy gallons of it to take home. Heidi Templeton, who bought what had become known as Torri's Ice Cream Parlor in 2004, no longer makes her own (she gets Sisler's ice cream from Ohio), but maintains a vintage sweetshop charm that makes this old place worth a visit. The wall behind the counter is occupied by a big 1950s wooden menu that lists hamburgers for 25¢ and banana splits for 35¢.

For years, the house slogan has been "Where Friends Meet." Torri's is the only place around serving breakfast (from 6 a.m.), so its tables and booths are where locals come to share morning conversation and to drink coffee served in a diverse collection of mugs. (We got ours in a Kinetico Water Systems mug and a Harley-Davidson Happy Holidays mug.) Torri's also is the only place in town with a dessert menu.

As much as we enjoyed spooning into a classic banana split, it was even more fun sitting at the counter watching it being carefully constructed. The woman who made it offered a running commentary about each step of the process, explaining how the two halves of the lengthwise-sliced banana were supposed to form a trough, damming up ice cream and sauce. She was crestfallen when, just before presenting her creation, the dam was breached by a spill of chocolate. Available ice cream flavors include all the usuals, plus black cherry, cotton candy, mango, and moosetracks.

The breakfast menu boasts that biscuits are made from scratch. Heidi said that they are indeed homemade, but not made here. We were puzzled but didn't pursue the question, as Heidi had her hands full, being both waitress and chef on the morning shift. Wherever it comes from, the biscuit is bland, a deficiency that can be remedied by having it split, buttered, and cooked on the grill, where it absorbs savory bacon-sausage-ham-and-eggs perfume. Ours came on the side of "loaded hash browns," which, calorie-wise, provide momentous bang for the buck: a pallet of crisp-fried potatoes topped with peppers, onions, mushrooms, and a mantle of cheese, all for $3.25.

VIENNA BEEF CAFÉ
viennabeef.com/cafemenu

2501 N. Damen Ave.	773-435-2309
Chicago, IL	**B L** (closed Sun)	$

Chicago hot dogs, aka red hots, are famous for the splendor of their condiments, but if the dog itself doesn't cut the mustard, condiments mean nothing. Most of the city's best are dense, garlicky, all-beef tube steaks made by Vienna Beef Company. Glory be, Vienna Beef happens to run its own factory-store café, where you won't find a more perfect version of the Chicago classic: a wiener steamed to bursting plumpness, the tenderest poppy seed roll, crisp pickle spears, tomatoes, and brilliant spicy-sweet piccalilli. Even the bright yellow mustard tastes like it was made that morning.

That's not all. Vienna Beef also makes superior corned beef, Polish sausages, pastrami, hard and soft salami, and Italian beef, all of which are on the lunch menu. The flagship item is a 3XL corned beef sandwich, nine ounces of spicy beef piled between slices of very good rye bread.

WEDRON OFFICE

2005 N. 35th Rd.	815-433-2974
Ottawa, IL	**L D** (closed Mon)	$

If you are driving along Thirty-Fifth Road north of Ottawa, you can't miss Wedron Office because there is absolutely nothing else to see other than acres of cornfields. A cool, dark, insulated haven of hospitality, it is as much a tavern as it is a restaurant. There is a pool table up front and overhead televisions are tuned to TruTV. As we dined, we watched a show titled *Busted in the Buff*, featuring criminals apprehended while naked.

Terrific fried chicken. Encased in a thin envelope of crust with trailing squiggles of crunchy batter all about, each piece oozing juice. Tasty as the meat may be, it is tempting to eat only crust, like having all the bacon off your breakfast plate but leaving behind the eggs, spuds, and toast.

While fried chicken is a staple of many LaSalle County restaurants, blue gill is not. In fact, it is a rarity because a large fish produces only a small fillet, and you need up to a dozen to make a meal. Wedron Office serves a plateful of little curls of the flaky white fish in a nutty, toasty crust—just salty enough to tease all the natural sweetness from this freshwater prize.

THE WIENER'S CIRCLE
wienercircle.net

2622 N. Clark St.   773-477-7444
Chicago, IL   **L D** | $

The name of the Wiener's Circle is etymological hijinks typical of Chicago, but there is nothing silly about the red hots served here. They are among the city's best, presented in steamy-soft Rosenbrand poppy-seed buns and topped with flawless condiments.

The mustard is classic yellow, the piccalilli is brilliant green and vividly pickly, the tomatoes are small and flavorful—four or five whole, fresh-cut discs per dog. And there are grilled onions or raw, sport peppers (hot!), and a sprinkle of celery salt. Have your frankfurter as you like it, from naked to loaded, and you will not be disappointed. The major decision to make is how you want your hot dog cooked: boiled, which yields plump, taut skin, or charred, which gives the dogs rugged crunch and smoky savor.

Don't get a hot dog without French fries. These are beauties: hand-cut, freshly fried, served in ridiculously large amounts that totally overflow their cardboard boat and fall all over the wax paper on which the boat is pushed toward you out the order window.

Dining is either at counter space inside or picnic tables overlooking Clark Street. Orders are taken and food delivered by one of several gals at the open-kitchen window. "Char Dog!" one calls out to a customer, using what he ordered as his name, then continuing her conversation as the bill is paid by calling him sweetheart, honey, and darling. On other occasions, it is not unheard-of for the staff to speak to customers the way Cubs fans yell at umpires who have made a controversial call. Such personality is an extra condiment that helps make Wiener's Circle hot dogs something special.

INDIANA

CONEY ISLAND WIENER

fortwaynesfamousconeyisland.com

131 W. Main St.   260-424-2997
Fort Wayne, IN   **L D | $**

Coney Island wiener shops abound throughout the
heartland, "Coney Island" being the old term for hot
dog, which once was a signature dish of New York.
Fort Wayne's Coney Island, a Main Street storefront formally known as the Famous Coney Island
Wiener Stand, was established in 1914, and has built
its reputation on the classic Greek-American frankfurter: a modest-sized bright-pink weenie nestled in
a steamed-soft bun and topped with Coney sauce,
which is a fine-grind chili with a rainbow of seasonings and fetching sweetness. Although all condiments
are technically optional, everyone orders their hot
dogs with Coney sauce, as well as a line of mustard
and a sprinkle of chopped raw onion. The only other
things on the menu are baked beans, chili (more a
soup than a stew), and hamburgers. Coke comes in
classic small bottles.

Seating is at small tables along the wall and at
counter stools. Stools up front offer a nice view not
only of the doings behind the counter and between
staff and customers, but also through the big window
out onto Main Street.

Tipster Brett Poirier, who encouraged us to
seek these fine weenies, pointed out that Fort Wayne
makes a great way station for anyone traveling

America's original coast-to-coast thoroughfare, the
Lincoln Highway.

★ GRAY BROTHERS CAFETERIA

graybroscafe.com

555 S. Indiana St.   317-831-7234
Mooresville, IN   **L D | $**

Gray Brothers is a gigantic cafeteria with deluxe
décor. Expect it to be crowded, but this is one time
when a slight delay is worthwhile. It gives you time to
study the dozens of food items from which you will
soon be choosing.

Among the most memorable dishes are chicken
and homemade noodles, meat loaf with mashed potatoes, smoked sausage with baked beans, and roast
pork with corn bread dressing. Tell the server what
entrée you want; she puts it onto a flower-patterned
plate then slides the plate to the vegetable area,
where it is weighted with whatever sides you desire.
Mac 'n' cheese, au gratin potatoes, cheesy broccoli
and cauliflower, and melted-marshmallow yams all
are standouts. The salad selection includes carrot-
raisin-marshmallow, creamy pea, three-bean, and, of
course, Jell-O.

Desserts are dazzling, whole pies arrayed on
shelves below the individual slices (many pies get
bought and taken home). Fruit pies abound, and there
are swell butterscotch, banana cream, and pumpkin
flavors, but the Indiana favorite, and a specialty of

Gray's, is sugar-cream pie . . . as simple and pure and good as the name suggests.

HOLLYHOCK HILL

hollyhockhill.com

8110 N. College Ave.   317-251-2294
Indianapolis, IN   **D** (closed Mon) | $$

--★-- Big chicken dinners once were a signature of
HOT Indianapolis, a fact easy to believe when you
TICKET
--★-- visit Hollyhock Hill. Originally opened in 1928 as the Country Cottage, it offers a feast, served family-style in bowls and on platters that diners pass around the table. You start with innocuous pickled beets, cottage cheese, and a head lettuce salad. Then comes the chicken, skillet fried until crunch-crusted, served with pan gravy. Whipped potatoes, green beans, buttered corn niblets, and warm biscuits with apple butter come alongside and are replenished as long as the table keeps eating. They're fine, but it's the chicken that will make you want to return to Hollyhock Hill. (Chicken frowners can choose from among shrimp, fried cod, broiled orange roughy or haddock, and steak.)

For dessert, make your own sundae. Sauces of butterscotch, crème de menthe, and chocolate are provided. The normal flavor is vanilla, but true Hoosiers opt for the state favorite, peppermint.

JOE HUBER'S

joehubers.com

2421 Engle Rd.   812-923-5255
Starlight, IN   **L D** | $$

Joe Huber's is not a charming little town café. It is a tourist attraction. But we defy you to sink your teeth into the crust of the fried chicken, or gather a silky dumpling from its chicken broth, or fork up some of those real mashed potatoes and not concur with Joe Huber's many fans that it is a worthy Roadfood destination. And the fried biscuits? Inspired! Roadfood.com contributor Cecif described them as "similar to beignets . . . but a bit less greasy and very fluffy and light." With or without the apple butter that comes alongside, they are impossible to stop

eating. And that's a problem, because as soon as your biscuit basket looks empty, you will be served more.

There are other items on the menu, including pork chops, steak, and catfish, and groups of people can have the chicken served family-style along with slices of honey ham and a constellation of slaw, potatoes, gravy, green beans, corn and, of course, biscuits. Desserts include fruit cobblers and cream pies as well as miniature versions thereof for those of us without remaining appetite but with a demanding sweet tooth.

JOHN'S FAMOUS STEW

1146 Kentucky Ave.   317-636-6212
Indianapolis, IN   **B L D** | $

A few years ago, Roadfood.com team members Bruce Bilmes and Sue Boyle noted that stew happened to be an especially popular dish in Indianapolis, where more than a few taverns and sandwich shops make it a specialty. When we arrived at John's Famous Stew midafternoon, Pauline, who has been a waitress in this dark, adults-only tavern for a few score years, had some time to chat. She clued us in to the difference between stew and goulash (the latter has more vegetables) and told us that John's stew is available ladled on top of a stuffed pepper or a fried pork tenderloin. She also warned us that we did *not* want the hottest of the three degrees of stew available.

"We like hot," we insisted.

Pauline shook her head pityingly, insisting ours be medium, but she advised her sister in the kitchen, Phoebe, to elevate the heat level a few notches.

"How do you do that? Add more hot sauce?" we inquired.

"I can't tell you that!" Pauline answered, taken aback by our nerve even in asking. Apparently the stew recipe goes back to the original John, long since passed away, and imparted only to cooks who can be trusted.

Pauline spoke with authority about barbecue, fried chicken, and southern vegetables, and as we forked into a gigantic bowl of just-a-bit-hot comfort food, praising the big, lovely butter beans on top of the hugely meaty stew, she admitted that they normally do not appear on stew; they crown John's almost equally famous goulash.

KING RIBS BAR-B-Q

kingribsbarbq.com

3145 W. 16th St.   317-488-0223
Indianapolis, IN   **L D** | $

King Ribs' house motto is "Fit for a King." The ribs are regal. They are tender enough so that the meat pulls from the bone in heavy strips, barely glazed with sauce but chewy enough that the pork flavor resonates forever. It is a pure, sweet flavor, just faintly tingling with smoke. The house sandwich is known as pork on a bun, and that is what it is: an outlandishly messy load of hacked-up pork dripping with sauce and surrounded by a bun too messy to be hoisted by hand. The sleeper on the menu is chicken: slow-cooked to fallapart tenderness, its meat moist and smoky.

Side dishes include mac 'n' cheese that is as thick as pudding and intensely cheesy, with noodles so soft they are almost indistinguishable from the cheese. Also: baked beans, fine-cut slaw, and white bread for mopping. For dessert, there is a choice of sweeties: chess pie or sweet-potato pie.

LEMON DROP

1701 Mounds Rd.   765-644-9055
Anderson, IN   **L D** | $

Roadfood stalwart Cliff Strutz (aka Buffetbuster) pointed the way to the oldest restaurant in Anderson, Indiana—the Lemon Drop—where the citrus theme includes bright yellow paint on the outside walls, lemon drop candies at the cash register, and lemon milk shakes.

Headliners are the toasted cheeseburger, sandwiched between tiles of buttered grilled toast instead of a bun (buns also are available) and the onion-burger, which is made by folding onions right into the ground meat before it gets fried. Cliff noted that most customers get their onionburger on grilled toast too; he suggested that those with a big beef craving get a couple of burgers, as these patties are fairly thin, pressed flat on the grill.

If for some reason you don't want a lemon milk shake (you do!), Cokes are available doctored-up with chocolate or vanilla syrup.

MR. DAVE'S

102 E. Main St.   260-982-4769
North Manchester, IN   **L D** (Tues–Sat) | $

The tenderloin, formally known as a breaded pork tenderloin sandwich, sometimes abbreviated BPT, is a slice of pork pounded flat and wide, breaded and fried, and sandwiched in a bun, preferably with pickle slices and mustard. There are few restaurants as proud of this heartland treasure as Mr. Dave's, where the tenderloins are neither too thin nor ridiculously wide (as so many are). Four-ounce boneless pork medallions are cut and pounded out so there is still good heft to the meat; they are breaded in cornmeal and fried, coming out crunchy, tender, and piggy-sweet—just right inside a bun with lettuce, tomato, and mustard.

Although tenderloins have been its glory since "Mr. Dave" Clapp opened up in 1962 (the business is now run by his son Kevin), there is a full menu to make all but a strictly kosher traveler happy. You can get your pork tenderloin grilled rather than fried, and there is pulled-pork barbecue as well. Cheeseburgers, broasted chicken, and corn dogs fill out the menu.

Mr. Dave's used to do a brisk mail-order business selling breaded, frozen, and ready-to-fry tenderloins to homesick Hoosiers but a dozen years ago elected officials protected us against such evil by ruling that pork cannot be shipped without federal inspection.

MUG 'N' BUN

mug-n-bun.com

5211 W. 10th St.	317-244-5669
Indianapolis, IN	**L D** | **$**

The mug is root beer, the bun a Hoosier tenderloin; together they are a paradigmatic Midwest drive-in meal. This timeless joint not far from the Indianapolis Motor Speedway gives customers a choice of eating off the dashboard or at outdoor picnic tables umbrella'd by radiant heaters for cold weather. In-car diners blink their lights for service and food is presented by carhops on window trays. People seated at tables summon the kitchen by using a buzzer that adjoins the posted menu.

We were tipped off to Mug 'n' Bun by writer Dale Lawrence, who described its root beer as "legitimately creamy, yes, but also smoky, carrying hints of vanilla fudge and molasses, as rich and smooth as a dessert wine." In other words, not your average soda pop! It is served in thick, frosted mugs and in sizes that include small, large, giant, quart, half gallon, and gallon. As for the tenderloin, it too is big, if not the juiciest in town. We were more fond of the Super Burger, which is two patties, cheese, and bacon, served triple-decker-style: bun halves on top and bottom, a slice of toast separating the two burgers. Onion rings are very good: thick, crisp, and sweet.

NICK'S CHILI PARLOR

nickschiliparlor.com

2621 Lafayette Rd.	317-924-5005
Indianapolis, IN	**L D** | **$**

Thanks to Ben Morton and Rick Garrett for alerting us to this happy chili parlor on a rather unhappy stretch of recession-blighted shopping centers. For anyone on a budget, it is an especially worthwhile place, offering good, filling meals for $5 or less. These include five-way chili, chili dogs with cheese, burgers with and without chili, hot tamales, and fillet o' fish.

While Nick's hot dogs themselves are nothing special, the chili does add panache that makes them into the sort of food that never makes one say, "Wow, this is delicious" but nevertheless somehow completely vanishes from the plate, inducing temptation for just one more.

Service is cafeteria-style, giving customers an opportunity to kibitz with the high-spirited guys behind the counter. While the staff all are African Americans, the clientele when we dined at Nick's was a racial rainbow that included youth in hip-hop uniforms and geriatric couples with matching walkers.

★ NICK'S KITCHEN

nickskitchen.net

506 N. Jefferson St.	260-356-6618
Huntington, IN	**B L D** (closed Sun) | **$**

With a history dating back to 1904, when Nick Freienstein started frying breaded pork cutlets to sell in sandwiches from a street cart in Huntington, Nick's Kitchen claims with some authority to have invented the tenderloin—a sandwich of crisp-fried pork. Whether or not the history is accurate, this is certain: Nick's twenty-first-century tenderloin is stupendously good. It is built around a wavy cutlet that extends a good two to three inches beyond the circumference of a five-inch bun, virtually eclipsing its plate. Soaked in buttermilk that gives a tangy twist to the meat's sweetness and tightly cased in a coat of rugged cracker crumbs (not the more typical fine-grind cracker meal), the lode of pork inside the crust fairly drips with moisture. Proprietor Jean Anne Bailey tells us she buys the meat already cut and cubed, then pounds, marinates, breads, and fries it.

Nick's Kitchen isn't only a tenderloin stop. It's a wonderful three-meal-a-day town café with big breakfasts and a noontime blackboard of daily specials. We loved our plate of ham, beans, and corn bread, and we have been bowled over, time and again, by Jean Anne's pies. Made using a hand-me-down dough recipe that incorporates a bit of corn syrup, her fruit pies have a flaky crust that evaporates on the tongue, melding with brilliant-flavored rhubarb or black raspberries. Butterscotch pie—which she learned to cook from her grandmother—is more buttery than sweet, nothing at all like cloying pies made from pudding filling. Sugar-cream pie, an Indiana signature dessert, is like cream candy in a savory crust.

SHAPIRO'S
shapiros.com
808 S. Meridian St.   317-631-4041
Indianapolis, IN   **B L D** | **$**

Shapiro's serves deli meals cafeteria-style. In addition to a full repertoire of traditional kosher-style fare such as gefilte fish, matzoh ball soup, and piled-high smoked-meat sandwiches, its menu includes specialties unique to the Midwest: perch plates every Friday, Hoosier sugar-cream pie, and Vernor's ginger ale. The corned beef sandwich is one of the best anywhere, the meat cut lean but not too much so. Each slice is rimmed with a halo of smudgy spice and is so moist that it glistens. The beef is mounded between slabs of Shapiro's own rye bread that has a shiny, hard, sour crust. Slather on the mustard, crunch into a dill pickle to set your taste buds tingling, and this sandwich will take you straight to deli heaven.

Get some latkes (potato pancakes) too. They are double-thick, moist, and starchy: great companions to a hot lunch of short ribs or stuffed peppers; Shapiro's supplements ordinary latkes with cinnamon-scented ones—wonderful with sour cream. And soup: bean, lentil, split pea, and chowder are daily specials; you can always order chicken noodle or borscht.

TEIBEL'S
teibels.com
1775 Route 41   219-865-2000
Schererville, IN   **L D** | **$$**

Teibel's is one of a handful of restaurants that continues to serve the favorite big-eats Sunday-supper sort of meal so beloved in northern Indiana: boned and buttered lake perch. When it opened in 1930, it was a mom-and-pop café, and today it is a giant-sized dining establishment (run by the same family), but the culinary values that made it famous still prevail.

The feast starts with a relish tray—scallions, olives, celery, and carrots—followed by a salad (superfluous), then a plate piled high with tender fillets of perch glistening with butter. It is a big portion, and this fish is full-flavored; by the time our plate was empty, we were more than satisfied. Our extreme satisfaction was due also to the fact that we ate an order of Teibel's fried chicken too. Perhaps even more famous than the perch, this chicken is made from a recipe that Grandma Teibel brought from Austria many years ago. It is chicken with a crumbly, red-gold crust and juicy insides, in a whole other league from the stuff that comes in a bucket from fast-food franchises. Some other interesting items from Teibel's menu: frog legs (another local passion), walleye pike, and shrimp de Jonghe. For fish and frog frowners, there is a turkey dinner.

After a family-style feed, what could be nicer than a hot apple dumpling? The flake-crusted, cinnamon-scented dumpling is served à la mode with caramel sauce on top.

VILLAGE INN
107 S. Main St.   574-825-2043
Middlebury, IN   **B L D** (closed Sun) | **$**

If you are looking for a meal fitted to the mighty caloric needs of the Amish farmers who live around Middlebury, we recommend a booth at the Village Inn. Of course you can have eggs and potatoes and toast, just as in any regular town café, but you can also plow into a vast plate of cornmeal mush, accompanied by head cheese. Lunches are huge too: chicken and noodles or meat loaf or beef stew and mashed potatoes, smothered steaks and stuffed peppers, all served with richly dressed slaws and salads and well-cooked vegetables fattened up with bread crumbs, butter, and cheese.

The chief reason to come to the Village Inn is pie. If you really love pie of all kinds, three times a day, this place is the Promised Land. A typical day's selection includes Funeral Pie (made of raisins), OF Cream (meaning "old-fashioned" cream, made of little more than brown sugar and cream), cherry, peach, pineapple, banana cream, custard (white sugar and milk), and peanut butter/powdered sugar. One time several years ago, we felt a little gluttonous ordering four pieces for the two of us. But then we noticed two giant-sized bearded gents in overalls topping off their hearty chicken-and-noodles lunch with an entire funeral pie, split half-and-half between them.

WORKINGMAN'S FRIEND

234 N. Belmont Ave.   317-636-2067
Indianapolis, IN   **L D** (closed Sun) | **$**

The name is no affectation. Surrounded by industry, priced for people with large appetites but small wallets, with Bud on tap (in immense chalices) and its barroom TV always tuned to a sports event that matters, the Workingman's Friend is a no-bull tavern without a speck of snark or sass. Burgers are pressed flat on the grill so they develop a crusty edge but still glisten with juice. They are small enough that everybody gets a double, and most come with the works, which includes a couple of slices of cheese, of course, as well as lettuce, tomato, and pickles. Burgers star, but the limited menu also includes sandwiches of braunschweiger, smoked sausage, tenderloin (pork, of course), and hot ham. There's bean soup and chili and fried sides like cheese sticks, onion rings, and mushrooms (all unremarkable). If you don't drink beer, there is good sweet tea.

Since it is a tavern, no one under twenty-one is allowed inside.

IOWA

ARCHIE'S WAESIDE

archieswaeside.com

224 4th Ave. NE   712-546-7011

Le Mars, IA   **D** (Tues–Sat) | $$$

A steak-eaters' destination since Archie Jackson started it in 1949, Archie's is now run by grandson Bob Rand, who is a fanatic for excellence and produces some of the best steaks anywhere in America. They arrive a little crusty on the outside, overwhelmingly juicy and bursting with the resonant flavor of corn-fed, dry-aged beef. Even the filet mignon, usually a tender cut that is less flavorful, sings with the authority of blue-ribbon protein. Bone-in rib eye is deliriously succulent. And an off-the-menu item called the Benny Weiker (named for a good customer of years ago who was a famous cattle buyer in the old Sioux City stockyards) is simply the most handsome piece of meat we have ever seen presented on a plate: an eighteen-ounce, center-cut, twenty-one-day dry-aged filet mignon.

Archie's is a sprawling restaurant with wood-panel décor that seems not to have changed since the 1970s. Its capacious booths are filled with happy customers who come from miles around to enjoy the beefy pride of Siouxland.

B&B GROCERY

bbgrocerymeatdeli.com

2001 SE 6th St.   515-243-7607

Des Moines, IA   **B L** (Tues–Sat) | $

At Des Moines's B&B Grocery, you will enjoy insanely wide tenderloins while dining elbow-to-elbow with lunching locals. When we ate here, a group of police officers took great delight in demonstrating how to fold the meat over once or even twice inside the bun to make it easier to handle. Although this is a relatively thin tenderloin, inside its crisp, golden crust is a vein of pork that remains sweet and juicy.

B&B also is known for heroic "killer sandwiches," such as the Dad's Killer, which is roast beef, turkey, ham, and corned beef with three kinds of cheese, lettuce, tomato, pickles, mustard, Miracle Whip, and Italian dressing. The burger selection ranges from one-third-pounders to multilayer burgers, all the way up to a four-patty Quadzilla with the works.

For ambience, B&B can't be beat: It is an old grocery store with a makeshift eating annex of counter and stools. The butcher is the real deal, offering everything from a pound of ground chuck to halves of cows and hogs cut into steaks, chops, ribs, and roasts.

BAUDER PHARMACY

bauderpharmacy.com

3802 Ingersoll Ave.   515-255-1124
Des Moines, IA   **B L | $**

Many Iowans who have never been to Bauder Pharmacy know and love its ice cream because it is a regular attraction at the annual state fair, where peppermint ice cream bars, made with an Oreo crust, are a highlight of the endlessly good grazing grounds near the show pavilion. In addition to its own ice cream, Bauder's serves such nostalgic soda-fountain treats as a cherry Coke, a Green River, and a lime phosphate. There are fine sundaes, shakes, malts, sodas, and floats of every stripe. Summer is an especially good time to visit when the ice cream flavor rotation includes fresh strawberry and peach.

The savory menu includes classic lunch-counter sandwiches such as grilled cheese and a hot Reuben, as well as a "Roosevelt Special" of turkey, Swiss, and mustard grilled on a long roll.

Bauder Pharmacy was founded in 1922 by Carolyn Bauder, a pharmacist whose motto was "Cleanliness. Order. Service." Ice cream became part of the pharmacy repertoire shortly after World War II.

BIRDSALL'S ICE CREAM CO.

518 N. Federal Ave.   641-423-5365
Mason City, IA   **L D | $**

Opened in 1938, Birdsall's is a Mason City magnet for ice cream lovers. When she visited in the summer of 2014, Roadfood.com contributor Shiree Schade described the signature peach ice cream as having "excellent texture and tremendous flavor," and recommended having it with chopped fresh peaches on top. "Manna from Heaven!" she declared. A nice alternative if you crave a different kind of manna is to have it topped with Johnston's hot fudge. The ice cream has a powerful enough flavor to maintain its peachy nature even under a blanket of the velvety fudgy topping.

When peach ice cream is not in season, we recommend banana fudge ice cream, which contains real bananas. Birdsall's also offers a full menu of turtle sundaes, banana splits, cones, cups, shakes, and sodas.

★ BOB'S DRIVE-INN

Highway 75 S.   712-546-5445
Le Mars, IA   **L | $**

You will not find loosemeats listed on the menu that hangs above the order window at Bob's Drive-Inn. That is because it goes by one of its several aliases, a "tavern." The dish is so heralded hereabouts that Bob's doesn't even offer a hamburger. If you want beef, you get loosemeats. Browned, strained of fat, then pressure-cooked with sauce and spice, this meat is moist, full-flavored, and deeply satisfying. Each sandwich is made on a good-quality roll that proprietor Myles Kass secures from Le Mars's own Vander Meer Bakery.

If for some reason you don't want loosemeats, or if you want to sample every good hot dog, get a couple of franks. They are natural-casing Wimmer's-brand beauties made in Nebraska. In the best-of-both-worlds department, have a Bob Dog, which is one of these snappy franks topped with loosemeats. The preferred side dish is cheese balls, which are deep-fried cheese curds.

Root beer is house-made, and fruit shakes are made from real summer fruit.

CANTEEN LUNCH IN THE ALLEY

canteenottumwa.com

112 E. 2nd St.   641-682-5320
Ottumwa, IA   **L D** (closed Sun) **| $**

For a few years in the early 1990s, Canteen Lunch in the Alley was famous as the inspiration for a diner opened by the television character played by Roseanne Arnold (née Barr) in her eponymous sitcom. But for nearly a century it has been known and loved by real people for its version of Iowa loosemeats. This local specialty is a bunned sandwich that contains a heap of crumbly steamed and seasoned burger meat (preferably with pickle chips and a slice of orange cheese). The Canteen Lunch version is a nice little package, presented in a wax-paper wrap to hold the inevitable spillage.

Now nearly swallowed up by a large parking garage that went up around it, Canteen Lunch is a hole in the wall with room for not much more than a dozen customers at its low counter.

THE CHATTERBOX

| 120 N. Division St. | 712-563-3428 |
| Audubon, IA | **B L D** (closed Sun) \| $ |

What an awesome tenderloin, one of Iowa's finest. It overhangs its bun, but it is neither fun-house wide nor parchment thin. It is a perfectly balanced combo of tender pork and crunchy crust. It comes accoutered with pickle chips and a slice of white onion. Apply your own mustard and/or ketchup. We appreciate the audacity of the Chatterbox's "hamberloin," which piles a hamburger atop the fried pork patty in a bun, but as much as we like burgers in nearly every form, the combo doesn't do beef justice. Compared to the pork it crowns, the red meat is cloddish, adding only avoirdupois to what is, without the burger, a rather elegant sandwich.

The Chatterbox is open for three meals a day, and many regulars come to have coffee and conversation throughout the day.

★ COFFEE CUP CAFE

coffeecupcafe.com

| 616 4th St. | 641-594-3765 |
| Sully, IA | **B L D** (closed Sun) \| $ |

--★-- **LOCALS** **LOVE IT** --★-- If you are southeast of Des Moines looking for the sort of town café where locals come to eat and schmooze, here's the place. Breakfast is dandy—plate-wide golden pancakes and big rounds of sausage; there are eggs and potatoes of course, and sticky pecan rolls and cinnamon buns with a translucent sugar glaze, served warm with butter. Menu pillars at lunch include hot beef sandwiches (on made-here bread), tenderloins, meat loaf, and roast pork. And there is one square-meal special every day—we have fond memories of baked ham with mashed potatoes and apple salad. Dutch lettuce is a unique concoction of crisp, cold iceberg leaves bathed in a warm sweet-and-sour creamy mustard dressing with pieces of bacon and hard-cooked egg.

No matter what meal you eat, or what time of day you eat it, you must have pie at the Coffee Cup Cafe. Iowa is major pie country, and it is in just such inconspicuous small-town cafés that some of the very best are eaten. Looking for a good cream pie? Have a wedge of Coffee Cup banana cream. It quivers precariously as the waitress sets it down on the table, the custard jiggling like not-quite-set Jell-O below foamy white meringue. The crust doesn't *break* when touched with a fork; it *flakes*. The whole experience of cutting a mouthful, raising it to one's mouth, and savoring it is what we imagine it would be like to eat pastries on the moon or some planet where gravity is only a fraction of Earth's, for the word "light" barely does justice to the refinement of this piece of pie.

DAIRY SWEET

| 118 Iowa Ave. | 712-643-5116 |
| Dunlap, IA | **L D** \| $ |

It is likely the breaded pork tenderloin sandwich was invented in Indiana (see the review of Nick's Kitchen, p. 268), but the state that has taken the tenderloin most to heart—where hogs really ought to be the state animal—is Iowa. (Curiously, Iowa has no official state animal.) From border to border, but most especially in the land west of Des Moines, countless cafés and taverns make a specialty of tenderloins. Dairy Sweet's has won the Pork Producers' Association award as the state's best—a broad cutlet that is fairly thick compared to others and therefore very juicy. It is hand-breaded and shockingly irregular—a great wavy shape that seems far too large for its bun, the crust that hugs it seasoned to a fare-thee-well.

There is a nice short-order menu beyond tenderloins: burgers, broasted (pressure-fried) chicken, wings, and tacos on Tuesday. As the name of the place suggests, ice cream is a specialty. House motto: "Always a Sweet Deal."

DARRELL'S PLACE

darrellsplaceiowa.com

4010 1st St.   712-563-3922

Hamlin, IA   **L D** (closed Sun) | **$**

Darrell's Place looks more like a large utility shed than a restaurant; but aficionados of the tenderloin know that it is a culinary gem. Winner of the 2003 Iowa Pork Producers Association Award for the best tenderloin in the state, Darrell's serves tenderloins that are thick and juicy, enveloped in a wavy, thousand-facet crust that hugs the luscious lode of pork within. The band of meat is a good half-inch thick, making for an ultra-opulent eating experience. Unlike many of Iowa's best tenderloins, which are ridiculously large, this crisp-edged patty barely extends beyond the bun, meaning you can easily pick it up, even with one hand.

Darrell's rhubarb pie, made using stalks from customers' gardens, is peerless, piled into a master-class crust, its tantalizing sugar-tart filling balanced by a cascade of soft-serve vanilla ice cream.

GROVE CAFE

grovecafe.com

124 Main St.   515-232-9784

Ames, IA   **B L** | **$**

When you say "pancake" at the Grove Cafe, you might want to separate the word. In this place, a pancake is a *pan cake*—a good-sized layer of cake that has been cooked in a pan, or in this case, on the grill. Nearly an inch thick in its center, it is as wide as its plate—a round of steamy cooked batter that has an appealing orange hue. It comes with butter and a pitcher of syrup (all of which this cake can absorb with ease). With some peppery Iowa sausage patties, one of these cakes is a full-sized meal. Two of them, listed as a "short stack," are a breakfast for only the tallest of appetites.

Grove Cafe also offers omelets with hash browns and happy little slices of French toast for breakfast, as well as hamburgers, hot beef, and meat loaf at lunch. But for many of its longtime fans, including hordes of Iowa State alumni who have consumed tens of thousands of calories in these bare-tabled booths and at the low stools at the counter, pancakes are all that matter. To its most devoted fans, Grove Cafe is a pancake parlor.

IN'T VELD'S MEAT MARKET

intvelds.com

820 Main St.   641-628-3440

Pella, IA   **L** (closed Sun) | **$**

Most customers come to In't Veld's to shop for meat rather than to eat, and even those of us who are just passing through will find such good travel companions as summer sausage, dried beef, and wax-wrapped cheeses. For those in search of regional specialties, the meat to eat is ring bologna, also known as Pella bologna because this town is the only place it is made. It is a tube of sausage about as thick as a pepperoni stick, curled into a horseshoe shape—cured, smoked, cooked, and ready to eat. It is delicious sliced cold with a hunk of cheese and a piece of bread; it's even better when you can warm it up and cut it into thick discs like kielbasa.

For travelers, what is especially good about In't Veld's Market is that you can sit down right here and have a hot bologna sandwich: several thick slices on a fresh bakery bun . . . pass the mustard, please! In fact, a whole menu of meat-market sandwiches is available for eating here (or taking out) until midafternoon each day. In addition to the famous bologna (wonderful when paired with Gouda cheese), you can have house-dried beef on a bun, homemade bratwurst with sauerkraut on a hoagie roll, ham and Swiss, Reubens, and wraps. For dessert, we suggest a walk across the square to Jaarsma Bakery, a Dutch-accented shop with beguiling pastries, sweet cakes, and the alphabet-shaped cookies known as "Dutch letters."

IOWA MACHINE SHED

machineshed.com

11151 Hickman Rd.   515-270-6818
Urbandale, IA   **B L D** | $

The handful of Machine Shed restaurants in and around Des Moines are scrupulously planned to evoke idealized twentieth-century farm life. The one in Urbandale, at the edge of the city, is huge, its dining-room walls crowded with vintage farm implements, seed bags, and advertisements for country-style products. The staff dresses in farmhand attire (but clean!). While the menu has something for everyone, its highlights are big-food bonanzas that theoretically provide enough calories for a long day's work but, in fact, make us need to take a nap.

Hamburgers are a nice eight ounces each, and the chicken potpie is a beauty; but the meat to eat is pork: crisp-fried tenderloins made into sandwiches, stuffed loin of pork, and best of all, the Iowa pork chop. Iowans make an issue of pork chops, differentiating between ordinary pork chops and Iowa chops, the latter cut so thick that the meat takes on the character of a roast. At the Machine Shed, we ate the thickest pork chop we have ever seen . . . and topped it off with mighty hunks of pie and cake.

Breakfast is hugely hearty, featuring cinnamon rolls as big as a bread box and fruit-filled sweet rolls dripping with frosting. The variety of pig meat to accompany eggs is complete, and pancakes are plate-sized.

Unlike most Roadfood restaurants, the Machine Shed is a highway-exit tourist attraction with an entire front room devoted to selling rustic-themed souvenirs and snacks. Don't expect small-town charm, but do expect a true Iowa meal as big as the outdoors.

JESSE'S EMBERS

theoriginaljessesembers.com

3301 Ingersoll Ave.   515-255-6011
Des Moines, IA   **L D** (closed Sun) | $$

Jesse's Embers is the sort of supper club you don't find much anymore: dark and cool, home of expertly made cocktails and high-quality meat-and-potatoes meals. Ensconce yourself at a comfy table and start with a pile of kettle-hot onion rings and an iceberg lettuce salad topped with creamy garlic dressing and croutons.

Although the menu lists fish and chicken, Iowa pork chops, and baby-back ribs, it seems wrong not to get red meat: a sirloin, rib eye, or shockingly flavorful filet mignon. Beef is what has made Jesse's a beloved destination since the early 1960s. Seared over an open flame, steaks have a succulence that satisfies hunger with great waves of flavor. On the side, you want cottage-fried potatoes or a baked spud loaded with butter and sour cream.

LARSEN'S PUB

4206 Main St.   712-764-4052
Elk Horn, IA   **L D** | $

Winner of the 2007 Iowa Pork Producers Association Award for the state's best tenderloin, Larsen's Pub makes one that is approximately a half pound of meat, pounded tender so that it extends beyond its bun in all directions, but still so thick that the big vein of pork within the golden crust spurts juice when you sink your teeth into it. Spread with mustard and bunned with lettuce, tomato, and pickle chips, this fine sandwich is a good explanation for why the tenderloin has earned such stalwart devotees.

Larsen's is an extremely inconspicuous storefront tavern in a Danish-ancestored town known also for its authentic Danish windmill, the Danish Inn (*frikadeller* meat balls, *medisterpolse* sausage, and *smørrebrød* sandwiches), and its annual end-of-May Tivoli Fest, featuring folk dancers, a costumed parade, and Danish-themed food vendors.

MILES INN

2622 Leech Ave.   712-276-9825
Sioux City, IA   **L D** | **$**

--★--
LOCALS
LOVE IT
--★--

In northwest Iowa, taverns (also known as loosemeats) are more popular than hamburgers. Dozens of restaurants serve them, and each has its own twist on the basic formula, which is ground beef that is gently spiced and cooked loose so it remains pebbly when put upon a bun. The meat is generally garnished with pickle chips and mustard, often with cheese, and the sandwich is almost never served on a plate.

Miles Inn calls its taverns Charlie Boys after Charlie Miles, who was founder John Miles's son. Served in a wax paper wrap, taverns are well fatted with a concentrated beef flavor that even a sirloin steak cannot match. (Raise your hand if you agree with us that the one meal that most fully satisfies the deepest hunger for beef is a great burger, even more than a great steak.) Two or three Charlie Boys make a hearty lunch, and the right libation is a schooner of beer from the tap.

Built in 1925, the Miles Inn is a sturdy neighborhood gathering place that sells suds by the case as well as by the draught. Seating is at tables or the bar, and if the Hawkeyes are playing, you can be sure the game will be on all house TVs. Charlie Boys are the only available hot food.

MILWAUKEE WIENER HOUSE

301 Douglas St.   712-277-3449
Sioux City, IA   **L D** (closed Sun) | **$**

Milwaukee Wiener House specializes in Coneys, formally known as Coney Island hot dogs, which are franks blanketed with chili. You see them marshaled on the grill by the window as you walk in. The formation is impeccable: row upon row, side-by-side, identical in shape, not one out of place. All condiments are available, but connoisseurs know there is only one way to go: mustard, chili, and chopped raw onions. Each dog comes fitted in a warm bun so soft and fresh that it shows finger-mark impressions from the gentlest grasp. The hot dogs themselves are pale pink tube steaks well complemented by the cinnamony zest of the house-made fine-grind beef chili. Three or four such steamy babies make a nice meal. Hamburgers and loosemeats are available for wiener frowners.

The Milwaukee Wiener House is a big rectangular dining room with rows of booths to which you tote your own meal after ordering at the counter. It opens at six in the morning, as it has done for nearly a century (its original location was nearby on 4th Street). Old advertising posted on the wall boasts that it has served 4 million hot dogs, but about eight years ago we were told that the tally had already topped 10 million.

MR. BIBBS

2705 6th Ave.   515-243-0929
Des Moines, IA   **L** | **$**

Mr. Bibbs lacks all the usual markers for charm, even those one might apply to a diner. It is no-frills stark, a kind of neighborhood miniature mess hall with booths lined up like desks in a humorless teacher's classroom. But check out these onion rings: hot from the fry kettle, each individual hoop is a circle of luscious crust that melts on the tongue. And the chocolate malt is terrific, just thick enough to make straw-sucking seem like athletic activity.

The main reason you want to come to Mr. Bibbs is its tenderloin. Four kinds are offered: regular (undressed), unbreaded, chili-topped, and deluxe. Deluxe is the way to go: a thin, double-wide loin garnished with lettuce, pickle chips, chopped raw onions, sliced tomato, mustard, and ketchup. It's a winning combo of crunch and oink, all the condiments tickling the taste buds the way only a fully dressed tenderloin can do.

SMITTY'S TENDERLOIN SHOP

smittystenderloins.com

1401 SW Army Post Rd.   515-287-4742
Des Moines, IA   L D (Tues–Sat) | $

"Home of the REAL Whopper" says a cartoon on Smitty's wall, and if you know the taste of Iowa, you know that in this case "Whopper" does not refer to a hamburger. It means a tenderloin: pork tenderloin, pounded thin and plate-wide, breaded and fried crisp and sandwiched in a bun. Smitty's Tenderloin Shop has been a tenderloin lovers' destination since 1952.

Like all top tenderloin tenderers, Smitty's is a humble setting. It has a scattering of tables and a friendly counter where locals sit and shoot the breeze at lunch hour. Although the menu includes a handful of other lunch-counter meals—hamburgers, double hamburgers, Coney Island hot dogs—"King Tenderloin" is the dish to eat. Available in small or large sizes (small is large; large is nearly a foot across), Smitty's tenderloin is served on an ordinary burger bun, which it dwarfs. Even a person with abnormally long fingers could not pick it up like a normal sandwich, but it is brittle enough to easily tear off and eat pieces from the circumference until the bun is reachable. Twice breaded with cracker meal, then cooked in soybean oil ("for the flavor," says third-generation chef Ben Smith), Smitty's King is all about the crunch that envelops a slim ribbon of juicy pork.

ST. OLAF TAP

106 S. Main St.   563-783-7723
St. Olaf, IA   L D | $

A sign outside the St. Olaf Tap advises, "Put Something Big Between Your Buns." It refers to the one-and-a-quarter-pound hunk of pork tenderloin that gets pounded out until it becomes a ragged-edged circle larger than a dinner plate, then breaded and fried crisp. The colossal hunk of food is presented between two halves of a hamburger bun that appears so relatively small that it reminds us of a tater tot. You can ask for it between halves of two buns, or three or four. Even a quartet is dwarfed by the meat within.

Without question, St. Olaf Tap serves the biggest of all tenderloins in the southern Midwest's tenderloin belt; it is also one of the most delicious: a savory balancing act of crunchy crust and succulent white pork, beautifully abetted by jumbo onion rings and/or corn fritters. Half-size and quarter-size versions also are available, but if you are more than one person (or if you have an insatiable appetite), we highly recommend getting the super jumbo; it's an only-in-Iowa dining experience.

TASTEE INN & OUT

tasteeinnandout.com

2610 Gordon Dr.   712-255-0857
Sioux City, IA   L D | $

Tastee Inn & Out is strictly takeout. Meals are procured at either a walk-up or drive-through window, and they are eaten either in the car or at a picnic table in the parking lot. Run by the Calligan family for over a half century now, this ingenuous eatery specializes in what it calls a Tastee sandwich, known elsewhere in northwest Iowa as a tavern or a loosemeats: made with finely ground beef that is seasoned and barely sauced, it is steam-cooked then shoveled into a bun with a slice of bright orange cheese, pickle chips, and onion. It is sloppy and unjustifiable by Cordon Bleu standards but hard not to like. Its only possible companion is an order of onion chips, which are bite-sized, crisp-fried petals of sweet onion, served with a creamy dip that eaters in the Plains farther west would recognize as a variant of fry sauce.

TC'S POINT AFTER

719 6th Ave.   563-659-8188
DeWitt, IA   L D | $

With its neon beer signs, Chicago Cubs memorabilia décor, and televisions everywhere (including the men's room), TC's Point After does not scream "Roadfood." But thanks to Dale Fine, who goes by the screen name Wanderingjew and has made a point of eating his way around Iowa, we recommend it wholeheartedly for its BPT, aka breaded pork tenderloin. Listed on the menu as Chuckie's Famous Tenderloin (after founder Chuck Cox), this tender cut comes enveloped in a crunchy, vividly seasoned crust, typically dressed with mustard, pickle, and onions. If you order it as a platter, you get thin, crisp French fries and extraordinarily creamy house-made coleslaw on the side. The tenderloin stars, but TC's menu also includes steaks, burgers, wings, and various deep-fried veggies that go well with beer and watching the game.

WILTON CANDY KITCHEN

wiltoncandykitchen.com

310 Cedar St.   563-732-2278
Wilton, IA $

We've never sampled Hadacol, the high-proof patent medicine that Colonel Tom Parker used to hawk before he became Elvis Presley's manager. But we do endorse the teetotaler's version of it made at the Wilton Candy Kitchen—an essential stop for anyone in search of small-town America the way it used to be.

Fiz-biz historians trace a fountain on this spot to the mid-1880s; today's Candy Kitchen dates back to 1910, when a young immigrant named Gus Nopoulos came to town and rented the place to make candy and sell soda and ice cream. The Candy Kitchen is a trip back to a world of long-forgotten concoctions such as a pink lady (strawberry, cherry, and vanilla flavoring), an oddball (strawberry and vanilla), and a dipsy doodle (six different flavors). Cokes and cherry Cokes are mixed to order, using water carbonated on-premises and Coke syrup. The late grandson of Gus, George Nopoulos, told us that Coke syrup, once a fountain staple in every American town, is getting hard to find. "We've got to go all the way to Cedar Rapids for it now," he lamented. That syrup is half of the formula for the Nopoulos family version of the Hadacol (cola plus root beer), the name of which George explained to us thusly: "They 'hada call' it something."

MICHIGAN

BORTELL'S FISHERIES

5528 S. Lakeshore Dr.   231-843-3337
Ludington, MI   **L D** (summer only) | **$**

You catch it, they'll cook it at this 1898 fish market and smokehouse that has all the exterior charm of a roadside garage. If you do not BYO seafood, you'll have a choice of walleye, smelt, catfish, trout, and whitefish from nearby waters. Bortell's also imports ocean perch and Alaskan salmon. Smoked fish is sold by the piece or pound; fried fish comes picnic-ready with French fries or onion rings and coleslaw. Step up to the counter, place your order, and pay. There is no dining room and business is strictly takeout. Once you get your fish, find a picnic table just outside or across the road at Summit Township Park on the Lake Michigan shore.

★ THE CHERRY HUT

cherryhutstore.com

211 N. Michigan Ave.   231-882-4431
Beulah, MI   **L D** (Memorial Day–mid-Oct) | **$**

Opened as a farm stand in 1922, the Cherry Hut moved to its present location in 1937. It has since become a restaurant with a repertoire of terrific comfort food: turkey with dressing, meat loaf with mushroom gravy, roast pork, and a different home-made soup every day. Cherry-centric dishes include turkey salad brightened up with cherries, a cherry jelly and peanut butter sandwich, and a cherry sundae. But it is pie that is the destination dish. A single serving is one-quarter of a full-sized pie; spilling out its sides are bright red, locally grown cherries with a sweetness balanced by a beguiling tart undertone. The crust is melt-in-the-mouth savory. Topped by a scoop of creamy vanilla ice cream, it's a perfect, all-American dessert.

Dining facilities include outdoor as well as indoor tables, and part of the Cherry Hut experience is buying things to take home. The restaurant shop sells not only whole fresh pies but also jellies, jams, and a wide array of Cherry Jerry, the Happy Pie-Faced Boy souvenirs.

CROSSROADS LOUNGE

900 County Rd. 480   906-249-8912
Marquette, MI   **B L D** | **$**

★ LOCALS LOVE IT ★ Crossroads Lounge opens at 7 a.m. and serves food until 10 p.m. (after which the bar stays open). It is locally famous for its Friday-night fish fry, but it also hosts a regular clientele of breakfasters who come for big omelets served in a skillet. Yoopers (that's people of the Upper Peninsula, aka the UP) come for half-pound hamburgers, pizzas, sandwiches, and a bargain lunch of bottomless soup-salad-breadsticks for $6.99. But the real deal here is the pasty.

It was on a pasty hunt that we were directed to this sociable outfit on the outskirts of the city by a man up Houghton way who told us that Crossroads' pasty was the best in the UP. We do not agree that it's the best, but it's definitely *one* of the best, packed with both beef and pork, as well as carrots in addition to the customary rutabaga, potato, and onion. While a common fault of inferior pasties is that they can be bland and/or dry, this one sings with spice and is moist enough that gravy is redundant.

Crossroads Lounge is all set up for takeout pasties: hot and ready to eat, cool and ready to heat, or frozen and ready to bake.

DON'S DRIVE-IN

donsdriveinmi.com

2030 N. US Hwy. 31   231-714-9993
Traverse City, MI   **L D | $**

Don's opened the year Elvis joined the army. Selections on its jukebox evoke days of American mid-century car culture at its prime, and the ambience is vintage rock-and-roll: hubcaps and album covers decorate the walls and you can dine inside or in your car, where meals are served on window trays. The menu is basically burgers and fries, featuring the old-fashioned "basket" presentation, meaning a sandwich sided by French fries and coleslaw.

The tough decision to make at Don's is whether to get a hamburger or a brace of Coney Island hot dogs. The burger is thick and juicy; a Coney, topped with chili sauce, is a Midwest paradigm. Whatever you get to eat, there should be no question about the beverage. Make it a milk shake. Don's blends its shakes to order, either large or small, both big enough to fill at least a couple of glasses, and both thick enough to require powerful suction with a straw. Chocolate and vanilla shakes are good all the time; in the summer, order a cherry shake—it is made with fresh local cherries.

GUSTAFSON'S

gustafsonssmokedfishinc.com

W. 4467 US-2   906-292-5424
Brevort, MI   **L | $$**

Michigan's Upper Peninsula lends itself to waterside picnics. A few chaws of beef jerky, a hunk or two of smoked freshwater fish, a stack of saltine crackers, a bag of cheese curds, and a few beers, plus the scenic beauty of Lake Michigan: What's better than that? And where better to get them than at Gustafson's, a gas station and party store that has it all ready-to-eat but does not offer full-service meals.

Even with your eyes closed, you'll find Gustafson's as you cruise along the shore road (we don't recommend driving this way) because a sugar maple haze from a quartet of smoldering smokers outside clouds the air with the unbelievably appetizing smell of whitefish, trout, menominee, chub, and salmon turning gorgeous shades of gold. Inside, coolers are arrayed with the firm-fleshed beauties, which you can buy by the piece, wrapped in butcher paper. Utensils and plates are unnecessary; it's a pleasure to use one's fingers to pick flavorful chunks of fish straight from the paper.

The beef jerky is top round, cut into strips, marinated, then slow-smoked over maple. You can get it Cajun-spiced, barbecue-flavored, or traditional smoky-sweet. Jerky is available through the mail, by the pound.

IRONTOWN PASTIES

irontownpasties.com

801 N. Teal Lake Ave.   906-475-6828
Negaunee, MI   **L D | $**

On the exterior wall at the back of Irontown Pasties is a very old sign, partially gone now to make way for a new window. Its only completely legible letters are the last three: I-E-S, but you don't have to be a professional semiologist to know that the first four letters are P-A-S-T. This sign out of the past is a reminder that the building that now houses Irontown Pasties has purveyed the Upper Peninsula's favorite meat pies for a long, long time, its most recent prior incarnation being Grandma T's Pasty Shop. The current owners, John and Lori Cizek, bought Grandma T's, along with the recipes; then, as Mr. Cizek jokes, they "changed everything."

You still can get a typical pasty here, and it is a dandy: beefy comfort food in a lovely tender crust—satisfying plain, but exciting when decorated with one of the three degrees of hot jalapeño ketchup Irontown offers. Other pasty choices include vegetarian with cheese, vegan with no lard or suet, spicy beef, and chicken potpie pasties. When served on premises, they come with a fork, but Irontown's pasties would be easy to eat with your hands.

For dessert, have either Cedar Crest ice cream (a northern Midwest brand) or fruit turnovers that look a lot like pasties but are filled with compote of blueberry, raspberry, apple, or cherry.

THE JAMPOT

societystjohn.com/store

6559 State Hwy. M-26   No phone
Eagle Harbor, MI   **L** (mid-June–mid-Oct) | **$**

---★--- **VEGETARIAN-** **FRIENDLY** ---★---
In a fairy-tale hut in the Eagle Harbor forest of Michigan's Upper Peninsula, monks of the Society of Saint John make cookies, muffins, cakes, and breads. Simply stepping out of the car in the Jampot parking lot can be dizzying from the warm smell of Jamaican black cake soaked with liquor and filled with fruits marinated in wine and rum. As its name suggests, this place also is renowned for jams and jellies made from Keweenaw's wild fruits: thimbleberry, strawberry, raspberry, bilberry, blueberry, dewberry, cokecherry, pincherry, sugarplum, blackberry, and apple.

There is no place to eat at the Jampot, other than one of the most beautiful dining spaces on the planet: the great outdoors of Michigan's Upper Peninsula. We grabbed a big, muffin-shaped banana-walnut bread packed with blueberries, a bag of molasses-powered gingerbread cookies, and a lemon-frosted pumpkin muffin, then drove to a nearby snacking spot overlooking achingly beautiful Lake Medora.

Gazing at the opposite shore, where autumn trees were perfectly mirrored on the still blue waters, we were in heaven, thanks in no small part to the monks.

★ JEAN KAY'S

jeankayspasties.com

1635 Presque Isle   906-228-5310
Marquette, MI   **L D** | **$**

Having had its ups and downs, Jean Kay's pasty shop currently is flying high. It was started by the Harsch family in 1975 in Iron Mountain and, as Jean Kay's Sweet Shop, its specialty was donuts. But then Mr. Donut came to Iron Mountain. Tourists favored the franchise, and when donut sales plummeted, Jean Kay Harsch suggested they make pasties. She felt the Upper Peninsula could use a place that made the British Isles meat pies the way her grandmother used to do it back when they were a staple in the diet of the region's Cornish settlers, who were known as Cousin Jacks and Cousin Jennies.

If you want to know what Grandmother's pasties were like, visit Jean Kay's of Marquette, a restaurant started by Jean Kay's son Brian, sold to someone else, then rebought by Brian when he came to believe that his successor's pasties were not up to snuff. Here you will savor a classic, made with steak (not burger meat) and suet (not lard). Although rutabaga-free pasties are available, Brian explained the value of rutabagas in the filling—an ingredient frequently ignored by Jenny-come-lately bakers. "It is an amazing vegetable," he enthused. "Aside from its own flavor, it works with whatever else is in there to keep the moisture flowing. It is a conduit."

While Jean Kay's is a small storefront with a few tables inside and out, the pasty-making part of the operation is big. Being USDA-approved, it can FedEx half-baked, frozen pasties coast-to-coast, anytime between September and May. Varieties include steak, veggie with cheese, and mini pasties that make wonderful hors d'oeuvres.

JOHNNY'S HAM KING

8209 E. 8 Mile Rd.   586-920-2571
Warren, MI   **B L | $**

Now that Motor City muscle has atrophied and Motown is ancient history, we suggest Detroiters find pride in their ham. Thanks to a truck driver named Joe, who tipped us off to what he called "out of this world" ham, we discovered that this is a city where little diners make a big deal of ham at low prices. Mike's Famous Ham Place in Corktown and Johnny's Ham King in Warren are the Big Two, where the pinkest part of the pig is sliced to order and sizzled on the griddle, served on the side of eggs for breakfast or sandwiched, still warm, in soft onion rolls for lunch.

Gearjammer Joe, who especially recommended Johnny's four-egg omelet with ham and buttery, extra-crisp potatoes, noted that a swivel stool at the long counter was the place to sit. Here is where you get to watch Pete, a short-order cook with a quarter century of experience, wield his spatula like a samurai sword and entertain customers with impassioned political soliloquies. In addition to the Ham King, ham and bean soup is a must.

★ KRAZY JIM'S BLIMPY BURGER

blimpyburger.com
304 S. Ashley   734-663-4590
Ann Arbor, MI   **L D | $**

When the University of Michigan muscled Krazy Jim's Blimpy Burger off the property it had occupied since opening in 1953, burger fans throughout the nation wept. Was this the end of Blimpy? Blessedly no. A new location now serves the last word in good, greasy, griddle-fried hamburgers.

Service along the line is still fast and furious. "Want fried?" someone behind the counter demands. The question refers to side-dish vegetables, including broccoli stalks reminiscent of muscular tempura, cream-centered steak fries, and big, irregular onion rings in self-detaching crust. Moments after the fried food goes into boiling oil and a yard farther down the line, the cook spins around from the griddle and makes eye contact so he can find out how many patties you want. Say a number from two to five. At ten-to-a-pound, two is minimal. Ice-cream-scoop-sized spheres of chuck, ground that morning, are slapped down onto the grill in doubles, trios, quartets, and quintuplets. Next, name your roll: Kaiser, regular, or onion? Want cheese? Say Cheddar, Swiss, provolone, American, blue, or feta. Fifth question: Any extras on top? These include fried eggs, bacon, salami, grilled onions, banana peppers, and mushrooms. Finally, when everything else is settled, give the assembler a list of condiments you want applied, naming the wet ones first. By this time, you are at the cash register at the end of the line. The fried things have arrived in overflowing cardboard boats, and your burger, precisely built to your specifications, is wrapped in wax paper and ready to go.

According to generally accepted burger-making rules, Blimpies are cooked all wrong. As soon as a sphere of meat hits the iron, it is squished flat, slapped and flipped, sometimes hit so vigorously that it disintegrates like Iowa loosemeats (but it's reintegrated with a deft spatula), and finally leaned on hard before getting topped with cheese et al and bunned. Call it burger abuse, but these hamburgers are fatty enough to take it and still come off the griddle oozing juice. No doubt, a single plain Blimpy on a bun would be boring. But no one gets a single, and only an ascetic would get one plain. A triple, quad, or quint, layered with cheese (on each of the patties), piled with onions, bacon, banana peppers, or olives (green or black), festooned with romaine leaves, tomato slices, mustard, mayo, and pickles, and sandwiched in a superb onion roll, is an enormous feast that transcends greasy-spoon ignominy.

LAFAYETTE CONEY ISLAND

118 W. Lafayette Blvd.   313-964-8198
Detroit, MI   **L D | $**

Although the term Coney Island comes from the Brooklyn beach resort where the hot dog supposedly was invented in 1867, you will find nothing called a Coney Island hot dog in the New York area. And the Coneys you do find nearly everywhere else in the nation bear only scant resemblance to the hot dogs of New York. While Coneys vary, their common denominator is chili topping, which never was part of the boardwalk formula. About 99 percent of them also are served with mustard and chopped raw onions.

Nowhere is the passion for Coneys more intense than Detroit, where an adjoining pair of rival storefront doggeries known as American Coney Island and Lafayette Coney Island serve franks that might look pretty much alike to the casual observer but are cause for adamant partisanship. We like them both, but last time we compared, Lafayette won.

Make no mistake, Lafayette's Coneys are not aristocratic; they are plebeian. But the harmony of spicy hot dog, soft white bun, smooth chili, bright yellow mustard, and crisp onions (and maybe shredded cheese too) is culinary magic. When the craving for one (or, more likely, four) of them strikes, Kobe beef wouldn't satisfy. It is possible to order one with "heavy chili," but we believe that throws the precious balance off. Better to have your extra chili blanketing French fries or cheese fries. The appropriate beverage with Detroit Coneys is a can of Vernor's ginger ale.

LAWRY'S PASTY SHOP

lawryspasties.com

2381 US 41 W.   906-226-5040
Ishpeming, MI   **B L D | $**

The sweet roll at Lawry's Pasty Shop is among the nation's pastry behemoths, approximately six inches square with enough white icing for a birthday cake. It's pretty good for that kind of thing, but heaven forbid you expend all of your appetite eating one. A healthy appetite is essential for enjoying Lawry's real specialties: pasties and *cudighi*.

One look at the semi-open kitchen behind the order counter provides evidence of the menu's claim that "We still make our pasties with pride every day just like our grandmother did when she started this business in 1946." They are fine, hefty, hand-formed pastry pockets packed with suet-saturated beef, potato, onion, and rutabaga. Succulent as it is, Lawry's pasty is portable enough that a half-eaten one can be put back into the paper bag in which it's served for a nice car snack later in the day.

Lawry's also makes an amazing *cudighi*, which is the sandwich made from pattied Italian sausage by the same name. A passion in the central UP, *cudighi* (the sausage) is distinguished by its use of such floral spices as nutmeg, clove, and allspice. Put between slices of flatbread along with onions, peppers, mushrooms, Italian sauce, and grated cheese, it is a colossal meal.

NORTHSIDE GRILL

northsidegrill.com

1015 Broadway St.   734-995-0965
Ann Arbor, MI   **B L | $**

The Northside Grill is not a pancake house. The popular pine-paneled café has a full menu for breakfast and for lunch, but other than drinking lots of its really good coffee, we've not been able to get much beyond the superb pancakes. Best of the bunch may be the apple–oat bran 'cakes with their rugged, apple-chunk texture and cinnamon twist. A similar configuration is available with blueberries. Plain buttermilk pancakes are too dairy-delicious to be called plain. Potato pancakes are crunchy on the outside but creamy within, and sparkling with herbs and spices, topped with grilled red onion and accompanied by ramekins of sour cream and applesauce.

We loved our Big Easy Omelet made with andouille sausage and a full measure of Cajun spice, and did manage to sample a piece of masterful apple pie, but there are so many subjects for further study, including cinnamon-swirl French toast and breakfast burritos, not to mention a good-looking lunch repertoire of burgers, chili, Mexican plates, and salads.

RALPH'S ITALIAN DELI

ralphsitaliandeli.com

601 Palms Ave.   906-485-4557
Ishpeming, MI   L D | $

Across the street from the US Ski & Snowboard Hall of Fame and cattycorner from a boring Pizza Hut, you will find Ralph's Italian Deli. It is anything but boring; it is an Upper Peninsula gem.

From the house bakery come sweet rye, cardamom loaves, and Italian breads, as well as enormous frosted apple-cinnamon rolls for breakfast. The butchers in back make sausage of all kinds, including the local fave, *cudighi*. Pronounced cud-a-gee with a hard *g*, it is such a specialty of Ralph's that there is a map posted on the back wall of the dining room where pushpins indicate all the places in the United States and beyond to which the butchers have shipped their sausage, titled "Where Has All the Cudighi Gone?"

A *cudighi* (sandwich) is available with a grilled patty of mild, medium, or hot sausage on a housemade white or whole-wheat roll. Standard dressing at Ralph's is mozzarella, mustard, ketchup, and onion. It's a strange combination of condiments, but somehow on this dense, crusty-edged sausage with perfumy seasoning, it works. For those interested in reducing their calorie intake, Ralph's also makes turkey *cudighi*.

SUOMI HOME BAKERY & RESTAURANT

54 Huron St.   906-482-3220
Houghton, MI   B L | $

More people of Finnish descent live in Michigan's Upper Peninsula than anywhere outside of Europe, so it is hardly affectation that the menu of the Suomi Home Bakery & Restaurant lists dishes in Finnish with English translations. You can get familiar *voileivät* (sandwiches) for lunch, and rice pudding or banana cream pie for *jälkiruoat* (dessert), but we recommend *aamiainen* (breakfast—served all day), for which *nisu* bread, perfumed with cardamom, is made into Finnish French toast, and *pannukakku* is the star attraction. Described as a Finnish pancake, *pannukakku* puts us in mind of a crustless egg-custard pie—sweet, creamy, fundamental. One large cake, about

a half inch thick, is baked in a glass tray and served in sunny yellow four-by-four-inch squares along with warm raspberry sauce. The sauce is wonderful, but we used it on *nisu* toast, unwilling to modify the pancake.

In some ways, Suomi is a classic American town café, where locals come to share morning coffee and regulars are well known by the staff. But the chatter, like the unusual food, lets you know you are someplace different. On our first visit one morning, it took a while to realize that cross-table conversations in the spacious dining area actually were in English rather than some Scandinavian language. It was the dialect known as Yooper, from UP (Upper Peninsula), a curiously musical blend that sounds Finnish and German and a bit Canadian and is especially strong northwest of Marquette.

The bill of fare at this handsome place, decorated with vintage photographs of copper-country history, is not all exotic. You can get bacon and eggs for breakfast (better yet, sausage and eggs; the dense, herby sausage links are made across the Keweenaw Waterway in Hancock) and hamburgers and ordinary sandwiches at lunch. And of course you can have a pasty filled with rugged clumps of beef and little irregular nuggets of potato and rutabaga. For a Finnish finish, end a meal with a bowl of cooked, cooled dried fruit known as *visku vellia*.

TONI'S COUNTRY KITCHEN

79 3rd St.   906-337-0611
Laurium, MI   B L D | $

Toni's is a few blocks off US 41, the main road leading up through the Keweenaw Peninsula. We likely never would have found it if an enthusiast we met in Houghton hadn't told us that his wife used to make *nisu* and saffron bread until they discovered Toni's, where the bread is so good that his wife hung up her apron. Those loaves, made by many Finnish bakeries in northernmost Michigan, are just two of the memorable eats.

Sticky buns: We smelled them the moment we walked in the front door. Three big round clusters of pull-apart buns were set on a rack atop the glass bakery case to cool. Each roll severed from the motherloaf was modest-sized but big-flavored. Just inside the front door, to the left, we peeked into the semi-open kitchen, where bakers were rolling dough on a floured table and another woman was plowing forearm-deep to hand-mix a big pan full of ingredients destined to be the filling of pasties. Toni's pasties are handsome fellas, light and elegant yet profoundly beefy.

It was late fall when we stopped in. The modest, one-room café was buzzing with conversations among locals who were reminiscing about the summer and anticipating the snows to come. When we ordered pasties, the waitress beamed with pride and exclaimed, "The best, ever!" We left with bags full of oven-warm molasses cookies and a loaf of *povitica,* a nut-rich sweet bread of central European heritage.

Note: Toni's closes just before Christmas and reopens at the end of January.

TRENARY HOME BAKERY

trenaryhomebakery.com

E2918 State Hwy. M-67   906-446-3330
Trenary, MI   **B** (closed Sun) | **$**

-- ★ --
LOCALS
LOVE IT
-- ★ --

Like biscotti and zwieback, Trenary Toast is a brittle, twice-baked bread that is ideal for dunking. But unlike the first two, both of which literally mean twice-baked in their countries of origin (Italy and Germany), Trenary Toast is named for the one and only small-town bakery that makes it: Trenary Home Bakery in Trenary, Michigan. Available plain, sugared, or cinnamon-sugared, it is—like Vernor's ginger ale and Detroit-style square pizza—treasured by those who grew up with it.

Trenary Toast can be found in markets and delis throughout the central Upper Peninsula, as well as at a few places in lower Michigan. Although it virtually never gets stale, it is a special pleasure to get some straight from the source—a charming little bakery-café that also offers breads, cinnamon rolls, and cookies, along with coffee for sit-down snacking on the spot.

YESTERDOG

yesterdog.com

1505 Wealthy St. SE   616-336-0746
Grand Rapids, MI   **L D** | **$**

Courteous service? No way. Comfortable, modern accommodations? Not here. Neat and tidy meals? Not a chance! Snappy-skinned boiled hot dogs loaded into steamed buns and smothered with sloppy chili sauce, cheese, onions, mustard, pickles, sauerkraut, and just about any other condiment you can name? This is the place. Chili is pretty much de rigueur; you can pick your toppings one by one or simply ask for an ultra, which is some of everything.

Yesterdog has been around since 1976, and today it is a self-consciously retro place with vintage advertising signs sharing wall space with pictures of happy customers wearing Yesterdog T-shirts and a pre-electric cash register. It is almost always crowded, so much so that there is frequently a mob of people out on the sidewalk waiting to get in, and it doesn't empty out until long after midnight. Tips are given to the staff by tossing coins into the bell flare of an old-time gramophone horn.

ZINGERMAN'S DELI

zingermansdeli.com

422 Detroit St.   734-663-3354
Ann Arbor, MI   **B L D** | **$$**

It started small, but Zingerman's has become a culinary colossus that includes a mail-order business, creamery, bakehouse, coffee shop, and estimable full-service roadhouse (at 2501 Jackson Ave.). While not every success proves the adage that they must be doing something right, the fact is that Zingerman's doesn't merely do something right; it does everything fantastically well.

Sandwiches are our favorite things, made with such top-notch ingredients as Nueske's bacon, Amish free-range chicken, Niman Ranch pastrami, Michigan-grown vegetables, Italian salami, Arkansas ham, and smoked salmon from Maine. They are assembled on the best bread in the Midwest: world-class baguettes, the best old-fashioned double-baked

Jewish rye in the nation, sourdoughs, chile-Cheddar, pecan raisin, or challah. And let's not even get into such peripheral (*not!*) items as excellent pickles, olive tapenade, smoked fish salads, and multiple cheese spreads, including pimiento cheese that competes with anything in the South.

Obtaining lunch can be confusing. You enter the surprisingly small deli, which is a retail operation selling meats, breads, cheeses, and so on, and browse a menu posted all over the wall. While you are figuring out what you want, a server will approach to take your order and your name. Find a seat (lots of nice ones outdoors for fair-weather dining), to which your food will soon be brought. The staff is extremely friendly and patient, and they are full of helpful recommendations if you can't decide between, say, halloumi and Muenster cheese.

Zingerman's is more expensive than an average sandwich shop. A BLT is $9.50–$10.99, depending on size; grilled cheese is $6.50–$7.99. But what you get is far superior to, and considerably bigger than, an average sandwich. Roadfood omnivores will find it frustrating because a single visit, no matter how much you order, will provide only a glimmer of all the good things there are to eat . . . and to see and to smell.

MINNESOTA

AL'S BREAKFAST

413 14th Ave. SE   602-331-9991
Minneapolis, MN   **B** | **$**

Al's is open year-round, but the coziest time to eat in this pint-sized diner near the University of Minnesota is from October through April, when the windows cloud with breakfast-scented steam from the well-seasoned griddle where pancakes, eggs, hash browns, and corned beef hash sizzle. It is impossible to convey the joie de vivre at Al's, where a patron once rhapsodized to us, "Al's is an organism. It is not some soulless concept restaurant that a corporate idea man at a drawing board designed. Good things happen here; people's lives change. If you want a car, or an apartment, or a sweetheart, come in and sit at the counter. Come in, have coffee, and chat a while. Pretty soon, I promise, you will get what you need. Al's has a life of its own, above and beyond any of us. I truly believe it is a crossroads of the universe."

OK, then, how about those buttermilk pancakes? They are broad, thin, and slightly sticky inside, with a good, sour smack. Rivulets of butter and sweet syrup complete their flavor perfectly; or you can get them made with blueberries or giant blackberries. The other basic batter variation is whole wheat, which has a wholesome, earthy flavor; either batter can be studded with corn kernels or walnuts as the pancakes cook. For garnishing these distinguished flapjacks, you can choose extra-cost maple syrup, sour cream, or bowls of berries. Beyond pancakes, Al's offers perfectly poached eggs, well-oiled corned beef hash, omelets, and crunchy hash browns.

BETTY'S PIES
bettyspies.com

1633 Hwy. 61   218-834-3367
Two Harbors, MN   **B L D** | **$**

Betty's sports a full menu of walleye sandwiches, hamburgers, wraps, salads, and Upper Peninsula pasties, but its reputation was earned by pies. Pies still are the reason to visit. Fruit pies are heavyweights, cream pies thick and creamy, and a few years ago Betty's introduced an item called a pie shake. Yes, it is what it sounds like. One entire piece of pie of whatever flavor you choose is blended with ice cream and milk! Our waitress dissuaded us from getting one made with fruit pie, as it would have too grainy a texture, so we chose banana cream, which made us think of pie à la mode in a tall glass. Pieces of banana and bits of crust inevitably clogged the straw, making it a drink that must be gulped or spooned.

Betty's is famous enough that it can get crowded in the summer when travelers come to enjoy the beauty of Lake Superior's North Shore. Although remodeled since its opening in 1956, and now under new management with Betty retired, it remains a charming place with blue-and-white kitchenette décor and waitresses who are outspoken in the best diner tradition.

Note: Betty's has limited hours in winter months; be sure to call ahead.

BLOEDOW BAKERY

bloedows.com

451 E. Broadway   507-452-3682
Winona, MN   **B** (closed Sun) | **$**

Minnesota foodlore tells the story of the little, home-grown bakery (in business for some eighty years) that ran Krispy Kreme out of town. It was back in '03 that the national chain moved in, setting up its products throughout town in groceries and convenience stores. But the interloper donuts did not impress Minnesotans who knew better. In less than two years, KK had vanished from the shelves and Bloedow reigned supreme.

It's a sweet story for those of us who prize eateries with genuine character, and the glazed and cake donuts, sweet rolls, maple-frosted long johns, and cookies at Bloedow (rhymes with Play-Doh) deserve their renown. Tipster Vanessa Haluska recommended Bloedow's peanut butter roll—a big, circular pastry made with sweet dough and swirled with peanut butter where you might expect cinnamon.

Note: In a 2012 poll conducted by Minneapolis's WCCO-TV, viewers elected Bloedow Bakery the Best Donut Shop in Minnesota.

BREAD & CHOCOLATE

breadandchocolatebakery.com

867 Grand Ave.   651-228-1017
St. Paul, MN   **B L** | **$**

Across the street from its parent eatery, Cafe Latté (right), Bread & Chocolate is an informal bakery and espresso shop open early every day for breakfast. There is lunch, which is mostly sandwiches on Cafe Latté bread, but it's the morning pastries that draw us near. Big croissants are available plain or filled; they are as flaky as possible, lightweight yet luxurious. It's astonishing how many blueberries get packed into the blueberry muffin, which is made from creamy batter that is an ideal medium for the fruit. Scones are moist and tender, like cake but not as sweet; tart lingonberries are an inspired inclusion, especially when the scone is topped with slivered toasted almonds.

A squared-off pastry called a "cinnamon swirl" is what you want a Cinnabon to be, but Bread & Chocolate's is no dyspepsia-inducing disappointment. The soft dough is butter-fresh and swirled with thick veins of cinnamon; the fine-textured icing makes sugar seem like health food. Best of everything is the sticky caramel roll: crisp-edged, enrobed in amber glaze, and studded with pecan halves.

Bread & Chocolate espresso is especially delicious: opaque and earthy. Next visit, we need to try the turtle latte listed on the coffee menu. The Twin Cities, after all, are in the running for Turtle Capital of America.

CAFE LATTÉ

cafelatte.com

850 Grand Ave.   651-224-5687
St. Paul, MN   **B L D** | **$$**

There isn't anyplace in America that can top Cafe Latté when it comes to cake temptation. Triple-layer beauties include orange blossom, German chocolate, and turtle—an intense mountain of the moistest possible cake interleaved with fudge, caramel, and meaty pecan halves. Among notable double-layer cakes are très leches, pumpkin pecan, lemon blueberry, and pear ginger. And there are cheesecakes, bundt cakes, tortes, and tarts.

Pre-cake, Cafe Latté is a great place for soup, sandwiches, and salads. There are all kinds of Caesar salad variations—the classic version as well as a Caesar supplemented by artichoke hearts, Greek olives, or sliced tomatoes. Or how about a chicken Caesar pasta salad? Each individual one is made to order (service is cafeteria-style), so you can specify if you want a little more of this or that. In the adjoining wine bar, you'll find beautiful pizzas, from classic margherita to barbecue chicken potato.

CAROL'S

11888 Aberdeen St. NE 763-757-9700
Blaine, MN **B L D** | **$**

Handicap parking spaces abound in the parking lot. A large number of regular customers are seniors, and we saw not a single millennial anywhere in the house. Nothing on the menu is edgy. In short, Carol's is the most unhip restaurant imaginable. But for Midwest comfort food prepared entirely from scratch (even the white bread), using humble recipes without a hint of drama, no place is better.

Amish chicken, for instance, made from a recipe that Carol found long ago in a self-published cookbook, is as mild as a dish can be, cooked low and slow in a buttery milk bath until the meat is excruciatingly tender. It is plated Sunday-supper-style, with herby dressing, lumpy mashed potatoes, cranberry sauce, and a mélange of garden-fresh braised cabbage and carrots. On the side comes a soft, nutty-sweet Nova Scotia roll. Hot turkey sandwich (locally known as a "commercial") is another tenderhearted meal, made with large pieces of white and dark meat from a house-roasted bird, accompanied by all the Thanksgiving fixins. (Carol's meat loaf comes in a similar configuration.) House-made hash is the leading light at breakfast; and while the menu is mostly classic square meals, there also is a small selection of such timid exotica as Mexican egg rolls and Oriental chicken salad. For dessert: blue-ribbon pies. We especially recommend the springtime delight, rhubarb-cream pie. It is a tart-luxe conundrum in a shattering-crisp lard crust.

CHET'S LAKESIDE INN

15681 County Rd. 102 NE 218-943-2471
Parkers Prairie, MN **D** (closed Mon & Tues) | **$$**

Devoted fans know Chet's Lakeside Inn as Chet's Chicken Shack, and while there is a broad menu of seafood, steaks, and chops, and the prime rib is famous, it's that chicken that puts Chet's on the Roadfood map. Battered and seasoned with what the management bills as a "secret Swedish recipe," it sports a thin, brittle crust with countless crunchy little shards that easily break off and melt in your mouth. Inside that elegant casing is meat that is wildly juicy, though not the least bit greasy. On the side come massive and equally excellent onion rings and access to a Midwest-large salad bar, where the offerings range from iceberg lettuce to chocolate pudding.

Located on the shore of Lake Irene, Chet's serves its fine chicken in a restaurant that harkens back to the mid-twentieth century with a rustic waterside theme of fishing nets and tackle and booths upholstered in aqua leatherette. It is still run by the same family who opened it 1953.

CONVENTION GRILL

conventiongrillmn.com
3912 Sunnyside Rd. 952-920-6881
Edina, MN **L D** | **$**

A Convention Grill hamburger won't win kudos from the nutrition police, but for us it inspires hash-house rapture. Sizzled to crisp-edged succulence on an oil-glistening grill, it oozes juice, and is complemented by melted cheese, lettuce, tomato, and mayonnaise (known as California-style). Fries are picture-perfect honeytone brown, a satisfying mix of crunch and spuddy creaminess. You also can order a Plazaburger with sour cream, chives, and chopped onions in a dark bun, as originated at the Plaza Tavern in Madison, Wisconsin.

Such a classic American meal demands a thick malt. Flavor choices include chocolate, wild blueberry, butterscotch, strawberry, coffee, banana, vanilla, caramel, honey, hot fudge, Butterfinger, mint, and Reese's Peanut Butter Cup. For 50¢ extra, you can have fresh banana added. If one of these malts doesn't satisfy your ice cream cravings, have a hot fudge sundae. It is served with a good portion of fudge underneath the ice cream, plus more fudge in a pitcher to pour on as you plow through.

★ HELL'S KITCHEN
hellskitcheninc.com

80 S. 9th St.   612-332-4700
Minneapolis, MN   **B L D** | $$

Our first visits to Hell's Kitchen were for breakfast—some of the best breakfasts anywhere. Every table is supplied with the late chef Mitch Omer's magnificent preserves and marmalade and extra-luxurious chunky peanut butter, which are themselves a compelling reason to eat at this downtown hot spot. Among the stars of the morning menu are huevos rancheros of the gods—a huge plate of food that includes spicy beans, eggs, cheeses, sour cream, and fresh salsa on a crisp flour tortilla. Rosti potatoes come alongside too, and they are available as a dish unto themselves. Chef Omer's rostis are less like the Swiss spuds that are their namesake than they are glorified hash browns, shreds of potato mixed with bacon, onions, chives, and scallions and grilled in sweet cream butter. A few other breakfast specialties: lemon ricotta hotcakes, maple-glazed bison sausage, and a quarter-pound caramel pecan roll with a refined glaze that is a sweet tooth's dream.

No one should have breakfast at Hell's Kitchen without a serving of Mahnomin Porridge, a recipe that the promethean Mr. Omer came up with from reading trappers' accounts of native Cree Indian meals that featured wild rice. He supplements the Native meal of rice, hazelnuts, cranberries, and maple syrup with a full measure of warm, heavy cream, making this the most lavish hot cereal imaginable.

The lunch menu is every bit as inviting. How about a walleye BLT made with cornmeal-dusted fillets and lemon tartar sauce instead of the homemade mayo the kitchen uses on its regular BLT? Who cannot love the ham and pear crisp sandwich on sourdough bread, draped with a mantle of Swiss and fontina cheeses? We instantly became addicted to the house Bread Bucket, which is all the chewy, freshly made baguette you can eat, served along with sweet cream butter, Omer's preserves, and peanut butter.

We once were asked: "If you had time for only one meal in Minneapolis, where would it be?" Our immediate response was Hell's Kitchen. But the more we thought about it, the more we didn't like that answer. Only one meal would be insanely frustrating—there are too many fabulous things to eat.

JOHNSON'S BACON & EGG CAFE

513 40th Ave. NE   763-789-4544
Columbia Heights, MN   **B L** | $

We originally came because we liked the name of this place, and we were extra-amused when we arrived and saw the sign outside announcing that it is "Home of the Big Johnson." But for all that superficial allure, we became real fans of Johnson's because of its unexpectedly excellent food. Pancakes are big softies from a batter that is just slightly sweet. Potato pancakes are a variation on the theme, nothing like crisp-edged latkes, but rather very tender and made from that same fresh batter laced with tender hash browns. Warm syrup is presented in a squeeze bottle.

Chicken-fried steak, which all too often is a hash-house disaster, here is Texas-good: tender meat encased in luxuriously crisp crust and topped with unctuous pepper gravy. On the side come good hash browns or home fries and a pair of buttery eggs. As for the famous Big Johnson, that's an oversized meal of eggs, toast, potatoes, pancakes, spuds, and a length of buff, smoky sausage.

Although it's just minutes from downtown Minneapolis, Johnson's has the easygoing vibe of a small-town café. Natalie, our friendly waitress, was at the table constantly to refill coffee cups, happy to chat with us and with a cadre of regulars sitting at the counter or in booths. Décor includes hundreds of chicken figurines.

Note that business is cash only.

★ LANGE'S CAFE

110 8th Ave. SE, Rt. 23   507-825-4488
Pipestone, MN   Always open | $

LOCALS LOVE IT The moment we walked into Lange's Cafe, we looked at the case of caramel rolls and knew we had hit pay dirt. Sure enough, as we ate our way through as much of the menu as possible, we swooned with pleasure over and over again. Roast beef is the entree not to miss. It is pot-roast tender, available with mashed potatoes, green beans, and gravy, or as "hot beef," which is a sandwich with mashed potatoes on top and gravy all over. Mashed potatoes are the real thing; dinner rolls are freshly baked.

The caramel rolls that so many people eat for breakfast must be sampled any time they are available. They are immense blocks of sweet, yeasty dough—about three inches square—and they are bathed in buttery warm caramel syrup that has a burnt smack to its sweetness.

Sour cream raisin pie, a specialty of bakers in Minnesota, Wisconsin, and Iowa, is at its best at Lange's. The custard base is dense, packed with raisins, creamy and sweet with the sour-cream edge that makes its sweetness all the more potent. The meringue is air-light; the crust flakes when poked by a fork. It was our supremely lucky day, for we walked into Lange's at about 10 a.m. and the pie was out of the oven only a short while. Our pieces were faintly warm, like baby food, and we declared this the best sour cream raisin pie ever made . . . 10 on a 1-to-10 scale.

LINDSTROM BAKERY

12830 Lake Blvd.   651-257-1374
Lindstrom, MN   B (closed Sun) | $

A Lindstrom Bakery Scandinavian donut is similar to a regular donut, but eggier, oilier, darker, and with a crisp tan surface. Proprietor Bernetta Coulombe, known to all as Bernie, said that her late husband endlessly fussed and fiddled with the recipe until he got it right. When he died, regular customers were concerned that his secrets went with him, but Bernie quickly assured them that she has what it takes to continue his legacy.

We wonder: "Why are they called Scandinavian?"

She answers: "Because I am Scandinavian and I make them."

In any case, they are pretty much the opposite of sissy donuts such as Krispy Kreme. Nothing wimpy or dainty about these sinkers. They come plain and glazed, coated with cinnamon sugar or drizzled with chocolate. In addition, Lindstrom makes donut holes and all sorts of more ordinary (that is, less substantial) donuts as well as Swedish white bread, caraway limpa bread, raisin rye, caramel rings, cookies, and coffee cakes. Lindstrom also makes a breakfast toast that is similar to Michigan's Trenary Toast (p. 285): baked-hard slices dusted with cinnamon sugar, ideal for soaks in morning coffee.

MATT'S BAR

mattsbar.com

3500 Cedar Ave.   612-722-7072
Minneapolis, MN   L D | $

Waitresses at Matt's Bar wear T-shirts that warn "Fear the cheese." That's good advice when eating a Jucy Lucy (Matt's spelling), the inside-out cheeseburger that is all beef on the outside and a lode of hot molten cheese within. An overeager first bite makes the burger erupt and its hot cheese flows everywhere. It tastes especially good with optional grilled onions added underneath the patty. Eateries all over the Twin Cities now feature a Jucy Lucy (or as others spell it, Juicy Lucy). Matt's is one of at least two places in town that claims to have invented it.

The beef itself has the taste and texture of an old-fashioned lunch-counter patty, griddle-sizzled until the outside turns crisp. Combined with cheese—either inside, Jucy Lucy–style, or on the top—it delivers glistening-good beef satisfaction.

Matt's has earned special notoriety on TV shows that like to highlight outlandish eats. Despite its fame, it remains a dimly lit dive bar with a very limited menu (burgers and French fries) and greasy-spoon ambience. Seating is at booths and tables and on a few stools at the counter.

Business is cash only.

MAVERICK'S

mavericksroastbeef.com

1746 N. Lexington   651-488-1788
Roseville, MN   L D (Tues–Sat) | $

Maverick's doesn't look like much—an inconspicuous storefront in a strip mall—but its roast beef sandwich is extraordinary: pink, velvety slices cut to order and piled into a soft white bun while the meat is still hot and moist. Rick Nelson of the *Minneapolis Star-Tribune* told us that the restaurant concept was inspired by the proprietor's desire to improve on Arby's. If that was the goal, he has more than succeeded, for this is a super roast beef sandwich—simple, pure, and satisfying.

It is served cafeteria-style, along with a short menu of other beefy things, including brisket (offered on a dark pumpernickel bun) and barbecued beef, plus pulled pork, ham, chicken, and fish fillets. When we stopped by, open-face roast beef sandwiches were the day's special: the same good beef piled on a plate with the roll on the side and a couple mounds of mashed potatoes. While the beef in this one was the same as in the simple sandwich, we much preferred Maverick's crisp French fries to the ersatz mashed potatoes.

Once you get your food, stop by a condiment bar, where the choices range from horseradish and horseradish cream to hot peppers, ketchup, mustard, and pickles. Find a place at one of the four-tops along the side of the room or at the long banquet table in the middle. We walked out happy and satisfied.

M&H RESTAURANT

510 Main Ave.   218-233-5510
Moorhead, MN   B L D | $

Thanks to "ndrose89," who sent us a note that began, "Hello from Fargo, ND!!" and went on to recommend M&H in Moorhead for "awesome chicken . . . SO much better than that 'chain.'" Technically speaking, the chicken is not fried like the chain does it, but broasted, meaning that it is pressure-cooked in hot oil. The process forces extra lusciousness into the crisp skin as well as into the meat below, resulting in thighs, breasts, and drumsticks that are to ordinary fried chicken what baby back ribs are to spare ribs: more tender and easier to eat, albeit lacking rugged personality. For comfort food, this stuff can't be beat.

The location is quite literally convenient, as the chicken is cooked and presented in the convenience-store part of the M&H gas station, which has all the sundries one expects as well as a handful of places to sit and eat. M&H is a local chain, but this is the one with extraordinary chicken. (And if you do need to compare and contrast, there is a KFC just up the road and across the street.)

NORTHERN WATERS SMOKEHAUS

northernwaterssmokehaus.com

394 Lake Ave. S., Ste. 106   218-724-7307
Duluth, MN   L D | $

Before he came to Duluth, Eric Goerdt was a fisherman in Sitka, Alaska, where he perfected his techniques for smoking fish as well as meats. When you listen to him talk about the firm luxury of a hunk of salmon that has been hand-trimmed, marinated, and smoked over maple wood, you are hearing a man on a mission to make delicious smoked food. Mission accomplished! His little smokery in the DeWitt-Seitz Marketplace in Canal Park is a culinary gem for passersby as well as lovers of smoked fish and meats who wish to mail-order their favorites.

It is a tiny retail store with a few tables for sitting down and eating such fine sandwiches as bison shoulder braised in Schlitz and barbecue sauce on a bun; wild Alaskan sockeye gravlax with pickled ginger, vegetables, and wasabi mayonnaise on a baguette; and an insanely opulent gloss on the traditional Reuben, this one made of hot bison pastrami, caramelized onions, pepperoncini, mayonnaise, and provolone on a crusty hard roll. We also treasure this place as a source of provisions. It is a secure feeling to hit the road with a stack of saltines and hunks of perfumy Lake Superior whitefish and smoked salmon for noshing between meals.

PUMPHOUSE CREAMERY

pumphouse-creamery.com

| 4754 Chicago Ave. S. | 612-825-2021 |
| Minneapolis, MN | **L D** \| $ |

If proof is needed that Minnesota is a great dairy state, we recommend a visit to Pumphouse Creamery. It is a parlor devoted exclusively to ice cream. Made using cream and milk from a single farm, it is angelic stuff, ascending to stratospheric goodness when flavored with the freshest possible ingredients. Banana ice cream sings of ripe bananas; coconut ice cream is genuinely tropical and crowded with almonds and large chocolate chips; caramel ice cream is laced with crunchy praline pecans; cherry ice cream is made with Door County (Wisconsin) sour cherries that are stunningly offset by their creamy medium.

This is not ice cream for kiddie tastes. Nothing is flamboyant or affected; the butterfat content isn't overwhelming; flavors are not insanely rich or supersweet. House-made cones are modest little cookies, crisp and tasty, and the scoops that get put on top of them (or in a cup) are not silly-large. Order a sundae—one scoop or two—and it comes in a little plastic cup. Whipped cream is cream that is whipped, nothing more or less.

Pumphouse is a narrow storefront—more ice cream kitchen than serving area—with a single large table up front and a bench and a few seats out on the sidewalk.

SWEDISH CROWN BAKERY

swedishcrownbakery.com

| 530 W. Main St. | 763-427-0506 |
| Anoka, MN | **B L** (closed Sun) \| $ |

"I don't churn the butter," co-owner Eva Sabat once told a reporter. "Otherwise, everything is made from scratch." It tastes it. Here are baked goods of the highest quality, made with real butter and organic cream and nothing artificial. There is no microwave oven or deep fryer in this bakery, where the specialties are Scandinavian.

Honey-tweaked Bavarian cream in a little sandwich known as the Swedish Beehive is whipped-that-morning fresh, all the more scrumptious for the two crisp, almond-dotted puff pastry discs that surround it. Veins of rhubarb and strawberry that swirl through a pastry called Spring in Sweden taste like essence of fruit. Cardamom buns are fragile and fragrant. Vanilla and chocolate-swirled meringues, known as Icelandic Lava, shatter into ethereal flavor at first bite.

Swedish Crown Bakery is a tiny place in a shopping center with hardly any seating. But for car snacks (or baked goods to eat at home), it is a destination to treasure. In addition to its repertoire of inviting pastries, the menu includes paninis and regular sandwiches, soup, and salad.

TAVERN ON GRAND

tavernongrand.com

| 656 Grand Ave. | 651-228-9030 |
| St. Paul, MN | **L D** \| $$ |

—★—— OPEN LATE ——★— There is more to eat than walleye at "Minnesota's State Restaurant Serving Minnesota's State Fish," but the moist white fish is so rare anywhere else that it behooves the culinary traveler to focus on it. Walleye cakes (like crab cakes, served in a spill of Béarnaise sauce) or a basket of deep-fried walleye bites make fine hors d'oeuvres. Many regular customers come for a walleye sandwich—a grilled or fried fillet on French bread. Probably the best way to savor the flaky fineness of the locally loved fish is to have it simply grilled, served on a plate with some vegetables. It comes with tartar sauce, but it's a shame to smother so delicate an eating experience with anything. Surf 'n' turf types can get the Lakeshore Special—a single fillet accompanied by a half-pound sirloin steak. You can even get walleye in the Minnesota fair-goer's favorite configuration, served on a stick like shish kebab. To round out a regional meal, there is wild rice turkey soup.

With interior appointments reminiscent of a hunting lodge in the North Woods (but comfortable!), Tavern on Grand feels like the right place to enjoy a Great Lakes meal. Wherever you sit in the bar, you will have a good view of the TV and whatever game is currently on.

WORLD'S BEST DONUTS

worldsbestdonutsmn.com

10 E. Wisconsin St.	218-387-1345
Grand Marais, MN	**B L** (mid-May–mid-Oct) | **$**

"The only donut that has ever rivaled my late grandmother's donuts," wrote tipster Paul Swindlehurst, attributing the excellence of World's Best Donuts to its frying medium: lard. "Best when warm," Mr. Swindlehurst advised. Heeding his advice, we arrived shortly after the shop opened at 4:30 one spring morning. Amen and hallelujah! Still warm from the fryer, these circular sylphs are donut royalty. We were awestruck by the plain cake donut, a hand-cut beauty that is substantial but in no way leaden, sweet enough and yet with deep, savory satisfaction. Chocolate-frosted and cinnamon-sugar cake donuts are simple and unimprovable, and the locally loved skizzles (similar to elephant ears), which are deep-fried dough discs smothered with sugar, provide a great way to maximize the joy of lard cooking.

Regulars keep their cups on the mug shelf so they can pour their own while waiting in line to place an order. Registered donut eaters (sign up for free) are entitled to a free donut when they return.

MISSOURI

AMIGHETTI'S

amighettis.com

5141 Wilson Ave.   314-776-2855
St. Louis, MO   L D (closed Sun) | $

Amighetti's is a serve-yourself sandwich shop that
has become a beloved culinary institution on "The
Hill," St. Louis's old Italian neighborhood. Eating
here is casual and fun, especially on a pleasant summer day. Place your order at the window and wait for
your name to be called. Find yourself a seat on the
sunny patio, and feast on a legendary Italian sandwich. Next door to the restaurant, Amighetti's bakes
its own bread—a thick-crusted loaf with sturdy
insides ready to be loaded with slices of ham, roast
beef, Genoa salami, and cheese, garnished with
shreds of lettuce and a special house dressing that is
tangy and a little bit sweet. All kinds of sandwiches
are available, including a garlicky Italian hero, roast
beef, and a three-cheese veggie sandwich—all recommended primarily because of the bread.

Each sandwich is wrapped in butcher paper
secured by a tape inscribed with Amighetti's motto:
"Often Imitated, Never Duplicated."

ARTHUR BRYANT'S

arthurbryantsbbq.com

1727 Brooklyn Ave.   816-231-1123
Kansas City, MO   L D | $$

Arthur Bryant used to shock reporters by calling his
esteemed barbecue restaurant a "Grease House."
Although the master of Kansas City barbecue passed
away in 1982, his business heirs, bless them, never
tried too hard to shed that moniker. The original
location of the "House of Good Eats" (another of
Mr. Bryant's appellations) remains a cafeteria-style
lunchroom with all the decorative charm of a bus
station. (There are branches at the Kansas City
Speedway, Ameristar Casino, and the airport.)

Because Arthur Bryant and his brother Charlie
(who started the smokehouse) hailed from Texas, it
makes sense that smoked brisket—a Texas passion—
is the best meat in the house. It drips flavor. Have it
in a sandwich or if you come as a large party, order
a couple of pounds of beef and a loaf of bread and
make your own at the table. Pork ribs are wonderful
too, glazed with blackened burnt edges and loads of
meat below their spicy crust. Skin-on French fries are
bronze beauties, and the goopy barbecue beans are
some of Kansas City's best.

What makes Arthur Bryant's unique is the
sauce. It is beautiful—a gritty, red-orange blend of
spice and sorcery that is not at all sweet like most

barbecue sauces. It packs a hot paprika wallop and tastes like a strange soul-food curry that is such a nice complement to any meat. Once you've tasted it, you'll understand why this old Grease House is a foodie legend.

BOOCHES

| 110 S. 9th | 573-874-9519 |
| Columbia, MO | L D | $ |

A billiard parlor/tavern where the beverages of choice are beer (in a bottle) and iced tea (in a pitcher), or maybe Coke in a paper cup, Booches is a magic name to hamburger aficionados. The hamburgers—known among old-timers as "belly bombers"—are small but juicy, maddeningly aromatic, and served unceremoniously on a piece of wax paper. They are available with or without cheese, and the condiments are onions, pickles, mustard, or ketchup; yet their smoky/meaty flavor is extraordinary from first bite to last. In 1999, Booches won kudos from the *Digital Missourian* as an Earth-friendly eatery, not only because each hamburger is cooked to order (thus, no meat is wasted), but because "no one can leave a Booches burger half-eaten."

Some of the food's charm is no doubt due to the offhand way in which it is served in colorful surroundings. Booches is the oldest pool hall in Columbia, and it is likely that your burger—or good chili dog—will be eaten to the wooden clack of pool shooters as well as the noise of whatever sports event is blaring on the television. Décor is a combination of sports memorabilia, praise from famous artists who have enjoyed the beer and burgers, and some delightful politically incorrect humor, including one sign that advises, "Parents . . . keep your ankle-biting little crumb-gobblers on a leash or I will put them in the cellar to play with the rats."

C&K BARBECUE

candkbbq.com

4390 Jennings	314-385-8100
Station Rd.	L D	$
St. Louis, MO	

Barbecue is a big deal in St. Louis, and there are several trendy outfits where you'll wait in line for a precious place to eat; but none of the Johnny-come-latelies can hold a candle to the grand old C&K. In fact, there is no place to eat at C&K, except for a single table outside with two chairs. Everything is take-out. And you will wait awhile, because every order is scrupulously prepared, served hot and sauced and divinely delicious.

The menu oddities are wonderful, if you like oddities: gelatinous pig ears, billed as "juicy," which they are; snoots, which are basically crisp-fried fat that is unspeakably luxurious when bathed in C&K's superb, complex, spicy sauce. Another curiosity only recently added to the menu is "turkey ribs"—large pieces of moist white meat infused with smoke. The soul-food smokehouse standards are glorious: rib tips bursting with flavor, pulled pork, hunky spare ribs, thick pork steaks, hot links, and whole chickens. Must-eat on the side: pickly smashed potato salad. And for dessert: lemon cake or gooey butter cookies.

For genuine St. Louis barbecue, C&K has no peers.

CARL'S DRIVE-IN

| 9033 Manchester Rd. | 314-961-9652 |
| Brentwood, MO | L D (closed Sun & Mon) | $ |

A sixteen-stool diner on old Route 66, Carl's is the place to belly up for elegant-oily hamburgers and foot-long hot dogs smothered with chili. The burgers are mashed flat on the grill so that their edges turn into a crisp filigree of beef, and they are thin enough that a double or a triple makes good sense, as does the addition of cheese.

Burgers are the main attraction, but Carl's is also a source for three-way chili and tamales topped with chili or sauce. Shoestring French fries are a great companion for any meal, and the thing to drink is house-brewed root beer drawn straight from the barrel, served in a frosted mug. (Milk shakes, available in only two flavors, vanilla and chocolate, are the real deal.)

Expect to wait for a seat at lunchtime, but not too long. The turnover is quick, and it is an amazing thing to watch the staff juggle.

CHRIS' PANCAKE & DINING

chrispancakeanddining.com

5980 Southwest Ave.   314-645-2088
St. Louis, MO   **B L D** | **$**

If you wake up in St. Louis one morning with an appetite that won't quit, we recommend a visit to Chris' Pancake & Dining. Here you find a breakfast titled Top of the Hill, which in fact is over the top: a hamburger crowned with eggs, chili, hash browns, cheese, and onions. Connoisseurs of St. Louis gastronomy will recognize it as a slinger, the kill-or-cure dish in the same over-copious genre as a Nick Tahou Garbage Plate (p. 104) or a Springfield (Illinois) horseshoe.

Not quite as immense, but immensely satisfying, is a Summer Omelet of tomatoes, bacon, spinach, and cheese. The menu lists it as coming with Provel cheese—a processed mix of Cheddar, Swiss, and provolone frequently found on St. Louis pizza—but single-origin cheese also is available: feta, Cheddar, or American. Salsiccia is another winner—muscular, fennel-spiked Italian sausages served in pairs with eggs, hash browns, and toast or pancakes.

Lunch and dinner options include half-pound burgers, pork steaks, fried chicken, and Cheeseburger Macaroni, a "Chris' original": ground beef, Cheddar jack cheese, tomatoes, onions, and basil tossed with macaroni and marinara sauce and baked. Should you doubt that you are in St. Louis, the appetizer menu includes such local likes as deep-fried, breaded Provel cheese sticks and deep-fried "toasted" ravioli.

CROWN CANDY KITCHEN

crowncandykitchen.net

1401 St. Louis Ave.   314-621-9650
St. Louis, MO   **L D** (closed Sun) | **$**

The Crown Candy Kitchen is an old-time sweet shop that makes its own chocolate candy and serves all kinds of malts, shakes, sodas, and sundaes. We are especially fond of the chocolate banana malted and the hot fudge malted. The house policy is to give five malts free to anyone who can consume them in thirty minutes (except during the lunch-hour rush).

Other than excellent ice cream treats, Crown has a nice lunch-counter repertoire of sandwiches, tamales, chili, and chili mac. Items of special interest from the kitchen are what the menu calls a Heart Stopping BLT, loaded with bacon and guaranteed to be made with Miracle Whip, and house-made chicken salad, available only on Tuesdays and Thursdays.

DONUT STOP

thedonutstopinc.net

1101 Lemay Ferry Rd.   314-631-3333
St. Louis, MO   **B** | **$**

A stark-white building, the Donut Stop has been earning loyal customers since 1953. Glazed donuts are lightweight beauties, and there are five kinds of fruit-packed fritters, a variety of fried pies, twists, cream-filled long johns, French crullers, and cinnamon rolls. The single item that makes us dream of coming back is what is known as a Cinnamon Glob, a hole-less pastry with egg-rich insides and an exterior with mouth-watering sugar crunch.

GOODY GOODY DINER

goodygoodydiner.com

5900 Natural Bridge   314-383-3333
Ave.   **B L** | **$**
St. Louis, MO

Breakfast is served all day (until closing midafternoon) Wednesday and Friday at the Goody Goody Diner, and other days until 11 a.m. The menu is vast, ranging from omelets, pancakes, waffles, and French toast to boneless catfish fillets with eggs and one amazing dish known as the Wilbur. Known in other local diners as a slinger, the Wilbur is an omelet filled with chili, fried potatoes, peppers, onions, and tomatoes.

Goody Goody's chili is stout and salty, made with chunks of beef, and it is the fundamental element in a once-popular but now rare Midwestern diner dish, chili mac. Goody Goody's chili mac is prepared with blunt hash-house style: well-cooked spaghetti noodles are crowned with chili and a mass of shredded Cheddar cheese.

"We have changed many items on our menu over the years," the Goody Goody credo goes. "But the way we prepare our Certified Angus Beef hamburgers will never change. They're not fancy. Just *Really* Good." We agree. Regulars and doubles, patty melts and cheeseburgers, slawburgers and barbecue slawburgers are all outstanding, available with sides that include onion rings, French fries, cheese fries, and, of course, chili. Each burger is mashed down hard enough on the grill that it becomes a thin, rugged patty with a lacy-crisp circumference.

HODAK'S
hodaks.com

2100 Gravois Ave.	314-776-7292
St. Louis, MO	L D | $

Hodak's is a tavern with a full menu, including steaks, frog legs, sandwiches, and toasted ravioli. Most customers come for fried chicken, made from a recipe used by the Hodak family since 1962 (and voted #1 by St. Louisans for decades). Meals come as half chickens, four drumsticks, five wings, or chicken livers. Pay 40¢ extra and you will get an order of Hodak's excellent hot barbecue sauce for dipping.

Nearly everybody waits for a table at mealtimes. Despite its modest appearance and location in a blah neighborhood, Hodak's attracts hordes of hungry families from miles around. If you are having a party, the kitchen offers up to a two-hundred-piece fried chicken package for $236.

JESS & JIM'S
jessandjims.com

517 E. 135th St.	816-941-9499
Kansas City	L D | $$$
(Martin City), MO	

HOT TICKET

Jess & Jim's, a Kansas City landmark that opened in 1938, is all about beef. This is apparent even from a distance, when you spot the huge statue of a bull atop the roof. Steaks arrive from the kitchen exuberantly sputtering, crusty from an iron griddle. The pound-and-a-half Playboy Strip is two inches thick, and unlike the super-tender bacon-wrapped fillets, it demands some chewing. Not that it is tough; but neither is it a cut for milquetoasts. Dense and intense, this is steak lover's steak, which is not to say that the T-bones, porterhouses, and strips are anything less than excellent.

On the side of regal meat, excellent potatoes are essential. There are cottage fries and French fries and immense bakers available, of course, with sour cream, bacon, and shredded cheese as condiments. The sleeper on the menu here is fried chicken. It's a reminder that as much as it always has been Beef Central, Kansas City also is a noteworthy fried chicken town.

Be aware that on weekends especially, this place gets very crowded. Call-ahead seating is available . . . and much advised.

LC'S BARBEQUE
lcsbarbq.com

5800 Blue Pkwy.	816-923-4484
Kansas City, MO	L D | $$

LC's sandwiches are presented in little trays because they are too messy for a flat plate. Sauce-sopped meat is piled in outlandish measure onto a puny slice of white bread and topped with another slice. The bread underneath disintegrates before it arrives at your table. Eating is done either with plastic utensils or picking at the sandwich by hand and unrolling plenty of paper towels that are supplied to every table by the roll.

From the barbecue pit behind the counter come beef, ham, turkey, pork, sausage, and ribs, as well as burnt ends. These are luscious nuggets cut from the outside edges of smoked brisket. Many pieces are laced with an obscenely delicious amount of fat; there are chewy pieces and crunchy pieces, the whole she-bang fairly glowing with LC's thin, powerfully peppery, celery-seed-accented barbecue sauce. First-rate French fries come alongside.

Luxurious as the food may be, LC's is a stark place, décor consisting of a television set up in the corner of the dining room and a few dusty game-animal heads on the wall. Place your order and pay for it at the counter, and it will be delivered to your table posthaste.

NATALIE'S CAKES & MORE

nataliescakesandmore.com

100 S. Florissant Rd.   314-801-7064
Ferguson, MO   (closed Sun) | $

Starting in 2014, the name of Ferguson, Missouri, conjured up dreadful images of urban riots, but since 2016, when we discovered Natalie's Cakes & More, it makes us think of the prettiest possible caramel cake. Sold whole or by the slice, baker Natalie Dubose's version of the teatime classic is modest, tender, soft-spoken yellow cake with its edges removed and a fine gold film of soft caramel covering the top and dripping down its edges. Both the cake and the caramel are as buttery as they are sweet, and the experience of forking up a soft piece inspires reveries of an era when neighborhood bakeries were isles of civility treasured by customers.

In addition to the signature caramel cake, the bakery makes pies, cookies, brownies, and a wide array of other loaf cakes and cupcakes from red velvet and orange dream to pineapple coconut. The menu, written in pink, advises, "If there's a flavor you want but don't see, it never hurts to ask!" Visitors are invited to take (for free) bags of cake crust cut from the yellow cake.

NIECIE'S

nieciesrestaurant.com

6441 Troost Ave.   816-444-6006
Kansas City, MO   B L D | $

Niecie's is a soul food café opened by Denise Griffin Ward in 1985. Since then it has become a sort of community center, and every morning except Sunday you can expect to see a table with a dozen or more Baptist and Holiness Church pastors gathered for breakfast. As we sat down in a booth one day, a couple nearby were praying over their pork chops before digging in.

We really like the breakfast of chicken and waffles: three jumbo wings, fried with lots of gnarled crisp skin, along with a waffle and a plastic jug of Hungry Jack syrup. Other breakfast choices include pancakes, country ham, and eggs with grits. Roadfood.com's Buffetbuster described Niecie's biscuits as "more like grilled corn cakes." Topped with peppery sausage gravy, he deemed them "simply the best I have ever had."

Among the daily lunch specials are salmon croquettes on Monday, a legendary smothered chicken Tuesday, short ribs Friday, and fried catfish Saturday. If you do have lunch, be sure to reserve enough appetite for dessert. Layer cakes—chocolate or caramel-frosted—are memorable.

The most exotic item on the menu, at least for those of us who don't have easy access to southern Midwest soul-food specialties, is the pig ear sandwich. "You get two ears!" beamed waitress Ms. Myra C., whose badge identified her as having nineteen years of service at Niecie's. Yes, indeed; it is two whole ears in a bun. We got ours with the works: lettuce, tomato, onion, and horseradish. We've got to admit that ears are a little scary, not so much because they're the worst part of the pig—there are plenty of parts far worse even to think about. The problem is that they look exactly like what they are: large, pointy porker ears. Their taste is not objectionable; it's something like the fatty parts of bacon or streak o' lean; but the gelatinous texture is, to say the least, a little weird.

O'CONNELL'S PUB

4652 Shaw Ave.   314-773-6600
St. Louis, MO   **L D** | $

Plates are paper. Service is blunt. The menu is short. Prices are low. The roast beef sandwich is a thing of beauty: abundant slabs of full-flavored beef, glistening with juice, available on whatever bread you like, but best on a length of French bread sturdy enough to withstand all that succulence. If you like it really wet, 25¢ side orders of au jus are available for dipping. Hamburgers, priced in the mid-single-digit range, are awe-inspiring nine-ouncers, beautifully charcoal-cooked. On the side you want French fries or fried mushrooms, along with house-made Mayfair sauce. Mayfair is an O'Connell's trademark, a garlicky ranch-type dressing that is fine as a dip, on salad, and a quirky condiment for roast beef or burgers.

O'Connell's menu is limited to sandwiches and a few daily specials, such as Monday baked ham, Thursday roast pork, and Saturday rib tips. It really is a pub with a vast inventory of single-malt Scotch, Irish whiskey, and bottled and draft beers. And no surprise since it is in St. Louis: You can have a gooey butter cookie for dessert.

RILEY'S PUB

3458 Arsenal St.   314-664-7474
St. Louis, MO   **L D** | $

——★—— St. Louis–style pizza is characterized by
OPEN LATE unleavened, matzoh-thin crust and
——★—— Provel cheese—a made-in-Wisconsin product that is a combination of provolone, Cheddar, and Swiss. Provel is essential because it tends not to weep oil when it cooks, thus helping keep the crust good and crisp. You can get this pizza at a chain called Imo's, at an Italian neighborhood place called Rigazzi's, and at Riley's Pub. Not exactly the place you'd expect to find memorable pizza, Riley's is a corner bar complete with darts, live music, Tuesday-night karaoke, and half-price pizza Monday and Tuesday.

The pizza is cut into little squares wieldy enough to hold in one hand while grasping a schooner of beer in the other. Completely unlike pies that are thick or chewy, it is easy to eat without worrying about drippage or crust collapse. In fact, it is rather amazing how the fragile-seeming crust stays crisp under toppings that can include sausage, pepperoni, buffalo chicken, and barbecue chicken. If this strange style of pizza is not your cup of tea, Riley's has a full pub menu that includes ribs, steaks, burgers, and sandwiches.

★ SNEAD'S

sneadsbbq.com
171st & Holmes   816-331-7979
Belton, MO   **L D** (closed Mon) | $$

Of all the many good smoke-cooked meats on Snead's menu, our favorites are beef and/or ham brownies, which are the crusty, smoky chunks stripped from the ends and tips of the meat—the best burnt ends imaginable. They aren't as soft as the ordinary barbecue, but they fairly explode with the flavor of meat and smoke. Sliced pork does not pack the potency of brownies, but it is hugely satisfying and sensuously tender. Beef brisket is shockingly fatless, and sauce is a natural companion. Snead's offers two variations: a slightly sweet mild sauce and a vigorously peppery orange brew that is reminiscent of Arthur Bryant's, not at all sweet. Then there are log sandwiches, named for their shape: tubular mixtures of finely ground barbecued beef, turkey, and ham, all minced together and wedged into a long bun. The result is a salty, powerful mélange reminiscent of a Maid-Rite. On the side: hand-cut, freshly made French fries, barbecue beans, and finely chopped coleslaw that is perfectly suited to brightening a fatigued tongue.

A low, rustic dining room decorated with quilts, farmy pictures, and a small collection of vintage wooden coat hangers, Snead's is way out in the country, where urban sprawl hasn't yet arrived. Opened in 1956 on Bill Snead's farm, it is, in our book, one of the greats, if not the greatest, among Kansas City barbecue restaurants.

★ STROUD'S

stroudsnorth.com

5410 NE Oak Ridge Dr.   816-454-9600
Kansas City, MO   **D** Mon–Thurs; **L D** Fri & Sun
(Sat open from 2 p.m.) | $$

Stroud's location on Oak Ridge Drive lacks the tumbledown charm of the original restaurant Mrs. Stroud opened in the 1930s on the location of the family fireworks stand, but the modern place has its own assets: an expansive frontier farmhouse with dining tables overlooking green grass on the rolling countryside. What better spot on Earth could there be to enjoy the ultimate fried chicken dinner?

The chicken is slow-sizzled in an iron skillet, emerging with a coat of gold that is noisy to crunch and not the least bit bready; there is just enough of it to shore in all the juices. Once you break through, those juices flow down chin and fingers and forearm. Side dishes are straight from heaven's table. Pour some peppery cream gravy onto the thick cloud of mashed potatoes; tear off a piece of warm, buttery cinnamon roll; spoon into chicken soup with homemade noodles. Even the green beans, which left al dente far behind, pack surprising porky sparkle.

Meals are served family-style. Stroud's is hugely popular and most of the time you will have to wait for a table, then wait while your chicken is fried. You will be glad you did.

A second location is at 4200 Shawnee Mission Parkway, Fairway, KS (913-262-8500).

★ TED DREWES

teddrewes.com

6726 Chippewa St.   314-481-2652
St. Louis, MO   (closed in winter) | $

For anyone in search of America's most delicious ice cream (and who is not?), here's a name to put on the short list of candidates for greatness: Ted Drewes. Technically, Drewes' product is not ice cream. It is frozen custard, meaning it is egg-rich and ultra-creamy. There's nothing more purely dairy-delish than vanilla, but you can mix it with flavoring agents from chocolate and strawberry to fudge, cherries, cookies, nuts, and candy bars.

The best-known dish in the house is called a concrete, which is a milk shake so thick that the server hands it out the order window upside down, demonstrating that not a drop will drip out. Beyond concretes, there are sundaes, cones, floats, and sodas.

Ted Drewes has two locations (the second is at 4224 S. Grand Boulevard, phone: 314-352-7376), both of them thronged all summer long with happy customers spooning into huge cups. In autumn, the custard operation closes and Ted goes into the Christmas tree business.

If you are far away and seriously crave this superb super–ice cream, Ted Drewes is equipped with dry ice to mail-order its custard.

OHIO

AGLAMESIS BROS.
aglamesis.com

3046 Madison Rd. 513-531-5196
Cincinnati, OH **L D** | $

Anne Mitchell, former dining editor of Cincinnati's alt-weekly newspaper *CityBeat,* informed us that Queen City ice cream connoisseurs tend to come down strongly in favor of either Aglamesis or Graeter's. It is her opinion that the decision depends on whether you like maximum butterfat (which Graeter's delivers) or extreme sweetness (an Aglamesis trait). It's a fine difference, and both are so good that we'd be hard-pressed to choose. But since Graeter's is a big chain and there are only a couple of Aglamesis Bros., the latter gets our nod.

Aglamesis's pumpkin ice cream, an autumn-only flavor, is as dark as Indian pudding, a just-right balance of spice and cream. Fresh banana delivers real tropical fruit flavor and can be haloed magnificently by a generous application of house-made bittersweet chocolate sauce. Dense-bodied whipped cream and a hail of chopped pecans complete the picture of perfection.

In addition to being an ice cream parlor (accoutered all in pink), Aglamesis is a complete chocolate shop with cases full of barks, clusters, truffles, and turtles. There is a second location at 9899 Montgomery Road, Cincinnati (513-791-7082).

★ AL'S CORNER RESTAURANT

151 2nd St. NW 330-475-7978
Barberton, OH **L** (Mon–Fri) | $

This immaculate storefront luncheonette, open only for weekday lunch, is a treasure trove of blue-plate Hungarian meals at blue-collar prices.

Choices are limited, but we've yet to find a clinker among such Old World stalwarts as cabbage and dumplings, pierogies, stuffed cabbage rolls, and Al's sausages, which are available in two variations—mild Slovene and spicy Hungarian. Made down the street at Al's Quality Market, the sausages are dense and big flavored (even the mild). Paprikash is creamy with a real paprika punch, the chicken falling-off-its-bone tender. For an accompanying starch, the choice is daunting: buttery dumplings, mashed potatoes and gravy, or *halushka,* which is a savory mix of cabbage and noodles. For dessert: beautiful strudel (apple, cherry, or cheese).

AVRIL-BLEH & SONS
avril-blehmeats.com

33 E. Court St. 513-241-2433
Cincinnati, OH **L** (closed Sun & Mon) | $

Avril-Bleh & Sons has been in the pork-packing business for well over a century (house motto: "A Link with the Past Since 1894"), and its display of tube steaks is a postgraduate education in oinky edibles. The curriculum includes bierwurst, bratwurst, knockwurst, bockwurst (spring only), yard sausage (with garlic), tiny links, oatmeal rings, liverwurst, kielbasa, wieners (natural casing or skinless), Cajun andouille, smoked Italian, chorizo, and *metts*. Short for *mettwurst*, a *mett* is a cured, deeply smoked, rugged-grind sausage about twice as large as a regular hot dog, firmly packed inside natural casing. *Metts* are also sold by street carts around town.

While most of what Avril-Bleh sells is meat to take home and cook, the shop does maintain a cook-cart out on the sidewalk as well as a handful of chairs for alfresco dining. The cart's menu is minimal: kielbasa, Italian sausage, chorizo, brats, cheeseburgers, hot dogs, and three kinds of *mett* (regular, hot, and Cheddar), all available in a bun with peppers, onions, kraut, and condiments. The Cheddar *mett* is magnificent. The skin audibly crackles when severed by teeth; its interior, while not oozy, is radiant with sweet pork flavor and a fusillade of spice.

BALATON

balaton-restaurant.com

13133 Shaker Sq.   216-921-9691
Cleveland, OH   **L D** (closed Mon & Tues) | **$$**

Great Hungarian food is one of Cleveland's culinary assets, and there is no better place to enjoy that fact than at a table in the Balaton. We've seen it described as a home-cooking restaurant, and dining here could be like coming home for supper, but only if you were lucky enough to have a mom who cooked brightly spiced and velvety paprikash (chicken or veal), crunch-crusted wiener schnitzel, and potato pancakes energized with a jolt of pepper. No mom we've known makes so magnificent a version of *lecso*—rugged smoked sausage atop a stew of yellow peppers, tomatoes, and onions.

Expert as it is, there really is something motherly about this food. It is so nurturing, so real, so down to earth. The hearty fare is well abetted by the setting, a handsome space that once was a men's clothing store, and by the staff, who all seem to be family (or act like it), including the small boy who was doing his homework at a back table when we stopped in for lunch.

The drink menu includes Hungarian wine as well as tart cherry juice from northern Michigan. You will have to choose dessert from a mouth-watering roster of multilayer *dobos* torte, chestnut cream torte, sponge-cake dumplings tipsy with rum, and *palacsinki*, which are slim crepes rolled around filling of apricot, sweet cheese, walnut, or poppy seed.

BELGRADE GARDENS

belgradegardenschicken.com

401 E. State St.   330-745-0113
Barberton, OH   **D** | **$$**

Are you looking for fried chicken that is drippingly juicy with a dense, red-gold crust that crunches and melts into pure savory flavor? If so, come to Barberton, Ohio, where a handful of restaurants in the Akron suburb specialize in what is known as Barberton chicken. Belgrade Gardens, which opened in 1933 and is now a huge, happy function hall, is where this particular kind of chicken first gained popularity, and while the menu is vast—including steaks, chops, seafood, sandwiches, and some really good chicken paprikash—first-time visitors need to get the full chicken dinner. You can get white or dark meat or a combination or a plate of nothing but legs, thighs, backs, wings, or tenders. Each is available small, medium, and large.

The secret of this chicken's appeal is no secret at all: It is fried in lard, and only lard can yield the supersavor that defines it. All the local chicken houses make it the centerpiece of a ritual feast that includes a bowl of spicy tomato-rice hot sauce, sweet-tart coleslaw, French fries, and a basket of white and dark bread.

★ CAMP WASHINGTON CHILI PARLOR

campwashingtonchili.com

3005 Colerain Ave.   513-541-0061
Cincinnati, OH   Always open, except
          Sunday | **$**

OPEN 24/7 Camp Washington sets the standard for Cincinnati's unique style of chili—a layered mound of limp spaghetti noodles topped by vividly spiced ground beef, then kidney beans, raw onions, and, finally, a fluffy crown of shredded Cheddar cheese. Oyster crackers are used as a garnish and one traditional side dish is a Coney Island hot dog topped with chili, cheese, and onions.

The other notable Queen City specialty on Camp Washington's menu is the double-decker sandwich, the basic principle of which is similar to five-way chili: stacked ingredients as impressive for looks as for multileveled tastes. Possible double-decker ingredients range from eggs and breakfast meats to roast beef, ham, and cheese. While half of a well-made one can indeed be picked up in two hands, it cannot be eaten like a normal sandwich, with all strata going into the mouth at one time. It must be nibbled at in such a way that some bites are more the top layer and others more the bottom.

While proprietor John Johnson has expanded and modernized the open-all-night restaurant since taking over in 1977, he has—bless his soul—maintained the welcoming, democratic spirit of a great American urban diner.

CATHEDRAL BUFFET
cathedralbuffet.com

2690 State Rd.	330-922-0467
Cuyahoga Falls, OH	**L** (Tues-Fri); **D** (Fri-Sun) | **$**

If you are neither a devout Christian nor a student of heartland American foodways, you probably won't enjoy dining in this restaurant, which is one part of the vast Ernest Angley Ministries. Before or after eating in the thousand-seat mess hall, one can step into the basement and pay a dollar to walk through the life of Christ as depicted in dioramas at Barbie-doll scale that show his journey from Nativity to Resurrection.

As for the food, it is of the church supper genre. Grab a plate and help yourself to an awe-inspiring multiroom buffet, including a cheerfully named Talk-of-the-Town salad bar area arrayed not only with lettuce and such but with a shimmering, multihued Jell-O mold, butterscotch pudding, and chocolate ambrosia with broken-up cream-filled cookies. (All are considered salad in much of the Midwest.) Of the dozens of other dishes available, we have enjoyed such home-ec masterworks as turkey Tetrazzini, broasted chicken, noodles in broth, and fruit cocktail cake: soul food for squares.

CRABILL'S
crabillshamburgers.com

727 Miami St.	937-653-5133
Urbana, OH	**L** (closed Sun) | **$**

Once an accursed branch of hash-house gastronomy, the griddle-fried micropatty known as a slider has become strangely fashionable. We have encountered Kobe beef sliders as hors d'oeuvres in striving restaurants, and most people who eat out have likely come across non-beef, so-called sliders made of barbecue, crab cakes, or tuna tartare. Let us assure you that the sliders you will eat at Crabill's are not trendy or upscale, and they are made of ordinary hamburger beef (and optional ordinary cheese) on spongy little buns. Eating one (that's about two bites' worth) is a unique experience: Cooked in deep oil on the grill, it has an outside surface with formidable crunch, and it is so skinny that there is virtually no interior. Six singles or a trio of doubles make a decent meal, but you might want to try to beat a record, which, last we looked, was thirty-three singles in one sitting (by a man) and nineteen doubles in one sitting (by a woman).

ECKERLIN MEATS
eckerlinmeats.com

116 W. Elder St.	513-721-5743
(in the Findlay Market)	**L** | **$**
Cincinnati, OH	

Eckerlin is a fairly small retail butcher shop in the very large Findlay Market. Given its modest space, it does booming business. We first were directed to it by Roadfooder Marjorie Solomon, who said it made the best *goetta*, Cincinnati's beloved pork and pin oats breakfast meat. A man behind the counter said he would be happy to make us a *goetta* sandwich, as long as we had the patience for it to fry.

Even before frying, the preparation of *goetta* is a painstaking process. Eckerlin cooks it a full four hours in a Dutch oven where a bell goes off every twenty minutes to remind a member of the staff to stir it. Once it's done and made into a loaf, slices from the loaf are fried ten or twelve minutes until the outside gets crusty and the inside is cooked through.

Although condiments are available, we took our sandwich plain on buttered white toast and strolled into the market for coffee to accompany it. It is easy to understand why Eckerlin is considered the top of the line among *goetta* connoisseurs. Instead of being made from ignominious by-products—its original provenance as a thrifty dish—it is made from creamy pork shoulder and a rainbow of spice, its meaty intensity cheerily leavened by little earthy bits of oat. It deserves status right up there with ham and bacon as one of pork's glories.

FLURY'S CAFE

fluryscafe.com

2202 Front St. 330-929-1315
Cuyahoga Falls, OH **B L** (closed Sun) | $

This tiny diner seats scarcely over a dozen people and there is nothing revolutionary on the menu, but if you are in greater Akron and looking for a hospitable slice of Americana, we highly recommend it. There is always a pancake of the day—we enjoyed cornmeal and banana-nut—and lunch opportunities include meat-loaf sandwiches and mac 'n' cheese, preceded by proprietor Kim Dunchuck's homemade soup. All the usual milk shake flavors are available, plus blueberry, raspberry, cherry, and peanut butter. For dessert, choose from among Kim's homemade cookies and shortcake laced with blueberries or blackberries.

G&R TAVERN

gandrtavern.com

103 N. Marion St. 740-726-9685
Waldo, OH **B L D** (closed Sun) | $

Since 1962, the G&R Tavern has built its reputation on bologna sandwiches that put pale, thin-sliced supermarket bologna to shame. In this family-friendly sports bar, the bologna is dark and smoky, firm as a knoblewurst salami, and sliced as thick as a good-sized hamburger patty. It is fried until its exterior turns crisp, then loaded into a burger bun with sweet pickles and onion, or your choice of mustard, mayonnaise, or tomato. Fitting side dishes include a variety of deep-fried vegetables and curly fries.

G&R also offers a bologna salad sandwich, and because this bologna is so much better than the spongy packaged stuff, the salad reminds us of something made with ham. The dessert roster includes high-rise, high-calorie chocolate peanut butter cream pie.

HATHAWAY'S COFFEE SHOP

441 Vine St. (inside the 513-621-1332
Carew Tower Arcade) **B L** | $
Cincinnati, OH

Here's a good Cincinnati breakfast for you: Hathaway's French toast, bright with cinnamon flavor and dusted with powdered sugar and splotched with melting butter. On the side, the locally loved pork-and-pin-oats loaf known as *goetta,* sliced thin and fried crisp. To drink: a bottomless cup of coffee, never allowed below half-full by the watchful waitstaff.

Located on the first level of Carew Tower, Hathaway's is one of a nearly extinct species: the downtown coffee shop. Seating is at one of three U-shaped counters or at a steel-banded dinette table against the wall. In addition to plate lunch, sandwiches, and well-respected hamburgers, there's a full soda-fountain menu of sundaes and banana splits, plus traditional malts and yogurt shakes. These latter include a banana whisk, a pink cloud (made with strawberries), and a crème sickle (orange juice and milk). The yogurt shakes evoke an era when yogurt was an alternative to normal food. The menu touts them as "Healthful Pick Me Uppers," for when one needs that sweet boost in the middle of the shopping day.

★ HENRY'S

6275 Route 40 614-879-9321
West Jefferson, OH **L D** | $

No traveler in a hurry wants to be on Highway 40, the side road parallel to I-70, but anyone with an appetite for home cooking needs to make the detour. Here, set back from the south side of the road is a defunct gas station. The pumps are long gone, but the on-premises restaurant is alive and well—a generous serving of Roadfood at its finest.

The meals are country-style fare: baked ham, hot roast pork sandwiches with mashed potatoes and gravy, creamed chipped beef on corn bread. But it's not the savories that put this unlikely knotty-pine-paneled roadside café on the map. It is pie. Here are some of the best pies in Ohio, in the Midwest, any-where: peach, banana, chocolate, peanut butter, cherry, coconut, et cetera. The butterscotch pie is thick and dense, full-flavored the way only real but-terscotch can be. Custard pie is modestly thin, a sunny yellow wedge dusted with nutmeg. It is melt-in-the-mouth tender. The flavor of the rhubarb pie is as brilliant as bright summer sun, intensely fruity, sweet but just-right tart, supported by a crust that flakes into buttery shards.

KENNEDY'S BAR-B-QUE

taggartsicecream.com

1420 7th St. NW
Canton, OH   330-454-0193
                          L (closed Sun) | **$**

Relish the relish! Whichever barbecued meat you get in your sandwich at Kennedy's, you must get it topped with cabbage relish. Vaguely similar to the slaw that goes into a pig sandwich in the South, but more pickly than sweet, the relish is bright and refreshing. And oh, what lovely pork this is: Tender with occasional chewy shreds, it is piled so high and huge in a bun that well over half the sandwich must be eaten with a fork or fingers. That much tumbles out if you try to lift it by hand.

Other pit-cooked meat choices are ham (fabu-lous), beef (yet to be tried), and turkey (not impres-sive). The rest of the menu is chili and bean soup, plus corn bread and Amish pies. That's the extent of it. The connoisseur's choice, other than a sandwich, is a bowl of bean soup loaded with chunks of pit ham and crowned with crumbled corn bread.

A Canton landmark since 1922, when it opened as Spiker's, the minuscule eatery was bought and renamed in 1960 by Jack Kennedy, who ran it for forty-nine years. After Mr. Kennedy died in 2009, it was taken over by Ernie Schott, proprietor of

Canton's superb Taggarts Ice Cream (p. 310). Mr. Schott extended the lunch hour to late afternoon but otherwise made no changes in the time-honored formula.

LIBERTY GATHERING PLACE

111 N. Detroit St.   937-465-3081
West Liberty, OH   **B L D** | **$**

"We have girls who come in at four in the morning to make the coleslaw and macaroni salad," a Gathering Place waitress boasted when we asked if the side dishes were good. "Good" turned out to be not a good enough word to describe them, for the little bowl of macaroni salad set before us was inspired: blue-ribbon, church-supper, Independence-Day-picnic fabulous! It was creamy with a pickle zip, dotted with hunks of hard-cooked egg and a few crunchy shreds of carrot, the noodles cooked just beyond al dente but not too soft.

Noodle rapture proved to be a paradigm for the dining experience at what appears to be a typical Main Street café, but is in fact an extraordinary one. During a week we spent in Dayton having suppers at the Pine Club (p. 307), the Gathering Place became our destination lunch stop for moist ham loaf and deep-flavored smoked pork chops sided by mashed potatoes and bread-crumb-enriched escalloped corn. We were astounded by the fried tenderloin sandwich—totally unlike the brittle-crisp, foot-wide 'loins typical of Midwest cafés. Here, the tenderloin is a thick pork steak with only a hint of crust—a slab of meat that is folded over inside the bun so you get a double layer of pork as juicy as a pair of chops. For dessert, we had cool coconut and peach crunch pie, the latter served hot and veined with melted butter.

LITTLE POLISH DINER

5772 Ridge Rd.   440-842-8212
Parma, OH   **L D** (Tues-Sat) | **$**

The name of the Little Polish Diner is not a cute affec-tation. It is really little: six counter stools and five tables in a space about the size of a walk-in closet. And it is really Polish, too; its motto: "Our Food Is Just Like Mom Used to Make." How we wish we had a mom who made such fine pierogies, *golabki* (stuffed cabbage), and pork-and-kraut *bigos* (hunter's stew).

We stopped in on a Wednesday, when the special lunch was a Warsaw Combination Plate, consisting of a crisp breaded boneless pork chop, stuffed cabbage glistening with sweet-tart sauce, a serving of *bigos,* and mashed potatoes. The soup of the day was chicken noodle, which was homey to the nth degree, filled with savory dark meat and spoonfuls of vegetables. We also got what the menu calls a Polish Boy—a length of kielbasa with sauerkraut in a roll; the sausage was bursting with juice and flavor. We want to return on a Saturday, when the special is chicken paprikash.

NEW ERA RESTAURANT

thenewerarestaurant.com

10 Massillon Rd.   330-784-0087
Akron, OH   **L D | $**

Since 1938, the New Era Restaurant has been a gathering place for Canton Serbs and others who like Serbian food. The well-weathered old facility was replaced in 2005 by a somewhat sterile, spanking new building; but even if architectural charm is lacking, the staff remain avatars of Old World charm and, more important, the kitchen continues to serve classic Middle European fare of the highest order.

"Where do you get your strudel?" we asked a young waitress when it came time to order dessert. She looked at us like we were crazy and pointed to the New Era kitchen. "We get it from there," she answered. "My grandmother makes it." Its spectacularly flaky dough encloses warm apple compote that is fruit-sweet more than sugar-sweet.

Unlike the more common Hungarian paprikash that is creamy-rich, New Era's is more a thin broth, insinuating its pepper flavor into the little dumplings that surround chicken pieces on the plate. The menu refers to it as "Our 75-Year-Old Signature Dish." We love the *cevapi,* skinless Serbian sausages with a good chaw and a pepper bite. Side them with mashed potatoes and rich brown gravy with a scattering of crisp chopped onion and you have a New Era Old World meal to remember.

NEW SANDUSKY FISH COMPANY

235 E. Shoreline Dr.   419-621-8263
Sandusky, OH   **L D | $**

Virtuoso Roadfooders Bruce Bilmes and Sue Boyle turned us on to this little takeout-only shack that offers sandwiches and whole dinners at single-digit prices. Located on Lake Erie's southern shore, it boasts fresh yellow perch and walleye fried to golden-crusted tenderness and piled into buns with abandon, as well as catfish and bass fillets. Frog legs are available at dinner along with fries, onion rings, hush puppies, et cetera.

Many customers are anglers who bring their catch here to have it cleaned (in a building out back) and have a sandwich while they wait. While all business is takeout, travelers who prefer outside-the-car dining will find nice bench seats in a gazebo across the street.

PERLA HOMEMADE DELIGHTS

perlahd.com

5380 State Rd.   216-741-9222
Parma, OH   **B** (closed Sun) **| $**

The Cleveland suburb of Parma is a bright star in northern Ohio's firmament of European food. In the neighborhood known as Ukrainian Village, Perla Homemade Delights mostly sells prepared meals to take home and heat—the pierogies are legendary, always winning #1 at the local pierogie festival—but for those of us passing through and demanding instant gratification, there are a couple of tables and an enthralling pastry case. Have a Lady Lock (a cream-filled puff pastry horn), a piece of strudel or nut roll, or, best of all, a slice of supremely refined *dobos torte,* a twelve-layer sponge cake ribboned with chocolate buttercream and capped with caramel.

THE PINE CLUB

thepineclub.com

1926 Brown St.   937-228-7463
Dayton, OH   **D** (closed Sun) **| $$$**

-- ★ --
HOT TICKET
-- ★ --
The Pine Club is a true Midwest supper club, open only in the evening, until midnight on

weekdays, 1 a.m. on Friday and Saturday. No reservations, no credit cards, no nonsense. Fantastic steak. You have your choice of filet mignon, porterhouse, or sirloin, each cut and aged on premises and grilled so the outside gets crunchy but the inside is swollen with juice.

Regulars begin a meal with Nantucket Bay scallops—sweet, firm nuggets with a pale light crust and smouldery sea taste. All meals are served with a basket of dinner rolls, and steaks come with a handful of onion straws and choice of potatoes that includes Lyonnaise: a crunchy, plate-wide pancake of shredded spuds woven with veins of sautéed onion. The traditional Pine Club salad is iceberg lettuce—cold, crisp chunks served "red and bleu," which is French dressing loaded with enormous clods of dry blue cheese. Those not wishing to spend $30+ on a cut of beef can get a terrific hamburger for one-third the price. One other favorite sandwich among longtime customers is sardines on rye.

PRICE HILL CHILI

pricehillchili.com

4920 Glenway Ave.   513-471-9507
Cincinnati, OH   **B L D** | **$**

Price Hill Cincinnati chili is prudently spiced and perfectly constructed: up to five layers, starting with spaghetti noodles and meat sauce on the bottom. But chili is only a fraction of what makes Price Hill a longtime favorite among Cincinnatians. Other dishes served with high style include Coney Island hot dogs (topped with the same meaty chili), double-decker sandwiches, and *goetta* (a locally preferred breakfast loaf made of pin oats, onions, and pork that is grilled to a crisp). Price Hill will serve *goetta* as a side with any meal or in a sandwich on rye, white, or whole wheat toast.

An amiable, family-friendly diner (with a larger cocktail lounge adjacent), Price Hill is open from dawn to late at night and has a full menu of typical sandwiches, hot dinners, salads, and breakfast omelets. The homemade soup of the day, in our experience (Monday chicken noodle and Tuesday beef barley), is fantastic.

PUTZ'S CREAMY WHIP

putzscreamywhip.com

2673 Putz Pl.   513-681-8668
Cincinnati, OH   **L D** (closed in winter) | **$**

Putz's is a drive-up stand with a menu of hot dogs, foot-long cheese Coneys, burgers, and barbecue, but everybody comes for custard. It is smooth and rich, an ivory-hued soft-serve product that is great swirled into a sugar cone or waffle cone or heaped into a cup and enjoyed for its pure, creamy goodness. Or you can have it whipped up for an extra-thick milk shake or malt or mixed into a soda.

The way we enjoy it most is in a sundae or banana split, the latter made in a long plastic boat that holds three mounds of ice cream, plus all the toppings. Best of all sundaes is the turtle, for which the bottom of a cup is filled with caramel, the caramel is topped with custard, then the custard topped with chocolate syrup. The chocolate syrup is mounded with whipped cream, chopped nuts, and a cherry.

Putz's is just off the highway in a little grove all its own (on a street that was rechristened to honor the longtime favorite destination-dessert place). There are pleasant picnic tables alongside that are an ideal place to spoon into creamy-whip perfection.

SLYMAN'S RESTAURANT

slymans.com

3106 St. Clair Ave.   216-621-3760
Cleveland, OH   **B L** (closed Sun) | **$$**

--★--
LOCALS
LOVE IT
--★--

A vintage near East Side deli where the corned beef slicing machine never stops, Slyman's is open only for weekday breakfast and lunch, the morning menu including a dandy corned beef, egg, and cheese breakfast sandwich. At lunch, there's a full menu but corned beef stars—on rye, of course. The sandwich is very big, the meat sliced thin. It is extremely tender and somewhat lean, lacking the lasciviousness of fatty corned beef. That is exactly why Slyman's Reuben is so popular. The addition of cheese and sauerkraut, plus a crisp crust of griddled rye, add the reckless luxury that lean beef does not deliver.

On the menu is a lexicon of slang unique to Slyman's sandwich-makers. Mummy = mustard + mayonnaise. Special K = hold the sauerkraut. Cake = mayonnaise + horseradish. Grill Brick = grilled bread only. Waitresses are no-nonsense, and the guys behind the counter are full of joie de vivre. Curiously, the menu is classic Jewish deli, but brochures at the cash register invite customers to know Allah better and the menu includes praise to Jesus in the form of a reference to John 3:16.

SOKOLOWSKI'S UNIVERSITY INN

sokolowskis.com

1201 University Rd.	216-771-9236
Cleveland, OH	L (Mon–Fri); D (Fri & Sat)
	| $$

It's a hearty appetite's dream to walk along the cafeteria line of this 1923-vintage tavern and gaze upon pans full of pierogies, kielbasa, sauerkraut, breaded lake fish, and stuffed cabbage. Pierogies are the most famous dish in the house: big, tender pockets filled with cheese and smothered in onions with which they are sizzled in butter until the onions turn caramel-soft and sweet. The kielbasa is as buff as a sausage can be, nearly too muscular for the flimsy cafeteria knife and fork provided, and it delivers megatons of smoky, piggy, spicy flavor. We especially like the balance of Sokolowski's *halushka,* which is a mix of salubrious sautéed cabbage and little squiggles of dumpling. On Friday nights, the menu features beer-battered cod and Lake Erie perch, with live piano music to dine by. Sokolowski's is open for supper only Friday and Saturday nights, when the menu expands to include grilled rainbow trout, prime rib, and chicken paprikash.

To drink, you can pluck a bottle of beer from one of the coolers, domestic and exotic kinds, and there is Vernor's ginger ale on tap. For dessert, we love the egg custard pudding dotted with fat grains of rice.

This is a hale, rollicking place. Our first visit was a few weeks before Christmas, when the sound system throbbed with familiar carols and holiday songs, all with a polka beat. In addition to the usual welcome signs in Polish and countless pictures of the celebrities who have come to enjoy this landmark restaurant, effigies of Santa and his elves were everywhere.

STATE MEATS

statemeats.com

| 5338 State Rd. | 216-398-0183 |
| Parma, OH | L (closed Sun) \| $ |

State Meats is a butcher shop and smokehouse, not a sit-down restaurant, but it is a godsend for sausage fans who are hungry and passing through Parma. Located in a shipshape neighborhood known as Ukrainian Village (and not far from swoonful pastries at Perla Homemade Delights [p. 307]), this family-run enterprise has a broad repertoire of kishka, rice rings, kielbasa burgers, Slovenian sausage, pork chops, and cottage hams that are smoked out back, and the porky, beefy, smoky aroma in here is a powerful appetite inducer for anyone of the carnivorous persuasion.

The one hot meal you can get to eat immediately (in your car, for there are no dining tables) is kielbasa. The big, taut, and brightly spiced sausage, complemented by delicious sauerkraut and packed into a hefty bun, is a terrific sandwich, although a challenge to eat without lots of napkins. Proprietor George Salo also gave us a few smokies, which he described as his favorite car snack. Smokies are thin, chewy, garlic-packed salami sticks that were a pleasure to gnaw out of one hand while swilling from a bottle of State Meats–brand root beer with the other (and steering with the third).

SWENSONS

swensonsdriveins.com

| 40 S. Hawkins Ave. | 330-864-8416 |
| Akron, OH | L D \| $ |

King of the menu at this curb-service drive-in is the Galley Boy, a double cheeseburger dressed with two sauces, one mayonnaisey with bits of onion added, the other zesty barbecue. Optional condiments include ketchup, relish, sweet pickles, horseradish, Worcestershire, Tabasco, cocktail, honey mustard, tartar, and Cajun spice. Garnish choices are tomato, lettuce, olives, grilled onions, hot peppers, bacon, Coney sauce, and coleslaw.

Beyond hamburgers the menu lists a quarter-pound all-beef bologna sandwich, salads, soups, fried chicken, and shrimp. Among the beverages are milk shakes and malts, something called a California (reminded us of Kool-Aid), and half-and-half (iced tea and lemonade). Onion rings are a brittle-crusted joy. French fries, which we didn't try, are listed as "Only Idaho's," the dubious apostrophe apparently having migrated from the restaurant name, which doesn't contain one on the outdoor sign or menu.

Swensons has no indoor seats. Meals to be eaten here are presented on sturdy trays that clip onto the inside of car windows in such a way that it's possible to dine in comfort even when it's raining.

TAGGARTS ICE CREAM

taggartsicecream.com

1401 Fulton Rd. NW   330-452-6844
Canton, OH   L D | $

Taggarts's hot fudge is the consistency of chocolate syrup, deeply fudgy-flavored, served just warm enough to dramatically pair with cool ice cream. Although Taggarts is an unassuming Midwestern ice cream parlor that goes back to the early twentieth century, there is something sophisticated about this hot fudge. Elegant. Suave. It comes topped with whipped cream and a cherry and perfectly roasted pecan halves salted just enough to create taste-bud buzz with the hot fudge and ice cream. Turtle sundaes and banana splits also benefit from the first-rate nuts.

The signature concoction is known as a Bittner, named for a customer back in the 1930s who dared the mixologists to create a milk shake so thick that a spoon would stand upright in it. Made from three-quarters of a pound of vanilla ice cream and chocolate syrup, it resembles concrete, but comes heaped with those good roasted pecans as well as whipped cream.

Ice cream is Taggarts's claim to fame, but there also is an inviting roster of sandwiches and short-order fare reminiscent of times gone by. We've tried the wonderfully old-fashioned olive-nut cream cheese on toast as well as a grilled cheese sandwich with bacon, and both were great. But it's hard to pay attention to the main course when dessert is so compelling.

TUCKER'S

1637 Vine St.   513-721-7123
Cincinnati, OH   B L | $

— ★ —
LOCALS
LOVE IT
— ★ —
Tucker's opened for business in 1946, and while some things in the humble Over-the-Rhine hash house have no doubt changed since then, its ambience remains more mid-twentieth-century than early twenty-first. Joe Tucker, who runs the place with his wife, Carla, grew up with it.

Along with hash browns and a sumptuously loaded vegetable omelet, we had a tile of *goetta*, the only-in-Cincinnati breakfast meat made from pork, beef, onions, pin oats, and spice. Joe slices his loaf of *goetta* thin and grills it a good long while (this is not fast food) until the outside is crunchy and glistening but the interior stays succulent.

Everything Tucker's does is first-class. An omelet comes scattered with eye-opening fresh snips of basil. Biscuits are from scratch; corn bread is Mid-South-style, in the form of a pancake. French toast comes decorated with fresh fruit. Last we looked, Tucker's neighborhood is on the skids, but the restaurant remains a bastion of hospitality.

WHITE HOUSE CHICKEN

whitehousechicken.com

180 Wooster Rd. N.   330-745-0449
Barberton, OH   L D | $$

White House chicken is for skin lovers. Each piece is enveloped in a chewy, spicy, supersavory coat so thick that the meat inside—white as well as dark—yields no juice until the envelope is breached. While we would hesitate to call any chicken too juicy, the soft, moist meat simply cannot compete with the assertive crust around it. In fact, nice as the meat is, we find that a full plate of this fine chicken with the works, which means French fries, spicy rice, coleslaw, and bread, has so much of that good, red-gold skin on it that we might leave meat behind just to make sure we get all the really good stuff.

What makes White House chicken skin such a marvel is that the frying medium is lard, insinuating every bite with wanton luxe. Like all the Barberton chicken houses, White House cuts its bird the old-fashioned way into wing, drumette, breast, leg, thigh, and back, an economical technique left over from Depression days when cooks tried to maximize the number of pieces they could get from one bird. When you sink your teeth into a piece, you may find meat where you don't expect it or not enough meat where you want it (in the back), but who cares when the additional pieces mean more of that can't-stop-eating skin.

The original location is a big white corner building with a neighborhood-tavern feel; the last time we ate here, a kindly old lady walking out the door smiled at us, poked a finger in our direction, and said, "You found it!" We have yet to visit any of the other Akron-area locations of the White House, which apparently is looking to franchise nationally.

WHITE TURKEY DRIVE-IN

whiteturkey.com

388 E. Main Rd.   440-593-2209
Conneaut, OH   **L D** (Mother's Day–
                                Labor Day) | **$**

"If you find yourself along Lake Eerie in the northeast corner of Ohio, pull into the White Turkey, a seriously vintage drive-in." So wrote a Roadfood tipster in a note with no return address and no ID. So we don't really know who to thank for this suggestion, but we sure would like to! This Richardson's Root Beer stand is a fine Roadfood stop along old US-20, offering seats at high stools where you can feel a lake breeze and watch the cars cruise past while you dine on true mid-American, midcentury drive-in fare. Its namesake turkey sandwich is the real thing, loaded with shredded meat. No compressed loaf here! You can get a plain one or a Large Marge, which also includes cheese and bacon. Beyond turkey, there are double and triple cheeseburgers, hot dogs, and chili cheese dogs.

While only vanilla ice cream is available, the variety of soda fountain drinks and desserts is mesmerizing. Of course there are cones, shakes, and malts; there are sundaes topped with pineapple, cherry, chocolate, hot fudge, homemade peanut butter, caramel, butterscotch, or blueberry. You can get a black cow (here, a blend of root beer and ice cream). And the root beer floats are divine, available in sizes from kiddie (80¢) to Super Shuper, created with a quart of root beer and a quantity of ice cream to match.

YOUNG'S JERSEY DAIRY

youngsdairy.com

6880 Springfield-   937-325-0629
Xenia Rd.   **B L D** | **$**
Yellow Springs, OH

Young's Jersey Dairy, which opened in 1968, is a farm-themed amusement park that includes a goat-petting zoo, a gift shop, a miniature golf course named Udders and Putters, and a summertime art exhibit of statuary cows painted by local artists. A few years back, a gourmet coffee shop with espresso drinks and Wi-Fi access was added. But of all its many attractions, the one that will keep us coming back is ice cream. They blend their own, and at 15 percent butterfat, it is rich but not insanely so. There is a different featured flavor every week of the year, from peaches and cream to espresso chocolate crunch and caramel cookie dough. Of all the ones we have tried, the one distinguishing characteristic is their balance. None is too sweet or overflavored. All are just right for eating multiple scoops.

Milk shakes, made in sizes from Calfshake to Cowshake to Bullshake and Lotsa Bullshake start with French vanilla ice cream and are available extra-rich, with malt powder. Gelato and sorbet also are available. You can eat a meal here: a basic menu of eggs and pancakes from 7 a.m. to 2 p.m. and burgers, hot dogs, soup, salad, and sandwiches for lunch. Plus excellent fresh cheese curds befitting of a real dairy farm.

WISCONSIN

ANCHOR BAR

anchorbarandgrill.com

413 Tower Ave.   715-394-9747
Superior, WI   **L D | $**

————★——— The Anchor Bar is a spare-looking tav-
OPEN LATE ern in an industrial non-neighborhood
——★——— near the Duluth shipyards. The inside is
nearly pitch-dark. Customers at the bar and big round
tables include rugged-looking seamen having
rugged-sounding conversations. The aroma of grilling beef is irresistible. The Anchor Bar is a destination
hamburger lovers need to know.

Each burger is a thick, hand-formed patty made
of meat fat enough to weep juice into the bun even
before you lift it. It is not high-end prime beef, but
its stout, blue-collar satisfaction is undeniable. And
its proletarian price is irresistible. A single burger,
served in over a dozen guises, including topped with
cheeses, hot sauces, even pineapple or cashews,
costs less than four dollars. A heap of hot-from-the-
kettle golden fries—big square, spuddy logs laced
with lots of crisp squiggles and burnt bits—adds
$1.25 to the price. An amazing five-dollar meal (not
counting beer)!

The menu makes fun of the few non-burger items
available, noting that the ham sandwich is "great if
you like ham" and the BLT is "not blueberries, liver,
and truffles."

BEERNTSEN'S CONFECTIONARY

beerntsens.com

108 N. 8th St.   920-684-9616
Manitowoc, WI $

In the back of Beerntsen's, through an elaborately
carved archway, handsome wooden booths are occupied by customers who come for such ice cream
fancies as a Sweetheart (caramel, vanilla ice cream,
marshmallow, crushed nuts) or a Sunset (strawberry and vanilla ice cream, pineapple, marshmallow,
crushed nuts). Hot fudge sundaes are served with the
fudge in a separate container, allowing customers to
pour it on as they eat.

Up front are more than a hundred different kinds
of hand-dipped candy, including a chocolate cosme-
tology set (brush, mirror, hair dryer), smoochies (like
Hershey's kisses, but bigger), raspberry and vanilla
seafoam dainties, and—the pièce de résistance—a
bonbon known as fairy food, which is a two-inch
square of brittle spun sugar shrouded in deep, dark
chocolate. We are very happy we live nowhere near
Manitowoc, Wisconsin, and that fairy food is too delicate to be shipped; otherwise, we'd be addicts.

BENDTSEN'S BAKERY

bendtsensbakery.com

3200 Washington Ave.   262-633-0365
Racine, WI   (closed Sun) | $

Bendtsen's calls its kringle "the world's finest Danish pastry," a claim with which we would not disagree. If you don't know what kringle is, think of an ordinary Danish, like you have with morning coffee. Now imagine its crust buttery and feather-light, almost like a croissant, and fill it with a ribbon of pecan paste and chopped nuts, or a layer of almond macaroon paste, or a tunnel of cherry and cheese. Picture it as big as a Christmas wreath, about a foot and a half across and iced with sugar glaze or flavored frosting. Have it warm with butter melting on top, accompanied by a leisurely pot of coffee. There you have one of the great breakfast (or teatime) treats in America, a dish that has become the signature of Racine, Wisconsin.

Bendtsen's has pictures on the wall that show the time they made the world's largest kringle, but size isn't what makes their pastry so wonderful. Each kringle made here, whether simply filled with apricot jam or fancy-filled with a mash of cranberries and walnuts, is a beautiful sight—a broad oval rather than a perfect circle, quite flat, and ready to slice into small pieces (of which you'll want three or four).

There is no place to eat at Bendtsen's, although samples of kringle are often available for tasting on the counter.

BENJI'S

benjisdeliandrestaurant.com

4156 N. Oakland Ave.   414-332-7777
Milwaukee, WI   B L D | $$

Benji's is an old-school Jewish-Midwestern delicatessen. Its menu ranges from corned beef sandwiches on rye to Friday-night fish fries, from blintzes filled with sweet pot cheese to a Cobb salad. We like it because it is one of the few restaurants in the Midwest that serves the old farmhouse meal called hoppel poppel— a griddle-cooked, kitchen-sink breakfast of salami, scrambled eggs, and potato chunks. Super hoppel poppel adds peppers and mushrooms and blankets the whole thing with melted cheese.

Of course, it is a good place for piled-high deli sandwiches, lox-and-bagel platters, sweet-and-sour cabbage borscht, and crisp potato pancakes served with applesauce. For dessert, we recommend noodle kugel (a cheesecake-rich block of cooked egg noodles and sweetened cheese), served hot with sour cream. And for a beverage to drink with your meal, Benji's offers true melting-pot variety: domestic or imported beer, kosher wine, Dr. Brown's in cans, Sprecher's soda in bottles, and chocolate phosphates (seltzer water and chocolate syrup).

CHARCOAL INN

charcoalinn.com

1313 S. 8th St.   920-458-6988
Sheboygan, WI   B L D (closed Sun-Mon) | $

The Charcoal Inn is a leading source of the great Wisconsin sausage known as a brat (rhymes with "hot," short for bratwurst). It is served as a sandwich, wrapped in wax paper, delivered without a plate. Each brat is slit and flattened before getting grilled, which makes for easy stacking in the bun if you get what many regulars get: a double brat (with pickle chips and raw onions). The sausages are generously spiced and deeply perfumed with the sizzle of a charcoal fire. Thick and resilient but thoroughly tooth-tender, they are as savory as sausage can be, oozing a delectable blend of meat juice and the melted butter with which they are basted.

While brats are the star attraction, burgers are big here too, and although the beef is not prime, it is plenty rich because it also gets basted with butter. A double burger with cheese is plush beyond measure.

For dessert you need a torte. Different days bring different flavors, from Old World poppy seed to modern American Oreo. Each piece is a square about four by four inches wide and two inches high. It is dense and smooth, sitting on a pallet of graham cracker crumbs, tasting like a pint of cream that has been reduced, thickened, flavored, and sweetened. It is similar in texture to a cheesecake, but so pure and rich you'll want to call it cream cake.

CHILI JOHN'S

519 S. Military Ave.   920-494-4624
Green Bay, WI   L D (closed Sun) | $

In 1916, "Chili John" Isaac devised a recipe for ground beef cooked with a fusillade of spice. His recipe featured an eye-opening measure of peppery oil, but the way he served it at his little eat place, in concert with spaghetti noodles, beans, and cheese, the heat became part of a well-balanced plate of food. Although some locals still call the multilayered configuration Texas-style chili (an appellation Texas chili-heads no doubt would abhor), variations of the formula are now known throughout the state as Green Bay–style chili, and the chili parlor has become a culinary guiding light.

JACK PANDL'S WHITEFISH BAY INN

jackpandls.com

1319 E. Henry Clay St.   414-964-3800
Whitefish Bay, WI   L D | $$

Jack Pandl's (since 1915) serves German-flavored Dairyland cuisine in a friendly, wood-paneled dining room with a wall of windows that look out over elegant Lake Drive. Waitresses wear dirndl skirts and there is lots of Old World memorabilia for décor (including a tremendous collection of beer steins), but the menu is at least as Midwestern as it is Middle European. At lunch, when the steel-banded tables are set with functional paper place mats, you can eat a julienne salad or a Reuben sandwich made with Wisconsin cheese, or pork chops, or a Denver omelet. In addition to broiled whitefish ("always purchased fresh," the menu guarantees), there is that lean but luscious local specialty, walleyed pike, filleted and broiled to perfection. This being Milwaukee, Friday is fish-fry night, of course. Pandl's perch is very nice—whole fish filleted so their two halves hold together, encased in a golden crust and accompanied by first-class potato pancakes.

We love *schaum torte* for dessert. That's a crisp meringue dolloped with freshly made custard. On the other hand, we never can resist the German pancake. It's not really a dessert item, and many people have it as their main course, but somehow it makes a grand conclusion to a meal. This gorgeous edible event, a Jack Pandl's specialty, is a big puffy cloud of batter similar in texture to Yorkshire pudding, but slightly sweeter. It arrives at the table piping hot and shaped like a big bowl, its circumference crisp and brown, risen high in the oven, its center moist and eggy. Dust it with a bit of powdered sugar and give it a spritz of lemon, creating a sophisticated syrup, then dig in immediately. It is a big plate of food, maybe enough to share.

JAKE'S

jakedelimke.com

1634 W. North Ave.   414-562-1272
Milwaukee, WI   L (closed Sun) | $

It took us a long time to realize that Milwaukee was a major corned beef city, but if we had any doubts, Jake's erased them. Here is a vintage urban deli where the hand-sliced corned beef is steamy-moist, unspeakably tender, and vivid-flavored.

The beef is sliced medium-thick, then piled into slick-crusted, Milwaukee-made Miller Bakery seeded rye: not an outrageously huge sandwich like you might get in Chicago or New York, but in no way skimpy, either.

There are a few other items on Jake's menu: pastrami, turkey pastrami, hard salami, hot dogs, and soups like Mama should have made, and you can have the corned beef as part of a Reuben with sauerkraut and cheese. But for us, and for generations of Milwaukeeans, Jake's is synonymous with corned beef on rye.

With its pale yellow walls, its tables topped with worn linoleum, its ancient wood booths equipped with out-of-order buzzers once used to summon service, Jake's exudes faded charm. It has been around since 1955, and now there are two other locations in Milwaukee, in the Grand Avenue Mall and the Southridge Mall.

JO'S CAFÉ

3519 W. Silver Spring Dr.   414-461-0210
Milwaukee, WI   **B L | $**

Hoffel poffel (aka hoppel poppel) isn't widely known anywhere in the United States. The few restaurant examples we have found are in Iowa and Wisconsin. It is one gigantic breakfast plate of eggs scrambled with chunks of potato, onions, and, at Jo's, lots of nuggets of spicy salami and, optionally, some cheese on top. The only reason we would recommend not getting it for breakfast at Jo's is that the *other* kind of potatoes—the thin-cut hash browns—are delicious. Cooked in a flat patty until brittle-crisp, they too are available under a mantle of melted cheese. Actually, either sort of potato dish will leave precious little room for Jo's pecan rolls and cinnamon rolls. Nor should one abjure toast. Roadfood warrior Cliff Strutz declared, "No matter what kind of bread you get with your breakfast, you must cover it with the homemade apple jelly sitting out on the counter." (There is a different kind of homemade jelly every week.)

We generally think of Jo's for breakfast, but lunch is good too. Blue-plate cuisine is the order of the day, including such daily specials as meat loaf, beef stew, pork chops, and country-fried steak with real (of course!) mashed potatoes, homemade gravy, and a yeasty fresh-baked dinner roll. Every day you can order barbecued pork ribs or chicken.

KLINGER'S EAST

920 E. Locust St.   414-263-2424
Milwaukee, WI   **L D | $**

-- ★ --
LOCALS
LOVE IT
-- ★ --
Klinger's East does not look like a promising eatery. It is a shadowy bar and pool hall where you might not expect anything but beer nuts and potato chips, and where, at first glance, you have to wonder if newcomers will be made to feel, shall we say, unwelcome. But in fact, it is a comfy place, even for strangers, and its customers include wholesome-looking families you'd never see dining in such an establishment in other parts of the country. But in Milwaukee, taverns aren't just for drinkers; they are community centers. We recommend it for the Friday fish fry, which is ridiculously inexpensive and unexpectedly good. Of course cod is on the menu, sheathed in a crunchy coat of beer batter. Bluegill sometimes is available. And you usually can get smelt (pronounced "shmelt" hereabouts)—a fish lover's fish with unabashed oily character—crunch-coated two-inch sprats well accompanied by a short stack of silver-dollar-size potato pancakes.

KOPP'S CUSTARD

kopps.com
5373 N. Port Washington   414-961-3288
Rd.   **L D | $**
Glendale, WI

Kopp's is a good place to stand and have a cooked-to-order double butter cheeseburger (there are no table seats), but it is better known for custard, not ice cream. You can see it pour in thick cascades from great silver machines behind the order counter. It is ivory-white, rich, and densely flavorful.

Plain vanilla is so, so pure—the true choice of a serious custardhead. No matter what else we get, we always need to dip a spoon into one dish of that. Beyond vanilla, Kopp's makes a new and different flavor every single day of the year. Among our fondest memories are caramel-apple with mixed nuts, Key lime pie, and Snickers chunky cheesecake. The menu also includes a milk shake of the day (mocha coconut frappe, for instance) and a featured sundae. "Magic flavors" are composed of several varieties mixed together, such as Cherry Bomb, a swirl of burgundy cherry, Key lime pie, and passion fruit.

There are two other Kopp's locations: 18880 West Bluemound Road, Brookfield (262-789-9490) and 7631 West Layton Avenue, Greenfield (414-282-4312).

★ LEON'S

leonsfrozencustard.us
3131 S. 27th St.   414-383-1784
Milwaukee, WI   **$**

There is no place to eat at this Eisenhower-era hangout other than in your car or standing in the neon-lit parking lot along with other pilgrims who have come for frozen dessert. Leon's menu is all custard: cones, cups, sodas, sundaes, malts, pints, and quarts. (Hot dogs are available, but irrelevant.)

Milwaukee is fanatical about custard, which is heavy, smooth, and pure—denser than the richest super-premium ice cream and nothing like wan frozen yogurt. As made by Leon's, it is egg-rich, sweet but not cloying, and uncomplicated. No mix-ins, no silly names for flavors, no cookie dough or brownie chunks. Choose vanilla, chocolate, strawberry, or butter pecan. Have it in a cone or cup. Or have a sundae topped with sauce of your choice and delicious toasted nuts: pecan halves that have a wicked crunch, a salty punch, and an earthy flavor that accentuates the superior custard.

MAGGIE'S
maggies-bayfield.com

257 Manypenny Ave.   715-779-5641
Bayfield, WI   **L D** | $$

Snowy whitefish fillets, which come sautéed in butter, seem almost too tender to attack with a fork. On most Friday evenings, Maggie's offers a special of headless but otherwise whole whitefish with all its bones, skin, and fins. Even if you've never faced a whole fish like this, getting the meat is a snap. The waitstaff will show you how to peel back the skin, then start at the top and easily separate moist forkfuls from the bone. The flavor of whole whitefish is not significantly different from those that are filleted and broiled or sautéed, but the presentation adds fish-camp fun to the dining experience.

On the subject of fish-camp vittles, how about a plate of whitefish livers? Because it takes a lot of fish to gather a small amount of livers—they're about the size of a quarter, and a dinner of them might include fifteen or twenty—mongers who sell to local restaurants and markets traditionally have thrown them away. But old-time fishermen have long considered them a delicacy, and in recent years as Bayfield has gone from quiet fishing village to popular tourist destination, livers have begun to appear on menus of a handful of plain and fancy restaurants. Like the flesh of the whitefish, the livers' most distinguishing characteristic is their inland water taste, more mellow than chicken liver but definitely an organ meat. Maggie's rolls them in spiced flour and sautés them with peppers, onions, and mushrooms until their outsides have a crunch and the inside of each turns melting-soft.

Remember that the northern Midwest is apple country. Maggie's apple cake is not to be missed, especially served warm and à la mode.

MAZO'S
mazoshamburgers.com

3146 S. 27th St.   414-671-2118
Milwaukee, WI   **L D** (Mon–Sat) | $

One of Milwaukee's lesser-known culinary attractions is excellent hamburgers. Many connoisseurs believe Mazo's serves the best. It is a tiny place, now run by Nick Mazo, whose grandparents started it in 1934, and if you come at lunchtime, prepare to wait a while once you find a precious seat in the dining room. These burgers are *not* fast food, but they are worth the wait. They are normal-sized patties of good ground beef in toasted buns, but what sends them into orbit is the fact that they are garnished with butter—the Milwaukee way!—resulting in a confluence of the two most wickedly good fats: meat and dairy. Available toppings include fried onions, sautéed mushrooms, and of course a layer of cheese. Other choices for dressing up the burger are bacon, lettuce, and tomato as well as thousand island dressing. On the side, have coleslaw, French fries, or baked beans.

Bonus: Mazo's is directly across the street from the excellent Leon's custard stand (p. 315).

★ MCBOB'S
mcbobs.com

4919 W. North Ave.   414-871-5050
Milwaukee, WI   **B L D** | $$

We first came to McBob's for its fish fry. Every Friday, there are three choices: perch, walleye, or grouper; or you can have a combo of perch and walleye, or a super combo of all three. With the fish come American fries or potato pancakes, coleslaw, and bread. Each fish fillet is encased in a highly seasoned, fragile crust. The walleye is light and ephemeral; the grouper is mild with a sweet, oily flavor. The perch is snowy white. If you get the meal with potato pancakes—you must!—the pancakes are fanned out on the plate as a kind of edible trivet for the fish. They are laced with bits of onion and have a potato flavor that perfectly complements the crisp fish.

If you happen to be a Friday fish-fry frowner, do not ignore McBob's! Every day of the week it is a source of A-1 corned beef. Big chunks of steamy-hot meat from a super-tender spiced brisket are piled into a sandwich of plain rye or in toasted rye with sauerkraut, horseradish mustard, and Swiss cheese (a Reuben). The meat is extraordinarily lean and yet dripping with flavor. The ideal condiment is horseradish mustard. The next morning, McBob's turns the corned beef into some of the best hash we've ever eaten.

MR. PERKINS' FAMILY RESTAURANT

2001 W. Atkinson Ave.   414-447-6660
Milwaukee, WI   B L D | $

Mr. Perkins' is a city lunchroom with a mostly African American clientele. It is a good place to know about even if you don't have a taste for such soul-food standards as neckbones and chitlins. Who couldn't find comfort in this baked chicken with dressing? Fried chicken bears a gorgeous golden crust; meat loaf is firm and satisfying; fried perch, three boneless fillets encased in a sandy cornmeal crust, is amazingly juicy with flavor as lusty as beefsteak.

One of the most delightful aspects of lunch and supper at Mr. Perkins' (which also serves breakfast) is choosing side dishes. Mac 'n' cheese is a duet of tender noodle and crusty edge; fried okra retains tremendous vegetable salubrity; fried green tomatoes are tangy and brittle-crisp; there are pot-likker-sopped turnip greens *or* turnip bottoms, made into an intriguing squashlike mash with butter and sugar. Corn bread is Tennessee-style—that is, a griddle-cooked cake that is buttery, tender, golden-colored, and an ideal tool for mopping gravy and vegetable drippings from a plate. Desserts include luxuriant

banana pudding, individually sized fried peach pies, sweet-potato pie, and cool lemon icebox pie. To drink, the beverages of choice are lemonade and iced tea, both served southern-style: *sooo-eeeet!*

PLAZA TAVERN

theplazatavern.com
319 N. Henry St.   608-255-6592
Madison, WI   L D | $

Some people go to the Plaza Tavern to drink or play pool. We come for the Plazaburger. What makes it different from a regular hamburger (which is also available) is the secret-sauce condiment that drenches the patty to a degree that it seems to seep right into it. Based on a combo of sour cream and mayonnaise, it is thinner than ketchup and its texture reminds us of an odd barbecue sauce, although it has neither vinegar tang nor peppery spice. In addition to infusing the meat with its flavor, it gets deeply imprinted into the dark bun. Connoisseurs have it on their French fries too.

The Tavern menu is an otherwise unremarkable array of sandwiches, plus, of course, deep-fried cheese curds. Beers are sold by the pint and pitcher. Ambience is pure Midwest saloon: long bar, tight booths, and wall murals showing scenic Wisconsin.

REAL CHILI

419 E. Wells St.   414-271-4042
Milwaukee, WI   L D | $

Real Chili, which dates back to 1931, serves an only-in-the-Midwest kind of chili, a layered affair of cheese atop beef atop beans atop spaghetti noodles, with oyster crackers and raw onions on the side. You can get it mild, medium, or hot; you can ask for sour cream on top; and if you are a chili *bec fin*, you can doctor it up with a spritz of sweet or hot vinegar, both of which are supplied on Real Chili's tables.

The déclassé joint that serves this witch's brew is the kind of beanery you once could find in cities throughout the Heartland. With the exception of Cincinnati, the Midwest has lost most of its chili parlors, and although this style of chili gets no respect from purists, it is a culinary adventure you don't want to miss. Uniformed waitresses dole out second helpings at half price, and the preferred beverages are beer or Coke.

There is a second location at 1625 West Wells Street (414-342-6955).

RING'S BAR

950 Alma Ave.	608-546-9231
Plain, WI	L D | $

Have a seat on one of the high-back counter stools in this third-generation town tavern and prepare to tuck into what Roadfood.com contributor Stefan Osdene described as "butter broiled perfection." The hamburger is what's broiled, at a temperature high enough to sear the exterior of the seven-ounce patty and seal in massive amounts of juice. Once cooked to your specifications, the burger is topped with a pat of butter that melts instantly into the crevices of meat, adding even further succulence; then it is put into a tall, heavy-duty bun. Thick slices of Wisconsin Cheddar or pepper jack cheese and bacon from the butcher across the street are worthy options. Pickle chips, broiled onion slices, and a fried egg also are available. "Nowhere else will you find greater butter burgers," Mr. Osdene declared.

Other than burgers, the Ring's Bar menu is limited to a soup of the day and chili when the temperatures drop.

★ SOLLY'S GRILLE

sollysgrille.com

4629 N. Port	414-332-8808
Washington Rd.	B L D | $
Milwaukee, WI	

Hamburgers are a passion in Milwaukee, where butter is the staff of life. Ergo, the butter burger. At Solly's, it is a medium-thin patty of beef, cooked through, served on a bun and saturated with unconscionable amounts of melted butter. Not margarine, not flavored oil: pure, dairy-rich, delicious butter. There is no hamburger we know so wickedly indulgent. You can get a Super Solly Burger (two patties, and a good idea—a single is overwhelmed by its bun) or a

Super Special, which adds lettuce, tomato, and mayo to the mix (also a good idea), as well as cheeseburgers and burgers topped with onions, mushrooms, and Monterey Jack cheese. The biggest of all is the Cheesehead—a half pound of sirloin with Swiss and American cheese, stewed onions, raw onion, and mushrooms.

There are other sandwiches on Solly's menu, none of which we've tried, also omelets and fish fries, excellent crinkle-cut French fries, and made-here pie. If you've got a sweet tooth, apply it to a milk shake, which is Dairy State–rich and made in flavors that include chocolate, hot fudge, strawberry, pineapple, vanilla, and the superb fresh banana malt. Another confectionery alternative is a black cow, made with Sprecher's root beer. And, this being a city where ice cream is as beloved as butter burgers, there is a full array of sundaes too.

Seating is at two horseshoe-shaped counters, and the staff of uniformed waitresses go about their business with well-seasoned hash-house élan.

SPEED QUEEN

speedqueenbbq.com

1130 W. Walnut St.	414-265-2900
Milwaukee, WI	L D | $

Speed Queen's neighborhood is iffy, but the barbecue is definitive. Pork, beef, and turkey are slow-cooked and glazed with sauce, either mild—robust and slightly sweet—or hot, which is an explosive, dark-orange emulsion reminiscent of Arthur Bryant's in Kansas City. For many customers, the mild is a little too mild, the hot is too lip-burning, so it is not uncommon to hear orders for "half and half." (Sauce is sold in bottles to take home: *highly recommended!*)

There are two kinds of pork available: shoulder or outside meat. Shoulder is thick slices that are almost chunks, tender as velvet. Outside meat is a motley pile of nearly blackened shreds and nuggets, some of which are tender, some of which are crusty, and some of which quite literally melt on the tongue. It is smokier-tasting than inside meat, like essence of barbecue. A favorite way to eat at Speed Queen is to order a half-and-half plate (ribs and outside, rib tips and shoulder, et cetera) that consists of meat, sauce, a couple slices of spongy white bread (necessary for sopping sauce), plus a cup of coleslaw. Beans and potato salad cost extra. You can also get a sandwich; but beware: these "sandwiches" are lots of meat and sauce piled onto white bread in such a way that it is inconceivable to hold it in your hands.

Everything is delivered at the order window in a Styrofoam container, and while most business is takeout, Speed Queen offers a row of functional booths for dining-in. Décor is minimal, consisting of two identical photomurals of the Wisconsin Dells on opposite walls. While there is a jukebox, it seems seldom to be plugged in or playing. Room tone is a hush punctuated by lip-smacks, sighs of pleasure, and the quietest kind of reverential conversation—the pensive hush induced by good barbecue.

★ STOCKHOLM PIE COMPANY

stockholmpieandgeneralstore.com

N2030 Spring St.   715-442-5505
Stockholm, WI   **L | $**

A corner store in a sweet little hamlet on the shore of Lake Pepin, the Stockholm Pie Company has quickly become a Roadfood legend for its cream pies, fruit pies, and savory pies.

Among the savories are sausage apple Cheddar, bacon pear blue cheese, and chicken potpie. They're very good, especially because of the flaky, melting-rich crust. With a locally bottled Spring Grove root beer—not too sweet, very spicy—one such pie is a memorable meal.

Sweet pies are swoonfully good. There are full-sized pies, six-inchers suitable for two, and at least a dozen pies available by the slice. The inventory varies day to day, including such seasonal specialties as mincemeat, pumpkin, rhubarb, and eggnog custard. Among year-round favorites are caramel apple crunch, sour cream apple, peanut butter fudge, banana cream, and a stunning double lemon that is a ribbon of citrus-specked curd atop creamy lemon chess. If you love genuine, from-scratch butterscotch pie and know you are coming to Stockholm, call ahead and they will make one for you.

THREE BROTHERS

2414 S. St. Clair St.   414-481-7530
Milwaukee, WI   **D** (closed Mon) | $$

LOCALS LOVE IT Branko Radiecevich's Serbian restaurant, which his father named for Branko and his two brothers, is a Milwaukee landmark that attracts eaters from all walks of life and all ethnic groups. Accommodations are polite but humble. Start with lemon-and-wine-marinated rice-stuffed grape leaves served with black olives and firm sticks of nut-sweet *kashkaval* (a goat's milk cheese) or a "Serbian salad" of tomatoes, green peppers, and onions veiled with a web of finely grated *bryndza*, a soft goat's-milk cheese.

One autumn several years ago when we came for supper, Branko reminded us that it was leek season and brought out a savory pastry pie layered with caramelized peppered leeks. He was even more enthusiastic about roast lamb, a Three Brothers signature dish that is basted four hours in its own juices with tomato, pepper, onion, and garlic, and served *just barely* on the bone. Poke it and bite-sized hunks of meat separate from the haunch and fall into the juice. The menu describes it as a must for the lamb lover; but we suspect that even non–lamb lovers might find its refined taste irresistible.

The building in which Three Brothers serves its superlative meals is a corner tavern that was built in 1897 and for decades was owned and operated by the Schlitz Brewing Company. The Schlitz insignia—a globe—still crowns the peak of the roof. There are no longer seats at the old bar, which runs the length of the front room and is now a service area, but the wood-floored saloon retains the warmth of a community gathering place.

WHITE GULL INN
whitegullinn.com

4225 Main St.   920-868-3517
Fish Creek, WI   **D | $$**

When it's summer in Wisconsin, vacation fancies turn to Door County, a slim peninsula of natural beauty that juts into Lake Michigan east of Menominee and north of Sturgeon Bay. The meal to eat in Door County is a fish boil, and no one does it with more panache than the White Gull Inn. Guests who are staying at the White Gull and visitors who reserve a place well in advance enjoy not only eating a fish boil but watching it being prepared—and that is half the fun. Into a hot-water cauldron over a campfire go small red potatoes, then onions, then fish steaks and salt. As the meal cooks, fish oil rises to the surface of the boiling water, and about ten minutes after the fish goes in, the "master boiler" tosses kerosene on the flames below. The burst of fire is spectacular and causes what is known as a boil-over, spilling unwanted fish oils over the rim and leaving the fish chunky, moist, and flavorful. The whole meal is then bathed in butter and concluded with a slice of cherry pie made, of course, from local cherries.

Andy Coulson, proprietor of the White Gull Inn, points out that for the old-time fishermen who likely invented the ritual, as well as for crowds of contemporary visitors who come north to enjoy the cool breezes that waft in off Lake Michigan every summer, one big appeal of the fish boil is the camaraderie it inspires among large groups of people. The bonfire and boil-over bring strangers together in an ebullient mix of awe and hunger. "As a meal for six, it is inefficient," Coulson says. "But for a dozen or more, it's a thing of beauty. This is Door County's answer to the all-American barbecue."

SOUTHWEST

★

NEVADA

UTAH

COLORADO

KANSAS

ARIZONA

NEW
MEXICO

OKLAHOMA

TEXAS

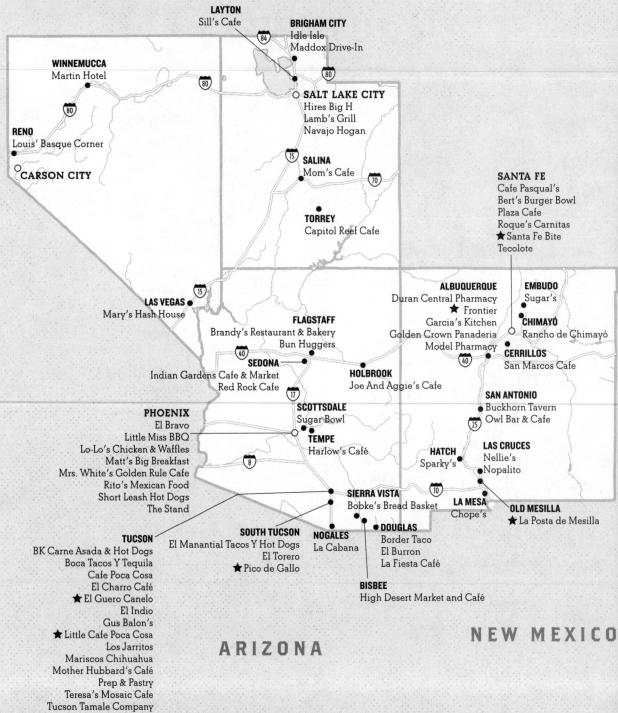

NEVADA

UTAH

NEW MEXICO

ARIZONA

LAYTON
Sill's Cafe

BRIGHAM CITY
Idle Isle
Maddox Drive-In

WINNEMUCCA
Martin Hotel

RENO
Louis' Basque Corner

CARSON CITY

SALT LAKE CITY
Hires Big H
Lamb's Grill
Navajo Hogan

SALINA
Mom's Cafe

TORREY
Capitol Reef Cafe

SANTA FE
Cafe Pasqual's
Bert's Burger Bowl
Plaza Cafe
Roque's Carnitas
★ Santa Fe Bite
Tecolote

ALBUQUERQUE
Duran Central Pharmacy
★ Frontier
Garcia's Kitchen
Golden Crown Panaderia
Model Pharmacy

EMBUDO
Sugar's

CHIMAYÓ
Rancho de Chimayó

LAS VEGAS
Mary's Hash House

FLAGSTAFF
Brandy's Restaurant & Bakery
Bun Huggers

SEDONA
Indian Gardens Cafe & Market
Red Rock Cafe

HOLBROOK
Joe And Aggie's Cafe

CERRILLOS
San Marcos Cafe

SAN ANTONIO
Buckhorn Tavern
Owl Bar & Cafe

SCOTTSDALE
Sugar Bowl

PHOENIX
El Bravo
Little Miss BBQ
Lo-Lo's Chicken & Waffles
Matt's Big Breakfast
Mrs. White's Golden Rule Cafe
Rito's Mexican Food
Short Leash Hot Dogs
The Stand

TEMPE
Harlow's Café

HATCH
Sparky's

LAS CRUCES
Nellie's
Nopalito

SIERRA VISTA
Bobke's Bread Basket

LA MESA
Chope's

OLD MESILLA
★ La Posta de Mesilla

SOUTH TUCSON
El Manantial Tacos Y Hot Dogs
El Torero
★ Pico de Gallo

NOGALES
La Cabana

DOUGLAS
Border Taco
El Burron
La Fiesta Café

TUCSON
BK Carne Asada & Hot Dogs
Boca Tacos Y Tequila
Cafe Poca Cosa
El Charro Café
★ El Guero Canelo
El Indio
Gus Balon's
★ Little Cafe Poca Cosa
Los Jarritos
Mariscos Chihuahua
Mother Hubbard's Café
Prep & Pastry
Teresa's Mosaic Cafe
Tucson Tamale Company

BISBEE
High Desert Market and Café

COLORADO

KANSAS

DENVER
Biker Jim's Gourmet Dogs
Buckhorn Exchange
Duffeyroll Café
La Fogata

MISSION
RJ's Bob-Be-Que Shack

JOHNSTOWN
Johnson's Corner

TOPEKA
Porubsky's Grocery

KANSAS CITY
★ Woodyard Bar-B-Que

ABILENE
Brookville Hotel

HAYS
Al's Chickenette

SEDALIA
Bud's Bar

SALINA
Cozy Inn

COUNCIL GROVE
Hays House

BUNKER HILL
Bunker Hill Cafe

FRONTENAC
Barto's Idle Hour

NEWTON
The Breadbasket

DURANGO
Durango Diner

WICHITA
Nu Way

PITTSBURG
Chicken Mary's

BARTLESVILLE
Dink's Pit Bar-B-Que
Murphy's Steak House

PERRY
Kumback Lunch

VINITA
Clanton's

OKARCHE
Eischen's Bar

CLAREMORE
Hammett House

CLINTON
Jigg's Smokehouse

STROUD
Rock Cafe

ELK CITY
Country Dove Tea Room

EL RENO
Johnnie's
Robert's
Sid's

SHAWNEE
Hamburger King
★ Van's Pig Stand

LAWTON
The Meers Store

TULSA
Cancun
Coney I-Lander
Freddie's Hamburgers
Hank's Hamburgers
Ike's Chili
Linda-Mar Drive-In
White River Fish Market
Wilson's B-B-Q

OKLAHOMA CITY
Cattlemen's Steakhouse
Classen Grill
Leo's
Nic's Grill

OKLAHOMA

TEXAS

AMARILLO
The Big Texan
Golden Light Cafe

LUBBOCK
Tom & Bingo's

CANUTILLO
★ Little Diner

EL PASO
H&H Coffee Shop

PONDER
Ranchman's Cafe

GRAPEVINE
Bartley's Bar-B-Q
Tolbert's

TEXARKANA
★ Bryce's Cafeteria

FORT WORTH
Angelo's
Cattlemen's Fort Worth Steak House
Paris Coffee Shop

DALLAS
Fuel City
Highland Park Soda Fountain
Norma's Cafe
Sweet Georgia Brown

WEST
Village Bakery

MARBLE FALLS
Blue Bonnet Cafe

GEORGETOWN
★ Monument Cafe

TAYLOR
★ Louie Mueller Barbeque

JOHNSON CITY
Hill Country Cupboard

ELGIN
Southside Market

ROUND TOP
Royer's Round Top Cafe

BLANCO
Blanco Bowling Club Cafe

DRIFTWOOD
Salt Lick

CONROE
Vernon's Kuntry Katfish

BANDERA
Ost

LULING
City Market

HOUSTON
Avalon Diner
Goode Co. Texas Bar-B-Q
La Mexicana

KYLE
Texas Pie Company

LA GRANGE
Weikel's Store and Bakery

SAN ANTONIO
Chris Madrid's
Green Vegetarian Cuisine
Taco Garage
Taco House
★ Taco Taco

AUSTIN
Hoover's Cooking
Hut's Hamburgers
Threadgill's

LOCKHART
Black's Barbecue
Kreuz Market
Smitty's

ARIZONA

BK CARNE ASADA & HOT DOGS

bktacos.com

5118 S. 12th Ave.   520-295-1176
Tucson, AZ   **B L D** | $

America's most flamboyant wiener, the Sonoran hot dog, starts as a simple beef frank. It gets wrapped in bacon and grilled alongside other bacon-sheathed hot dogs whose grease drippings make the process very much like deep-frying. Bacon flavor melts into the dog, leaving the outside patched with streaks of lean that provide marvelous chewy contrast to the frank they embrace. Stuffed into a substantial, yeasty *bolillo* roll, the frank is topped with tomatoes, pinto beans, onions, mustard, hot green jalapeño sauce, and mayonnaise. On the side comes a roasted guero pepper, which is about the same size, shape, and heat level as a jalapeño, but more yellow than green. At BK, you eat this hot dog on a covered patio and accompany it by cold beer or the refreshing Mexican rice drink known as *horchata*.

While Sonoran hot dogs are the featured attraction, the other part of the restaurant's name requires attention. BK's carne asada is some of the best in Tucson: tender strips of grilled flank steak that are spicy, smoky, and hugely beefy. Order the meat in a taco and it arrives plain in a corn or flour tortilla (your choice), but its flavor is pronounced enough that it flourishes when you dress it to the nines at the copious salsa bar, which includes chunky guacamole as well as salsa verde, chopped tomatoes, pico de gallo, onion, radish, lime, and sliced cucumber.

BOBKE'S BREAD BASKET

355 W. Wilcox Dr.   520-458-8580
Sierra Vista, AZ   **B L** | $

Because Sierra Vista's Fort Huachuca is a large military installation, it attracts people from around the world, and many of its personnel spend time in other countries. That is why this desert town in the middle of nowhere has an amazing array of interesting foreign food, including at Bobke's Bread Basket, where the motto is "When the schnecken beckons" and where the staff communicates with each other in German. A local favorite now for twenty-three years, Bobke's is an immaculate little bakery-café with a huge selection of cakes, pretzel rolls, cookies, bars, strudels, puffs, and stollen. It also has a lunch menu that includes hot brats on freshly baked rolls and fine wiener schnitzel with spaetzle and puckery-sweet cucumber salad. Salads, soups, and sandwiches also are available. Dining accommodations, across from the deli counter, include about a half-dozen tables outfitted with festive tablecloths.

When we perused Bobke's pastry case in search of car snacks, waitress Monika suggested we pay special attention to the apple fritters. "We make those in the deep fryer," she boasted. They are like the best fun food on a state-fair midway: wanton, sweet luxury with just enough fruit to add a vaguely healthful mien. A short while later on Highway 90 to Bisbee, we swooned over Bobke's cherry star—a buttery little pastry filled with sour fruit—and a big, toothsome macaroon. And although Bobke's does not sell its bundt cakes by the slice, the whole ones are so perfectly beautiful that we took a marble pound with us. It was butter-rich, moist, and exactly sweet enough to be an ideal coffee companion, one of the best pound cakes we've ever eaten.

BOCA TACOS Y TEQUILA

bocatacos.com

828 E. Speedway Blvd.	520-777-8134
Tucson, AZ	**L D** | **$**

Boca Tacos y Tequila is a punk joint with graffiti on the walls, outside lavatories, and a smart-ass attitude expressed by the overhead sign that crows "Our salsas are hotter than your wife." Rude and crude all that may be, but the people who work here are nice when they explain the kitchen's unique dishes, and, more important, those dishes are very, very good.

Chef Maria José Mazon guarantees that her tacos contain no yellow cheese, ground beef, or iceberg lettuce. They are elegant little pockets, available on either a homemade corn or flour tortilla, and nearly all of them adorned with cabbage and guacamole. Grilled octopus, squash, fire-roasted corn, and *barbacoa* are some regular fillings, and every Wednesday Mazon offers exotic-meat night, featuring anything from silkworms to snapping turtle to elk. "If it's already dead, I can make it into a taco," she once joked to a reporter.

With tacos come extraordinary salsas, an ever-changing repertoire that includes chipotle, mango-habanero, watermelon-pepper, pickled carrots, and ginger-wasabi. A special treasure on the menu, listed as an appetizer, is Mazon's Boca ball—a sphere of mashed potatoes infused with chipotle peppers, rolled in panko crumbs, deep-fried, and served with chile sauce that is a balance of cream and spice.

For customers watching their waistline, "taco lites" are available—the ingredients you like wrapped in lettuce instead of a tortilla.

BORDER TACO

103 E. 5th St. #3	520-364-6196
Douglas, AZ	**B L D** | **$**

We haven't actually measured, but it looks like Border Taco is the Arizona restaurant closest to the Mexican border. Virtually all conversations among staff and customers are in Spanish, and it was a bit of a challenge to communicate with the order taker when we stepped up to the counter. Although the setting is in an utterly boring mall and the spacious dining room is so clean it seems on the verge of being sterile (but is, in fact, charmingly personal), the food made here is colorful, soulful, and delicious.

We knew we were on the right track the moment we stepped inside and sniffed the perfumes of *menudo* simmering, beef grilling, and roasted hot chiles sweetening the air. Local tipster Patty Ortiz directed us here with the promise, "It's like grandma is in the kitchen." We only wish our grandmas had made tacos this scrumptious: shredded pork *carne adovada* bright red and smoky; chile verde replete with vegetable flavor; *barbacoa* (beef) dark and profound. The list of potential ingredients is long, including beef tongue, beef head, beef rind, shrimp, and steak, and all are available in big burritos as well as modest-sized tacos.

Those who come as a foursome can avail themselves of a family platter (steak, chicken, shrimp, salad, chili, rice, beans, and tortillas) at under $10 per person.

BRANDY'S RESTAURANT & BAKERY

brandysrestaurant.com

1500 E. Cedar Ave.,	928-779-2187
Ste. 40	**B L** | **$**
Flagstaff, AZ	

Brandy's is a busy strip-mall café that makes its walls a venue for exhibits of local artists' work. It used to be a three-meal-a-day place but now serves only breakfast and lunch. "Best of Flagstaff" awards all over the wall testify to breakfast's success. We recommend the kitchen's Swedish oat pancakes, which are so soft and tender that they are reminiscent of spoonbread. They come with hot cinnamon-apple topping and can be filled with apples, bananas, blueberries, or chocolate chips—but it's the pancakes themselves that make this a memorable plate of food.

From the bakery come bagels, absurdly sticky sticky buns, big brownies and blondies, muffins, scones, coffee cake, and fruit Danishes. An entire menu card is devoted to espresso variations such as Baja Mocha made with Mexican chocolate, Café Aloha with cream of coconut, and red velvet mocha. We were delighted with a regular Café Mocha, which is an expertly concocted triple-whammy of cream, chocolate, and espresso.

BUN HUGGERS

901 S. Milton Rd.   928-779-3743
Flagstaff, AZ   L D | $

Located just off Historic Route 66, Bun Huggers sports fraternity house décor, its walls covered with a discordant hodgepodge of road signs, old tools, neon, and flea market finds, its wooden booths carved with years' worth of graffiti. Since it opened in 1977, it has been a favorite haunt of students from nearby Northern Arizona University.

They come for meat cooked on a mesquite-fired grill. One-third-pound hamburgers are the main attraction—glistening and crusty-edged, perfumed by smoke. They are not extraordinary burgers as you get them, with or without cheese on a grill-toasted bun (there are juicier patties in town at Diablo Burger). But near the grill is a large buffet of condiments where customers are free to dress their burgers to the nines with lettuce, tomato slices, relish, mustard, ketchup, pickles, jalapeño chips, chopped onions, and mayonnaise. That's the fun part of burger eating here.

What draws us back to Bun Huggers are the steak sandwiches. Unlike the burgers, these sirloins are cooked to order, and while they aren't pillow-thick, they do have enough substance that degree of doneness is an issue. Several variations are available, with mushrooms, peppers, onions, and so on. We recommend the one titled Sonoran Steak, which includes grilled onions and pepper jack cheese, plus a whole roasted chile pepper that adds a halo of gentle heat to the package.

CAFE POCA COSA

cafepocacosatucson.com
110 E. Pennington St.   520-622-6400
Tucson, AZ   L D (Tues-Sat) | $$$

Many years ago when we first came upon Cafe Poca Cosa, it was the dining room of a crappy hotel and its décor was standard-issue Mexican fiesta. It now inhabits ultramodern quarters with objects of Mexican art displayed as in a fine museum. Ambience has turned from fiery to cool. But one thing hasn't changed. Meals still are innovative, unpredictable, and impossible-to-categorize Mexican fare like you will eat nowhere else. There are no printed menus because the kitchen's yield changes as ingredients get used up and new ones come into play. Once you are seated, you will be shown a portable blackboard menu on which nearly every item needs explaining. Nothing chef Suzana Davila makes is familiar; certainly, there are no tacos, enchiladas, or burritos! Neither are there lists of appetizers and side dishes from which to choose. Each dinner is presented on a plate exactly how, and with what, Ms. Davila believes it should be served.

There always are at least a couple of chicken molés, or perhaps the variant of molé known as *pollo en pipian,* for which boneless chicken is cosseted in sauce made from bitter chocolate, crushed red chiles, Spanish peanuts, pumpkin seeds, and cloves. Tamale pie is a menu regular too, and while it is a vegetarian alternative, please do not let your love of meat dissuade you from ordering it. As tender as a soufflé, it comes in many variations. We have had it topped with hot green chile purée, with mango sauce, with curried carrots, and with a zesty tomato paste reminiscent of Italian marinara.

There is shredded beef (*deshebrada*) infused with smoky chili flavor; there are seafood dishes and pork too. Each entree shares its plate with a bright, fresh salad, so that whatever your main course is, it mixes with the greens and makes a happy mess of things. On the side come small warm corn tortillas, and for dessert, there's Mexican-flavored chocolate mousse (is that cinnamon we taste?) and a sultry square of flan, floated on a dish of tremendously sweet burnt-sugar syrup.

EL BRAVO

elbravoaz.wordpress.com

8338 N. 7th St.   602-943-9753

Phoenix, AZ   **L D** (closed Sun) | $$

Chuck Henrickson recommended we visit El Bravo for the "best tamale in Arizona." Thumbs-up to that! The chicken and green corn tamales we sampled are earthy, just zesty enough to perk up the taste buds, and impossible to stop eating until appetite has become only a dim memory.

Add to that the other AZ-Mex fare on this merry menu and you have a restaurant that is hard to resist. It's not much for looks: décor is piñatas and beer signs. But who needs mood-making ambience when you can choose from among chiles rellenos, enchiladas, burros and burritos, and a fragile-crusted Navajo red beef popover that are all dishes to remember? On the side come supersavory refried beans. We are especially fond of the *machaca*, aka dried beef, that is available in tacos, burritos, and flautas. For dessert? How about a chocolate chimichanga?

Service is homey, meaning sometimes slow and sometimes brisk. Grandma is friendly, but not cloyingly so.

EL BURRON

elburron.com

1008 Cochise Ave.   520-805-0141

Douglas, AZ   **L D** | $

Aside from being home of the majestic Gadsden Hotel with its forty-two-foot Tiffany stained-glass mural of Southwest desert life, Douglas, Arizona, is not a major tourist destination. That fact is reflected in a population of unassuming restaurants that serve inexpensive food to locals at moderate prices. How local is El Burron? If you don't speak Spanish, prepare to use sign language.

But really, how hard is it to order a hamburger? It was a tipster's recommendation of the hamburger that brought us here, and while we thought the burger was OK, if boring, what will bring us back are the burros, sized from normal to large to very large to ridiculously large. Our favorite filling is carne asada, the grilled, shredded beef in which the idea of well-done is turned on its head and becomes glistening succulence. Other burro fillings are *carne adovada* (chile-marinated beef), chicken, and tripe, as well as strictly beans, and it is possible to add melted cheese to the interior. Ours came plain and would have been dauntingly stark if all we did was eat it end to end. But before the tortilla wrap is torn and the burro opened, a pilgrimage to El Burron's condiment bar is in order. Here we found a rainbow of fresh, beguiling salsas, pickled onions, various vegetables, and condiments. We tried to ask what, exactly, some of the more complex ones were, and although the staff tried valiantly to explain, their English turned out to be no better than our Spanish.

EL CHARRO CAFÉ

elcharrocafe.com

311 N. Court   520-622-1922

Tucson, AZ   **L D** | $$

El Charro is a century-old mission-style home now expanded into a multiroom restaurant, bar, and gift shop, a fortress of Southwestern foodways.

The tostada grande, created here by founder Tia Monica Flin, is a broad cheese crisp like a Mexican pizza. Most people get it with a thin veneer of creamy melted cheese on top; other options include green chiles, guacamole, air-dried beef, and refried beans. El Charro's round-the-world version is a majestic appetizer, served on a pedestal and garnished with fresh basil leaves.

Carne seca is a Tucson passion. El Charro's is cured high above the patio in back of the restaurant, where strips of thin-sliced tenderloin hang in an open metal cage. Suspended on ropes and pulleys, the cage sways in the breeze, wafting a perfume of lemon and garlic marinade into the fresh Arizona air. Sautéed after it is air-dried, *carne seca* is customarily served in concert with sweet onions, hot chiles, and tomatoes, making an explosion of flavor like no other food. El Charro has a full menu of tacos, enchiladas, and chiles rellenos, plus such rarer regional specialties as enchilada Sonorese (a patty of fried corn meal garnished with chili) and chalupas (small corn meal canoes filled with chili, meat, or chicken and whole beans). Beyond these hearty meals, the kitchen offers a full repertoire of nutritionally enlightened fare—lo-cal, lo-fat, good-for-you, and good-tasting!

El Charro is noisy and sociable, almost always packed with tourists, Tucsonians, health nuts, and burrito hounds who spoon up fiery salsa picante with corn chips and drink Tecate beer. Mariachi music sets the mood as the sturdy wood floors rumble with the crowds and the air fills with the aroma of hot tostadas grandes. Wall décor is a kaleidoscope of vintage south-of-the-border advertisements, straw sombreros, and years' worth of El Charro calendars, which feature melodramatic scenes of Mexican horsemen (known as *charros*), proud steeds, and pretty maidens all making flirty eyes amid stormy landscapes.

★ EL GUERO CANELO

elguerocanelo.com

5201 S. 12th Ave.	520-295-9005
Tucson, AZ	**B L D** | $

More than any of the hundred places that sell Sonoran hot dogs in and around Tucson, El Guero Canelo deserves the credit for making it popular. Opened in the 1990s, when the "hot-dog estilo Sonora" was strictly a street-cart affair, it is a happy urban picnic more than a restaurant, its outdoor dining area shaded by a canopy with nozzles all along the rim that rain down mists of cool water to hydrate savage desert air. Hot dogs are assembled at a cart adjoining the patio; other Mexican dishes are cooked in a separate kitchen. After you get your meal but before you take a seat, you can gather condiments from the salsa bar to dress your caramelo, taco, torta, or quesadilla with salsa verde, chopped tomatoes, pico de gallo, onion, radish, lime, or sliced cucumber.

But you do not dress your Sonoran hot dog. That is done by the hot dog man, and it is almost always done exactly the same way. A beef frank, wrapped in bacon and grilled in a trough, is inserted in a big, soft Mexican bun, then dressed with chopped tomatoes, a scattering of pinto beans, grilled or raw onions, a line of yellow mustard, a green ribbon of hot jalapeño sauce, and an artistic squiggle of mayonnaise.

On the side comes a roasted guero pepper, which looks like a pale jalapeño (*guero* = "blond") and can be every bit as hot. It would be possible to omit one of the ingredients—onions, beans, or jalapeño sauce, perhaps—but that would be wrong. A Sonoran hot dog with everything is unimpeachable harmony. If you really love the hot dog and bacon duet, El Guero Canelo's cook can make you a Sammy Dog, which is two in one bun, equally well-accoutered—a reasonable idea, considering the dogs are modest-sized and the bun capacious.

EL INDIO

elindiomexicanfood.com

3355 S. 6th Ave	520-620-0504
Tucson, AZ	**B L D** (closed Tues) | $

Sharing a parking lot with a Circle K gas station-convenience mart, El Indio looks like a hundred other Mexican restaurants in Tucson. Its big, open dining room is decorated in Incan kitsch: stormy, bodice-ripping pictures of Indian musclemen and maidens and snorting stallions along with handsome crockery and green plants. At the door, a wooden Indian stands with a sign around its neck inviting customers to seat themselves. Waitresses scurry around the dining room, pushing carts to deliver food to customers.

Meals start with tortilla chips and a ramekin of purplish bean dip that is porky and flowery-spiced. Rich as it is, it is easy to keep eating until the meal arrives. Cool *horchata* (sweetened rice milk) is thin and refreshing, generously spiked with cinnamon.

If you have only one meal here, make it green chili. We were clued into it by culinary sage Randy Spalding, who said that El Indio is "the only place in Tucson I know that makes green chili in the traditional way, with pork." Three different kinds of chile peppers thread through the viscous liquid and cling to the small cubes of tender pork. It is a rich, radiant dish with a swirl of flavor that is hot with a sour twist that teases taste buds, nothing like chili that is cloddish and hammering.

The Tucson signature dish *topopo* salad is not the typical tower, but rather a more traditional salad presented in a tortilla bowl. The bowl is thick but frail, freshly fried, and it breaks easily into pieces for plowing into all the goodies it holds.

One item on the menu we did not try, but might if we are in an adventurous mood next time we visit, is *menudo*. Served every day, it is available red or white, with or without hooves and tendons.

EL MANANTIAL TACOS Y HOT DOGS

Park Ave. & 36th St.   520-429-4248
South Tucson, AZ   **L D** | $

We cannot guarantee El Manantial will be found at Park Avenue and 36th Street in South Tucson. It is a mobile food truck and the location is a vacant lot. If the proprietors find a better location, the truck may relocate. That's the nature of dozens of itinerant vendors who sell good Mexican food in the Old Pueblo. But El Manantial has been in its current spot for quite a while and it seems extremely popular, so if you are on the hunt for one of the city's best Sonoran hot dogs, it is worth seeking out.

Like the more permanent places that sell Sonoran hot dogs, El Manantial is two kitchens: one for tacos, burros, caramelos, tortas, and quesadillas, the other a small adjoining wagon dedicated to hot dogs. The dog is swaddled in bacon, nestled in a fresh bun, and dressed with the full galaxy of condiments—tomatoes, beans, mustard, mayo, and very hot jalapeño sauce. The roasted guero pepper that accompanies all of Tucson's Sonoran dogs is wrapped in smoky bacon. As happens on the wiener, the cooking process glues the bacon to the outside of the pepper, creating a lusty laminate of chewy pork and firm-walled vegetable. The bite of the pepper is offset by a droplet of creamy melted cheese stuffed inside the pod.

Dine at picnic tables with a canopy for protection from the desert sun.

EL TORERO

231 E. 26th St.   520-622-9534
South Tucson, AZ   **L D** (closed Tues) | $$

South Tucson is surrounded by the city of Tucson but is legally and culturally separate. In this part of town, buildings are festooned with brilliant painted tiles, streets hum with low riders cruising in their chopped-roof custom *caruchas,* and at least a dozen different restaurants serve Mexican food that most of us gringos never know.

One of the best is El Torero, a place so inconspicuous that you likely will drive right past it. Once you do walk in, you know you have entered Mexican-food paradise. The jukebox will be belting out party tunes; the bar you walk past to get inside will be occupied by happy people knocking back long-neck beers; at tables in the brightly lit dining room, where the walls are decorated with bullfighter paintings and one large stuffed swordfish, people plow into expertly prepared Sonoran-style food.

Start with a wafer-thin tortilla crisp of cheese and green chile strips, presented on a silver pedestal so all at the table can pull away slices. This crisp is among the thinnest and tastiest in a neighborhood full of excellent crisps. The main menu offers familiar Sonoran Mexican dishes, such as tacos, burros, enchiladas, and chimichangas, plus a few items that are truly special. These include off-the-bone turkey topped with a spicy molé sauce or, on occasion, the similar sauce known as *pipian,* which includes pumpkin seeds. Also noteworthy is the *topopo* salad, named for its resemblance to a volcano. It is a Devil's Tower–shaped mound of lettuce, peas, carrots, et cetera, packed with chicken, *carne seca,* or whatever floats your boat, its sides bolstered by columns of hard cheese.

GUS BALON'S

gusbalonsrestaurant.com

6027 E. 22nd St.   520-747-7788
Tucson, AZ   **B L** (closed Sun) | **$**

Gus Balon's is a cut above in every way. Seemingly ordinary breakfast sandwiches are elevated to excellence by Gus's homemade bun. Eggs come with American fries freckled with crunchy bits from the griddle. The pancakes, which look ordinary, are light and delicious—far better than you'd expect. Gus's sweet roll is outlandishly huge, served warm with a big schmear of butter.

Aside from breakfast and inexpensive lunches served in a bare-bones coffee-shop setting (counter and booths), Gus's is known for pies. It's hard to choose among them (although the freshly made butterscotch is pretty hard to resist), because they all look good. A few years back, we took inventory of one single day's list: banana, chocolate banana, chocolate peanut butter banana, chocolate peanut butter, chocolate, coconut, lemon, butterscotch, blueberry, peach, raspberry, peanut butter, pineapple, apple, cherry, raspberry, peach, and raisin. Plus crumb-topped apple-cranberry, peach, raspberry, apple, apple-raisin, cherry, and pumpkin!

Waitresses are diner pros who pour coffee and bring food almost faster than you can speak the words to order it.

HARLOW'S CAFÉ

1021 W. University Dr.   480-829-9444
Tempe, AZ   **B L** | **$**

Breakfast is served any time until the 2 p.m. closing, and it is impressive. Eggs Maximilian stars: a large flour tortilla heaped with savory hash browns, three eggs, onions, zesty diced green chiles, and (optional) chorizo sausage, the whole caboodle crowned with sour cream and salsa. Crisp, easy-to-slice chicken-fried steak is available as breakfast or lunch. Other choices include an assortment of Benedicts, pancakes, creamed chipped beef, and huevos rancheros. Starting at 11 a.m., lunch is served. We have enjoyed an immense fried fish sandwich and a decent charbroiled bacon cheeseburger but did not like the desiccated French dip.

Harlow's is a happy, high-energy joint, its wood-paneled walls covered with pictures of local and national sports heroes, "Best of Phoenix" awards, and vintage movie memorabilia, especially pictures of Jean Harlow. Seating is in booths and at a short counter that offers a glimpse of short-order cooks doing twelve things at once.

HIGH DESERT MARKET AND CAFÉ

highdesertmarket.net

203 Tombstone Canyon   520-432-6775
Bisbee, AZ   **B L D** | **$$**

★
MOUNTAIN
VIEWS
★
One of the most sensible spelling rules, to which we consciously refer almost every time the issue arises, is that the word "dessert" (what you have after a meal) contains two *s*'s because you want a double portion, whereas "desert" (dry, hot, sandy) contains a single *s* because you want to stay there only briefly.

The High Desert Market and Café tests that rule. Located in the old mining town of Bisbee in the hills just east of the Sonoran Desert, this restaurant serves portions of dessert that are literally quite high. High as in huge: Great wedges of coconut cream pie rise three or four inches off the plate, their abundant filling crowned by a thick ribbon of cream. All this goodness rests upon a flaky crust that has just enough savory presence to make everything on top taste extraordinarily coconutty. A block of chocolate sour cream cake is big enough for two, the cake itself a titillating balance of sweetness and sour cream, all under a soaring mantle of whipped cream. Key lime pie is high too: the classic formula of sweetened condensed milk and tart lime, but taller than most with a double-thick graham-cracker crust.

Sky-high dessert is just one of the many reasons we like this colorful café/bakery/coffeehouse/juice bar/grocery/wine shop/crafts gallery/cosmetics emporium/town gathering spot. The High Desert Café is a place to come for three meals a day, to eat on premises (inside or on the patio), or to takeout. It opens at 7 a.m., serving morning rib-stickers like egg-loaded burritos, Indian-spiced scramble with house-made chutney, and sweet-potato pancakes, as well as an array of pastries that are baked here every day. Of the muffins, biscuits, sweet rolls, and cookies, the one we cannot resist is the scone. Like High Desert pies and cakes, it is an immense piece of food—tall and craggy, butter-rich and jam-packed with whatever ingredient is featured, from chocolate chips to cranberries.

INDIAN GARDENS CAFE & MARKET
indiangardens.com

3951 N. State Route 89A   928-282-7702
Sedona, AZ   **B L** | **$**

Indian Gardens Cafe & Market is a culture fusion of vintage roadside Americana and modern culinary values. In this 1940s-era general store with supplies for adventurous travelers, you'll find artistic lattes, smoothies, and craft beers, kale salad and house-made granola, vegan and gluten-free options, and fresh-pressed organic apple cider. We love the Super Greens Smoothie, which is as thick as a good milk shake but made of spinach, kale, banana, cucumber, avocado, and apple cider. Despite its good-for-you ingredients, it is flavorful and satisfying. There are berry smoothies and smoothies made with granola as well.

Breakfast is swell: pancakes, *chilaquiles* (a dolled-up version of *migas*), chorizo and egg tacos, and a healthful and yummy item called Grains & Greens Bowl. That's roasted butternut squash, quinoa, a couple of eggs cooked to order, sliced avocado, and sautéed kale, accompanied by a ramekin of house-made hot sauce to make it buzz. Whether eating here or getting provisions for the road, do treat yourself to a loaf of sturdy, house-baked sourdough bread.

Despite its modern take on eating, the place maintains an old-time feel, well-worn and hospitable; and the setting is wondrous, on the graceful winding road that threads through Oak Creek Canyon.

JOE & AGGIE'S CAFE
joeandaggiescafe.com

120 W. Hopi Dr.   928-524-6540
Holbrook, AZ   **B L** (closed Sun) | **$**

Despite the interstate replacing Route 66, Holbrook remains a town where you can get a good feel for what life was like along western roads in the two-lane days. It still has the famous "Sleep in a Wigwam" motel; there are some fascinating pawnshops and Native American jewelry emporia; and at Joe & Aggie's—the oldest restaurant in town, since 1946—you can have a real old-fashioned roadside diner meal.

Tables are outfitted with squeeze bottles of honey for squirting onto sopaipillas (puffy triangles of fried bread), and meals begin with a basket of chips and an empty bowl in which you decant some hot, pepper-flecked hot sauce for dipping. The sign on the front window boasts of "Mexican and American food," but in fact, the menu at Joe & Aggie's is not quite either; it is a blend of Mexican and American that is unique to the Southwest. After the chips and salsa, you move on to such meals as enchiladas made with red or green chili, burros, tacos, or chicken-fried steak with potatoes and hot sopaipillas on the side. Roadfood.com user "icrmg" posted a ravishing photo showing breakfast of green chili–topped huevos rancheros sided by a cake of hash browns and a side of cheese-dripping refried beans.

LA CABANA

840 N. Grand Ave. #12   520-287-3249
Nogales, AZ   **B L D** | **$**

La Cabana is a cozy cantina in a cluster of shops on the main drag. It is outfitted with tables and a couple of comfortable booths. For serious eating, we recommend a booth, where you can lounge like royalty.

Start with made-to-order guacamole. Spruce it up with a dab of the hot salsa provided to every table, as well as a spritz of tiny Mexican limes. The border-town menu includes corn tamales, enchiladas, corn-crusted tacos, and a beef burrito filled with meat that is moist and pot-roast tender. Chiles rellenos are packed with deep green-chile flavor, oozing melted cheese, and enrobed in crisp-fried crust. Among the most memorable flavors on the table are the simple flour tortillas: warm, delicate, with an earthy wheat flavor so rich they taste pre-buttered.

LA FIESTA CAFE

1844 E. 10th St.   520-805-0033
Douglas, AZ   **L D | $**

Over the years, La Fiesta on 8th Street has built a solid reputation for serving exemplary Sonoran-style Mexican food. Now carrying on that tradition (with a sign overhead announcing "La Tradicion") is this new La Fiesta—a friendly, one-room eatery with oilcloth-covered tables and festive south-of-the border décor. Here you will find green corn tamales, rolled enchiladas filled with tender shreds of chicken and topped with exquisite green tomatillo sauce, and, of course, broad flour tortillas served warm with every meal.

Everybody starts with chips and a salsa whose stealthy pepper punch is more reminiscent of New Mexico and its chile culture than of the milder Sonoran style. One other New Mexico twist to the menu comes in the form of chiles rellenos that, while rather soft and bland themselves, sport a lively salsa on top. But most of what is served here reflects the taste of Tucson and its surroundings. The burros are grand, the burritos not so grand but equally tasty, the chimichangas are crisp and loaded, there are all manner of cheese crisps, and even well-apportioned taco salads.

When it comes time for dessert, consider stepping across the street to La Nueva Michoacana, which boasts "the best artisan ice cream in southern Arizona." There are custard, ice cream, Jell-O, and freezer cases loaded with *paletas* (ice pops) of endless variety.

★ LITTLE CAFE POCA COSA

151 N. Stone Ave.   No phone
Tucson, AZ   **B L | $**

——★——
VEGETARIAN-
FRIENDLY
——★—— Little Cafe Poca Cosa, just down the street from Suzana Davila's magnificent Cafe Poca Cosa (p. 327), shares the same culinary values, but the ambience is totally different and the prices are low. This colorful, party-time place, run by Suzana's sister Sandra, is strictly a breakfast-and-lunch establishment, closing midafternoon, and it has its own way of doing everything. It has no phone number and no website. Reservations are not accepted. Business is cash only.

Breakfasters come for handsome huevos rancheros, the eggs enveloped in colorful red chile sauce, served with rice, lettuce, and a brace of fruit: pineapple, strawberry, and watermelon. Huevos Mexicanos, scrambled with tomatoes, onions, and chiles, is a great way to start the day, as is *machaca con huevo*, which mixes moist shreds of beef with bits of green chile in a veil of scrambled egg.

When gazpacho is on the blackboard menu at lunch, it's a must. Sandra tells us she makes it with roasted poblano chiles and roasted tomatoes. When we dip up a cool spoonful and audibly swoon at its smoky vegetable intensity, she advises that her secret is to not peel the roasted peppers. "To me," she says, "the burnt part of the skin is what has all the good flavor."

Another delectable creation is shredded pork simmered in achiote berry sauce. It is sweet and luscious with a subtle citrus twist. Sandra suggests that we bring its flavor to fruition by squeezing on a few drops of fresh lime juice from the halves provided with the dish.

Little Cafe Poca Cosa is a restaurant where vegetarians can eat very well. We rarely can resist at least one order of the *tamale de elote*—a soufflé-like swirl of cornmeal, sweet corn, green chiles, and cheese steamed to comforting warmth inside a corn husk. Chiles rellenos is another meatless meal, served in a mild salsa ranchero redolent of tomatoes. Vegans with big appetites will want to know about the Gigantic Vegan Tostada, which is a great spill of pinto beans and seasonal vegetables atop a broad fried corn tortilla. Salsa ranchero comes on the side.

Those who have a hard time deciding what to choose from the endlessly inviting menu can ask for the Plato Poca Cosa, aka Surprise Plate. You get three items off the menu—"whatever the gals in the kitchen feel like giving you," Sandra says, adding that no two Surprise Plates are alike.

LITTLE MISS BBQ
littlemissbbq.com

4301 E. University Dr.	602-437-1177
Phoenix, AZ	**L D** (until meat runs out)
	(Tues–Sat)	$$

-- ★ --
HOT TICKET
-- ★ --
Little Miss rightfully could be called artisan barbecue—everything is done the old-fashioned way using the finest obtainable ingredients—but don't worry; there is nothing precious about this authentic eatery, other than seats, which are scarce, and meats, which can sell out by midafternoon.

The style is Texas meat market. Sandwiches and plates with side dishes are available, and it's also possible to buy brisket, sausage, ribs, or pulled pork by the pound and have it served on butcher paper atop a plastic cafeteria tray.

Brisket is out of this world, smoke-cooked in a coat of coarse pepper that partners so deliciously with the protein wallop of the beef. When you order some, you'll be asked if you want lean or fatty. The lean slices virtually melt in your mouth. The fat ones literally do. Heaven!

Sausages are sold either whole or sliced—plump tubes of beef and pork and enough hot pepper to give every bite a buzz. Pulled pork is as soft as butter, subtly smoky, wanting only a dash of house-made sauce to bring it to perfection. For us, the brisket is too succulent and too scrumptious as-is to need any sauce at all.

Side dishes are no afterthought. Beans are so freighted with meat (cutting-board scraps of beef and pork) that the beans themselves become a secondary note. Thick, creamy grits are enriched with Cheddar cheese and spiked with bits of jalapeño pepper. For dessert there's individual smoked pecan pies with wicked-crisp crust and powerhouse filling, topped with a handsome formation of pecan halves.

Though located in a fairly stark industrial part of town, Little Miss BBQ has been discovered and is almost always crowded enough that you will wait in line to place an order and get your food. After that, you can enjoy it at one of a handful of indoor tables or at al fresco picnic tables out back.

LO-LO'S CHICKEN & WAFFLES
loloschickenandwaffles.com

1220 S. Central Ave.	602-340-1304
Phoenix, AZ	**B L D**	$

It wasn't long after Larry White, grandson of the esteemed Mrs. White of Mrs. White's Golden Rule Cafe, opened Lo-Lo's in 2002 that you could barely get in. This soul-food beacon in downtown Phoenix quickly became such a magnet for visiting celebrities as well as locals that there always was a line outside. Mr. White expanded to the current former warehouse, and although there is now a second location (3133 North Scottsdale Road in Scottsdale), you still can expect to wait for a table at either place.

The popularity is well deserved, especially for the signature dish, chicken and waffles. Lo-Lo's waffles are thin and crisp, served hot enough that big balls of butter melt fast into the treads, along with pieces of whatever chicken parts you desire. The dish is most commonly had with gravy and sautéed onions, but some devotees actually use syrup. Beyond chicken and waffles, the menu includes salmon croquettes (which the menu attributes to one Aunt Hattie) and biscuits and gravy (a recipe from "Yo Mama"). There also is a full roster of good side dishes such as peppery collard greens, mac 'n' cheese, candied sweet potatoes, fried okra, cheese grits, and buttered corn.

LOS JARRITOS

losjarritosmexicanfood.com

4832 S. 12th Ave.   520-746-0364
Tucson, AZ   **B L | $**

Los Jarritos, a tiny Twelfth Avenue café, always has green corn tamales on the menu, and they are some of the best anywhere, a swirl of sweet corn and hot pepper flavors steamed to a point of opulent harmony. Order at least a couple of them to accompany such classic Sonoran meals as carne asada, *nopalitos con chili* (prickly pear cactus with chili Colorado), and red or white *menudo* available in sizes from a pint to a gallon. Most meals are ordered to take out and most tamales are sold by the dozen, but a couple of tables inside and a few on a small patio out front give regulars the opportunity to linger over long breakfasts of huevos rancheros with house-made chorizo and carry on conversations with one another and with strangers.

Note to alcoholics: Los Jarritos sells *menudo* "ready to cook." For $35 you get the essential fixins needed to make a large vat of the traditional Mexican hangover cure: eleven pounds of tripe, two beef feet, and five pounds of *nixtamal* (treated corn).

MARISCOS CHIHUAHUA

mariscoschihuahua.com

2902 E. 22nd St.   520-326-1529
Tucson, AZ   **L D | $$**

Mariscos Chihuahua is a big place with sunlight streaming in picture windows all around, illuminating a tempestuous seascape mural that covers one wall. The staff are friendly, and the sound system belts out Mexican tunes that make every meal feel like a celebration. Seafood stars: oysters raw or cooked, fish grilled or fried, stews and soups. And oh, such shrimp! The menu lists a dozen different styles, including cool cocktails and "drowned raw," meaning ceviche-style—cooked by immersion in a lime marinade.

We are partial to shrimp *endiablados,* which means devilishly hot. They come strewn across a bed of French fries on a broad, fish-shaped plate that also holds a mound of rice, a green salad, and a warm tortilla wrapped in foil. This way of plating the shrimp ensures that whatever they are sauced with, be it garlic butter, soy sauce, oyster sauce, or that wicked *endiablados,* seeps down and flavors the French fries that are their bedding. That means that as you approach the end of your shrimp, you then get to savor crisp fries infused with whatever flavor it was that gave the shrimp their character.

Beverages include excellent presweetened (and lemon-flavored) iced tea as well as *horchata* (sweetened rice milk). A large cooler in the dining area holds bottles and cans of Dos Equis, Tecate, Corona, and Bud and Bud Lite.

There now are several Mariscos Chihuahuas in Tucson. The Twenty-Second Street shop is the original.

MATT'S BIG BREAKFAST

mattsbigbreakfast.com

825 N. 1st St.   602-254-1074
Phoenix, AZ   **B L | $**

For breakfast in Phoenix, Matt's can't be beat. Hash browns are among the best anywhere: Cooked on the griddle as a big, flat pancake, they are sectioned into rectangles for each serving. Wickedly crisp, a perfect balance of crusty edge and spuddy middle, they are good not only alongside breakfast but as a side dish for one of Matt's superb butter-grilled hamburgers at lunch. On the subject of potatoes, while home fries don't have the charisma of hash browns, they have a fine subtle charm of their own. They are soft and luxurious, laced with limp caramelized onions and perfumed by rosemary, and delivering tremendous potato flavor.

What else is excellent? Bacon is extra-thick and profusely peppered. Pancakes and waffles come with real maple syrup. Several flavors of freshly squeezed lemonade are available every day. Matt's salami scramble is a knockout: velvety eggs laced with long twigs of soppressata salami that is full-flavored, rank, and chewy. One other can't-miss plate is a "chop and chick" breakfast that features a skillet-cooked Iowa pork chop, with thick-cut toast and house-made preserves alongside.

Matt's has a stylish urban-renewal look with exposed ductwork and concrete flooring that looks like a vintage garage, but the vibe is classic diner. Many regular customers and their orders are well-known to the staff, and service is brisk and informal. Seating is at two counters, one of which looks outward onto 1st Street, and at several bare wood tables.

There are two other locations of Matt's Big Breakfast in Phoenix: 3118 E. Camelback Road (602-840-3450), and at Gate B5, Terminal 4 in Sky Harbor Airport.

MOTHER HUBBARD'S CAFÉ

14 W. Grant Rd.   520-623-7976
Tucson, AZ   **B L | $**

When the craving for contemporary interpretations of traditional Nahuan cuisine strikes, the place to go is Mother Hubbard's Café in Tucson. Having no idea at all what Nahuan cuisine is, let alone its contemporary interpretations, we approached this restaurant with some trepidation. Worries of it being pretentious proved to be unfounded. Mother Hubbard's is in fact a humble storefront diner that serves friendly Southwestern/Native American/Mexican comfort food.

As delivered here, contemporary Nahuan cuisine includes blue corn and pine nut waffles, green corn waffles topped with red or green chili, huevos rancheros, chorizo omelets, and buckwheat pancakes made from a recipe that dates back to 1896. Much of what's served is familiar non-Nahuan fare, but kicked up a notch. The ham used for eggs Benedict is smoked on premises, sliced thin, and soft as velvet. Hollandaise on top is the consistency of light cream, pure and buttery. The English muffin underneath is made from a spectacularly sour sourdough that the menu advises is seventy-five years old. Even the coffee is something special—a custom roast that proprietor Kelzi Bartholomei worked on for weeks to get just right.

Mother Hubbard's has the feel of a good old-fashioned diner, but with charming interior décor that includes tables covered with flower-pattern oilcloth and whimsical Day of the Dead skeleton art hung on brightly painted yellow walls.

MRS. WHITE'S GOLDEN RULE CAFE

808 E. Jefferson St.   602-262-9256
Phoenix, AZ   **L D** (until 3 a.m. Fri & Sat nights) | **$$**

Here is a soul-food restaurant that attracts a rainbow of customers at lunch. It can get crowded, but waiting a while for a seat is an incredible appetizer. Sniffing the food from this kitchen makes the time joyful. Mrs. White's is one of the best-smelling restaurants we know.

The menu is a soul-food party: fried chicken, catfish, oxtails, and two kinds of pork chops—smothered and simply fried. Other choices include catfish and crunchy-crusted fried chicken, all of them accompanied by corn bread. A list of the day's vegetables is written directly on the wall, which is like a chalkboard. They include sweet yams, black-eyed peas, mac 'n' cheese, and (weekends only) okra gumbo. For dessert, there are sweet-potato pies, layer cakes, and four-star peach cobbler.

Mrs. White's normally closes at 7 p.m., but on Friday and Saturday nights, it reopens at 9 p.m. and stays open until 3 a.m. The late-night menu is streamlined to catfish, wings, hot links, and burgers.

★ PICO DE GALLO

2618 S. 6th Ave.   520-623-8775
South Tucson, AZ   **L D | $**

This informal serve-yourself eatery started as a street-corner taco stand and has grown into several small dining rooms. Nothing about the increase in size has affected its magnificent food. Tacos, constructed in rugged, made-here corn tortillas, are among the best anywhere, available with carne asada and *birria* or more exotic ingredients such as tongue, manta ray, and beef cheeks. We love the *coctel de elote* (corn cocktail), which is not quite the beverage its name suggests. It does come in a large Styrofoam cup, the cup filled with an extraordinary stew of warm corn kernels, drifts of soft melted cheese, hot chili, and lime. Spoon it up like soup; it is corn-sweet and lime-zesty. The menu also lists burros, quesadillas, and tamales by the dozen.

In other regions, "pico de gallo" refers to salsa that serves as a condiment; but here the restaurant's namesake is an astonishing fruit cocktail: chunks of watermelon, coconut, pineapple, mango, and jicama, all spritzed with lime and sprinkled with salt and exclamatory chile powder. The red-hot spice elicits the fruit's sweetness and packs its own lip-tingling punch. It is a heady culinary collusion like nothing else we've ever eaten.

PREP & PASTRY

prepandpastry.com

3073 N. Campbell Ave.   520-326-7737
Tucson, AZ   B L | $

One half of the Prep & Pastry menu is devoted to drinks: teas and juices, of course, but also wine and Champagne, cocktails and beer, and eleven different takes on the mimosa. Yes, Prep & Pastry, open for breakfast, brunch, lunch, and weekday afternoon tea, is a place to kick back and imbibe.

It also happens to be a very good restaurant, with breakfast specials like sweet-potato hash, berry compote French toast, and Cheddar biscuits with sausage and duck fat gravy. The biscuit is extraordinary—vividly herbed, rich, and savory. Duck confit hash is shreds of luxurious meat laced with shallots, spinach, and raisins, crowned with a fried egg and goat cheese mousse. It is gluten-free, as is sweet-potato hash, a rainbow presentation that includes corn, asparagus, mushrooms, and leeks.

Swine-o-philes should note the pork belly breakfast sandwich, a thick slab of the ultra-piggy meat, braised to fall-apart tenderness, sharing space on an artisan roll with shaved apple and fennel, greens, and a fried egg.

A comfy, faux-rustic restaurant with bare wood tables and exposed beams, Prep & Pastry offers tables inside and out, as well as a counter/bar well suited to single diners.

RED ROCK CAFE

redrockcafeaz.com

100 Verde Valley School   928-284-1441
Rd., Ste. 107   B L | $
Sedona, AZ

The scene-stealer at the Red Rock Cafe is its cinnamon roll—a plate-sized monument of food that is tall and puffy, veined with buttery ribbons of cinnamon and raisins and smothered with an unconscionable amount of icing. It's more than a meal for one (a monomaniacal meal, for sure) and is better enjoyed if split among two to four people as a side dish.

We love the Southwestern breakfasts in this easy-going town café, especially the very pretty plate of huevos rancheros built on a foundation of blue corn tortillas. Two eggs, melty cheeses, black beans, and zesty ranchero sauce are festooned with crisp ribbons of different-colored tortillas. The chicken-fried steak is a beauty, arriving under a blanket of melted cheese, that same good ranchero sauce, and a sprinkle of green onions. On the side you get a choice of potatoes (hash browns or home fries), toast, biscuit, beans, or a pancake.

Whether you come for breakfast or lunch, do save room for pie. A couple of pies are available every day. They are expertly baked by Red Rock waitress Laura Anair.

As beautiful as the red rocks around Sedona are, the cafe is located in a totally bland shopping center. The dining area is clean and friendly. When we stopped in on a weekday morning, the clientele was a mix of regular locals and a few savvy travelers. We were told there usually is a wait for a table on weekends.

RITO'S MEXICAN FOOD

ritosmexicanfood14st.com

907 N. 14th St.   602-262-9842
Phoenix, AZ   L D (closed Sun) | $

We list Rito's for its grand burrito, served enchilada-style. That means it comes blanketed with melting orange cheese and your choice of red or green chile sauce. It is a substantial plate of food, brilliantly flavorful thanks to the hot red or hotter green chili that smothers it. Inside are beef or vegetarian mixes of beans and/or rice. The rest of Rito's menu is classic Sonoran fare: tacos, chimichangas, enchiladas, and tostadas.

Located in Tucson's Garfield neighborhood, which is listed on the National Register of Historic Places for its multitude of vintage homes from throughout the twentieth century, Rito's is a tiny place, more kitchen than order area. All on-premises seating is outdoors on one of two patios. Everything is sold in take-away containers.

SHORT LEASH HOT DOGS

shortleashhotdogs.com

110 E. Roosevelt St.   602-795-2193
Phoenix, AZ   L D | $

Short Leash hot dogs come wrapped in naan bread, tortillas, or pretzel rolls. Condiments range from mango chutney and peanut butter to chipotle cream cheese and avocado sauce. The tube steaks themselves can be all-beef, chicken dogs, spicy-beer hots, brats, or meat-free.

It is possible to select a wiener—all-beef, chicken, brat, vegetarian—and have it dressed and bunned exactly as you like. You even can ask for a standard-issue beef-and-pork frank topped with only yellow mustard. But at Short Leash Hot Dogs, it's the wild combos that win our attention. The Devil Dog, for instance, comes with roasted red peppers, green chiles, sautéed onions, sriracha, melted Cheddar cheese, and enough chopped-up jalapeños to clear the sinuses. It is bedded in a round of naan bread, which is a welcome fire-dampening agent for the tongue. Then there's the Sunny Dog: a chicken wiener topped with grilled fruit, prosciutto, goat cheese, honey, and

peppery arugula. It is a whirl of flavors that does not quite scratch a hot-dog itch, but it satisfies hunger in a completely unexpected way. A somewhat more traditional choice is Short Leash's chili dog, an all-beef frank topped with vegetarian chili, grated Cheddar cheese, and chopped raw onions. The chili coat is more cumin-flavored than fiery, cradled in a round of buttery naan bread.

Side dishes include mild mac 'n' cheese with crunch from its bread-crumb top, thin French fries that arrive well-peppered and salted, and fried pickles that teeter-totter between sweet and sour inside their crisp coat.

THE STAND

thestandbnt.com

3538 E. Indian School   602-314-5259
Rd.   L D | $
Phoenix, AZ

The setting—a former soft-serve ice cream outlet—is bare-table plebeian, including a drive-through window, but the hamburgers and tacos at the Stand are patrician. Burgers come as doubles. Cheese, bacon, butter-caramelized onions, and roasted jalapeño peppers all cost extra, but unless you say otherwise, each "Standard" comes accoutered with lettuce, tomato, crisp onion slices, kosher dill pickle chips, and a lather of Stand sauce, which looks like a dark version of thousand island dressing but is spicier and not as sweet. This all makes for one stupendous burger, the meat itself fresh and full-flavored. That same Stand sauce makes a worthy dip for the kitchen's thin, skin-on French fries.

Three kinds of tacos are served: chicken, veggie, and short rib. That last one is outstanding. A pair of soft corn tortillas are piled with fall-apart-tender, intensely beefy shreds, along with pickled red cabbage, cotija, chopped onion, and cilantro. Ingredients of the vegetable taco vary with the season, but always include quinoa, beans, and red cabbage.

Drinks are delightful. House-made *horchata* is smooth and cinnamony. Jamaica (hibiscus tea) is an exotic shade of deep purple. Milk shakes are scrupulously blended to order. Banana shakes are so thick that they barely make it up their extra-wide straw. They are made with freshly peeled banana, banana custard, and vanilla ice cream—an extraordinary beverage!

SUGAR BOWL

sugarbowlscottsdale.com

4005 N. Scottsdale Rd.   480-946-0051
Scottsdale, AZ   **L D | $**

Few restaurants are as pure in spirit and intention as the Sugar Bowl, which seems like it might not have changed at all since opening day in 1958. With its pink-upholstered booths and swift young staff who look so cheerful carrying Raspberry Glaciers (Sprite and sherbet), Golden Nuggets (Sprite, sherbet, and ice cream), and Turkish coffee sodas, it is the archetypal ice cream parlor. In particular, we recommend Camelback sodas, made with either vanilla or coffee ice cream, "extra luscious malts," for which glasses are lined with your choice of marshmallow, hot fudge, or caramel sauce, and the tin roof sundae, made with excellent chocolate syrup and a bounty of redskin Spanish peanuts.

There are sandwiches, soups, and salads too, and those we've tasted are very good; but in truth, when we walk into this happy place, we instantly become too obsessed with ice cream to think much about anything else.

TERESA'S MOSAIC CAFE

teresamosaiccafe.com

2456 N. Silver Mosaic   520-624-4512
Dr.   **B L D | $**
Tucson, AZ

Teresa's Mosaic Cafe bills itself as Oaxacan, and there are some less familiar Mexican dishes on the menu—chile rellenos stuffed with shredded chicken, marinated pork loin fillets served with squash, and smoked and pickled pasilla chiles that make a spot-on garnish for anything savory—but much of what's offered is familiar border cuisine (tacos, burros, chimichangas, enchiladas). And Tucson's own personality is reflected in such specialties as *topopo* salad and cheese crisps. Corn and wheat tortillas are made at the back of the dining room and arrive at your table griddle-hot. We love the chunky guacamole and mini chimichanga appetizers, and the green corn tamales, dotted with fresh kernels, are classic Sonoran desert fare.

We found this inconspicuous diner thanks to Roadfood.com team members Chris Ayers and Amy Breisch, who proclaimed Teresa's breakfast worthy of exaltation: "Amy dubbed the huevos rancheros the best ever, while Chris made the same claim for the cheese enchilada." The latter is available as part of a combination plate that also includes eggs and a hot tamale. The former, without being outlandish or unique, truly is the model for the way huevos rancheros ought to be: the eggs glistening with butter and perched atop a tortilla that is crisp but also a bit chewy, the salsa hot enough to make you grab for a tortilla from the accompanying basket to tamp your tongue and yet not so hot that the tomato, pepper, egg, wheat, and cheese don't each sing their essential notes loud and clear.

TUCSON TAMALE COMPANY

tucsontamale.com

2545 E. Broadway   520-305-4760
Tucson, AZ   **L | $**

—★— **VEGAN FRIENDLY** —★— Todd Martin is a man on a mission: to celebrate tamales. He makes fine versions of familiar green corn tamales and cheese and jalapeño tamales, but also has invented countless variations on what he sees as an opportunity for invention. Among his creations are vegetarian tamales, vegan tamales, gluten-free tamales, and breakfast tamales such as the Denver (ham, red pepper, onion, cheese) and the Tubac (chorizo, potato, cheese). We love the Arizona tamale—roasted sirloin and smoky chipotle chiles—and the Santa Fe tamale, made with pork loin and green chiles. A few other wonders: the Little Italy tamale, loaded with spicy sausage, pepper, and cheese; the Thanksgiving tamale, which is basically a full turkey dinner enrobed in sage masa; and the New Delhi tamale, which is a cornucopia of carrots, corn, potato, and onions flavored with curry powder and coconut milk. There even is an ode to Tucson's notorious Sonoran hot dog: the dogmale (say "dog-molly"), which is an all-beef hot dog, bacon, beans, and salsa enveloped in corn masa.

"Simplify, Sustain, and Celebrate" is the motto of Martin's sunny little storefront, which vends hundreds of dozens of tamales every week—by mail and takeout for cooking at home and warm for eating on premises at a handful of tables (along with housemade salsas in three heat levels). "People think of the tamale as a Mexican thing," Martin says, "but it goes back to pre-Columbian Mesoamerica, long before the Spanish. So many cultures around the world have their own take on the concept."

COLORADO

BIKER JIM'S GOURMET DOGS

bikerjimsdogs.com

2148 Larimer St. 720-746-9355
Denver, CO **L D** | **$**

OMG, what a menu! If, like us, a restaurant with too many tempting choices induces anxiety—which of all of these inviting things should I order?—Biker Jim's could make you catatonic. But what delicious madness! A printed menu does help the decision-making by organizing your thoughts into a step-by-step process. First, choose a dog. The dozen-plus available can be as basic as an all-beef frank or it can be a sausage made of elk, rattlesnake/pheasant, reindeer, buffalo, or duck. There's a vegan one too.

Having selected a tube steak, you then peruse available toppings: wasabi aioli, New Jersey chili, caramelized apple, roasted cactus, Coke-marinated grilled onions, and so on. Next: side dishes. There are fine homemade fries and hand-cut potato chips, plus mac 'n' cheese, baked beans, and fried green tomatoes. Far be it from us to recommend one combo over another, but we will say that the recommendation of Roadfood.com's Cliff Strutz and Cousin Johnnie made us very happy: a wine-laced pork sausage on a pretzel roll topped with Dijon cream, crunchy squiggles of beer-battered onion, toasted sauerkraut, and a dusting of tomato bacon powder. It's called a Waatlander Dog.

BUCKHORN EXCHANGE

buckhorn.com

1000 Osage St. 303-534-9505
Denver, CO **L D** | **$$$**

--★-- **HOT TICKET** --★-- Holder of Colorado Liquor License #1 (issued in 1893), outfitted with a few museums' worth of antique firearms and furniture, and hung with a menagerie of some five hundred game animal trophies shot by former owner Shorty Zietz, the Buckhorn Exchange is no mere frontier-themed restaurant for tourists. It happens to be a fine place to eat the cuisine of the Rockies.

At lunch, hamburgers, salads, and sandwiches are consumed without ado by a cadre of regular customers inured to the stare of a thousand glass eyes and the creak of wood floors where Buffalo Bill once trod. Tourists like us cannot help but gape and wonder . . . and then tuck into a seriously carnivorous meal. Those who want to eat really Wild Western fare can start with Rocky Mountain oysters (deep-fried calf testicle) or rattlesnake marinated in red chile and lime. Less daunting hors d'oeuvres include the Buckhorn's legendary bean soup and smoked buffalo sausage with red chile polenta. For the main meat you can choose buffalo tenderloin, elk medallions, Colorado lamb, beefsteaks, baby-back ribs, or Gramma Fanny's Pot Roast, made from a recipe that dates back to 1893. If there's more than a single passionate meat-eater at the table, the dish to have is the

Big Steak, carved tableside. It's a strip steak available in sizes from one and a half pounds (for two) to four pounds (for five). The latter sells for $199.

Top it all off with a broad slab of hot crumb-topped apple pie with cinnamon rum sauce, and you will have eaten a true-West meal.

BUD'S BAR

5453 Manhart St.	303-688-9967
Sedalia, CO	**L D** | **$**

Bars tend not to be great places to look for excellent food, but if it's a hamburger you seek, they're worth putting on the hit list. For a rewarding bar burger, we suggest heading south on Highway 85 out of Denver to the town of Sedalia and finding a mid-twentieth-century watering hole named Bud's. Here is served what tipster Mindy Leisure described as "one of the best burgers you will ever eat." It is juicy with a good crust, modest-sized, nothing fancy. You have a choice of a single or a double with or without cheese. Pickles and onion are the only garnishes available. There's no deep-fryer on premises, so the menu advises patrons, "We don't have no damn fries." Instead, you get a bag of potato chips.

As you might guess by the extremely limited menu—there's nothing to eat other than burgers—Bud's attracts a lot of people for whom the hamburgers are a side dish to the main course, which is beer.

DUFFEYROLL CAFÉ

duffeyrolls.com

1290 S. Pearl St.	303-953-6890
Denver, CO	**B L** | **$**

Colorado is rich in cinnamon rolls. The most famous is the enormous, plate-sized megaroll at Johnson's Corner truck stop up in Loveland (p. 343). The most elegant is the one at the Duffeyroll Café in Denver. Actually, there are several Duffeyrolls available—crisp-edged swirls of dough drizzled with maple, orange, even Irish cream frosting, but it's our firm belief that such drippy indulgence, while a welcome addition to big, doughy rolls, overwhelms the fragile texture of a plain Duffeyroll. Oh, we do like pecanilla

crunch and English toffee, which are applied judiciously and add a nice extra note. But the regular roll is so perfectly sugary and cinnamony and buttery that we are loath to adulterate it.

If you do need something denser and more substantial, have a pecan sticky bun, stuck with a thick blanket of nuts. Sandwiches, wraps, soups, and salads are available at lunch.

There are three other locations: in Denver, 4994 East Hampden Avenue (303-753-9177) and 1601 Blake Street (303-623-0654), and in Englewood, 5198 South Broadway (303-996-5900).

DURANGO DINER

durangodiner.com

957 Main Ave.	970-247-9889
Durango, CO	**B L** | **$**

It was pancakes that made us fall in love with the Durango Diner—plate-wide pancakes, preferably with blueberries, glistening with butter and running rivers of syrup. We branched out to other breakfasts, and liked them plenty, especially the "half and half" plate of biscuits with gravy and green chile, and the big warm cinnamon roll. You will share breakfast in this Main Street hash house with some locals who claim to have been having coffee an' at these seats since opening day in 1965.

If you are a connoisseur of hamburgers, put Durango on your treasure map, for its Bonus Cheeseburger Deluxe: one-half pound of meat under a mantle of melted Swiss cheese and diced green chiles, French fries on the side. We love the Durango Diner's bacon double cheeseburgers almost as much as we love the chiliburgers (available red or green), and although some customers combine all these toppings on one mound of meat, we must confess that bacon and chili together atop a cheeseburger is just too much for our delicate palates.

JOHNSON'S CORNER

johnsonscorner.com

2842 SE Frontage Rd.   970-667-2069
(Exit 254 off I-25)   Always open | $
Johnstown, CO

A favorite truckers' stop along Highway 87 between Denver and Cheyenne since before there was an interstate, Johnson's Corner serves breakfast (and lunch and supper) around the clock, and is famous for its colossal cinnamon roll. The roll is OK—probably the most bang for your buck, but when we seek maximum flavor along with maximum calories, we prefer Johnson's chicken-fried steak with eggs, crunchy hash browns, and a biscuit with gravy. The breakfast menu contains all the usual suspects—omelets, pancakes, corned beef hash—as well as buffalo sausage and a breakfast burrito. Non-breakfast highlights include pot roast dinner, hot turkey sandwich, steaks, and pork chops. A full-service soda fountain offers shakes, floats, malts, and one heck of a handsome banana split.

Recently remodeled, the dining area sports hugely spacious booths and counter service. And for truckers and other travelers who want to stay connected, it is a Wi-Fi hot spot.

LA FOGATA

la-fogata.com

5670 E. Evans Ave.   303-753-9458
Denver, CO   B L D | $

La Fogata means "the bonfire," however the green chile bowl (available with or without pork) served in this bilingual establishment isn't really all that hot. But it is quite delicious: zesty, glowing with sunny chile flavor, and packed with the punch of cumin. If you are looking for excellent Mexican food in Denver, this is the place to be.

Many items on La Fogata's menu are nationally familiar Tex-Mex staples—enchiladas, chiles rellenos, tamales—expertly made and served in abundance, but this is also an opportunity to be adventurous. If you are blasé about beef in your taco, you can order tacos filled with crisp-roasted pork (wonderful!), tacos with beef tongue (spicy!), or ceviche tostadas; or you can spoon into the bowl of the tripe and hominy stew known as *menudo*. To drink, there are imported beers, plenty of tequila cocktails, and the true-Mex non-alcoholic favorite, *horchata*, which is sweet rice milk.

This is a fun place to dine, where the crowd is equal measures downtown business executives, blue-collar beer drinkers, and foodies who appreciate a taste of high-quality but unpretentious Mexican food.

Two other locations: 8090 East Quincy Avenue, Denver (720-974-7315) and 16600 Washington Street, Thornton (303-252-5530).

KANSAS

AL'S CHICKENETTE

700 Vine St.   785-625-7414
Hays, KS   **L D | $**

If you are traveling in western Kansas along I-70 with any degree of appetite as you approach Hays, do yourself a favor and find Al's. It will be especially easy to find if it's after dark, for this sixty-year-old eatery has a beautiful vintage neon sign glowing outside. Indoors, the walls are covered with evocative pictures of Kansas railroad history and a huge collection of chicken figurines.

Of course, the thing to eat is chicken. Fried. You can buy it by the quarter or half bird, tenders or nuggets, a breast fillet or a giblet dinner of livers and/or gizzards. This is not fast-food chicken. It will take a while for your order to cook, which is one reason it is so good. As your teeth crack through the chicken's crunchy skin, aromatic steam erupts into the air. It is delicious plain, but the way Al's customers know to eat it is to drizzle some honey across the crisp skin (as well as on the excellent French fries). The honey's sweetness sings mellifluous harmony with the chicken's salty crust.

BARTO'S IDLE HOUR

210 S. Santa Fe St.   620-232-9834
Frontenac, KS   **D | $$**

Even before goofball TV found its way to the fried chicken restaurants in and around Pittsburg, Kansas, and made a big deal of the rivalry among them, food writers tended to concentrate only on the big two: Chicken Mary's (p. 346) and Chicken Annie's. Considering they are within spitting distance of each other and they were the first to specialize in full-bore chicken dinners, the concentration made sense. But in fact there are six restaurants in the area that specialize in fried chicken, and to many of those who have tried them all, Barto's Idle Hour stands supreme.

It is relatively new, opened as a music hall in the 1950s and finally taking up the fried-chicken gauntlet in the 1960s. When Roadfood.com's Chris Ayers and Amy Breisch visited in 2010, this is what they had to say: "The fried chicken skyrocketed to the top of our list, having exceeded all necessary criteria from the crispy-without-being-overly-greasy skin to the melt-in-your-mouth juiciness of the meat. Pieces of white and dark meat can be ordered individually, but to do so would mean missing out on the traditional sides that are inextricably tied to chicken dinners in this region. As opposed to the mayonnaise-laden potato salads and coleslaws most familiar to the American palate, local menus offer these side dishes German-style (vinegar and oil–based). The result is nothing short of *wunderbar,* as both sides are both delightfully zesty and highly addictive. Those looking to emphasize the 'fried' in fried chicken dinner are encouraged to pay the supplemental charge and add a side of homemade onion rings to the mix. Their fragile crusts make these rings indeed unforgettable. Each table also gets a basket of bread freshly baked by the Frontenac Bakery, which services all of the chicken restaurants in the area."

Chris and Amy, who have been to nearly all the great Roadfood restaurants coast to coast, concluded their review by saying that Barto's "ranks among our most memorable Roadfood stops of all time."

THE BREADBASKET

newtonbreadbasket.com

| 219 N. Main St. | 316-283-3811 |
| Newton, KS | **B L D** \| $ |

Roadfood.com's Dale Fine, who goes by the screen name Wanderingjew, came across the Breadbasket while hunting *bierocks.* Also known as cabbage burgers and a very close cousin to the trademarked Runza of Nebraska, a *bierock* is a pocket of dough filled with beef, onions, cabbage, and spices and cooked until golden brown. The Breadbasket's version is a Jayhawker treasure—a whole comfort-food meal in a single sandwich (or, better yet, two sandwiches; they are not very large).

As is true of so many worthy heartland cafés, the salad bar here is a cut above: not just ingredients for putting a salad together, but also several composed salads, including pea salad, macaroni salad, carrot-raisin salad, and several slaws. The bread selection does justice to this restaurant's name: Six or seven fresh-baked loaves are available—pumpernickels and ryes and whole wheats, cinnamon-raisin, white and brown bread, all presented whole so the slice you cut for yourself is absolutely fresh.

Then there's pie, all kinds of it. Dale chose Toll House pie, which he said tasted "like a big, soft chocolate chip cookie." All sorts of cream and meringue pies also are available. And if you happen to be allergic to pie, come on a Friday or Saturday night and try some cherry moo. That is a Mennonite soup made with cream and sweet-tart cherries. It makes a sweet finish (or start) for those evenings' German buffets, where you can fill a plate with sausages and baked ham, hot potato salad, chicken borscht, and zwieback with apple butter.

BROOKVILLE HOTEL

brookvillehotel.com

| 105 E. Lafayette Ave. | 785-263-2244 |
| Abeline, KS | **L D** (closed Mon & Tues) \| $$ |

Buffalo Bill slept at the Brookville Hotel in the small town of Brookville, as did untold numbers of drovers when Kansas was the end of the line for trail drives up from Texas. It was opened in 1870 and has built a reputation for its bountiful family-style chicken dinners since 1915.

It was a sad day when it closed in 1999 and moved to Abeline. While the new setting lacks the charm of the old railhead town of Brookville, great pains were taken to make the building look like the old facility. Even if it is more like a theme park than a century-old restaurant, the Brookville Hotel continues to serve the meal that has made it a destination for generations of hungry Kansans who think nothing of driving two hours each way for Sunday supper. As always, fried chicken is the main attraction—a half a bird, skillet fried and served with mashed potatoes and cream gravy, with creamed corn, cottage cheese, baking-powder biscuits with sweet preserves, sweet-and-sour coleslaw, and ice cream for dessert.

BUNKER HILL CAFE

| 609 Elm St. | 785-483-6544 |
| Bunker Hill, KS | **D** (Thurs–Sat) \| $$$ |

The Bunker Hill Cafe is a rugged limestone building that opened as a drugstore then became a pool hall. Today it is a destination steak house, open for supper only Wednesday through Saturday. It's a small place, no more than a dozen tables, with a menu that includes shrimp, catfish, and chicken, although nearly everybody comes for steak. Filet mignon is available in sizes that range from two to sixteen ounces, sirloin from four to sixteen. There's also bacon-wrapped ground beef and, on occasion, Kansas elk and buffalo. Our sirloins were laden with juice, tender but not at all tenderized, a joy to slowly savor. It was late summer, and on the side came beautiful, full-flavored tomatoes and corn on the cob, as well as the house specialty, honey bread (available for purchase by the loaf).

Décor is Plains rustic: lots of mounted trophies and naturalist pictures on the wall and a couple of wood-burning stoves for warmth in cool weather. As seating is limited, reservations are advised.

CHICKEN MARY'S

1133 E. 600th Ave.   620-231-9510
Pittsburg, KS   **D | $$**

The narrow lane off Highway 69 between Frontenac and Pittsburg, Kansas, is known as the Chicken Dinner Road, home of two flourishing restaurants—Chicken Mary's and Chicken Annie's—that specialize in nearly identical dinners of deep-fried chicken.

Mary and Annie have long ago gone to their reward, and many years ago Mary's son—no spring chicken himself—explained to us that in the hard times of the 1930s, his father and Annie's husband both worked in a nearby mine. In 1934, Annie's husband lost a leg in a mine accident. To make ends meet, Annie opened a little restaurant and served her specialty, fried chicken. Only a few years after that, Mary's husband had to quit work too, because of a bad heart. "There were three of us kids to feed," the old man recalled. "And my mother could see how well Annie was doing selling chicken dinners out here. She took a hint and opened her own place, Chicken Mary's, just down the road."

A tradition was begun. The rivalry has made this unlikely farm road a chicken lover's mecca for six decades. The meals are ritualized family-style feasts, centered on chicken that arrives glistening with grease. The skin is chewy and luxurious, the meat below moist and tender. You can order whichever parts you want in whatever quantity: dark, white, wings, backs, even livers, gizzards, or hearts. On the side you want German potato salad and/or coleslaw. Poultry frowners can order chicken-fried steak.

Note: Chicken Annie's is a few hundred yards up the road, at 1143 East 600th Avenue (620-231-9460). We've never eaten at both in the same trip, nor have we done enough research to rate one place above the other.

COZY INN

cozyburger.com

108 N. 7th St.   785-825-2699
Salina, KS   **L D | $**

--★--
**LOCALS
LOVE IT**
--★--
When the McDonald brothers opened their first hamburger restaurant in California after World War II, the Cozy Inn had already been around a quarter century. This is one of America's original hamburger stands, and although its management has changed over the years and it was threatened with extinction (but saved by a consortium of local hamburger patriots), it serves burgers that are pretty much the same as they were in 1922.

They are archetypal sliders. The first great thing to praise about them is their smell. As you approach the diminutive diner, the scent of grilling onions and beef with a hint of dill pickle tickles your senses like exotic hash-house perfume. There is a window for takeout orders, but for full enjoyment, sit inside at the counter on one of six stools. Here, the ten minutes to have lunch of maybe a half dozen sliders and a bag of potato chips will ensure that the Cozy aroma will saturate your clothes and stay with you the rest of the day. Freeze a bag of Cozies, heat them in the microwave oven six months later, and their scent will billow out.

The second exceptional thing about them is their taste. These are no Salisbury steaks or quarter-pounders. They are thin-as-a-nickel, one-ounce patties in little buns that somehow form a perfect combination with pickle, mustard, and ketchup. It is a configuration so consecrated that, according to Cozy Inn folklore, some years ago when a Cozy cook tried to put a piece of cheese on his own personal burger, he was fired on the spot.

HAYS HOUSE

hayshouse.com

112 W. Main St.   620-767-5911
Council Grove, KS   B L D | $$

Hays House has had its ups and downs since Seth Hays started serving food here in 1857. We occasionally read good reports about it from travelers passing through Council Grove, but its kitchen was destroyed by fire in 2011. When the place reopened in 2012, it was run by a consortium of locals, and it has since regained its status as a destination restaurant for anyone traveling the old Santa Fe Trail in search of hearty country food.

It is great to start the day here with breakfast of French toast made with house cinnamon bread or biscuits with meaty sausage gravy. On the side, you definitely want a sweet roll, especially if you arrive near opening at 6 a.m., when it still will be oven-hot. At lunch and supper, there is an effulgent salad bar featuring not just rabbit food but also ambrosia, macaroni salad, potato salad, pasta salad, and the like. Nebraska-made Dorothy Lynch dressing always is available. Entrees range from traditional (rib-eye steak, fried chicken, and a marvelous chicken-fried steak that is cooked in chicken fat) to modernities like mango-glazed salmon and pasta à la vodka. Ice cream is made on premises, as are such specialty pies as grasshopper, Kahlúa, and cran-strawberry, which all come topped with freshly whipped cream.

NU WAY

nuwayburgers.com

1416 W. Douglas Ave.   316-267-1131
Wichita, KS   L D | $

We don't know of another American food with as many names as loosemeats. That is what Heartland eaters call a sandwich of spiced, unpattied, and unsauced beef that usually is served in a bun with pickle and onion, sometimes with cheese, and sometimes mustard (but never ketchup). Its native habitat is Iowa, where it also goes by the brand name Maid Rite; up in Siouxland, you'll find it listed as a Tavern, Charlie Boy, Big T, or Tastee.

In Wichita, Kansas, the sandwich is called a Crumbly Burger or, eponymously, a Nu Way, after the place that serves it. Nu Way's Nu Way is available medium or large (twice the amount of crumbly burger on a big bun), arriving wrapped in wax paper and already cut in half for easy eating without too much of the beef falling out when you pick it up. The meat is moist with temperate beefy taste, well abetted by onion, pickle, and mustard.

While the beef tends toward bland, Nu Way's garlic salad is alarmingly flavorful, a creamy slaw with garlic pungency that tastes nearly radioactive. If you don't love garlic, you won't like it, and even if you do love garlic, it can be overpowering. You definitely do want Nu Way onion rings, which are big hoops crusted with fragile batter, and sweet, dark, brewed-here root beer. Limeade, regular or cherry-flavored, is squeezed to order.

There now are six Nu Ways in Wichita. The West Douglas Avenue location is the original, dating back to 1930. It was opened by Tom McEvoy, who came to Kansas from (no surprise) Iowa.

PORUBSKY'S GROCERY

508 NE Sardou Ave.   785-234-5788
Topeka, KS   L (Mon-Sat) | $

-- ★ --
LOCALS
LOVE IT
-- ★ --
For more than half a century, customers have been coming to the Little Russia neighborhood of North Topeka to eat Porubsky's chili (during chili season only—October to March) and cold-cut sandwiches. Regulars include a blue-collar crowd, traveling trenchermen, and politicians who want to be photographed in a setting that makes them look like normal people.

The sandwiches are no big deal—ordinary lunch meats on regular bread—but the extras are outstanding. The most famous of these are Porubsky's pickles. They are big, firm discs that start as dills but are then infused with horseradish, mustard, and hot peppers to become an eye-widening garnish guaranteed to snap taste buds to attention. They are a favorite complement, along with crumbled saltine crackers, atop a bowl of Porubsky's chili. Before the hot pickles are applied, the chili is a fine bowl of Heartland comfort:

ground chuck cooked with a measure of chili powder and other spice, then added to a battered old pot of simmering beans.

RJ'S BOB-BE-QUE SHACK

rjsbbq.com

5835 Lamar Ave.   913-262-7300
Mission, KS   **L D** (breakfast on weekends)
                                   | $$

There was a time when burnt ends were nothing but bits, scraps, and shreds gathered from the cutting board after barbecued brisket had been sliced. A duet of rugged crunch and melting fat, these traditional burnt ends, once a delicacy known only to barbecue devotees, are now a smokehouse menu staple. The meal that used to be debris has become so popular that contemporary barbecue restaurants cut tidy little chunks off the edge of the brisket so that burnt ends can be a regular, everyday menu item. That's not necessarily a bad thing; modern burnt ends, although leaner and therefore less lascivious, can still deliver tremendous flavor. RJ's Bob-Be-Que Shack proves the point. Available here as pork or beef burnt ends, these nuggets of meat are available in a sandwich, on a platter, and—Saturday and Sunday only—as the anchor of burnt-end hash, a tangle of pork or brisket with onions, peppers, mushrooms, and bacon.

RJ's menu beyond burnt ends is vast, including four kinds of ribs by the rack (spare, St. Louis, baby backs, and lamb ribs), barbecued chicken, Polish sausage, and a butt burger. That last one is a half pound of ground pork butt, pattied and smoked. Interesting side dishes include a cheesy corn bake and potato chips drizzled with truffle oil and balsamic vinegar.

★ WOODYARD BAR-B-QUE

woodyardbbq.com

3001 Merriam Ln.   913-362-8000
Kansas City, KS   **L D** | $$

The Woodyard is in fact a woodyard selling hickory, cherry, pecan, and applewood logs to pitmasters and backyard barbecuists. It is also a restaurant that serves first-rate Kansas City barbecue, which you can enjoy at tables inside a country wood-frame house or on a patio built around an open-air smoker. From the smoker emerge splendid baby-back ribs sheathed in meat that pulls right off the bone in big, juicy ribbons.

Smoke profoundly infuses the Woodyard's burnt ends (tips, squiggles, shreds, and nuggets of barbecued meat), which are available in a sandwich or on occasion as the topping for multi-bean chili. Burnt ends are powerful stuff. For those less extreme in their barbecue lust, the pulled pork here is nothing short of magnificent, just-right smoky and so full of juice and flavor that sauce is entirely optional. Other items on the menu include hot legs—like wings, but meatier—and a Friday special of pecan smoked salmon.

NEVADA

LOUIS' BASQUE CORNER

louisbasquecorner.com

301 E. 4th St.   775-323-7203
Reno, NV   **L D | $$**

We ate at Louis's Basque Corner on our first trip across the USA in the early 1970s. At the time, the place was five years old—Mr. and Mrs. Louis Erreguible, who had only recently come to Reno from southern France, were ebullient hosts in their new-world dining room. After supper, we walked out utterly inspired, thinking that *someone* really ought to be writing about marvelous local restaurants in unlikely places across the country. We've been writing about such restaurants ever since, and Louis' Basque Corner continues to serve what Mrs. Erreguible described long ago as "simple food cooked to perfection."

By average-American-meal standards, the food at Louis' is far from simple. What you eat at the long, family-style tables are copious feasts that start with soup, salad, bread, and beans, then move on to a plate of beef tongue, paella, oxtails, lamb stew, or Basque chicken. That's the *first course*! After that comes the serious eating: an entree of sirloin steak, paella, pork loin or pork chops, lamb chops, or a fish of the day.

Louis's is a colorful place with waitresses outfitted in native attire and walls decorated with travel posters of the Pyrenees as well as pottery from Ciboure. Its clientele is a mix of travelers passing through for whom a meal here is a special treat as well as plenty of locals who make Louis' a regular part of their regimen.

MARTIN HOTEL

themartinhotel.com

94 W. Railroad St.   775-623-3197
Winnemucca, NV   **L** (Mon-Fri) **D | $$**

Bring plenty of appetite if you plan to eat dinner at the Martin Hotel, which has been serving Basque feeds to locals for well over a century. The copious meals start with soup, salad, herbed carrots, Basque beans, garbanzo beans with sausage, garlic mashed potatoes, and bread, all accompanied by basso profundo burgundy wine. Next, you have a steak, lamb shank, pork chops, pork loin, sweetbreads, or salmon, accompanied by excellent French fries cut from local potatoes. There is good bread pudding for dessert, and you must also consider a glass of Picon Punch, the bittersweet Basque digestif.

The hotel is a humble stucco building that still has hitching posts outside. Dining is at long communal tables that seat up to a dozen people. At lunch, normal-sized plates of food are served.

MARY'S HASH HOUSE

hashouse.net

2605 S. Decatur, Ste. 103   702-873-9479
Las Vegas, NV   **B L | $**

If we were sticklers for our own rules, one of which defines Roadfood as fare of the region where the restaurant is located, Mary's Hash House would not be included in this book. It's in Las Vegas and boasts of serving Midwestern food. But because Las Vegas is a city where normal rules of life don't apply and, more important, because it is a city with a dearth of normal restaurants (what is native Las Vegas cuisine, anyway?), we include it here as a service to hungry travelers in search of something other than an all-you-can-eat buffet or yet another celebrity chef's high-priced eating shrine. (Please, do not confuse it with Hash House A Go Go at the Imperial Palace on the Strip.)

We'd never have found it were it not for the intrepid appetites of Roadfood.com's Bruce Bilmes and Sue Boyle, who wrote, "The simple, unflashy home-cooking, served in a simple, unflashy room, plays well in mega-flashy Vegas." They noted that it really is a hash house, its breakfast-all-day menu featuring corned beef hash, ham hash, roast beef hash, and chicken hash, as well as Super Hash, which blends them all. A good-sized portion, including a couple of side dishes (fried potatoes, grits, fresh fruit, toast) will get you change from a ten-dollar bill: one of the city's true dining bargains. Bruce and Sue emphasized that just about everything at Mary's is made right here: The hash, of course, which you can have with or without peppers, onions, mushrooms, or even eggs scrambled in, but also an amazing array of jellies and jams, including hot habanero, not-quite-as-hot jalapeño, peach, strawberry, and watermelon.

The menu extends far beyond hash. Omelets, pancakes, waffles, eggs Benedict, Alaskan salmon, and perch with eggs for breakfast; soup, salad, sandwiches, fried chicken, and hamburgers for lunch.

BUCKHORN TAVERN

buckhornburgers.com

68 US Hwy. 380   575-835-4423
San Antonio, NM   **L D** (closed Sun) | $

Buckhorn Tavern's green chile cheeseburger is a swirling combination of beef, melted cheese, hot green chile, lettuce, tomato, and pickle chips on a broad, tender bun. There are more elegant GCCBs in New Mexico and there are some that are beefier or oozier; this one earns kudos for harmony.

Buckhorn's Fritos pie is another example of multiple-ingredient poise, the corn chips an agreeable medley of tamale-soft and hard-breaking crisp. Chile cheese fries are also a good ensemble idea, but the ones we ate were limp and not cooked through. Maybe it was just a bad deep-fryer day, or perhaps our arrival at the very start of lunch hour meant the cooking oil wasn't yet hot enough.

Buckhorn Tavern got a lot of attention on TV food shows a few years ago, meaning that even though San Antonio, New Mexico, is in the middle of nowhere, it usually is so crowded that you will wait in line for a seat. The place opens at 11 a.m.; a 10:45 arrival puts you in the first wave.

CAFE PASQUAL'S

pasquals.com

121 Don Gaspar Ave.   505-983-9340
Santa Fe, NM   **B L D** | $$

Pasqual's looks like a modest corner café and in some essential way it is. But the food is too good to be modest and while breakfast or lunch won't break the bank, dinner for two can cost north of $50. At any mealtime in the crowded, split-level dining room, you are lucky to find a seat at a small table or at the large shared one, where a local or a stranger from just about any part of the world might break bread with you.

At breakfast, we love the chunky corned beef hash, the pancakes, the blue and yellow cornmeal mush, big sweet rolls, and giant bowls of five-grain cereal with double-thick cinnamon toast on the side, accompanied by immense bowls of latte. And for lunch, we can never resist the expertly made soups. Little things mean so much: fresh bread for sandwiches, flavorful chiles on quesadillas; even the coffee is a tasty surprise.

CHOPE'S

16145 S. Hwy. 28   575-233-3420
La Mesa, NM   L D (Tues–Sat) | $

You'd expect this kitchen's work with chiles to be good; many of its regular customers are planters whose business is to grow the legendary New Mexico peppers. There is no better way to taste the long greens of the Mesilla Valley than as Chope's chiles rellenos. Stuffed with mild cheese, battered, and crisp-fried, the fleshy walls of the pod have a strapping vegetable punch.

As for red chiles, their quintessence can be tasted in the cream-thick, bright vermillion purée that is scrupulously handmade in the kitchen. It is pretty darn hot, the kind of lip-searing hot that any restaurant outside New Mexico would warn customers about. But in this area, it's normal. The really hot stuff on the table is green salsa, made entirely from Mesilla Valley jalapeños. Chope's will oblige those who insist on maximum heat by offering special four-alarm chile in a bowl or on enchiladas. The chilecentric menu also includes gorditas, tacos, plates of chile con carne, tamales, and green chile-draped cheeseburgers.

DURAN CENTRAL PHARMACY

durancentralpharmacy.com
1815 Central NW   505-247-4141
Albuquerque, NM   B L | $

One of our favorite views in the scenery-rich Southwest is from a stool at the lunch counter in Duran Central Pharmacy. To the right is the kitchen, where you can view one of the staff using a dowel to roll out rounds of dough into broad flour tortillas that are perfect tan circles. Straight ahead is the grill where they are cooked. To see them puff up from the heat and blister golden-brown, then to smell the warm, bready aroma filling the air, is to know for certain that good food is on its way.

These superlative tortillas, available plain or glistening with butter, come on the side of most lunches, including the wondrous Thursday-only *carne adovada*. They are used to wrap hamburgers and as the base of quesadillas. We like them best as a dunk for Duran's red or green chile, which is available either plain (nothing but chiles and spice) or loaded with your choice of ground beef, beans, potatoes, or chicken. The green is hugely flavorful, hot and satisfying with an earthy character; the red is pure essence of plant life, liquefied with a full measure of sunshine.

Duran, by the way, is a full-service pharmacy.

★ FRONTIER

frontierrestaurant.com
2400 Central SE   505-266-0550
Albuquerque, NM   (5 a.m.–1 a.m. daily) | $

—— ★ —— The Frontier boasts that it is
OPEN EARLY AND LATE "home of the latest in broiled food
—— ★ —— and the Frontier sweet roll." We're not up on broiled food trends, and the famous Frontier sweet roll, while awesomely sized, is not on our top ten list. Nevertheless, we love this place—not only because it is cheap, informal, and open twenty-one hours a day, but because the New Mexican food is first-rate.

At breakfast, huevos rancheros are available with a choice of four toppings: salsa, green chile stew, red chile, and green chile. The last one is the hottest, with a full-tilt chile punch, giving the plate a roasted, earthy aroma that is insanely appetizing. Cheddar cheese should not be left out of this big platter that looks like a mess but eats like a dream. On the side comes a puffy, just-cooked flour tortilla (you can watch the man make them behind the counter) that is almost too hot to handle. Orange juice is fresh-squeezed. Quart carafes of coffee are available for $2.

The lunch menu includes such Land of Enchantment specialties as a *carne adovada* burrito, green chile stew, and, naturally, a chile cheeseburger, here dubbed the Fiesta Burger. Homemade lemonade is available to drink.

One thing that makes dining at the Frontier fun is its breakneck pace. Because meals are ordered fast, cooked fast, and served instantaneously, you are guaranteed that things that are supposed to be hot are piping hot; we've gotten hamburgers still sizzling from the grill. Although many customers linger over coffee, it is possible to be in and out, with a good meal under your belt, in five minutes. The system is serve-yourself. While you wait in line, study the overhead menu and make your decision. When the green light flashes, indicating someone is ready to take your order, step up to the counter and say what you want. Approximately two minutes later, you are carrying your meal to an open table.

GARCIA'S KITCHEN
garciaskitchen.com

1113 4th St. NW
Albuquerque, NM

505-247-9149
B L D | $

Garcia's Kitchen has been around since 1975 and there now are seven locations in Albuquerque. All are bright and gay, from Fiestaware dishes to colorful murals on inside and outside walls. The menu is big, including such New Mexico signature dishes as blue corn enchiladas, green chile cheeseburgers, and stuffed sopaipillas. There are Tex-Mex chili con carne and true-Mex *menudo,* as well as a full array of burritos available "chili in," "chili and cheese over," or "smothered."

Whatever else you get, we highly recommend a bowl of *chicharrones,* which are a bacon lover's fantasy: whole nuggets of crisp fried pork rind that are about half-meat, half-fat—unbelievably delicious when eaten still melt-in-the-mouth warm, still irresistible as we devoured the last of them at the end of the meal, appetite only a memory but taste buds still ravening. It was especially fun to tear off a small piece of sopaipilla, insert a single *chicharrone,* then drizzle on some honey: sweet, wheat, and meat all in one!

Glorious *carne adovada:* hunks of pork saturated with sunny chile flavor and bathed in red purée—so much purée that the yolks of two sunnyside-up eggs on the plate barely poke up through the chile. On the side come good fried potatoes and lard-rich refritos. Huevos rancheros is an equally overabundant plateful. You get your choice of red or green chile; say "Christmas" and you get both—two soupy brews that magically arrive perfectly separated on the plate but then swirl together as soon as you attack with a fork. A huge breakfast burrito is available similarly dressed.

GOLDEN CROWN PANADERIA
goldencrown.biz

1103 Mountain Rd. NW
Albuquerque, NM

505-243-2424
B L D (closed Mon) | $

Not far from Albuquerque's Old Town, the Golden Crown is a full-service bakery making everything from *biscochitos* cookies (the official state cookie of New Mexico) to bread loaves shaped like turkeys. Artisan pizzas are available on regular "peasant dough" or on a New Mexico green chile crust. The toppings roster includes green chiles and jalapeños.

Aside from fascinating pizza, must-try breadstuffs include green chile bread. It is made with bits of tomato, green onions, cilantro, grated cheese, and ribbons of smoke-scented roasted green chile pods. Hot stuff . . . but not ferocious. Chris Ayers and Amy Breisch of Roadfood.com said that this bread, toasted and buttered, is so good that "time may actually stand still."

Other menu notables: fruit-filled empanadas, sugary flautas, and cinnamon-sugared tostadas.

★ LA POSTA DE MESILLA
laposta-de-mesilla.com

2410 Calle de San Albino
Old Mesilla, NM

505-524-3524
B L D | $$

La Posta is one of the grand old Mexican-American restaurants of the Southwest. Opened in 1939 by Katie Griggs, and now run by her descendants, it is a sprawling, multiroom place that attracts a lot of tourists and is well worth the trip for anyone with a hankering for authentic regional food.

When we say authentic, we mean *tostadas compuestas,* a dish that became a standard throughout the Southwest after it was invented here. It is a crisp-fried corn tortilla cup into which is ladled red chili con carne, beans, cheese, lettuce, and tomato. Other expertly made native dishes include folded and rolled tacos, flautas, green chile enchiladas, sunset-hued *carne adovada,* and steak smothered in green chile and melted cheese. No matter what you order, you will get a basket full of warm sopaipillas for mopping up every last good bit of food off the plate.

MODEL PHARMACY

modelpharmacy.com

3636 Monte Vista
Blvd. NE
Albuquerque, NM

505-255-8686

L (closed Sun) | $

You enter this neighborhood pharmacy past the drug counter, navigate among perfumes, soaps, and sundries, then find the little lunch area: a few tables and a short marble counter with a Pueblo-deco knee guard of colorful enamel tiles. If you are like us, your attention will be drawn to the right of the counter, where the cobblers are displayed under a spotlight. Three or four are made every day—geological-looking strata of flaky crust atop syrupy tender hunks of apricot, peach, blackberry, or a mix thereof—and they are available warm or with a globe of ice cream melting on top.

The soda fountain is impressive: a fully stocked armory of milk-shake mixers, syrup dispensers, and soda nozzles, plus a modern espresso machine (so you can get an espresso milk shake—mmm). As for lunchtime entrees, locals love the walnut chicken salad, and some come to eat hamburgers and cold-cut sandwiches, but we'll choose green chile stew every time. It is more a soup, actually, chockfull of carrots, tomatoes, and bits of green chile with good flavor and alarming heat.

NELLIE'S

1226 W. Hadley Ave.
Las Cruces, NM

575-524-9982

B L | $

Inside this snug, cozy cinder-block and glass-brick restaurant, a sign on the wall clearly declares the kitchen's priorities: "A day without chile is like a day without sunshine." Danny Ray Hernandez, Nellie's son, makes vivid salsas using five to seven different types of chile and specializes in such eye-opening breakfasts as huevos à la Mexicana (scrambled with jalapeños) and eggs with chile and meat. For the latter you can get red or green or the combination of both, known as Christmas. The red tastes of pure pod; the green is hot enough to require tongue-tamping with the kitchen's pulchritudinous sopaipillas.

Years ago, Nellie's and its offspring, Little Nellie's Chile Factory, served dinner. Today it is strictly a breakfast-and-lunch eatery.

NOPALITO

nopalitorestaurants.com

310 S. Mesquite St.
Las Cruces, NM

575-524-0003

L D (closed Wed) | $

Las Cruces is in the heart of chile-growing country and Nopalito is a family-run restaurant (actually two restaurants; the other is at 2605 Missouri Avenue) where you can count on excellent chile-based food. It is neither Tex-Mex nor Arizona-Mex nor California-Mex nor Sonoran Mex but the unique cuisine of New Mexico. That means that nearly every meal poses the question: red or green chile? There is no rule about which is hotter. The day we came to Nopalito (which means "little cactus"), the waitress assured us that green was the hot stuff but that red was more delicious. What to do? "Christmas!" she replied, which is the term for a dish topped with both.

Before the main course come crisp, warm tortilla chips and a set of salsas, red and green. The green is served hot (temperature-wise), but is fairly mild. The red is served cool but is very, very hot. To tamp down tongue fires, there's practically nothing better than a tall glass of the rice milk drink called *horchata*. Nopalito's is smooth and just-right sweet.

The building that houses Nopalito originally was built as a church. Its mission décor and spacious dining room provide a broad, comfortable environment well suited for quiet contemplation of commendable local food.

OWL BAR & CAFE

77 Hwy. 380
San Antonio, NM

575-835-9946

B L D | $

The Owl Bar is a watering hole to which many customers come first thing in the morning to start their day with cans of Bud. It also just might be the place where the green chile cheeseburger was invented. The story is that when the atom bomb was being tested at nearby White Sands, scientists would repair here for after-work drinks and thermonuclearly hot hamburgers. Whether or not that's true, the Owl Bar's green chile cheeseburger is a good one, built upon a crusty patty of beef covered with only moderately hot chopped green chiles, then bright orange cheese that melts down to blanket everything. Raw onion, lettuce, tomato, and pickle chips are the standard-issue condiments. Monomaniacal chiliheads can accompany their GCCB with a plate of French fries smothered with chopped green chiles.

PLAZA CAFE

thefamousplazacafe.com

54 Lincoln Ave.   505-982-1664
Santa Fe, NM   **B L D | $**

Although many of the businesses that now surround Santa Fe's plaza are trendy and high-priced, the Plaza Cafe, established in 1905, is what it's been all along— a three-meal-a-day town café frequented by locals as well as travelers, who come for dishes that range from American cheeseburgers to Greek souvlaki to New Mexican green chile stew. The sopaipillas that come with the stew are hot from the fry kettle, perhaps the best in town, and please have the quesadilla, a griddled tortilla sandwich filled with soft, shredded pork and little nuggets of caramelized garlic.

RANCHO DE CHIMAYÓ

ranchodechimayo.com

300 Juan Medina Rd.   505-351-4444
Chimayó, NM   **L D | $$**

--★--
HOT
TICKET
--★--
In the 1970s, when we pondered the feasibility of a guide to restaurants that serve great regional food around America, our first dinner at Rancho de Chimayó was strong persuasion to proceed. Here was—and continues to be—a fount of New Mexican fare at its finest, served in a setting that is nothing less than magical. Candlelit tables are arrayed on a stepped patio outdoors, strolling guitarists strum Southwestern tunes, and the air smells of sagebrush and native cooking.

New Mexicans seldom sit down for a "bowl of chili," but there are few dishes here in which the chile pepper doesn't play a vital role, foremost among them *carne adovada*, which is pork marinated in chile purée and sizzled until it glistens red. The marinade turns it tender, and its pepper heat is balanced by a serving of posole (hominy corn). For something less incendiary, consider sopaipillas rellenos, in which the triangular fried breads are stuffed with beef, beans, tomatoes, and Spanish rice, and topped with red or green chile sauce. There are flautas too—rolled corn tortillas filled with chicken or pork and fried crisp, topped with cool sour cream.

The drive to Rancho de Chimayó through the foothills of the Sangre de Christo Mountains in the cool of an autumn evening is a Roadfood trip to remember. Chile *ristras* (wreaths) decorate adobe homes, and late-day light makes sagebrush shimmer.

ROQUE'S CARNITAS

San Francisco St. & Old   No phone
Santa Fe Tr.,   **L** (closed in winter) | $
on the Plaza
Santa Fe, NM

Roque's is a jolly little chuckwagon that serves a sandwich folded inside a sturdy flour tortilla that has been heated on a grate over a charcoal fire. Inside the warm tortilla is succulent beef, and plenty of it—top round steak thinly sliced and marinated, sizzled on a grate along with onions, chiles, and fiery jalapeño salsa. As soon as you peel back the foil and try to gather up the tortilla for eating, chunks of salsa tumble out, meat juice leaks, onions slither, and plump circles of earth-green chile pepper pop free. In the past, customers dined standing over open garbage cans to catch the spillage, but recently Roque has started bringing little yellow stools where people can sit and take advantage of having a lap to catch all that drops. There also are dining facilities in the form of park benches in the Plaza.

If you are allergic to beef, chicken carnitas are available, as are green chile-cheese tamales (vegetarian) and pork red chile tamales.

SAN MARCOS CAFE

3877 NM 14   505-471-9298
Cerrillos, NM   **B L | $**

The San Marcos Cafe is a popular destination eatery and feed store that is a convenient stop for folks on their way to Cerrillos or Madrid. Cinnamon rolls are taller than they are wide, and rather than being dense and doughy like so many others, they are lightweight, almost croissant-like in character. Other dandy breakfast items are "eggs San Marcos," which is a large serving of scrambled eggs wrapped inside a tortilla and sided by beans, chili, and guacamole under a mantle of melted cheese; biscuits topped with spicy sausage gravy; and *machaca* (beef and eggs with pico de gallo).

A cozy, charming ranch house decorated in country-kitchen style (old enameled stoves, wooden cupboards, knickknacks galore), the café also happens to be a veritable bird jungle. Peacocks and peahens, wild turkeys, and roosters all cavort around the front and back, and while they are not allowed inside the restaurant, there are pictures of the most famous chicken of them all, a leghorn rooster named Buddy who served long tenure as unofficial maître d'. Dressed in black tie, Buddy cheerfully greeted guests and crowed through the breakfast hour. Years ago, when Buddy passed away, customers mourned. Although a few other roosters have been named to take his place, none has ever shown the people skills that Buddy had.

★ SANTA FE BITE

santafebite.com
311 Old Santa Fe Trail   505-982-0544
Santa Fe, NM   **B** (Sat & Sun only) **L**
                             D (closed Mon) | **$**

A measure of neon roadside charm was lost when John and Bonnie Eckre moved from their old roadhouse at the edge of Santa Fe to Garrett's Desert Inn, but the green chile cheeseburger that put Bobcat Bite in the firmament of brilliant Roadfood is as good as ever—maybe the best burger of any kind, anywhere.

While some hash slingers put chiles on top of cheese to make green chile cheeseburgers, Santa Fe Bite secrets a lode of sunshine-flavored chopped chile underneath the cheese. The creamy cheese melts among the peppers and into the crevices of the crusty, juice-laden burger down below to create a beef-heat-dairy fusion that is pure Land of Enchantment. It's an impressive hunk of meat, ten ounces of freshly ground chuck and sirloin, set into a tall-domed bakery bun able to absorb the inevitable flood of savory juices. Burger nirvana!

SPARKY'S

sparkysburgers.com
115 Franklin St.   575-267-4222
Hatch, NM   **L D** (Thurs–Sun) | **$**

Sparky's is loud, both figuratively (wild, crazy pop-culture signage) and literally (live music in the Green Chile Room). It is a coffeehouse with a wide array of espresso drinks, a soda fountain (green chile shake, anyone?), a barbecue parlor that slow-cooks both pork and beef the slow old-fashioned way, and—dearest to our hearts—home of a fine green chile cheeseburger. The heart of the burger is a seven-ounce patty that is juicy enough to completely disintegrate the bun bottom on which it sits—a delicious situation made even messier if you get the outlandish double green chile cheeseburger. The hot Hatch chiles topping the burger have a woodsy twist that is well complemented by lavish amounts of orange cheese.

If a green chile milk shake (or normal-flavored milk shake) or coffee drink is not what you want to drink, Sparky's also offers freshly squeezed lemonade and, of course, green chile lemonade. Hatch, after all, has proclaimed itself the Chile Capital of the World.

SUGAR'S

1799 State Rd. 68   505-852-0604
Embudo, NM   **L D** (Thurs–Sun) | **$**

Fusion cuisine: Texas and New Mexico. The Texas part is brisket: thick flaps of juice-heavy beef so painfully tender that they fall apart when handled, pervaded by sweet smoke and rimmed with an edge that is blackened, crisp, and succulent. The New Mexico contribution is roasted green chiles with sunny flavor and the kick of capsicum. Intertwine these two items with cheese that melts because of the meat's heat and roll them inside a soft, flaky flour tortilla and you have a magically delicious burrito that is a prototypical wrap.

Eat this superb sandwich at a picnic table adjoining the tin-sided trailer that is Sugar's kitchen, or ensconced in your vehicle. There are no indoor seats at this remote Land of Enchantment gem. Sugar, by the way, was a bulldog bitch whose progeny you might see in the yard to the left of the tin trailer. Sugar's picture adorns the wall-mounted menu, which is a roadside roster of burgers and green chile cheeseburgers, corn dogs, burritos, and of course, Fritos pie.

TECOLOTE

tecolotecafe.com

1616 St. Michaels Dr.   505-988-1362
Santa Fe, NM   **B L** (closed Mon) | **$$**

Santa Fe has many places that serve good breakfast. Breakfast is Tecolote's raison d'être. Our favorite thing to eat is pancakes made with blue cornmeal and studded with roasted piñon nuts. Pale blue inside with a faintly crusty exterior from the grill, each cake is ethereally fluffy, and gosh, what joy it is to bite into a little lode of those roasty-rich nuts! There are blueberry pancakes too, made with a similar, from-scratch batter, Toll House chocolate chip pancakes, fresh strawberry pancakes, and plain ones that are anything but plain—each available singly, as a short stack (two), or a full stack (three).

Of course, there are omelets galore and eggs of every kind, including shirred on a bed of chicken livers; as the crown of corned beef hash; rancheros-style—fried on a corn tortilla smothered in red or green chile and topped (at your request) with cheese. One nontraditional meal we hold dear at Tecolote is a gallimaufry called "sheepherder's breakfast"—new potatoes boiled with jalapeño peppers and onion, cooked on a grill until crusty-brown, then topped with two kinds of chile and melted Cheddar cheese.

OKLAHOMA

CANCUN

eatatcancun.com

705 S. Lewis Ave.   918-583-8089
Tulsa, OK   **L D** (closed Weds) | **$$**

Cancun is a neighborhood Mexican restaurant where English is a second language. It is a welcoming little place with a handful of tables, those along the front window offering a view of the bumpers of cars in the parking lot. We plowed into a super burrito stuffed with carnitas (shredded pork), rice, and beans; smothered with shredded cheese and warm salsa; and decorated with dabs of sour cream and guacamole. It's a grand meal, the savory roast pork packing heaps of flavor. On the side you can have *horchata*, the cool, sweet rice beverage that is so refreshing with spicy food; Jarritos-brand mandarin orange soda; or, of course, beer.

The menu is frustrating for anyone with time for only a single meal. Beyond the big burrito, choices include tacos filled with a wide range of ingredients from spicy pork to tongue, cheek meat, tripe, fish, chicken, and goat. Other temptations: enchiladas, chile verde and chili Colorado, fajitas, and chimichangas. Seafood specialties include *camarones al Tequila* (shrimp with green salsa and tequila) and *pescado frito* (whole fried fish).

CATTLEMEN'S STEAKHOUSE

cattlemensrestaurant.com

1309 S. Agnew Ave.   405-236-0416
Oklahoma City, OK   **B L D** | **$$**

The neon sign outside says "Cattlemen's Cafe," and yes, indeed, this is the café to which people who work in and around the Oklahoma stockyards come for a 6 a.m. breakfast of calf brains and eggs (or, of course, steak and eggs). It is also a top-end steak house, serving some of the best cuts of beef you will find in the West. Top-of-the-line is a big, boneless prime sirloin that comes from the kitchen alone on a white crockery plate, surrounded only by a puddle of its translucent pan juice. It is charred on the outside, but not drastically so, and you can see by its glistening, pillowy form—higher in the center than around the rim—that this hefty slab has been seared over a hot flame. Cattlemen's provides each customer a wood-handled knife with a serrated blade. The blade eases through the meat's crust and down into its warm red center—medium-rare, exactly as requested.

If you are an adventurous eater, you probably want to know that Cattlemen's makes a specialty of lamb fries—that is, nuggets of deep-fried testicle. They are served as an appetizer: a mound of them on a plate with a bowl of cocktail sauce for dipping and half a lemon to squeeze on top. They are earthy-tasting inside their golden crust, the exquisite organ meat quivery and moist, with nut-sweet savor.

While you easily can spend $50 on a steak dinner, lunch can be one-quarter of that price. We like the steak burger in particular. It is juicy and radiant with big beef flavor. Dinner patrons tend to be a dress-up group, but the crowd at lunch is a mix of ranchers in $1,000 beaver hats and fancy boots, huge blue-collar guys in overalls, and skinny blue-haired ladies out with their friends.

CLANTON'S

clantonscafe.com

319 E. Illinois Ave.   918-256-9053
Vinita, OK   B L D | $

Clanton's makes its chicken-fried steak by dipping a well-tenderized cube steak in a mixture of egg and buttermilk, then dredging it once and only once (any more and you will smother the beef with crust). Cooked in vegetable oil until crisp and palomino gold, it is tender enough that a knife is superfluous. The edge of a fork is all you need to sever a mouthful. With the steak comes a globe of mashed potatoes smothered with peppery cream gravy and a side of palate-refreshing coleslaw. There are many other good things on Clanton's menu—we love the chicken and sage dressing, but whatever else you eat, save room for pie: chocolate cream, coconut cream, or banana cream, all poised atop the most fragile foundation of crust.

Route 66 sightseers often find their way to Clanton's, which is one of the oldest continuously operating restaurants along the old Mother Road. (It's not the original building, though. That burned down and was rebuilt.) When Sweet Tater Clanton opened for business in 1927, most of the highway was not yet paved, and it is said that to attract customers Mr. Clanton used to walk out the front door and bang a pot and pan together when he spied someone about to drive past.

CLASSEN GRILL

okcmexicanrestaurant.com

5124 Classen Cir.   405-252-1322
Oklahoma City, OK   B L | $

We love to start the day at Classen Grill with a glass of fresh-squeezed orange juice and a plate of *migas*, the Mexican egg scramble that includes strips of tortilla, chunks of tomato, nuggets of sausage, and a mantle of melting shredded cheese. Chinook eggs are salmon patties topped with poached eggs and accompanied by a block of cheese grits. Taquitas are tortilla-wrapped packets of eggs, cheese, and vegetables. The chicken-fried steak is nearly as big as its plate. It is tender enough that the knife provided seems irrelevant. When we arrive with insatiable appetites, we go for "biscuits debris"—two big ones split open and smothered with gravy chockablock with ham and sausage chunks, cloaked with melted Cheddar cheese.

On the side of breakfast, enjoy significant potatoes—either home fries or the specialty known as Classen Grill potatoes, which are mashed, seasoned with garlic and rolled into little balls, then deep-fried until brittle gold on the outside. The result is a kind of prairie knish—but not so heavy.

The place is an ultra-casual, one-room café with paintings of fruit and other gastronomical items posted on its pink stucco walls. Early during Sunday breakfast, nearly half the customers sit at tables reading the morning paper while leisurely enjoying their meals. By brunchtime, the place is too crowded for casual reading.

CONEY I-LANDER

coneyi-lander.com

7462 E. Admiral Pl.   918-836-2336
Tulsa, OK   L D | $

Dating back to 1926, Tulsa's Coney I-Lander (of which there are a few outlets in the city) is among the nation's first Coney Island restaurants, specializing in plump little hot dogs in steamed buns, dressed with mustard, onions, and a finely ground, elaborately spiced, but ultimately mild meat sauce. At some point in hot dog history, shredded orange cheese became a popular addition, and here in Tulsa, many folks get theirs with a sprinkle of cayenne pepper. The dogs are small enough so that one or two are a snack, four or six a meal. It is not uncommon to see a runner from a nearby business walk out with dozens to take back for lunch with colleagues.

Ambience is fluorescent-light divey. Service is immediate. The menu is minimal. Coney I-Lander's one dandy alternative to a hot dog is the Southwest's beloved hot lunch, a Fritos pie.

COUNTRY DOVE TEA ROOM

610 W. 3rd St.   580-225-7028
Elk City, OK   **L** (closed Sun) | **$**

The recognized glories of Oklahoma cuisine tend to be rugged, manly, and beef-centric. Country Dove Tea Room is something else. A charming little destination, it is an opportunity to enjoy heartwarming examples of that bygone genre known as ladies' lunch, served with grace and good manners in an old country home. Creamed soups are accompanied by heart-shaped muffins and honey butter; little squares of Jell-O are known here as "Jell-O salad," presented on a lettuce leaf. The house specialty is chicken-avocado salad, which is the two elements pulverized together with mayonnaise and served on either a croissant or grilled wheat bun.

It is such a nice, polite repertoire of dishes . . . until you get to dessert and French silk pie, which is a powerhouse: lasciviously chocolaty, smooth, dense, topped with a frothy ribbon of whipped cream and mounted on a plush nut crust. Proprietors Glenna Hollis and Kay Farmer, who opened the tearoom over a quarter century ago, blush when they recall the author who came through many years back and later wrote that he wasn't sure if he should eat the pie or smear it all over his body.

Glenna and Kay are kind hosts who made us feel like we had come to a family reunion. They delighted in showing off their kitchen, which is little more than the original home kitchen, including the four-burner electric stove. Beyond two small dining rooms, the first and second stories of the house serve as a Christian bookstore and country décor emporium.

DINK'S PIT BAR-B-QUE
dinksbbq.com

2929 E. Frank Phillips   918-335-0606
Blvd.   **L D** | **$$**
Bartlesville, OK

Dink's barbecue selection is broad. Hickory-cooked pig dinners (pork loin), ham, turkey, chicken, sausage, spare ribs, brisket, and back ribs all are available, and while the menu advises that brisket is the specialty, we like pork better. The brisket can be dry—not a horrible problem, considering that Dink's red-orange sauce beautifully revives it and adds a welcome tangy punch. The spare ribs were so good that we left only bare bones on the plate, and the pig dinner is succulence squared. Each dinner comes with a choice of two side dishes from a roster that includes baked beans, fried okra, pinto beans, green beans, coleslaw, curly-Q fries, baked potato, potato salad, and cottage cheese, plus bread, pickles, green onion, and sauce.

A Bartlesville fixture since 1982, Dink's is a family-friendly, multiroom establishment with buckaroo décor: steer horns, pictures of hunters, cowboys, and Indians, and displays of the "Barbed Wire that Fenced the West."

A second Dink's in Bentonville, Arkansas, is at 3404 Macy Road (479-657-6264).

EISCHEN'S BAR
eischensbar.com

109 S. 2nd Ave.   405-263-9939
Okarche, OK   **L D** (closed Sun) | **$$**

--★--
LOCALS
LOVE IT
--★--

Opened in 1896 and touted as the state's oldest bar, Eischen's is a Wild West destination a half hour northwest of Oklahoma City. The brick-front bar is patronized by locals at lunch and is almost always crowded with pilgrims at suppertime, especially weekend nights when it is not uncommon for strangers to share the big tables in the back dining room. Everybody comes for fried chicken of succulent meat and bacon-rich skin that is made to be eaten by hand (plates and silverware are nonexistent). The chicken comes with pickles, onions, and bread as well as fried okra. The beverage of choice is cold beer from the tap. The only other thing on the menu is chili-cheese nachos, another no-utensil food.

Classic road-trip tunes blare from the jukebox, and when you wait for a seat, avail yourself of one of two available pool tables to pass the time.

Business is cash only.

FREDDIE'S HAMBURGERS

802 S. Lewis Ave.   918-585-3544
Tulsa, OK   **L D** (closed Sun) | $

The complex of condiments, the audacity of magnitude, and the quotient of fat in Freddie's bunned hamburgers put all the national chains to shame. You don't have to get the Double Jumbo, which is a pair of one-third-pound patties, to see what we mean. Take the Double Deluxe basket: two quarter-pound patties that are dripping cheese, garlanded with a bouquet of lettuce, tomatoes, pickles, fresh onions, fried onions, and mustard (plus mayonnaise if requested), all stacked in a soft, oversized bun. It is a challenge to one's burger-handling skills. When you first pick it up, you instantly become aware of just how tender and pliable the bun is—a wonderful textural note in the whole package. But its very feel foreshadows catastrophe: The glistening patties want to slide out whichever side of the bun your fingers aren't gripping, lettuce shreds start to fall, pickles and onions slip and squiggle, mayo oozes. It is an outstanding burger-eating adventure, one of the best in Tulsa, which is one of Oklahoma's several nuclei of hamburger greatness.

The place itself has personality to spare. At first glance, it looks a bit disreputable and, indeed, the counter in the front room does tend to attract fringy types; counter seats also guarantee that you will smell of grilling beef and onions for hours afterward. But around to the right are a series of little dining rooms—spare places that double as storage areas—where tables and chairs are set up for a more gracious mealtime experience. Here we saw nice couples and families downing the mighty burgers (and also Fritos pies and Coney dogs). "Delicious as usual!" chirped one white-haired granny as she and a couple

generations of her family exited, politely returning their emptied plastic baskets to the burger makers up front.

HAMBURGER KING

322 E. Main   405-878-0488
Shawnee, OK   **L D** (closed Sun) | $

We love the look of this 1927 lunchroom with its tall ceiling and long rows of tables, each equipped with a direct phone line to the open kitchen. The menu refers to this as the "electronic order system." On the walls are pictures that show the history of Oklahoma in general and Hamburger King in particular, the show-stopper being a blown-up photo of founder George Macsas flanked by King of Western Swing Bob Wills and movie star Jack Hoxie. Wills once wrote a song to celebrate his favorite eatery:

> When you're feelin' blue, and hungry too
> Here's a tip to make you sing.
> Pick up your hat, close your flat
> Go down to the Hamburger King.

Right up front behind the counter and cash register where broad, medium-thick burger patties sizzle on the grill, you can watch each one being assembled by a cook skillful enough to bun, dress, and garnish one faster than it takes to name its components. The result is a classic lunch-counter hamburger: not too thick, not thin, oily enough to flavor the bun with juice, crusty enough to provide textural contrast to the lettuce, tomato, and pickle on top.

HAMMETT HOUSE

hammetthouse.com
1616 W. Will Rogers   918-341-7333
Blvd.   **L D** (closed Mon) | $
Claremore, OK

Thanks to intrepid Roadfooders Howard Baratz, Cliff Strutz, and Cousin Johnnie for clueing us in to the pies at Hammett House. In Cliff's words, the banana cream pie "had wonderful real banana flavor, plus lots of small cut-up bits of banana. The filling was thick but still airy and just about the perfect texture. All housed in a buttery, flaky crust: a high-quality slice of pie." As for peanut butter chocolate chip, Cliff described it as "smooth, airy, with strong peanut butter flavor"; sour cream raisin pie struck "that perfect balance between the sweet and sour"; and buttermilk chess ("the best of the best") was "soft [with] buttermilk tang, plus a strong cinnamon taste."

Other choices in the pie repertoire include coconut cream (Hammett House's bestseller), chocolate cream, lemon pecan, and sour cream cherry. But suppose you are in the mood for something pre-pie? Chili is available with and without beans; "pamper-fried" chicken, served with cream gravy, is a specialty; and testicle lovers have their choice of lamb fries or turkey fries or a combo plate of both. There are steaks and chops and sandwiches and salads and a menu of half-pound hamburgers, plus child-sized sliders.

Last we looked, Wednesday was cinnamon roll day. The first hundred customers in the door after opening at 11 a.m. get one free.

HANK'S HAMBURGERS

8933 E. Admiral Pl.   918-832-1509
Tulsa, OK   L D (Tue–Fri) | $

Burger central: have a single, a double, a triple, a Big Okie (four patties), or a Hank's Burger, which is a single half-pound patty. While the heft of a Hank's Burger is impressive, we prefer the multiple-patty configurations. The interleaved meat and cheese provide a textural adventure that a large single patty cannot. Standard condiments are mustard, pickle, grilled onion, raw onion, lettuce, and tomatoes.

Hank's is a tiny place with just a few booths around the counter, which is high enough that no seat affords a good view of Mr. Felts, chef and owner, orchestrating events at the griddle. We recommend standing up, or going to the walk-up to-go window at the front, because watching him create his burgers is short-order ballet. Onions are pressed hard onto the surface of each patty before it hits the hot surface so that as the burger cooks under a heavy iron, the onions caramelize and virtually become one with the hamburger itself. When the iron is lifted and the burger is flipped, Felts sprinkles on some of his secret seasoning, then cheese. If he is creating a double, triple, or quadruple, he applies the bun top to one patty, uses a spatula to lift it onto another, and so forth until the pile is ready to be placed onto the bottom half of the bun, which has been arrayed with all other condiments.

"Please allow us a few minutes to prepare your order for you because we don't cook ahead," the menu asks. "Please call early and tell us what time you would like your order. We will try our BEST to have it ready for you right on time and FRESH off the grill." A sign above the counter advises, "We will call your name & bring your food to you as fast as possible . . . Hank's a lot."

IKE'S CHILI

ikeschilius.com

1503 E. 11th St.   918-838-9410
Tulsa, OK   L (Mon–Sat) D (Mon–Fri)
                          (closed Sun) | $

According to a 1936 article in the *Tulsa Daily World*, reprinted on the back of Ike's menu, "When the original Ike Johnson established his first modest little 'parlor' down by the old Frisco depot twenty-five years ago, there was no lowlier food than chili. . . . It was openly sneered at by the Social Register and the hot dog was much higher up on the social scale." To this day, chili maintains a plebeian aura, and there's no better place to savor that aura, and a classic bowl of chili con carne, than Ike's. We thank Tulsan Jim Oakley for tipping us off to this excellent Southwestern chili parlor.

Made from a recipe supposedly secured from a Hispanic Texas employee named Alex Garcia, Ike's chili is a viscous dish of ground beef and a peppery jumble of spice. It comes plain in a bowl, with spaghetti noodles, or three-way, meaning with noodles and beans. Cheese, jalapeño peppers, and onions are extra-cost options, but even a double three-way with everything is scarcely more than five dollars. Chili is also the star of Ike's Fritos pie and Coney dog, described as being built upon a "large Oscar Meyer."

JIGG'S SMOKEHOUSE

jiggssmokehouse.com

Exit 62 off I-40   580-323-5641
Clinton, OK   **L** (Tues–Sat) | **$**

Jigg's beef jerky is one tough chaw, and that's the way it is supposed to be. Slices of loin as big as a handkerchief are desiccated in a dry mix of brown sugar, garlic, and cayenne pepper, then slow-smoked over coarse-ground hickory sawdust for up to twenty-four hours. The result? Gnarled burnt-sienna-colored patches that pack a resounding harmony of beef, pepper, and smoke. Chew, chew, chew: The waves of flavor are relentless.

Unlike the mighty jerky, Jigg's barbecue is tenderness incarnate, although some of the specialty sandwiches are a real challenge to eat. The Wooly Burger, for example: thirty-one ounces of smoked ham and summer sausage, Cheddar cheese, chow-chow relish, mayonnaise, and barbecue sauce. The menu calls it "2 lbs of fun!!!" Jigg's pigsickles, which are slabs of rib meat (no bones) with Cheddar cheese and sauce, come as doubles and triples. Normal-sized sandwiches also are available; sausage and beef brisket are exemplary. Sides are beans, potato salad, and potato chips.

Accommodations in the weather-beaten Okie snack shack include a front porch where you can sit in the shade and interior dining rooms decorated with countless business cards, portraits of meat-eating heroes John Wayne and Marty Robbins, and—noted on a recent visit—a Christmas wreath made of green and red shotgun shells.

JOHNNIE'S

301 S. Rock Island Ave.   405-262-4721
El Reno, OK   **B L D** | **$**

A sphere of beef is slapped onto a hot griddle. Onto the beef goes a fistful of ultrathin-sliced yellow onions—about the same cubage as the beef. The grill man uses a spatula to flatten the onions and the meat together, creating a broad circular patty with an uneven edge; he presses down three or four times, slightly changing the angle of attack with each press, and pressing only one-half to two-thirds of the patty each time. The ribbons of onion get mashed deep into the top of the soft, raw meat, which assumes a craggy surface because of the uneven, overlapping use of the spatula. Once the underside is cooked, the burger is flipped. The air around the grill clouds with the sweet steam of sizzling onions. After another few minutes, the hamburger is scooped off the grill with all the darkened caramelized onions that have become part of it, and it is put on a bun, onion side up. Lettuce, tomato, mustard, and pickles are all optional if you like them, but no condiment is necessary to enhance this simple, savory creation.

Johnnie's also makes a great El Reno–style Coney Island hot dog, topped with meaty chili and a strange, soupy slaw that local epicures hold dear. (Some customers get this slaw on their burger too.) We also like breakfast at Johnnie's, when the little place is packed with locals eating Arkansas sandwiches (that's a pair of pancakes layered with a pair of eggs) and all-you-can-eat platters of biscuits and gravy. It was at breakfast one day that we decided we had to stick around El Reno for a midmorning pie-break, for as we were finishing our coffee, in walked Everett Adams, Johnnie's baker, wedging his way through the thirty-seat restaurant toting a battered tray above his head on which were set the coconut meringue pies and Boston cream pie he had made that morning for the lunch crowd.

KUMBACK LUNCH

625 Delaware St.   580-336-4646
Perry, OK   **B L D** (closed Sun) | **$**

Kumback Lunch was founded in 1926 in a town created by the 1893 Cherokee Strip land run. Its walls
are covered with pictures and memorabilia of "Perry
Heroes," including local athletes, several governors
of the state, and Oklahoma Highway Patrol officer
Charlie Hanger, who captured Oklahoma City bomber
Timothy McVeigh and brought him to the county jail
in Perry.

History and beautiful art deco façade aside,
Kumback Lunch is a swell place to eat. And everyone
in the town of Perry (and beyond) seems to know
that fact, because the place always is crowded with
happy eaters and coffee drinkers. For breakfast, we
recommend blueberry and pecan pancakes, swirly
warm cinnamon rolls, biscuits and gravy, egg-stuffed
burritos, and crisp-crusted chicken-fried steak. That
steak also makes a fine lunch or supper, or you can
choose from among a dozen different hamburgers, barbecued ribs and brisket, and a selection of
Mexican meals that includes a baked potato stuffed
with seasoned beef, cheese, and salsa.

LEO'S

3631 N. Kelley Ave.   405-424-5367
Oklahoma City, OK   **L D** (closed Sun) | **$**

Leo's barbecue beef is coarsely hacked so that a portion of it, on a platter or sandwich, contains some
outside chunks with crunchy blackened edges and
others that are soft and dripping natural juice. Sauce
is dark and spicy with a vinegar punch, good not only
on the meat but on the buttery baked potato half that
can be had with sandwiches and entrees. Leo's also
offers magnificently meaty pork ribs, hot links that
are seriously hot, and a locally favored treat, bologna.
Before you dismiss barbecued bologna as a smokehouse aberration, you need to try it here. This is not
bubble-gum-colored supermarket lunch meat; it is a
thick-sliced slab with wicked zest—dense and smoky.
We don't like it better than the beef or ribs, but it *is*
interesting.

Undecided types can order meals that combine
all meats and a couple of side dishes (sweet and porky
beans and cool potato salad are recommended), but
such bet-hedging does run the risk of discovering that
you love the ribs (or links, or brisket) most of all, and
you are getting only a partial portion thereof. Meals
come with dessert: a slice of wonderful frosted yellow
layer cake topped with bananas, strawberries, and a
sweet sugar glaze.

Located in an old gas station, Leo's looks a little
scary, but the people inside are as friendly as can
be. You do need to be careful, though. "Due to high
humidity, please watch your step," a sign on the front
door warns. The humidity, a good portion of which
comes from years' worth of fatty meats cooking over
smoldering coals, makes the floors slick and slippery
the way Arthur Bryant's of Kansas City used to be.

LINDA-MAR DRIVE-IN

1614 W. 51st St.   918-446-6024
Tulsa, OK   **L D** (closed Sun) | **$**

The Andy Griffith Show plays continuously on a TV
in the corner of the dining room, which is decorated
with NASCAR mementoes. The crowning piece of
Americana comes from the kitchen and is known as
the Westsider. Named for the neighborhood in which
this quick-eats joint is located, it is two seared quarter-
pound beef patties, each topped with cheese, served
between a couple of slabs of buttered and grilled-crisp
Texas toast, preferably with the works, which means
chopped lettuce, sliced tomato, grilled onion, mustard, pickle chips, and—if requested—mayonnaise.
It is a two-fisted, fat-glistening sandwich, the kind of
wanton pleasure that anhedonic nutrition prigs abhor
and robust eaters find immensely satisfying.

Bunned singles, doubles, and triples also are
available, as are Fritos pie and Coney dogs. O-rings
and fries are nothing special, but if you are on a
burger-eating mission, Linda-Mar deserves attention.

There is a second location at 5941 E. Admiral
Place (918-933-6360).

THE MEERS STORE

meersstore.com

26005 Hwy. 115   580-429-8051
Lawton, OK   L D (closed Tues–Wed) | $

Tulsa World magazine once declared the hamburger at the Meers Store the best burger in Oklahoma, which is a bold pronouncement. Border to border, Oklahoma is crazy for all kinds of interesting and unusual burgers, including the unique giants—seven inches across—known as Meersburgers.

A Meersburger is special not only for its size but because it is made exclusively from Longhorn cattle that are locally raised. Longhorns are less fatty than usual beef stock and supposedly have less cholesterol than chicken, and yet the meat has a high-flavored succulence. In addition to Meersburgers, Meerscheeseburgers, and Seismic Meersburgers (topped with bacon, cheese, jalapeño peppers, relish, mustard, pickles, tomatoes, onions, and lettuce), the Meers Store has a menu of steak, chicken-fried steak, prime rib, and barbecue, plus a salad bar.

The town itself is a sight. In the southwest corner of the state, it sprung up in the wake of a gold strike in the 1890s but is now populated by exactly six citizens—the Maranto family, who run the Meers Store. The Store is the only open business, located in what was once a mining-camp emporium. Its walls are blanketed with antiques, memorabilia, pictures of famous and not-so-famous customers, and business cards left behind by happy eaters.

MURPHY'S STEAK HOUSE

1625 SW Frank Phillips   918-336-4789
Blvd.   L D | $
Bartlesville, OK

LOCALS LOVE IT What Roadfooder could resist a menu whose motto is "Gravy Over All"? When you tell the waitress you want a hot hamburger, that is what she will ask: "Gravy over all?" The correct answer is yes.

Gravy is what makes Murphy's signature dish, the hot hamburger, special. Nothing like a regular bunned burger, a hot hamburger is in fact more like a Springfield, Illinois, horseshoe sandwich: a real plateload. Its foundation is a couple of slices of toasted white bread. Atop the bread goes a hamburger that's been hacked up into chunks of beef. Atop the deconstructed burger go French fries. And the whole shebang is crowned with a spill of dark, velvety gravy. It's a transcendent combination: crisp logs of fried potato softened where the gravy blankets them, imbibing a rich, beefy savor for which squiggles of onion (an optional component) are an ideal accent. Even people who come for steak get a side dish of fried potatoes with gravy.

Don't let the words "steak house" lead you to think that Murphy's is in any way high-end. It is in fact more like a diner, complete with counter, bare-topped tables, a walk-up window for carry-out orders, and reasonable prices. (A hot hamburger is under $10; a T-bone is under $20.)

NIC'S GRILL

1201 N. Pennsylvania   405-524-0999
Ave.   B L (closed Sat & Sun) | $
Oklahoma City, OK

When Roadfood.com's always-reliable "Wandering-jew" (Dale Fine) took a trip to the Plains states a few years back, he ate many fine meals in Kansas and Oklahoma. He declared the best of them to be a hamburger at Nic's Grill: an "incredibly big, thick, juicy onion burger." He commented, "It's no wonder that Oklahoma is truly the burger belt of our great nation."

It is a gorgeous mess: a raggedy half-pound mass of ground beef, fatty enough to glisten and ooze juice, its edges slightly crisped from the flat-top grill, the whole thing smothered in onions, some of which are translucent and limp, others caramelized amber, a few sizzled to delectable crunchiness. The package (which should include pickle chips and may also be festooned with a couple of slabs of bright orange cheese) is barely contained in a bun that gets steamed soft when placed atop the cooking burger.

Nic's is known, rightly, for its burgers, but it is also a place to have a breakfast of eggs, pancakes, or chicken-fried steak. It is less crowded in the morning (total seats: fifteen), and since it's been featured on TV, it gets mobbed by noon. Burgers are the #1 thing to eat, but regulars also come for daily specials of pork chops on Tuesday, fried chicken on Thursday, and meat loaf on Friday.

ROBERT'S

300 S. Bickford Ave.	405-262-1262
El Reno, OK	B L | $

El Reno is a hub of hamburger culture in Oklahoma, which has a higher hamburger consciousness than any other state. Of its several burger joints, Robert's is the oldest, dating back to 1926, and it is a virtual museum piece—the sort of eatery that makes Route 66 such an interesting trip. The menu does not list an onion-fried burger, but burgers cooked with onions are such a pillar of local gastronomy, that is what you automatically will get: a burger melded with a tangle of caramelized onions. The cook forces the onions right into the patty by squishing them down as the burger sizzles.

In addition to serving what may be the best onion-fried burger in Oklahoma (and therefore the best on Earth), Robert's makes a wicked Coney Island—the El Reno way, of course, which means the chili sauce is topped with a spill of coarse, pickly coleslaw.

ROCK CAFE

rockcafert66.com

114 W. Main St.	918-968-3990
Stroud, OK	B L D | $

The Rock Cafe opened in 1939 when the last stretches of the Oklahoma section of Route 66 were paved. So much of the historic road from Chicago to Los Angeles has vanished, as have the colorful tourist courts, service stations, and short-order diners that once made it a bonanza of highway kitsch, but this solid little restaurant is a vision out of the past. Even a devastating fire in 2008 couldn't keep it down. Left with little more than its four rock walls, proprietor Dawn Welch re-created it once again.

Just as those heavy sandstone walls endured the fire, so did the café's original grill, named Betsy, which cook and proprietor Dawn Welch describes as having been "seasoned for eternity." She credits the old grill—one of the very first made by Wolf—with the shattering-crisp crust that hugs her chicken-fried steak as well as with the dripping moistness of the thick ribbon of beef inside. "The moment you put something in a deep fryer [the typical way to make a bad chicken-fried steak], you can see the juice start coming out of it," she says, adding that the traditional version, made with beef, shares the menu with a similar dish, made with pork. Although it sounds similar to the tenderloins popular in the Midwest, this one is thicker and spicier and fathomlessly juicy, sporting a complex bouquet of flavor from its tenure on the venerable grill. Dawn told us that she graces everything possible with a spell on the grill: chili to top burgers, ham for ham and beans, even sauerkraut and spaetzle to accompany the no-beef, all-pork chicken-fried steak.

Dawn says that several years ago a rich woman from New York offered to buy the grill so she could bring it back east with her. The offer was generous, big enough to buy a modern replacement, but Dawn refused what she considered a Faustian bargain. The soul of the Rock Cafe was not for sale.

SID'S

300 S. Choctaw Ave.	405-262-7757
El Reno, OK	B L D (closed Sun) | $

Sid's is one of El Reno's legendary hamburger restaurants, where onion-fried burgers are cooked so that onions mashed into the patty of meat get charred from their time on the grill, giving the sandwich a sweet and smoky zest. Burgers are available regular and king-sized, with cheese, bacon, chili, slaw, lettuce, tomato, and jalapeño peppers. Non–burger eaters get two or three Coney Islands, which are bright-red weenies topped with chili and a superfine slaw that is sweet but also packs mustard punch. Milk shakes are thick enough to require a spoon as well as a straw.

Sid's is noteworthy for its amazing interior décor, which is a virtual museum of El Reno history. Using eleven gallons of clear epoxy to seal some 450 pictures onto the top of the counter and the tops of tables, proprietor Marty Hall has arranged his gallery in chronological order starting at the far left of the restaurant. Here are pictures of the Oklahoma land lotteries and cowboys on horseback, as well as ephemera from the early days of car culture, when El Reno was a major stop along Route 66. No matter where you sit at Sid's, images of olden days in Oklahoma will surround you.

★ VAN'S PIG STAND

pigstands.com

717 E. Highland St.   405-703-3000
Shawnee, OK   **L D** | **$$**

This rustic, wood-paneled eatery, where tables are outfitted with rolls of paper towels and sheaves of toothpicks and woodwork covered with volumes of graffiti, is the oldest barbecue in Oklahoma, and one of the best anywhere. It offers a large menu of smoked meats, hamburgers, and Sunday chicken dinners, but the essential thing to eat is pork, either as ribs that are crusty with glaze and packed with flavor, or in a pig sandwich, which is vividly sauced hacked hunks of pork in a bun with Van's own zesty relish. Superb sides include "Curlie Q fries," which are a variegated tangle of honeytone twigs, and a bacon-flavored, twice-baked potato invented by the current Van's grandma and listed as "Vanized" on the menu.

"The pie lady goofed," said the girl taking our order at Van's counter. "She put coconut meringue on the chocolate pie and regular meringue on the coconut pie." This heinous error—which, in fact, made the chocolate pie extra-good—was the worst thing that happened during a magnificent meal at one of the great barbecue outposts of the Southwest. Opened in 1928 in Wewoka, Van's has five locations in Oklahoma, including one in Norman, one in Moore, one in Purcell, and another in Shawnee.

WHITE RIVER FISH MARKET

whiteriverfishmarket.com

1708 N. Sheridan Rd.   918-835-1910
Tulsa, OK   **L D** (closed Sun) | **$$**

—★—
LOCALS
LOVE IT
—★—
Surrounded by light industry and warehouses, the White River Fish Market is not where anyone would expect to eat well. Outside, it looks like a hardware store in a strip mall; there is no printed menu—just a posted list of items on the wall above the counter where customers stand in line to place orders. Meals come at fast-food speed to boomerang-pattern Formica tables, some of which are private, some communal; the brightly lit dining room sounds like a rowdy factory mess hall, occupied by blue collars and Oxford shirts, blacks and whites and native Americans. For all its indecorous democracy, this outpost is an aristocrat among seafood restaurants.

At the order counter just inside the front door is a long glass case with trays of raw sea scallops from Boston, catfish live-hauled from Arkansas, rainbow trout from Idaho, red snapper, frogs' legs, colossal shrimp and popcorn shrimp, salmon steaks, tilapia, orange roughy, perch, and whole Gulf Coast flounders. Select the item you want and tell the server your preferred cooking method. If you want it fried, the piece or pieces you have chosen are immediately dipped into salted cracker meal; if it is to be broiled, your selection is put directly onto a broiling tray. The ready-to-cook order is then handed through a large pass-through portal straight to the kitchen. Meanwhile, you pay and find a seat. The servers will make note of where you've gone, and by the time you're comfortable and sipping sweet tea, the meal will be carried from the kitchen trailing wisps of savory smoke.

The dish at the top of our must-eat list is broiled flounder. It is one big fish, weighing over a pound and wider than a large dinner plate. Its flesh is scored in a diamond pattern, making the display of several raw ones on ice in the glass case resemble a shimmering ocean jewel box. When broiled, the flesh firms up and forms a pattern of bite-sized diamonds of meat arrayed neatly atop the skeleton. The tail, hanging over the side of the large oval plate on which it is served, is blackened by flame and provides its own smoked scent; each juicy nugget you lift—using the gentlest upward pressure of a fork—has a delicate ocean sweetness that disallows fancying up.

WILSON'S B-B-Q
jbwilsonsbbq.com

| 1522 E. Apache | 918-425-9912 |
| Tulsa, OK | L D | $ |

A recording of Chicago blues floats into the parking lot at Wilson's on East Apache, a Tulsa street that sports a handful of interesting barbecue parlors. Inside the door, the blues are louder, but another rhythm is even more compelling: the whack-thud-whack of a meat cleaver hacking hickory-cooked beef into shreds. "U Need No Teeth to Eat Our Beef" is one of Wilson's several mottos (others being "U Need a Bib to Eat Our Ribs" and "U Need No Fork to Eat Our Pork"), and sure enough, that hacked-up beef

is preposterously tender. Moist, velvet-soft shreds are interspersed with crusty strips from the outside of the brisket. Wilson's sauce is tongue-stimulating hot with vintage savor that reminded us of fine old bourbon.

Hot links are terrific: snapping-taut, dense, and peppery. Another house specialty is a huge smoke-cooked spud that is presented splayed open and lightly seasoned, available "plain" with just butter and sour cream, or stuffed with your choice of brisket, cut-up hot links, or bologna.

Wilson's is a modern two-room eat place with wood-paneled walls, table service, and a counter where people come for takeout orders. Décor includes signs that read, "Our cow is dead. We don't need no bull" and "The bank and I have an agreement. They will not sell bar-b-que and I will not lend money or cash checks." Tulsa law enforcement officials who dine at Wilson's are entitled to a 10 percent discount for their public service.

TEXAS

ANGELO'S

angelosbbq.com

2533 White Settlement   817-332-0357
Fort Worth, TX   **L D** (closed Sun) | **$**

Angelo's, which dates back to 1958, has become one of the most respected barbecue parlors in the Metroplex. It is a large dining hall with a remarkable exhibition of game-animal trophies, including big fish and brown bears, one of which wears a souvenir T-shirt.

When you stand at the order counter, you can watch brisket being carved. As the knife severs the dark crust and glides into the meat's tender center, each slice barely stays intact enough to be hoisted onto a Styrofoam plate, where it is sided by beans, potato salad, coleslaw, a length of pickle, a thick slice of raw onion, a ramekin of sauce, and two pieces of the freshest, softest white bread in America. Tote your own meal to a table.

The hickory pit also yields pork ribs with meat that slides easily off the bone, as well as hot link sausages, ham, and salami. In the relatively cooler months of October through March, Angelo's serves chili. It is an unctuous soup/stew of ground beef and plenty of pepper. Most people get an order to accompany a rib or beef plate or sandwiches . . . along with a few of Angelo's huge, cold mugs of beer.

AVALON DINER

avalondiner.com

2417 Westheimer Rd.   713-527-8900
Houston, TX   **B L** | **$**

Although it is in the deluxe neighborhood of River Oaks and extravagantly manicured ladies come to lunch, the Avalon Diner isn't the least bit fussy. Eating here is a taste of lunch-counter democracy.

It is the place to get to know Texas drugstore chili or to sample such Dixie delights as smothered pork chops, chicken-fried steak, or a pimiento cheese sandwich. Hamburgers are short-order classics, just thick enough that a hint of pink remains in the center, their crusty outsides glistening with oil from the griddle. The configuration is deluxe, meaning fully dressed with tomato, lettuce, pickle, onion, mustard, and mayonnaise, and the bun has been butter-toasted crisp on the inside but is ineffably soft outside.

Avalon serves elegant, small-tread waffles, all the better to hold countless pools of swirled-together syrup and melted butter. Not-to-be missed beverages include vibrant squeezed-to-order lemonade and milk shakes served in the silver mixing can.

Note: There are two other Avalon Diners, in Stafford, at 12810 Southwest Freeway (281-240-0213) and at 8823 Katy Freeway (713-590-4377).

BARTLEY'S BAR-B-Q

bartleysbbq.com

413 E. Northwest Hwy.   817-481-3212
Grapevine, TX   L D (Tues–Sat) | $

The sight of Bartley's, in a strip mall next to a Laundromat, will not set anyone's Roadfood radar beeping. This house of meats has none of the visual charisma of the tumbledown pits of the barbecue belt east of Austin. But inside the door, the air is righteously perfumed by smoke and the decorative theme is Mythology of the West: horseshoes, steer horns, Navajo rugs, a saddle or two, and a portrait of John Wayne.

Service is cafeteria-style, and the selection of meats is broad: brisket, ribs, hot links, Polish sausage, and thick slices of bologna. Tell the extremely friendly guy at the cutting block what you want—specify how fatty you like the brisket, whether you want the ribs severed or slabbed—and he accommodates, all the while keeping up a nice conversation with customers.

If we had a quibble with the food at Bartley's, we would say that the ribs might be *too* tender, not quite buff enough to reward a good chew. Brisket, on the other hand, feels just right, and while it tends toward dry when sliced, application of the house's good sauce fixes that instantly. Side dishes include giant baked potatoes (stuffed or not), collard greens, and braised cabbage. For dessert, pecan cobbler is richer than the richest bread pudding—without doubt the perfect food for anyone seeking to grow a huge ass.

THE BIG TEXAN

bigtexan.com

7701 E. Hwy. 40   806-372-6000
Amarillo, TX   L D | $$$

-- ★ --
HOT While it does not fit any reasonable definition
TICKET of a Roadfood restaurant, the Big Texan is an
-- ★ -- experience that every traveler should have at least once. It is brash and touristy, and although the featured meal is a gimmick worthy of P. T. Barnum, the steaks are really good!

The Big Texan's trick is that if a single person eats a seventy-two-ounce sirloin in an hour—along with a shrimp cocktail, salad, a baked potato, and a dinner roll with butter—it is free. More than forty thousand people have tried since the offer began in 1960, and fewer than one in five has succeeded. You don't just sit at your table and eat it. You go onstage, where other diners get to watch you eat it. In other words, you become the evening's entertainment. Even if that is acceptable to you, the big problem is that among the four and a half pounds of red meat is enough marbling so that even if you could devour, say, three pounds of steak in a single sitting, you also must consume a pound of fat. Not that there's anything wrong with fat. It is what makes this steak, as well as the Big Texan's normal-sized cuts, taste good. A while back, when one of us Sterns took the challenge, he got rather close to consuming all the best parts of the steak, but there had to be a couple of pounds left on the plate that became a blubbery Waterloo.

BLACK'S BARBECUE

blacksbbq.com

215 N. Main St.   512-398-2712
Lockhart, TX   L D | $

Black's, since 1932, boasts that it is Texas's "oldest and best major BBQ restaurant continuously owned by the same family." Whatever its provenance, of this we are certain: It is one of the top destination barbecue parlors in the heart of Texas and therefore one of the great barbecues in this solar system. Its pit-cooked sausage rings veritably burst with flavor and its brisket is unspeakably succulent.

Black's differs from the other exalted barbecues in Lockhart because it actually has quite a menu beyond meat. Stroll through the short cafeteria line and choose among hard-boiled eggs stuck on toothpicks, little garden salads in bowls, and fruit cobbler for dessert. There are pit-cooked potatoes loaded with chopped meat; there even is sure-enough Lone Star chili. It is possible to have the man behind the counter put your meat into a sandwich and your sandwich on a plate—a deluxe presentation unheard-of in more traditional barbecues where meat is sold by the pound and accompanied by a stack of white bread or saltine crackers. Furthermore, Black's dining room has décor—another smoke-pit oddity—in the form of game trophies and pictures of the high school football team on its knotty pine walls.

Black's will ship ribs overnight to most places in the United States. Although the cost of sending them is about the same as the ribs themselves, this is a good emergency source to know about when the craving strikes.

BLANCO BOWLING CLUB CAFE
blancobowlingclub.com

| 310 4th St. | 830-833-4416 |
| Blanco, TX | B L D \| $ |

The Blanco Bowling Club Cafe menu offers a nice selection of burgers, sandwiches, tacos, chalupas, and enchiladas, and a recent visit at breakfast time featured huge warm biscuits. But it's for the pies that we will be returning, especially for the meringues that rise three times as high as the filling they top. And the fillings are delicious. Coconut pie has an indescribably creamy flavor, accented by little bits of toasty coconut scattered across the top of the meringue. Fudge pie is dense, rich, and super-chocolaty. If you are a pie fancier, put this bowling alley on your must-eat list.

It really is a bowling alley where the nine-pin league rolls at night. During the day the alleys are curtained off, although customers in the back dining room do enjoy such décor as bowling trophies, racks of balls, and ball bags piled atop league members' lockers. Accommodations are basic: wood-grain Formica tables set with silver wrapped in paper napkins. There is a short counter in the front room with a view of the pass-through to the kitchen and one big table where locals come and go for coffee and cinnamon buns and glazed donuts all morning.

BLUE BONNET CAFE
bluebonnetcafe.net

| 211 Hwy. 281 | 830-693-2344 |
| Marble Falls, TX | B L D \| $ |

The Blue Bonnet Cafe can satisfy any sort of appetite, whether it's for a modest salad or an immodestly large plate of chicken-fried steak or pot roast. With big meals come choices from a roster of such sides as fragile-crusted fried okra, pork-rich pinto beans, and butter-sopped leaf spinach. Lunch and supper begin with a bread basket that includes four-by-four-inch yeast rolls with a bakery sweetness that perfumes the whole table as soon as you tear one apart. With the rolls are rugged corn-bread muffins. At breakfast (served all day), eggs are accompanied by hash brown potatoes or grits and your choice of thin toast, biscuits, or double-thick Texas toast.

The only problem with eating breakfast at the Blue Bonnet Cafe is that the pies may not be ready to serve until after 11 a.m., and in this place it behooves diners to heed the sign posted on the wall that implores "Try Some Pie!" Eight or ten are available each day, plain or à la mode, and while we enjoy the apple pie and pecan pie, the one we'll come back for is peanut butter cream. Smooth and devilishly rich, topped with a thick ribbon of white cream, it is accompanied by a small paper cup full of chocolate sauce. It is up to you to decide whether you want to pour the chocolate all over the slice or to dip the pie into the cup, forkful by forkful.

Monday through Friday from 3 p.m. to 5 p.m., the Blue Bonnet Cafe features "pie happy hour" at which a slice and a cup of coffee go for $3.50.

★ BRYCE'S CAFETERIA
brycescafeteria.com

| 2021 Mall Dr. (I-30, Exit 222) | 903-792-1611 |
| Texarkana, TX | L D \| $ |

Here is cafeteria quintessence, featuring more vegetables than most Yankees see in a year: purple-hulled peas, fried green tomatoes, red beans, turnip greens cooked with chunks of ham, and a full array of potatoes, ultracheesy macaroni casseroles, rice casseroles, buttered cauliflower, sauced broccoli, pickled beets, et cetera, et cetera.... Main course highlights include fried chicken that is stupendously crunchy and big slabs of sweet ham sliced to order. There are roast beef and gravy, chicken and dumplings, turkey with all the fixins, fried and broiled fish. Among the multitude of pies, we like Karo-coconut pie and chess. Excellent alternatives include hot fruit cobbler and traditional banana pudding made with meringue and vanilla wafers.

Bryce's has been a Texarkana landmark since it opened downtown in 1931. Now in modern quarters with easy access from the interstate, it remains a piece of living culinary history. They don't make restaurants like this anymore! Among amenities are a smartly uniformed dining-room staff (to carry your tray and place all dishes from it on the table when you arrive at your chosen place) and servers who address men as "sir" and ladies as "ma'am." Bryce's also offers drive-through service, which, although convenient for travelers in a hurry, eliminates the joy of browsing along one of the nation's most appetizing cafeteria lines.

CATTLEMEN'S FORT WORTH STEAK HOUSE
cattlemenssteakhouse.com

2458 N. Main St.   817-624-3945
Fort Worth, TX   L D | $$$

-- ★ -- Portraits of monumental Herefords, Anguses, **HOT** and Brahmans decorate the walls at Cattle**TICKET** men's Fort Worth Steak House, located in the -- ★ -- historic stockyards district since 1947. At the back of the main dining area, known as the Branding Room, raw steaks are displayed on a bed of ice in front of a charcoal fire where beef sputters on a grate. Before placing a dinner order, many customers stroll back toward the open broiler to admire the specimens on ice and compare and contrast rib eye and T-bone, demure filet mignon and ample porterhouse, KC sirloin strip and pound-plus Texas strip.

Texas sirloin is the steak lover's choice, a bulging block of aged, heavy beef with a charred crust and robust opulence that is a pleasure simply to slice, and sheer ecstasy to savor. About the Heart O' Texas Rib

Eye the menu warns, "Not to be ordered by those who object to heavy marble." Sweet dinner rolls make a handy utensil for sopping up juices that puddle onto the plate. Start with a plate of lamb fries—nuggets of testicle sheathed in fragile crust—get the zesty house dressing on your salad, plop a heap of sour cream into your baked potato, and accompany the big feed with frozen margaritas, long-neck beers, or even a bottle of Texas's own Llano Estacado Cabernet Sauvignon. It's one grand cowtown supper.

CHRIS MADRID'S
chrismadrids.com

1900 Blanco Rd.   210-735-3552
San Antonio, TX   L D (closed Sun) | $

An efficiency expert might blow a gasket looking at Chris Madrid's, a chaotic, multiroom tavern/burger joint where the modus operandi makes no sense but works beautifully. First, squeeze into a line that heads toward the order counter, where you tell the lady what you want and pay for it. You are given a vibrating pager, and while the food is being cooked, you hunt around for space at a table (outdoors or in). When the pager vibrates, return to the pick-up counter and carry trays full of burgers back to the dining room.

Madrid's hamburgers are broad and beautiful, not too thick, but juicy enough to ooze the moment finger pressure is applied to the big-domed bun that holds them. Several variations are available, including a flaming jalapeño burger, a Porky's Delight layered with bacon, and a super-goopy Cheddar Cheezy, but the house specialty, not to be missed, is a Tostada Burger. Silky refried beans and massive amounts of Cheddar cheese form a luxurious crown for the big hamburger, also layered with a sheaf of tortilla chips that offer earthy corn flavor and intriguing chewy crunch. The great condiment is salsa, to which customers help themselves near the pickup window. French fries are fresh-cut and delicious. Among wine, beer, and cocktails, a favorite among many customers is Madrid's mango margarita.

Chris Madrid's is loud, boisterous, and colorful, something like a cross between a frat party and a family reunion. Décor is beer signs and signed T-shirts;

when it's really crowded (it usually is), strangers share tables.

CITY MARKET

633 E. Davis St.   830-875-9019
Luling, TX   **L D** | **$**

The dining area at the City Market in Luling is cool and comfortable. To fetch the food, however, you must walk into hell. A swinging door leads into a back-room pit—a shadowy, cavelike chamber illuminated by the glow of burning logs in pits on the floor underneath the iron ovens. It is excruciatingly hot, but apparently at ease in their sweltering workplace, pit men assemble meats on pink butcher paper with gracious dispatch. They take your money, then gather the edges of the paper together so it becomes a boat-like container you easily can carry back into the cool, pine-paneled dining room.

The brisket is terrific, as are pork ribs, but City Market's great dish is a sausage ring. Even when the long communal tables are crowded and a dozen conversations are in full sway all around, you cannot help but hear the crunch and snap as diners' teeth bite into the unbelievably taut casings of a City Market sausage ring. These horseshoe-shaped, string-tied guts are a lean, rugged grind with only the echo of pepper laced through their mineral-rich muscularity.

Uncharacteristically (for Texas), the City Market also makes significant barbecue sauce—a spice-speckled, dark-orange emulsion so coveted by customers that signs above every booth implore "Please Leave Sauce Bottles on Tables."

FUEL CITY

fuelcity.com

801 S. Riverfront Blvd.   214-426-5124
Dallas, TX   **B L D** | **$**

--★--
OPEN
24/7
--★--
We do not recommend Fuel City only because it is a takeout window in a gas station, open twenty-four hours a day, seven days a week. Neither is our enthusiasm for the tacos prejudiced by the longhorn cattle out back or the cart outside serving delicious cups of warm corn mixed with cheese, sour cream, and hot sauce. Yes, the ambience is sensational, but it really is the tacos that make Fuel City worth a visit.

Between 5 a.m. and 10 a.m., tacos are available filled with eggs, along with bacon, chorizo, and/or potatoes. Non-breakfast varieties include picadillo (spicy ground beef with diced potatoes), beef or chicken fajita (sautéed with onions), *barbacoa* (roast beef), and *pastor* (pork). Standard garnishes include chopped raw onions, cilantro, hot sauce, and a wedge of lime. They are modest-sized so that three or four make a meal.

Even if they were served on fine china in a linen-table dining room at $5 apiece with a wine list instead of beer, we would give the thumbs-up to these tacos. Their authenticity goes beyond the no-nonsense setting. The cilantro is fresh and overwhelmingly green-flavored; onions are crisp and sweet. *Barbacoa*, cooked so long it has lost all resistance, delivers baritone beef satisfaction with a sweet-meat edge; *pastor*, which is chunky and chewier than *barbacoa*, is sneaky-hot, creating ecstatic mouth glow; picadillo is as consoling as Mom's casserole.

GOLDEN LIGHT CAFE

goldenlightcafe.com

2906 SW. 6th Ave.   806-374-9237
Amarillo, TX   **L D** (Mon–Sat) | **$**

The Golden Light really does glow in the afternoon light along old Route 66. The oldest restaurant in Amarillo, it originally opened as a hamburger joint and although the menu has expanded, burgers are still the big allure. They are not hoity-toity burgers, mind you. The medium-thin patties come off the vintage grill cooked through but still juicy enough, at their best when topped with cheese and chiles (hot jalapeños or milder greens) and sided by thin-cut French fries. An alternative is to have the burger wrapped in a giant tortilla along with hot sauce and sour cream. We are also big fans of the Fritos pie (here known as Flagstaff Pie)—a large oval plate of Fritos chips topped with the stout house red chili, cheese, and onions. What's great about Fritos pie is how different every chip is, depending on how close it gets to the chili. Those corn ribbons that are totally smothered turn to soft, salty cornmeal; some remain untouched and crisp; most are half-and-half crisp and tender, or on their way to delicious disintegration.

Next door to the café is the Golden Light Cantina, a live music venue that features Texas red dirt band music.

GOODE CO. TEXAS BAR-B-Q

goodecompany.com/restaurantbbq1

5109 Kirby Dr.   713-522-2530
Houston, TX   **L D** | $$

To Houstonians, Goode Co. means good food. Driving south on Kirby from the city center, you pass Goode Co. Seafood and Goode Co. Taqueria, and there is another branch of Goode Co. Bar-B-Q on Katy Freeway. The place on Kirby is a large eating barn (with a nice covered outdoor patio) surrounded by stacks of wood and the perfume of smoldering mesquite. Inside, there's always a line leading to the cafeteria-style counter. The line moves fast because nearly everyone knows exactly what they want. Once you've eaten at Goode Co. barbecue, chances are good you will return for more.

Long-smoked brisket is velvet-soft and so moist that sauce is superfluous. You can get the beef as part of a platter with superb, slightly sweet baked beans, potato salad, and jambalaya, or you can have it in a sandwich. While blah bread is de rigueur in most great barbecue parlors, Goode Co. offers a fantastic alternative: thick slices of fresh, soft jalapeño corn bread that make a first-rate mitt for the smoky beef. Brisket frowners (if there are such creatures in Texas) have the option of getting pork sausage, pork ribs, ham, chicken, duck, or turkey. Brazos Bottom Pecan Pie is legendary.

GFRAP (the Gluten Free Restaurant Awareness Program) has given its blessing to many of the items on Goode Co.'s menu, including most of the meats and many side dishes. Rubs and seasonings are certified gluten-free. The special menu does advise, "Ask to have the cutting board wiped with a clean cloth before they cut your meat!"

GREEN VEGETARIAN CUISINE

eatatgreen.com

200 E. Grayson St.,   210-320-5865
Ste. 120   **B L D** (closed Sat) | $
San Antonio, TX

—★— **VEGETARIAN-FRIENDLY** —★— For eating meat, San Antonio is hard to beat. Soul-food barbecue and border-town *barbacoa, menudo* at the taquerias and macho burgers at Chris Madrid's (p. 372), Tip Top chicken-fried steak and Barn Door T-bone: It's a carnivore's delight. And so it was that after four days of doing our damnedest to deplete the population of Texas cows, we actually found ourselves craving a moo-less meal. As far as we could discover, there is one game in town—Green Vegetarian Restaurant—and it is a doozy.

The day's special veggie drink was a Ginger Bomb of apple juice, carrot juice, beet juice, and ginger. When he saw our waitress bring it, co-owner Chris Behrend came by the table to remind us that it needed to be shaken or stirred before every pull on the straw because the juices almost instantly want to separate. Momentarily forced together, they sure sing a happy tune.

At lunch or supper, you can have gluten-free sushi vegetable rolls, grilled portobellos that are designed to remind you of steak, even chicken-fried steak made of "wheat meat." Chili, available as a side with other meals, does a yeomanly job of impersonating real chili, albeit not authentic *Texas* chili, as it contains beans. But the spices are right and it is extremely hearty.

Among pseudo meats, few are weirder than wham, a ham substitute that has a smoky flavor and texture something like tender pastrami. It's the star of a tremendously satisfying sandwich named Mike (for chef and co-owner Mike Behrend), which contains jaw-stretching strata of avocados, cucumbers, sprouts, spinach leaves, tomato slices, purple onion, sliced tomato, and jalapeño jelly—all on thick slices of fresh, rugged-grained bread.

There is a second location of Green at 10003 Northwest Military, Suite 2115, San Antonio (210-233-1249).

H&H COFFEE SHOP

701 E. Yandell Dr.　　　915-533-1144
El Paso, TX　　　　　　**B L | $**

If you are hungry and your car is dusty from traveling Southwest roads, the place to go is the H&H Coffee Shop, where table seats in the little café afford a view of the adjoining car wash where your vehicle gets scrubbed and dried. We prefer counter stools with a vista of chiles rellenos getting battered and fried and huevos rancheros being topped with a curious buttery gravy flecked with onions and hot peppers. Artemisa, who has been a waitress here for years, frequently conjures up her own special salsa, which capsicum addicts know to request. "It will hurt you," warns proprietor Kenny Haddad, who offers curious visitors a few spoonfuls in a saucer. It is flecked with seeds and pod membrane (the hottest parts) and glistens seductively. Artemisa, who is normally a stern sort of person, broke into a broad grin when she watched us wipe the last of it up with warm tortillas, then wipe the beads of perspiration from our brow with napkins.

Not everything posted on the H&H wall menu is four-alarm. You can eat ordinary eggs for breakfast or a hamburger for lunch (the café closes at 3 p.m.). Burritos are available seven ways: stuffed with chile rellenos, egg and chorizo sausage, picadillo, red chile, green chile, *carne picada,* or beans. Specials include chicken molé, red and green enchiladas, and—always on Saturday—*menudo,* the tripe and hominy stew renowned for its power to cure a hangover.

Hospitality at the well-worn cookshop is enchanting. If you speak Spanish, so much the better: you will understand the nuances of the chatter. But if, like us, you are limited to English, you will still be part of the action. The day we first visited, many years ago, we were wearing ten-gallon hats, so we soon became known to one and all as the cowboys. *"Vaqueros,"* called a waitress as we headed out the door, *"vaya con dios."* With our car newly cleaned and the radio tuned to the rollicking Mexican polka rhythms of Tejano music, we highballed north along the Rio Grande.

HIGHLAND PARK SODA FOUNTAIN

highlandparksodafountain.com
3229 Knox St.　　　　214-521-2126
Dallas, TX　　　　　　**B L | $**

LOCALS LOVE IT Whereas the Highland Park neighborhood of Dallas is sleek and swanky, the Highland Park Soda Fountain, located in the Highland Park Pharmacy, opened in 1912, is a humble relic. Perhaps only a very well-heeled community has the luxury of letting such low gross-income real estate remain unexploited. Whatever the reason, this time-worn eatery that takes up more than one half of a working drugstore continues to serve inexpensive, unfashionable food to fashion-conscious shoppers, nearly all of the distaff persuasion. The menu posted above the counter lists grilled pimiento cheese sandwiches, hot dogs and chili dogs, chicken salad sandwiches on white or whole wheat, and a full battery of soda fountain drinks, fizzes, and sundaes.

In the second decade of the twenty-first century, how many eateries in upscale locations do you know that offer a choice of a phosphate, a cooler, a freeze, a float, or a soda? This is one of the few places we know that serves what chili guru Frank X. Tolbert used to refer to as drugstore chili: thick and meaty, just a bit pepper-hot, eager to be complicated with shredded cheese and raw onions or to serve as the soul of a Fritos pie.

Chocolate sodas are expertly concocted: First, chocolate syrup is squirted into a tall glass; then a stream of soda gets jerked in, hitting the syrup hard enough that no spoon is needed to mix it; finally the whole foamy brew is topped with a couple scoops of vanilla ice cream. The Highland Park Soda Fountain business card boasts that its lunch counter is "home of the best milk shake in Dallas."

HILL COUNTRY CUPBOARD

101 S. Hwy. 281   830-868-4625
Johnson City, TX   **B L D** | **$**

Chicken-fried steak is bedeviling. There are so many bad ones that a person could lose faith. But then you come across one such as that served at the Hill Country Cupboard and you are a believer once again. This big barn of a restaurant claims to serve the world's best. Two sizes are available: regular and large, the latter as big as its plate. Neither requires a knife; a fork will crack through a golden-brown crust that is rich and well spiced, a perfect complement to the ribbon of tender beef inside. Alongside the slab of crusty protein comes a great glob of skin-on mashed potatoes and, of course, thick white gravy blankets the whole kit and caboodle.

Beyond chicken-fried steak, Hill Country Cupboard has a full menu of Southwest eats: barbecued beef, sausage, turkey, and ribs; catfish fillets; grilled chicken with jalapeño cheese sauce. There are even salads, available topped with hunks of chicken-fried steak or chicken-fried chicken!

HOOVER'S COOKING

hooverscooking.com

2002 Manor Rd.   512-479-5006
Austin, TX   **L D** | **$$**

Chef Hoover Alexander says, "I am an Austin native with deep central Texas roots that run from Manchaca and Pilot Knob to little o' Utley, Texas. All of the recipes we use here were inspired by both my mother Dorothy's good cooking and the styles and spices native throughout Texas itself. I grew up on home cooking—nicely seasoned vegetables, smoked foods, pan-fried dishes, and spicy foods with a nod toward Tex-Mex and Cajun. I also have never forgotten eating a lot of Mom's fresh-baked rolls, corn bread, and desserts. . . . After you've had one of our freshly made meals and washed it down with a nice cool beverage, you'll understand why I like to call the restaurant my Smoke, Fire, and Ice House!"

Hoover's has its own smokehouse, perfuming the parking lot outside, from which come pork ribs, Elgin sausage, highly spiced Jamaican jerk chicken, and lesser-spiced (but nonetheless delicious) regular-spiced barbecue chicken. In addition to smoked fare, the menu lists chicken-fried steak (perhaps the best one anywhere), meat loaf, catfish, and an array of sandwiches that range from a meatless muffuletta (made with a portobello mushroom) to half-pound hamburgers. On the side of any meal, choose from a large selection of vegetables that include chunky mashed potatoes, mac 'n' cheese, black-eyed peas, sweet and hammy mustard greens, crisp-fried okra, and jalapeño-accented creamed spinach.

HUT'S HAMBURGERS

hutsfrankandangies.com

807 W. 6th St.   512-472-0693
Austin, TX   **L D** | **$**

Hut's is a burger joint with nineteen different varieties of hamburger listed on its menu (not to mention the options of buffalo meat, chicken breast, or veggie burgers), each one topped with a different constellation of condiments that range from hickory sauce (delicious!) to cheeses of all kinds to guacamole to chipotle mayonnaise. We recommend the Buddy Holly Burger (American cheese, mayo, mustard, onions, pickles, lettuce, tomato), the double-meat Dag Burger (also with the works), and the Mr. Blue (blue cheese dressing, Swiss cheese, bacon, lettuce). Monday nights, meat frowners can get two veggie burgers for the price of one. French fries are very good, available on a half-and-half plate with onion rings that have a peppery zest: a joy to overeat. There are other sandwiches, a different blue-plate special every day (chicken-fried steak, meat loaf, catfish, et cetera), and beverages that include cherry Coke, pink lemonade, and a root beer float.

Decorated to the rafters with neon beer signs, team pennants, and clippings celebrating its long-standing fame—since 1939—it is a small place that is always overstuffed with people, with noise, and with a spirit of fun. You will likely wait for a seat in the small vestibule or on the sidewalk outside, but once seated, the food comes fast.

KREUZ MARKET

kreuzmarket.com

619 N. Colorado St.   512-398-2361
Lockhart, TX   **L D** | **$$**

Kreuz (rhymes with "bites") started as a downtown meat market more than a century ago, and it was one of the places that defined Texas barbecue. Several years ago, owing to a complicated family feud, it moved out of town to an immense roadside dining barn with all the charm of an airplane hangar. Ambience notwithstanding, one cannot deny that its fatty—OK, we'll say "well-marbled"—slabs of pit-cooked prime rib are among the most carnivorously satisfying foodstuffs on Earth. And despite the modern facilities, Kreuz has maintained the pit-cook tradition of tote-your-own service from a ferociously hot pit where meat is sliced to order and sold by the pound. While the prime rib is a splurge (at nearly $20 per pound), the more familiar meats (priced about half that) are superb in their own right: beef brisket and shoulder, pork chops, ribs, ham, and sausage rings. In a nod to convenient dining, there is a separate counter where ice cream can be purchased and small servings of banana pudding are available for dessert.

LA MEXICANA

lamexicanarestaurant.com

1018 Fairview St.   713-521-0963
Houston, TX   **B L D** | **$$**

La Mexicana started more than thirty years ago as a corner grocery store and now offers sit-down meals in a festively decorated dining room and bar as well as takeout meals from a cafeteria line, and all sorts of interesting pastries from the in-house bakery. In fact, this is a good place for breakfast, starting at 7 a.m. In addition to baked goods, the choices include all sorts of huevos rancheros, eggs scrambled with chorizo (Mexican sausage), *migas* (a sort of tortilla omelet), and, on Saturday and Sunday only, *menudo,* which is a bowl of stewed honeycomb tripe. *Menudo* is Mexican folklore's hangover cure. Every morning from 7 a.m. to 9 a.m., customers are welcome to "jump start happy hour" with $3 mimosas and $8 jumbo margaritas.

When you sit down for a lunch or dinner, a waiter (outfitted in white shirt and tie) brings a basket of thin, elegant tortilla chips, still warm, along with a mild red sauce and a hotter, lime-tinged green pepper sauce. The chips are large and somewhat fragile; if you eat your way through half the basket so that only smaller, broken half-chips remain, the old basket is whisked away and a new one of full-sized, warm chips takes its place.

The menu is huge, including fajitas à la Mexicana, for which the beef is stewed rather than grilled, tacos, flautas, tamales, enchiladas, and chiles rellenos. We love the fish tacos, made not the typical way with fried fish but with succulent strips of grilled mahimahi. They are light, refreshing, and hot (if you ask for them that way), the fish, cabbage, tomato, and cilantro laced with little nuggets of tongue-searing pepper. Alongside come Mexican rice and a bowl of creamy-smooth, blue-black refritos.

No matter how much we eat, it is hard to pass up the likes of chocolate cake topped with flan, or at least a few fudge-coated coconut macaroons. For the road we always take a bag of heart-shaped cinnamon-sugar cookies.

★ LITTLE DINER

littlediner.com

7209 7th St.   915-877-2176
Canutillo, TX   **L D** (closed Wed) | **$**

Lourdes Pearson's Little Diner, also known as the Canutillo Tortilla Factory, is far off I-10 in an obscure residential neighborhood north of El Paso, but her crisp-skinned gorditas (stuffed cornmeal pockets) are worth getting lost to find. The normal filling is ground meat, but the great one is chili con carne. Tender shreds of beef become an ideal medium for the brilliant red chile that surrounds them with a walloping flavor of concentrated sunshine. You can also get the chili con carne in a bowl—one of the few classic "bowls of red" still to be found in all of Texas. Its flavor is huge, and you wouldn't think of adding beans or rice to this perfect duet. Of course, you do want to tear off pieces from Lourdes's wheaty flour tortillas to mop the last of the red chili from the bottom of the bowl.

We love everything about this friendly diner, where you step up to the counter and place your order before sitting down. The tortilla chips that start each meal have an earthy corn character and are scarcely salty—all the better to taste the essence-of-red-chile salsa served with them. Flautas are crunchy little fried tortilla tubes (like flutes, which is what the name means) packed with moist shreds of chicken or succulent pot roast. The last time we visited, the green chili was even hotter than the red (this varies with the harvest); it adds potatoes and onions to the basic meat-and-chiles formula.

The broad Tex-Mex menu includes burritos, enchiladas, tapatias, and tacos. Tamales—red chili pork, green chili cheese, green chili chicken, and green chili chicken cheese—are generally made once a week, but Lourdes told us that in December, they are a menu item every day.

★ LOUIE MUELLER BARBEQUE
louiemuellerbarbecue.com

| 206 W. 2nd St. | 512-352-6206 |
| Taylor, TX | L D (closed Sun) \| $$ |

Several years ago, Louie Mueller's, which we have long considered the best of all Texas barbecue parlors, added a modern dining room that lacks the smoky patina of the original brick-walled restaurant; but no matter where you eat in this august temple of meat, the flavor is historic. Here is a restaurant where beef brisket (as well as sausage, ribs, and mutton) are cooked and served the way Texas pitmasters have been doing it for decades. Step up to the counter that separates dining tables from the smoke pits. Place your order by pound or plate. Carry it yourself to a table.

The brisket is a thing of beauty. It is sliced relatively thick, each individual slice halved by the ribbon of fat that runs through a brisket, separating the leaner, denser meat below from the more marbled stuff on top. Wayne Mueller, Louie's grandson, and now master of the barbecue domain, told us that no spices go into or onto his briskets other than salt and pepper. Add time and smoke to those two elements, plus a pitmaster who knows how to move the meat around in the pit to take maximum advantage of hot spots, cool spots, and drafts, and the result is brisket that is impossibly juicy and huge-flavored. By comparison, prime sirloin and Wagyu kobe filet mignon are wimpy. There is sauce reminiscent of jus, but it is irrelevant. Meat is what you want to eat: brisket, with perhaps a side of all-beef sausage.

★ MONUMENT CAFE
themonumentcafe.com

| 500 S. Austin Ave. | 512-930-9586 |
| Georgetown, TX | B L D \| $$ |

Three meals a day are served at the Monument Cafe, and we have enjoyed everything from a grilled cheese sandwich to chicken-fried steak; but it is breakfast we like best. The kitchen's *migas* are perfect: eggs scrambled with cheese, diced tomatoes, and small ribbons of tortilla that variously soften and turn crisp depending on where they are in the pan, giving the dish an earthy corn flavor. On the side come peppered bacon and refried beans, plus red salsa to heat it up if desired. Pancakes and waffles are of the highest quality, as are the big squarish biscuits. The pastry we'd kill for is sour cream coffee cake, its top blanketed with sugar and frosting, its inside layered with local pecans.

"We make our own desserts, from scratch, every day," the menu notes. "And we use only real ingredients: real whipping cream, real butter, real yard eggs." Of these boasts, you will have no doubt if you order a piece of cream pie. Here is some of the best pie in Texas, some of the best *anywhere*! Chocolate pie with a toasted pecan crust is inspired and devilishly chocolaty. Coconut cream pie is equally amazing, but angelically light, silky, fresh, and layered on a flaky gold crust.

Oh, one more thing: lemonade, limeade, and orange juice are *fresh*.

NORMA'S CAFE

normascafe.com

1123 W. Davis St.   214-946-4711

Dallas, TX   **B L D** | $

An overarching 1950s consciousness and the house slogan, "Life Is Short—Eat Dessert First," suggest that Norma's Cafe is trying awfully hard to be a down-home diner. It needn't try; it is the real deal. It dates back to 1956; modern website notwithstanding, it remains a sprung-spring-booth and worn-counter hash house with cop and blue-collar clientele, breakfast with gravy over everything, and no-bull waitresses pouring bottomless coffee.

Biscuits arrive all warm and friendly, fairly reeking buttermilk tang, needing neither the margarine nor jelly that are supplied, and just right for mopping up cream gravy. Loaded with gnarled chunks of sausage, the gravy is light on pepper and heavy on cream.

A sign hanging over Norma's dining room proclaims "Pie Fixes Everything." If you eat nothing else in this place, you must eat some, for these pies are made by masters. Peanut butter chocolate is an exquisite balance of those two oh-so-complementary elements that make Reese's candy right, neither layer hogging attention, both cool and silky, their frothy white crown dotted with enough nutmeat to provide happy crunch. The crust is sturdy and serviceable, more like a cookie than the flaky pastry of aristocratic pies.

While there are plenty of booths, counter seats provide an opportunity to kibitz with the staff and also to look into the kitchen's pass-through window, where cooks are busy cutting up fatback for cooking vegetables, icing cinnamon buns, and seasoning pots of soup and gravy destined to be lunch.

There are three other locations. Another Norma's, in Farmer's Branch, is not related.

OST

305 Main St.   830-796-3836

Bandera, TX   **B L D** | $$

OST (Old Spanish Trail) has been Bandera's town café since 1921, and its roomy cypress booths and barstools made of western saddles make it an especially appealing destination for hungry travelers in search of cowboy culture. One whole room is devoted to images of John Wayne; its spur collection includes rowels dating back to frontier days; and the buffet is set out under a downsized covered wagon. The buckaroo trappings make a lot of sense in Bandera, which is surrounded by dude ranches and has proclaimed itself the Cowboy Capital of the World.

The number one cowboy dish in these parts is chicken-fried steak, and OST makes a good one: a tantalizing balance of crunch and tenderness with gravy that is cream-soft but pepper-sharp. The menu highlights include such Tex-Mex stalwarts as enchiladas, fajitas, and chiles rellenos. Old-fashioned buttermilk pie is the great dessert; blackberry cobbler is excellent too.

PARIS COFFEE SHOP

pariscoffeeshop.net

700 W. Magnolia Ave.   817-335-2041

Fort Worth, TX   **B** (Mon–Sat) **L** (Mon–Fri) | $

The day starts early in cattle country, so it should be no surprise that Fort Worth has always been a good breakfast town. By 7 a.m., the Paris Coffee Shop is bustling. A convivial, wood-paneled room with a counter, booths, and tables, it smells delicious in the morning, its air fragrant with the piggy perfume of sausages, bacon, and pork chops, as well as biscuits smothered with gravy. Beyond biscuits, breadstuffs include soft, glazed cinnamon rolls and a choice of eight-grain, sourdough, or sun-dried tomato toast.

The Paris Coffee Shop is also a legendary lunchroom (since 1926), known for meat loaf, fried chicken, and chicken-fried steak with mashed potatoes and gravy, as well as one of the best bowls of chili in the Metroplex. The café's signature dish is an Arkansas Traveler: hot roast beef on corn bread, smothered with gravy. Such Lone Star comfort fare is accompanied by your choice from a wide variety of southern-style vegetables such as turnips and/or turnip greens, pole beans, and butter beans.

Any meal *must* be followed by a piece of Paris pie. One morning, when we spotted a single piece of custard pie we wanted behind the counter and ordered it for breakfast, the waitress warned, "It's not today's." (Today's pies were still in the oven.) But then she agreed with our choice, declaring, "Hey, yesterday's egg custard pie is better than no pie at all!"

RANCHMAN'S CAFE (AKA PONDER STEAKHOUSE)

ranchman.com

110 W. Bailey St.   940-479-2221
Ponder, TX   **L D** (reservations advised)
          | **$$$**

★ In a sleepy encampment by the train tracks at
LOCALS the northern fringe of the Dallas/Fort Worth
LOVE IT Metroplex, the Ponder Steakhouse (actually
★ named Ranchman's Cafe) has been a meat-eaters' destination since 1948. Indoor bathrooms were added many years ago, but the steaks are still hand-cut, and the ambience is Lone Star to the core.

The menu ranges from quail quarters and Rocky Mountain oyster hors d'oeuvres to fabulous made-from-scratch buttermilk pie. It is big, glistening steaks that motivate us for the drive. Porterhouse, T-bone, club, rib eye, and sirloin are sizzled on a griddle until they develop a wickedly tasty crust. Although tender, they are steaks of substantial density that require a sharp knife and reward a good chew with tides of flavor. French fries come on the side, but if you call ahead, they'll put a baked potato in the oven and have it ready when you arrive. Pies, made from scratch, include apple, strawberry-rhubarb, buttermilk, chocolate, coconut, and pecan.

ROYERS ROUND TOP CAFE

royersroundtopcafe.com

105 Main St.   979-249-3611
Round Top, TX   **L D** (closed Mon–Wed) | **$$**

Bud Royer has described his menu as "contemporary comfort food" but no single category of cuisine begins to describe his kitchen's boundlessly creative bent. Yes, there are familiar square meals: filet mignon, rack of lamb, a fourteen-ounce pork chop, and Sunday's garlicky, buttermilk-battered fried chicken, but nearly everything has a Royer twist. Grilled pork tenderloin is topped with a peach and pepper glaze, quail comes stuffed with shrimp and wrapped in bacon, Bud's salad includes both grilled beef and bacon.

If you know Royers Round Top, you know we haven't yet mentioned its flagship dish: pie. Bud (who goes by the moniker Bud the Pieman) offers big country-style classics with ribbons of baked fruit oozing out over the edge of knobby crusts as well as several pies of his own design. We believe the pecan pie, made with giant halves of Texas-grown nuts, is the best anywhere—a perfect balance of toasty nut flavor and syrupy sweetness. And the chocolate chip pie, loaded with pecans and super-chocolaty—really more a huge, thick cookie than a pie—is nothing short of devastating.

Royers is so deeply into pies that the menu threatens to charge customers 50¢ extra if they do not get it à la mode. "It is so wrong to not top your pie with Amy's ice cream!" (Amy's is an Austin brand started in 1984 by Amy Miller, who earned her chops working at the legendary Steve's in Boston.) If you come with a group, you can order a pie sampler for dessert: four different kinds à la mode. Those who cannot come should know that Royers is set up to ship pies anywhere in the United States, and pie devotees can enroll in one of the café's Pie-of-the-Month plans. They range from six pies delivered every other month for a year to Pie-for-Life!

SALT LICK

saltlickbbq.com

18300 FM 1826   512-858-4959

Driftwood, TX   **L D** | $$

Our first review of the Salt Lick, in the earliest edition of this book, described a place that began with neither four walls nor a restroom—just a smoke pit and makeshift tables on Thurman and Hisako Roberts's six-hundred-acre ranch. My, how it's grown! Located in the Hill Country west of Austin, it has become a theme park of barbecue with seats for two thousand, its limestone buildings surrounded by rough-hewn log fences, the air smelling of slow-smoked meats. Compared to the region's back-of-the-butcher-shop barbecue parlors, it's a refined place with ambience you might call Rustic Deluxe. There is a printed menu, there is waiter service, and the kitchen's repertoire includes all sorts of side dishes and dessert.

One other element that separates the Salt Lick from the primal parlors: sauce. Unless you ask to have your meat dry, it comes already painted with sauce. Not that the meat needs it—it's moist and full-flavored—but it does happen to be really tasty sauce, a tangy-sweet glaze with perhaps a hint of mustard. In fact, the sauce is good enough to use as a between-meat dip for the slices of good white bread that come alongside the meal. The sausage is smoky and rich, made from equal amounts of pork and beef. Brisket, slow-smoked for sixteen hours, is lean and polite (unless you request fattier slices), and if it lacks a certain succulence, Salt Lick sauce is an instant fix. Pork ribs drip juice from the tender meat at the bone and deliver a stupendously concentrated smoke-pit flavor in the chewy burnt ends.

Among the worthy side dishes are an intriguing cabbage slaw flecked with sesame seeds and cool, German-style potato salad. And of course, pickles and sliced raw onions are available with every meal.

Business is cash only.

SMITTY'S

smittysmarket.com

208 S. Commerce St.   512-398-9344

Lockhart, TX   **L D** | $$

The atmosphere at Smitty's backroom barbecue is tangible: eye-stinging clouds of smoke rise from wood fires around the indoor pit where you order meat by the pound. It is cut and assembled and wrapped in butcher paper so you can carry it to a communal table in the dining room. The pork chop is swell, but the Texas beef is definitive. Brisket is indescribably tender. Barbecued boneless prime rib (cut extra-thick, please) has got to be the ultimate in pit-cooked luxury, pink in its center, saturated with juice, and giddy with carnivorous energy. The sausage rings are insanely succulent, so loaded that if you plan to snap one in half, you must be sure to push out and away from you, lest its juices splatter your shirt.

Smitty's operates from the oldest barbecue facility in Lockhart, the building in which Charles Kreuz opened his grocery store more than a century ago. In 1948 Kreuz sold the business to the Schmidt family, but several years back, a feud split the Schmidts and sent the Kreuz Market out to a big new building (p. 377). Smitty's retains a charismatic historic feel; to walk in off Commerce Street through the age-burnished dining room with its benches along the wall is to see a virtual museum of Texas foodways. The room, now idle, was still in use when we first dined at Smitty's in the 1970s. The long counters were equipped with sharp knives attached by chains long enough for customers to cut their meat but too short for a knife fight.

SOUTHSIDE MARKET

southsidemarket.com

1212 Hwy. 290   512-281-4650

Elgin, TX   **L D** | $

In the geography of American sausage, no town holds more respect than Elgin (with a hard *g*, as in "gut"), known for hot beef sausages ever since the Southside Market fired up its smoke pit in 1882. One hundred and ten years after opening day, the sawdust-floored house of meats moved to a huge, spanking-clean, barn-sized building on the outskirts of town. While the new place lacks the charm of a well-aged and dilapidated barbecue parlor, it maintains a working butcher shop, and it still smokes sausage and beef brisket the old-fashioned way, in big iron pits over slow-smoldering post oak wood. Order your meat by the pound and carry it to a table.

The sausage is some of the best anywhere, a crazy-moist balance of spicy pyrotechnics and stalwart beef. Beyond the signature sausage, this is a good place to eat such Lone Star smoke-pit standards as brisket (regular or lean), and one of four kinds of rib: mutton, pork, beef, and baby back. Bread is sold by the slice (10¢) or loaf ($1.99); jalapeño peppers cost 39¢ apiece.

SWEET GEORGIA BROWN

2840 E. Ledbetter Dr.   214-375-2020
Dallas, TX   L D | $$

Mac 'n' cheese alert! Toothy elbow noodles are bound in a dense emulsion that is far from soupy, but more like custard. It is thick mac 'n' cheese that you actually chew, albeit barely. If you request or happen to receive a portion with reefs of edge and topskin, you seriously will chew it, for these elastic sections do require jaw work. In return they provide intense cheesy satisfaction.

Sweet Georgia Brown is a soul-food restaurant serving mostly African Americans. It is best known to its corps of loyal customers for barbecue. Here you will eat brisket and ribs, hot links and Polish sausages that are deliriously fatty and inescapably delicious. With a meal of one, two, or three of these meats, or with catfish, smothered chicken, meat loaf, or beef tips, each customer selects from an array of about a dozen different side dishes, macaroni being one of them. Other choices include collard greens, sautéed corn, fried okra, braised cabbage, beans and peas of various size and color, and a broccoli casserole in which pieces of the vegetable exist only to provide something firm amidst a dish that is really all about melting cheese.

Do bring plenty of appetite to Sweet Georgia Brown. A full meat-and-three meal weighs more than five pounds and will serve at least two large hungry people, meaning that the $10–$15 price is a bargain. (BBQ sandwiches also are available at about $7; they too are big.)

TACO GARAGE

8403 Broadway   210-826-4405
San Antonio, TX   B L D | $

With plenty of open space and, one trusts, good ventilation, an old service station garage makes a nice restaurant dining room. At San Antonio's Taco Garage, once a Break Check shop, the automotive theme endures in the form of front door handles that are little chain-link steering wheels. Out back, a forlorn VW microbus echoes hippie times with faded flowers painted on its body panels. The front of the menu advertises "Tex-Mex Cruizine."

There is a connection between custom cars and tacos—both are fields in which Mexican craftsmen excel—but once you are seated in this place, the food commands serious attention while the car stuff seems like fluff. As soon as you sit down, salsa is brought to the table. Dark and smoky, hot enough to make sure every taste bud is wide-awake, it keeps you eating as long as there are chips in the basket, or until meals arrive. Made with corn tortillas that have been rolled out and cooked just moments earlier, the tacos are sure proof of San Antonio's hegemony in the taco world. Cooked either flat or puffy (the latter quickly deep-fried), they can be filled with crisp-broiled shrimp and cabbage, ground beef, or chicken and cheese, or, for breakfast, huevos à la Mexicana. In fact, the menu lists twenty-six different kinds of taco, plus enchiladas, nachos, flautas, fajitas, and even hamburgers.

Drinks include "high horsepower" margaritas as well as "unleaded" (non-alcoholic) Mexican sodas.

TACO HOUSE

6307 San Pedro Ave.   210-341-3136
San Antonio, TX   B L | $

In some places, breakfast tacos are a novelty. In San Antonio, they are a staple, served in dozens of little eateries all over the city. The best of the taquerias use tortillas that are rolled out and griddle-cooked on the spot, just minutes before construction. Taco House, which has been a destination for decades, offers more than a dozen different kinds, from bacon and egg to *carne guisada* (gravy-sopped beef) and *lengua* (tongue). Fresh, chewy flour tortillas make a big difference, delivering even the most plebeian filling with high honors. But Taco House's plebeian fillings are far from drab. Eggs are buttery; bacon is thick and smoky; nuggets of potato are cooked to a perfect point of inside creaminess and outside crunch.

If you're going to have only one breakfast, consider chorizo and eggs, which, per local custom, is not eggs with a side order of chorizo sausage but rather eggs scrambled with ground-up sausage to become an entirely new and different food: juicy, spicy, and cream-rich. It's great on a plate with refried beans and potatoes or as the filling of a taco.

Lunch is a full roster of Tex-Mex fare, including tacos, enchiladas, flautas, and chicken molé. If you order chili, you will be asked whether or not you want beans. Say no and you are presented with an enormous bowl of true chili con carne, a minimalist dish of meat and red chile. Fajitas, like tacos, are available with crisp or puffy tortillas, the latter another San Antonio fave—quickly fried so they blow up like a flat sopaipilla.

★ TACO TACO

tacotacosa.com
145 E. Hildebrand Ave.   210-610-2795
San Antonio, TX   B L | $

Service is swift at Taco Taco, but if you come at peak hours for breakfast or lunch, you will have to wait for a table. The goodness of its tacos is no secret among San Antonio Tex-Mex aficionados, who have a huge number of excellent taquerias from which to choose. As in all the good places, Taco Taco rolls out its tortillas by hand and griddle cooks them. This means yours will be warm and fresh—delicious to eat with no filling whatsoever.

It is customary for local taquerias to offer *barbacoa* on the weekend, and it's hard to imagine a more delicious version than Taco Taco's. It is the tenderest, most unctuous smoky beef imaginable, slowly roasted and loaded into the taco in heaping shreds that audibly ooze when bitten. No other ingredients are warranted in this taco, as opposed to a chicken taco where a layer of refritos and a sprinkle of cheese are a nice complement, or a potato and egg breakfast taco gilded with the kitchen's marvelous salsa. Puffy tacos, a San Antonio passion, also are available—the same ingredients but enveloped in a tortilla that has been fried just enough to swell and soften. Specialty tacos are made on tortillas that are double-wide. El Norteno contains sizzled chicken (or beef) with beans, slices of avocado, cheese, peppers, and onions. Fiesta is fajita-grilled chicken with chunky pico de gallo.

Meals begin with excellent tortilla chips and that house salsa—impossible to stop eating until all chips are gone or the main course arrives. Beyond tacos, the menu offers weekend *menudo* and such fine borderland dishes as chicken molé enchiladas, gorditas, and flautas.

TEXAS PIE COMPANY

texaspiecompany.com
202 W. Center St.   512-268-5885
Kyle, TX   L | $

There is no chance you will miss the Texas Pie Company if you drive through Kyle along West Center Street. Looming over the roof that shades the sidewalk is an immense 3-D sculpture of a slice of cherry pie. Behind that, the house motto is written in bright red letters: "Life Is Short. Eat More Pie!"

This dessert-focused café is especially convenient for travelers just passing through because it makes single-serving mini pies as well as big ones. Crusts are terrific—not all that pretty, but light and savory. Lemon chess pie radiates dazzling citrus flavor with a buttermilky cushion; coconut is supremely toasty, its fleshy white shreds packing full nutty richness; and the nuts that crowd the top of the pecan pie taste fresh enough to have just come out of their shell. We also highly recommend strawberry cake, which is delectably moist and crowned with a heap of fruit-flavored frosting.

In addition to dessert, the Texas Pie Company sells simple lunches to eat here, including sandwiches and salads, and sells hot meals to take home. Among the latter is that Texas home-ec specialty of chicken and canned soup, King Ranch casserole.

THREADGILL'S
threadgills.com

6416 N. Lamar   512-451-5440
Austin, TX   **L D** | $$

 In the years we've been eating at Threadgill's, portions have gotten noticeably smaller. Now one full meal is big enough to feed only a couple of people. Still, this boisterous restaurant remains a bonanza for endless appetites, particularly appetites ravening for southern and/or Texas cooking.

Side dishes are vital here, from virtuous (okra with tomatoes) to wicked (garlic cheese grits). Many fans come to Threadgill's to eat *only* vegetables, accompanied by big squares of warm corn bread. If you choose right, a meal of five vegetable selections is, in fact, every bit as satisfying as a few pounds of beef. Among the excellent choices from the regular list are the San Antonio squash casserole, turnip greens, and crisp-fried okra.

As for entrees, we tend to go for chicken-fried steak or an impossibly rich plate of fried chicken livers with cream gravy. Those of lighter appetite can choose a very handsome (albeit gigantic) Caesar salad piled with grilled chicken, and there are a couple of unfried fish items.

Aside from big, good food, Threadgill's is worth visiting for its history (the Austin music scene started here; Janis Joplin used to be a waitress) and its Texas-to-the-max ambience. Although the original beer joint/gas station that Kenneth Threadgill opened in 1933 burned down twice and virtually none of it remains, the restaurant today has the feel of an antique: creaky wood floors, wood-slat ceilings, and a devil-may-care floor plan that gives the impression the sprawling space just kept growing through the years. The decorative motif is beer signs.

TOLBERT'S
tolbertsrestaurant.com

423 S. Main St.   817-421-4888
Grapevine, TX   **L D** | $$

Downtown Grapevine is like a large living-history museum, populated with antiques stores and western-themed specialty shops. Among the reliquaries is a restaurant called Tolbert's. Named for the late Frank X. Tolbert, author of *A Bowl of Red,* the definitive book about traditional Texas cooking, it is run by his daughter and son-in-law. Tolbert's is one of the few places we know that serves a bowl of true chili con carne.

What is chili con carne? Literally, it is chili with meat. Texas loyalists will accept nothing else as genuine. No add-ins or add-ons are allowed. No beans, no tomatoes, no bell peppers or Yukon golds or ground turkey or soysage. Chili con carne, as served at Tolbert's, is a muscle-bound duet of beef and heat. It comes with tortilla chips on the side, as well as shredded cheese and chopped raw onions to sprinkle on top, but the diehard Texas chilihead can ignore those things and spoon into delicious purity.

Beyond chili con carne, Tolbert's offers a full menu that ranges from chicken wings and ballpark nachos to steaks, seafood, burritos, and chocolate mousse cake. You can even get a sacrilegious bowl of chili, made with pinto beans. On the menu, it is titled "North of the Border."

TOM & BINGO'S

tomandbingos.com

3006 34th St.   806-799-1514
Lubbock, TX   **L** (closed Sun) | **$**

A wood-slat shack surrounded by a parking lot, Tom & Bingo's serves tender, moist beef brisket in a bun. Everybody comes for the brisket; the only alternatives are a ham sandwich and a burger. Gluttons can get a sandwich of all three: brisket, ham, and burger on a bun. Side dishes are chips by the bag, pickles, and onions. Sauce is good, but hardly necessary to enhance brisket so succulent after its long hickory-smoke bath. Seating is spare, at school desks along the wall.

Whole briskets are available if you order in advance, and Meg Butler, who tipped us off to this place, reported that after she and her husband shared four sandwiches at Tom & Bingo's, they bought one to carry home. "Security screeners at the airport didn't blink," she said.

VERNON'S KUNTRY KATFISH

kuntrykatfish.com

5901 W. Davis St.   936-760-3386
Conroe, TX   **L D** | **$**

Hugely popular—you will wait for a table any weekday at lunch—Vernon's Kuntry Katfish serves not only Mississippi-raised catfish, but also a passel of country-style vegetables every day. Mustard greens or turnip greens, northern beans, field peas, fried okra, mashed potatoes, and cheese-enriched broccoli are some of the selections; and crunchy, dark-cooked hush puppies, studded with bits of onion and jalapeño pepper, are accompanied by bowls of pickled green tomatoes. If catfish is not your dish, try the chicken-fried steak. It's one to make Texans proud, gilded with pepper gravy and served with biscuits or cornbread squares on the side.

Dessert is significant: fruit cobbler, banana pudding, or an item known as Good Pie, which is a uniquely American pastry edifice of pineapple chunks, bananas, cream cheese, nuts, and chocolate syrup.

VILLAGE BAKERY

113 E. Oak St.   254-826-5151
West, TX   **B** (closed Sun) | **$**

The *kolache,* brought to Texas by immigrants from central Europe, has become a morning pastry more popular than donuts in some towns. It is like a fruit-filled Danish, but made with sweeter dough that is so delicate, you need to hold it tenderly lest you compress it with brutal fingers. For some of the best *kolaches,* go to the town of West, Texas, just off I-35, and visit the Village Bakery. "Kolače [Czech spelling] are sold warm from the oven," assures the movable-letter menu above the counter. Apricot, prune, and poppy seed are standard-bearers from the old country. More modern variations are fruitier, filled with apple, strawberry, or blueberry preserves. A recent special contained espresso-chocolate and cream cheese filling.

The Village Bakery added a Texas twist to tradition in the early 1950s when baker Wendell Montgomery asked his mother-in-law to come up with a snack-sized version that included the sausage links that are another passion of Eastern Europeans who settled the heart of Texas. Her creation was a gloss on Czech *klobasniki,* which are customarily made with ground sausage. Purists still refer to them as that or, possibly, as pigs in blankets, reserving the term *kolache* for those filled with fruit, cheese, or poppy seeds. Savory *klobasnikis* are now popular wherever *kolaches* are sold. The Village Bakery makes regular and hot sausage versions.

More a bakery than a full-service restaurant, this welcoming little shop will sell you a cup of coffee and offers three small dining tables and one circular ten-seat table occupied by gabbing townsfolk most mornings.

WEIKEL'S STORE AND BAKERY

weikels.com

2247 W. State Hwy. 71   979-968-9413
La Grange, TX   **B L | $**

——★——— **OPEN EARLY** ———★—— A Danish-like pastry with Czech lineage, the *kolache* has become a tasty symbol of the Eastern European roots that have helped make this part of Texas such a culinary adventureland. One of the least likely places to find superior *kolaches* is Weikel's, a convenience store attached to a gas station by the side of the highway. While it might at first look like any other quick-shop highway mart, bakery cases toward the back tell a different story. Here are handsome cakes, rolls, and cookies, plus several varieties of *kolache* from a house repertoire of about a dozen. Prune, cream cheese, apricot, and poppy seed are fluffy-crumbed superior coffee companions.

You know Weikel's is serious about its *kolaches* when you consider the house motto: "We Got'cha Kolache." In addition to its pastry treasures, one other house specialty worth sampling is the house-made pig-in-a-blanket. It is a taut-skinned, rugged-textured kielbasa sausage fully encased in a tube of tender-crumb bread that is finer than any hot dog bun we've ever eaten.

CAPITOL REEF CAFE

capitolreefinn.com

360 W. Main St. 435-425-3271
Torrey, UT **B L D** | $$

At the west end of the town of Torrey in the wilds of south-central Utah, the Capitol Reef Cafe is an oasis of good food and elevated cultural consciousness. It is not only a restaurant: It is an inviting (and inexpensive) motel with hand-hewn furniture in the rooms; it is a bookstore featuring practical and meditative volumes about the west; and it is a trading post with some intriguing Native American jewelry and rugs.

The restaurant serves three meals a day and appears to be as informal as any western motel dining room, except for the fact that you are likely to hear the gurgle of an espresso machine in the background and Bach played to set the mood. The house motto is "Local, Natural, Healthy," and while you can have a fine breakfast of bacon and eggs, you can also choose to have those eggs accompanied by smoked local trout, or you can have an omelet made with local cheeses . . . with fresh-squeezed juice to drink.

The Capitol Reef dining room is a blessing for traveling vegetarians. A few notable meatless menu items include spaghetti with marinara sauce (also available with meat), fettuccine primavera, and plates of steamed, stir-fried, or shish-kebab vegetables. Beef, chicken, and seafood are always available for vegetable frowners (that trout, broiled with rosemary,

is what we recommend), and desserts include a hot fudge sundae and apple pie.

HIRES BIG H

hiresbigh.com

425 S. 700 East 801-364-4582
Salt Lake City, UT **L D** (closed Sun) | $

Ever since the success of nickel-a-glass root beer at A&W stands during Prohibition, "the temperance beverage" has been an axiomatic drive-in drink. At Hires Big H, with three curb-service outlets in the Salt Lake City area, it comes in five sizes, from "kid" to "large," and of course there are root beer floats. Or you can sip a limeade or a marshmallow-chocolate malt. Lemon, lime, cherry, vanilla, and chocolate can be added at no charge.

The juicy quarter-pound Big H burger is available plain or topped with bacon, ham, pastrami, Roquefort cheese, grilled onions, or a trio of crunchy onion rings, and it is brought to the car in a wax paper bag that makes a handy mitt. The bun is gentle-tempered sourdough with a floury top (as opposed to what the combative menu describes as "some preservative-enhanced, wilted crust studded with obnoxious seeds"), and French fries and onion rings are served with fry sauce, reminiscent of French dressing. Correspondent Mel Fullmer informed us that Utah fry sauce was invented at the Arctic Circle Drive-In in 1948. It has since become a thing of pride among burger joints as far away as California, Oregon, and Washington.

Other locations: 835 East Fort Union, Midvale (801-561-2171) and 2900 West 4700 South, West Valley City (801-965-1010).

IDLE ISLE

24 S. Main St.   435-734-2468
Brigham City, UT   **B L D** | $

Ahh, idleberry pie! A sultry, dark extravaganza that resonates with the booming fruitiness of blueberries, blackberries, and boysenberries, all packed into a crust that complements the berries with savory luxury, this pie is so complete that even à la mode seems superfluous. That's the one dish for which we always will love Idle Isle.

But we love Utah's third-oldest restaurant (since 1921) for all sorts of other things, and not just the food that is served. This is the sort of cordial town dining room once found on Main Streets everywhere. In the twenty-first century, its charm is a rarity to treasure.

You can have a burger and a malt at the marble and onyx soda fountain, and there is a slightly more boisterous back room with oilcloth-covered tables where regulars congregate at noon, but the choice seats, at least for us travelers, are in polished wood booths up front, each outfitted with a little ramekin of Idle Isle apricot marmalade for spooning onto fleecy rolls. The rolls come alongside dinners that are blue-plate fundamentals, including divinely tender pot roast with lumpy mashed potatoes shaped like a volcano crater to hold gravy as well as such daily specials as Wednesday braised beef joints, Friday trout, and Saturday prime rib.

LAMB'S GRILL

lambsgrill.com
169 S. Main St.   801-364-7166
Salt Lake City, UT   **B L D** (closed Sun) | $$

Utah's oldest restaurant hasn't changed much since we first ate here some three decades ago, at which point it was celebrating sixty years in business. Liquor is more readily available (although you still have to make a special request to see the booze menu), but it remains a house of family-friendly, meat-and-potatoes classics, some of which have all but vanished from modern restaurants' repertoires. Poached finnan haddie, anyone? Beef tenderloin à la Stroganoff? None of it is self-consciously old-fashioned. These simply are dishes that never have been dropped from a menu that has indeed changed with the times to include the likes of Cajun salad with blackened chicken breast and portobello mushroom ravioli.

Still, it's the old-fashioned dishes we like to see on our plate at this well-aged diner/coffee shop in the heart of Salt Lake City: broiled chicken with lemon caper sauce, triple lamb chops, mountain trout, or chicken-fried steak with garlic-tinged whipped potatoes. Meals come with sesame-seeded Greek bread, which is at once wispy and chewy—great to use for mopping gravy or for eating with or without butter.

If Utah has one distinguishing culinary characteristic (other than scones and fry sauce to accompany French fries), it is a love of sweets. You will appreciate this at Lamb's in the dark, chocolaty five-layer cake thick with icing, in the homey baked apple, and in the unusually al dente rice pudding blanketed with powdered cinnamon.

MADDOX DRIVE-IN

maddoxfinefood.com

1900 S. Hwy. 89   435-723-5683
Brigham City, UT   **L D** (closed Sun & Mon) | **$**

The Maddox Drive-In, attached to the Maddox Steak House, serves lots of hamburgers but specializes in another drive-in delight, the chicken basket: fried chicken and French fries piled into a woven plastic trough. The beverage of choice is known as "fresh lime," which tastes something like lime-aided Sprite with extra sugar. The long, covered tramway where you park at Maddox is festooned with enthusiastic signs apparently meant to stimulate appetites: "We serve only grain-fed beef . . . We invite you to visit our entire operation." What we remember best is the huge sign high above the restaurant, where futuristic letters boast of MADDOX FINE FOOD.

There used to be a feed lot right in back, allowing customers at the adjoining steak house to look out the window at future steaks on the hoof as they dined. Today the cows are gone, but pound-plus T-bones remain the order of the day, accompanied by a basket of crunchy corn pones and glasses of pure drinking water drawn from Maddox's own well.

MOM'S CAFE

10 E. Main St.   435-529-3921
Salina, UT   **B L D** | **$**

--★--
LOCALS
LOVE IT
--★--
Salina is a dusty old cowboy town with a few thousand citizens; Mom's is on its Main Street, serving blue-plate meals since 1929. We included this place in the very first edition of *Roadfood* (1978), giving it only one star out of four because there was no Mom in evidence, and service, by a gaggle of goofy teenagers, was sloppy. But the hamburgers were hand-formed and the coconut pie was fine, and, frankly, there weren't a whole lot of other dining options in central Utah. "Next time around," we wrote, "we'll peek in the kitchen first. If Mom is there, we'll give it another try."

About fifteen years later, we didn't have to look in the kitchen because the current Mom oversaw the operation from a desk right out in the dining room.

Carolyn Jensen ran a tight ship. We were impressed by the efficiency of coffeepot-armed waitresses who wore blue uniforms that matched the aqua-blue upholstered booths, and more important, we had learned enough about Southwestern food to better appreciate a truly regional meal. Chicken-fried steak with pepper-cream gravy, biscuits with gravy . . . heck, nearly everything with gravy was (and remains) first-rate. Pies at Mom's are Roadfood paradigms: lovely apple and cherry and custards, blueberry sour cream that is extraordinary, and, on occasion, cherry sour cream too.

It was on that return visit to Mom's that we first tasted the kind of scone that is unique to Utah. Completely unlike the dense, English-ancestored quick-bread scone, a Utah scone is a flat disc of puffy fry bread—pliable, crisp-edged, and tender within. It is no doubt related to the sopaipilla of New Mexico, but customarily it is made with sweeter dough. All meals at Mom's come with kettle-hot scones accompanied by the Beehive State's favorite condiment, honey butter.

NAVAJO HOGAN

447 E. 3300 South   801-466-2860
Salt Lake City, UT   **L D** | **$**

Few foods served in modern restaurants actually are native to America; nearly everything we eat is the product of immigrants bringing their recipes (and sometimes their seeds, livestock, and spices) and mixing them with what's available across the fruited plains. Navajo Hogan's tacos are, in fact, exactly the sort of melting-pot dish that characterizes our nation's cuisine at its most exuberant: Mexican, New Mexican, and Utahan, with a measure of fast-food brio.

The Navajo taco, popular throughout the Southwest, is built upon fry bread: excellent stuff here, made using flour and cornmeal that gets slid into a pan of hot oil and fried into a pliable disc ready for anything. Atop the bread goes your choice of ingredients, ranging from what the menu calls "traditional" (beans, beef, lettuce, tomato, shredded cheese, and sour cream) to dessert versions topped with honey butter or cinnamon sugar. You can get green or red chili from New Mexico, vegetarian toppings, or grilled chicken. That is the extent of the menu, except for Saturday-only mutton stew, a true Navajo dish that goes back at least a millennium.

Roadfood.com contributor Dale Fine, whose screen name is Wanderingjew, noted that Navajo Hogan is the sort of place "you're likely to pass by without realizing it's there": a windowless cinder-block bunker with fabric signs hung outside. We thank Mr. Fine for discovering it.

SILL'S CAFE

335 E. Gentile St.   801-544-7438
Layton, UT   **B L D** | $

--★-- **LOCALS LOVE IT** --★-- We wouldn't suggest making a special trip to Sill's Cafe to eat fabulous food. The one unique-to-Utah item on the menu, a scone, is very good—especially so because the deep-fried disc of dough, vaguely reminiscent of a monstrous beignet, comes with a cupful of fine honey butter that melts immediately from the freshly fried scone's heat. Another notable specialty of the house, albeit not exclusive to the Beehive State, is the peppery SOS—a thick sausage gravy that is especially welcome as the blanket for a plateload of hash-brown potatoes. The cinnamon rolls are large and gooey, and there are pancakes and eggs for breakfast and hot beef sand-wiches with drifts of mashed potatoes, burgers, and such for lunch and supper.

If the meals are not necessarily tripworthy, the place is. Roadfood.com's Dale Fine nailed its appeal by noting that it is a restaurant that is very much part of its community. For more than fifty years now, Sill's has attracted a cadre of regulars who are served by a staff of professional waitresses in an interactive daily encounter that is the spirit of Layton. There are no bells and whistles (except maybe for that outstanding scone), but there is true satisfaction for the traveler in search of traditional small-town foodways.

GREAT PLAINS

MONTANA

SANDPOINT
Di Luna's
Old Tin Can
The Pie Hut

PONDERAY
Hoot Owl Cafe

DOVER BAY
Dish

COEUR D'ALENE
Fisherman's Market
Garnet Cafe
★ Hudson's Hamburgers
Java on Sherman
Jimmy's Down the Street
Meltz
Wolf Lodge Inn

LEWISTON
Effie's Tavern

GREAT FALLS
★ Eddie's Supper Club

LEWISTOWN
Dash Inn

BILLINGS
Rex Restaurant
Sarah's
Stella's

BUTTE
Matt's Place
Pekin Noodle Parlor

HELENA

WILLOW CREEK
Willow Creek Cafe & Saloon

RED LODGE
Red Lodge Cafe

STORY
The Wagon Box

CODY
Noon Break

GREYBULL
Lisa's

GILLETTE
Lula Belle's Cafe

BOISE
Goldy's Breakfast Bistro
Leku Ona
Westside Drive-In

KUNA
Enrique's

HUDSON
Svilar's

CHUGWATER
Chugwater Soda Fountain

CHEYENNE

IDAHO

WYOMING

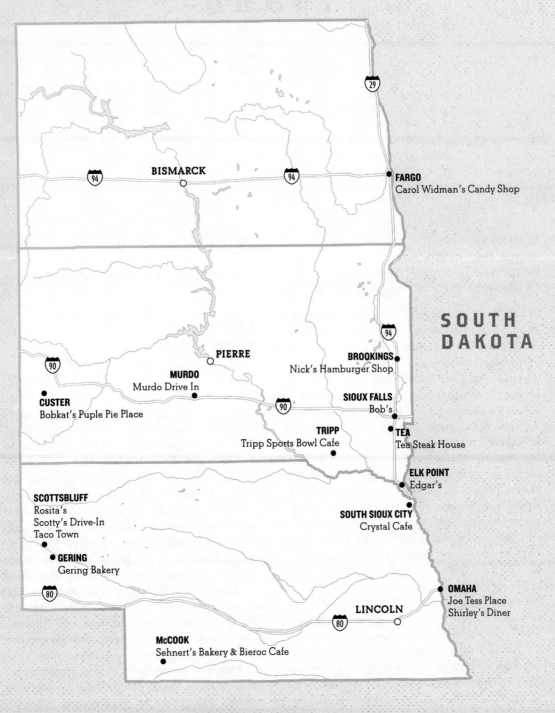

NORTH DAKOTA

🛣 29

🛣 94 BISMARCK 🛣 94 FARGO
Carol Widman's Candy Shop

SOUTH
DAKOTA

🛣 94

PIERRE BROOKINGS
Nick's Hamburger Shop

🛣 90 MURDO
Murdo Drive In

CUSTER SIOUX FALLS
Bobkat's Puple Pie Place Bob's

🛣 90

TRIPP TEA
Tripp Sports Bowl Cafe Tea Steak House

ELK POINT
Edgar's

SCOTTSBLUFF
Rosita's SOUTH SIOUX CITY
Scotty's Drive-In Crystal Cafe
Taco Town

GERING
Gering Bakery

OMAHA
Joe Tess Place
🛣 80 Shirley's Diner

🛣 80 LINCOLN

McCOOK
Sehnert's Bakery & Bieroc Cafe

NEBRASKA

IDAHO

DI LUNA'S

dilunas.com

207 Cedar St.
Sandpoint, ID

208-263-0846

B L D (Wed-Sun) | $

Di Luna's is a friendly town café, crafts gallery, and music venue that offers dinner concerts of jazz, country, and blues, and serves breakfast and lunch Wednesday through Sunday. We are fond of a morning meal called Three Sisters Skillet, which the menu advises is a gloss on a native Pend d'Oreilles tribe dish: a meatless medley of grilled polenta, roasted butternut squash, and white beans. The potato choice at breakfast is either regular hash browns, which are crisp and starchy, or sweet-potato hash browns, which are only barely sweet and agreeably oily. The breakfast called Sharp & Sweet tops those fine sweet-potato hash browns with sharp Cheddar cheese, accompanied by thick-sliced bacon, ham, or sausage.

There are regular eggs Benedict (albeit made with ham rather than Canadian bacon), salmon Benedict, veggie Benedict, and country Benedict, that last one being a split biscuit topped with sausage and smothered with sausage gravy. The gravy is substantial, served also as the companion for Di Luna's crunch-crusted chicken-fried steak.

At lunch, we have enjoyed beer-battered halibut and chips as well as an opulent steak and gorgonzola salad. The only clinker was a dish that duty demanded we try—the yakburger, made from locally raised yaks.

A few bites and we were very glad that good old beef cows are the nation's mainstay. The yakburger was sawdust-dry, like an imitation of overcooked, over-lean sirloin.

DISH

dishatdoverbay.com

651 Lakeshore Ave.
Dover Bay, ID

208-265-6467

L D (limited hours in winter)

| $$

★
WATER-FRONT
DINING
★

Dish is casual enough to feel like a shorts-and-sandals waterside grill, which in some ways it is, perched on the shore of breathtakingly beautiful Lake Pend Oreille. You can come for a hamburger, tacos, or fish and chips. On the other hand, there is serious kitchen wizardry going on, evident in the likes of buffalo meat loaf with chipotle barbecue sauce or sweet chili-glazed prawns with wasabi crème fraîche. Anyone looking for a big-deal culinary experience in the vicinity of Sandpoint won't find a better opportunity.

Dinners of steak, salmon, and buffalo meat loaf are accompanied by "smashed potatoes"—medium-size Idahos that are parboiled, iced, semi-flattened, then fried until their soft insides are enveloped in a well-salted leathery coat. This is spud heaven, especially when supplemented by a few strips of what the menu bills as "world-famous bacon"—mahogany ribbons that are smoky, peppery, and otherwise doctored up to give them succulence like the juiciest pork belly, but with all the crispy-chewy texture of thick-sliced bacon.

That same bacon also happens to be the unlikely star player in a lunch item that Dish offers: the vegetarian burger. Yes, according to proprietor Gary Peitz, three out of four veggie burgers served at Dish are ordered with bacon on top. Beefless they may be, but the bacon's piggy virtue is an intensely pleasurable animal-fat complement to the thick patty of root vegetables in which finely shredded beets do an amazing visual imitation of rare ground sirloin. The burgers come on pretzel rolls and are decorated with lettuce, tomato, onion, and jalapeño aioli.

If you come late summer, you can start the meal with a huckleberry mojito and finish it with ice cream blanketed with walnuts and freshly picked huckleberries.

EFFIE'S TAVERN

1120 Main St.   208-746-1889
Lewiston, ID   L D | $$

A tip of the hat to Lisa McDermott for directing us to Effie's, which she described as a "hole-in-the-wall dive—so right up your alley—and the plate-sized burgers are wonderful." Amen, sister! These are outlandish hamburgers, costing nearly $20 and weighing one pound each (unless you choose the one-and-a-half-pounder or the three-pound double). If size was their only claim to fame, we'd drive on; but, in fact, Effie's hamburgers are very good. They are wide, juice-laden, griddle-sizzled patties presented on truly plate-sized buns, available, of course, with cheese and bacon and all imaginable condiments. If the thought of a one-pound burger is daunting, know that many customers order a single burger for two and cut it into halves or quarters. Seasoned curly fries and beer-battered onion rings are available on the side.

As Lisa noted, Effie's is nothing fancy—it's a well-worn, wood-paneled café with a short counter in back and sets of upholstered booths up front.

ENRIQUE'S

enriqueskuna.com
482 W. Main St.   208-922-5169
Kuna, ID   L D | $

A cheerful restaurant whose name translates as "the fighting rooster," this Treasure Valley gem southwest of Boise and just a few minutes from I-84 serves superb true-Mex food. Start with *pozole* (hominy-pork soup), *campenchana* (octopus and shrimp in a garlic-lime marinade), or freshly made guacamole accompanied by chips and salsa. Quaff a Mexican beer or creamy-sweet *horchata* (rice milk), then move on to a beautiful plate of chicken molé blanketed with intense chile-chocolate sauce or fish tacos on soft tortillas. *Molcajetes*, served in lava rock bowls, are a dining event. Even the refried beans are extra-good, sprinkled with crumbled cotija cheese.

From what we could see on other people's tables, the more familiar Tex-Mex meals are mighty tempting: enchiladas, chimichangas, fajitas, et cetera. The little tacos, selling for a dollar apiece, are local legend. You can have them filled with steak, pork, goat, cheek, tongue, chicken, or tripe.

One reason people return again and again, other than the food, is the hospitality of Enrique Contreras, who is known for circulating around the dining room to say hello to old friends and welcome new ones.

FISHERMAN'S MARKET

215 W. Kathleen Ave.   208-664-4800
Coeur d'Alene, ID   L D (closed Sun) | $$

Most of what is served at the Fisherman's Market is handsomely displayed raw, on ice in glass cases for people to purchase by the pound and take home to cook: mahimahi, Alaskan cod, halibut, salmon, shrimp, oysters, scallops, and calamari. For those who come to eat in this spacious piscatorial dining hall, nearly everything in the case is available as the "fish" part of a fish and chips platter. Halibut and chips is the most expensive item on the menu (other than crab Louis), but it is well worth the premium price, falling into big, creamy flakes when you cut through the well-seasoned breading. (Grilled fish and chips is also available.) The chips are excellent freshly cut French fries. One of the fun things about any of the fried items on the menu is that you get to choose tartar sauces from a roster of eight. We love the Cabo (jalapeño and lime) and the Cap'n Dick's (horseradish and cocktail sauce). Also available: Rasta (jerk spices), Sicilian, Tokyo, Bombay, Cajun, and Traditional.

Other dishes of interest on the Fisherman's Market dine-in menu include oyster and catfish po' boys, seafood salads, coconut-crusted snapper, shrimp or fish tacos, a fresh Dungeness crab sandwich, steamed clams, and raw ahi tuna salad. The dining room includes a lively sushi bar, specialties of which include a North Idaho Roll, made with salmon, scallions, avocado, and cucumber, and a California roll made with real crab rather than surimi.

GARNET CAFE

garnetcafe.com

315 Walnut St.   208-667-2729
Coeur d'Alene, ID   **B L** (closed Mon) | **$$**

Named for Idaho's state gem, the Garnet Cafe really is precious. Proprietors Justin and Angeline McLane and chef Everett Fees have made it their mission to serve food that is caught, raised, or grown locally. In fact, much of what is cooked here is sourced directly from the McLane family farm. Bacon, sausage, and ham come from McLane hogs. Yogurt is made in-house from farm milk; duck and chicken eggs come from farm poultry. Seafood is wild-caught from Pacific waters, and while the McLanes don't raise mushrooms, the ones they use in the kitchen are foraged in the area and brought to the restaurant by their mycological friends.

While all of the above might imply that the Garnet Cafe is a stylin', pricey sort of place, nothing could be further from the truth. The fare is high quality and handsome, no doubt about that, but there's nothing the least bit pretentious about the meals or the service; it's easy to dine well here for under $15.

This is the only restaurant where we have eaten—and enjoyed—spaghetti for breakfast. Glistening al dente noodles are tossed with shreds of sun-dried tomato, roasted garlic, herbed goat cheese, Parmesan

cheese, and basil, the pretty medley accompanied by a pair of McLane Farm eggs and a hefty slice of buttered toast—sourdough, rosemary, or whole wheat. To enhance the terrific toast, diners are presented with a ramekin of what looks like honey butter but turns out to be sunshiny lemon curd.

Another fine breakfast/brunch/lunch plate is Bristol Bay (Alaska) sockeye salmon. A thick slab of it is glazed with marmalade that becomes a sweet halo for the luxurious pink protein. The salmon is presented atop a mound of sautéed vegetables: mushrooms, peppers, squash, onions, leafy greens, and herbs. It too comes with a pair of eggs and choice of toast.

A few other morning house specialties: duck confit, which is a leg slowly cooked in duck fat until fall-apart tender; green eggs and ham (pesto sauce provides the color); and French toast stuffed with Nutella and banana; oatmeal, made with extra-thick-cut Snoqualmie Falls oats that pack deep-roasted flavor. Perhaps the most curious dish available for breakfast, listed on the menu as Everyone's Favorite, is Spam and eggs.

GOLDY'S BREAKFAST BISTRO

goldysbreakfastbistro.com

108 S. Capitol Blvd.   208-345-4100
Boise, ID   **B L** | **$$**

Who couldn't love Goldy's "Create Your Own Breakfast Combo"? Select a main course, which can be eggs, chicken-fried steak, or a salmon fillet, then take your pick from long lists of meats, potatoes, and breads. Among the not-to-be-missed meats are habanero chicken sausage, Basque chorizo, and pork sausage infused with sage. The potato roster includes not only hash browns and sweet-potato hash browns but also red-flannel hash (spuds, beets, and bacon) and cheese grits. Among available breads are fresh-baked biscuits, sourdough, and cinnamon raisin walnut.

Hollandaise sauce is fantastic: smooth and fluffy with an ethereal lemon perfume. It comes on several variations of eggs Benedict. There's eggs Blackstone (Black Forest ham and tomato); a dilled salmon fillet blanketed with slivers of cucumber and sauce; even a veggie benny, which is sauce over broccoli, asparagus, and tomato. Other choice breakfast items: frittatas, breakfast burritos, cinnamon rolls, and sticky buns.

A stylish little place with an open kitchen, Goldy's can be maddeningly crowded, making meal service less than speedy, and on weekends expect to wait for a table. But if your goal is having the best breakfast in Boise, this is the place to go.

HOOT OWL CAFE

30784 Hwy. 200   208-265-9348
Ponderay, ID   **B L | $**

Looking for a unique local drink? Have a huckleberry lemonade at the Hoot Owl Cafe. Looking for a really hearty breakfast? Biscuits, made each morning, are served plain to go with eggs and such, or as a meal, smothered with sausage gravy. They also are the foundation for Redneck Eggs Benedict, in which sausage patties substitute for Canadian bacon and gravy replaces hollandaise. (Note: The day's supply of biscuits can be gone before lunch.)

Hoot Owl's rib-sticking gravy is also available atop an order of hash browns. If you want something seriously filling, consider Hash Browns Supreme: spuds and scrambled eggs, onions, peppers, tomatoes, mushrooms, spinach, zucchini, and chopped fresh garlic, with salsa on the side.

This is a made-from-scratch sort of place where nothing is trendy but everything is a cut above: fresh corned beef hash sizzled as crusty as you request, plate-wide pancakes, gnarled chicken-fried steaks. Vegans can order Hash Browns Supreme made without eggs.

The Hoot Owl opens at 5 in the morning, shortly after which it is populated by locals drinking coffee and enjoying one another's company.

★ HUDSON'S HAMBURGER'S

hudsonhamburgers.com
207 E. Sherman Ave.   208-664-5444
Coeur d'Alene, ID   **L | $**

--★--
HOT
TICKET
--★--
"Pickle and onion?" the counterman will ask when you order a hamburger, a double hamburger, or a double cheeseburger at Hudson's, a counter-only diner that has been a Coeur d'Alene institution since 1907, when Harley Hudson opened a quick-eats lunch tent on the town's main drag.

Your garnish selection is called out to grill man Todd Hudson, Harley's great-grandson, who slices the raw onion to order, using his knife blade to hoist the thin, crisp disc from the cutting board to the bun bottom; then, deft as a Benihana chef, he cuts eight small circles from a pickle and arrays them in two neat rows atop the onion. When not wielding his knife, Todd hand-forms each burger, as it is ordered, from a heap of lean ground beef piled in a gleaming silver pan adjacent to his griddle. All this happens at warp speed as customers enjoy the mesmerizing show from the sixteen seats at Hudson's long counter and from the small standing area at the front of the restaurant, where new arrivals await stool vacancies.

Each patty is cooked until it develops a light crust from the griddle but retains a high amount of juice inside. One in a bun makes a balanced sandwich. Two verge on overwhelming beefiness. Chef Hudson sprinkles on a dash of salt, and when the hamburger is presented, you have one more choice to make: which condiment? Three squeeze bottles are deployed adjacent to each napkin dispenser along the counter. One is hot mustard, the other is normal ketchup, the third is Hudson's spicy ketchup, a thin orange potion for which the recipe is a guarded secret. "All I can tell you is that there is no horseradish in it," the counterman reveals.

There are no side dishes at all: no French fries, no chips, no slaw, not a leaf of lettuce in the house. And other than the fact that a glass case holds slices of pie for dessert, there is nothing more to say about Hudson's. In the last century it has honed a simple perfection.

JAVA ON SHERMAN

819 Sherman Ave.   208-667-0010
Coeur d'Alene, ID   **B L** | $

When we first came across Java on Sherman a dozen years ago, it was primarily a place to get coffee along with some pretty darn good pastries. The coffee is as good as ever, as are the scones and muffins, but the food choices have improved tremendously.

The great leap forward took place in 2014, when Java moved to a new location up the street where a full kitchen gets a good workout every day through midafternoon. The lunch menu is a short one of sandwiches, paninis, and salads. Knife-and-fork morning meals include broad, fluffy pancakes, from-scratch granola and oatmeal, Benedicts and breakfast sandwiches, and sweet-potato hash that is laced with chewy squiggles of onion and bits of green pepper. Now that there's a deep fryer, Java also makes donuts. Made to order, they come by the dozen or half dozen, still too hot to handle, available plain or blanketed by cinnamon sugar or powdered sugar. Accompany these exemplary sinkers by a Bowl of Soul (Java's name for espresso, coffee, and cinnamon) or a Keith Richards (espresso, coffee, and Mexican chocolate) and you will walk away humming a happy tune.

A broad patio out front makes the new location a happy place to be when the weather is nice. Dogs are welcomed out here (but not inside).

JIMMY'S DOWN THE STREET

jimmysdownthestreet.com

1613 E. Sherman Ave.   208-765-3868
Coeur d'Alene, ID   **B L** | $

For a hearty breakfast in Coeur d'Alene, you can't beat Jimmy's Down the Street. Locals congregate at this welcoming counter-and-table town café for such rib-stickers as a chicken-fried steak skillet with chunky fried potatoes and cheese and a couple of eggs, plus oversized biscuits and cream gravy. Pecan rolls are big, flat mesas of cake-rich dough, topped with a slurry of caramel glaze and chopped nuts. French toast, made with sourdough bread, can be had stuffed with sweet cream cheese and topped with berries and whipped cream. The day we went, it was Meat Lovers Scramble Day—a scramble made with three eggs, bacon, ham, and sausage, topped with cheese.

Breakfast is served all day, and lunch begins at 10 a.m. There are seven-ounce burgers, including a summer-only chili cheeseburger and patty melt on grilled rye. The signature dish is chicken and dumplings, which is copious although fairly bland. A more exciting choice among gigantic lunch possibilities is the John Wayne sandwich, which is a half foot of chicken-fried steak, bacon, fried dill pickles, onion rings, and a bunch of condiments. Not a lot of finesse here, but plenty of flavors!

For dessert you can have a bowl of ice cream, an individually sized apple or pecan pie, or a deep-fried pecan roll.

LEKU ONA

lekuonaid.com

117 S. 6th St.   208-345-6665
Boise, ID   **L D** (closed Sun) | $$$

Located on what Boisians know as the Basque Block, Leku Ona is both a five-room boutique hotel and an adjoining restaurant celebrating the hearty, high-spiced cuisine of the people of the Pyrenees. Unlike many of the region's Basque restaurants, which serve only groaning-board, family-style meals, this Old World ode offers a regular menu from which each customer is free to choose an appetizer (perhaps Urdaiazpikoa, aka Serrano ham), a soup (red bean and chorizo, please), and an entree, which can range from whole squid cooked in its ink to honeycomb tripe or lamb shank. Prices are high on the Roadfood scale (dinner entrees in the $20+ range); service is suave and each dish is exemplary.

For those who want the more traditional Basque-hotel experience, Leku Ona does offer family-style feeds of soup, salad, and hot bread, followed by battered codfish and chef's paella, French fries, and your choice of lamb stew, pork chops, or roast chicken, sirloin steak, pork loin, or meatballs. Drink choices include Pagoa (a Basque beer) in lager, red ale, and stout. There's also a *pinxtos* (aka tapas) bar featuring small portions of such savories as leek pancakes, beef tongue, and cod croquettes. For dessert: *madari egosiak*, a lurid dish of sweetened pears poached in red wine.

MELTZ

meltzextreme.com

1735 W. Kathleen Ave.   208-664-1717
Coeur d'Alene, ID   **L D** | $

Meltz's mission statement is "Extreme Grilled Cheese." No kidding. The sandwich called Korean Krazy, for example, is provolone and pepper jack cheeses, barbecued beef, kimchi, crushed sesame sticks, scallions, hot pepper ketchup, and cilantro. Another eye-popping as well as palate-pleasing invention is the Oinker: barbecued pulled pork, Cheddar, Brie, roasted artichokes, red peppers, caramelized onions, garlicky spinach, grilled zucchini, and sun-dried tomatoes.

Simpler sandwiches of merely cheese also are available, with your choice of Cheddar, fontina, Monterey Jack, pepper jack, Colby, Swiss, provolone, mozzarella, gorgonzola, gruyère, Brie, blue, chèvre, American, and even Cheez Whiz.

Beyond the abundance of first-rate ingredients, what gives these sandwiches an edge is that they are made on thick-cut whole-wheat or sourdough bread that gets good and crunchy on the grill. It is not uncommon for cheese to ooze out and turn chewy or crisp during the cooking process, creating yummy little wings that extend beyond the bread. Because sandwiches tend to be complicated and are made to order, the wait time is a full ten minutes. When your order is ready, your name is called, and it is up to you to tote your tray to a table in the small, crowded dining area. To go with the sandwiches, Meltz makes thick-cut potato chips (from Idahos, of course) that are salted and brilliantly seasoned.

Meltz shares space in a modest strip mall with a gas station convenience store and a Take 'n' Bake pizza place. Its location and its fast-food looks do nothing to suggest that it is as interesting a restaurant as it actually is.

OLD TIN CAN

317 Oak St.   208-920-0596
Sandpoint, ID   **L** (spring–Oct) | $

The Old Tin Can is one of several food trucks that regularly park at Sandpoint's Oak Street Court across from Farmin Park. Dining is al fresco, at picnic tables under tents. While many of the trucks offer very good fare, from Thai banana crepes to Memphis barbecue, Old Tin Can hamburgers are the culinary standout. Big, irregular, hand-formed rounds of ground beef (from local cattle) are cooked to order; unless you're a well-done person, you can count on great rivers of juice to flow from the burger at the slightest squeeze and the first bite.

The standard cheeseburger is terrific, especially when fully accoutered with lettuce, tomato, onion, and various condiments; plus, you can count on at least one creative variation each day. A few such gems we've encountered are an avocado-Cheddar burger; a Cowboy Burger that includes bacon, Cheddar, barbecue sauce, and fried onion straws; a burger adorned with basil cream cheese, roasted red pepper, balsamic-tossed spinach, grilled onions, and local tomato; and a peanut butter, bacon, and Cheddar burger. The regular menu even lists a quinoa burger for vegetarians.

Created and helmed by Brad and Savannah Clark, the Old Tin Can gets its name because it is housed in a gleaming silver mid-twentieth-century Kit Companion travel trailer—a vintage vision of streamlined beauty.

THE PIE HUT

502 Church St.   208-265-2208
Sandpoint, ID   **L D** (closed Sun & Mon) | $

Sandpoint, Idaho, hosts a huckleberry festival every August, but the luminous maroon berries, which are the state's official fruit, start coming into town as early as the first week in July. Lucky for us, that's when we found the Pie Hut. In fact, proprietor and chef Heather Gross was busy at the end of lunch hour making crusts for her first-of-the-season huckleberry pies to be baked the next morning, ready to serve when she opened at 10:30 a.m.

Year-round, the Pie Hut serves a high-rise huckleberry Monte Cristo, which is an egg-dipped and griddle-fried sandwich of turkey, ham, and Swiss cheese topped with sweet huckleberry syrup. The emblematic fruit of the Idaho Panhandle is just one reason to visit this snug little diner where banquettes are upholstered in Fiestaware-colored leatherette. The Pie Hut is a worthy destination for all who appreciate superb pie of any kind—cream, fruit, nut, even a chockablock savory chicken potpie. Beyond precious huckleberry, the pie repertoire in early July included smooth sour cream lemon with sharp citrus zing, marionberry-apple in which the dark berry's complexity sings in harmony with the apples, and rhubarb that is the classic pie-plant pie with fruity ebullience in a savory crust that easily flakes when prodded with a fork.

Just as huckleberries are precious to Idahoans, so potatoes are their staff of life. In this department, the Pie Hut delivers the goods in the form of baked potato soup—a surprisingly spritely white potion garnished with scallions, herbs, and a scattering of Cheddar shreds. Other pre-dessert considerations include grilled sandwiches, French dip, the occasional gyro, and barbecued pulled pork with pineapple slaw.

WESTSIDE DRIVE-IN
mobi.cheflou.com

1939 W. State St.   208-342-2957
Boise, ID   **L D | $**

A drive-in owned by "Chef Lou" Aaron, who has a regular cooking segment on Boise's KTVB and is the creator of a dessert called the Idaho Ice Cream Potato, Westside is a place people come to eat (off their dashboards or on the patio's picnic tables) and to take home such Chef Lou specialties as prime rib, pastas, and salads. The drive-in fare includes crisp-fried shrimp and fish and chips and a roster of extraordinary made-to-order hamburgers that are thick and crusty and juicy inside, nothing like franchised fast-food junkburgers. There are doubles, deluxes, Cajun burgers, guacamole burgers, and Maui burgers. We like a good ol' cheeseburger, preferably with lettuce and tomato. It comes wrapped in wax paper for easy eating. With French fries, you get the sweet dip called fry sauce . . . which many like on burgers too.

In honor of his home state, Chef Lou offers "the biggest bakers in the valley," which are one-pound Super Spuds available simply saturated with butter or loaded with chili, cheese, and onions. To drink, there are fine milk shakes, including huckleberry and black raspberry.

WOLF LODGE INN
wolflodgecda.com

11741 E. Frontage Rd.   208-664-6665
(Exit 22 off I-90)   **D | $$$**
Coeur d'Alene, ID

Here are meat-and-potatoes meals of Homeric scale. A vast red barn-board roadhouse just yards from the highway, this exuberant Wild West domain features oilcloth-clad tables and walls festooned with trophy animal heads, bleached bovine skulls, antique tools, old beer posters, and yellowing newspaper clippings of local-interest stories. It is a sprawling place with miscellaneous booths and dining nooks in several rooms; at the back of the rearmost dining area is a stone barbecue pit where tamarack firewood burns a few feet below the grate. On this grate lie sizzling slabs of beef, ranging from a ten-ounce filet mignon to the Rancher, which is forty-four ounces of porterhouse and sirloin. (Seafood is also available, cooked over the wood.)

Cowboy-cuisine aficionados start supper with a plate of "swinging steak"—sliced and crisp-fried bull testicles, served with cocktail sauce and lemon wedges. We relished a bowl of truly homey vegetable beef soup that was as thick as stew with hunks of carrot, potato, beef, green pepper, and onion. Dinners come with saucy "buckaroo" beans, a twist of *krebel* (fried bread), and baked or fried potatoes, the latter excellent steak fries, each of which is one-eighth of a long Idaho baker that has been sliced end-to-end and fried so that it develops a light, crisp skin and creamy insides.

There is a second Wolf Lodge Inn in Spokane, Washington.

MONTANA

DASH INN

207 NE Main St.   406-535-3892
Lewistown, MT   **L D** | **$**

Long before foodies knew about paninis, the Dash Inn made its reputation on a burger known as the Wagon Wheel: a beef patty that gets cooked and put between slices of bread, then grilled until the bread gets crisp. There are singles, doubles, cheese Wagon Wheels, and Western Wagon Wheels; there also are regular bunned hamburgers, twin burgers, triple burgers, and pizza burgers. If for some reason you are not in the mood for a hamburger, the Dash Inn also serves many other sandwiches, including the Montana-born Pork Chop John sandwich and a Sourdough Dash that is Swiss cheese, bacon, tomato, and mayonnaise on grilled sourdough bread. Fried chicken is sold by the piece and bucket.

On the side, choose from among tater tots, French fries, curly fries, and potato wedges, and while there are smoothies, milk shakes, and floats to drink, do consider soda pop. Offering both Coke and Pepsi products, the Dash Inn will doctor up your favorite drink with flavored syrup, including lime, chocolate, and cherry. Blythe Butler, who first alerted us to this jolly place, wrote that the most popular potation was Coke with Hot-N-Tot, which is cinnamon syrup. She also suggested rum syrup in Mountain Dew.

The Dash Inn is strictly drive-through, all food served in paper bags. There is plenty of space around the restaurant to park and eat.

★ EDDIE'S SUPPER CLUB

3725 2nd Ave. N.   406-453-1616
Great Falls, MT   **L D** | **$$**

Eddie's is supper-club dining at its finest, patronized since 1944 by generations of Montanans who come to have cocktails and steaks in comfort.

There are two halves to it: a coffee shop, which is lighter-feeling, more casual, and with a menu that includes sandwiches, and the more serious restaurant, which has a big-deal menu of beef and seafood.

We like sitting in the supper club if only for its décor: large, handsome pictures of horses, all kinds of them: trotters in action, a bucking horse tossing a cowboy, western horses at work tending cattle. The picture at the back of the room, which has a horse's head in the foreground and a herd of cows in back, is especially beguiling. "We call him Mr. Ed," our waitress said. "His eyes follow you all around the room."

Booths are comfortable, lights are low, and the staff are able pros. Steaks are grand. "Tastes just like that old Marlboro Cowboy cooked it over the campfire," advises the menu. Our waitress told us that the secret of the steaks is not the fire, but the house's special wine marinade. This seeps into the meat and gives it a special tang, also coating the surface so the exterior of the steak develops a crunchy, caramelized crust as it cooks. The T-bone we ate was spectacularly good. And an off-the-menu hamburger, which has the marinade folded into the meat, was wild.

MATT'S PLACE

2339 Placer St.	406-782-8049
Butte, MT	**L D**	**$**

A virtual time machine, Matt's of Butte, Montana, looks like it might not have changed at all since opening in 1930. The state's oldest drive-in has a short, curved counter and a bright-red, waist-high Coke machine from which you fetch your own bottle from icy waters. Hamburgers sizzle in the back kitchen; milk shake mixers whir, and soda jerks ply seltzer and syrup dispensers to brew effervescent potions. If you are not in the mood for a pork chop sandwich (Montana's passion) or an ordinary hamburger, Matt's offers custom burgers, including one topped with fried eggs and a "nutburger" spread with mayonnaise and a fistful of chopped peanuts.

PEKIN NOODLE PARLOR

117 S. Main	406-782-2217
Butte, MT	**D**	**$**

Pekin Noodle Parlor is a relic of Butte's boom days as a mining town, when the small street out back was known as China Alley. An ancient sign on the wall says, "Famous Since 1916." Climb a small dark staircase to the second floor and you will be escorted to your own curtained dining cubicle. The setting suggests exotic intrigue, like an old Montana version of the *Shanghai Express*. When the food comes from the kitchen, it is announced by the rumble of the waitress's rolling trolley along the wood-plank floor; the curtain whisks aside, and behold! Here is a vista of foreign food the likes of which most devotees of Asian cookery forgot about fifty years ago.

Chop suey and chow mein are mild, thick, and harmless; fried shrimp are girdled by a pad of breading and served on leaves of lettuce with French fried potatoes; sweet-and-sour ribs drip pineapple-flavored syrup; and the house specialty—noodles—come in a shimmering clear broth with chopped scallions on top. Get the noodles plain or accompanied by strips of pork, beef, or chicken served on the side in a little bowl with half a hard-boiled egg.

The after-dinner drink menu that time forgot includes Separators, Stingers, White Russians, and Pink Squirrels. The thing to drink before a meal is a Ditch—Montanese for whiskey and water.

RED LODGE CAFE

16 S. Broadway	406-446-1619
Red Lodge, MT	**B L D**	**$**

Come for breakfast and you can have a jumbo omelet, ham steak, or blueberry buckwheat pancakes and sip coffee long enough to eavesdrop on the conversations of locals and passers-through. Lunch is such stalwart items as country-fried steak and potatoes and buffalo burgers, as well as deluxe hamburgers. For dessert, everybody has pie: apple or berry pie or, best of all, banana cream pie, so jiggly that it eats better with a spoon than a fork.

The Red Lodge Cafe is eager to please with all modern facilities, yet ingenuous like a mid-twentieth-century tourist stop. It has a western theme, but there is something for everyone from morning to night: keno, weekend karaoke, and the strangest-shaped pool table we've ever seen. Lighting fixtures above the dining room are made of wagon wheels, the ceiling is stamped tin, and the walls are bedecked with painted wooden totem poles and spectacular murals of scenery along the 11,000-feet-above-sea-level Beartooth Highway that leads from here to Yellowstone. The two-lane highway is closed by snow in the winter, but once it's open, it is a spectacular trip.

REX RESTAURANT

therexbillings.com

2401 Montana Ave.   406-245-7477
Billings, MT   **L D | $$**

Montana Avenue in Billings has become a restaurant row with a handful of trendy places drawing people back downtown for dinner. One of the old reliables in the area is the Rex, a vintage hotel dining room that has been cleaned up but not drastically modernized to be one of the city's most respected upscale eating establishments. Unless you sit on the breezy patio, accommodations are dark and clubby, all varnished wood, brass, raw brick, and cut glass under an old stamped-tin ceiling.

Start with immense, thick-cut onion rings or a hunk of iceberg lettuce blanketed with blue cheese or thousand island dressing. Then move on to beef. Prime rib is a beauty: thick, juice-laden, and full-flavored. For those not intent on ingesting maximum red-meat protein, the broad menu includes pizzas made to order, sandwiches and big salads, shrimp, crab, salmon, and lobster. Lunch can be as inexpensive as a $10 half-pound bar burger or an $8.50 Caesar salad; beef dinners range to near $40.

We were introduced to the Rex many years ago by a local saddle maker whose doctor had told him he needed to eat less beef, so he ordered cream-sauced pasta, which looked to us like it was richer than a rib-eye steak!

SARAH'S

sarahsmexfood.com

310 N. 29th St.   406-256-5234
Billings, MT   **B L D | $**

Sarah's is a little hard to figure out, but worth the effort for some of the best Mexican food in the Plains. Here's the way it works. Upon entering, go to the back of the room to an order window. At the right of the window is a large posted menu. Choose your burritos, tacos, or enchiladas and tell the nice lady who steps out of the kitchen what you want. Then go to the cash register and pay for it. Now move over to the condiment bar and help yourself to Styrofoam cups full of hot sauce or mild sauce, onions, or jalapeños to carry to a table, where a basket of chips is set out along with lots of napkins. When you are halfway through the chips, the meal arrives.

We especially love the taquitos, which would be called flautas in much of the Southwest: tightly wrapped, crisp-fried tortilla tubes containing moist shredded beef. They are served with a cup of garlicky guacamole. The red smothered beef burrito is a mighty meal, loaded with big hunks of beef. Our one complaint is that the plastic forks provided are only barely up to severing the tortilla wrap and beef inside.

STELLA'S

2525 1st Ave. N.   406-248-3060
Billings, MT   **B L | $**

Stella's is a large bakery that supplies breads, cakes, cookies, bagels, and rolls to local restaurants and stores, but if you're in town for breakfast, why not eat at the source? Stella's cinnamon rolls are monumental, each one bigger than a softball. The rolls are made fresh each day, but when you order one, it is microwaved so a big glob of butter set atop it is melting when the roll arrives at the table. Heating also tends to give the caramel glaze on top a chewy texture that makes it a fork-and-knife pastry. Even bigger than the cinnamon roll is Stella's giant white caramel roll—fourteen ounces of sweet dough served with a small tub of whipped butter.

Everything is large at Stella's, especially pancakes, which are known as monster cakes. "You've got to see 'em to believe 'em," the menu boasts. Each one is a good twelve inches, edge to edge, and yet they have a nice light texture that makes it easy to eat a couple, or maybe even three. You have your choice of buttermilk or wheat batter, and if you can polish off four of them in a single sitting, you get a free cinnamon roll! We are especially fond of the very small print underneath the pancake listing on the menu: "Diet Smuckers jelly & syrups available upon request." So these would qualify as diet food?!

There are normal-sized breakfasts at Stella's: omelets, hot cereals (oatmeal, seven-grain, and Stella's homemade grits), and egg sandwiches; the lunch menu includes such regular-sized items as club and sub sandwiches, chili by the bowl, and a French dip, as well as hamburgers that range up to the half-pound Ziggyburger, served on an outsized bun to match.

For dessert? Bread pudding made with Stella's homemade breads, please.

WILLOW CREEK CAFE & SALOON

21 Main St.   406-285-3698
Willow Creek, MT   **D** (reservations advised) | **$$**

Reservations advised? In Willow Creek, population 209?

You bet. Here is a way, way out-of-the-way restaurant that attracts customers from Three Forks and Manhattan, MT, even Bozeman, some fifty miles away. They come for pillowy beef steaks and chicken-fried steaks, hamburgers and homemade soups, pies and cakes made that day, even such upscale suppers as pork marsala and saltimbocca. There's always prime rib on weekend nights, but the one never-to-miss meal is barbecued ribs, anointed with a brilliant honey-mustard glaze that teases maximum flavor from the pork. A chalkboard lists the day's specials and featured wines, which oenophile friends tell us are a good deal.

The place itself is a hoot: a sunflower-yellow house that started life in 1912 as the Babcock Saloon and has been a pool hall, barber shop, and a butcher shop. Dining facilities are small indeed, with room for only a few dozen customers at a time. The old-fashioned print wallpaper and antique wood fixtures make it feel like a trip back in time. If you're heading for Willow Creek, don't worry about finding it. It is the only business in town.

NEBRASKA

CRYSTAL CAFE

4601 Dakota Ave.   402-494-5471
South Sioux City, NE   Always open | $

--★-- OPEN 24/7 --★-- At 8:30 in the morning at the Crystal Cafe, men and women who are starting the day (and some finishing a long night) converse about issues that include jackknives, deadheading, log books, and speed traps. They are professional truckers; the Crystal Cafe is where they come not only to eat but for fuel and over-the-road supplies. It is an open-all-night truck stop just west of the Missouri River.

Each place is set with a coffee cup and a water glass. The waitress flips your cup right-side up and pours coffee and refills throughout breakfast. The cuisine is haute highway: big food, served in abundance. Plate-wide buttermilk pancakes, chicken-fried steak with a patty of oily hash browns, sausage gravy on big, crumbly biscuits are some of the morning specials. The morning item we especially like is the caramel sweet roll, which is thick and goopy. At lunch, you can have a breaded pork tenderloin, a bowl of chili, or a ten-ounce king-of-the-road Texaco Burger. Crystal Cafe's sour cream raisin pie is one of the Midwest's best: dense, creamy, and sweet, crowned with ethereal meringue.

GERING BAKERY

geringbakery.com
1446 10th St.   308-436-5500
Gering, NE   **B L** (closed Sun) | $

A small sign in the window of the Gering Bakery advertises cabbage burgers. Considering that we were in Nebraska, home of the *runza* and the *bierock*—bread pockets stuffed with ground beef, cabbage, and spice—the sign caused us to come to a sudden halt and investigate. *Runzas* and *bierocks* are nineteenth-century immigrant fare, but in the mid-1950s, the name Runza was trademarked and is now the lead item at the eponymous restaurant chain. Runza's Runzas are OK, but the monotony of the identical restaurants makes us depressed.

Gering Bakery, on the other hand, is the real deal. Sure enough, the advertised cabbage burger is a non-corporate *runza*, bigger and more delicious. Available in bulk or singly, heated up by the kind lady behind the counter, they are fully enclosed pillows of tender bread inside of which is a spill of juicy beef and peppery bits of cabbage and onion. Delicious, real comfort food.

Our hearts won over by the cabbage burger, we had to sample some of the good-looking sweet pastries on the bakery shelves. We liked the crisp-edged old-fashioned cake donuts and fell instantly in love with something called a peanut butter pretzel. That's a twisted piece of pastry dough generously frosted with sweet peanut butter icing.

Most business is takeout, but Gering Bakery offers a few window tables as well as help-yourself coffee and a cooler full of soda.

JOE TESS PLACE

joetessplace.com

5424 S. 24th St.   402-733-4638
Omaha, NE   **L D** (closed Mon) | **$**

Roadfood warriors Bruce Bilmes and Sue Boyle pointed us to Joe Tess Place (no possessive apostrophe), which bills itself as "Home of the Famous Fish Sandwich." It is a restaurant, tavern, and fresh seafood market on the south side of Omaha that serves a fish little known on dining tables outside the region: carp. Like the herring that swim upriver in North Carolina, carp are fish-flavored fish that get deep-fried long enough that their fine bones become part of the soft, juicy flesh underneath the crunchy batter crust. The fried pieces of carp are available on rye in the famous sandwich or doubled up in the double fish sandwich. (The connoisseur's condiment is hot pepper sauce.) Or you can have a dinner-sized portion bedded on rye on a plate with coleslaw and discs of fried potato, the latter known here as jacket fries. Catfish is another specialty. Like the carp, mudpuppies are trucked in live from Minnesota and you can see them swim in the tanks of the live fish market. For those with a less adventurous palate, the Joe Tess menu offers chicken (white or dark), grilled salmon, and fried shrimp.

There is a full bar's worth of beverages to drink, plus the western working man's version of a Bloody Mary, known as red beer: beer and tomato juice. Bruce and Sue noted, "Any restaurant that serves upside-down cake gets bonus points from us." Besides pineapple upside-down cake larded with pecans, the dessert menu includes a swell cream cheese bundt cake.

Ambience is all-fish, all the time and everywhere. The bar is shaped like a boat and walls are decked with taxidermied fish of every size and shape as well as pictures, posters, and nautical memorabilia.

ROSITA'S

1205 E. Overland   308-632-2429
Scottsbluff, NE   **L D** | **$**

Here are great corn chips, nearly as three-dimensional as a sopaipilla, fried so they puff up and become airy triangles with fragile skin. An order arrives almost too hot to handle; they come plain or as the foundation for the house specialty called panchos—a circle of them topped with frijoles, melted cheese, guacamole, and jalapeños. Panchos are like nachos, but the chips' refined texture and their perfect poise between breakable and bendable give panchos character far more satisfying than any bar grub.

The same quick-fry technique makes Rosita's taco shells an ideal crispy-chewy wrap for beef or chicken with plenty of garnishes; flat tostadas are made the same way, and even taco salad includes the fine, fluffy chips.

Proprietor Rosemary Florez-Lerma credits her mother-in-law with the recipes that make this friendly Mexican café a standout in an area with an abundance of Mexican restaurants (the legacy of fieldworkers who came to pick beets). The cinnabar-red, garlic-charged salsa that starts every meal and chunky pico de gallo that dresses up any dish with a stunning spicy punch are especially memorable. We also are fond of Rosita's garlicky *menudo*, thick with puffs of *posole* and strips of tripe, sparkling with fresh lemon.

SCOTTY'S DRIVE-IN

618 E. 27th St.   308-635-3314
Scottsbluff, NE   **L D** | **$**

Scotty's menu features a picture of an anthropomorphic serving of French fries talking to an equally humanoid beverage, the scene captioned, "This spud's for you." These are indeed very good potatoes: thin and crisp-edged. They're an ideal companion for burgers that range from singles to bacon-double-cheese to quarter-pounders and half-pounders and a Bluff Burger that is three meat patties, cheese, and all appropriate condiments.

The menu lists lots of sandwiches beyond burgers, including fish, chicken, pork, and shrimp. The most interesting alternative is Scotty's Tasty Tavern, a sloppy joe that echoes the passion of neighboring Iowa's Siouxland for ground meat sandwiches. Scotty's Taverns are small (and cheap, at about $1 each); we saw a group of large local boys each ingesting a half dozen of them along with a family pack of French fries for supper.

Roadfood.com contributor Buffetbuster, whose sweet tooth is infallible, says that his favorite items at Scotty's are the extremely thick milk shakes.

SEHNERT'S BAKERY & BIEROC CAFE

bieroccafe.com

312 Norris Ave.	308-345-6500
McCook, NE	**B L** (closed Sun) | **$**

-- ★ --
LOCALS
LOVE IT
-- ★ --
Sehnert's is a full-service bakery with donuts, crème horns, apple fritters, cinnamon buns, peanut-butter-frosted sweet rolls, and bread by the loaf. Just before Christmas, fruited stollens are a specialty, available by mail order.

Locals are the clientele; they come to chat 'n' chew, drink coffee and espresso, and eat such sandwiches as the Apple Planter (turkey, bacon, provolone, and apples with honey mustard on focaccia bread) and the Happy German (a Reuben, available in a lettuce wrap as well as on rye). For Roadfood devotees in search of unique regional specialties, the star attraction is a unique Great Plains pocket meal known as a *bieroc*—a packet of soft bread enclosing seasoned ground beef and your choice of either sauerkraut or cabbage. In the same genre as an Upper Peninsula pasty, a Cajun meat pie, and a Mexican empanada, the *bieroc* is moist and satisfying—truly homey.

Sehnert's also is a live music venue. For an up-to-date schedule of performers, visit their website.

SHIRLEY'S DINER

shirleysdiner.com

5325 S. 139th Plz.	402-896-6515
Omaha, NE	**B L D** | **$**

If you haven't spent some time in Omaha, or if you are not a devoted visitor to Roadfood.com, you might not know about a specialty unique to cafés and diners in eastern Nebraska known as the Frenchie: a cheese sandwich that is batter-dipped and deep-fried.

At Shirley's it is spelled Frenchy, and the batter dip includes crumbled cornflakes, adding extra crunch to what becomes a crisp coat surrounding an interior of Texas toast and a molten mix of jack and American cheese. Frenchys are available for breakfast as well as lunch and dinner.

The rest of the menu is familiar heartland fare: pork tenderloin sandwiches, hot beef and hot turkey sandwiches, and an "atomic" chicken-fried steak, so named because it gets a hot-sauce dip. Desserts include deep-fried Oreos. Breakfast at Shirley's is a big deal, featuring hash browns that can be ordered country-style, topped with sausage gravy.

This restaurant is completely uninviting from the outside: a bland storefront in Millard Plaza. Inside, it is a hospitable town café with nostalgic 1950s décor.

TACO TOWN

1007 W. 27th St.	308-635-3776
Scottsbluff, NE	**L D** | **$**

Since the mid-twentieth century, Taco Town has been a favorite gathering place for locals, many of whom are descendants of the Mexican families who settled here to work on the vast beet farms surrounding Scottsbluff. While the inside seats are frequently buzzing with table-to-table conversations (a sign outside boasts "We're the Tac-O the Town!"), many customers simply drive through and pick up food at the window just as one would do at any humdrum junk-food franchise.

Despite a corporate appearance, Taco Town definitely is not Taco Bell. Pork chili, sold by the pint and quart, is a full-flavored homey stew. There are handsome plates of burritos, enchiladas, and flautas, and for $6.75 you can have a combo meal with all of the above plus rice and beans. The regular taco is a simple delight, its earthy corn shell audibly crisp but pliable enough that it doesn't shatter, loaded with a heap of ground beef filling that is creamy-rich and peppery. Each taco comes wrapped in paper that is twisted tight at both ends to keep it secure until you've found a parking place and are ready to unwrap it and dine off the dashboard. Soft-shell and super-soft-shell tacos also are available.

NORTH DAKOTA

CAROL WIDMAN'S CANDY SHOP

carolwidmanscandy.com

4325 13th Ave. S.   701-281-8664
Fargo, ND   (closed Sun) | $

Widman's has been the big name in Red River Valley candy for more than a century. It is especially well known for its unusual chocolate-covered savories that represent some of North Dakota's crops: wheat nuts, soybeans, sunflower seeds, and—best of all—potato chips. The chocolate-covered chips are called chippers, and they are an unlikely but compelling harmony of sweet and salt, melting chocolate and crunchy fried potato. Chippers are available enrobed in milk chocolate or semisweet dark chocolate, as well as strawberry, peanut butter, and butterscotch.

It is a joy to stop into the candy store in Fargo to inhale its chocolaty aroma and sample some of everything. If you are not coming to Fargo, Widman's will mail chocolates by the pound and gift-box. Because chocolate melts in hot weather, mail-order sales are available only between October 1 and May 1. As the lady behind Widman's counter told us, "If you are comfortable, the candy will be too."

SOUTH DAKOTA

BOBKAT'S PURPLE PIE PLACE

purplepieplace.com

19 Mt. Rushmore Rd. 605-673-4070
Custer, SD **L D** (closed in winter) | $

Yes, the restaurant is shockingly purple. And yes, pie is its specialty—really good pie. Sour cream raisin comes with a Cool Whip top, but once that's pushed aside, it's a just-right balance of sour cream and the sweetness of raisins and custard. Sturdy-crusted fruit pies are available filled with rhubarb, apple, and berries of all kinds; there is one called bumbleberry, which is a crazy-good mix of pretty much all the fruit in the house. Of course, fruit pies are better à la mode—maybe with huckleberry ice cream, when available. Better still if they are warm, which is achieved by briefly nuking a slice—not the best crust conditioner, but not a disaster, either.

Pie's the thing here, but there is a dining room in back and a pre-pie menu of sandwiches, soup, chili, and barbecue.

BOB'S

bobscarryout.com

1312 W. 12th St. 605-336-7260
Sioux Falls, SD **B L D** | $

Bob's was known as the Pickle Palace when it opened in 1944. Having gained fame as a hamburger destination, it became Ray's Drive-In, then finally Bob's in 1951. In 2000, Bob sold the business to Ben Weiland, who kept the name, which now in the twenty-first century is as well known for broasted chicken as it is for burgers.

Hamburgers start as round balls that get placed on the griddle then flattened with a spatula—but not too hard—to form thick patties with a good crust and a load of juice. If you are very hungry, you'll want to know about the Mega Bob Meal, which is a three-quarter-pound hamburger, along with three-quarters of a pound of French fries, a twenty-ounce soda, and a couple of cookies. You can buy broasted chicken by the piece, in a basket with spuds, slaw, and a roll, or as a 250-piece order to feed a hundred. Anyone who eats an entire chicken platter in an hour gets the meal free, plus a Bob's T-shirt and a $50 Bob's gift certificate. A platter is sixteen pieces, five potatoes, and rolls, along with a pint of gravy.

Breakfast is swell, especially when enjoyed from a stool at the curvy counter with a view of the grill. Of special note is a meal called Hash Browns Delight, which augments the crisp-fried spuds with steak, peppers, onion, mushrooms, and cheese. Thursday (and only Thursday) is caramel roll day.

EDGAR'S

edgarssoda.com

107 E. Main St.	605-356-3336
(Bus. Rt. 29)	**L** | $
Elk Point, SD	

With its pink-and-white tin ceiling, vintage wood booths, and steel-rod chairs for a scattering of tables, Edgar's is a charming little sweetshop where mixology is an art. Order a soda and observe: First, syrup is combined with a dab of ice cream at the bottom of a tulip glass, forming a sweetshop roux; next, soda is squirted in and mixed vigorously; penultimately, a globe of ice cream is gingerly floated on top; finally, a crown of whipped cream is applied and, to that, a single cherry. It's a beautiful sight, and while much of the soda will drip down the sides of the glass as soon as it is touched by a spoon, one cannot help but admire the confectionery perfectionism.

The same high standards apply to sundaes, malts, and shakes, and a long roster of more elaborate and daring delights that range from the relatively familiar turtle sundae (vanilla ice cream with hot caramel, chocolate syrup, and pecans) to the Rocket—an astonishingly vertical banana split that the menu promises "will send you for a blast!"

Edgar's menu includes practical how-to articles taken from the 1906 *Standard Manual of Soda and Other Beverages*. Among the suggestions are that a soda fountain attendant "should never stand watching the patrons drinking," and "should study each customer's desire and endeavor to remember the particular way in which he likes his drinks mixed and served." The year all this was written, the *Centerville Journal* declared Edgar's soda fountain one of the finest in the state, and over a century later, it has no peers.

MURDO DRIVE IN

murdodrivein.com

212 Kennedy Ave.	605-669-2972
Murdo, SD	**L D** (summer only) | $

Just a hop off Interstate 90 in the relatively food-barren middle of South Dakota, this eat shack serves nothing that is especially regional, but the burgers, chicken, and turtle ice cream are definitely worth a stop.

The menu is emblazoned with these watchwords: "We are not fast! We are good. We are cheerful. We are courteous. But we are not fast. For fast, go to Chicago. Here we are north of the 'tension line.' So relax." If you order broasted chicken, you will have a good twenty minutes to relax, because it is cooked to order and arrives at your place still sizzling hot. Likewise, burgers are not from pre-pressed patties, and the dessert/drink cyclones, which are something like milk shakes, are actually made with real fruit when available. Hans Bauman, who reviewed the friendly place at Roadfood.com, noted that his rhubarb cyclone was "delicious, from its creamy substrate to the tangy threads of freshly harvested rhubarb." Less crop-dependent cyclone flavors include banana split, banana pudding, Oreo, chocolate-covered cherry, and peanut butter crunch.

NICK'S HAMBURGER SHOP

nickshamburgers.com

427 Main Ave.	605-692-4324
Brookings, SD	**B L D** (closed Sun) | $

Nick's is a Roadfood landmark for the itty-bitty hamburgers it has served since the early days of the slider, in 1929. The price of a Nickburger has gone up from a nickel to well over a dollar in the last fourscore and five years, and the restaurant, officially listed on the National Register of Historic Places, has gotten bigger; but the burgers are still buy-'em-by-the-sack lovelies, hand-formed and cooked on a grill with so much oil that they are virtually deep-fried. Onions are part of the formula, so the burger as well as Nick's itself is perfumed with the sweet smell of them caramelizing. They're small and wieldy enough that plates are extraneous; Nickburgers are presented on wax paper. We'd say three to five or a couple of doubles makes a nice meal. The ingestion record is thirty-four in a single sitting, set by a student from South Dakota State. Whoever beats the record eats free.

TEA STEAK HOUSE

teasteakhouse.webs.com

215 S. Main St.   605-368-9667
Tea, SD   **L D** (closed Sun) | **$$**

The cushiony pound-plus T-bone oozes juice at the first poke of a knife. It's a good thing to order hash brown potatoes on the side to soak up the beef's seepage; crisp and oily, they are fine potatoes in their own right (much better than the foil-wrapped baked potato or uninteresting French fries). We also ordered filet mignon, which came splayed open and wrapped in bacon, and it was amazing just how different these two cuts of beef were: each excellent, but while the T-bone had a vivid, almost gamey smack and tight-knit texture that rewarded serious chewing, the filet was cream-gentle in flavor and wanted to melt on the tongue.

The Tea Steak House serves more than steak. You can eat chicken or ham, halibut, perch, lobster tails, or a Saint & Sinner supper of one lobster tail and one small sirloin. Don't ask us how any of that stuff tastes. When we're in Tea, we'll eat beef. Dessert is limited to cheesecake and ice cream.

The restaurant motto: "We're Glad You Brought Your Sugar to Tea."

TRIPP SPORTS BOWL CAFE

210 S. Main St.   605-935-6281
Tripp, SD   **L | $**

-- ★ --
LOCALS
LOVE IT
-- ★ --
Tripp, South Dakota, population 631, is a small town in big country. A short jog off the highway takes you to Main Street, where the bowling alley and town café are one. We love this place where the locals eat (few travelers pass through Tripp at all), and where décor includes not only the bowling alleys themselves but trophies won by the likes of Doug Janssen (a 300 game!) and Dorothy Schnabel (267). The day we visited, a blackboard in the dining area listed the day's special as creamed chicken on toast—quintessential comfort food—but we were also intrigued by an item called the Dakota Burger.

The Dakota Burger turned out not to be a hamburger at all—at least if you define hamburger as a patty of ground beef—but rather, Tripp's version of that upper Midwest pleasure, hot beef. Junellia Meisenhoelder, chef and proprietor at the Sports Bowl Cafe, didn't tell us why the sandwich is known as a burger, but there is no point quibbling about labels; it is swell. Hot beef served with mashed potatoes and gravy is a frequent daily special at the Sports Bowl Cafe, and the Dakota Burger is a somewhat more wieldy variation on the theme: chunks of ultra-tender roast beef, warm enough to melt a slice of bright orange cheese placed atop them, piled into a grill-warmed bun. Simple and excellent!

WYOMING

CHUGWATER SODA FOUNTAIN

chugwatersodafountain.com

314 1st St.   307-422-3222
Chugwater, WY   **B L D | $**

The year 2014 marks the hundredth anniversary of
the storefront that houses Chugwater Soda Fountain,
which lays claim to being the oldest operating soda
fountain in Wyoming. A seat at the counter affords
a view of Wendell the Elk (a trophy dating back to
the 1940s) and an assortment of vintage milk-shake
mixers, plus the opportunity to enjoy silver-beaker
shakes and malts, sundaes, sodas, flavored Cokes,
and ice cream served in cones and cups.

The town of Chugwater, population 244, has
gained some fame as the home of Chugwater chili.
Made from a Wyoming State Championship recipe
purchased in 1986 by a group of townsfolk, there are
two varieties available at the soda fountain: red and
green. Both are more soup than stew, the red a mild
mix of ground beef and beans in cinnabar broth, the
green made with chicken in a bisquey liquid that does
pack a half-alarm of heat.

Chugwater Soda Fountain also has a summer
beer garden and a small package store.

LISA'S

lisaswesterncuisine.com

200 Greybull Ave.   307-765-4765
Greybull, WY   **L D | $$**

★
MOUNTAIN
VIEWS
★

As you travel west out of the Big Horn
Mountains—or prepare to head east
into them—the town of Greybull offers
all sorts of attractions. These include a sprawling
Museum of Flight and Aerial Fire Fighting with
decommissioned airplanes on display, a museum of
taxidermy, and Lisa's.

"In Wyoming when we say hearty, we mean
hearty!" Lisa's menu crows. But it isn't so much the
generous size of meals that makes this a worthwhile
stop; it is the taste. Breakfasts include chunky corned
beef hash, warm biscuits with luxurious sausage
gravy, "puff scrambles," which are eggs stuffed into
puff pastries and topped with hollandaise sauce,
and side orders of crisp Indian fry bread. Breakfast
Charlotta is a tortilla stuffed with potato hash,
scrambled eggs, cheese, and pico de gallo, sided by
beans and hash browns.

Lunch features such Southwest and Tex-Mex
dishes as fajitas, enchiladas, chimichangas, and chiles
rellenos, plus a catalog of sandwiches, half-pound
hamburgers, salads, and a soup of the day.

We love the watchwords on Lisa's menu: "The
original chefs of the Big Horns were of course the
Native Americans. Cattle drives brought more South

American influences such as pinto beans and peppers. At Lisa's, aromas of the past prevail . . . paying tribute to our Western Plains heritage and original chefs. Not all chefs live in the city!" Décor includes Navajo rugs, Mexican tiles, and walls of stucco and wood; a tree-shaded outdoor patio offers the opportunity to dine in crisp mountain air.

LULA BELLE'S CAFE

101 N. Gillette Avenue   307-682-9798
Gillette, WY   **B L | $**

We love so many things about Wyoming, but the Cowboy State presents a challenge to a traveler in search of restaurants worth remembering. Prolific Roadfood.com correspondent Cliff Strutz most assuredly met the challenge when he found Lula Belle's Cafe in Gillette. Cliff, who goes by the handle Buffetbuster, is an omnivore, but his specialty is pie, so let's start with that. Hawaiian pie, for instance, is a variety we've never seen elsewhere, a combo of pineapple, banana, and coconut with a toasted-coconut crown. "A good slice of pie," Cliff wrote, "but nothing earth shattering." On the other hand, the Dutch apple pie is, in this pie connoisseur's words, "Fantastic! Tall stack of fresh fruit, thick apple-crisp-like crumb top, just the right amount of cinnamon on a flaky, buttery crust."

Pre-pie recommendations include taco soup that is really more a Plains chili, topped with shredded cheese, sour cream, and a few tortilla chips, and an entree listed on the menu as SC Pot, which translates as scalloped potatoes and ham. "Strikes me as much more a dish you find in a home and not a restaurant," Cliff reported, concluding that it "brought back fond memories of my mother's cooking." Other notable lunch items include French dip, Indian tacos, meat loaf, and hamburgers.

Breakfast is a big deal here, featuring large, gooey caramel rolls, biscuits and gravy, and especially good crisp-fried hash browns to accompany eggs.

Note: As of 2016, smoking is permitted at Lula Belle's. Those bothered by secondhand smoke will likely be unhappy.

NOON BREAK

noonbreak.com
2619 Sheridan Ave.   307-578-7247
Cody, WY   **B L** (closed Sun & Mon) | $

Steve Rankin's Noon Break used to be our favorite place to eat in Cody, Wyoming. But then it went out of business and came back as a food truck. Not that we have anything against food trucks, but we tend not to include them in Roadfood because they are, by definition, ephemeral. Then, late in 2015, Steve found a storefront home for his deliciousness. Primary question: Is he still serving his wonderful Code Ten Chili? Answer: Yes, indeed. It is not the sort of chili you eat as a main course, but rather as the star element in several specialty dishes, including a chili relleno plate, an enchilada plate, a burrito, and a walking taco (aka Frito pie). It's even prominent at breakfast, as the adornment for huevos rancheros, which are presented atop a blue corn tortilla.

What is special about Code Ten? It is radiant in two ways: with the sunny flavor of the chile pepper and with the intense heat thereof. It contains no beans or beef. It is pork and green chile peppers, a viscous taste sensation for chili lovers only.

SVILAR'S

173 Main St.   307-332-4516
Hudson, WY   **D** (closed Sun & Mon) | $$$

Hudson, Wyoming, is hours from any interstate on the south edge of Wind River Reservation, where shaggy horses graze the flatlands by the Little Popo Agie River and derelict oil works are strewn across the hills. It is nothing but a short strip of bedraggled buildings with businesses that look to be defunct. But in the evenings, Friday and Saturday in particular, the old Main Street comes alive. A sign in one parking lot boasts "Welcome to Hudson: World's Finest Food." An overstatement, perhaps, but High Plains folk who travel the two-lanes through the land of the Arapahoe to dine at Svilar's gladly attest to the fact that the little community is home to the finest beef in the Cowboy State.

Svilar's, a supper club that has been a culinary High Plains magnet since the middle of the last century, serves a full-course dinner that starts with relish tray and salad, then moves on to a hot-appetizer course of ravioli and stuffed cabbage (Serbian-style). Although chicken, shrimp, and lobster tails are available, the only appropriate entree is red meat, either steaks available in cuts from wee filet to multipound rib eye or great mesas of prime rib large enough to overhang a dinner plate. Maybe there's dessert, maybe not. We've never bothered to inquire, figuring that if we have any appetite at the end of the meal, we probably didn't order a large-enough piece of cow.

THE WAGON BOX

wagonboxinn.com

103 N. Piney Rd.   307-683-2444
Story, WY   **L D** (closed Mon) | $$$

A rustic inn with cabin accommodations, The Wagon Box also is a restaurant that attracts beef eaters from miles around. Start with a salad dressed with huckleberry vinaigrette, then plow into such big cuts of cow as prime rib up to a pound, filet mignon wrapped in bacon, and rib-eye steaks served with sautéed garlic and mushrooms. On the side, you can have potatoes your way: baked, mashed, baby reds, French fries, or made-to-order chips. There are all kinds of surf 'n' turf options and beef frowners can choose from a menu of shrimp, salmon, lobster tails, and crab legs. Whatever else you get, we highly recommend starting with prime rib mushroom soup when it is available. Cousin Johnny of Roadfood.com said it reminded him of beef Stroganoff in a bowl.

Dining facilities include a big stone fireplace and a cool outdoor patio surrounded by fragrant Ponderosa pines. Lunch can be had for $10–$15. Dinner tends to be north of $25.

WEST COAST

★

WASHINGTON

OREGON

CALIFORNIA

CALIFORNIA

MARSHALL
The Marshall Store

SAN FRANCISCO
Bi-Rite Creamery
Sam's Grill
Sears Fine Food
★ Swan Oyster Depot

○**SACRAMENTO**

●**LOCKE**
Al's Place

MIDPINES
June Bug Cafe

HALF MOON BAY
Barbara's Fishtrap

BERKELEY
Bette's Oceanview Diner
Ici
Rick and Ann's

PESCADERO
Duarte's Tavern

CASMALIA
The Hitching Post

SANTA BARBARA
La Super-Rica

NIPOMO
Jocko's Steak House

HOLLYWOOD
Musso & Frank Grill

LOS ANGELES
★ Apple Pan
Canter's
★ Du-par's
Original Pantry
Pann's
Philippe the Original
The Waffle

LAGUNA BEACH
Orange Inn

INGLEWOOD
Harriet's Cheesecakes Unlimited
Philip's Bar-B-Que
Randy's Donuts
Serving Spoon

SAN JUAN CAPISTRANO
El Campeon

SANTA YSABEL
Julian Pie Company

MANHATTAN BEACH
The Kettle
Uncle Bill's Pancake House

LA JOLLA
★ The Cottage

RAMONA
Ramona Cafe

OCEAN BEACH
★ Hodad's

SAN DIEGO
D.Z. Akins
El Indio
Hob Nob Hill

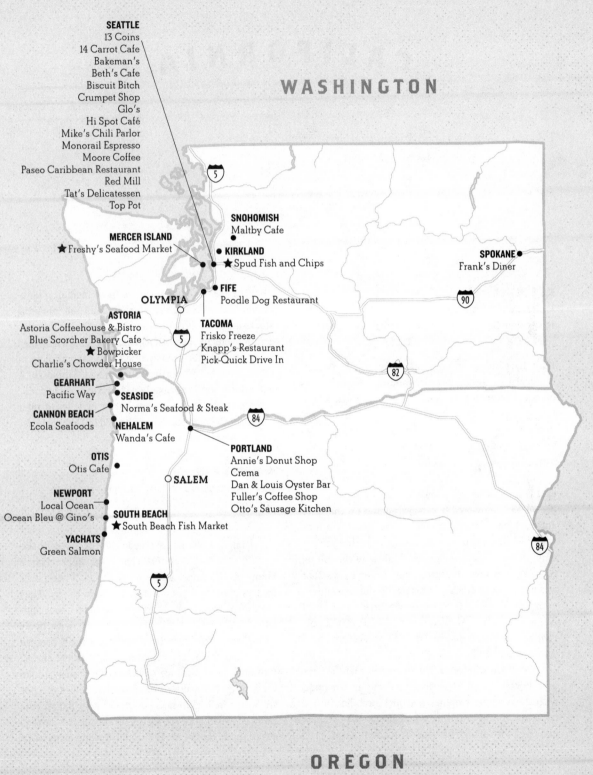

WASHINGTON

SEATTLE
13 Coins
14 Carrot Cafe
Bakeman's
Beth's Cafe
Biscuit Bitch
Crumpet Shop
Glo's
Hi Spot Café
Mike's Chili Parlor
Monorail Espresso
Moore Coffee
Paseo Caribbean Restaurant
Red Mill
Tat's Delicatessen
Top Pot

SNOHOMISH
Maltby Cafe

MERCER ISLAND
★ Freshy's Seafood Market

KIRKLAND
★ Spud Fish and Chips

SPOKANE
Frank's Diner

OLYMPIA

FIFE
Poodle Dog Restaurant

ASTORIA
Astoria Coffeehouse & Bistro
Blue Scorcher Bakery Cafe
★ Bowpicker
Charlie's Chowder House

TACOMA
Frisko Freeze
Knapp's Restaurant
Pick-Quick Drive In

GEARHART
Pacific Way

SEASIDE
Norma's Seafood & Steak

CANNON BEACH
Ecola Seafoods

NEHALEM
Wanda's Cafe

OTIS
Otis Cafe

PORTLAND
Annie's Donut Shop
Crema
Dan & Louis Oyster Bar
Fuller's Coffee Shop
Otto's Sausage Kitchen

SALEM

NEWPORT
Local Ocean
Ocean Bleu @ Gino's

SOUTH BEACH
★ South Beach Fish Market

YACHATS
Green Salmon

OREGON

CALIFORNIA

AL'S PLACE

locketown.com/als.htm

13936 Main St.   916-776-1800
Locke, CA   **L D** | **$$**

Built by Chinese immigrants early in the twentieth century, the old levee community of Locke was
once notorious for its gambling halls, brothels, and
last—maybe least—of its pleasures, Cantonese food.
Locke's weathered Main Street of wood-plank side-
walks and swayback second-story balconies remains
a magical sight. In the middle of it is Al's Place.

The building housed a regular Chinese restaurant from 1915 to 1934, when Al Adami, fresh out of
prison as a convicted bootlegger, came up the river
and took over. Al had no menu—he asked you how
you liked your steak, which was the only thing to eat
amid the slot machines and card tables in the dining
room behind the front-room bar. Legend says that
at some point in time, a hungry crop duster came in
with jars of peanut butter and marmalade and asked
Al for some toast. Al liked the idea, and started putting peanut butter and marmalade on every table, a
tradition that endures.

Al's Place still feels illicit. You enter past the beer
and shooter crowd who occupy a dimly lit bar hung
with dusty game trophies and memorabilia, into a
backroom dining area lined with worn laminate tables
equipped with shared benches instead of chairs.

The menu remains simple, now including hamburgers, cheeseburgers, steaks, and one amazing
steak sandwich. It is amazing because it is only barely
a sandwich. In fact, what it is, is a sandwich-sized
steak on a platter accompanied by a second plate of
toasted pieces of sturdy Italian bread. Horseradish
and minced garlic are available to spread on the meat.
Most people put the peanut butter or jelly on their
toast, but the management informed us that some use
it to garnish their steaks.

★ APPLE PAN

10801 W. Pico Blvd.   310-475-3585
Los Angeles, CA   **L D** (Tues-Sat) | **$**

——★——— Legendary hamburgers. Four-star pies.
OPEN LATE Hash-house joie de vivre at a twenty-six-
——★——— seat counter. That's the Apple Pan, a
landmark Los Angeles eatery since 1947. What makes
its hamburgers so wonderful? It's hard to say. They
are thin patties, cooked through, not huge or outlandish in any way, but juicy and humming with beefy
savor. They come beautifully and bountifully dressed
with crisp fresh lettuce, tomatoes, pickles, cheese
(optional), and a choice of house-made sauces. Like
the burger, the sauces in and of themselves are not
stellar. There is chili sauce on the hickory burger (the
meat of which gets smoky seasoning) and a savory-
sweet relish on the steak burger. No one element of

these packages is sensational, but in each, the combo is greater than the sum of its parts.

There is no mystery about the pies' distinction. Made daily from scratch using old family recipes, they are nothing short of magnificent. Apple pie, loaded with hugely fruity apples well-spiced and still a bit al dente, is sandwiched by a crisp, savory crust that would be delicious to eat simply as a not-so-sweet cookie. Have the apple à la mode, and you're in fruit-pie heaven. The same fine crust supports Apple Pan's outstanding cream pies: banana cream made with thick, ripe (but not overripe) slices of banana, fresh custard, and pure cream; and coconut pie crowned by a fluffy sprinkle of toasted coconut shreds.

BARBARA'S FISHTRAP
barbarasfishtrap.com

281 Capistrano Rd.   650-728-7049
Half Moon Bay, CA   L D | $$

Barbara's makes fish and chips with rock cod, aka Pacific snapper, that is cut thick enough to remain extremely moist, its natural sweetness underscored by a gold coat with light, oily crunch. You get four large tiles, hot from the fryer, accompanied by thick fried potatoes. Tartar sauce is unnecessary with fish so flavorful, and ketchup for the fries is irrelevant. (Malt vinegar is supplied for the spuds too, but why moisten their crisp skin?)

To precede fish and chips, you want a cup or bowl of clam chowder. This is good stuff, its heartiness very much of the Pacific variety, meaning it is creamless but nearly fork-thick, loaded with large pieces of tender clams as well as potatoes and celery: a winning balance of elements.

Barbara's menu is big, including linguine served with your choice of clams, mussels, prawns, or calamari, as well as full-bore cioppino with Dungeness crab. There are shrimp and/or crab Louie and vegetable plates that come steamed, sautéed, or tempura-fried. Meals begin with baskets of fresh, chewy sourdough. At a little over $10, fish and chips is the most affordable meal on the menu. Most entrees are in the $20 range.

Barbara's is casual with a charming nautical dishevelment about the décor, and it is small enough always to seem crowded. It offers a pleasant view overlooking the boats in Pillar Point Harbor. But windows remain closed. It became obvious why, when, mid-meal, we watched a very large seagull swoop down and perch on a rail just outside. It seemed all too clear that he had come to watch us with his beady, greedy little eyes.

BETTE'S OCEANVIEW DINER
bettesdiner.com

1807 4th St.   510-644-3230
Berkeley, CA   B L | $

We first found Bette's Oceanview Diner while looking for macaroons at Bette's to Go, the bakeshop next door. Aside from the magnificent macaroons and trompe l'oeil chocolate espresso Twinkies (the finest snack cake on earth), the bakery shelves' delights include pecan-topped red velvet cake and twin-layer lemon bars (creamy on top, crunchy below).

Anyone with an appetite and a functioning olfactory system would be hard-pressed to visit the bakery without being seduced by aromas from the diner next door: potato pancakes grilling to a crisp, waffles pried fresh from the irons, and eggy, oven-baked pancakes.

All these and a full menu of diner classics are dished out in a restaurant that is a savvy gloss on the vintage diner. We usually are skeptical about retro restaurants, diners in particular. Even if their heart is in the right place, all too often the food is not. But a first meal at Bette's disabused us of all prejudice. Here is a modern diner with classic values . . . and really good buttermilk pancakes, usually available in a special flavor each day. For our first visit, around Christmas, the day's pancake (and waffle) was eggnog. Mm-mm-good. The extra egginess was quite subtle, adding an intangible richness to the cakes, all the better when drowned with real maple syrup.

Another compelling breakfast highlight is scrapple, which is some of the best anywhere, including the Delaware Valley. Part of a "Philadelphia breakfast" with poached eggs, it is made from pork butt and hock meat, cornmeal, sage, and plenty of pepper, and sliced thick enough that while the outside gets nice and crisp, the interior virtually melts into nothing but flavor. If you get a fruit salad, fruits are cut and peeled to order. Muffins are available . . . made with donut batter: genius!

BI-RITE CREAMERY

biritecreamery.com

3692 18th St.   415-626-5600
San Francisco, CA   **L D | $**

We've never had a banana split we did not like. And we've never had one in the same league as the one made at Bi-Rite Creamery. The vanilla ice cream is a shocking reminder that it is, in fact, chilled cream, suffused with liquor of vanilla beans. The chocolate sauce is cocoa turned to liquid velvet; the bananas are caramelized in amber syrup; the whipped cream—out of Straus Family Dairy cows that graze on grass above Tomales Bay—is as dense as crème fraîche. Dazzling!

Boasting that it makes "small-batch, artisanal ice creams," Bi-Rite offers such unusual flavors as salted caramel, strawberry balsamic, and honey lavender, as well as a sundae made with bergamot olive oil(!), and a lemon-gingersnap pumpkin ice cream sandwich. Still, we recommend you start with vanilla ice cream . . . and the best banana split in the universe.

CANTER'S

cantersdeli.com

419 N. Fairfax Ave.   323-651-2030
Los Angeles, CA   **B L D | $$**

OPEN 24/7 Opened in 1931, Canter's is a delicatessen that smells of salami and corned beef and pickles and is staffed by take-no-prisoners guys and gals who are equal parts service and entertainment. Open all night, it serves excellent kosher-style (but not actually kosher) fare. This includes the full repertoire of cured meats and smoked fish, matzo ball soup, noodle kugel, and a variety of deli pastries including hamantaschen, rugelach, and black-and-white cookies. Hot entrees range from corned beef and cabbage to chicken in a pot, and the sandwich selection is epic. We like traditional corned beef (on rye), the meat briny and just fatty enough to feel

slightly sinful. Another good sandwich ingredient is chopped liver enriched with plenty of schmaltz for a just-right rugged/smooth balance. Chicken soup is like what an idealized grandmother might make. Add a big, soft, flavorful matzo ball and you have a supreme bowl of Jewish-style comfort food.

★ THE COTTAGE

cottagelajolla.com

7702 Fay Ave.   858-454-8409
La Jolla, CA   **B L; D** (Fri-Sat) **| $$**

Here is Southern California at its brightest: fresh and casual and delicious. On a quiet corner in the village of La Jolla, the Cottage offers vibrant meals in either a sun-drenched dining room or on the breezy patio outdoors.

Breakfast is especially wonderful. As you walk in the door, look right. There's the bakery case holding the nut-topped cinnamon rolls, muffins, and buttermilk coffee cake with cinnamon and walnut crumb topping. The pastries are superb . . . but so are hot meals. In particular, we recommend Cottage Irish oatmeal, served with a full complement of brown sugar, sliced bananas, raisins, milk, and a dish of sensational sticky-crunchy caramelized walnuts. Also grand are meat-loaf hash crisped with cottage-fried potatoes and topped with eggs, French toast stuffed with strawberry compote and mascarpone, and crab Benedict, which is like eggs Benedict, but heaped with pure rock crab instead of Canadian bacon. Cottage granola is extra-special—dark and toasty, a delightful chew.

Lunch is an opportunity to taste a high-tone version of San Diego's favorite fast food, the fish taco, here built around grilled mahimahi, dressed with cilantro-avocado sauce and accompanied by bowls of creamy black beans and chunky papaya relish. The pork and beef chili has a true Southwest pepper zest, and the hamburger is a SoCal classic, served with an abundance of Cheddar cheese, tomato, lettuce, onion, and mayo. The BLT, augmented with avocado, reigns supreme.

The restaurant is in a bungalow that was built early in the twentieth century and served as a private home in the days when La Jolla was a little-known community of sun-and-surf worshippers. It still exudes edge-of-the-continent charm that once made California so appealing.

DUARTE'S TAVERN
duartestavern.com

202 Stage Rd.	650-879-0464
Pescadero, CA	**B L D** | $

We weren't yet driving around looking for Roadfood in 1894 when the Duarte family opened a tavern in Pescadero (neither were there any automobiles to drive around in; it was a stage stop); but we can tell you that the rugged old tavern hasn't changed much at all since we first happened upon it in the mid-1970s. It is still a place where locals come for coffee and three square meals a day at mismatched tables and chairs in a knotty pine-paneled dining room or at the short counter opposite the kitchen.

Travelers have come to know it for its artichokes, which are farmed just south of Pescadero around Castroville, and which grow into gorgeous globes in the Duarte family's abundant garden behind the restaurant. The pick of the backyard crop is available simply steamed—you won't believe how much flesh you can scrape off each petal—and you can have artichokes stuffed with fennel sausage, in breakfast omelets, or as the foundation of blissful cream of artichoke soup.

Most of the menu is down-home dining, California-style: pork chops with homemade applesauce and chunky mashed potatoes, chicken and dumplings, roast turkey with sage dressing. Even the house salad—a perfunctory gesture in so many restaurants—comes topped with beets and tomatoes that come directly from the family garden. The kitchen's respect for its provender's seasonal correctness rivals that of any highfalutin bistro in wine country. Ron Duarte, who took over the business in the 1950s from his parents (and whose kids, Kathy and Tim, now run it), cannot hide his happiness as Dungeness crab season starts in November, because that means the restaurant's legendary cioppino will be at its best. "We don't buy frozen or precooked," he says. "We like to get them live."

To conclude any meal at Duarte's, you must have pie. We are gaga over the one made using olallieberries from nearby Watsonville; but they have a short season early summer, so after that, they are replaced by marionberries from farther north. The last time we visited, Ron showed off a big box of just-picked pears and a handsome pie the kitchen staff had made from them.

★ DU-PAR'S
dupars.net

6333 W. 3rd St.	323-933-8446
Los Angeles, CA	Always open | $

OPEN 24/7 There's a lot of fashionable cooking in Los Angeles, but if you are looking for a place that reflects California cuisine when the Golden State was the end of the rainbow, you won't find a more perfect example than this coffee shop in the Farmers Market (and a few other locations).

It is always open, 24/7/365, offering a menu of such comfort food as savory potpies, Welsh rarebit, corned beef hash, turkey with all the trimmins, and meat loaf. Desserts are wonderful, including pecan, lemon, and coconut custard pie as well as several puddings. Regular customers time their lunch visits according to the immemorial daily specials: Monday fried chicken, Tuesday turkey, Wednesday pot roast, Thursday liver and onions, Friday meat loaf—all accompanied by freshly mashed potatoes.

Breakfast is best of all, especially the pancakes. You can get a single, a short stack (three) or a full stack (five). These are some of America's finest flapjacks, fairly thick but not heavy, sizzled on a slick grill so they develop a glistening, fragile crust. They come with plenty of syrup as well as a good-sized pitcher of melted butter. The 'cakes already are buttery; pour on the extra butter, swirl in some syrup, and you're in breakfast paradise.

The meals are served in spic-and-span surroundings by professional uniformed waitresses who see your half-full cup of coffee as half-empty.

D.Z. AKINS

dzakinsdeli.com

6930 Alvarado Rd.   619-265-0218
San Diego, CA   **B L D | $$**

As folks who frequently complain that urban delis aren't what they used to be, we were thrilled several years ago the moment we walked into D.Z. Akins. The air was perfumed with spiced beef and the bakery shelves up front held a handsome array of ryes, pumpernickels, bagels, hard rolls, and challahs, plus countless macaroons and cookies, all baked right here. The sandwiches we got were fantastic: hot, fat-striated corned beef radiant with flavor, cut thick and piled between slices of old-fashioned deli rye, soft inside with a sour smack and a tough, savory crust. Roast beef was presented in a poppy-seed-spangled hard roll. At breakfast you can feast on matzoh brei, blintzes, or bagels and lox. Nothing is short of excellent.

The full-service restaurant also features a soda fountain, the menu of which includes sundaes and sodas of all kinds, from a traditional banana split to one called Prenatal Silliness: chocolate ice cream and pickles, with your topping of choice!

EL CAMPEON

31921 Camino   949-489-4078
Capistrano #12   **L D | $**
San Juan Capistrano, CA

Located in a nondescript Orange County shopping center, El Campeon is a large, bustling cafeteria, bakery, and fresh juice source specializing in sleeves-up Mexican food. The menu is displayed on the wall above a service line where meats and garnishes are arrayed in pans, ready to be stuffed into tacos, tortas, or burritos. Options include *cabeza de res* (beef head), *birria* (goat meat), and more familiar meats such as carnitas (roasted pork), *barbacoa* (sauced roast beef), chicken, and ham. Burrito fillings include red or green chili (along with arroz, frijoles, *cebolla*, cilantro, and ensalada).

The carnitas are moist and robust, especially well complemented by hot green salsa available at a serve-yourself bar in the center of the dining area. *Barbacoa*, in the form of massive shreds, delivers big beef flavor,

sopped with spicy sauce. Carne asada, sprinkled with cilantro (which the server does not apply unless you give him the green light) can be rather dry, a condition beautifully remedied by an application of vivid red salsa. To drink: *horchata* (rice milk), cinnamon-sweet and perfumy.

Seats are limited to counter stools, so some customers simply dine while standing either indoors or on the shopping-center sidewalk. A lot of business is takeout.

EL INDIO

elindiosandiego.com

3695 India St.   619-299-0333
San Diego, CA   **B L D | $**

Meals are served on Styrofoam plates with throwaway utensils at this cafeteria-style taqueria adjacent to Interstate 5. There are a few seats at a counter and some tables to the side of the order line, but many people choose to eat on the fenced-in patio across the street. Here, one is serenaded by vehicles passing on the raised highway.

The menu is Cal-Mex. An on-premises tortilla press turns out warm, wheaty ones for burros and chimichangas; there are freshly fried, hot corn tortillas and deliciously crunchy taquitos, and there are all sorts of combo plates topped with gobs of sour cream. El Indio's fish taco is a hefty meal served in a foil wrapper along with a wedge of lime. When the foil is pulled back, you find a double layer of warm corn tortillas loosely wrapped around a log of crisp-fried cod with a golden crust. The fish sits on a bed of ruggedly shredded cabbage, a few tomato shreds, and a faintly peppery pink sauce. Give it a spritz or two from the wedge of lime provided—an ideal complement for the sweet meat of the white fish and its savory crust.

Above the windows where you order your food at El Indio are portraits of fierce Mayan gods, including the god of war, the gods of rain and wind, and the god of Mexican food, who, according to this portrait, goes by the name of El Indio. We are not up-to-date on our Mayan theology, but one cannot deny that El Indio is indeed a deity in San Diego's food scene.

HARRIET'S CHEESECAKES UNLIMITED

1515 Centinela Ave.   310-419-2259
Inglewood, CA   (closed Sun & Mon) | $

Harriet's is not a sit-down restaurant. All business is takeout, and cheesecake is the only thing available. Oh, what cheesecake it is! Fresh, dairy-pure, and nearly as dense as modeling clay, it raises a new bar of radical richness among all desserts. With a full repertoire of more than five dozen varieties, Miss Harriet's offers about a dozen and a half different types each day. The best seller is praline, a caramel-draped wedge of cake scattered with candied nuts on a crust that seems at least 50 percent brown sugar—soft and crumbly. The crust under a spicy sweet-potato cheesecake is similar, but because the sweet-potato cake is less gooey, the crust stays more intact. The banana pudding cheesecake rests on a more traditional graham-cracker crust. Supporting the cookies 'n' cream cheesecake, which is absolutely chockfull of thick chocolate veins, is a crust that is like the cookie part of an Oreo, but more intensely chocolaty.

Great news for the traveler—all of Harriet's cakes are available as individual slices as well as whole.

THE HITCHING POST

hitchingpost1.com
3325 Point Sal Rd.   805-937-6151
Casmalia, CA   D | $$$

Unlike barbecue in the South and Southwest, where meat is cooked for hours in the smolder of hardwood coals, Santa Maria barbecue is always done in the open on a grate over flaming red oak logs. While much of it is served from mobile cookeries in local parking lots, the best restaurant source is the Hitching Post, where T-bones, sirloins, and filet mignons anchor full dinners that start with a relish tray and shrimp cocktail and include a head lettuce salad, garlic toast, and potatoes either baked or French fried (the latter are wonderful). The meat glows with the flavor of the fire and with the piquant smack of a wine vinegar and oil marinade applied as it cooks. "The trick is in how the steaks are handled," proprietor Bill Ostini explained. "You've got to know how to cook which steak which way—some are made to be cooked rare, some well-done; it depends on the marbling and how much age they have. It takes two to three years to train a cook to do it the right way."

Ambience in this old, family-run roadhouse evokes a forgotten California, when the Golden State was cattle country and its people were frontier types. Above the bar, a TV is always playing; the mirror is plastered with decals from NASA, *Voyager*, and the Army Corps of Engineers; a bison head on one wall wears a Buffalo Bills cap. In the dining room, which affords a view of the kitchen, there are mounted deer heads and old black-and-white family photos of the proprietors on hunting and fishing trips. The hallway that leads to the restrooms is lined with cattle hides.

HOB NOB HILL

hobnobhill.com
2271 1st Ave.   619-239-8176
San Diego, CA   B L D | $

The California coffee shop is a unique style of square-meal restaurant, but there aren't a lot of them left. Hob Nob Hill pretty much defines the genre: a three-meal-a-day place where the food is homey, the service fast, and the prices low. You may have to wait in line, especially at breakfast. But the line moves quickly, and once you are seated you are set upon by a team of waitresses who could not move faster if they flew through the aisles—taking orders, filling coffee cups, making sure everyone is happy.

The kitchen's offerings are broad, and there isn't a clinker on the menu. Breakfast items include pecan waffles, pigs in blankets (buttermilk pancakes rolled with ham, sausage, and sour cream), blueberry hotcakes, grilled smoked pork chops, et cetera—plus a bakery's worth of coffee cakes, muffins (try carrot), and a not-to-be-missed pecan roll. Even the little amenities are special: syrup is served warm; jelly comes in hollowed-out orange halves; coffee is strong and rich.

At dinner, it's meat-and-potatoes time: leg of lamb with sage dressing and mint jelly, chicken and dumplings, roast tom turkey with giblet gravy, corned beef and cabbage, pot roast and buttered noodles. There are turkey croquettes with cranberry sauce, a nursery-nice breast-of-chicken curry, and baked ham with fruit sauce and yams on Thursday. Accompaniments are such comfort-food side dishes as warm applesauce (homemade, of course), marinated bean salad, and puffy yeast rolls.

★ HODAD'S
hodadies.com

5010 Newport Ave.   619-224-4623
Ocean Beach, CA   **L D** | $

There isn't a restaurant more casual than Hodad's, where a sign notifies patrons: "No Shirt, No Shoes, No Problem." The place throbs with wave-riders' music and its walls are plastered with hundreds of decommissioned vanity license plates, their meanings ranging from silly (Texas OI VEY) to provocative (California I LUV SX). Hodad's has no silverware and no written menus; the one hot meal cooked in its kitchen is a hamburger.

Oh, what a hamburger: the most awe-inspiring one we have ever seen, a paragon of SoCal burger culture, a joy to behold and an adventure to eat. Nothing casual or slapdash about this bunned beauty! The burger itself is swell—good and juicy with a savory crust—but it's the way it's built that puts it in a class by itself. It comes with the works, unless you say otherwise, and that means mayo, mustard, raw onion, ketchup, pickle slices, sliced tomato, and shredded lettuce, plus bacon and/or cheese if desired. All these elements are piled high and handsomely to create a sandwich so strapping that no human jaw could possibly enclose it top to bottom.

Beautiful hamburgers aside, we love Hodad's for its infectious joie de vivre. Seating includes not only booths and one long communal table where stoked bros congregate and swap great-wave stories, but also an entire front section of a VW Microbus with seating for two and a table where the dashboard used to be, plus a counter up front where the stools offer a ringside view of Newport Avenue. A latter-day Haight-Ashbury, this amped artery of Ocean Beach includes surf shops, head shops, bead shops, and juice bars. This off-the-wall burger joint fits right into the high-attitude avenue.

ICI
ici-icecream.com

2948 College Ave.   510-665-6054
Berkeley, CA $

First, a warning: If you want an ice cream cone or cup, you almost surely will wait in line at Ici. The line moves slowly because once a person gets to the head of it, he or she is allowed—even encouraged—to try little spoonfuls of different kinds of ice cream before committing to one. This is a very good thing, because so many of Ici's flavors are ones you would likely never have tried, such as mocha salted almond, sesame praline, Santa Rosa plum, and peach habanero sorbet. If that is off-putting, we have an insider's tip: Those with ice cream hunger so great that it precludes waiting can bypass the line and step right up to the counter, where they are free to buy and instantly consume an ice cream sandwich, such as fudge-streaked vanilla ice cream between two devil's food cookies or lemon ice cream sandwiched in tiles of gingerbread.

Still, the weird and original flavors are good enough to wait for. And they demand slow savoring. As much as we like ice cream cones (Ici's are particularly nice: homemade, of course, with a nugget of rich chocolate in the point at the bottom), we suggest getting your chosen flavor in a cup. That allows for very slow licking—an unnatural act that is well worth practicing, for as this ice cream warms, its flavors blossom.

JOCKO'S STEAK HOUSE

125 N. Thompson Ave.   805-929-3686
Nipomo, CA   **B L D** | $$

We found Jocko's many years ago while we were students at Gary Leffew's bull-riding school north of Santa Barbara. When the week of riding was over, cowboys who hadn't broken too many bones and had some jingle in their jeans headed for Nipomo to eat beef at Jocko's on Saturday night.

When you walk into this place, you might have to remind yourself that yes, you are in California. For this is a California very different from the sad, broke, troubled cities and suburbs in the news. It is a California populated by country folk whose idea of fun is to come to this tavern, quaff beers under taxidermized animal heads, and eat red meat. Although the steaks are first-class, the experience of dining at Jocko's is absolutely nothing like a meal in one of the high-priced, dress-up steak house chains. Wear your jeans and boots and Stetson or farm cap and you'll be right at home.

Beef, pork, and lamb are what there is to eat. (One Roadfooder wrote to us suggesting that this must be the place where bad vegetarians go when they die, for it truly is a kind of beef frowners' hell, where smells of roasting meat permeate the air.) Shockingly thick steaks and hefty lamb chops and pork chops are cooked on an open pit over oak wood and served Santa Maria–style, accompanied by tiny pinquita beans and salsa. It's a great, filling meal, and even if you get a relatively modest-sized filet mignon, chances are you'll be taking meat home in a doggie bag.

JULIAN PIE COMPANY
julianpie.com

21976 Hwy. 79	760-765-2400
Santa Ysabel, CA	$

Apple pie is the specialty of the Julian Pie Company, a sweet oasis at the base of Volcan Mountain, where the climate is perfect for growing tasty apples. The handle on the front door advises, "Begin Smelling." Indeed. Walk in and you will be bowled over by one of the best smells there is: apple pies baking in the oven. You can watch the pies being made behind the counter; you can buy whole pies to take home; or you can get a single slice and a cup of coffee and find a seat at the counter and indulge.

There are many different variations available, including Dutch apple, strawberry apple, and apple rhubarb. Non-apple pies include peach, blackberry, and pecan. But for us, it's basic apple pie every time.

It is perfect, with a flaky crust and filling that is big-flavored and very sweet—fruit-sweet more than sugar-sweet.

One other item we love at this place: pie crust. Yes, crust, just crust. These are heart-shaped morsels made from dough that is baked in a veil of cinnamon sugar to become cookies that fall into flakes as you bite.

The other store is at 2225 Main Street in Julian (760-765-2449).

JUNE BUG CAFE
yosemitebug.com/cafe.html

6979 Hwy. 140	209-966-6666
Midpines, CA	B L D | $

If you are coming to Yosemite to hike, bike, swim, or savor the wilderness, but want to stay in a room or tent cabin for the evening, you won't do better than the Yosemite Bug Mountain Resort. And if you're looking for a nice place to eat other than around a campfire, the Cafe at the Bug is swell.

It's a three-meal-a-day place with outdoor patios and a glassed-in deck for scenic dining and a menu with choices that range from carnivorous to vegan. You can start the day with a giant buckwheat pancake (available vegan or not), muesli, eggs, or tofu egg substitutes. And while you are having breakfast you can have the kitchen prepare a boxed lunch for the trail. We relished our dinner of stuffed trout with rice and seasonal vegetables and a handsome sirloin steak with potatoes. We were especially fond of the chocolate cake served for dessert; while we cleaned the last of it from our plates, we listened to neighbors rave over their cheesecake.

Service is casual, semi-cafeteria-style. Order at the counter and pick your table. It is customary for customers to bus their own tables.

THE KETTLE

thekettle.net

1138 Highland Ave.   310-545-8511
Manhattan Beach, CA   **B L D** | **$**

--★--
OPEN
24/7
--★--
Open all night and serving breakfast all day, the Kettle is a thriving example of the ever-more-rare category of restaurant: the Southern California coffee shop. Not coffee HOUSE, as in cappuccinos and lattes, but coffee SHOP, as in three square meals a day in a polite, handsomely decorated, well-upholstered space where the coffee is never fancy but is diligently brewed and refilled constantly.

From the griddle come bananas Foster French toast and stacks of big, handsome pancakes, including a winning combo of blueberry buttermilk pancakes with house-made cranberry-maple granola. Benedicts include California (with avocado), smoked trout, and crab cake Benedict with an orange-cilantro-infused hollandaise. Other enticements from the breakfast menu include *oeufs pain perdu*, buttermilk-honey fried chicken and biscuits, and a "hangover scramble" of eggs, chiles, bacon, cheese, avocado salsa, and sour cream.

The only bad thing about the hangover scramble is that it doesn't come with muffins, which are a must-eat item at the Kettle. Moderate in size, they are plated in pairs, preferably warmed up if not oven-warm at that moment. We like honey bran best—they're sweet and oily with especially broad, crisp-edge tops—but other winners include carrot-raisin, banana-nut, and blueberry crumb. Whatever else you eat here, try some of these.

As is true of so many great coffee shops, interior décor is stylin'. In this case, the style is an eclectic mix of western arts-and-crafts rustic, including counter armchairs fashioned from carved logs, as well as elaborate chandeliers, extra-plush booth upholstery, and, oddly enough, large vintage posters for French libations. It's an especially fun place to come in the wee hours of the morning, when clientele includes local cops on a break, dating couples rounding out their night, and a motley collection of well-behaved insomniacs.

LA SUPER-RICA

622 N. Milpas St.   805-963-4940
Santa Barbara, CA   **L D** | **$**

La Super-Rica is barely a restaurant. It is a taco stand where service is do-it-yourself and customers are expected to clean their own place when they're finished eating. All plates and utensils are disposable, and seating is at wobbly tables on a semi-alfresco patio.

Using made-here tortillas, tacos can be had with beef, with green chile and cheese, or as a "chorizo especial" of spicy sausage, melted cheese, and tomato. We are especially fond of the taco *adobado* (grilled pork) and the frijol Super-Rica (chorizo and pinto beans with bacon and chile). In addition to tacos, La Super-Rica makes gorditas, quesadillas, cheese-stuffed pasilla peppers, and what Julia Child once proclaimed to be her favorite tamales. Each of the three kinds of salsa is excellent: chunky tomato, spicy red chile, and even spicier green chile. Beverages include *horchata* (sweet rice milk), hibiscus, and Mexican beer.

Since Isidoro Gonzalez opened for business in 1980, this extremely modest eatery has built a huge reputation, meaning you will wait in line at mealtime. In one way, the line is a good thing: La Super-Rica has no signs outside, so the crowd of people you see on North Milpas Street is the sign that lets you know you have arrived.

THE MARSHALL STORE

themarshallstore.com

19225 State Rt. 1   415-663-1339
Marshall, CA   **L** (closed Tues) | **$$**

----★----

WATER-FRONT
DINING
----★----
The Marshall Store, which gets provender from the Hog Island Oyster Company up the road, brushes just-opened oysters on the half shell with butter and cooks them on a grate only until they are warm. They are then dabbed with barbecue sauce and served with garlic toast. There are few simple pleasures as right as this, the experience amplified by the casual magic of the dining facilities, which are boards set out on wine

barrels where the Tomales Bay breeze wafts over your meal.

There is more on the Marshall Store menu, including raw oysters on the half shell, chowder (dip your own), sandwiches, and salads. It's those barbecued oysters that will keep us coming back.

MUSSO & FRANK GRILL

mussoandfrank.com

6667 Hollywood Blvd.   323-467-7788
Hollywood, CA   **L D** (closed Mon) | **$$**

When Musso & Frank opened for business in 1919, Hollywood was young and fresh and Hollywood Boulevard was a magic address. The boulevard went to honkytonk hell in a handbasket and is now trying to rebirth itself with entertainment complexes and shopping malls that compete for attention with hookers' wig shops, but the moment you step inside Hollywood's oldest restaurant, the battle of the lifestyles is left behind.

In fact, whenever meat and potatoes are decreed by food oracles to be having a renaissance (perhaps once every seven years), this vintage eatery almost seems trendy. Musso is known for dowdy kinds of meals: thin flannel cakes (for lunch), Welsh rarebit, chicken potpie on Thursday, classic corned beef and cabbage every Tuesday, lamb shanks, baked ham, chiffonade salads. Ten different kinds of potato occupy the menu, from mashed and boiled to Lyonnaise and candied sweet. Steaks and chops—cooked on an open broiler where those sitting at the counter can watch—are splendid. From the dessert list, note bread and butter pudding, and its deluxe variant, diplomat pudding—topped with strawberries.

Many adventurous gourmets of our acquaintance do not understand the appeal of Musso & Frank. They compliment its antique Tudor décor and comfortable red leather booths but complain that the food is ordinary. Yes, indeed! It is some of the tastiest ordinary food anywhere.

ORANGE INN

cafelagunabeachca.com

703 S. Coast Hwy.   949-494-6085
Laguna Beach, CA   **B L** | **$**

Whether or not the smoothie was invented at the Orange Inn is debatable. The goodness of its smoothie, however, is indisputable. The Pacific Coast Highway shack, first opened in 1931, does put a trademark sign in superscript next to the listing on its menu. More important, this smoothie tastes like the original intent. Nothing about it is outlandish or exotic, at least by twenty-first-century standards. It is elemental, a blend of strawberries, bananas, dates, juice, and ice, topped with a sprinkle of bee pollen. It tastes quite healthful and it is refreshing in two ways: first for its cool, fruity flavor, but also for its simplicity. The date shake is another old-time drink made here without folderol.

Beyond whirled drinks, the Orange Inn serves fine coffee with or without espresso and has an inventory of beguiling pastries. Among the latter are gnarly muffins with tops that are chewy and dense. On the counter above the morning muffins, we spotted a tray of brownies that were billed as "extra-chewy [with] a thick crispy edge … baked in Great-Grandma's glass baking dishes." God bless Great-Grandma and whoever makes these dark-brown monuments today. Taste in brownies varies tremendously; some like them light and feathery-textured, others want them as intense as a chocolate truffle. We think Orange Inn's are a perfect balance: powerfully chocolaty and offering serious tooth resistance but more like cake than fudge.

The one other item we need to recommend is granola. Like the smoothie, it contains nothing surprising, but it is a masterful mix of nuts, grain, and fruit, just barely sweet and perfectly complemented by a dab of plain yogurt.

ORIGINAL PANTRY

pantrycafe.com

877 S. Figueroa St.   213-972-9279
Los Angeles, CA   Always open | $

OPEN 24/7 — ★ — Not far from the Staples Center, the Original Pantry is a choice stop for fans after Lakers games. Never having closed its doors since opening in 1924, this round-the-clock temple of honest eats is renowned for hotcakes and full-bore egg breakfasts accompanied by sourdough toast, thick slabs of bacon, and piles of excellent hash brown potatoes. OJ is fresh-squeezed and the coffee keeps coming. At supper, you can't go wrong with a steak platter or such stalwarts as roast beef or short ribs, and the favorite dessert is hot apple pie with rum sauce. Sourdough bread and coleslaw are served with every meal.

When the Original Pantry was threatened by developers in 1980, former mayor Richard Riordan bought it, and Hizzoner's aura helped make it a destination for city politicians, bigwigs, and wannabes, especially at breakfast, when people-watching is a sport. A relatively small place, it is always bustling and service, by hash-house pros, is nearly instantaneous.

PANN'S

panns.com

6710 La Tijera Blvd.   323-776-3770
Los Angeles, CA   B L D | $

Pann's is like the polymorphous Flubadub on the old *Howdy Doody* TV show: a single entity composed of wildly different characters. In this case, the culinary crazy quilt is part medieval grotto (ponderous stone walls), part spaceship-boomerang panache, and part tailfin automobile upholstery. In other words, it is a perfect example of what is known as Googie-style, aka Do-Wop design, that thrived in mid-twentieth-century America.

Like the place itself, the menu is a nostalgic wonderland of such coffee shop classics as roast turkey with corn-bread stuffing, liver and onions, chicken and waffles, mile-high layer cakes, and tapioca pudding. Beverages include milk shakes and malts, strawberry lemonade, and root beer floats. If you order coffee, a uniformed waitress will top it off approximately every ninety seconds.

Fried chicken is a house specialty. It comes enveloped in a dark-gold crust as unctuous as crisp bacon. Mashed potatoes are available with white gravy, brown gravy, or country sausage gravy. Pann's is proud of its buttermilk biscuits, served with butter and bubble packs of honey. Unlike fluffy southern-style biscuits, these are dense and heavy. But we don't mean that in a bad way. Their avoirdupois is a style unto itself.

PHILIPPE THE ORIGINAL

philippes.com

1001 N. Alameda St.   213-628-3781
Los Angeles, CA   B L D | $

Genesis, according to Philippe's: One day in 1918 Philippe Mathieu was preparing a beef sandwich at his proletarian eat place when the roll fell into gravy. Fetched out with tongs, the drippings-sopped bread looked good enough that an impatient customer said, "I'll take it just like that." And so the French dip sandwich was created.

Philippe's moved to its current location in 1951, but it remains a sawdust-on-the-floor, people-watcher's paradise. Place your order with a carver at the counter, then carry it to a communal table, where your dining companions will range from tourists to refugees from the nearby courthouse to SoCal creative types seeking a dose of old-fashioned reality.

Dips are made from pork, beef, ham, lamb, or turkey. The beef is soft and tender, the pork even tenderer. The sliced meat of your choice is piled into a fresh roll and sopped with gravy that is radiant with protein. You can get cheese on top, which we consider superfluous; but you must apply some of Philippe's hot mustard, a roaring-hot emulsion that is meat's best friend. Beyond the famous dips, there is a full menu of breakfasts, salads, sandwiches, and two soups each day. The price of coffee remains 9¢ per cup.

PHILLIPS BAR-B-QUE

1517 Centinela Ave.   310-412-7135
Inglewood, CA   **L D** (closed Sun) | $$

Phillips is a soul-food barbecue parlor (actually three parlors in the L.A. area) that offers little in the way of hospitable charm, no accommodations (it's all take-out), and an uncompromising menu of smoke-cooked meats. Its character is mirrored by its sauce: a tart, tangy red emulsion with no sweet charm but with plenty of spicy authority. Even the mild version, while lacking pepper punch, does nothing to amuse a light-weight palate. The hot version is at least three-alarm. An in-between "mixed" sauce is classic urban 'cue.

Unless you specifically request to have it on the side, Phillips's serious sauce is automatically applied to any meat you get, which can be pork ribs, baby backs, beef ribs, links, or chicken. As a result, eating is a roll-up-the-sleeves, finger-licking mess, albeit a mighty tasty one. Top of the line are pork ribs: giant bats with chewy meat that resonates smoky-sweet character. There are baby backs too: more meat, more tender, less flavor. The chicken is moist and flavorful, although it tends to be overwhelmed by the sauce. It is fun to chew the rugged beef links, which come pre-sliced, but let's be frank—in this venue, pork is king. While beans and potato salad are merely serviceable, macaroni and cheese is a cut above, creamy and rich and a marvelous counterpoint to the power-packed meat and sauce. It is based on the large, fall-apart noodles that are typical of soul-food mac 'n' cheese in this part of the country.

For dessert: sweet-potato pie, peach cobbler, banana pudding, or sock-it-to-me cake.

Note: The two other Phillips are located at 4307 Leimert Boulevard in Los Angeles (323-292-7613) and 2619 S. Crenshaw Boulevard, Los Angeles (323-731-4772).

RAMONA CAFE

theramonacafe.com
628 Main St.   760-789-8656
Ramona, CA   **B L D** | $$

Here is a menu that respects potatoes. No mere side dish, Ramona Cafe's glistening chunks of home-fried potato are the underpinnings of whole breakfasts piled into ceramic skillets. Design your own, selecting toppings from a list that includes ham, bacon, taco meat, chorizo sausage, four kinds of cheese, crushed garlic, and jalapeños. Or choose the Kitchen Sink, which is a panful of hunky home fries loaded with some of everything, including sausage gravy and a couple of eggs, and sided by an immense squared-off biscuit. If you want a meal that is less complicated but perhaps even more filling, consider Ramona Cafe's cinnamon roll: a half-pound circle of hot, sweet pastry veined with cinnamon sugar and accompanied by two paper cups of butter. It's really enough for two, or three, or four.

Among the many omelets available, of special note is the Gilroy Omelet, named for the California town that has proclaimed itself the garlic capital of the world: ham, bacon, mushrooms, Cheddar, and jack cheese, plus lots and lots of garlic.

Lunch is big too. There are good-sized cheeseburgers, hot meat loaf sandwiches with good mashed potatoes and gravy, turkey potpie, and fried chicken that is crusted with breading made from the café's breakfast biscuits. If you are looking for pie (and who is not?), the list of pies is a long one, including boysenberry crunch and apple crunch, coconut cream, and chocolate peanut butter cup.

RANDY'S DONUTS

randysdonuts.com
805 W. Manchester Ave.   310-645-4707
Inglewood, CA   Always open | $

OPEN 24/7 With a two-story-tall donut perched upon its roof, Randy's has long been a favorite location for movies and TV shows that want a background of roadside kitsch. It is a good example of what became known in the mid-twentieth century as vernacular architecture, a term that, in the world of gastronomy, refers mostly to buildings that are shaped like the food they serve.

Architectural significance aside, Randy's also happens to be a fine place to get donuts at any time of day or night. Varieties include honey-glazed, chocolate-covered, jelly-filled, powdered, frosted, and filled with crème. Glazed twists and sugar twists are lighter than the standard sinkers, and the maple bars are superb. Randy's also offers very good cinnamon rolls, apple fritters, and bear claws.

Note to those arriving at LAX: Randy's is a five-minute drive from the airport.

RICK & ANN'S
rickandanns.com

2922 Domingo Ave.	510-649-8538
Berkeley, CA	**B L** | **$$**

Rick & Ann's is not Bay-Area hip, so we really like it. Hey, what's not to like about a place proud of fried chicken supper with mac 'n' cheese and corn bread?

We are not its only fans. Crowds come to this spot across from the Claremont Hotel, especially on weekends. (There is a communal table that is great for singles or those in search of conversation.) Breakfast is the beacon meal, featuring gorgeous red-flannel hash made with sweet and new potatoes and enough beets to turn it brick-red. With eggs and toast, it is part of a breakfast known as the Northeast, but you'd be hard-pressed to find red-flannel hash this good in New England. As devoted waffle folks, we heartily endorse the thin, crisp gingerbread-corn waffles (regular buttermilk waffles also are available), and on a return visit, we swooned over the fragile, flavorful lemon ricotta pancakes. For dinner, if fried chicken is not your idea of comfort-food bliss, how about chicken potpie or meat loaf with mashed potatoes?

Rick & Ann's website changes each day to list such specials as shrimp tacos, summer caprese salad with heirloom tomatoes, and springtime crepes with roasted artichokes, fava beans, asparagus, portobello mushrooms, and goat cheese. And let's have a plum strawberry tart for dessert!

SAM'S GRILL
samsgrillsf.com

374 Bush St.	415-421-0594
San Francisco, CA	**L D** (Mon–Fri) | **$$$**

Food trends come and go, and hot restaurants appear and fizzle. Sam's never seems to change. Tracing its history back to the 1860s, it is at once deluxe and informal, featuring high-priced, top-quality groceries prepared simply. It looks the way you want a great old California restaurant to look: outfitted with yards of thick white linen, brass hooks for coats, and private wooden dining booths for intimate meals.

The daily printed menu is divided into such enticing categories as "Fish (Wild Only)" and "From the Charcoal Broiler," and the big rounds of sourdough bread brought to table at the beginning of the meal are among the best anywhere. The menu lists so many things that are intriguing, from the unknown (what is chicken Elizabeth? what are prawns Dore?) to such bygone classics as hangtown fry and mock turtle soup to ultra-exotica (fresh abalone meunière). It is possible to order charcoal-grilled steaks and chops, sweetbreads done three ways, short ribs of beef with horseradish sauce, or just bacon and eggs, but nearly everybody comes to Sam's for the seafood. Our favorites have all been sole: rex sole fillets glistening with butter (perhaps the tenderest seafood we've ever slid onto the tines of a fork), charcoal-broiled petrale sole, and delicately fried fillets.

Sam's is open only on weekdays, only until nine at night, hours aimed at customers who work downtown and come every day for lunch, or for an early dinner before heading home. At noon, it is mobbed with successful-looking types jockeying for a table, or crowding three deep against the bar. Once you are seated, it is an immensely comfortable place to eat. The impeccably dressed waiters are consummate professionals, treating out-of-towners in jeans with as much respect as high rollers in business suits.

SEARS FINE FOOD

searsfinefood.com

439 Powell St.   415-986-0700
San Francisco, CA   B L D | $$

While not the most exciting or innovative restaurant in town, nor an undiscovered gem, this comfortable storefront facing the cable cars on Powell Street has been Old Reliable since it opened in 1938, especially for breakfast. In fact, three meals a day are served and the lunch and dinner menus are extensive; but like most other tourists who find their way here, when we think of Sears we think of little Swedish pancakes served eighteen to a plate, sourdough French toast as tender as custard, non-Belgian waffles (from an old Fannie Farmer cookbook recipe) and thick, crisp bacon or plump sausage links alongside.

SERVING SPOON

theservingspoon.net

1403 Centinela Ave.   310-412-3927
Inglewood, CA   B L | $

The Serving Spoon bills itself as "An Urban Eatery," which means that it is a high-energy breakfast-and-lunch coffee shop specializing in soul food. On a podium up front, a sign says if there will be a wait for a table and how long it might be. When your time comes, you will be directed to a booth or table or armchair seat at a long diner-style counter. ESPN plays on a few overhead TVs, but unless an important event is on, it is totally drowned out in a room that bustles with ebullient conversation, music, and good vibes. Everyone who eats here seems very happy to be doing so, and that good cheer is amplified by a staff who all seem equally happy to be on the job.

The menu features such homespun items as chicken and waffles, pork chops, catfish, and vegetables galore. The fried chicken is wonderful, but there's nothing wrong with altogether circumventing entrees and going for an all-vegetable plate including, for instance, yams spiced like Christmas and soft, clumpy collard greens that are a little bitter and barely sweet. Available pseudo-vegetables on a four-item, no-entree plate can include mac 'n' cheese, which is spicy, rich, and satisfying, and thick, brightly spiced seasoned beanless chili con carne. On the side of meals comes a slab of corn bread nearly as sweet as pound cake. To conclude: syrupy peach cobbler that is more about pastry than fruit or, of course, sweet-potato pie.

Note: Serving Spoon's location makes it an ideal first or last stop on the way from or to LAX.

★ SWAN OYSTER DEPOT

sfswanoysterdepot.com

1517 Polk St.   415-673-1101
San Francisco, CA   L (closed Sun) | $$

Swan's is an urban seafood shack that is a combination oyster bar and storefront market. Seating is limited to a nineteen-seat counter, where your chances of finding a seat at mealtime are near zero. It is relatively expensive, uncomfortable, and noisy. And yet somehow its inconvenience is part of its charm (as is the ebullience of the Sancimino family, who have run the lunch counter since 1946). For devotees, it is simply the best place in San Francisco to eat fresh seafood. Fans have been crowding in for nearly a century to feast on oysters from the East and West Coasts, whole lobsters, salads of shrimp or crab, and smoked trout or salmon. Also, New England–style chowder, which is so right with hunky sourdough bread. The marble counter is strewn with condiments: Tabasco sauce, lemons, oyster crackers.

Dungeness crab is served in season (generally, mid-November through May), available "cracked," meaning sections of cooked, cooled claw, leg, and body ready to be unloaded of their sweet meat. Crab Louie is a regal dish in which large chunks of crab are cosseted in a condiment made from lemony mayonnaise spiked with relish and olive bits, enriched by hard-cooked egg.

UNCLE BILL'S PANCAKE HOUSE

unclebills.net

1305 Highland Ave.   310-545-5177
Manhattan Beach, CA   B L | $

OCEAN-VIEW DINING

Uncle Bill's is an indoor/outdoor café that does serve lunch but is known to fans for eggs, pancakes, waffles, and marvelous potatoes, like Potatoes Stroganoff. That's a mountain of crisp-edge hash browns that get sautéed with bacon and melted cheese and topped with sour cream: endless satisfaction. Add peppers, onions, and avocado, and the dish becomes the even more lavish Potatoes del Riego.

Waffles are of the small-tread variety, arriving not-quite crisp but not the least bit doughy. You can have them plain or infused with cheese, pecans, raisins and cinnamon, blueberries, or bacon, and topped with strawberries, whipped cream, or even ice cream. Pancakes come regular- or dollar-sized in quantities of six or twelve. As for eggs, name your pleasure. Accompanied by bacon or sausage or corned beef hash or pork chops, they're beautiful plates of food. We're especially fond of a meal called Mitch's Scramble, a mix of eggs, mild chiles, and cream cheese. And one day we will try the emblematic beachside item listed as Body Builder's Power Breakfast: banana-nut buckwheat pancakes and five egg whites.

Happy, busy, sunshiny, and within a few steps of the ocean, Uncle Bill's is a memorable taste of classic Southern California.

THE WAFFLE

thewafflehollywood.com

6255 W. Sunset Blvd.   323-465-6901
Los Angeles, CA   B L D | $

OPEN LATE

The Waffle stays open past midnight on weekends. Apparently the squareness of its menu has garnered a retro-chic admiration society. But you'll see little stylin' if you arrive at what most people consider normal breakfast time. After the sun comes up and before the cool crowd wakes up, this place could pass for a regular diner. Coffee is presented with a stirrer already in the mug, and it gets topped off with hash-house regularity.

The Waffle's waffles are big Belgian rectangles but light and crisp rather than doughy, and they have the eggy flavor that morning meals want. Each comes with a couple of little butter tubs, and although the butter is soft, there is no way to easily spread it on a tile with treads so big. Some holes get more, others less or none. Each trough holds massive amounts of syrup. All sorts of waffles are available, two to an order, including ones with pecans or bacon baked in, multi-grains, gluten-frees, a red velvet waffle, and a rather ridiculous sticky-bun variation, which is a plain waffle topped with the sort of goo that adorns Cinnabons: unjustifiable by any meaningful culinary or nutrition standards, but good to eat.

There are plenty of non-waffle breakfasts as well as a full menu of sandwiches, soups, and milk shakes. Vegan and vegetarian options are available.

OREGON

ANNIE'S DONUT SHOP

3449 NE 72nd Ave.   503-284-2752
Portland, OR   **B | $**

——★——— There's been a donut renaissance in the
OPEN EARLY Pacific Northwest. Seattle and Portland
——★——— are bonanza cities for sinker lovers,
especially those who like their morning pastry with
excellent coffee. For all the new, fashionable, retro,
vegan, and Goth donuts available in both cities, we
have a soft spot for traditional ones that cost less
than a dollar and go so well with morning coffee (not
latte!). These you will find at their best at Annie's.
They are fresh and the variety is tremendous. Old-
fashioned cake donuts have the double-circle crown
profile so popular in the Northwest that provides
twice the crunchy exterior of a simple round one.
Glazed and maple-frosted OFs are especially swell,
and although the price is plebeian, the taste and
mouthfeel are aristocratic. Cream puffs are light and
impeccably fresh-flavored, the only way a cream puff
ever should be. The wickedest variety we sampled
was a raspberry fritter—unctuous, super-sweet,
slightly fruity, and monumentally filling. And if you
need something really outrageous, try Annie's
chocolate-glazed peanut-butter fritter.

Annie's has none of the amenities of upscale coffee and donut shops: no art on the walls, no Wi-Fi, no
couches or lounge chairs and, of course, no baristas.
You sit in molded plastic booths that look out on the
parking lot and are served by a staff with no attitude
other than pride in the donuts.

ASTORIA COFFEEHOUSE & BISTRO

astoriacoffeehouse.com
243 11th St.   503-325-1787
Astoria, OR   **B L D | $$**

Coffee hounds know that America's caffeine consciousness is at its zenith in Seattle, Portland, and
throughout the Northwest—all the way to Anchorage,
which has more coffee shops per capita than any
other American city. One nice piece of evidence is the
Astoria Coffeehouse & Bistro in the northwestern-
most part of Oregon. The coffee poured is Caffé Vita-
brand from Seattle, and in addition to all the usual
espresso drinks are such exotic lattes as lavender
vanilla, cardamom mocha, salted caramel, and maple
brown sugar.

Actually, the food at breakfast wowed us more
than the coffee. Smoked salmon hash is a mélange of
bite-sized salmon, potatoes, and peppers, topped with
eggs and sided by a buttermilk biscuit. We savored
an almond paste–filled croissant and a slice of moist
chocolate cake. There are *aebleskivers* (Danish pancakes), cardamom bread French toast, and biscuits
topped with bacon gravy.

You can have an over-$20 meal for supper, which
the menu describes as "neo-regional cuisine using
direct caught seafood, all natural meats and wild local

produce 'foraged' from the area." These items include Cajun oysters, chickpea and tabouli salad, pork molé, paella, steak frites, French dip, sushi rolls, and pad Thai. We are a little confused about the concept of neo-regionality, but the goodness of the salmon hash and freshness of the rhubarb scones make us want to discover exactly what it means.

BLUE SCORCHER BAKERY CAFE
bluescorcher.coop

1493 Duane St.   503-338-7473
Astoria, OR   **B L** | $

Operating as a workers' collective with noble principles that include the use of actual cloth napkins and non-disposable flatware to minimize waste, gluten-free Fridays for people who are allergic, and a seasonal-local vegetarian menu, the Blue Scorcher has some of the best pastries anywhere. To wit: chocolate babka cupcakes, Irish brown butter cake with mascarpone filling, and mixed-fruit ginger custard tartlets.

Must eat: extremely moist chocolate chip applesauce cake, full of little melting chips. Must eat #2: chocolate gingerbread that delivers sharp ginger snap as well as a tsunami of chocolate flavor. The intensity of the latter could easily induce taste-bud overload were it not for the palliating globe of pure (organic) whipped cream offered on top.

We were so busy eating cakes and drinking good espresso that we did not even think to order from an interesting breakfast selection that includes house-made Northwest cherry hazelnut granola, the Breakfast of Wonder (poached eggs on greens with tempeh and toast), frittatas, and "huevos scorcheros." Lunch items include pizza and calzones, veggie burgers, soups, and salads. Based on the goodness of the pastries, these are all worthy of a return visit. We did manage to come away with a loaf of asiago sourdough bread that was memorably delicious.

★ BOWPICKER
bowpicker.com

1634 Duane St.   503-791-2942
Astoria, OR   **L D** (Wed-Sun) | $

Bowpicker is not a building but a former fishing vessel now landlocked and serving some of the best fish and chips anywhere on the West Coast. It is a small craft, scarcely more than a kitchen and cash register. There is no indoor seating and only a couple of picnic tables around it. Most customers get their meal to take somewhere else, if only to the dashboard of a car.

We highly recommend eating your meal soon after you get it. The gossamer beer-batter crust on this fish demands immediate indulgence. Enveloped inside are trapezoidal hunks of albacore tuna dense with seafood-richness (as opposed to the more typical fried-fish oily-crust richness). French fries are very good, but we found ourselves pretty much ignoring them, not wanting to use up any appetite while there was still superlative fish to eat.

By the way, the first syllable of the restaurant's name is pronounced "bough," like the front of a boat off of which fish are picked from the net.

CHARLIE'S CHOWDER HOUSE

1335 Marine Dr.   503-741-3055
Astoria, OR   **L D** | $$

At the northernmost end of Route 101 in Oregon, the city of Astoria lacks the pristine beauty that defines so much of the state's coast, but it has a gritty, seaside-city appeal that is hard to resist. Charlie's Chowder House is a good example, where the word "eclectic" does not do justice to the ambience and décor. Every table is arrayed with a different salt-and-pepper set and a diorama in the window shows a Barbie Doll mermaid hovering over a pile of pirates' bones while a school of sharks swims close.

All that is immaterial to the fact that Charlie's chowder is terrific. Its identity at first seems ambiguous, listed on the menu as "Astoria's own" but on the wall as "New England clam chowder"; one bite tells you the former is true. This chowder is thick and peppery, enriched not by cream but by massive amounts of bacon. Its bounty of chopped clams is so tender and savory-sweet that sometimes you think you have hit a nugget of bacon when in fact you are enjoying a morsel of clam. After the taste-bud rapture of this chowder, everything else we ate, while perfectly fine, lacked punch. If you must have something beyond chowder, we recommend the grilled mahimahi tacos.

CREMA

cremabakery.com

| 2728 SE Ankeny St. | 503-234-0206 |
| Portland, OR | **B L** \| $ |

Crema is among the crème de la crème of Portland coffeehouses. It features French-press coffee brewed so strong that hot water is available for those who need to weaken it. The espresso is thick and syrupy, black as licorice, and among the fancy drinks is a dazzler called Spanish latte, which is made with sweetened condensed milk, adding extra body and luxe. Were the espresso not so strong, the supermilk might be overwhelming, but the two extremes form an infinitely satisfying yin-yang morning beverage. As gilding for this lily, the baristas at Crema know how to add the foam on top in exquisite patterns, making each drink a potable work of art.

We also like this large, enthusiastically caffeinated coffeehouse for its pastries. Among the wide assortment of sweet ones are Mexican chocolate cupcakes, green tea cheesecake, orange cinnamon buns, cranberry-caramel pecan bundt cake, chocolate bread pudding studded with bananas, and a double-chocolate, powdered-sugar-dusted earthquake cookie complete with fault lines. There are all sorts of savory breakfast pastries made with eggs and veggies, our favorite being the ruggedly handsome Cheddar corn biscuit, a squat circle that is all crusty and chewy with baked cheese and dotted with sweet corn kernels.

DAN & LOUIS OYSTER BAR

danandlouis.com

| 208 SW Ankeny St. | 503-227-5906 |
| Portland, OR | **L D** \| $$ |

Oyster stew at Dan & Louis is little more than warm milk, melted butter, and lots of small Yaquina oysters, which are sweet and mild and ideal participants in a bowl full of warm comfort. If we are really hungry, we'll follow stew with a plate of pan-fried oysters. Yaquinas fry up beautifully with a toasty golden crust. They are sent to the table with ramekins of tartar sauce and thousand island dressing, as well as a pile of lettuce shreds heaped with small shrimp and a length of chewy sourdough bread.

Among non-oyster items on the menu, we are fond of the dowdy creamed crab on toast, a dish that one might expect to have been served in a department store lunchroom seventy-five years ago. You'll also find cracked Dungeness crab, shrimp Louis, and halibut fish and chips.

The interior of Dan & Louis is mesmerizing, its handsome sailing-ship wood walls bedecked floor to ceiling with an inexhaustible accumulation of nautical memorabilia and historical pictures, notes, and maps that tell of Portland since Louis started serving food here.

ECOLA SEAFOODS

ecolaseafoods.com

| 208 N. Spruce St. | 503-436-9130 |
| Cannon Beach, OR | **L D** \| $$ |

Cannon Beach is one of the most picturesque places on the Oregon coast, known for the awe-inspiring haystack-shaped rock just offshore. It is a quiet hamlet and a grand destination for eaters because of Ecola Seafoods (named for nearby Ecola State Park). Ecola is total Roadfood—extremely casual and extremely local, a no-frills seafood market and restaurant where fresh is all. We love simply browsing the cases of Dungeness crab, oysters, scallops, and flat fish that we seldom see back east. For those who arrive with a good appetite, what fun it is to choose from a broad menu of "fish and chips," the former part of the equation including Willapa Bay oysters, Oregon Albacore tuna, razor clams, or troll-caught Chinook salmon. Plus Pacific cod, halibut, jumbo prawns, and ocean scallops. Each is available as a lunch or dinner (bigger portion), and you can get the cod, halibut, salmon, or oysters fried up and put into a toasted, buttered bun with lettuce, tomato, and a couple of lemon wedges.

We feasted on a crab cocktail, which was cool, pearly meat in a bowl along with zesty red cocktail sauce. And we liked the chowder too: fine-textured and creamy, its ocean savor highlighted by a jolt of pepper.

The market's own *F/V Legacy* brings in wild salmon that can be had in the form of a grilled salmon taco, a salmon burger (a couple of big chunks in a bun), topped with mango salsa, or encased in crusty batter on a fish and chips plate. Smoked Chinook salmon is dense and heavy, falling into moist, bite-sized forkfuls as fully satisfying as prime aged beefsteak. A sign on the wall warns, "Friends don't let friends eat farmed salmon."

For picnickers, sandwiches and whole ready-to-eat dinners are available to go, as are all manner of cook-it-yourself fish.

FULLER'S COFFEE SHOP

| 136 NW 9th Ave. | 503-222-5608 |
| Portland, OR | **B L | $** |

Off the tourist path but loved by locals, Fuller's is the sort of high-quality urban hash house now nearly vanished from most American cities. A man sitting near us at one of the two U-shaped Formica counters mopped the last of some yolk off his plate with a forkful of pancake and declared that he used to eat at Fuller's nearly every day thirty-two years ago, and as far as he could see, nothing's changed but the prices. "This is a diner where they know how to fry bacon!" he declared. Yes, indeed. An order of bacon is four medium-thick ribbons that are crisp but retain enough pliability so they don't break at first bite. And the hash browns are a short-order delight, fried so they are a mix of golden crust and soft, spuddy shreds of buttery potato. The pancakes are good too, and the cinnamon roll, baked fresh each day, is yeasty and tender.

Our favorite thing at Fuller's is the bread. It's not artisan bread; it's not fancy at all. You get white or whole wheat. These slices are simple and perfect, especially so when toasted and buttered and accompanying a well-rounded breakfast. Jelly and marmalade are set out along the counter.

Lunch is such short-order classics as chicken-fried steak, French dip, hot beef and gravy (on the good bread), and ham and/or cheese sandwiches. There always is interesting seafood: salmon steaks in season; batter-dipped fish and chips; fresh-fried oysters; and big, slightly scary (but easy to eat) egg-battered, fried razor clams with French fries and coleslaw.

GREEN SALMON

thegreensalmon.com

| 220 Hwy. 101 N. | 541-547-3077 |
| Yachats, OR | **B L | $** |

———★——
**VEGETARIAN-
FRIENDLY**
——★——
The Green Salmon serves great coffee and espresso, but that's just the beginning. How about a Cafe Oregonian with hazelnut milk, a Cafe Mexico with pepper, brown sugar, and cocoa, or a Kopi Jahe, which is a double-strength brew infused with the sparkle of ginger and sweetness of cane sugar?

Good coffee, great pastries. Muffins, scones, and croissants are all hale and hearty. Breakfast opportunities include a panini-grilled Sicilian egg sandwich on multigrain bread, granola baked with maple syrup and moistened with steamed milk, and a wide-bodied croissant frosted with a thick glaze of maple (the Pacific Northwest is crazy for the flavor of maple). On a recent visit, we enjoyed a sensational (if irregular) plate of lox and bagel: gorgeous, glistening-pink ribbons of smoked Pacific salmon accompanied by a whole-wheat bagel and cream cheese infused with matcha tea. Plus, of course, capers, tomatoes, and chopped onions.

Crowded and sociable, the Green Salmon is more for lingering than for a quickie coffee. Partly, this is because drinks and hot dishes all are made to order; but also because the place is infused with the life-savoring rhythms of the slow food movement . . . despite all the caffeine consumed on premises.

LOCAL OCEAN

localocean.net

213 SE Bay Blvd.   541-574-7959
Newport, OR   **L D | $$**

Local Ocean is a loud and lively place staffed by a crew who are fully aware that they are operating what is the cutting-edge seafood place on Bay Boulevard. The attitude is more one of confidence than arrogance, so we won't hold it against them; neither will we be bothered by fairly high prices. The fact is that you get your money's worth here: some of the finest seafood meals in a region replete with really fine seafood meals.

Dungeness crab soup glows warm with roasted garlic; crab cakes come with crunchy fennel slaw; a handsome crab po' boy is dressed with green chile avocado purée and is sandwiched in a loaf crusted with parmesan cheese. Fish tacos, which include a wild pickly hot salsa, are made with the catch of the day; it was ling cod when we last stopped in: white, smooth, and flaky. Salads may be enriched by house-smoked salmon and toasted Oregon hazelnuts, or you might want a halibut panzanella salad made with crisp-grilled ciabatta bread and roasted vegetables. Dessert is nothing short of sensational: lemon shortcake smothered with local berries and whipped cream.

Local Ocean also is a seafood market, each kind of raw fish in the case marked with a placard that tells which vessel caught it, using what fishing technique.

NORMA'S SEAFOOD & STEAK

normasseaside.com

20 N. Columbia St.   503-738-4331
Seaside, OR   **L D | $$**

When we first came across what was then known as Norma's Ocean Diner, we knew we were going to like it as soon as we saw the chalkboard near the pass-through window to the kitchen. It lists which fresh seafood is available and where it is from: wild salmon from the Oregon coast, steamer clams and oysters from Willipa Bay (Washington), halibut from Alaska, razor clams from Washington, and prawns from the Gulf of Mexico.

The waitress congratulated us on our choice of petrale sole mid-April: "Oooo, it's in season right now," she said. And it was wonderful: delicate-flavored, buttery-rich, ocean-sweet. Nor could we resist Dungeness crab, which is available here in all sorts of ways. We chose the Louis presentation, which turned out to be about a dozen big, pearly hunks of white meat arrayed atop a pile of lettuce with all the proper garnishes, plus garlic toast made from fresh-baked bread, and a ramekin of excellent house-made thousand island dressing.

People at a nearby table were all eating fish and chips. The menu lists cod, salmon, halibut, and even albacore available as the fish part of the equation. We asked our dining-room neighbors how they liked it. Between bites, they were able to exclaim that this is the best fish and chips they have eaten anywhere, any time.

And how about warm marionberry cobbler topped with Tillamook ice cream for dessert?

OCEAN BLEU @ GINO'S

oceanbleuseafoods.com

808 SW Bay Blvd.   541-265-2424
Newport, OR   **L D | $$**

Newport's harbor is filled with fishing boats. Bay Street, along the waterfront, abounds with good restaurants that serve what they catch. One such place is Ocean Bleu @ Gino's.

The lunch and dinner menu is a bonanza of coastal specialties. Fish-and-chips is available with everything from rockfish and wild salmon to popcorn shrimp and local tuna. Onion rings are made from sweet Walla Wallas. Tiny Yaquina oysters are harvested just upriver; black cod, salmon, and sable are smoked in-house; Dungeness crabs are kept live in a seawater tank. Newport being the Dungeness Crab Capital of the World, it behooves visitors to tuck into Ocean Bleu's "sea pups," which are cornmeal fritters like Yankee clam cakes but laced with cracked crab and jack cheese. (*Sea Pup*, by the way, is the restaurant's own fishing vessel.)

As for the name of the place, it began as a fish market called Gino's. It remains a market as well as a restaurant, the house motto: "Live Free, Love Often, Eat Wild."

OTIS CAFE

otiscafe.com

1259 Salmon River Hwy.   541-994-2813
Otis, OR   **B L D** | $

The Otis is an undersized roadside diner serving over-sized meals. Located next to the post office, featuring a picnic-table patio as well as counter-and-table seats inside, the modest eat place has received national acclaim for great pies, and lumberjacks' (or more accurately in this case, fishermen's) breakfasts. Sourdough pancakes have a tang beautifully haloed by lots of melting butter and a spill of syrup. Eggs come with hash browns, the potatoes blanketed with melted cheese and green onions (known as German potatoes), and excellent homemade black molasses bread or a jumbo cinnamon roll.

One great lunch is the BLT made with full-flavored slices of beefsteak tomato, plus a bonus layer of cheese. We also recommend the one-third-pound cheeseburger, a goopy affair on a hefty bun with Otis's homemade mustard. On the side come dreamy griddle-fried potatoes or potato chips. (Otis Cafe does not have a deep-fryer; hence, no French fries.)

Pies are gorgeous, especially the West Coast rarity, marionberry. A more intense, supremely aromatic blackberry, the marionberry was made to be put in a pie. The crust here is crisp and aristocratic, making it all the more excellent a dessert.

OTTO'S SAUSAGE KITCHEN

ottossausage.com

4138 SE Woodstock Blvd.   503-771-6714
Portland, OR   **L** | $

While it is a full-scale meat market and smokehouse with cold cuts and sausages of all kinds to take home and cook, Otto's is also a dandy place to eat lunch—either deli sandwiches (the Reuben is grand) or hot dogs. Whether you choose an ordinary beef-and-pork frankfurter (with snap to its skin that is far from ordinary) or an extra-large sausage made from chicken or pork, you might just find yourself amazed by just how much better these fresh, homemade tube steaks taste than factory-made ones. The progeny of Otto Eichentopf, who opened this neighborhood meat market in 1927, maintain the highest standards of Old World sausage making. The beauty of the links they make for lunch is that you really taste the meat of which they are made. Spices are used to accent rather than overwhelm the primary ingredient. Served with a choice of onions, kraut, relish, mustard, or ketchup for you to apply yourself, Otto's sausages can be enjoyed with a beverage chosen from a cooler full of local soft drinks and interesting beers.

Dining facilities are nothing more than a bunch of wooden tables arranged on the sidewalk outside, as well as a handful of places to sit indoors. It's a neighborhood picnic every lunch hour.

PACIFIC WAY

pacificwaybakery-cafe.com

601 Pacific Way   503-738-0245
Gearhart, OR   **B L D** (Thurs–Mon) | $$

— ★ —
LOCALS
LOVE IT
— ★ —

Pacific Way actually is two places: a friendly little bakery where locals hang out every morning sipping espresso drinks and eating muffins, croissants, and casual breakfasts, and a restaurant for sit-down, multicourse meals next door. The restaurant starts things off with a terrific bread basket—slices of Cheddar-basil onion, oatmeal molasses, and French bread—and we liked the restaurant's pear and gorgonzola salad. As for Dungeness crab pizza, the crab gets outshouted by sun-dried tomatoes and sweet, creamy cheese.

It's the coffee shop that won our hearts—a cozy spot with a couple of chairs and a few counter stools, plus outdoor tables under and around which customers' dogs goof off and hunt crumbs. Conversations fly through the air at this perpetual town party, and when we stood at the counter trying to decide which pastry to get with our coffee, a flash of group consciousness arose among the indoor diners, who determined it must be the multi-fruit Danish—a bouquet of Oregon berries on a pallet of flaky crust. On a coast rich with first-rate pastries, this one really stood out. Gearhart, incidentally, is the town where culinary Zeus James Beard was raised.

★ SOUTH BEACH FISH MARKET

southbeachfishmarket.com

3640 South Coast Hwy.   541-867-6800
South Beach, OR   L | $$

South Beach is a picnic-style café and fish market attached to a convenience store where you can buy a souvenir T-shirt that tells the world, THE 2ND AMENDMENT IS MY GUN PERMIT. The store sells some scary food: movie-theater hot dogs kept warm on rolling dowels for who-knows-how-long, sports-stadium nacho trays, and Crock-pot chili, plus an immense inventory of energy drinks and beer. Honky-tonk it may be, but the restaurant on premises serves magnificent seafood. Dungeness crabs are cooked in cauldrons by the highway out front; chunks of their cooled meat are piled into a cup with no adornment other than a wedge of lemon (and, if you wish, horseradish hot sauce) to become an impeccable Pacific cocktail. Salmon, tuna, sturgeon, mussels, oysters, and sable are marinated and smoked using hickory and alder wood. Wild Chinook king salmon is made into "candy" by glazing nuggets of smoked pink meat with pepper and brown sugar. Each firm, moist piece packs a provocative sweet and savory punch.

South Beach fried seafood, veiled in tempura batter laced with garlic, has few equals anywhere. Jumbo wild prawns offer two levels of crunch: first, the crackle of the crust that surrounds them, then the dense snap of the meat itself. Salmon, tuna, oysters, and calamari all are available as fish and chips, as is snow-white halibut. While the French fries are fine, we highly recommend paying a few dollars more for onion rings too. Along with perfect O-ring circles, each basket also contains frail squiggles of batter that are merely onion-flavored and several hoops of onion with hardly any batter: It's all good. Dishware at South Beach is paper and plastic, and you may have to dispose of not only your own trash but also of that left behind by the last people who used the picnic table you claim for yourself.

WANDA'S CAFE

wandascafe.com

12870 H St.   503-368-8100
Nehalem, OR   **B L** (closed Wed & Thurs)
                         | $$

Decorative diversity rules at Wanda's. A few details: souvenir plates all over the walls, vintage radios and toasters on display in every nook and cranny, old vinyl record album covers tacked up among the plates, a few hundred different salt-and-pepper sets on shelves throughout the main dining area, one corner of which is occupied by a dinette set with steel-banded double-leaf table and matching canary-yellow chairs as well as a mid-twentieth-century television set.

If all that doesn't wake you up, have a cup of Oregon-excellent Sleepy Monk espresso. Irish coffee or a Bloody Mary will open your eyes, as will a Laughing Wanda, which is vodka with orange juice and peach nectar.

Cookies, scones, coffee cakes, brownies, and biscotti all are alluring, but we went for the hot-breakfast menu and a plate of huevos rancheros: beans, eggs, cheese, and chopped onions crowned with spectacularly fresh salsa. Oregon being biscuit country, we also ordered biscuits and gravy. The biscuits are huge, dense, and delicious; the gravy is rib-sticking thick, loaded with hunks of spicy sausage.

We arrived at Wanda's on a weekday, just after opening at 8 a.m., and were seated right away, but there can be a long wait for a table, especially on weekends. Lunch also is served (Wanda's closes at 2 p.m.), the menu featuring sandwiches made on multigrain, sourdough, rye, or polenta bread.

WASHINGTON

13 COINS

13coins.com

125 Boren Ave.   206-682-2513
Seattle, WA   Always open | $$

--★--
OPEN
24/7
--★--

At 13 Coins, you can spend $15 for breakfast or $150 for dinner and fine wine, and you can do either 24 hours a day, 7 days a week, 365 days a year. Opened over forty years ago, this favorite haunt of journalists from the nearby *Seattle Times* is not for trend seekers or effete gourmets. But if you appreciate a square meal composed of quality ingredients cooked and served by pros, there's no finer place north of Hollywood's Musso & Frank (p. 427).

Décor is a jaw-dropping anomaly of Tudor weight with mid-twentieth-century frivolity. Booths have upholstered backs that soar toward the ceiling; counter seats are not stools but rather huge padded thrones that swivel to make for easy conversation with a neighbor and provide full-access vision of the short-order chefs at work in the open kitchen. It is a pleasure to watch the cuisiniers shuffle sauté pans on the stove, poach eggs, grill meats, and griddle-cook potatoes.

The menu is gigantic, ranging from a grilled cheese sandwich to surf 'n' turf, including likeable versions of the West Coast specialties Joe Special (ground sirloin, spinach, and eggs topped with shredded Parmesan cheese) and Hangtown Fry (oysters, bacon, and eggs, here cooked frittata-style).

The one must-eat dish, whatever else you get, is hash brown potatoes. They are cooked on the griddle with plenty of clarified butter in cakes thick enough for the outside shreds to turn hard and chewy while the inside softens but doesn't become mush. Other allures from the multipage menu include French onion soup, a Joe special made with sausage, Dungeness crab Louie, chop-chop salad, and smoked Cheddar and prosciutto macaroni.

14 CARROT CAFE

2305 Eastlake Ave. E.   206-324-1442
Seattle, WA   B L | $

Casual and comfortably disheveled, nutritionally enlightened, and perfumed inside and out by coffee, here is an echt-Seattle dining experience. Although lunch includes excellent salads and soups as well as vegetarian plates and no-beef hamburgers, most fans of the 14 Carrot Cafe consider it a breakfast place. Omelets are big and beautiful, served with good hash browns and a choice of toast, English muffin, or streusel-topped coffee cake. The coffee cake itself is something to behold: a moist crumble-topped block, served with a sphere of butter as big as a Ping-Pong ball. Other notable breadstuffs include blueberry muffins and cinnamon rolls. The latter, described as "large and gooey" by our waiter, is a vast doughy spiral with clods of raisins and veins of dark sugar gunk packed into its warm furrows.

One of the best-known specialties of the house is Tahini toast, gilded with a thin layer of sesame butter. Hotcakes come sourdough or regular, with sliced bananas, apple slivers, or blueberries, with bacon on the side or cooked into the 'cakes. If you are in a cereal mood, you can get homemade granola or hot oats with soy milk, dates, and cashews.

BAKEMAN'S
bakemanscatering.com

122 Cherry St.   206-622-3375
Seattle, WA   **L** (Mon–Fri) | $

A working-class cafeteria with a menu that is pretty much limited to soup, sandwiches, and salads, Bakeman's is open only for lunch, 10 to 3, Monday through Friday. Its claim to fame is the turkey sandwich on white or whole wheat. The bread is homemade, stacked up at one end of the cafeteria line. It is not artisan bread, just good sandwich bread: tender slices that come to life when spread with mayo, mustard, cranberry, and/or shredded lettuce, then heaped with turkey or—almost as wonderful—slabs of meat loaf.

The meat loaf is tightly packed but tender, gently spiced, and with a delicious aroma. As for turkey, get it any way you like, because this is superb, *real*, carved-from-the-bird turkey with homey flavor. The dark meat is lush; the white meat is moist and aromatic; either variety has an occasional piece of skin still attached, a nice reminder of just how real it is. The way we like it is, in the words of the countermen who hustle things along, "white on white; M & M," which means white-meat turkey on white bread with mustard and mayonnaise. Turkey sandwiches get no better than this!

Bakeman's offers three or four good soups each day, such as turkey noodle or beef vegetable, plus a nice chili, or, on one memorable occasion, Chinese eggflower—an egg-drop variation. There are other sandwiches—tuna, egg salad, baked ham, et cetera—and a few salads, but they aren't all that interesting. Dessert can be wonderful—carrot cake, cookies, or cake of the day, such as lemon poppy seed cake, sliced like bread.

BETH'S CAFE
bethscafe.com

7311 Aurora Ave. N.   206-782-5588
Seattle, WA   Always open | $

--★--
OPEN
24/7
--★--
Are you hungry? Really hungry? If so, eat at Beth's. Order the twelve-egg omelet. Yes, that's an even dozen, served not on a puny plate but on a pizza pan. If you're only half-hungry, Beth's offers six-egg omelets. Each comes piled onto a heap of hash brown potatoes and, if desired, bacon strips that have been cooked under a weight so they arrive flat and fragile. Biscuits-and-gravy is another of Beth's monumental meals, but if you arrive with only a tiny appetite, the menu offers mini breakfasts that are merely a single egg with hash browns and your choice of bacon or sausage.

The flagship meal at lunch is a half-pound Mondo Burger with cheese, bacon, lettuce, and tomato, fries on the side. There's a big Reuben sandwich as well as normal-sized burgers, BLTs, and French dips.

Beth's is open 'round the clock and is not a place to please the fastidious epicure. It is what some have called an "alternative greasy spoon," attracting wee-hours diners from the fringes of city life. And in Seattle, those fringes are pretty far out!

BISCUIT BITCH
biscuitbitch.com

2303 3rd Ave.   206-728-2219
Seattle, WA   **B L** | $

The biscuits are very good—blocky and crusty-topped—but gravy is the star at Biscuit Bitch, the sarcastic motto of which is "Trailer Park to Table." Vividly peppery and crowded with crumbled sausage, this gravy belies the restaurant's ironic redneck pose. It is in fact a poised kitchen tour de force, perhaps best savored in the Straight-Up Bitch, which is simply a gravy-topped split biscuit. Fancier presentations include a Hot Mess Bitch, which includes eggs, garlic grits, cheese, a hot link, and jalapeño peppers; a Smokin' Hot "Seattle" Bitch, for which the biscuit is topped with a hot link, cream cheese, and grilled onion; and a Cheesy Pork n' Bitch featuring bacon and melted Cheddar cheese.

Gravy options include vegetarian and gluten-free shiitake mushroom, but if gravy is too substantial for your breakfast appetite, consider the Bitchwitch, this kitchen's version of a breakfast sandwich: egg, cheese, a choice of sausage, Spam, or bacon, plus a measure of house-made Bitchy Sauce. The sauce, a sort of tomato-pink aioli with eye-opening kick, is a great complement for biscuits that are dense and dry enough to demand some kind of lubricant.

Biscuit Bitch closes midafternoon, and the only meal served is breakfast. Those in need of something sweet can order a Nutty Bitch made with Nutella, banana, and whipped cream, a Buttered Up Bitch (butter and jam or maple peanut butter), or, on occasion, a strawberry shortcake biscuit with whipped cream. Coffee is known as Bitch Blend, roasted by Seattle's Seven Roasters, and it is kick-ass good.

CRUMPET SHOP

thecrumpetshop.com

1503 1st Ave.   206-682-1598
Seattle, WA   **B L** (closed Tues) | **$**

At the entrance to the Pike Place Market, the Crumpet Shop is a small café that serves crumpets for breakfast, brunch, and lunch. A crumpet is thick like an English muffin but poured out and cooked on a griddle, coming off chewy and rich-flavored with a craggy-textured surface that begs to be spread with butter and fruit-clotted marmalade. You can have one simply buttered, with butter and maple syrup, or with your choice from among nearly two dozen different sorts of sweet and savory toppings, including honey, Nutella, local jams, ham, cheese, and smoked salmon. On the side, have espresso, cappuccino, or, better yet, imported tea. If crumpets are not your cup of tea, the Crumpet Shop also bakes terrific loaves of bread, including a rugged groat bread that is an apt foundation for a hefty sandwich.

FRANK'S DINER

franksdiner.co

1516 W. 2nd Ave.   509-747-8798
Spokane, WA   **B L D** | **$**

Located in Seattle from 1931 to 1991, then trucked to its current location in Spokane, Frank's really did start life as a railroad car. For the last several decades it has served as a hash house with a traditional counter providing a view of the short-order cook at work.

The breakfast menu includes waffles, blueberry muffins, French toast, Benedicts, corned beef hash, and what the menu assures are "authentic fried green tomatoes" topped with hollandaise sauce. Omelets are especially handsome. Our fave is the Italianate meal known as a New Joe Special, which is three eggs scrambled with seasoned beef, sausage, spinach, and onion, flavored with Parmesan cheese.

We were clued in to Frank's Diner by a Washington State tipster named Charlie, who told us that breakfast is the best meal to eat at Frank's; but lunch has never let us down. It includes a terrific hot turkey sandwich, made from turkey roasted in Frank's kitchen, as well as a grilled meat loaf sandwich on Texas toast, turkey potpie, and giant-sized burgers made with assorted combinations of cheese, bacon, and even pineapple.

A second Frank's Diner is located at 10929 North Newport Highway in Pinewater Plaza, North Spokane (509-465-2464).

★ FRESHY'S SEAFOOD MARKET

freshysseafoodmarket.com

2411 76th Ave. SE   206-232-3028
Mercer Island, WA   **L** | **$$**

In the middle of Lake Washington on the outskirts of Seattle, Mercer Island is a paradisiacal community with a heavenly seafood restaurant. That's heavenly on the Roadfood scale, meaning it is inexpensive, local, and situated in a former gas station. Inside what used to be the gas station's office is a seafood market selling oysters, Dungeness crab, salmon, tuna, halibut, and swordfish as well as crab cakes ready to cook and a variety of smoked fish. Proprietor Bryce Caldwell has been a fisherman all his life, and he knows exactly how and where to get the best of the best.

Dungeness crab, for instance, gets no more delicious than what you will eat here. A crab cocktail is a boatload of big, pearly white hunks of sweet meat that is perfectly tender and resilient, redolent of clear ocean waters. Of course, cocktail sauce and tartar sauce are available, as are aioli and Freshy's smoky tartar sauce, but this crab needs absolutely nothing to improve it. Eating it pure and plain is a primary pleasure that cannot be enhanced.

Fish and chips are available made with true cod, salmon, prawns, clams, calamari, scallops, oysters, or halibut. That last, the halibut, is heavy and moist, all its milky juices shored in by a shatteringly crisp crust. Fish tacos come festooned with shredded cabbage and pico de gallo and/or pineapple salsa and can be made using cod, grilled blackened salmon, ahi tuna, prawns, or rockfish. Onion rings are a necessary side dish. They are a little scary at first: big and dark. They look heavy. In fact, they are featherlight, crunching into nothing but luxurious flavor.

Eating at Freshy's couldn't be more casual. Place your order and pay at a walk-up window and dine from cardboard boats and plastic baskets while seated at a picnic table.

FRISKO FREEZE

| 1201 Division Ave. | 253-272-6843 |
| Tacoma, WA | L D \| $ |

We thank Roadfood correspondent Allie Spangler for clueing us in to this good old drive-in with its mid-twentieth-century vibes and well-dressed burgers. Even those who don't usually get cheese on their patty should do so here, Allie suggested, because it melts with the boatload of other condiments to make this burger into a fine jumble. Those other toppings include pickles, onions, ketchup, lettuce, and a slightly sweet mayonnaise sauce, all of which add luster to a hamburger that would otherwise be only OK. On the side you want French fries, which, like the burger, are served in wax paper bags that in fact do very little to keep cooking oil off hands, fingers, and car upholstery.

Do plan to dine in the car, as there is no indoor seating and only a few precious benches next to the order window. While the cuisine may not be memorable, a visit to this blast from the past definitely is. In fact, Allie noted that the meals are so extremely aromatic that their scent will linger in the car's interior for the rest of the day, even with the windows down.

GLO'S

gloscafe.com

| 1621 E. Olive Way | 206-324-2577 |
| Seattle, WA | B L (plus extended late-night weekend hours) \| $$ |

———★———
VEGETARIAN-
FRIENDLY
———★———

We are told that Seattle's Capitol Hill neighborhood is trendy, which would be one reason Glo's is almost always crowded. The other, better reason is that it serves a terrific breakfast. Not trendy breakfast, mind you, but good old square-meal breakfast. Glo's calls itself "an original coffee shop," the word "original" a bit baffling. Etymology aside, the cuisine really is classic coffee shop, but with a twenty-first-century Seattle twist.

Modernity is most evident in the profusion of vegetarian options. These include hearty biscuits served with meatless mushroom gravy, a grilled vegetable frittata, and an Aaron's Special of sautéed vegetables atop hash browns. It is available cheeseless, for vegans, or draped with Cheddar or jack cheese for animal-product-eating vegetarians. You certainly don't have to be a vegetarian to appreciate Glo's gorgeous fruit-topped Belgian waffle, presented under a mountain of summer-fresh blueberries, strawberries, blackberries, raspberries, and slices of banana plus garnish of pink grapefruit. If you need meat to go with the waffle, there's a crusty-edge patty of pulverized corned beef hash (also available as a main course) or, of course, bacon or sausage. By the way, the sweetness of the fruit atop the waffle may dissuade you from pouring on the syrup that comes with it. That would be a mistake. It's real maple.

Of course, omelets and scrambles abound, but Glo's makes a specialty of eggs Benedict. Variants include Benedict with smoked salmon, with spinach and bacon (Eggs Blackstone), and the sunny Eggs Californian, which is made with abundant avocado and slices of grilled tomato. Topped with the kitchen's superb hollandaise—smooth and buttery with a vivid citrus twist—the California version is simply brilliant. Although this kitchen isn't the least bit fussy or faux artistic, every plate of food it produces is wonderful simply to look at: bright, festive, and appetite provoking.

Meals are served at a brisk diner pace, but everything is made to order and there always seem to be customers out on the sidewalk hoping for a table inside to open up soon. Waiting is part of the Glo's experience.

HI SPOT CAFÉ

hispotcafe.com

1410 34th Ave.   206-325-7905
Seattle, WA   B L | $$

Upon entering this popular neighborhood café, glance right. Here you see the pastries, which are a primary Hi Spot attraction: huge flavor-packed scones, huger buttermilk biscuits, and ridiculously huge cinnamon rolls that are crammed with sugar and slivered nuts. Attractive as the jumbo breadstuffs may be, it's the omelets that won our hearts, especially El Pacifico, which is full of smoked salmon, dill cream, capers, and scallions and topped with more dill cream. The Round-Up is another winner, built of chicken sausage, goat cheese, tomatoes, and basil. Both come with home fries and toast. Egg dishes are served until closing at 2:30 p.m. The lunch menu, which becomes available at 11:30 a.m., includes soups and salads and sandwiches on superb Macrina Bakery rolls.

Among the attractive drink options are freshly squeezed limeade, mimosas, and Fonte coffee. Fonte is a local microroaster; the espresso we had was chocolaty, dark, and smooth.

KNAPP'S RESTAURANT

2707 N. Proctor St.   253-759-9009
Tacoma, WA   B L D | $

All kinds of people give us suggestions of places to eat; but when one of the nation's great restaurateurs tells us where to go, we pay special attention. It was Hap Townes, who for many years ran a grand lunchroom in Nashville, Tennessee, who tipped us off to Knapp's. "It's your kind of place," Hap said with assurance born of watching us eat many of his fine meals.

The setting of Knapp's in the Proctor district helps create an aura of small-town charm in the midst of big-city life. Walking into the old brick building is like going back in time. (Knapp's dates back to 1933.) The dining room is patrolled by teams of waitresses—pros who refill coffee and replace needed silverware with the grace of a four-star sommelier.

The menu is nostalgic too. This is a place to have a platter of liver and onions or turkey with sage-flavored dressing and a pile of mashed potatoes with a ladle of gravy on top. Every Tuesday, Knapp's serves corned beef and cabbage; every Wednesday, roast pork loin. Weekend dinner specials include roast pork and dressing, old-fashioned pot roast, and Sunday fried chicken. Begin your meal with homemade soup (clam chowder on Friday) and top it off with homemade peach pie. It is an all-American experience, not necessarily for the fussy epicure, but a treasure for aficionados of square meals.

MALTBY CAFE

maltbycafe.com

8809 Maltby Rd.   425-483-3123
Snohomish, WA   B L | $

If ever we write a book called *Really Big Food*, the Maltby Cafe would be featured for breakfast. Its cinnamon roll is less a roll than a loaf—a massive circular coil of sweet, walnut-enriched pastry smothered with drippy icing that comes on a dinner plate, which it fits edge-to-edge. It is a couple of breakfasts unto itself.

While other items on the menu are not so flabbergastingly immense, they are satisfying in the extreme. The Maltby omelet, for example, is another plate filler, loaded with ham, beef, peppers, and onions. The Maltby prime rib omelet includes plenty of beef, plus mushrooms, peppers, onions, tomatoes, olives, and two kinds of cheese: Cheddar and Swiss. The Whole Hog omelet features bacon, sausage, and ham, plus Tillamook Cheddar. Oatmeal is served with melted butter running all over the top of the bowl; the French toast is double-thick; and, lest we forget, the strawberry jam on every table is homemade and especially delicious when liberally spread on a big, oven-warm biscuit along with—are you ready?—crème fraîche.

Lunch is big too, especially the half-pound burgers. There are French dips, chicken-fried steak with mashed potatoes and biscuits with sausage gravy, and a prime rib stir-fry. Desserts include hot apple strudel, pie à la mode, and a Maltby sundae, which is a Maltby Bar (oatmeal, chocolate chips, walnuts) with ice cream, chocolate sauce, and whipped cream.

Maltby is a nostalgic little town with an allegedly haunted cemetery. Its cafe is located in a former school gym and cafeteria built in 1937.

MIKE'S CHILI PARLOR

1447 NW Ballard Way   206-782-2808
Seattle, WA   **L D | $**

Outfitted with a billiards table, video games, an ATM station, and pull-tab lotto, decorated with beer signs and festooned with announcements warning that only cash is accepted and touting such specials as a Big Ass Bowl of Chili, Mike's is an in-your-face chili parlor. Seats are available at a couple of communal tables in the center of the room, at the counter, and in a few booths. Customers are a tough bunch, and the staff can seem tougher. In fact, among the "extras" listed on the menu, such as jalapeño peppers (25¢) and onions (25¢), is "abuse" (free). You must be twenty-one to enter.

The chili is a he-man brew of coarse-ground beef with bright Greek seasonings, saturated with enough grease that when it is served by the bowl, your spoon will slide through a glistening layer on top before it hits meat. (Oyster crackers are provided, and they are the connoisseur's way to soak up the oil.) Beans are optional, as are grated cheese and chopped onions.

You can have this stout stuff in a cup or bowl, as the dressing for burgers, hot dogs, and steak, and in concert with spaghetti noodles. You also can buy it by the gallon (at about $50), but for that you must bring your own container.

MONORAIL ESPRESSO

510 Pike St.   206-422-0736
Seattle, WA   **B | $**

Coffee is not the only reason we love Seattle, but its abundance and goodness sure add to the appeal. A person could travel around the Emerald City and drink five different cups a day for a month and still not feel that all the good brews have been sampled. Still, it is hard to imagine finding a cup as perfectly satisfying as the double-shot espresso at Monorail Espresso. Velvet smooth, ink-dark, and as bracing as a bitch slap, this little cup of joe is surely a benchmark of perfection. Lattes are peerless, made in such flavors as toasted coconut, caramel mocha, lavender, and burnt crème. To eat with one's coffee, there are locally baked scones, coffee cake, banana bread, and chubbies (little cookies good for dunking).

Monorail Espresso is descended from Seattle's first espresso stand, opened just down the block in 1980. It is a walk-up window with no indoor seating, but a few sidewalk bench seats are available nearby.

MOORE COFFEE

moorecoffeeshop.com
1930 2nd Ave.   206-883-7044
Seattle, WA   **B L | $**

The #1 reason to come to Moore Coffee is the latte. Even if you don't particularly like lattes, come. Look. It is stunning. Latte art, in which practitioners carefully apply steamed milk onto the surface of a cup of espresso, creating designs or pictures, is a big deal in Seattle and beyond. Nowhere is it as polished a craft as it is in this little café at the old Moore Building in Belltown. In a minute or so, the baristas transform an ordinary-looking drink into a work of art: a feline or canine face, a heart, a tulip, a bunny, a butterfly. Similar designs, but on a green surface rather than brown, are available on matcha tea.

Even we non–latte lovers must say that these are some delicious drinks: rich, creamy, and intensely dark. Beyond familiar lattes, Moore coffee makes a wide variety of more exotic caffeinated beverages, including a *horchata* latte (using sweetened rice milk), Mexican mocha (with chocolate and spice), cafe Madrid (an especially sweet latte), and Nutella mocha.

The food menu includes breakfast pastries, sandwiches on sourdough or French bread, and tamales. In the tiny dining area next to the room where the coffee is made, waffle irons are heated up each morning about eight, yielding waffles that are thin and crisp— a joy in and of themselves but especially wonderful in the apple-cinnamon incarnation we sampled. For this, a quartered waffle is topped with thin slices of crisp raw apple and a dusting of cinnamon; and in the middle of the plate comes a heap of apples that have been cooked until soft and caramel-sweet. The waffle menu includes sweet ones topped with the likes of Nutella, Brie and berries, or PB&J; and savory ones, such as the Monte Cristo (ham, Swiss, raspberry jam), the Caprese (mozzarella, tomato, basil), and one with bacon shreds and mascarpone.

Moore is a tiny place, often maddeningly crowded, and because each latte is made with care, it will take a while for the inevitable line to move along. There are a handful of seats indoors and some out on the sidewalk.

PASEO CARIBBEAN RESTAURANT
paseoseattle.com

4225 Fremont Ave. N.   206-545-7440
Seattle, WA   **L D** (closed Mon) | **$**

Behold the Caribbean Roast. Such an awe-inspiring sandwich: a great mound of marinated pork, roasted soft and dripping-moist, is dressed with aioli, cilantro, hot jalapeño chips, lettuce, and caramelized onions, and piled into a toasted baguette from Macrina Bakery. It is the most popular sandwich at Paseo, a brash and beloved eatery in the Fremont neighborhood of Seattle.

Those onions in the Caribbean Roast really are extraordinary, so sweet on the tongue. They are special enough that another popular sandwich here is a meatless wonder known as Onion Obsession: a great oily tangle of them along with garlic tapenade, cilantro, and jalapeño peppers. Other compelling sandwiches on the Paseo menu include sautéed prawns, chicken thighs or breast, and even tofu made into something wonderful with plenty of the garlic tapenade. Top-of-the-line among sandwiches is the Paseo Press, close cousin of the classic Cuban: roast pork, smoked ham, and Swiss cheese augmented by sweet banana peppers and caramelized onions, all close-encounter-melded in the sandwich press known as a *plancha*.

Sandwiches star at Paseo, but the menu also includes platters of roast pork, scallops, prawns, chicken thighs, and fish in red sauce as well as vegetarian rice bowls topped with black beans.

Dine in the rough. Paseo is a small shack with such limited seating that many customers eat outside on the sidewalk or in their cars, or take their inevitably messy sandwiches elsewhere.

PICK-QUICK DRIVE IN

pick-quick.com

4306 Pacific Hwy. E.   253-922-5599
Fife, WA   **L** (closed Dec 1–Feb 1) | $

Here's a roadside blast from the past (1949, to be precise), especially alluring when you can sit outside and enjoy a nice double bacon cheeseburger deluxe, chili fries, and chocolate malt . . . all of that for well under $15.

The hamburgers are medium-thin, crisp-edged, modest-sized, and of uniform shape with a moist savor from the well-aged grill that imprints itself into the toasted bun. Grilled onions are a popular topping. For 20¢ extra, the deluxe version includes lettuce, tomato, onion, pickle, and Pick-Quick sauce. French fries, made from spuds cut right here, are very good, and the milk shakes can be extraordinary, as they are made from fresh fruit in season—strawberries, blueberries, blackberries, cherries, raspberries.

Pick-Quick is a minuscule establishment that originally served as the canteen for a now-defunct drive-in movie theater. There is plenty of dining room in the great outdoors with picnic tables of all shapes and sizes.

There is a second Pick-Quick at 1132 Auburn Way North, Auburn (253-248-1949), which is open year-round.

POODLE DOG RESTAURANT

poodledogrestaurant.com

1522 54th Ave. E.   253-922-6161
Fife, WA   **B L D** | $

The Poodle Dog has been serving three meals a day to passersby and Tacoma locals since 1933. The one recommended to us by Roadfood correspondent Allie Spangler is breakfast, in particular the butterhorn, a sweet crescent roll that is formally listed on the menu as Miss Jane's Oven-Baked Butterhorn. Made fresh to order, it is as wide as a dinner plate with a fine glaze of sweet frosting and a scattering of slivered almonds on top. It is served warm with a ramekin of butter, but it is so buttery that the extra butter is almost superfluous. Poodle Dog's full morning meals include eggs Benedict, French toast made from butterhorns, a Landmark Breakfast of three eggs, three breakfast meats, hash browns, immense skillet-full of chicken-fried steak atop hash browns topped with gravy, scrambled eggs, and Cheddar cheese.

Lunch and supper meals are mostly meat and potatoes, including weekend specials like old-fashioned pot roast, turkey and dressing, and Sunday fried chicken. For dessert: strawberry rhubarb cobbler, served warm and à la mode.

RED MILL

redmillburgers.com

1613 W. Dravus St.   206-284-6363
Seattle, WA   **L** (closed Mon) | $

There was a diner called the Red Mill in Seattle for thirty years starting in 1937. Twenty-seven years after it closed, a new Red Mill opened in Phinney Ridge, and a hamburger legend was born. No doubt, Seattle is a significant burger city, and many of its connoisseurs believe Red Mill's rate near the top. Flame-broiled to a smoky savor, they come in many configurations, including patties topped with blue cheese, barbecue sauce, and/or peppery bacon. You can get a double—that's a half pound of meat—and you even can get a meatless garden burger. We are fond of the verde burger with roasted green chiles, jack cheese, red onion, lettuce, tomato, and the Red Mill's proprietary sauce. Condiments and dressing are applied in abundance, so while the meat patty itself is good, the extras put it over the top.

On the side, onion rings are essential. They are big crunchy rounds with thick ribbons of sweet, caramelized onion inside. And there is a whole menu of milk shakes and malts, plus fresh-squeezed lemonade.

As if burgers, O-rings, and shakes weren't enough to love this place, we should also add that it has a strict *no cell phone* policy, allowing all of us to dine well and in peace. If you do need to take or make a call, there's a Starbucks right next door.

Seattle's first Red Mill is in Phinney Ridge at 312 North 67th Street (206-783-6362).

★ SPUD FISH AND CHIPS

spudfishandchips.com

9702 NE Juanita Dr.   425-823-0607

Kirkland, WA   **L D | $**

When he found out we were in the Seattle area, Roadfood.com contributor Wanderingjew sent us an urgent note advising we head to Kirkland for fish and chips. We now pass along this advice to anyone eager for cod, halibut, shrimp, scallops, or oysters hand breaded and fried in fresh oil until crisp, served alongside first-rate French fries. Spud Fish and Chips, a local destination since 1935, has a limited menu, with salad and chowder just about the only non-fried items, but you can be sure these folks know how to fry. The crust on each piece of fish is thin and crunchy; the cod is cream-moist; the halibut falls into elegant flakes; the shrimp snaps. Onion rings also are excellent: individual circles with severely crunchy exteriors holding ribbons of onion that have caramelized to tender sweetness. You will pay extra for tartar sauce (25¢), but it's worth the splurge; this homemade stuff is studded with al dente bits of pickle. While the iced tea and lemonade are fine, we also recommend the milk shakes, which are too thick for a straw.

Service is do-it-yourself. Place your order at the counter, pay, then wait until the order is put on a tray and ready for you to carry it to a booth inside or to the exterior counter and picnic tables. Signs atop each napkin dispenser ask customers to please bus their own tables when they've finished.

TAT'S DELICATESSEN

tatsdeli.com

159 Yesler Way   206-264-8287

Seattle, WA   **B L** (closed Sun) **| $**

By strict Roadfood rules, Tat's does not belong in this guidebook, the goal of which is to direct readers to local eats. Tat's is a Seattle restaurant that aims to deliver what it calls "East Coast steaks and subs." The steaks are Philadelphia-style cheesesteaks; the subs include Delaware Valley hoagies, a "New Yorker" of corned beef, pastrami, and Swiss cheese, and a traditional Italian-American chicken parm.

The sandwiches are good enough that we break the rules to include Tat's as a Roadfood choice. (That's a perk of having written the rules.) Foremost among the worthy sandwiches is the Tat'strami, which is pastrami, melted Swiss cheese, coleslaw, and Russian dressing. The pastrami itself is extraordinary: tender and moist, vividly spiced, and deliriously smoky. The sandwich is an impossible mess—and irresistible. A more familiar corned-beef Reuben also is available on rye bread. And there are subs of sausage, fried chicken, eggplant Parmesan, meatballs, and hot roast beef.

Cheesesteaks come with one's choice of cheese (provolone, Swiss, Cheddar, pepper jack, mozzarella, and, of course, Whiz) and options of marinara sauce or lettuce, tomato, and onion. The beef in these sandwiches is full-flavored and butter-tender, and the rolls are good and chewy . . . if not quite up to the lofty standards of the best steak shops of New Jersey and Pennsylvania. All sub sandwiches are available as eight- or twelve-inchers.

Tat's is a boisterous joint, crowded and cheerful. Order food by stepping up to the counter, after which you find a seat indoors or out on the sidewalk and then are called to fetch your sandwich.

TOP POT

toppotdoughnuts.com

2124 5th Ave.   206-728-1966
Seattle, WA $

Top Pot has grown into a Seattle-area empire, but conspicuous success has not diminished the excellence of its donuts. First and foremost, there's the crunch of the skin on the old-fashioneds—crisp enough to feel like your teeth are breaking something, after which they slide into the creamy cake interior just below the golden crust. Now, encase the top half with silky dark chocolate, maple frosting, or a glistening thick sugar glaze, and these modest-sized circular pastries become ecstasy.

The kitchen has a repertoire of forty different kinds, not all of which are always available. Some of our favorites are the cinnamon old-fashioned, the maple bar, and the apple fritter, which is chockfull of hunks of caramelized apple. However they are dressed, even with multicolored jimmies or coconut shavings, there is nothing froufrou or pretentious about these lovelies. They are good ol' donuts, the kind you want to have with morning coffee. By any meaningful standard—taste, texture, heft, even good looks—they are world-class, far superior to any of the national chains, as well as to their doppelgängers sold around the country.

RESTAURANTS
BY REGION
AND STATE

NEW ENGLAND

Connecticut

Abbott's Lobster in the Rough ▪ Noank, 21
Al's Hot Dog Stand ▪ Naugatuck, 21
Big Dipper ▪ Prospect, 22
Blackie's ▪ Cheshire, 22
Carminuccio's ▪ Newtown, 22
Clamp's Hamburger Stand ▪ New Milford, 23
Coffee An' ▪ Westport, 23
Colony Grill ▪ Stamford, 23
Denmo's ▪ Southbury, 23
Doogie's ▪ Newington, 24
Dottie's Diner ▪ Woodbury, 24
Dr. Mike's ▪ Bethel, 24
Five-O ▪ Fairfield, 25
Frank Pepe Pizzeria Napoletana ▪ New Haven, 25
Gluten Free Oasis ▪ Brookfield, 25
Harry's Drive-In ▪ Colchester, 26
Kamp Dog ▪ New London, 26
K. LaMay's ▪ Meriden, 27
Kitchen Little ▪ Mystic, 27
Lakeside Diner ▪ Stamford, 27
Laurel Diner ▪ Southbury, 27
Lenny & Joe's Fish Tale Restaurant ▪ Madison, 28
Lenny's ▪ Branford, 28
Letizia's ▪ Norwalk, 29
Lobster Landing ▪ Clinton, 29
Louis' Lunch ▪ New Haven, 29
The Lunchbox ▪ Meriden, 30
Mamie's ▪ Roxbury, 30
Modern Apizza ▪ New Haven, 30
O'Rourke's Diner ▪ Middletown, 31
Pizzeria Lauretano ▪ Bethel, 31
Rawley's Drive-In ▪ Fairfield, 31
Ridgefield Ice Cream Shop ▪ Ridgefield, 32
Roseland Apizza ▪ Derby, 32
Sally's Apizza ▪ New Haven, 32
Sea Swirl ▪ Mystic, 33
Shady Glen ▪ Manchester, 33
Speedy Donuts ▪ Norwalk, 33
Stanziato's ▪ Danbury, 34
Super Duper Weenie ▪ Fairfield, 34
Sycamore Drive-In ▪ Bethel, 34
Ted's ▪ Meriden, 35
Wethersfield Pizza House ▪ Wethersfield, 35
Zuppardi's Apizza ▪ West Haven, 36

Maine

Beal's Lobster Pier ▪ Southwest Harbor, 37
Becky's ▪ Portland, 37
Bet's Famous Fish Fry ▪ Boothbay, 38
Bob's Clam Hut ▪ Kittery, 38
Clam Shack ▪ Kennebunkport, 38
Cole Farms ▪ Gray, 38
Congdon's Doughnuts ▪ Wells, 39
Dolly's ▪ Frenchville, 39
Doris's Café ▪ Fort Kent Mills, 39
Five Islands Lobster Co. ▪ Georgetown, 40
Flo's ▪ Cape Neddick, 40
Harmon's Lunch ▪ Falmouth, 41
Harraseeket Lunch & Lobster ▪ South Freeport, 41
Helen's ▪ Machias, 41
Hodgman's Frozen Custard ▪ New Gloucester, 42
Jordan's Snack Bar ▪ Ellsworth, 42
Lobster Shack ▪ Cape Elizabeth, 42
Long Lake Sporting Club ▪ Sinclair, 43
Maine Diner ▪ Wells, 43
Moody's Diner ▪ Waldoboro, 43
Nunan's Lobster Hut ▪ Kennebunkport, 44
Pemaquid Lobster Co-Op ▪ Pemaquid, 44
Rock's Family Diner ▪ Fort Kent, 44
Sea Basket ▪ Wiscasset, 45
Shaw's Fish & Lobster Wharf ▪ New Harbor, 45
Shaw's Ridge Farm ▪ Sanford, 45
Waterman's Beach Lobster ▪ Thomaston, 46
Young's Lobster Pound ▪ Belfast, 46

Massachusetts

Baxter's Fish & Chips ▪ Hyannis, 47
Christina's Homemade Ice Cream ▪ Cambridge, 47
Clam Box ▪ Ipswich, 48
Donut Dip ▪ East Longmeadow, 48
Durgin-Park ▪ Boston, 48
Elisabeth's ▪ Fairhaven, 49
Essex Seafood ▪ Essex, 49
Graham's Hot Dogs ▪ Fall River, 49
Hartley's Original Pork Pies ▪ Fall River, 50
J.J.'s Coney Island ▪ Fall River, 50
Kelly's Roast Beef ▪ Revere, 50
The Liberal Club ▪ Fall River, 51
Marguerite's ▪ Westport, 51
Marzilli's Bakery ▪ Fall River, 51
Mee Sum Restaurant and Lounge ▪ Fall River, 52
Nick's ▪ Fall River, 52
Nick's Famous Roast Beef ▪ North Beverly, 53
Oxford Creamery ▪ Mattapoisett, 53
Red Skiff ▪ Rockport, 54
R.F. O'Sullivan & Son ▪ Somerville, 54

MID-SOUTH

Kentucky

Bell's Drug Store ▪ Sebree, 124
Hall's on the River ▪ Winchester, 124
Heaton's ▪ Princeton, 125
Homemade Ice Cream and Pie Kitchen ▪ Louisville, 125
Leigh's Barbecue ▪ Kevil, 125
Marion Pit ▪ Marion, 125
Mike Linnig's Place ▪ Louisville, 126
Moonlite Bar-B-Q Inn ▪ Owensboro, 126
Mr. D's ▪ Henderson, 126
Nord's ▪ Louisville, 127
Peak Bros. ▪ Waverly, 127
Thomason's Barbecue ▪ Henderson, 127

North Carolina

Allen & Son ▪ Chapel Hill, 128
Bar B Q King ▪ Charlotte, 128
Bill Spoon's ▪ Charlotte, 129
Bridges Barbecue Lodge ▪ Shelby, 129
Brownie-Lu ▪ Siler City, 129
Bum's ▪ Ayden, 130
Bunn's Bar-B-Q ▪ Windsor, 130
Cypress Grill ▪ Jamesville, 130
Dame's Chicken & Waffles ▪ Durham, 131
Flo's Kitchen ▪ Wilson, 131
Jay Bee's ▪ Statesville, 132
Keaton's ▪ Cleveland, 132
Lexington Barbecue #1 ▪ Lexington, 132
Long Creek Fish Fry ▪ Dallas, 133
Lupie's ▪ Charlotte, 133
Mama Dip's Country Kitchen ▪ Chapel Hill, 133
Nana's Soul Food ▪ Charlotte, 134
Parker's ▪ Wilson, 134
Price's Chicken Coop ▪ Charlotte, 134
R.O.'s Barbecue ▪ Gastonia, 135
Short Sugar's ▪ Reidsville, 135
Skylight Inn ▪ Ayden, 136
Snappy Lunch ▪ Mount Airy, 136
South 21 Drive-In ▪ Charlotte, 137
Stamey's ▪ Greensboro, 137
Sunrise Biscuit Kitchen ▪ Chapel Hill, 137
Wilber's Barbecue ▪ Goldsboro, 137
Zada Jane's Corner Cafe ▪ Charlotte, 138

Tennessee

400 Degrees ▪ Nashville, 139
A&R Bar-B-Que ▪ Memphis, 139
Alcenia's ▪ Memphis, 140
Arnold's Country Kitchen ▪ Nashville, 140
Beacon Light Tea Room ▪ Bon Aqua, 140
Bluegrass Grill ▪ Chattanooga, 141
Bolton's Spicy Chicken & Fish ▪ Nashville, 141
Bozo's Hot Pit BBQ ▪ Mason, 142
Bryant's Breakfast ▪ Memphis, 142
Coletta's ▪ Memphis, 142
Cozy Corner ▪ Memphis, 143
The Cupboard ▪ Memphis, 143
Dyer's Burgers ▪ Memphis, 144
Ed's Fish & Pizza House ▪ Nashville, 144
Elliston Place Soda Shop ▪ Nashville, 144
Germantown Commissary ▪ Germantown, 145
Gus's Fried Chicken ▪ Memphis, 145
Hot Stuff Spicy Chicken & Fish ▪ Antioch, 145
Interstate Barbecue ▪ Memphis, 146
Leonard's ▪ Memphis, 146
Little Tea Shop ▪ Memphis, 146
Litton's ▪ Knoxville, 147
Loveless Cafe ▪ Nashville, 147
Merridee's Breadbasket ▪ Franklin, 148
Nikki's Drive-In ▪ Chattanooga, 148
Pancake Pantry ▪ Nashville, 148
Payne's ▪ Memphis, 149
Pepperfire Spiced Chicken ▪ Nashville, 149
Prince's Hot Chicken Shack ▪ Nashville, 149
The Rendezvous ▪ Memphis, 149
Ridgewood Barbecue ▪ Bluff City, 150
Rotier's ▪ Nashville, 150
Swett's ▪ Nashville, 151
TJ's BBQ & Fish ▪ Nashville, 151
Zarzour's ▪ Chattanooga, 151

Virginia

Ace Biscuit and Barbecue ▪ Charlottesville, 152
The Apple House ▪ Linden, 152
Barbeque Exchange ▪ Gordonsville, 153
Brown's ▪ Charlottesville, 153
Brownsville Shell ▪ Crozet, 153
Charlie's Café ▪ Norfolk, 154
The Chicken Coop ▪ Lovingston, 154
Chutzpah ▪ Fairfax, 155
Dixie Bones BBQ ▪ Woodbridge, 155
Doumar's ▪ Norfolk, 155
Dr. Ho's Humble Pie ▪ North Garden, 156
Exmore Diner ▪ Exmore, 156
Franklin Restaurant ▪ Rocky Mount, 157

Georgia

Louisiana

Mississippi

Abe's Bar-B-Q ▫ Clarksdale, 222
Abe's Grill ▫ Corinth, 222
Big Bad Breakfast ▫ Oxford, 223
Blue & White Restaurant ▫ Tunica, 223
Crystal Grill ▫ Greenwood, 224
Dilworth's Tamales ▫ Corinth, 224
The Dinner Bell ▫ McComb, 224
Doe's Eat Place ▫ Greenville, 225
The Elite ▫ Jackson, 225
Fayard's ▫ Biloxi, 225
Giardina's ▫ Greenwood, 226
Hicks' ▫ Clarksdale, 226
Leatha's Bar-B-Que Inn ▫ Hattiesburg, 226
Lusco's ▫ Greenwood, 227
Peggy's ▫ Philadelphia, 227
Phillips Grocery ▫ Holly Springs, 228
Ramon's ▫ Clarksdale, 228
White Front Cafe ▫ Rosedale, 228
White Trolley Cafe ▫ Corinth, 229

South Carolina

82 Queen ▫ Charleston, 230
521 BBQ & Grill ▫ Fort Mill, 230
Beacon Drive-In ▫ Spartanburg, 231
Bertha's Kitchen ▫ North Charleston, 231
Betsy's On the Corner ▫ Aiken, 232
Big Boys Original Smokehouse ▫ Columbia, 232
Bowens Island ▫ Charleston, 233
Bush's ▫ Graniteville, 233
Cahill's Chicken Kitchen ▫ Bluffton, 234
Carolina Bar-B-Que ▫ New Ellenton, 234
Charlie's Fish Market ▫ Aiken, 235
City Billiards ▫ Aiken, 235
Dave's Carry-Out ▫ Charleston, 235
DeShawn's Seafood and Chicken ▫ North Augusta, 236
Dukes ▫ Aiken, 236
Evo ▫ North Charleston, 236
Fishnet Seafood ▫ Johns Island, 237
Freeman's Bar-B-Q ▫ Beech Island, 237
Grits & Groceries ▫ Belton, 238
Hilltop Café ▫ Salley, 238
Hite's Bar-B-Q ▫ West Columbia, 239
Hominy Grill ▫ Charleston, 239
Hot Dog Cafe ▫ South Lyman, 239
Hyman's Seafood ▫ Charleston, 240
Jackie Hite's Bar-B-Que ▫ Leesville, 240
Juniper ▫ Ridge Spring, 240
The Kingsman ▫ Cayce, 241
La Cantina ▫ Clarks Hill, 241
Martha Lou's Kitchen ▫ Charleston, 242

Middleton Place Restaurant ▫ Charleston, 242
Northgate Soda Shop ▫ Greenville, 243
Peaches 'N' Such ▫ Monetta, 243
Ray's Diner ▫ Columbia, 243
Rockaway Athletic Club ▫ Columbia, 244
Scott's Bar-B-Que ▫ Hemingway, 244
SeeWee Restaurant ▫ Awendaw, 244
Sgt. White's ▫ Beaufort, 245
Shealy's Bar-B-Que ▫ Leesville, 245
Southside Smokehouse ▫ Landrum, 245
Summerton Diner ▫ Summerton, 246
Track Kitchen ▫ Aiken, 246
Triangle Restaurant ▫ Johnston, 247
True BBQ ▫ West Columbia, 247
WildFlour Pastry ▫ Charleston, 247
The Wreck ▫ Mount Pleasant, 248

MIDWEST

Illinois

Al's #1 Italian Beef ▫ Chicago, 253
Byron's Hot Dog Haus ▫ Chicago, 253
Charlie Parker's ▫ Springfield, 254
Corned Beef Factory ▫ Chicago, 254
Cozy Dog ▫ Springfield, 254
D&J Café ▫ Springfield, 255
Doughnut Vault ▫ Chicago, 255
Freddy's Pizza ▫ Cicero, 255
Garrett Popcorn Shop ▫ Chicago, 256
Gene & Jude's ▫ River Grove, 256
Green Gables ▫ Hudson, 257
Harry Caray's ▫ Chicago, 257
Hoosier Mama Pie Company ▫ Chicago, 258
The Igloo ▫ Peru, 258
Joe Rogers Original Recipe Chili Parlor ▫ Springfield, 258
Johnnie's ▫ Elmwood Park, 259
Lagomarcino's ▫ Moline, 259
Lem's ▫ Chicago, 259
Manny's ▫ Chicago, 259
Merichka's ▫ Crest Hill, 260
Mr. Beef ▫ Chicago, 260
Paradise Pup ▫ Des Plaines, 261
Poochie's ▫ Skokie, 261
Rip's ▫ Ladd, 261
Shannon's Five Star ▫ Bloomington, 262
Smitty's Tap ▫ Leonore, 262
Superdawg ▫ Chicago, 262
Torri's Ice Cream Parlor ▫ Ladd, 263
Vienna Beef Café ▫ Chicago, 263
Wedron Office ▫ Ottawa, 263
The Wiener's Circle ▫ Chicago, 264

Indiana

Iowa

Michigan

Minnesota

Missouri

Amighetti's ▪ St. Louis, 295
Arthur Bryant's ▪ Kansas City, 295
Booches ▪ Columbia, 296
C&K Barbecue ▪ St. Louis, 296
Carl's Drive-In ▪ Brentwood, 296
Chris' Pancake & Dining ▪ St. Louis, 297
Crown Candy Kitchen ▪ St. Louis, 297
Donut Stop ▪ St. Louis, 297
Goody Goody Diner ▪ St. Louis, 297
Hodak's ▪ St. Louis, 298
Jess & Jim's ▪ Kansas City, 298
LC's Barbeque ▪ Kansas City, 298
Natalie's Cakes & More ▪ Ferguson, 299
Niecie's ▪ Kansas City, 299
O'Connell's Pub ▪ St. Louis, 300
Riley's Pub ▪ St. Louis, 300
Snead's ▪ Belton, 300
Stroud's ▪ Kansas City, 301
Ted Drewes ▪ St. Louis, 301

Ohio

Aglamesis Bros. ▪ Cincinnati, 302
Al's Corner Restaurant ▪ Barberton, 302
Avril-Bleh & Sons ▪ Cincinnati, 302
Balaton ▪ Cleveland, 303
Belgrade Gardens ▪ Barberton, 303
Camp Washington Chili Parlor ▪ Cincinnati, 303
Cathedral Buffet ▪ Cuyahoga Falls, 304
Crabill's ▪ Urbana, 304
Eckerlin Meats ▪ Cincinnati, 304
Flury's Cafe ▪ Cuyahoga Falls, 305
G&R Tavern ▪ Waldo, 305
Hathaway's Coffee Shop ▪ Cincinnati, 305
Henry's ▪ West Jefferson, 305
Kennedy's Bar-B-Que ▪ Canton, 306
Liberty Gathering Place ▪ West Liberty, 306
Little Polish Diner ▪ Parma, 306
New Era Restaurant ▪ Akron, 307
New Sandusky Fish Company ▪ Sandusky, 307
Perla Homemade Delights ▪ Parma, 307
The Pine Club ▪ Dayton, 307
Price Hill Chili ▪ Cincinnati, 308
Putz's Creamy Whip ▪ Cincinnati, 308
Slyman's Restaurant ▪ Cleveland, 308
Sokolowski's University Inn ▪ Cleveland, 309
State Meats ▪ Parma, 309
Swensons ▪ Akron, 309
Taggarts Ice Cream ▪ Canton, 310
Tucker's ▪ Cincinnati, 310
White House Chicken ▪ Barberton, 310

White Turkey Drive-In ▪ Conneaut, 311
Young's Jersey Dairy ▪ Yellow Springs, 311

Wisconsin

Anchor Bar ▪ Superior, 312
Beerntsen's Confectionary ▪ Manitowoc, 312
Bendtsen's Bakery ▪ Racine, 313
Benji's ▪ Milwaukee, 313
Charcoal Inn ▪ Sheboygan, 313
Chili John's ▪ Green Bay, 314
Jack Pandl's Whitefish Bay Inn ▪ Whitefish Bay, 314
Jake's ▪ Milwaukee, 314
Jo's Café ▪ Milwaukee, 315
Klinger's East ▪ Milwaukee, 315
Kopp's Custard ▪ Glendale, 315
Leon's ▪ Milwaukee, 315
Maggie's ▪ Bayfield, 316
Mazo's ▪ Milwaukee, 316
McBob's ▪ Milwaukee, 316
Mr. Perkins' Family Restaurant ▪ Milwaukee, 317
Plaza Tavern ▪ Madison, 317
Real Chili ▪ Milwaukee, 317
Ring's Bar ▪ Plain, 318
Solly's Grille ▪ Milwaukee, 318
Speed Queen ▪ Milwaukee, 318
Stockholm Pie Company ▪ Stockholm, 319
Three Brothers ▪ Milwaukee, 319
White Gull Inn ▪ Fish Creek, 320

Oklahoma

Cancun ▪ Tulsa, 358
Cattlemen's Steakhouse ▪ Oklahoma City, 358
Clanton's ▪ Vinita, 359
Classen Grill ▪ Oklahoma City, 359
Coney I-Lander ▪ Tulsa, 359
Country Dove Tea Room ▪ Elk City, 360
Dink's Pit Bar-B-Que ▪ Bartlesville, 360
Eischen's Bar ▪ Okarche, 360
Freddie's Hamburgers ▪ Tulsa, 361
Hamburger King ▪ Shawnee, 361
Hammett House ▪ Claremore, 361
Hank's Hamburgers ▪ Tulsa, 362
Ike's Chili ▪ Tulsa, 362
Jigg's Smokehouse ▪ Clinton, 363
Johnnie's ▪ El Reno, 363
Kumback Lunch ▪ Perry, 364
Leo's ▪ Oklahoma City, 364
Linda-Mar Drive-In ▪ Tulsa, 364
The Meers Store ▪ Lawton, 365
Murphy's Steak House ▪ Bartlesville, 365
Nic's Grill ▪ Oklahoma City, 365
Robert's ▪ El Reno, 366
Rock Cafe ▪ Stroud, 366
Sid's ▪ El Reno, 366
Van's Pig Stand ▪ Shawnee, 367
White River Fish Market ▪ Tulsa, 367
Wilson's B-B-Q ▪ Tulsa, 368

Texas

Angelo's ▪ Fort Worth, 369
Avalon Diner ▪ Houston, 369
Bartley's Bar-B-Q ▪ Grapevine, 370
The Big Texan ▪ Amarillo, 370
Black's Barbecue ▪ Lockhart, 370
Blanco Bowling Club Cafe ▪ Blanco, 371
Blue Bonnet Cafe ▪ Marble Falls, 371
Bryce's Cafeteria ▪ Texarkana, 371
Cattlemen's Fort Worth Steak House ▪ Fort Worth, 372
Chris Madrid's ▪ San Antonio, 372
City Market ▪ Luling, 373
Fuel City ▪ Dallas, 373
Golden Light Cafe ▪ Amarillo, 373
Goode Co. Texas Bar-B-Q ▪ Houston, 374
Green Vegetarian Cuisine ▪ San Antonio, 374
H&H Coffee Shop ▪ El Paso, 375
Highland Park Soda Fountain ▪ Dallas, 375
Hill Country Cupboard ▪ Johnson City, 376
Hoover's Cooking ▪ Austin, 376
Hut's Hamburgers ▪ Austin, 376
Kreuz Market ▪ Lockhart, 377

La Mexicana ▪ Houston, 377
Little Diner ▪ Canutillo, 377
Louie Mueller Barbeque ▪ Taylor, 378
Monument Cafe ▪ Georgetown, 378
Norma's Cafe ▪ Dallas, 379
OST ▪ Bandera, 379
Paris Coffee Shop ▪ Fort Worth, 379
Ranchman's Cafe ▪ Ponder, 380
Royer's Round Top Cafe ▪ Round Top, 380
Salt Lick ▪ Driftwood, 381
Smitty's ▪ Lockhart, 381
Southside Market ▪ Elgin, 381
Sweet Georgia Brown ▪ Dallas, 382
Taco Garage ▪ San Antonio, 382
Taco House ▪ San Antonio, 383
Taco Taco ▪ San Antonio, 383
Texas Pie Company ▪ Kyle, 383
Threadgill's ▪ Austin, 384
Tolbert's ▪ Grapevine, 384
Tom & Bingo's ▪ Lubbock, 385
Vernon's Kuntry Katfish ▪ Conroe, 385
Village Bakery ▪ West, 385
Weikel's Store and Bakery ▪ La Grange, 386

Utah

Capitol Reef Cafe ▪ Torrey, 387
Hires Big H ▪ Salt Lake City, 387
Idle Isle ▪ Brigham City, 388
Lamb's Grill ▪ Salt Lake City, 388
Maddox Drive-In ▪ Brigham City, 389
Mom's Cafe ▪ Salina, 389
Navajo Hogan ▪ Salt Lake City, 389
Sill's Cafe ▪ Layton, 390

GREAT PLAINS

Idaho

Montana

Nebraska

North Dakota

South Dakota

Wyoming

WEST COAST

California

If you have a restaurant you want to review or recommend, or if you have a comment about one that we have recommended, please visit Roadfood.com and let the world know, or get in touch with us directly at info@roadfood.com.

DESTINATION:
ANTARCTICA

Inset Map (top left)

P. of Cap

Antarctic Circle

Sea

PALMER PENINSULA

Weddell Sea

Ross Sea

SOUTH + POLE

ANTARCTICA

NEW ZEALAND

Tropic of Capricorn

of Capricorn

Ocean

CAPE OF GOOD HOPE

TASMANIA

AUSTRALIA

Indian Ocean

NEW GUINEA

MADAGASCAR

AFRICA

© RM&N&Co.

uator

32   160°   33

180

35

34

150°

140°

Main Map

Antarctic

Circle

THURSTON I.   C. FI

DEMAS ICE TONGUE

Amundsen Sea

CAPE DART

THWAITES ICE TONGUE

Peacock Bay

Wrigley Gulf

+ MT. SIPLE 10,171 FT.

WALGREEN

ELLS

GETZ ICE SHELF

EXECUTIVE COMMITTEE RANGE

M A R I E

CORDELL HULL GLACIER

MT. SIDLEY + 13,717 FT.

ROCKEFELLER PLATEAU

B Y R D

EMORY LAND GLACIER

120°

BALCHEN GLACIER

EDSEL FORD RANGES

L A N D

WHITMO MOUNTA

140°

Sulzberger Bay

EDWARD VII PEN.

C. COLBECK

Kainan Bay

Prestrud Inlet

160°

ROOSEVELT I.

SCOTT GLACIER

Pacific

Little America Bay of Whales

ROOSEVELT I.

AMUNDSEN GLACIER

Discovery Inlet

ROSS ICE SHELF

80°

QUEEN NA

+ MT. FR 13

R o s s

(A)

+ MT. WAD 14,078 F

180°

+ MT. KIRKPATRICK 14,600 FT.

+ BEARDMORE GLA

(D)   80°   (C)   SCOTT   70°   S e a   (B)

MT. MARKHAM 14,272 FT.

Ocean

MT. EREBUS 12,280 FT.

MINNA BLUFF

LADY NEWNES ICE SHELF

ROSS

McMurdo Sound

McMurdo

160°

+ MT. ALBERT MARKHAM

C. COTTER

C. HALLETT

C. ADARE

Robertson Bay

+ MT. SABINE 12,631 FT.

MT. LISTER 13,350 FT.

+ MT. MC CLINTOCK 11,844 FT.

VICTORIA   LAND

A N T A

C. WILLIAMS

LILLIE GLACIER TONGUE

BALLENY IS.   *Rennick Bay*

CAMPBELL (N.Z.)

WILLIAMSON HEAD

W   I   L   K   E   S

140°

C. FRESHFIELD

GEORGE V COAST

120°

AUCKLAND IS.(N.Z.)

Deakin Bay

NINNIS GLACIER

MERTZ GLACIER

L   A   N   D

MACQUARIE (AUSTL.)

SOUTH MAGNETIC POLE

Commonwealth Bay +

ADELIE COAST

C. BICKERTON

Davis Bay

Porpoise Bay

NORTHS HIGHLAND

CAPE GOODENOUGH

SABRINA COAST

BUDD COAST

QUEEN

DENN

GLAC

MA

Vincennes Bay

KNOX COAST

I   n   d   i   a   n

SCOTT TONGUE

MAN GLACIER

TONGUE SHACKLETO

ICE

DESTINATION: ANTARCTICA

by ROBERT SWAN

photographs by Roger Mear, Robert Swan, and Rebecca Ward

SCHOLASTIC INC.

New York Toronto London Auckland Sydney
Mexico City New Delhi Hong Kong

ISBN 0-439-08777-5

12 11 10 9 8 7 6 5 4 3 2 1   9/9 0 1 2 3 4/0

Printed in the U.S.A.   14

Reissued by Scholastic, May 1999

I would like to thank
Barry Denenberg for his invaluable help
in the preparation of this book.
—R.S.

Preface

IT WAS spring of 1912. Robert Scott and his companions had been expected back eight months earlier.

Scott and his party had set out to be the first men to reach the South Pole. At the time, the way to reach the South Pole was on foot, sometimes with the help of dogs, through nearly nine hundred miles of ice, wind, and snow. It was a long and dangerous trek through the frozen continent of Antarctica.

On January 17, 1912, Scott and his party finally did reach the South Pole, only to find a Norwegian flag planted by Roald Amundsen. Scott's team arrived five weeks too late.

Several months later, the eleven-man search team came upon a mound of snow. "It is the tent," said one of the men. They dug out the tent and discovered the bodies of Bowers, Wilson, and Scott wrapped in their reindeer-skin sleeping bags.

Next to Scott was a tin with a lamp wick, which he probably used for light when he made entries into his diary. The last entry was on March 29:

> Since the twenty-first, we have had a continuous gale from the west southwest and the southwest. We had fuel to make two cups of tea apiece and have food for two days on the twentieth. Every day, we have been ready to start for our depot eleven miles away, but outside the door of our tent, it remains a scene of whirling drift. I do not think we can hope for any better things now.

The search team collapsed the tent over the
bodies and built an eight-foot mound of snow; they
made a cross out of a ski.

"This must last for many years," said one of
the search team. But the monument was never seen
again. Sun and snow would cause it to sink beneath
the surface, where the bodies, preserved by the
snow, will remain until one day an iceberg breaks
from the edge and carries them north.

Seventy-four years after Scott began his final expedition, Roger Mear, Gareth Wood, and I, Robert Swan, embarked on a trek dedicated to Scott's memory. Without the help of animals, machines, or radios, we manhauled food, gear, and supplies over the same route Scott took. Our expedition was named "In the Footsteps of Scott," and this is our story.

Men Wanted for Hazardous Journey

FOR AS long as I can remember, I have enjoyed studying history. I like learning about other places and times. Even more, I am fascinated by individuals and what they accomplished.

To tell the truth, though, something always bothered me. I didn't want to spend my whole life reading about things that other people did. I wanted to do them myself. It was that simple. I wanted to *write* history, not read it.

One day, when I was twenty-one, I was spending a long morning in the library at the University of Durham. I had been in the ancient history stacks for hours when I wandered to a section on polar exploration. I pulled out one of the books, opened it, and was attracted by an extraordinary photograph. It was of the men who were with Captain Robert Scott on his tragic journey to the South Pole. The look in their eyes made an impression on me. I decided right then that I wanted to experience what they had experienced. I wanted to go where they had gone, do what they had done, and see what they had seen. I decided I would do whatever I had to. I was going to the South Pole.

From that time forward, my life was different. I felt excitement and anticipation. I knew I had lots to do, and I began immediately. I started by reading books about the history of the exploration of Antarctica: about Scott and his gallant crew; about Ernest Shackleton, another British polar explorer; and about Roald Amundsen.

I decided I really needed to experience Antarctica firsthand before I could begin to make preparations for the expedition. So in 1979, I presented myself at the Cambridge offices of the British Antarctic Survey, which maintained a year-round base of operations in Antarctica in a place called Rothera. I told them that I wanted to join them at Rothera. I asked them how I could make myself useful there, and they told me.

For a year and a half, I worked at one job after another, learning the various trades that the people at BAS told me were important. I learned to fix motors, mend machines, climb mountains, and mix concrete. In September 1980, I returned to the same BAS offices and soon was on my way to Rothera Base, Antarctica.

On the trip, I got to know Roger Mear, whom I had met earlier at a BAS conference. Roger was already recognized as one of a handful of world-class mountaineers. His still-growing list of firsts included successful challenges of the world's highest and most forbidding mountains. Roger usually chose to scale their sheerest slopes, often in winter and sometimes in darkness. He was more at ease facing step-by-step dangers on an icy mountainside than strolling to the corner store for the Sunday paper. I was sure that this was the person I wanted in charge in Antarctica.

At first, to use his word, he was "under-whelmed" with the idea. After careful consideration he agreed, but with one provision: that we did it his way. "We must make a one-way journey to the Pole together yet alone. Without depots, dogs, or outside assistance of any kind. We will not take radios or rescue beacons. We will start with as much food and fuel as we can haul, and once past the halfway mark, it will be the South Pole or nothing."

After our stay in Rothera, Roger returned to his mountaineering life and studied the particular techniques we would need to cope in the Antarctic. I returned to England in 1981, when I set out to gather what was needed for the expedition: people, food, equipment, money, a ship.

I decided to run the ad that Ernest Shackleton had run in a newspaper over seventy years ago when he, too, was planning an attempt to reach the Pole:

> Men wanted for hazardous journey. Small wages, bitter cold, long months of complete boredom, constant danger, safe return doubtful. Honor and recognition in case of success.

Thanks to the Shackleton ad and stories about the expedition that appeared in newspapers and occasionally on television, we received over four thousand applications. From those, and from people whom Roger and I knew, we chose the twenty-five members of our expedition. All would make the boat trip to Antarctica, though only Roger and I planned to walk to the South Pole.

Gareth Wood, a thirty-four-year-old Canadian, was among the twenty-five. Roger had climbed with him many times. Gareth had left his life on rural Vancouver Island to organize all aspects of our base. Gareth's courteous manner seemed to be a good balance to my natural brashness and Roger's closed-book personality.

Gareth was a welcome and critical addition to the team, as was Michael Stroud, whom Roger and I met on our trip to Rothera Base. Michael was to be our doctor, assuring us of proper medical care. Dr. Michael would be able to combine two things he enjoyed: adventure and medicine.

Though our ad stated "Men wanted," we had three women among the crew, including Rebecca Ward, who joined our team as a photographer.

John Tolson, a thoughtful person who has a tendency to reserve judgment, became our cameraman, shooting over twenty-six hours of film that would become a fifty-two minute documentary of our journey.

We set up operations in a warehouse located in Shed 14 on the London docks. It was just yards away from where Scott's ship, the *Terra Nova*, was loaded. Now that we had a warehouse, we needed to fill it. I planned to ask men and women who ran companies for money and supplies, and I put together a presentation for that purpose.

Sir Peter Scott, Robert Scott's son and co-founder of the World Wildlife Fund International, is widely respected by conservationists. In early 1982, he gave us his full support. As I had suspected, it made things quite a bit easier. Companies would listen to me with Sir Peter Scott's support.

We soon began to make headway. We received assurances from Shell that they would supply our fuel. Rolex supplied our watches; Leica, our cameras; Bow Water-Scott, our toilet paper. Before we would set foot on the continent of Antarctica, we would raise three and a half million dollars in money and supplies that represented the good wishes of over two thousand companies, schools, and individuals.

My friend Peter Malcolm joined us in search of a ship that was capable of navigating the icy and treacherous Antarctic seas (or could be made capable) and also within our budget. Peter found a gleaming red and white vessel that we later named the *Southern Quest* after Shackleton's ship, the *Quest.*

At the end of March 1984, the ship accidentally crashed into the wharfside London docks, scattering bricks, wood, and the welcoming party in all directions. I tried to see it as a good omen. "That, Ladies and Gentlemen, was a demonstration of her ice-breaking capabilities."

It took nine months of professional refurbishing to insure that the *Southern Quest* was in condition for the hazardous journey. Finally, on November 10 at nine o'clock in the morning, preparations came to an end. With a small group of friends and well-wishers bidding us farewell, we set sail for Antarctica. My dream was becoming a reality.

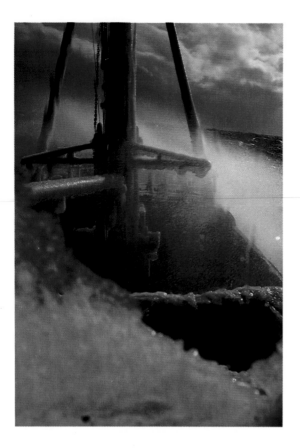

Bound for Antarctica

T HE ROUTE of the *Southern Quest* followed Captain Scott's: from London to Cardiff, where we
picked up sixteen tons of coal (as Scott had), then
on to Cape Town, South Africa.

Lyttelton, New Zealand, was our last port of
call before Antarctica. We set sail on January 30
after a two-week stay. We were escorted through
the still waters of the channel by the tug *Lyttelton*,
which had escorted Scott's ship, *Terra Nova*,
seventy-four years earlier.

Five days later, we passed through some of the
roughest seas in the world. We entered waters that
were 36°F. There were icebergs and snow.

On February 7, we sighted Mt. Erebus, the
active volcano. It seemed to keep watch over the
Antarctic landscape.

All of us were aware of the problems that could be caused by the unpredictable waters of McMurdo Sound. A ship might pass through unharmed at one point, only to be immobilized in pack ice at the next, frozen solid for a year or more.

When we finally landed, we had little time for rejoicing or resting. The Antarctic summer was ending, and the pack ice that had let us in was already reforming. We had no time to spare.

Gareth supervised setting up the base. He went about his job with the precision and preparation that we had come to expect. Twenty-five of us took eight 15-hour days to unload the cargo, all fifty tons of it.

Our evenings were spent eating and enjoying each other's company. Resting our tired bones, we moved as little as possible.

Gareth's plans were well thought out, and we were able to erect our hut, which came in pre-fabricated sections, in only four days. We named our base after Sir Jack Hayward, one of our sponsors.

Scott's hut stood two hundred yards from our base. Clothes, boots, socks left for drying, books, and photographs of loved ones remained where they had been when abandoned three quarters of a century earlier. The food and fuel that Scott had so desperately needed was still there in its original abundance.

Over the past eight years, I had studied the photographs of Scott and his men. Now, standing where they had spent so many hours, I felt their presence. The sound of my boots on the floorboards startled me. For a moment I thought one of Scott's men was there, about to ask just what in the world I was doing and who I was.

I returned to our hut and lay awake for quite a while thinking about what we were going to attempt and about those who had gone before us.

Antarctica has few plants and animals. Microscopic life, moss, lichens, tiny wingless insects, and two types of flowering plants live on the land. Penguins, seals, and the skua (a bird) also inhabit the continent, but they spend only part of the time on land. These animals depend upon the sea for their food.

A small human population of mostly research scientists also lives in Antarctica. The scientists are from several nations that have agreed to share their discoveries.

McMurdo, an American base, is heated and lighted by a small power plant. People, supplies, and mail are transported by airplane.

A Long Wait

THE SUN doesn't appear at all for four months during the height of the Antarctic winter; the weather is brutal.

We arrived in Antarctica at a time when the *Southern Quest* could enter McMurdo Sound. Now Roger and I had to wait until the following summer, when the sun would return and the weather become milder, to walk to the South Pole. Gareth Wood, Dr. Michael Stroud, and John Tolson waited out the nine months with us. Meanwhile, Dr. Michael did medical research, and John filmed our activities.

The temperature had been dropping almost daily since we arrived. The Antarctic winter was approaching. On February 23, the *Southern Quest* departed for the warmth of Sydney, Australia, where she would spend the winter. Roger, Gareth, Michael, John, and I stood at the shoreline and watched the others disappear across the bay. The five of us would spend the next nine months together in a space that measured sixteen by twenty-four feet.

We entered our hut through a porch, where we kept coal, skis, and sleds. Just inside the door was the bathroom/storeroom. The toilet used biodegradable chemicals, and the contents were emptied into the sea each day.

We kept most of our food outside, but food to be used in the next few days and food that could not be frozen was in the pantry. Our living room contained a coal-burning cooker that doubled as a heater, a dining room table, a kitchen sink, and water tanks for melting blocks of snow thrown in through a hatch from outside.

There was also space for Gareth's radio equipment, a computer that was kind enough to play chess with Roger, Dr. Mike's medical equipment, and a darkroom for developing film. Our bedrooms were upstairs in an atticlike space below the roof.

The most critical feature upstairs was the window that opened in case of fire. Outside, we erected a tent, stocked with emergency supplies as a precaution.

Fire is the single greatest hazard to huts in Antarctica, where it never rains and rarely snows. A piece of dry wood could be ignited by the smallest flame, and strong winds spread a fire. A dropped fuel can and a match carelessly tossed away could mean sudden and total disaster.

Antarctica forces you to think about everything you do. The extreme cold, the driving and relentless wind, and the foreign terrain will make you pay for any lapse in concentration.

Winter in Antarctica brings many extremes: temperatures that fall to −70°F and lower, winds that reach over a hundred miles an hour, terrain that is without life and appears forever frozen solid. But perhaps the most trying extreme is when the sun deserts the continent from the middle of May until the last days of July. During that time, only the moon lights up the sky.

It was interesting to watch everyone develop schedules for eating, sleeping, and working in a sunless environment. I preferred taking cat naps. I often woke at four in the morning and usually read until seven or so. Then I began my chores: burning the rubbish (we were committed to leaving the continent as unlittered as we found it), bringing in blocks of snow for drinking water, emptying the latrine. I also wrote many letters to people who were interested in our progress.

Roger never seemed to sleep at all. Staying up all night, he pored over his charts and maps and made certain that our plans for navigation were correct. Gareth kept to a more normal schedule.

I don't recall exactly when the tensions began to build, but by May it was clear that our original plan would not work. The problems that Roger and I encountered with each other's personalities caused enough distrust between the two of us to make a two-man walk dangerous. Choosing a third to join us was the only way to proceed. A third would relieve the tension and balance things out. There was little question that Gareth Wood was the most qualified to join us.

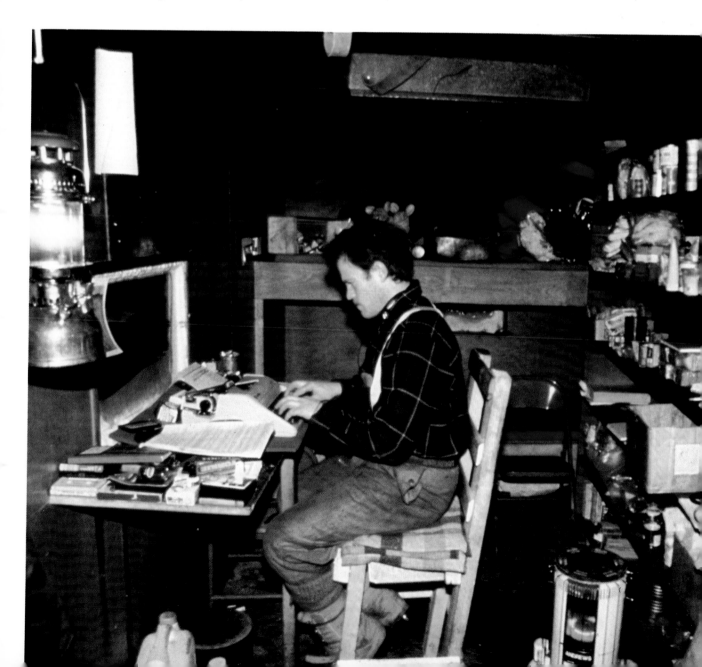

The South Pole or Nothing

W E SPENT the days before our trek calculating, weighing, and repacking our food. We did everything we could to reduce the weight. We even unwrapped 480 chocolate bars to save 26 ounces. But no matter what we did, we could not get our sleds to weigh less than 353 pounds. My sled turned out to weigh .2 pounds less than Gareth's and Roger's. Discovering this, Gareth said that they would let me get away with it this time.

John and Mike walked with us for fifteen miles from our base to Hut Point. They left us to begin our journey from Hut Point on November 3, the same location and day that marked the beginning of Scott's expedition. We were scheduled to arrive within eighty-three days. We had food for no more.

We didn't push ourselves those first few days. We knew that no matter how well-conditioned we were, it was best to let our bodies gradually get used to the shock of this kind of load. But somewhere along the way, we would have to make up for our slow initial pace in order to average the ten miles a day that were essential to cover the distance.

The wind blew from the south directly into our faces. The surface was very difficult. By day ten, we had traveled only 86 miles, an average of 8.6 miles a day. It was not good enough, so we pushed on.

But at least by now, we could no longer look back and see where we had come from.

We slept right next to each other, head to foot, in a small tent. Each morning, we were up at seven. Gareth, who slept in the middle, was the first to rise. The moment I opened my eyes, I felt as if I hadn't slept enough the night before.

There was barely enough room for us to sleep in the tent. Moving and putting on socks and shoes was even more difficult. Dressing was quite a gymnastic exercise. Though it was very cold, I couldn't dress too rapidly. Dressing for the day could actually mean the difference between life and death. It would certainly mean the difference between comfort and discomfort during the day's walk. I had to carefully apply antiperspirant to my feet to prevent sweating. Moisture in my shoes would freeze and give me frostbite. A wrinkle in a sock could cause a blister that would get worse every day. If I put on too much clothing, I would have to stop, take off the extra layer, and repack my sled. Then I would have to make up the time that I had lost.

After a quick breakfast of hot chocolate, oatmeal, biscuits and butter, we broke camp and were on our way. We would walk for three hours, rest for ten minutes, walk for three hours, rest for ten minutes, walk for three hours. During our rests, we would have a snack of chocolate and salami. After our last period of walking, we would set up camp and eat a freeze-dried dinner.

Each day, one of us would take a turn supplying the food we needed from his sled. This would make the sled six pounds lighter. It felt great every time my turn came. We carried our trash with us because we did not want to add to the pollution of Antarctica.

We were always hungry and often bored. To pass the time, I would pretend that the walk from one campsite to another was a stroll across London. One day I would walk from Hampstead Heath to Euston Station. Another day, I would walk from the Barbican to Westminster Abbey. I would try to remember every landmark and feature along the way. My problem was that I would also picture every restaurant, cafe, and food shop. I always finished my stroll hungrier than ever.

At night, it was all we could do to fight off exhaustion so that we could light our tiny portable stove and fix dinner. After dinner, Roger and Gareth worked on the navigation tables for the next day's march. Staying on course was one of our major concerns.

We carried only one book with us, Scott's diary. Each night, we would read the entry from the corresponding day of Scott's journey. Although sleep beckoned, we always took time to write in our own diaries.

Our first major obstacle was the four-hundred-mile Ross Ice Shelf, an immense plane of floating ice covered with ice ridges, crevasses (deep cracks), and snow crusts that could suddenly cave in from our weight. On skis, we pulled our sleds, each man lost in his own world. Each decided for himself when to stop to take a breather or adjust clothing or equipment. The slowest would catch up when it was time to set up camp.

The wind blew from the south at twenty-five miles straight into our faces. It did not let up. Spinning particles of frozen snow made it difficult to see and hear.

I was consistently falling behind. By the twenty-fifth day, I had fallen a full mile behind. Roger came to see if he could help. He pulled my sled and discovered it was harder to pull than his. After some investigation, Roger discovered the problem. The runners were on backwards. The difference was not apparent to the naked eye, but in

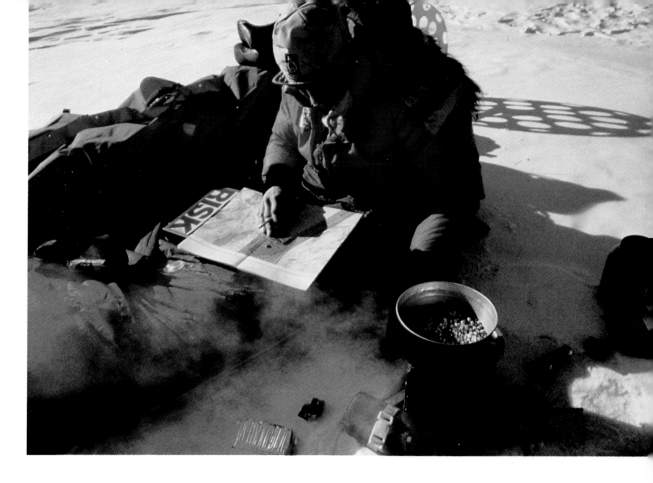

Antarctica, the most minute mistake could bring defeat or even death. Roger took the runners off and turned them around, and we were on our way.

After thirty-eight days and three hundred ninety-seven miles, we reached the end of the Ross Ice Shelf. Now we were ready to face the most dangerous terrain on the entire journey: the Beardmore Glacier. It was a nine-thousand-foot climb over a distance of one hundred thirty-six miles, with a surface of rugged ice covered by waves three and four feet across.

But in spite of the dangers, the Beardmore was a welcome sight. It symbolized the progress we had made. It meant there was a great deal behind us.

At the halfway point Roger, Gareth, and I had an important decision to make. If we chose to continue beyond this point, there would be no turning back. We had enough food and supplies to turn around *or* to continue to the South Pole; we did not have enough to turn back at a later date.

The decision was unanimous. It would be the South Pole—or nothing.

Roger saw them first: the tents, the helicopter, and the men. When I got closer, I took off my goggles and blinked to make sure that my eyes were not deceiving me. They were not. Four American geologists and one Russian scientist were surveying the area. They invited us to join them for an extravagant dinner of lobster and steak, and we accepted. The next day we rested, suffering from too much food and feeling disappointed that things had not gone as originally planned: that we would face the same challenges, including the same isolation, that Scott and his men had faced. We had not expected to meet other people until we had reached the Pole.

It happened on our forty-third day: what I had feared since the beginning of our journey. On December 15, I had an accident. My sled swung out of control and trapped my foot in a crack in the ice. The ligaments in my knee snapped as I fell. We still had four hundred seventy-one miles to go.

"You'll just have to go on at your own pace," said Roger. "Do your best, and we'll never separate too far from you. But we can't slow up at this point."

I agreed. My knee swelled within just a few hours, but I could still walk on it.

Though it took me longer, somehow I managed to cover the daily mileage. Every night, I caught up with my partners while they were setting up camp.

In spite of my injury, we scaled the Beardmore in only seven days, five days less than it took Scott and his party. I quoted the words John Mills spoke in the movie *Scott of the Antarctic:* "Barrier done. Glacier done. Plateau ahead."

We had less than three hundred fifty miles to go once we reached the Polar Plateau, an ice-covered flat surface at an altitude of ten thousand feet. The surface was smoother now, allowing us to return to our skis, but the wind once again blew directly into our faces. We feared that it would get worse and that blizzards would halt our progress. Navigation was becoming a critical problem nearly every step of the way. Roger continued to navigate in circumstances that seemed impossible.

Our bodies were sapped dry, and I could feel that I had dropped as much as thirty pounds. Our lips were cracked with vertical lines of blood, and there were circles around our eye sockets from our goggles.

We were drained mentally as well. I found myself talking to people who weren't there. I would have daydreams about sitting in a restaurant with people all around me eating sumptuous feasts—but no waiter would come to my table. My mind filled with nonsense as my imagination traveled to distant planets.

The terrain grew worse as we encountered sastrugi, windblown waves in the snow. To our weary minds, they seemed like an endless chain of mountains that had to be climbed one by one.

On January 10, we were only 11.27 miles from the Pole. By the next day, we were 8.79 miles away, but visibility had become so bad that Roger could no longer be sure that we were on course. We had to stop. The winds that night blew at thirty-six miles an hour, the strongest winds recorded since 1958. Fortunately, the blizzard lasted only a few hours, and we were marching once again, each thinking about the Pole, which was now within reach.

I thought I spied something, but I wasn't sure. I continued hopefully. It became clearer. It was the geodesic dome that capped the Amundsen-Scott South Pole Station. We were five days earlier than planned, and there was no one to be seen. Then I noticed movement. A hooded figure motioned for us to follow him. We went down the ramp that tracked vehicles used to go in and out of the station. We walked under a sign that read, "The United States Welcomes You to the South Pole." It was eleven fifty-three at night.

The manager of the station shook my hand. Gripping his, I felt overwhelmed by the knowledge that we had done it. We had reached the South Pole, following in the footsteps of Scott.

Epilogue

BUT ALSO like Scott and his party, disappointment would greet us at our moment of victory. After our handshake, the manager of the station quickly informed us of the disaster that had occurred only hours before. "Welcome," he said. "I'm glad you guys made it. I've got some bad news for you, though. The *Southern Quest* has sunk. It was crushed by pack ice. Fortunately, everyone is safe."

The *Southern Quest* had spent the winter in Sydney, Australia. In preparation for the trip south, the crew dismantled a small Cessna aircraft and loaded it on board. The plane was to fly us directly from the American base at the South Pole back to the *Southern Quest.*

On January 9, 1986, the *Southern Quest* encountered pack ice. The captain, Graham Phipper, decided there was little choice other than to look for an ice flow that was large enough to allow the crew to assemble the Cessna. An ice flow was found, but the pack ice continued to be a threat. The ship drifted with the ice. By January 11, it was clear they were stuck. All hands chopped ice and did what they could to free the ship. It was a gallant but hopeless effort. The ship was trapped and slowly crushed. Rivets popped; decks buckled. She went down slowly at first, then the process speeded up. The bold white letters spelling *Southern Quest* disappeared one by one, and she was completely engulfed.

I arranged for the crew of the *Southern Quest* to be flown to New Zealand. Roger and I joined them. Gareth Wood and two members of the crew volunteered to stay in the hut for the next year until I could arrange to clear the beach as originally planned. In December 1986, the three volunteers were picked up by a small twin-engine Otter aircraft. In February 1987, the hut and remaining supplies were taken away by ship, completing the expedition.

Though time has put a distance between me and the expedition, every day is filled with memories, both good and bad: the excitement during our many years of preparation; the thrill of the boat trip; the tensions that we felt in the hut during that brutal Antarctic winter; the great hunger, bitter cold, and frightening injuries that we endured during our trek; our first disappointment, our encounter with the scientists; our joy as we reached the South Pole; and our greater disappointment, the sinking of our ship.

We had experienced all that. And we had lived up to the epitaph of Scott and his men, a quote from Tennyson's "Ulysses": "To strive, to seek, to find, and not to yield."

Inset map (top left)

Tropic of Capricorn

Antarctic Circle

PALMER PENINSULA

Weddell Sea

Ross Sea

SOUTH + POLE

ANTARCTICA

Antarctic Ocean

Capricorn

NEW ZEALAND

CAPE OF GOOD HOPE

TASMANIA

Indian Ocean

AFRICA

AUSTRALIA

NEW GUINEA

MADAGASCAR

© RMGN&Co.

32   160°   33

Main map

THURSTON I.   C. F.

DEMAS ICE TONGUE

Antarctic

Circle

Amundsen Sea

CAPE DART

Wrigley Gulf

+ MT. SIPLE 10,171 FT.

GETZ ICE SHELF

THWAITES ICE TONGUE

Peacock Bay

WALGREEN

ELLS

M A R I E

EXECUTIVE COMMITTEE RANGE

MT. SIDLEY + 13,717 FT.

CORDELL HULL GLACIER

ROCKEFELLER PLATEAU

B Y R D

WHITM

MOUNT

EMORY LAND GLACIER

EDSEL FORD RANGES

L A N D

120°

BALCHEN GLACIER

140°

Sulzberger Bay

EDWARD VII PEN.

C. COLBECK

Kainan Bay

Prestrud Inlet

ROOSEVELT I.

SCOTT GLACIER

AMUNDSEN GLACIER

Little America

Bay of Whales

180°

QUEEN

NA

+ MT. F

P a c i f i c

R o s s

Discovery Inlet

ROSS ICE SHELF

+ MT. WA 14,078

D   80°   C   SCOTT   70°   S e a   B   80°   180°   A   MT. KIRKPATRICK + 14,600 FT.   + MT. F

BEARDMORE GLA

O c e a n

MT. EREBUS

LADY 12,280 FT.

C. COTTER

NEWNES

C. HALLETT

ICE SHELF

MINNA BLUFF

160°

MT. MARKHAM 14,272 FT.

ROSS •

C. ADARE

McMurdo Sound

• McMurdo

Robertson Bay

MT. SABINE 12,631 FT.

MT. LISTER + 13,350 FT.

+ MT. ALBERT MARKHAM 10,449 FT.

VICTORIA   LAND

MT. MC CLINTOCK 11,844 FT.

CAMPBELL (N.Z.)

C. WILLIAMS

LILLIE GLACIER TONGUE

BALLENY IS.   Rennick Bay

A N T A

140°

WILLIAMSON HEAD

GEORGE V COAST

120°

AUCKLAND IS. (N.Z.)

C. FRESHFIELD

Deakin Bay

NINNIS GLACIER

MACQUARIE (AUSTL.)

MERTZ GLACIER

W I L K E S

Commonwealth Bay

SOUTH MAGNETIC POLE +

ADELIE COAST

L A N D

C. BICKERTON

Davis Bay

NORTHS HIGHLAND

Porpoise Bay

CAPE GOODENOUGH

SABRINA COAST

SCOTT

GLACIER TONGUE

MAN GLACIER

TONGUE   SHACKLET

BUDD COAST

QUEEN

DEN

GLAC

MA

Vincennes Bay   KNOX COAST

I n d i a n